Contemporary Approaches to Psychotherapy and Counseling

The Self-Regulation and Maturity Model

Contemporary Approaches to Psychotherapy and Counseling

The Self-Regulation and Maturity Model

Joseph F. Burke

La Salle University and the University of Hartford

Brooks/Cole Publishing Company
Pacific Grove, California

Brooks/Cole Publishing Company
A Division of Wadsworth, Inc.

Printed in the United States of America
10   9   8   7   6   5   4   3   2   1

Library of Congress Cataloging-in-Publication Data
Burke, Joseph F.
    Contemporary approaches to psychotherapy and counseling : the self-
regulation and maturity model / Joseph F. Burke.
        p.   cm.
    Bibliography: p.
    Includes index.
    ISBN 0-534-10146-1 :
    1. Psychotherapy.   2. Counseling.   I. Title.
RC480.B779   1989
616.89′14—dc 19   88–39587
                                                                          CIP

Sponsoring Editor: *Claire Verduin*
Editorial Assistant: *Gay C. Bond*
Production Editor: *Penelope Sky*
Manuscript Editor: *Lynne Y. Fletcher*
Permissions Editor: *Carline Haga*
Interior and Cover Design: *Sharon L. Kinghan*
Art Coordinator: *Lisa Torri*
Interior Illustration: *Lisa Torri*
Typesetting: A-R Editions, Inc.
Cover Printing: *Phoenix Color Corporation*
Printing and Binding: *The Maple–Vail Book Manufacturing Group*
(Credits continue on page 410.)

Preface

This is not an ordinary textbook. For an introductory text, it is pretty demanding, and for a serious publication it has some funny, and even strange, moments. In short, it has a personality—my personality. In addition, though I try to be as comprehensive and as fair as possible, some substantial (and fairly obvious) biases and preferences come through, all of them as well-substantiated as I could make them. For example, I insisted on a chapter (Chapter 3) on the intellectual history of psychotherapy and counseling because I think understanding the *why* of our present state of affairs is important. A few advance reviewers have disagreed; I, in turn, have disagreed with them. Another example: I think that some form of **social learning theory** has a chance of being *the* theory to unify a good portion of the practice of counseling and psychotherapy. I could be wrong, but that's where I've made my bet. Finally, in this book, I introduce a model, the "self-regulation and maturity" model. In a very real sense, this is a working hypothesis about the practice of psychotherapy and counseling. Again, nothing substantial may come of it, but it may prove helpful even if its irrelevance is eventually established. On the hope that more than that may come of it, however, I include it in the book.

The Reach and the Grasp

Although this is an introductory text for courses in counseling and psychotherapy, it is intentionally geared to students who have backgrounds in academic psychology and who read at a fairly sophisticated level. Some readers will find that they have to reach a bit; specifically, they may have to consult their shelved "intro psych" text, learning theory book, or even a dictionary. This occasional scurrying to other sources seems a bit like scholarly activity and could even be undertaken with some enthusiasm—"learning for learning's sake," so to speak. On the other hand, readers with stronger backgrounds in psychology may find some of the information in this book nothing more than a review of what they have previously learned. Forbear your annoyance, if you will, with the understanding that repetition is an oft-underrated component in the pursuit of relatively permanent learning.

Organization

This book departs from traditional ways of organizing a psychology textbook. My goal was to let the form follow the demands of the content. The first three chapters provide an overall introduction to the nature and history of counseling and psychotherapy. Then, in keeping with the book's self-regulation and maturity model, I discuss approaches to self-regulation in Chapters 4 and 5, and those that emphasize maturity in Chapters 6, 7, and 8. Chapter 9 is about family therapy, which draws on the insights of many of the approaches introduced in the earlier chapters and contributes to those that follow it. In Chapter 10 I present the three approaches that most clearly reflect the self-regulation and maturity model and that from my perspective are at the cutting edge of individual psychotherapy and counseling. A short and important Coda follows.

Each chapter concludes with a point-by-point summary. The summaries serve as a source of review, although reading them does not adequately replace studying the chapters. Some students may use the summaries to prepare for the material covered in the chapters.

Throughout the text, some terms are set in **bold type** and are defined in the glossary at the back of the book. Some items were selected for the glossary because they appear throughout the book; others were chosen simply because at their first appearance in the text they require supplementary definition. Since the definitions in the glossary are necessarily terse, entries include references back to specific chapters where the topic is treated more thoroughly.

Acknowledgments

I greatly appreciate the contributions of the Brooks/Cole staff, including Claire Verduin, Gay Bond, Penelope Sky, Carline Haga, Sharon Kinghan, and Lisa Torri; manuscript editor Lynn Fletcher is also deserving of praise. Thanks are due to the following reviewers: Frederick Borgen, Iowa State University; James A. Boytim, Dickinson College; Patty Connor-Greene, Clemson University; Mitchell M. Handelsman, University of Colorado at Denver; David Kendall, State University of New York at Brockport; Wayne L. Lanning, University of Wyoming; Helen B. Moore, James Madison University; Don Sawatzky, University of Alberta; and Donald E. Ward, Pittsburg State University.

This book is lovingly and respectfully dedicated to more than a decade's worth of undergraduate and graduate students at La Salle University. Some of them have actually thought of me as a mentor, or at least as a cheerleader in their quest for knowledge. This book was written *for* them and, to some extent, *by* them, but they should not be held responsible for it. Nor should blame be directed at my understanding colleagues from La Salle University and the University of Hartford who have found so many nice ways to say, "Isn't that book done *yet*?"

Joseph F. Burke

Contents

CHAPTER 3

An Intellectual History of Psychotherapy and Counseling   *50*

CHAPTER 6

Maturity and Insight Therapy: Theoretical and Practical Foundations   *168*

CHAPTER 1

Introduction

> Psychology's present business then is still to clear away rubble, to take with it the insights of the everyday world, without its myths and fictions.
>
> **George Mandler**

Jack's Experience

I can still remember my second day of therapy. I was counting aloud—backwards—while lying on a gently vibrating chaise longue. I could hear the affable yet firm voice of my therapist coming through my earphones, I could feel the pull of the wires leading from my forehead to the black box in front of me, and I kept my eyes on the row of bright green lights that was gradually becoming shorter and shorter. I had come to therapy to rid myself of whatever was causing me to become anxious and worried at work and interfering with my sleep at night. I fully expected to have to talk about a lot of embarrassing things, and I had vowed to tell the therapist every secret ambition, every adolescent lust, every sordid memory that would help me find the answer to my life. But the therapist wanted me to "learn to relax," and I found myself wired to a biofeedback machine imagining myself on a desert island, in deep water, and floating upon clouds.

At first, it was just very strange and silly, although it felt good. After a while, though, I found that I could relax better at night doing relaxation exercises and listening to cassette tapes the therapist had made for me. The therapist spent some time talking with me about the situations at work that made me anxious and challenged me to determine how reasonable my fears were. At times, he even made me laugh as we talked about my fears. We began to talk about practical strategies I could use at work to minimize the number of situations in which I would become anxious, and he taught me some quick "head tricks" to think my way through the difficult moments. The therapist and I would reenact events that typically happened to me at work, and we would rehearse things I could do in future situations. We would talk about my attitude, and he would make me actually practice saying and doing things that I could use later at work. There were some awkward and embarrassing moments both in his office and on the job, but after a while it became easier, and I would go to him and try out different ways of acting to see how workable he thought they would be.

After eight months, I have found that I am able to function with only minor bouts with anxiety, and I am sleeping well. I no longer see my therapist on a regular basis, but when I encounter a problem, I make an appointment and we work things out. I continue to do the relaxation training he taught me.

Cindi's Experience

The main reason I went for counseling was pain—emotional pain. In the initial session, the counselor basically requested a life history from me—a 50-minute overview of everything that had happened to me practically since birth.

It seemed impossible to remember everything, but in retrospect, it seems that the situations I did relate to her were those that had had a significant impact on my experiences. I remember thinking to myself at the time, Why does she want to know about that? It happened such a long time ago that it can't possibly have anything to do with how bad I feel today!

Once we had touched on aspects of just about every relationship I had ever had with every family member and all of my close friends, the counselor began to point out specific patterns—certain situations would make me act the same way time and time again, and I had never realized it. I could not see the pattern until it was laid out before my eyes, and even then, it was still difficult to accept it.

Some revelations really hit me like a ton of bricks. I had blamed my parents for so very much in my life, and now I was forced to see the world from their perspective. The therapist taught me to take the role of a movie camera, affording me the luxury of being an unemotional, nonjudgmental piece of equipment that could look at important situations in my past, imagine the feelings and motives of others, and acknowledge how my own feelings colored everything else. I could no longer place blame so easily, and I began to feel sorry for my parents. However, as things went along, my anger reappeared, and I no longer wanted to forgive them that quickly. I had a constant battle between compassion and rage, as the counselor led me to responsibility for my own feelings and actions.

The relationship I have with my counselor is a very important one, and at times some of the feelings I have for my parents find their way into my dealings with the counselor. She points this out to me sometimes as a pattern I have to be attentive to. Some of our times together have been very emotional, very painful. At other times, I feel afraid of going on, afraid of what might be revealed. All in all, though, it is a journey I cannot turn away from. I am owning up to myself, and my counselor is an important part of that experience. I do not know how much longer it will take, but the investment is worth it to me.

Even the most casual student of psychology who pages through a collection of books on various approaches to psychotherapy, whether looking for a "cure" or a ready-made term paper, quickly becomes aware of the incredible diversity of ideas and techniques referred to as "therapy." A client can be invited to relax, ideate, or meditate; to imagine, dream, or analyze; or to associate, turn on, tune out, stretch, pull, punch, scream, dramatize, or chat with a father (or mother, sister, or brother) figure. In fact, the experiences of Jack and Cindi that open this chapter only hint at the variety of forms of counseling and psychotherapy that are available. This diversity amuses some people, angers others, and fascinates serious students of the art and science of applied psychology.

In this initial chapter, I lay the groundwork for understanding this diversity. I explain the relationship between theories and therapies, examine how eclecticism affects the selection of an approach to therapeutic intervention, and, lastly, outline a synthesis of self-regulation and maturity.

Although psychotherapy and counseling are often distinguished according to the training of the clinician and the severity of the client's distress, counselors and psychotherapists share the same goals, rely on many of the same theories and research, require mostly the same skills, and succeed under the same conditions. Therefore, *psychotherapy* and *counseling* will be used interchangeably throughout this text, and the term *practitioner* will be used to identify the person performing either one.

Theories and Therapies

Both counseling and psychotherapy can be defined as the artful application of scientifically derived psychological knowledge and techniques for the purpose of changing human behavior. The nature of art and science in therapy will be examined in some detail in Chapter 2, but several other terms in the definition are worth noting. *Knowledge* is specific information about something. For example, research has demonstrated the ways in which alcohol changes an individual's feelings, information that may be helpful in both understanding an individual client's behavior and educating the client. A *technique*, on the other hand, is a systematic procedure by which a task is completed. For example, a practitioner might learn how to demonstrate empathy, train a client to relax, or interpret a dream—all specific techniques from different therapies. *Behavior*, in the broad sense used here, includes "the totality of intra- and extra-organismic actions and interactions of an organism with its physical and social environment" (Wolman, 1973, p. 41). The behavior being changed thus includes actions, internal awareness of thoughts and feelings, unconscious factors, personality traits or patterns, and so on. In other words, behavior includes all *observable* (for example, compulsive actions, anxiety), *reported* (for example, fear, worry, headache), and *inferred* (for example, defense mechanisms) activities of the person.

All psychological knowledge and techniques applied in the clinical setting exist within a larger framework. In promoting a particular method of changing behavior, one makes statements about the origin, development, and malleability of human behavior in general. All approaches to psychotherapy, therefore, are really theory-therapies. Underlying any technique is a general theory of human behavior that answers (or addresses) such questions as: What determines how people behave? How predictable is human behavior? Can human behavior be changed? How? What factors affect personal development? What factors are involved in causing this particular behavior? Underlying any behavior theory is, necessarily, an even larger philosophical framework that addresses such questions as: What does it mean to be human? What is the meaning of life? Is there an ultimate reality? What is the individual's place in nature? What is good? What is evil? Implicitly or explicitly, all psychological approaches to human behavior represent philosophical positions, statements about the very nature of being human (Allport, 1960).

In evaluating a theory-therapy, the student of psychotherapy and counseling must look for several features. First, are the theory and therapy logically consistent? For example, if a theory of human behavior and its underlying philosophy proclaim the importance of the client's volition, then the techniques of that theory-therapy should allow the client to freely choose what to do rather than being manipulated, coerced, or drugged into a change of behavior.

A second consideration has to do with the verifiability or testability of the theory-therapy. As A. A. Lazarus (1976, p. 10) amusingly points out, our tendency to ascribe causative properties to the most recent event in a sequence often means that the causes of change in a client are ascribed incorrectly. He notes that should a client be rubbing her knee and tugging her ear at the same time she is relieved of a symptom, an attentive and enthusiastic practitioner is likely to "invent" a new technique: the knee-rubbing/ear-tugging technique! Clearly, the theory-therapy must be examined scientifically in order to tease out real causes of change. The methods used to test therapeutic approaches are varied and include experimental research, survey research, and clinical research. Traditionally, most therapies have relied on clinical research; that is, supporting data have come from individual cases dependent on interview techniques, psychological tests, and the judgment of the practitioner. Clinical methods of research have been criticized by more experimentally oriented researchers as being too subjective and unreliable. The problems associated with the scientific study of therapeutic outcomes stem from the fact that psychotherapy as an *application* of knowledge is *idiographic*; that is, it is geared to the individual person, the individual client. Practitioners are interested in particular people in particular sets of situations. Good experimental research, on the other hand, has traditionally been *nomothetic*; experimentalists strive for a generalized understanding of human behavior that will enable psychologists to predict and control behavior. Thus, what we have is a specific, idiographic art (psychotherapy) deriving its concepts and methods from a general, nomothetic science (psychology and related disciplines). This tension between the "pure" and the applied is at the root of our difficulties in testing the effectiveness of psychotherapy. However, emerging strategies for applying the experimental method in clinical settings, usually called **single-case experimental design,** may soon help to obviate some of the problems associated with verifiability (Barlow, Hayes, & Nelson, 1984; Hersen & Barlow, 1976).

A third consideration in evaluating the validity of a theory-therapy is its language. Does the theory-therapy use language that is consistent, comprehensive, and comprehensible? Do the words express the concepts economically and understandably? Do the language and concepts allow for the diversity of experiences expressed by the client? Is the language dynamic, changing as practitioners more precisely define their ideas and as clients more clearly express their experiences?

Of course, an approach to psychotherapy may have more than one language: Practitioners may use a precise, mutually understood language ("jargon" to some) among themselves that may not always be accessible to clients. At the same time, any psychotherapeutic approach must also have a more colloquial language, one that allows clients to express their experiences and allows practitioners to communicate their insights. As might be expected, the disparity between the professional idiom and the language used between the practitioner and client cannot be great or the richness of the theory will be lost, along with the effectiveness of the therapy.

The language of a theory-therapy is also important because the process of therapy often involves the exchange of one set of linguistic symbols for another. Take, for example, a client who describes his problem as "I'm just so bad that I can't stop myself from yelling at my kids." If the practitioner can help the client reframe his problem in other language—for example, "I sometimes cannot deal with the frustration I feel in my life, and I take it out on my kids"—the client may then be able to see the relationships between past experiences and current thoughts, feelings, and actions. Different therapies may have different ways of reframing the problem: In this greatly simplified example, aggressive behavior is explained in terms of a frustration model. Whatever the model used, a change in language—because it changes one's assumptions about the world—can lead to insight and, possibly, to a change in behavior.

Eclecticism

It is an old battle among practitioners: eclectic application of theories and techniques versus adherence to a single, comprehensive theoretical perspective and its corresponding techniques. The fruits of eclecticism, to borrow a celebrated phrase, can be both bitter and sweet (Allport, 1968, pp. 3–41).

A survey of clinical psychologists revealed that over 50% of the 855 respondents described their theoretical orientation as "eclectic" (Garfield & Kurtz, 1976, p. 4). Previous statistics indicate that this eclecticism may represent a trend. D. Smith (1982), analyzing responses to questionnaires sent to 800 clinical and counseling psychologists, found that more than 40% of his respondents described themselves as eclectic. What exactly is eclecticism? An examination of the literature reveals at least two different definitions of eclecticism.

First, eclecticism involves "strategies and methods from several approaches applied selectively to clients" (Brammer & Shostrom, 1982, p. 34). This is identical to what A. A. Lazarus (1967) has called "technical eclecticism," which emphasizes finding an appropriate technique for coping with the problematic behavior with minimal regard for the theory behind the technique.

A second definition of eclecticism, from Wolman (1973), is the "organization of compatible facts and positions from diverse sources and incompatible theories into a consistent system" (p. 112). Practitioners of this second kind of eclecticism attempt to create a consistent system that accommodates at least some theoretical fitting together of its diverse elements.

The benefits of eclecticism are readily apparent. A technique is applied to a problem with maximum regard for the specific needs of the client. Theoretical "fit," if you will, remains secondary. Changing the client's distress-producing behaviors is the practitioner's primary concern. Applied optimally, eclecticism allows the practitioner to select appropriate and tested means of intervention even when they do not fit neatly into a preferred model or theory of human behavior. Used carelessly, however, it can result in a jumbled collection of "hit parade" techniques, untested, learned inadequately, and often unrelated to the actual needs of the client. In such cases, the word *eclectic* masks trendiness and laziness—bedfellows of disaster.

Although contemporary practitioners are moving away from single-theory approaches, many are dissatisfied with an eclecticism that is subjective and unsystematic. Thus, as D. Smith (1982) notes, the current literature "indicates a trend in the direction of creative synthesis, masterful integration, and systematic eclecticism" (p. 802). The synthesis provided below is one such attempt at integration.

The Current Synthesis: Self-Regulation and Maturity

No specific school or approach to counseling or psychotherapy fully expresses the individuality of any practitioner. Each practitioner's approach is a unique hybrid of knowledge and techniques drawn from various theories and research sources. Ideally, each practitioner creatively develops an eclectic yet integrated approach to counseling or psychotherapy. In the present text, I propose a basic synthesis, a theoretical framework into which individual practitioners can integrate whatever particular elements of knowledge and technique they choose to use. This attempt, like any other, is bound by the insights, research, and opinions of the time, integrating approaches widely used by contemporary practitioners.

In summarizing the survey of orientations noted earlier (Garfield & Kurtz, 1976), Mahoney (1977) identified several important trends. First, though practitioners are increasingly eclectic in selecting what theories and techniques they use, many favor the theories and techniques of **behavior therapy** and **humanistic-existential therapies.** Second, practitioners are integrating two emphases that traditionally have been considered opposites, one focusing on overt behavior, the other on cognitive and affective processes. In accordance with these trends, I have tried in the present synthesis to incorporate the ideologies and techniques of both behavior therapy and humanistic-existential therapies. Further, noting the increasing emphasis on cognitive-behavioral approaches (Borgen, 1984; D. Smith, 1982), I emphasize therapies that integrate behavior theory with cognitive theory.

In the present synthesis, I propose a two-part model, consisting of **self-regulation** and **maturity.** This model derives from two different traditions in psychology. The first element, self-regulation, comes from the theories and techniques of behavior therapy and the philosophy of science known as **behaviorism.** Within this tradition of therapy and counseling, the emphasis is on identifying specific excesses or deficits of behavior (thoughts, feelings, or actions) in the client and applying specific intervention strategies to change the behavior. The second element, maturity, emphasizes intra- and interpersonal concepts and techniques and is a concept of introspective and interpersonal psychotherapies like **psychoanalysis** and **person-centered therapy.** Within this tradition of counseling and psychotherapy, the relationship between the practitioner and client is central, and **insight** leads to changes in the client's behavior. In their present forms, many of these introspective and interpersonal approaches to psychotherapy can be grouped with the philosophy of science associated with humanistic-existential psychology. Thus, as I will elaborate in later chapters, the present synthesis brings together two different approaches to therapy and two different philosophies of science.

Self-Regulation

Most of the numerous approaches to self-regulation, or self-control, as it is also called, depend on strategies from behavior therapy and are historically related to behaviorism. Yet, most contemporary approaches to self-regulation no longer accept the underlying assumptions of behaviorism. Rather, contemporary practitioners see a person's behavior and the environment as interdependent. This departs from the more traditional behavioristic conception of behavior as simply the product of rewards and punishment. The present perspective, referred to as **social learning theory,** emphasizes that people, in addition to being acted on by the environment, also act on the environment, thus altering the conditions that produce behavior. Contemporary approaches to psychotherapy that either implicitly or explicitly accept such a reciprocal relationship between the individual and the environment emphasize self-regulatory processes that are behavioral *and* cognitive-affective. As Bandura (1974) has pointed out:

> Contrary to popular belief, the fabled reflexive conditioning in humans is largely a myth. Conditioning is simply a descriptive term for learning through paired experiences, not an explanation of how the changes come about. Originally, conditioning was assumed to occur automatically. On closer examination, it turned out to be cognitively mediated. (p. 859)

Such an approach stresses the ability of the individual to develop a variety of controls over behavior. Self-regulation has been defined in the following manner: "a person displays self-control [self-regulation] when in the relative absence of external constraint, he [or she] engages in behavior whose previous probability has been less than that of alternatively available behaviors" (Thoresen & Mahoney, 1974, p. 12). In other words, we practice self-regulation when we voluntarily try new behaviors. Put another way, self-regulation is the ability to deal satisfactorily with the immediate and anticipated demands of life by exercising voluntary control over interfering actions, thoughts, and feelings.

The methods for gaining self-regulation are diverse and may involve behavior modification techniques, hypnotherapy, biofeedback, improved or restricted diet, imaginary rehearsal, and any number of other behavioral, cognitive, and medical techniques. All in all, a person's perception of his or her own powerfulness, that is, his or her ability to regulate actions, feelings, and thoughts, is fundamental to more internal developments like self-concept, maturity, awareness, growth, and the like. In other words, self-regulation is the foundation for future maturity.

Maturity

Over the past few decades, many practitioners have been part of a shift in the concepts and language used to describe the various problems humans have in coping successfully with life. For many years we talked about "emotional health," viewing psychological well-being in the same way we view physical well-being. Although for many political and economic reasons the medical language remains with us, many practitioners see concepts of illness and health as inappropriately applied to behavior problems. Such concepts are static, imply single causation of the "illness," and are too closely tied to the medical model of treatment. As Albee (1969) has noted, what has emerged is a model more accurately described as socioeducational, one that emphasizes developmental concepts and learning. This model describes human behavior in terms of its *adaptivity* or *maladaptivity* rather than its health or sickness. Patterns of behavior are evaluated according to their place along an adaptive continuum. Thus, one can ask, To what degree does this pattern of behavior help the individual deal effectively and rewardingly with life, and to what degree does this pattern of behavior limit the person, depriving her or him of opportunities for satisfaction and limiting his or her actualization of unique potentials?

An individual's ability to become maximally adaptive is a function of maturity, the second part of our model. The concept of maturity is taken from the work of Maslow (1970a). Beyond gaining control over actions, thoughts, and feelings, an individual can continue to mature—that is, become increasingly capable of successfully dealing with the demands of the environment. In ideal human development, psychological maturity keeps pace with chronological age; that is, as an individual becomes older, he or she becomes less self-conscious and self-centered, more capable of challenging limits, and more focused on realizing personal potentials that are beneficial to self and others at the same time. Approaches to psychotherapy that enhance maturity are numerous and encompass many theories and techniques; all, however, aim at providing or promoting improved *insight* on the part of the client, new understanding, new appreciation of some aspect of behavior. Insight is not enough, however. Insight that leads to maturity includes a movement toward action, toward change. As we will see in a later chapter, Maslow's conception of maturity is anything but passive insight; it is a call to productivity and competence. As such, insight that leads to maturity moves the client from *understanding* to *acceptance* to *determination* to *action,* as illustrated in Figure 1.1.

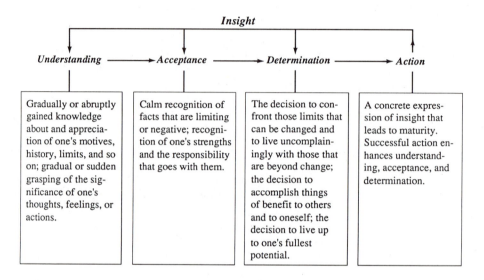

Figure 1.1 *The components of insight leading to maturity*

Self-Regulation and Maturity

For the most part, the initial goals of therapy are self-regulatory; that is, they relate to improving the client's capacity to interact successfully and rewardingly with the environment by gaining power or control over actions, thoughts, and feelings. Beyond these initial goals, clients usually also seek to understand the whys and hows of the situation they are trying to control; that is, they seek insight into their problems, a goal that leads to maturity. In addition, a certain level of maturity is necessary before a client can accomplish her or his therapeutic goals—a level usually present anyway when an individual elects to participate in counseling or psychotherapy. Both self-regulation and maturity are thus integral components of the goals of therapy. Table 1.1 lists several goals with their self-regulation and maturity components.

Some approaches to counseling and psychotherapy emphasize the importance of self-regulation, providing the client with specific techniques for changing behavior, while other approaches emphasize the importance of promoting the client's maturity through developing insight into the problems. An approach to counseling or psychotherapy that emphasizes self-regulation to the exclusion of maturity is likely to provide only temporary help; an approach that emphasizes maturity to the exclusion of self-regulation may prove interminable.

Table 1.1   *Self-Regulation and Maturity Components of Sample Goals of Therapy*

Sample General Goals	Self-Regulation Components	Maturity Components
reduction of major psychotic symptoms, improved capacity to live competently on a day-to-day basis	changes in body chemistry through chemotherapy; reduction of effects of stress by means of biofeedback training, progressive relaxation, or other techniques	interpersonal support and confrontation leading to INSIGHT, that is, an *understanding* of the disorder and of one's own and others' reactions, *acceptance* of the limitations imposed by the disorder, and *determination* to live as fully as possible
decreased shyness, decreased self-consciousness, and improved interpersonal relationships	reduced anxiety in social situations through assertiveness training, reduced anxiety by means of progressive relaxation, changes in awareness of self through cognitive restructuring	interpersonal support and confrontation leading to INSIGHT, that is, an *understanding* of self-defeating patterns of behavior and their development, *acceptance* of personal strengths and weaknesses, and *determination* to confront one's limits and capitalize on one's strengths
ability to cope effectively with periods of depression related to lack of success in school	decreased depression by disputation of irrational beliefs, increased knowledge through learning time management skills, increased ability to remain relaxed during tests through stress inoculation techniques	interpersonal support and confrontation leading to INSIGHT, that is, an *understanding* of the pattern of avoidance and any underlying insecurity, *acceptance* of responsibility for what ought to take place, and *determination* to successfully achieve the goals that are set

Summary of Chapter 1

This chapter presents a brief overview of the following ideas:

1. Students of psychotherapy and counseling, as well as practitioners, are faced with an often bewildering variety of therapeutic approaches and intervention techniques.

Theories and Therapies

2. Counseling and psychotherapy are both defined as the artful application of scientifically derived psychological knowledge and techniques for the purpose of changing human behavior. Behavior is defined broadly to include both internal processes and external actions.
3. No approach to psychotherapy or counseling is free of an underlying theory of human behavior, which is itself based on a more general philosophy. The degree to which there is "fit" among these elements is a test for the integrity of any approach to therapy.
4. The validity of a therapy is also evaluated in terms of the testability of its procedures. Although clinically generated research has been criticized because it has not been derived experimentally, single-case experimental design holds promise as a means of closing the gap between the nomothetic and the idiographic.
5. The comprehensiveness and comprehensibility of the language used in defining and applying a therapy is another criterion on which evaluation can be based.

Eclecticism

6. Many practitioners describe themselves as "eclectic"; that is, they draw on a variety of theories and therapies.
7. Applied optimally, eclecticism allows practitioners to select appropriate and tested methods with maximum regard to the needs of the client.

The Current Synthesis: Self-Regulation and Maturity

8. The current synthesis offers a theoretical framework within which practitioners can integrate disparate approaches. It unites the concepts of self-regulation and maturity and draws from both behavioral and humanistic-existential approaches to reflect the dominant thinking of the time.
9. Self-regulation, a concept derived from behavioral approaches and the theoretical foundations of social learning theory, emphasizes gaining or regaining control of thoughts, feelings, and actions as the client's primary concern.
10. Maturity, a concept from humanistic-existential approaches, comes from the work of Maslow and rests on a long clinical tradition. It is based on the idea that adaptive behavior is furthered by insight—that is, by understanding, accepting, and changing one's thoughts, feelings, and actions.
11. Most clients seek both self-regulation and maturity; that is, they want both control over their problems and fuller understanding and growth.

CHAPTER 2

The Therapeutic Process

> *T*hese disparate visions in their tension reflect the paradoxical truths of human experience—that we know ourselves as separate only insofar as we live in connection with others, and that we experience relationships only insofar as we differentiate others from self.
>
> **Carol Gilligan**

A common fantasy of a typical counseling or psychotherapy session might go something like this: An attractive, sexually provocative young person walks into your tastefully appointed office. Lounging comfortably in an overstuffed chair, admiring your numerous diplomas and license, the articulate prospective client outlines for you the difficulties that mar an almost perfect life. Sporting your most understanding face, you listen attentively, reinforce appropriately, and, finally, outline with enthusiasm your future sessions together. You can see quite clearly by this time the reason the client is having problems, and you pull a plan of action from your vast bag of tricks, anticipating with excitement the coming session with the client. The new client bounds out of your office confident in your skills, determined to change those nasty behaviors, half-cured through sheer optimism. You lean back in your swivel chair, filled with fantasies (most of them unethical), and bask in the knowledge that you are a worker of minor miracles in a suffering, abnormal world.

Though the preceding scenario has been exaggerated for effect, some beginning students of psychotherapy and counseling entertain similar expectations and fantasies. Although an occasional Fifth Avenue psychiatrist or Beverly Hills talent-agent-turned-sex-therapist may come close to fulfilling this stereotype, it has little to do with the real practice of therapy or counseling. "YAVIS" clients, as A. P. Goldstein (1971) has called them, are Young, Attractive, Verbal, Intelligent, and Successful. Frankly, few YAVIS clients find any long-term psychotherapy or counseling necessary, and when one does, the YAVIS glow is quickly lost in the dark despair the client experiences confronting the discrepancy between appearances and inner reality. More likely, the person who comes to your makeshift office, drab clinic, or antiseptic cubicle is anxious, uneasy, depressed, unsure, unhappy, or undone. Your client is, to use Frank's word, "demoralized." Frank (1973) defines **demoralization** as "a sense of failure or of powerlessness to affect one's life and one's environment" and identifies it as "a major source of the distress and disability of persons who seek psychotherapeutic help" (p. xvi).

Though an occasional client may be unusually attractive, articulate, or both, most are average in appearance, not exceptionally interesting to listen to, and often reticent to explore the central components of their distress. This does not mean, however, that the process of helping the client does not provide excitement, wonderment, and satisfaction. On the contrary, to witness, step by step, the demoralized client's progress toward a sense of power and competence is both exciting and wondrous, and the client's ensuing maturity is palpable—and satisfying—proof of the intervention's effectiveness. The satisfaction that comes with these changes, however, is the product of hard work and numerous frustrations.

For the most part, counseling and psychotherapy occur in less than ideal settings, with less than ideal clients, and practitioners often fail to establish the elementary relationship necessary for the intervention to progress. Even when such rapport does develop, few changes in behavior patterns are made easily.

other cases, clients have learned the cultural tools but find them no longer adequate for coping successfully. Such cases are particularly notable in our age of telecommunications, the computer, and nuclear warfare.

This brings us to a fundamental question for practitioners. Is one-on-one intervention the answer when culture is at the root of the problem? For example, anyone familiar with the demographics of schizophrenia and other major mental disorders in the United States can attest to the contribution of racism and poverty, as larger cultural realities, to mental illness (Kohn, 1976). Albee (1982) has argued that the culture (language, intervention methods, and so forth) of most mental health professionals is so solidly middle class that it is not appropriate for the needs of lower-class minorities in the United States. It may well be that only major changes in the culture (for example, legislation on housing, mass transit, education, and preventive and remedial health care) can make a difference in the problems confronting many Americans today. Therefore, though this book focuses on individual psychotherapy and counseling, it is important to realize that one-on-one intervention is far from the entire picture. In recognition of these realities, psychologists, counselors, and other professionals are moving toward models of training and intervention that recognize the broader cultural context in which behavioral problems emerge, with an increasing emphasis on the full range of services people need to overcome psychological problems (Levy, 1984). Also, as we will see in Chapter 9, the burgeoning popularity of *family therapy* is an important part of the response to our increasing awareness of the significance of cultural context.

From an anthropological point of view, we are talking about the way in which social, economic, and political realities shape or design a given culture. Some cultures allow individuals to develop successfully, others less so. It is possible to examine cultures as diverse as government, schools, or the family in terms of how well they provide for both the common good and the good of the individual. We turn now to a detailed discussion of **synergy,** a term used to describe the balance between personal and group needs.

The Concept of Synergy

I begin our discussion of synergy with an all-too-common vignette. You are a counselor at Allamerica Junior High School. A 12-year-old boy, Pete, is brought to your office because he has been "disturbing" the class. Apparently, he has been using vulgar and abusive language in responding to "kidding" from his classmates. Fellow students have been making humorous remarks about the fact that Pete is seriously overweight, and he has been returning barbs of his own, often humorless remarks about his classmates' heritage. The teacher assures you that the other students' comments are "relatively harmless" and "typical of kids that age." Now Pete sits before you, angry and hostile, and he breaks into tears. Not only is he hurt by the experiences in the classroom, not only does he feel worthless and stupid in his exchanges with the other students, but he desperately wants to be accepted by them. After some time with

Pete, you gain his confidence. Jointly you set up a plan to help him change his relationship with the class by (1) learning how to deal with their comments, (2) developing a stronger self-concept through encouragement and kindness, and (3) starting a weight loss program. Of course, as you inform Pete, it will be hard work, but, with the help of the school nurse, you are sure that in time Pete will look better, that this will make him feel better about himself, and that this will make him more acceptable to the class. It is a grand plan. It fails miserably. Let's trace what happens.

Initially, thanks to a well-trained and concerned school nurse, Pete starts a sound weight reduction program that involves exercise, restricted food intake, and conversations with and encouragement from the nurse and yourself. In class, Pete ignores the comments of his fellow students and forces himself to make an occasional positive comment to selected peers. In turn, perhaps due to the lack of reinforcement from Pete himself, the overt comments go underground. Pete occasionally hears a remark about his weight, but he ignores it. At your suggestion, he has thrown himself into making himself the person he wants to be. Eventually the class will come around.

After several weeks of modest advances on the weight front, and after several weeks of uneasy calm in the classroom, Pete is back in your office as a serious discipline problem. He has again "acted out" with other students, this time becoming physically abusive. Further, he has accused several classmates of plotting against him, of mocking him behind his back. A check with the nurse indicates that Pete has gained weight that week. It's back to the drawing board.

Perhaps, you think, you can get somewhere with Pete's family. Pete's mother agrees on the telephone to come and see you. She is a thin woman, soft-spoken, charming. She speaks lovingly of her son. Though she is shocked at Pete's behavior, she is not surprised: "He gets it from his father."

Let's fulfill every practitioner's fantasy and go invisibly into Pete's home. It is dinnertime, and Pete, his mother, his father, and his sister, Carol, are seated around the table. Dinner consists of dry, overcooked roast beef, mashed potatoes, canned carrots, doughy white bread, and margarine. There is instant pudding for dessert. Pete passes the potatoes and bread without taking any. It is the first day of his new diet, and he knows to limit his intake of certain items. He takes a modest piece of meat, a healthy amount of carrots, and as the heavy, floury gravy goes by, he puts a half tablespoon of it on the meat to provide some moisture. Mom, with a look of concerned horror, asks Pete if he is feeling sick. "Is there something wrong, dear?" Pete says he is on a diet; he wants to lose weight. Carol giggles. He ignores her. His mother says, "There's nothing wrong with your weight; you'll grow out of it. It's just baby fat." His father is silent. This recurs night after night. After almost a week of the diet, his father explodes: "I'll fix your plate, young man, and you'll eat what I put on it!" The diet has angered Pete's father, caused his mother to feel rejected, amused his sister, and deeply frustrated Pete. He adopts a tactic of "diet-all-day-stuff-by-night." His mother is relieved, his father appeased, his sister bored, and Pete unhappy (and still obese).

The design of cultures   In Pete's story we see two cultures, the school and the home, designed in such a way that they almost defy Pete to change his behavior. The way in which the classroom is organized and managed lets covert insults be accepted as appropriate but allows no mechanism whereby Pete can improve his relationship with the class. At home, Pete's parents, besides failing to realize the health dangers of their daily diet and the medical realities of Pete's obesity, tend to use food as a measure of love ("love me, eat my food") and to use anger and authority (on the part of the father, for example) as a solution to problems. An individual, Pete, is attempting to change his life in the isolation of the temporary culture called counseling. Unfortunately, Pete lives in a number of larger, more permanent, change-resistant cultures: the family and the school. Like all cultures, these are designed to maintain *low entropy. Entropy,* in the broad sense in which we are using it here, refers to the capacity for change, randomness, or chaos in a system. Thus, Pete's family system is designed to allow the least amount of change, randomness, or chaos. Low entropy, with its predictability and stability, is maintained through the products of culture. In any culture, whether as large as a nation or as small as a family, it is rituals, myths, beliefs, language, values, tools, and artifacts that ensure low entropy. Much of the design of any family cultural system, of course, has come from the larger culture. Table manners, ways of dealing with anger or of expressing love, restrictions on the use of certain words, ways of expressing religious beliefs, beliefs about race or creed, methods of coping with death—all of these come to each of us through the culture we call our family, from larger cultures like our neighborhood, ethnic group, and religious institutions (see again Figure 2.1).

What has happened to Pete's family culture? Like the school culture, it has developed over time for its own perpetuation. Everything is designed to function smoothly for the good of the group. But as Henry (1971) has pointed out in his studies of the families of institutionalized children, sometimes families develop low entropy cultures that are detrimental to the individual. These are pathological cultures, cultures that are, as Henry puts it, "pathways to madness." While Pete's school culture and his family culture may not deserve Henry's appellation, the same processes are at work, and the same potential exists for limiting the individual's growth.

Cultural relativism and the synergy model   One way of looking at the interaction between culture and the individual is the *synergy model* developed by Ruth Benedict and utilized by Abraham Maslow in his theory of **self-actualization.** While we will look at Maslow's theory in detail later, the notion of synergy is relevant to our current discussion.

The development of the synergy model can be traced to problems encountered by early students of anthropology. Anthropologists realized that it was necessary for them to get beyond the ethnocentrism that plagued most visitors to new and/or "primitive" cultures. *Ethnocentrism* is the evaluation of another culture according to the criteria of one's own culture. In other words, what is "good" in another culture is whatever is the same in one's own culture. What is "bad" in another culture is whatever is different in one's own culture. Infused with ethnocentrism, hundreds of thousands of explorers, missionaries, and soldiers have moved across several continents "improving" the cultures of primitive peoples. Native Americans were educated in the principles of private possession and land ownership, various peoples were indoctrinated into believing that true decency meant covering their nakedness, and religions thousands of years old were enlightened by mass conversion to Christianity, as interpreted variously by the French, Germans, Italians, Spanish, British, Portuguese, and Anglo-Americans.

Recognizing that they themselves are products of cultures, anthropologists developed methods of investigation designed to minimize ethnocentrism in their research. Though the specifics of that methodology are beyond the scope of our present discussion, the overall approach that developed is important to us. The concept that enabled anthropologists to overcome their ethnocentrism is known as *cultural relativism.*

The nature of cultural relativism has been outlined in various sources, including Boaz (1940), M. Harris (1968), and Lowie (1937). Essentially, to view a culture from a relativistic position is to recognize that all cultures develop patterns of behavior that ensure their own survival. Languages, myths, rituals, cosmology, customs, and so forth are designed to enable a specific population of people to adapt to a specific environment. Culture is thus a blueprint for successful integration into a total *ecosystem.* A group of people develops the tools, weapons, habitats, and food production methods its members need to survive in the immediate environment. In addition, the group develops rituals that express its members' collective beliefs about the nature of the universe and their place in it. Such rituals usually partake of religion as well as some system of governance. Often basic survival behaviors are celebrated in rituals said to have originated in divine revelation. Most cultures appear to operate in this way; a certain wisdom seems inherent in the suprapersonal nature of culture.

Simply stated, from the perspective of cultural relativism, "good" and "bad" are irrelevant to the study of cultures. If each culture is meeting its own adaptive requirements, then assigning value to specific rituals or behaviors within that culture is both ethnocentric and inappropriate. The role of anthropology and other social sciences, therefore, is not *evaluative* but, rather, *explicative.* The investigator's role is not to judge but to explain the complex interaction of ecosystem, group, and individual, and the resulting products of culture.

The concept of cultural relativism enabled social scientists to understand both the structure and function of complex cultures, but by the middle of this century, the limits of cultural relativism also had become apparent. First, in a world divided by technological sophistication, some important cultures were dying. The question of whether dying cultures should be saved as is or whether they should be given the advantages (and disadvantages) of technology presented a serious challenge to the assumptions of cultural relativism. Second, the emergence of Nazism and other destructive cultures also weakened the cultural relativists' position. Opponents of cultural relativism argued that social science that simply explains what happens without regard to the values inherent in the actions of a culture fails to contribute the full measure of its potential. The alternative, however, appeared to be ethnocentric dogma. The dilemma of how to objectively study human behavior and culture while not ignoring ethical and moral problems remains a serious challenge to social and behavioral science.

Synergy An important attempt to resolve this dilemma was made by Ruth Benedict, the noted anthropologist, in a 1941 talk at Bryn Mawr College (Maslow & Honigmann, 1970). In that presentation, Benedict outlined a way of looking at how societies are designed, a way of judging the strengths and limits of specific cultures. She used the concept of *synergy*, which has been elaborated by Maslow and others.

Synergy refers to the degree of mutuality that exists within a culture between the needs of the individual and the needs of the group. Benedict identifies two types of cultures: "cultures with low synergy, where the social structure provides for acts that are mutually opposed and counterproductive, and cultures of high synergy, where it provides for acts that are mutually reinforcing" (Maslow & Honigmann, 1970, p. 326). If we borrow Coleman's (1980, p. 14) use of the term *well-being*, we have the following reformulation of Benedict's thinking.

A culture is high in synergy to the degree that, when an individual acts to enhance his or her own well-being, the culture's well-being is also enhanced. Likewise, when the culture (through its laws, customs, and so forth) operates to preserve its own well-being, the well-being of the individual is enhanced. At the other end of the continuum, a culture is low in synergy to the degree that, when an individual acts to enhance his or her own well-being, the culture's overall well-being is in some way harmed or restricted. Likewise, when the culture operates to preserve its well-being, the well-being of the individual is in some way harmed or restricted. Looking back at Figure 2.1, we recall that the term *culture* can be used both in a broad sense (in describing, for example, a nation or group of nations) and more narrowly (in describing a social institution, ethnic group, neighborhood, or family). Maslow explains further:

> A synergic institution was one that arranged it so that a person pursuing his selfish ends was automatically helping other people thereby; and that a person trying to be altruistic and helping other people and being unselfish, was also automatically and willy-nilly helping along his own selfish advantages. That is to say, it is a resolution of the dichotomy between selfishness and unselfishness, showing very clearly that the opposition of selfishness and unselfishness or their mutual exclusiveness was a function of a poorly developed culture. (Maslow, 1965, pp. 88–89)

Well-being refers first of all to the meeting of certain needs. Some of these needs Maslow called *basic* or *deficiency needs*. These needs, whether within an individual or a culture, are lacks or deficiencies that someone or something in the environment must fill. Therefore, they are needs *for*. These include physiological needs (for example, food, water, and air), and the needs for safety and security, belongingness, and esteem. Above and beyond these are needs *to*—to create, to build, to seek justice, to perfect—needs that are unique to the individual person and the individual culture. These higher needs, related to self-actualization, pull the person beyond simply filling biological, social, and psychological gaps. They call the person to challenge limits and develop unique potentials of personality, social action, artistic or scientific talent, knowledge, beauty, truth, and so on. The basic, or deficiency, needs are common to all persons, and their overwhelming dominance as a motivator in adult life is one way of defining neurotic behavior. The higher needs take us beyond that; they call for the realization of our own unique personality, our own unique patterns of behavior, our own unique talents or abilities.

With some differences, we can talk about cultures in a similar way. Cultures, too, operate to meet the basic needs of their members. It seems possible, also, to talk about cultures that self-actualize. Some cultures achieve uniqueness, great productivity, or broad influence. The question synergy poses is, At what cost to the individual?

Cultures high in synergy are designed such that individual and group goals not only do not conflict but actually reinforce each other. By *design* I mean the complex of language, laws, customs, mythology, rituals, institutions, arts, sciences, and so forth that fits the culture into its ecosystem. Some cultures, for example, a family, may be designed such that self-actualizing is not possible. The restrictions on the culture may be economic, psychological, or linguistic, but whatever they are, the design allows only individuals' basic needs to be met. An institution may achieve greatness (financial, social, physical) by severely restricting the rights or individuality of members. Every culture—be it a family, a school, a religious organization, a Girl Scout troop, or a nation—has a design. Many of its elements may be borrowed from larger cultural circles, but each culture's design is unique. And every culture is characterized by low entropy. For the culture to endure, its art, language, laws, and customs must resist change. Regrettably, the cost of stability for all may be restriction for some.

The design of a culture is a central factor in the development, maintenance, and even the definition of psychopathology. Consequently, to deal with a client's behavior in individual psychotherapy without attending to changing the cultural milieu (be it family, institution, or nation) is at best a stopgap measure and at worst a promise of change impossible to fulfill. In talking about the design of a culture, it is important to realize that a person or group of persons rarely sits down and literally designs a culture. True, specific, deliberate individual or collective acts may significantly shape a culture, as the framing of the U. S. Constitution has shaped American culture. Yet, most cultural design is the product of complex interplay among individuals, groups, and environmental demands. Social, psychological, economic, and political variables may interact with each other to promote racial disharmony, poverty, alienation, or hostility without any identifiable "bad guy." In such cases, mental health professionals must shift their focus from the individual to the cultural conditions that foster and maintain maladaptive behavior. Though traditional psychologists and psychiatrists have made few inroads in this regard, the emerging interest in community psychology, for example, demonstrates an increased concern for the social context of behavior (Korchin, 1976). Practitioners are increasingly aware of the need to deal with the ravages of social injustice in new ways, and the ultimate hope of many is to design our cultures for higher synergy so that prevention of mental disorders replaces remediation.

The Individual and the Cultural Environment

The study of human behavior is essentially the study of how individuals adjust to their cultural environment; understanding that process of adjustment or adaptation is critical to understanding behavior.

Social learning theory   Social learning theory, introduced in Chapter 1, helps explain the process of adaptation. According to social learning theory, if you remember, behavior is more than the simple product of inborn or acquired mechanisms, conscious or unconscious. It is also more than the product of simple conditioning from the outside. Rather, social learning theory explains human behavior in terms that reflect the complex interaction that exists between the environment and the person.[1] Thus, psychological function is understood in relation to "continuous reciprocal interaction between behavior and its controlling conditions. . . . Behavior partly creates the environment and the resultant environment, in turn, influences the behavior. In this two-way causal process the environment is influenceable, just as the behavior it controls is" (Bandura, 1973, p. 43).

Social learning theorists allow for the complexity of human behavior by arguing that behavior is determined and controlled by stimuli, reinforcement, and cognition (Bandura, 1973, 1977b). In other words, behavior is produced and therefore changed by events outside and inside the organism (stimuli) and by rewards and punishments anticipated because of direct or vicarious experience (reinforcement); further, behavior is integrated, modified, and recalled in that most personal of computers, the human brain (cognition). We human beings think, feel, and act, are affected by the environment, and likewise affect the environment. In interacting with the various levels of culture surrounding us, we both determine ourselves and are determined. Within the confines of

---

[1]Social learning theory's emphasis on the reciprocal interaction between behavior and its controlling conditions was anticipated in the work of Kurt Lewin (1935). He argued that as a science matures it shifts from an Aristotelian view of science to a Galilean view of science and, in doing so, replaces a model of singular, unidirectional causation with one that emphasizes reciprocal causation. He anticipated that as psychology became a more mature science, it would turn from simplistic explanations of behavior like those proposed by traditional psychoanalysis and behaviorism, both of which attribute behavior to single unidirectional causation, either internal (through libidinal chicanery) or external (by simple, mindless conditioning).

our genetic givens and previous learning, we choose how to be, what to do, how to respond to our culture, and what changes to make in our actions, feelings, and thoughts. This is **self-regulation,** a daily practice in each of our lives and, as noted in Chapter 1, one of the ends of psychotherapy and counseling. Again, psychotherapy and counseling usually involve more than work on self-regulation; they also emphasize the development of greater **maturity.** To review Figure 1.2: First, the client seeks insight that will help in understanding the causes of the problems, the reasons for conflicting feelings, or the dynamics of troubled relationships. Second, the client accepts his or her limitations and accepts those symptoms that cannot be controlled, along with the inevitabilities of aging, sickness, separation, and death. Third, through gutsy determination, the client overcomes lethargy and hopelessness to act in more adaptive ways. The client's need for self-regulation or maturity is usually expressed as specific problems, but the consistent experience of all clients, regardless of the problem, is *demoralization.*

Demoralization and power   As a rule, people who come (or are sent) for professional help feel that their ability to live effectively in the world is somehow inadequate or unsatisfactory. Their difficulties may be primarily *situational*— that is, related to specific events. The death of a relative, loss of health, failure at an important task, loss of employment, divorce, family conflict—all of these situations create stress and cause discomfort or distress. Underlying a person's responses to such events, of course, are characteristics of personality, variables that can be called *dispositional.* Dispositions, or traits, are typical ways of acting, feeling, and thinking; they characterize an individual's behavior and provide predictability. Each person has a unique history; each person has learned, within his or her biological limitations, a unique set of coping skills, ways of acting, ways of feeling, ways of dealing with stressors. Some of these skills remain effective; some no longer work for the person. All, effective or not, form a part of the person's disposition. And, since behind even the most situational problem is a person with a developmental history, a person who either has or has not developed and maintained the personal resources to deal with the problematic situation, all problems have situational and dispositional elements.

Whether an individual's problem is more situational or more dispositional, the existence of the problem bespeaks demoralization. As noted earlier, individuals become demoralized when they are no longer able to successfully meet the demands that they and others expect them to meet. The resulting syndrome is characterized by "depression, self-blame, guilt, and shame," and the demoralized person often feels resentment toward and alienation from others who continue to expect successful behavior (Frank, 1978, p. 10).

Demoralization—that sense of a loss of power to affect one's environment—characterizes all problems, from stress-related dermatitis to schizophrenia to depression over a lost pet. Power, real or perceived, is key to an individual's well-being. Our culture, however, be it our family, school, government, or church, often controls our sense of powerfulness. Too little is known about power, but recently social psychologists have been looking at how power in the cultural system produces or at least promotes powerlessness in individuals. Zimbardo (1975) exaggerates little when he writes:

> Power dominates others not through physical might but through their control of sources of information which provide the cognitive bases for attitudes and values (such as ethnocentrism, bigotry, militarism, etc.). Those in power define reality for the rest of us; they do so not only through information control, but by limiting the range of alternatives we choose "freely" from, by providing convenient labels to take the place of explanations and understandings, and by sanctions for refusing to accept the world view. . . . "Madness" consists in redefining reality without having at least two other people to believe in that new order. With power, such madness may become the basis of scientific discovery, art, religion, social movements, and revolutions. (pp. 47–48)

Although counseling or psychotherapy can help an individual face and overcome the powerlessness that comes with sexism, racism, poverty, and other forms of injustice, ideal intervention works at ending the social conditions that maintain the client's distress. Although individual practitioners cannot single-handedly change their clients' environments and their accompanying sense of powerlessness, they can contribute to the pool of accurate information about human behavior, both through scientific research and by engaging in the therapeutic process. The forums through which such information is shared include professional publications, the popular media, teaching, and political action.

The Nature of the Process

Therapists and counselors, despite occasional appearances, do not drop from the sky. Like clients, they are products of and producers of cultures. Like clients, practitioners must learn to adapt to their environment; like clients, practitioners also experience demoralization. It is hoped that what differentiates the practitioner from the client is more than the outrageous temerity it takes to tamper with another person's life. Shakow (1976) proposed writing these words of Browning's, taken from "A Light Woman," above the doors of all schools of clinical psychology:

> 'Tis an awkward thing to play with souls
> And matter enough to save one's own.

Shakow goes on to point out that practitioners are humbled by the awareness that "even the most expert of us, with all the good will in the world, know little more than the ignorant, and we must depend on this knowledge for our expertness" (p. 555). The practitioner, therefore, must be alert to two realities: There is no freedom from the influence of culture, and the tools we currently have for changing behavior are primitive.

With this in mind, we turn to an examination of the nature of the therapeutic process.

Therapy as Art and Science

Psychotherapy is both an art and a science; thus, therapists and counselors exist at the interface between science and the humanities (Shakow, 1976). Earlier, psychotherapy was defined as "the artful application of scientifically derived psychological knowledge and techniques for the purpose of changing human behavior." Though the art and the science of psychotherapy may appear to be polar elements requiring very different strategies, a common purpose and some common basic characteristics lend the process of therapy an essential unity. The following discussion explains that common purpose and identifies some of the characteristics that art and science share.

A Common Purpose

Essentially, science is a kind of human behavior. More than the collection of data, science is first and foremost a way of dealing with experience. As anthropologist Leslie A. White points out, "The word may be appropriately used as a verb: one *sciences,* i.e., deals with experience according to certain assumptions and with certain techniques" (White, 1949, p. 3). Art, too, is a human behavior, a way of dealing with experience. When one *arts,* one deals with experience in a different manner. Art and science have a single purpose, however: "to render human experience intelligible" (White, 1949 p. 3). As White explains:

> But although working toward the same goal, science and art approach it from opposite directions. Science deals with particulars in terms of universals: Uncle Tom disappears in the mass of Negro slaves. Art deals with universals in terms of particulars: the whole gamut of Negro slavery confronts us in the person of Uncle Tom. Art and science thus grasp a common experience, or reality, by opposite but inseparable poles. (White, 1949, p. 3)

Psychotherapy and counseling are both science and art. The practitioner applies scientifically derived information about human behavior in an artistic way. As scientist, the practitioner moves from a specific client's experiences to the objective formulation of hypotheses and testing procedures until lawfulness emerges. The scientist-practitioner also consumes data generated by other scientists working in the same and related fields. As artist, the practitioner takes these data and applies them subjectively to specific individuals or groups of individuals. The objectivity of the scientific venture shifts to the subjectivity of artistic expression at the point where the practitioner applies the research-generated knowledge to the client. In this way, in the interplay of sciencing and arting, art and science work together for the common purpose of enlightening and enlivening human experience.

Despite their common goal, the artist and the scientist appear to rely on different tools, skills, and languages. The practitioner as scientist may need sophisticated electronic devices to measure muscle activity, a working knowledge of computer languages, and a familiarity with the intricacies of systematic desensitization. The practitioner as artist depends on the medium of personality and its palette of interpersonal skills. These skills are used to establish a workable relationship with the client. The literature has generally confirmed that the skill triad of *unconditional positive regard, empathy,* and *genuineness* is elemental to forming this therapeutic relationship, but recent studies point out the danger of psychotherapy that is just art, just the capacity to form relationships (Parloff, Waskow, & Wolfe, 1978). It now appears that a relationship characterized by empathy, unconditional positive regard, and genuineness is necessary but not sufficient to effect significant behavioral change (C. H. Patterson, 1980, p. 661). But if the art-without-science brand of psychotherapy is inadequate, so too is psychotherapy that is science without art. Apart from the changing of a few simple habits, all psychotherapy depends on persuasion or influence. No amount of scientific knowledge, equipment, or skill will produce change if the practitioner and client have not developed a relationship that fosters persuasion.

How can such disparate activities and skills be united in a single practice? Again, unity in the therapeutic process is possible for two reasons. First, both science and art, the two facets of psychotherapy, aim at the same purpose: making human experience intelligible. Second, at their cores, science and art possess the same four characteristics.

Four Common Characteristics

Art and science—and, specifically, the art and the science of psychotherapy—can each be judged according to four fundamental characteristics that they have in common: honesty, parsimony, duality, and insight. These qualities characterize both good art and good science and can be considered measures of their value. We will look at each in turn.

Honesty   Good art is honest art. Good science is honest science. Barron (personal communication, October 1979), after a number of years of studying creativity, has emphasized the honesty of the artist as a central factor in whether or not an artistic product has lasting value. A work of art, be it music, a painting, or a short story, must express some fundamental truth about human experience or, no matter how technically precise and skillful it may be, its power to move will not endure. Art will fail its ultimate tests—providing the audience with a re-creative experience and the artist with a sense of satisfaction—if the artist has not been honest. The scientist, too, must be honest. Careful research that is open to replication, generalizations made only within the confines of what can be confirmed—that is honest science.

Practitioners, as artists and scientists, require both types of honesty. Scientific honesty is easier to demonstrate. It means thorough reading of research, frank discussion of probable outcomes, and openness with other professionals. Artistic honesty in psychotherapy is an interpersonal phenomenon that is manifested as genuineness or authenticity on the part of the practitioner. The practitioner is, in a sense, transparent, demystified. The "transparent" practitioner, to use Jourard's (1971) term, is one who allows him- or herself to be known. Such *self-disclosure* is not to be understood as a contest with clients to see who can reveal the most or who has had the greatest problems, wildest fantasies, or most restricted childhood. While allowing clients to know certain facts about oneself may be important at times, a practitioner's transparency and genuineness go beyond factual information. They involve letting clients know that the practitioner does not walk on water, that she or he, like them, has experienced the emotions, disappointments, and difficulties that characterize human life. In essence, honesty is putting aside the professional persona while remaining professional. Honesty requires providing accurate, direct feedback to clients that does not brutalize but challenges and enlightens. This is risky business, of course. The practitioner must be personally secure, or honesty is impossible. Accordingly, since the practitioner learns the practical aspects of honesty through supervised clinical training, the sine qua non for venturing into supervision is the practitioner's psychological security.

Parsimony   Brahms reportedly said that the real trick in composing was not creating music but rather letting the superfluous notes fall under the piano. This is parsimony, and it is the second quality that art and science have in common. Parsimony in poetry, for example, means that no other words are better or more economically convey the experience. A paraphrasing of the poem will never equal the impact of the poem itself. Parsimony means that each brush stroke in a painting, each note in a sonata, each movement in a ballet, each breath in an aria is necessary, integral, and meaningfully related to the whole piece: Nothing can be taken away from the work without changing it, and nothing can be added without distorting the work.

   In science, the law of parsimony refers to the principle that states that "the simplest of alternative explanations of a situation or phenomenon is to be preferred" (Wolman, 1973, p. 270). Parsimony is perfect reductionism. It involves accounting precisely for the phenomenon by identifying and demonstrating the interaction of all the variables. Where there are intervening variables, care is taken to stick as closely as possible to an explanation that will be verifiable.

   As both science and art, psychotherapy requires parsimony in a number of ways. First, the practitioner is a scientist striving for the most parsimonious explanation of the complex patterns of the client's behavior. Second, the practitioner seeks the most parsimonious—in terms of money, time, and distress—and appropriate intervention strategies possible. Third, in applying the preferred strategy, the practitioner strives for a parsimony of language. The language of counseling or psychotherapy should be comprehensive and comprehensible. Precise vocabulary and syntax, free of abstractions and garbled elaboration must accommodate the client's experience and meaningfully describe the therapeutic process. The practitioner must constantly try to refine understanding by working with understandable constructs and making verifiable predictions. Fourth, psychotherapy requires emotional parsimony. The practitioner neither expresses nor elicits from clients emotions that are not immediately germane to the process of changing behavior. Such parsimony is intimately connected with the fundamental honesty that must inform the therapy. Emotion for the sake of emotion (or for the sake of the practitioner) is drama, not therapy. Since parsimony means neither too much nor too little, emotional avoidance also shows a lack of parsimony in withholding the level of feeling necessary for the most effective intervention.

Duality   Duality refers to the quality of being twofold. In the sense in which we are using it here, it involves an individual's capacity to express two different but essential affective responses. At one end of the affective continuum, evident in both science and art, are sensitivity, softheartedness, and vulnerability. Even the most precise and technical scientist or artist must be sensitive to subtleties of one sort or another, be able to become emotionally aroused about someone or something, and be capable of becoming completely engaged in and absorbed by some activity. At the other end of the continuum, is toughmindedness, tenacity, and the ability to disengage. An artist steps back, learns and practices a new technique, evaluates, criticizes, starts over and over again. A scientist plows on even after the initial thrilling insight is long gone. The qualities at this end of the continuum let unconfirmed hypotheses lead to new hypotheses rather than to a desperate leap from an ivory edifice.

Practitioners must also possess this duality. Practitioners must have the sensitivity to empathize, to feel with clients, to relate to their experiences, to have compassion for their distress, to share with them. But this must be balanced by a tough-minded desire to achieve goals, challenge clients, plan strategies, evaluate clients' progress, and disengage when appropriate. Practitioners with only one side of this duality become victims of their clients' problems. Either they cannot engage themselves in their clients' experiences, or they cannot regain perspective by disengaging themselves. In either case, long-term help for the client is unlikely, and disillusionment or exhaustion is the outcome for the practitioner.

Insight   Insight is the "activity of mediating processes leading to solutions of a problem, but especially the reorganization of such processes with sudden success" (Hebb, 1972, p. 302). The act of insight is not in itself learned but depends on previous learning. Essentially, it involves seeing new relationships, new uses, making novel that which is common. Previous knowledge, previous efforts, previous stores of information are recombined in a way that sparks new awareness. Insight is the moment when the metaphor blazes, the hypothesis clicks, the light bulbs flash, the melody sings forth. For practitioners, insight may be the pulling together of two different intervention procedures to fit a unique client problem, a witty comment that relaxes and enlightens the client, a sudden awareness of the function of complex client defense mechanisms, or a special understanding of the client that goes beyond mere words.

This discussion of the four characteristics common to art and science should demonstrate graphically that, despite the real differences and difficulties associated with the dual nature of psychotherapy, the process itself is necessarily both singular and creative. We now stop to look briefly at the nature of the creativity required of practitioners in the process of therapy.

Therapy as a Creative Process

Though Barron (W. Taylor & Barron, 1963) has noted that psychotherapy is a creative process, and though researchers have examined creativity in science (W. Taylor & Barron, 1963) and in art (Barron, 1972), far more research has been aimed at studying the relationship between creativity and mental illness (see I. Taylor, 1975, pp. 1–36 for a review of the research). Therefore, a statement on psychotherapy as a creative process is in order.

The client and the practitioner create a new culture. They join differing experiences of the world to form a temporary culture with its own unique rules, linguistic idiosyncrasies, response patterns, and rituals. This new culture is in essence a relationship, and like all relationships of love and caring, an initial "willing suspension of disbelief," to borrow from Coleridge's *Biographia Literaria,* must exist on the parts of both practitioner and client. Clients must suspend their disbelief in the possibilities of change. Practitioners must suspend their disbelief as well, stay any prejudices regarding their clients' character or appearance, and shelve any premature dismal prognoses. Inconsistencies in the client's story are let stand for the moment, and the practitioner actively seeks to believe. This is not pretense; it is the building up of a mutuality of trust that begins with a relationship that can imagine realistic change and that then grows in such a mammer that change can occur. The initial suspension of disbelief, of course, is gradually balanced by scientifically accurate evaluations and intervention procedures, but the bond of mutual trust formed in those initial sessions particularizes the science to the client working with this practitioner.

This act of particularizing treatment to the client forms the central focus of the practitioner's psychotherapeutic creativity. In the act of creating the therapeutic relationship, in the act of shaping theory and technique to the situation at hand, the practitioner relies, of course, on all four of the characteristics common to art and science: honesty, parsimony, duality, and insight. It should, therefore, be emphasized that the examples used to illustrate those qualities also serve to illustrate in detail the creative process that is psychotherapy.

Having described the creative aspect of the therapy process, we turn now to the subject of professional training.

We have established that psychotherapy in the last quarter of the 20th century is necessarily both a science and an art. The practitioner must be a trained and creative scientist and artist. As skilled scientist and creative artist, the practitioner shares with physicians and certain other professionals a dual responsibility in relation to continuing education (staying current with the professional literature) and character (integrity and honesty). In the education of mental health professionals, emphasis must be placed on both scientific training and the development of personal skills. One model for accomplishing this is know as the "scientist-professional model," to which we now turn our attention.

The Scientist-Professional Model

The *scientist-professional model* for the training of clinical psychologists was first proposed at the 1949 conference of the American Psychological Association in Boulder, Colorado, where contemporary clinical psychology was born, and a blueprint for the education of clinical and counseling psychologists was established (Barlow et al., 1984; Borgen, 1984). The Boulder model, with its emphasis on traditional scientific training as foundational to a practitioner's clinical training, has also influenced the education of professionals in social work, psychiatry, and counselor education (Barlow et al., 1984).

Nonetheless, the scientist-professional model has been criticized for being impractical. Critics point out that the scientific training is largely unused by the average practitioner. Alternate degree programs, some within universities and others with less independent programs of study, have developed more clinically oriented courses of study with less emphasis on research skills. Some of these programs offer a Psy.D. degree, Doctor of Psychology. These degrees are seen as more "applied," more practical. Perry (1979) has outlined the controversy and has made a strong case for maintaining the scientist-professional model as the dominant one. Phares (1979) points out that while some practitioners do not have the time or inclination to engage in research on a regular basis, they must be intelligent consumers of research or face obsolescence. The training of practitioners, whether or not it adheres strictly to the scientist-professional model, must, therefore, equip practitioners with this facility with research.

Scientist-professionals, Shakow (1976) reminds us, identify with their field and its history and, beyond that, with all science. The practitioner takes on Bronowski's "habit of truth," a habit manifested in "the constant effort to guide one's actions through inquiry into what is fact and verifiable, rather than to act on the basis of faith, wish, or precipitateness" (Shakow, 1976, p. 554). The practitioner is a person who has pulled together the intellectual pursuit of knowledge and the emotional pursuit of understanding and integrated them into a mode of operation that is sensitive and thoughtful at the same time. Strupp (1976), warning against anti-intellectualism, has demonstrated that the practice of counseling or psychotherapy is not a matter of choosing between "guts" and "head," but rather realizing that both are vital to effecting change. More recently, Barlow et al. (1984), calling the Boulder model the "scientist-*practitioner* model," argued that the reintegration of science and practice is at hand. Advances in research strategies appropriate to the study of individual client behavior make the practitioner's education in scientific psychology quite practical. Further, the increasing demand for accountability makes scientific verifiability imperative.

Considerations and Variables

Counseling and psychotherapy depend upon the development of a relationship between client and practitioner capable of changing the client's behavior. This relationship is essentially a process of interpersonal influence or persuasion that promotes self-regulation and maturity.

Healer and Sufferer

All cultures have identified someone to work with problems of behavior. Though not all cultures have separated the religious from the medical and the behavioral, someone has always been set apart. From Mesopotamia to Main Street, the same basic components are there. A person within the culture is identified as special, as a *healer*. The *sufferer* seeks relief from the healer. A structured series of contacts occurs between the healer and the sufferer, sometimes with the aid of the group, and the healer attempts to produce changes in the sufferer's emotional state, attitudes, and/or actions. All participants believe that such change is possible, and this belief is supported by the culture. While physical and chemical adjuncts may be used, words, acts, and rituals are basic to the change process (Frank, 1973). Essentially, it is a process of persuasion, a process of influence. The techniques may change, the healer's credentials may vary, and the language of labels may change from "possession" to "psychosis," but the basics remain the same.

  If all cultures have their equivalent to the modern practitioner, what differentiates the process of influence practiced today from that of a thousand years ago? Part of the answer to this question may come from looking at the following statement by Levi-Strauss about the primitive culture's *shaman,* a general term used for a healer, a manipulator of *mana,* an impersonal spiritual power or force:

> That the mythology of the shaman does not correspond to objective reality does not matter. The patient believes in it and belongs to a society that believes in it. The protecting spirits, the evil spirits, the supernatural monsters and magical monsters are elements of a coherent system which are the basis of the natives' concept of the universe. The patient accepts them, or rather she has never doubted them. What she does not accept are the incomprehensible and arbitrary pains which represent an element foreign to her system but which the shaman, by invoking the myth, will replace in a whole in which everything has its proper place. (Levi-Strauss, 1963, p. 192)

  Frank (1973, 1978) has pointed out that a loss of belief by many in our culture has driven many to replace religion with psychotherapy. Unlike religion, however, psychology and psychiatry do not have the comprehensive system of beliefs and myths and rituals that the shaman in the above quote does. Yet, faith is an element of psychology; faith exists on the parts of the client and the practitioner. Psychology also has rituals (intervention techniques are rituals), and myths, too. What makes counseling or psychotherapy increasingly different from the art of the shaman is, it is hoped, its reliance when possible on science. Although the scientific knowledge we have about human behavior is rudimentary at present, it does allow us to eschew simplistic explanations of human behavior based solely on preference, prejudice, or whim. The beliefs, myths, and rituals in which practitioners engage are constantly being refined by scientifically derived knowledge; our hunches and intuitions lead us to seek verification when that is possible.[2]

Psychological Influence

Psychotherapy and counseling involve personal interaction between client and practitioner capable of changing the client's behavior through influence or persuasion (Frank, 1973; Lewis, 1972; Strong & Claiborn, 1982). No matter what techniques a practitioner uses, counseling is a process that in essence involves initiating or sustaining a client's motivation to change. The interaction's potential for causing change depends on the client's belief in the healing abilities of the practitioner. Counseling and psychotherapy are planned activities during which one or more persons attempt to influence one or more other persons beyond the extent possible in a chance encounter (Pentony, 1981).The influence can occur one-on-one (*individual therapy*), in a group of unrelated individuals (*group therapy*), or in a social unit with one or more practitioners (*family therapy*). In all cases the purpose of the structured time together is for practitioners to influence one or more individuals.

Beyond these considerations, each approach to therapy will add a distinct flavor to the therapeutic process by its unique language, theoretical base, and techniques. Yet, a number of variables operate in all approaches to counseling and psychotherapy; we turn now to them.

The Relationship

Almost all approaches to psychotherapy and counseling emphasize the relationship between the client and the practitioner. If the initial sessions of therapy are characterized by mutual respect and positive feelings, the deepening relationship will probably allow the practitioner to become an agent of persua-

---

[2]Discussing the merits of scientific knowledge brings to mind a short poem by Emily Dickinson that usually serves to spark debate:

"Faith" is a fine invention
When Gentlemen can *see*—
But *Microscopes* are prudent
In an Emergency.

(Johnson, 1960, p. 87)

sion or influence for the client (Garfield, 1980). Even behaviorally oriented therapists, who have traditionally minimized the importance of relationship variables, have in recent years come to acknowledge them (Davison, 1980); Frank (1980) has gone so far as to say, "without being able to document it with scientific evidence, that much of the therapeutic power of the therapist lies in aspects of the therapists's personality, the patient's personality, and their fit, which probably cannot be conceptualized in objective terms" (p. 288).

Counselors and therapists from various approaches point to a working relationship or rapport as fundamental for the beneficial influence to take place. While there are various ways to describe the relationship, some of the literature of psychotherapy, primarily drawn from the work of Carl Rogers, suggests that a relationship characterized by unconditional positive regard, empathy, and genuineness is the effective cause of therapeutic change.

Do counseling and psychotherapy, without regard to other more specific techniques, work simply because of the positive, empathic, and genuine relationship formed between the practitioner and the client? Parloff et al. (1978) have pointed out that a large body of literature suggests just that and that an entire generation of practitioners has been influenced by that idea. However, these authors have also pointed out that a review of the literature indicates that such a conclusion is simplistic. More complex models have emerged, in which the therapeutic relationship is not dismissed "but is included in one of a number of important factors to be considered" (Parloff et al., 1978, p. 251). Viewed within a larger framework, the "goodness" of the relationship becomes *necessary but not sufficient* for effective behavioral change (C. H. Patterson, 1980, p. 661); that is, while the establishment of a relationship characterized by rapport is necessary for all psychotherapy, it is not in itself sufficient for most interventions. As Patterson points out, the presence of unconditional positive regard, empathy, and genuineness in the therapeutic relationship "leads the client to engage in the process of self-exploration. Clients learn to take responsibility for themselves when they are expected to and allowed to do so. They make necessary choices and decisions. They look for and obtain training in necessary and desirable skills" (p. 663).

Whatever the practitioner's personality characteristics, the client must in the end expect that change can occur. Rotter (1980b) points out that the effectiveness of the practitioner in achieving this expectancy depends on "(1) the therapist's strength as a reinforcer, (2) the degree to which he or she is thought of as being objective, i.e., not having some personal stake in the person's change, and (3) the degree to which the therapist is perceived as being knowledgeable, wise, and/or skilled" (p. 291). Thus, whether unconditional positive regard, genuineness, and empathy are more important than knowledge, wisdom, and skill or vice versa may well depend on the individual client.

Roles and Expectations

The process of psychotherapy involves the enactment of roles by the client and the practitioner. "The term role enactment refers to patterns of activity with a particular social position (e.g., physician), an informally defined social position (e.g., class clown), or a particular value (e.g., patriot)" (Spanos & Gottlieb, 1979, p. 528). Inherent within these roles are a set of expectations about what will happen during therapy, how the other will act, what attributes a good client or practitioner will have, and the like. Role enactment includes both external behavior patterns and patterns of subjective experience. To call a behavior role enactment, whether internal or external, does not mean that it is being faked or that the person does not truly believe in it. On the contrary, role enactment in psychotherapy requires belief for changes to be lasting.

The client comes to counseling or psychotherapy with expectations about both roles, that of client and that of practitioner. Likewise, the practitioner has expectations about their respective roles. These expectations about the roles each other must enact include minor variables like attire or office furnishings. More important variables, research indicates, include factors like attractiveness, sex, age, and social status of both practitioner and client. Some of the expectations of both clients and practitioners are simply stereotypes. For example, an attractive woman in her mid-20s, no matter how superb her scholarship and professional background, will fall outside the expectations of some clients—and some practitioners. An older man may appear fossilized to the client (unless he has a Viennese accent). Expectations work both ways; practitioners have their own stereotypes of clients based on age, gender, type of problem, and so forth.

Of critical importance are the expectations the client learns during the initial weeks of counseling or therapy. The practitioner guides the client in forming expectations about how therapy works, what happens during the sessions, how long the sessions will last, and a host of other things. The client moves from an "implicit personality theory" to one that is explicit (R. Jones, 1977) and answers such questions—often unarticulated—as What does it mean to be a person? How do people change? How do heredity and environment interact? How do situations and dispositions interact? These questions are answered formally and informally. Expectations expressed by the practitioner can lead to expectancy-fulfilling behavior change for the client, thus enhancing the seeming ability the practitioner has to predict. In fact, some changes in the client's behavior may occur simply because the practitioner has said they will occur.

Other Variables

The literature of counseling and psychotherapy identifies a number of other variables present in most forms of intervention. Garfield (1980, pp. 95–130) provides the following list:

1. the therapist-client relationship
2. interpretation, insight, and understanding
3. catharsis, emotional expression, and release
4. reinforcement
5. desensitization

6. relaxation
7. information
8. reassurance and support
9. expectancies as a therapeutic variable
10. modeling
11. facing or confronting a problem
12. time as a therapeutic variable
13. the placebo response

Several things about this list are noteworthy. First, each of the variables listed above is supported by the research literature. Second, while the language of certain variables (for example, *reinforcement*) may appear to fit only certain therapies (behavior therapy), these variables operate in most approaches to counseling and psychotherapy, whether explicitly or implicitly. Variations in technique and language often mask the similarities inherent in the various approaches, as theoretical differences often obscure the similarities among the therapies when they are actually practiced.

Steps in the Therapeutic Process

Though talking about steps or stages in the process of psychotherapy or counseling is somewhat artificial, it is often helpful for the beginning practitioner to keep some sort of model in mind. The model proposed here, shown in Figure 2.2, is based on one by Gottman and Leiblum (1974) and provides a guide for examining how therapy operates in practice. It is worth noting, however, that this model assumes a noncritical situation. The process and skills used in emergency situations may be quite different from those discussed here.

Initial Contact

The initial sessions with the client are extremely important in developing a working relationship and establishing roles and expectations. The first priority is the establishment of *rapport* between client and practitioner. Minimally, rapport exists when there is a "mutuality of purpose in a comfortable relationship" (Sundberg, Tyler, & Taplin, 1973, p. 203; quoted in Phares, 1979, p. 181). As rapport grows, pretense, inhibition, and self-consciousness decrease. As rapport grows, mutual trust, emotional expression, and the willingness to risk, on the part of both practitioner and client expressing thoughts and feelings that could be viewed by the other as negative or hostile, increase. Before client and practitioner can move out of this initial contact stage, minimal rapport must be established. Rapport continues to grow as the therapy progresses and is facilitated by the relational triad: unconditional positive regard, empathy, and genuineness. The goal of the initial contact sessions is to establish what has been called "the therapeutic alliance" (Horwitz, 1974). Though the clinical skills

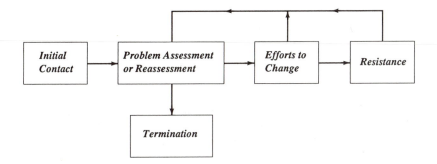

Figure 2.2 *Steps in the therapeutic process* (Adapted from Gottman and Leiblum, 1974)

necessary for forging this alliance depend on the individual personalities involved, some guidelines for this part of the process can be identified.

In the initial sessions of rapport development, the practitioner should allow clients to reveal themselves in their own ways, using their own language. The practitioner suspends judgment, suspends disbelief, and focuses on getting the client to communicate those experiences she or he sees as crucial. The practitioner minimizes the use of questions; this is not the time to learn the details of what has happened. Rather, through verbal and visual cues, the practitioner lets the client know that the practitioner is listening to and understanding what the client is saying and that the practitioner is willing to help him or her make constructive changes. The practitioner focuses on the emotional content of what the client is saying as well as on the factual content.

The practitioner is not passive. On the contrary, the role of the practitioner is to listen and reflect, behaviors that are very real and quite active. To listen actively is to hear not only what is being said but also the emotional tone in which it is said. Reflection involves accurately restating what the client has said, preserving both intellectual and emotional content. Through careful listening and reflection, the practitioner comes to know and empathize with the client, while demonstrating that knowledge and empathy to the client. Additionally, the practitioner and client develop a common understanding of what has happened and a common language for talking about it. Active listening requires an intensity that involves gestures, words, and tone of voice—all of which, since clients differ, must vary with the individual client. Skills important to this period of initial contact are best obtained through supervised training lest they become stylized and mechanical.

Some special demands of this therapeutic step deserve mention. During this initial period of psychotherapy or counseling, it is important to be attentive to the use of questions. Beginning practitioners tend to want to ask a string of questions during these early sessions. While the practitioner wants clear and accurate information, questions have inherent problems. The responsibility for revealing the problem belongs with the client. Questions tend to lead the client in particular directions and, often, reveal more about the practitioner than they do about the client. True, some details must be obtained by direct questioning. But such a strategy should be the exception and not the rule. Later, during assessment, detailed questions will become the norm, but by that time a working rapport will exist. Asking a lot of questions early in counseling may lead the client to expect and depend on questions to reveal information. When the practitioner quickly runs out of questions, the client is left hoping the practitioner will figure out what to ask! Other clients may see questioning as interrogation. Rapport is built on declarative sentences that assert the practitioner's willingness and ability to become involved in the client's demoralized reality, a complex reality that must be communicated by the client as he or she is experiencing it. Questioning as a pattern of interaction rarely, if ever, gets at that experience.

The initial contact period, whether it lasts for one session or five, is also a time to learn some of the client's expectations. The client's expectations about the process and outcomes of therapy must be explored, and practitioner and client must reach some mutual understanding. After a working rapport has been established, after the steps in the therapy have been explained to the client, after the client and practitioner have mutually declared their willingness to work together for the benefit of the client, then assessment begins.

Assessment

In general terms, clinical assessment refers to the process of determining the psychological status of the client. Determining the psychological status of the client involves identifying one or more of the following: patterns of external behavior; patterns of interpersonal activity; unrealized or partially realized perceptions of the self, others, or both; real, imagined, or unconscious conflicts, needs, or desires; and, possibly, an appropriate descriptive label or diagnostic category for the client or the behavior. The means of assessment may include oral, written, biological, or observational measures. While the term *assessment* is often used interchangeably with *diagnosis* or *psychodiagnosis,* it can be argued that assessment without a traditional diagnosis is possible (Brenner, 1982). In other words, a practitioner can assess a person's psychological well-being without assigning the client or the behavior a diagnostic category or label.

Clinical assessment is commonly an integral part of therapy and counseling, although there is considerable variation in its practice and disagreement about the extent of its usefulness. Indeed, practitioners of various persuasions argue cogently against extensive use of clinical assessment. Humanistic-existential practitioners see heavy use of psychological testing as reductionistic, relegating the complex person to the narrow confines of a diagnostic category.

Many have argued that the results of a battery of tests tend to become dispositional labels that trap the client into a diagnostic category, thus creating expectations about the client's behavior that are not warranted. The client's personal identity is replaced by a label, and the client becomes "a person with repressed anger," "a neurotic," "a borderline personality," "hypomanic," "schizophrenic," or "mentally retarded." Given a diagnosis and its attendant prognosis, practitioners may narrow their perception and behavior, letting them be shaped by expectations. Behavioral practitioners object to the fact that psychodiagnosis leads to the establishment of permanent, internal personality constructs as explanations of behavior. The dispositional orientation of a typical diagnosis does not fit traditional behavioral paradigms. Beyond these considerations, as Eysenck, Wakefield, and Friedman (1983) have noted, the diagnostic categories in use by most practitioners and mental health institutions, defined in the *Diagnostic and Statistical Manual of Mental Disorders* (DSM–III) (American Psychiatric Association, 1980), have not been scientifically derived, and the reliability of diagnoses using the categories of DSM–III are suspect.[3]

Minimal Goals of Assessment

Though psychological assessment can lead to unproductive and restrictive categorization of a client's behavior, assessment procedures can also provide a picture of the client's problems that can shorten the intervention process and help practitioners avoid using inappropriate procedures. A variety of assessment techniques exist, and a practitioner may use just a few or many of these procedures. Whether the assessment methods are highly formalized, as in the administration of many tests, or less formalized, as in a conversational question and answer session, several issues related to the client's problem should be addressed as fully as possible before beginning intervention.

Biological or behavioral? Though *mind* and *body* are convenient distinctions, the real world of clients' problems rarely yields such discrete categories. As our awareness of the complex relationship between biology and behavior increases, practitioners are being called upon to understand and utilize the findings, assessment procedures, and research methodologies of psychobiology and related fields (G. E. Schwartz, 1978).

One of the first things the assessor must know is the degree to which the cause of the client's distress is essentially biological or behavioral. This is rarely an easy distinction to make because of the complex interaction between the biological with the behavioral. In some cases, a client's inability to deal effectively with environmental stressors produces physical symptoms, for example, in psychophysiologic disorders. At other times, physical conditions produce behavioral manifestations that *appear* to be primarily psychological in nature—

[3]DSM–III is now DSM–III–R. It was revised in 1987 (American Psychiatric Association, 1987).

hyperthyroidism, for example, resembles anxiety, and biochemical depression resembles situational depression. Some problems are clearly medical; that is, they require the attention of a physician. Later, psychological help of some sort may benefit the client. Other problems are more clearly behavioral and are more appropriately dealt with by someone with training in counseling or psychotherapy. Still other problems may have multiple causes and require formal medical *and* psychological treatment. The point here is that knowing the degree to which the problem should be treated behaviorally or medically is absolutely necessary for appropriate treatment. Eight months of the best psychotherapy will not shrink a tumor; all the Elavil in the world will not create security in interpersonal relationships.

Understanding the client's history and culture   Though finding out about that early trauma involving Uncle Hans and the German shepherd may no longer be necessary, it is important to look at critical situations in the client's experience and to develop an understanding of the various levels of culture that the client has experienced. Very often clients have specific hypotheses about how their distress came about. There was the fire at age 7; there was the death of a parent at 12; there was the attempted rape at 14; there was the rejection by one's peers during high school; there was a cold, uncaring father and a self-seeking, absent mother; there was the illness, the car accident, the love affair, the court case, the evil professor! Clients have hypotheses—some correct, some not, most oversimplified, but all helpful to the practitioner. Sometimes clients' hypotheses are more general: "I'm this way because my parents were this way." "I'm this way because of the neighborhood I grew up in." It is important, therefore, to know the client's history, real and fanciful, coupled with as complete an understanding of the culture as possible. More immediately, why is the client coming for help? Is he or she seeking counseling voluntarily or being forced, either directly or by emotional blackmail? How does the client feel about being in the position of needing help? How does the client envision the "finished product" fitting in with her or his significant others? These can be critical bits of information in successful therapy.

Identifying specific behavioral manifestations   Clinical assessment is aimed at identifying as specifically as possible the symptoms or behaviors through which the client's distress is being manifested. Here the practitioner is looking to determine the frequency, intensity, and/or duration of any maladaptive thoughts, feelings, or actions, and in what situation(s) that behavior is likely to occur. To know a client is "shy" is one thing; to know in what specific situations she or he exhibits shyness, what sorts of physical states accompany it, and what thoughts go into the inhibition of action is quite another. Clients' descriptions of their problems are often vague and imprecise. Assessment procedures can answer questions of degree, kind, frequency, cognitive involvement, and formation. Manifestations of the often vague problems of the client may be found by noting the frequency and intensity of certain events, monitoring electrical activity, analyzing the blood or urine, observing the client in a new situation, or using a host of other methods for moving beyond the descriptions of the client. Increasingly, practitioners are using prepared forms to monitor deficient or excessive behavior (Cautela, 1977, for example, provides a volume of such forms). Additionally, assessment, intervention, and outcome evaluation can be integrated using self-monitoring techniques, direct observation, and other means of specifying behavioral manifestations (Barlow et al., 1984). The goal of assessment is to do justice to the complexity of the person by moving beyond general expressions of the problem to specific behavioral manifestations so that self-regulatory efforts can be initiated.

Clinical assessment thus answers some very basic questions, as well as fleshing out conversations the practitioner has had with the client during the initial contact period. Clinical assessment can also be a shortcut in the therapeutic process. If the practitioner uses effective measures expertly and judiciously and avoids overgeneralization, assessment can reduce the length and, thus, the cost of the therapy. Many practitioners, of course, would argue for significantly more assessment and much more encompassing goals. Psychological assessment is often viewed as predictive, and indeed there is reason to believe that some psychological tests serve as successful predictors of future behaviors. Additionally, some psychological measures and evaluation tools can be helpful in explaining things to clients. Careful explanations of assessment results can help clients concretize their experience and can provide insights that can further benefit them. What is described above are minimal goals.

Assessment Techniques

Phares (1979) describes four varieties of assessment techniques: the interview, life history data, tests, and situational observation. A brief look at each follows.

The interview An interview is an interaction between two persons that is overseen by one of them, the interviewer. The purpose of an interview may be to benefit the interviewee (a *clinical interview*) or to benefit the interviewer (a *research interview*). Of particular interest to us is the clinical interview. Phares (1979) points out that "all forms of professionally executed interviews are devoid of one feature that characterizes normal conversation. Interviewers are not using the interview to achieve either personal satisfaction or enhance prestige. They are using it to elicit data, information, beliefs, or attitudes in the most skilled fashion possible" (p. 167). Though there are a number of different types of interviews, we will concern ourselves with the type of interview designed to provide an historical profile of the client, a description of the complaint and its history, data about relatives, a catalog of important experiences, and other information pertinent to the client's problem. An interviewer may use questions, open-ended statements, or a combination of both to gather information. The interviewer is attentive to all kinds of physical cues: diverted eyes, handwringing, fluctuations in tone, and the like. The interviewer defines the situation to the interviewee as an information-gathering session, one that will ultimately benefit the interviewee. Therefore, the interviewer may take notes or record the session (with the client's permission). Some practitioners have shortened the interviewing process by providing the client a fairly thorough questionnaire to be answered at home. Such a questionnaire would include basic data (address, phone, marital status, education), clinical data (duration of problem, description of severity), historic and family data (occupations, siblings), sexual history, and the like. The use of a questionnaire saves time and money, and with many clients such a technique helps reduce anxiety. A questionnaire does not obviate an interview, but it does reduce the time needed. When minimal rapport has been established, a careful discussion during the interview of the client's answers to the questionnaire may yield rich clinical data.

Life history data   As noted above, valuable developmental information can be gathered by using a questionnaire. This can be supplemented by having the client provide a written or oral autobiography. Medical, legal, and educational documents may also prove helpful at times (Phares, 1979).

Tests   Most of the tests used in assessment can be described as either *projective* or *objective*. Tests that use projective techniques derive from the psychodynamic tradition in psychiatry and psychology. Wolman (1973) defines a projective technique as a "method used to discover an individual's attitudes, motivations, defensive maneuvers, and characteristic ways of responding to unstructured, ambiguous stimuli" (p. 291). Projective tests range from the inkblots of the Rorschach test to the narration of stories about pictures in the Thematic Apperception Test to drawings of a person, house, tree, or family. Some tests ask clients to describe faces, arrange pictures, or complete sentences. The basic assumption underlying these tests is that important psychic information (areas of conflict, self-perceptions, perceptions of others and of relationships, needs, desires, and so on) exists that the client is either unable or unwilling to provide. Projective tests may have a place in the assessment battery used by practitioners, but they also present dangers. Since projective tests require interpretation by the practitioner, they are sometimes more reflective of the conflicts, perceptions, and theoretical preferences of the practitioner than of the motivations, conflicts, and needs of the client. In addition, with some clients, the "hidden" information revealed by the tests is well-known and readily shared by the client. Still, projective tests can yield rich insight into the inner workings of the client, insights that often promote growth and maturity. Some of the potential problems with projective techniques can be avoided by using them in conjunction with interviews and objective measures and interpreting the results in a double-blind procedure with another professional.

Objective tests derive from psychology's long involvement with the quantification of behavior. Objective tests provide a numerical value according to which the client can be grouped or ranked. Though objective tests are quite diverse, practitioners most often use tests that measure intellectual functioning, personality traits, or psychopathology. Examples of each of these types follow.

The most widely used and most respected instruments for measuring intelligence are the Wechsler Intelligence Scales (Wechsler, 1958), which include these tests: the Wechsler Adult Intelligence Scale—Revised (WAIS-R), the Wechsler Intelligence Scale for Children—Revised (WISC-R), and the Wechsler Preschool and Primary Scale (WPPSI). Measures of intelligence and their uses have been controversial, but many practitioners feel that the WAIS, for example, yields valuable information about intellectual functioning in a number of different areas (such as comprehension of words, arithmetic skill, and ability to understand causal relationships) and, combined with other tests and experienced interpretation, reveal much more information about the client than that two- or three-digit number called an "I.Q." Such information can be critical: A client's intellectual strengths and weaknesses are sometimes directly related to the types of clinical strategies selected by the practitioner.

Measures of personality traits or characteristics can also be helpful in understanding the client. R. Meyer (1983) has argued that the most useful of these for assessment is the Cattell Sixteen Personality Factors Questionnaire, commonly referred to as the "16 PF" (Cattell, Eber, & Tatsuoka, 1970). Solidly researched and widely used, it measures relatively permanent aspects of personality, or traits, as well as conflicts. The 16 PF comes in several forms but typically consists of 187 items. The results indicate the relative strength of 16 polar traits, for example, reserved versus outgoing, lower ego strength versus higher ego strength, shy versus venturesome, and group adherence versus self-sufficiency. The 16 PF exemplifies a measure capable of providing a useful profile of a client's characteristic ways of thinking, feeling, and acting.

Still other psychometric tests measure psychopathology and provide a basis for assigning a diagnostic label. The most widely used of these tests is the Minnesota Multiphasic Personality Inventory, commonly called the "MMPI" (Hathaway & McKinley, 1951). The MMPI is a diagnostic instrument consisting of 566 true-false items. The measure is one of the most widely used and researched tests ever developed and provides a profile of the client according to 10 major scales (for example, hypochondriasis, paranoia, hypomania, and social introversion). The MMPI has been in use for over 40 years and has been used in thousands of studies. Many newer instruments evaluate their effectiveness by comparison with the MMPI. Though the MMPI may not be a good means of discrete diagnostic classification, a client's profile can be compared with the profiles of psychiatric patients to predict later behaviors like suicide or homicide. Such comparison, along with scoring the test, can be done quickly and reliably, on a computer. Using both the standard scales of the MMPI and the numerous research scales that have been developed, a practitioner can obtain relatively thorough descriptions of the client.

There are many other tests like those noted above, each designed to measure some trait, attitude, disorder, or the like. As outlined by R. Meyer (1983), a minimal diagnostic battery of tests might include the WAIS, the 16 PF, and the MMPI, for use in categorizing a client's problem according to the DSM–III.

A more typical battery for thorough assessment might augment these and other objective measures with one or two projective tests.

The increased use of computers for testing, scoring, and profiling holds both promise and foreboding. Great amounts of information can be accurately derived, integrated, and profiled, and elaborate and official-looking reports swiftly generated. The caveat remains: Psychological tests, no matter how impressive the computer graphics or how elaborate the printout, serve only as clues to the complexity of the client.

Situational observation The vast majority of the projective and objective tests used in clinical work measure some aspect of personality, a fact that indicates an emphasis on traits, or characteristic ways of thinking, feeling, and acting. In contrast, behaviorally oriented practitioners emphasize behavioral assessment over personality assessment.

Behavioral assessment techniques are characterized by an emphasis on actually observing behavior rather than on inferring motivations or historical causes. The client is observed or monitored in vivo, in a real-life situation. Goldfried and Lineham (1977) have explained that behavioral assessment focuses on determining what adaptive and maladaptive performance capabilities exist in the client's behavioral repertoire. Generally, behavioral assessment takes place in one of two ways: direct observation or interview (Kalish, 1981). The client or those around the client record the frequency of targeted behaviors and the conditions under which the behaviors occur. At times, experimental conditions are set in order to determine the potential of certain intervention techniques (Kalish, 1981). Where direct observation is not possible, interviews may be used to gather the same information. The essential factor is that *specific behaviors* are monitored in *specific situations* by the client or some other observer. Quantitative data on the frequency of the behaviors and the conditions under which they occur provide a baseline for monitoring improvement.

Through the interviews, historical data, tests, and situational observation, the practitioner is provided with tools for assessment and reassessment. Until recently, the idiographic goal of the practitioner, with its concern for individual behavior, and the nomothetic goal of the researcher, with its concern for accurate measurement and generalization, may have been irreconcilable. Specific behaviors across a population sample could be measured experimentally, but the experimental measurement of an individual's behavior over time seemed impossible. Recently, however, with the emphasis on behavioral assessment growing, researchers have developed the experimental method called **single-case experimental design** (Barlow et al., 1984; Hersen & Barlow, 1976; Kratochwill, 1978). Although these assessment strategies come out of a theoretical orientation that some practitioners may consider too narrow because it focuses on the quantification of identifiable behaviors, such strategies increase a practitioner's concrete information about the client and provide an indicator of change as well as a basis for research. Chapter 4 will provide specifics about single-case experimental design. Assessment within the eclectic model proposed here suggests the use of a number of assessment techniques in accordance with the nature of the problem, the needs and expectations of the client, and the practical limits of cost, time, and personnel.

Efforts to Change

As Figure 2.2 shows, the third step in the psychotherapeutic process is applying specific psychological techniques designed to change behavior. The eclectic model of self-regulation and maturity suggests a variety of strategies fitted to the specific needs of the client. Generally, clients whose problems involve initiating, eliminating, or modifying some pattern of action, thought, or feeling will respond well to specific, self-regulatory change strategies with measurable outcomes. Some clients' problems may require more than self-regulation and concern maturity—again, the increasing capacity to learn from and contribute to human existence because of improved understanding, acceptance, and determination. In these cases, a practitioner's approach should be more conversational, more improvisational, and less directed toward specific behaviors. Of course, individual clients rarely fit into only one part of this model. Rather, both components are usually involved, and effective change efforts will both improve self-regulation and enhance maturity.

As a preliminary to beginning the work of change, many practitioners find it helpful to formalize an agreement with their clients, specifying short- and long-term goals and, where appropriate, criteria for evaluation. For example, a client who has insomnia may establish as a short-term goal being able, after 10 therapy sessions using biofeedback and autosuggestion techniques, to relax sufficiently to fall asleep within 15 minutes after going to bed. Long-term goals, which concern general adaptive patterns, may be more difficult to specify, but definite dates for evaluating a client's progress can be set. Whether such an agreement is oral or written depends on the situation, the therapeutic approach, and the preferences of the practitioner and client, but if a formal written contract is not used, the practitioner should keep a record of the goals and time frames that are set.

Resistance

Since the idea of changing problematic behavior is more attractive than actually doing it, both clients and practitioners tend to resist it. Like all cultures, the therapeutic relationship tends toward low entropy; after rapport has been established a certain comfortableness and predictability take over, and the practitioner and client may find it easy to talk about things without pushing for change. It is the practitioner's primary responsibility to use persuasive skills and personal honesty to keep resistance from occurring.

The concept of resistance has its origin in Freud's psychoanalysis. Either consciously through *suppression* or unconsciously through *repression,* people avoid psychic materials that would cause anxiety if brought into the open. The psychoanalyst's goal, therefore, is to identify resistance, call it to the attention of the client, and discover why resistance exists in this client. Further, the client and the practitioner work through the resistance over a sustained period of time (Strupp, 1971, pp. 28–29). At times, the client is completely ignorant of the resistance and the reasons for it. At other times, he or she is partially aware of it, and sometimes, the resistance is purposeful. Some manifestations of client resistance include external behaviors like missing or coming late to sessions, telling irrelevant stories, elaborate use of humor, creating unreal problems, and focusing on the practitioner's life. The client may also get into the circular phenomenon of discussing the same topic each week or reliving the same emotional trauma.

Why do the clients resist? Sometimes, the issues at hand are just too painful or too embarrassing to discuss and so are avoided, at least temporarily. At other times, the problem lies in conflict between what the client would like to do and what the client believes others expect. Take, for example, a client who behaves obnoxiously at social events. Because such behavior has made her a social outcast among her peers, the client wants to change. Unfortunately, others in the client's life have come to expect that behavior. Also unfortunately, the client cannot predict how others will respond if she does change. From the client's perspective, choosing to continue self-defeating behavior to which the response is known is sometimes less threatening than trying new behavior that may find an even worse reception.

Some resistance has to do with the relationship between the client and practitioner. Given an unconditionally positive, genuine, and empathic relationship, a client often is afraid of disappointing or alarming the practitioner with some new memory, impulse, feeling, or act. Gottman and Leiblum (1974) point out some additional things that can happen. The client may fall in love with the practitioner and resist out of a desire to be loved back. The client may suspect that the practitioner is allied with significant others in the client's life and may resist because of that suspicion. In fact, the client may no longer really trust the practitioner but, because of role expectations, may maintain an external appearance of cooperation while resisting any real progress. Whether caused by love, hate, suspicion, doubt, fear, worry, or distrust, such resistance provides valuable information about how the client relates interpersonally. The relationship between the practitioner and the client is a microcosm of the way in which the client deals with relationships in everyday life.

Another form of resistance is practitioner resistance. Naturally, a very insecure, lazy, confused, or stupid practitioner can be so self-absorbed that resistance occurs because the intervention is not really focused on the client's priorities but on the practitioner's. More often, though, well-trained and well-motivated practitioners experience resistance for other reasons. The practitioner may realize that a certain insight is likely to hurt or anger the client and be uncertain how to respond to the client's anger or sadness. Or perhaps the practitioner perceives some larger issue toward which therapy should be working but is insecure about dealing with such a problem. Then again, the practitioner may be displeased with the client and reluctant to say so. Or the practitioner may have fallen head over heels in love with the client, a difficult position from which to conduct therapy.

Recognizing resistance should send the client and practitioner back to re-assessment to determine what strategies may improve the process. Eventually, of course, reassessment leads to termination.

Termination

Termination is hardly a perfect word to describe the end of psychotherapy—ideally, a new beginning for the client and the launching of a renewed person into a more independent and satisfying life. Appropriate or not, however, *termination* refers to the decision, one-sided or mutual, to stop counseling or therapy.

From one perspective, given the fact that we can always become more mature, more psychologically adaptive, psychotherapy need never end. Once the truly maladaptive behaviors are gone, we could spend a lifetime growing further. But, though prolonged therapy has some merit, it is neither realistic nor advisable for most people—if only for reasons of finance. More compelling reasons have to do with the focus required by therapy. Psychotherapy and counseling aim at making individuals more mature, and the process of maturing psychologically (self-actualizing) is characterized by decreasing self-consciousness and self-absorption. Psychotherapy and counseling, on the other hand, necessarily require a certain degree of self-consciousness, of preoccupation with the self. Ideally, we all grow psychologically throughout our lives and (for the most part) outside of the context of professional psychological assistance. Psychotherapy and counseling involve a certain degree of dependence. The client comes to rely on the practitioner, and if the process really works, the dependence eventually becomes mutual—that is, interdependent. Interdependent relationships are mutually supportive and characterized by affection, *not* fee-for-service. When the client has the resources to move beyond the support of therapy, when the client has achieved a self-regulated life and is engaged in living that furthers maturity, the client should leave therapy. Of course, this does not mean that clients cannot return. Clients may need occasional reassurance, assistance, or insight, but generally, life is best lived outside the context of therapy.

As Figure 2.2 shows, the process of psychotherapy sometimes ends immediately after clinical assessment. Either the client or the practitioner decides to terminate, usually because the client has decided to postpone working on his or her problems or because the practitioner has decided to refer the client to another, more appropriate professional (a neurologist, biofeedback expert, or family therapist, for example).

Ideally, of course, termination follows successful completion of the therapy process, but the ideal scenario—the client and practitioner mutually agree that the client no longer needs therapy and part with satisfaction—very well may not be the norm. Sometimes the client stops therapy believing, despite opposition from the practitioner, that it is no longer needed. Usually, in such cases, the client's situation has improved somewhat, enough to satisfy the client for the time being. Sometimes the client quits because the practitioner is simply inadequate—or too abrasive, too passive, too friendly; the practitioner fails, for whatever reason, to meet the client's needs or expectations. And sometimes the practitioner refers the client elsewhere, because the client, the practitioner, or both agree that it would be best for the client.

Summary of Chapter 2

This chapter examines various aspects of the therapeutic process, including the context in which therapy occurs, the dual nature of psychotherapy, variables common to most therapeutic approaches, and the steps of the process. The major ideas covered are:

The Context

1. The client comes to the process of therapy with a cultural history that has provided a variety of ready-made strategies for coping with life. The client has acquired and been shaped by language, myths, rituals, customs, and other expressions of culture from the family culture, and all the other agencies that maintain the culture (government, religion, education, and so on).
2. The client's family, itself a product of the cultures surrounding it, is built to maintain itself; that is, it, like all cultures, is designed for low entropy. This means that the client's culture often operates to sustain problems rather than letting change occur. Some cultures are designed to limit the client's ability to change.
3. One way to evaluate a culture is to look at it in relation to Ruth Benedict's synergy model. According to the synergy model, a culture is high in synergy to the degree that the actions of the group maintain or enhance the well-being of the individual and vice versa. Cultures that are low in synergy are detrimental to the individual and may cause or maintain maladaptive patterns of behavior.
4. In accordannce with social learning theory, the client's relationship to the environment is defined as reciprocal: The environment (culture) creates behavior, and individual behavior in turn creates the environment (culture). The client, because of life situations or because of personal traits developed over a lifetime, does not have the ability to cope successfully with the demands of the environment. This inability causes *demoralization,* a sense of powerlessness common to all clients.

The Nature of the Process

5. Psychotherapy is both an art and a science, and the practitioner works as both artist and scientist within the creative process called psychotherapy. As artist, the practitioner's medium is personality. As scientist, the practitioner applies and generates knowledge and techniques drawn from careful research.

6. Art and science share a common purpose—"to render human experience intelligible" (White, 1949, p. 3)—and four common characteristics— honesty, parsimony, duality, and insight. Effective counseling also has these characteristics since it is both an art and a science.

7. The scientist-professional model (the Boulder model) provides for training of the practitioner that reflects both the scientific and artistic aspects of the therapeutic process.

Considerations and Variables

8. The roles of healer and sufferer have a long history in human cultures and are always characterized by some form of psychological influence or persuasion.

9. Key in this process of influence is the relationship formed between the client and the practitioner. An effective therapeutic relationship is one in which *rapport* has been established. This relationship is characterized by *unconditional positive regard, genuineness,* and *empathy.* These conditions are viewed as necessary but not sufficient conditions for effective behavior change in most situations.

10. The process of psychotherapy or counseling involves the enactment of roles and the establishment of expectations. Understanding the roles and expectations that exist is important if the relationship is to prosper. Other variables common to most forms of psychotherapy and counseling are identified and listed.

Steps in the Therapeutic Process

11. The process of individual counseling or psychotherapy takes place in steps: (1) initial contact, (2) assessment, (3) efforts to change, (4) resistance, and (5) termination.

CHAPTER 3

An Intellectual History of Psychotherapy and Counseling

Research is sometimes more than a habit and it requires more than patience. It requires, among other things, an irresistible urge, bolstered up, I think, not so much by curiosity, as by egotism.

E. G. Boring

History is bunk—at least so Henry Ford was reported to have said. Those who agree may be tempted to skip this chapter or rely on the summary. This is ill-advised. A study of the diverse approaches used in contemporary counseling and psychotherapy would be incomplete and terribly confusing without a historical context through which to understand how the ideas and techniques evolved. In the present chapter, I highlight some of the events, persons, and trends that brought us to our current practices. I hope that what may appear at first to be a jumble of conflicting techniques, priorities, and ideas will, when viewed historically, show itself to be the product of logical progressions in intellectual development.

Psychotherapy and counseling are practiced by a variety of professionals with different academic degrees and credentials, including counselors, nurses, psychiatrists, psychologists, and social workers. Each of these professions has its own unique history; each emerges out of unique social, political, and economic conditions. Understanding what is unique to each is helpful in understanding the diversity of job descriptions, titles, income differences, and educational requirements that exist today, but beyond such concerns are historical factors that explain why fields with such different social histories use the same concepts and therapeutic strategies in their practice of psychotherapy and counseling. Practitioners in each of these professions are concerned with helping people change behavior. Therefore, each accepts certain assumptions about the malleability of human behavior, draws on sets of interrelated concepts, and employs many of the same techniques for changing behavior. All practitioners thus draw on a common intellectual history that is different from their professions' social histories. An examination of that common intellectual base will help us understand the diversity and occasional confusion within the practice of psychotherapy and counseling.

Science and Behavior: Basic Issues

Two fundamental issues underlying the scientific study of human behavior have shaped the intellectual history of all practitioners of counseling or psychotherapy. The first issue, vitalism versus mechanism, involves our understanding of the lawfulness of human behavior; the second asks what kind of science of behavior is possible, natural or human.

Vitalism versus Mechanism

In the 18th century, Voltaire challenged the wisdom of his day by pointing out how strange it would be for the little five-foot animals we call humans to act as they pleased while everything else in nature, even the planets, obeyed eternal laws. By the 19th century, this idea had taken root, and scientists were working to discover the lawfulness informing human behavior.

Until the 19th century, religious and philosophical assumptions had made the scientific study of human behavior improbable. Following Descartes and others, the prevailing assumption behind 19th-century thinking was that the human being possessed a rational soul and, like God, did not follow the mechanical laws of the physical world. Involuntary actions followed the laws of nature, but voluntary actions were governed by the mind or soul, which was not physical and not subject to the same predictability as events in the physical world. Even after scientific investigation of the human body became accepted, the belief that some élan vital, or "vital force," produced voluntary human behavior and that this force per se was beyond experimental science remained. Such a position, common in the early 19th century, is known as *vitalism*.

Vitalism can be defined as a "philosophical position that views life and psychological processes as caused and maintained by a living force or agency, separate and distinct from the physical mechanisms of the body" (Brennan, 1982, p. 362). Vitalistic positions explain human action in terms of concepts like free will, thus moving behavior outside of the realm of experimental science, which requires causes and effects that can be understood, predicted, and controlled. Vitalism did not go unchallenged in the 19th century.

The scientific study of human behavior developed in Europe during the second half of the 19th century. As Figure 3.1 illustrates (page 55), the experimental research tradition can be traced to Leipzig, Germany, and the clinical research tradition, to Vienna, Austria. The advent of these two traditions was heralded by a gradual shift from vitalistic assumptions to a new belief about human behavior known as *mechanism*. Mechanism, like vitalism, is a philosophical position. It is based on the assumption that the lawfulness governing the physical also governs our mental experience. Human behavior, from the workings of the nervous system to the most private thought, is held to be inherently lawful, and understanding, predicting, and controlling that behavior, within the realm of science. From the vantage point of the last quarter of the 20th century, this may not seem to be such a radical idea. After all, one version of mechanism would shape psychology in the experimental research tradition, while another version would inform the clinical research tradition. Consider for a moment the following passage from Boring's classic *History of Experimental Psychology* (1950). Here he recounts a meeting among four of the greatest scientists of the 19th century as they plot to subvert the ideas of the previous generation's master scientist, Johannes Müller (1801–1858).

> In 1845, eleven years before Freud's birth, four young, enthusiastic and idealistic physiologists, all pupils of the great Johannes Müller, all later to be very famous, met together and formed a pact. . . . They were, in order of age, Carl Ludwig, who was then twenty-nine, Emil du Bois-Reymond, Ernst Brücke and Hermann von Helmholtz, then twenty-four. They were joining forces to fight vitalism, the view that life involves forces other than those found in the interaction of organic bodies. The great Johannes Müller was a vitalist, but these men were the next generation. Du Bois and Brücke even pledged between them a solemn oath that they would establish and compel the acceptance of this truth: "No other forces than common physical chemical ones are active within the organism." It was in support of this

thesis that Helmholtz, two years later, read and published his famous paper on the conservation of energy, a paper which, along with some by other men, places the origin of this theory in the 1840s. Thirty-five years later, Helmholtz and du Bois at Berlin, Ludwig at Leipzig and Brücke at Vienna saw their aspiration well on its way to complete acceptance. Meanwhile Brücke had acquired a new student named Freud. (p. 708)

This story is more than an account of impassioned, young scientists. Each of these men advanced the science of physiology, and each had profound influence on the people who would shape the science of psychology. The mechanist position, in one form or another, is built into the assumptions of each of the traditions we will be examining. At the same time, the conflict between mechanist and vitalist positions has recurred in a number of forms and is related to a fundamental question about the science of psychology itself: Is psychology a natural science or a human science?

Natural Science or Human Science?

This may appear at first glance to be a rather silly question. Psychology must necessarily be both natural and human. All human behaviors are natural (despite the use of the term *unnatural* to describe certain sexual acts), and psychology, by definition, studies human behavior. Yet, if we look at these terms historically, we see a fundamental problem that has plagued the applications of psychology we know as psychotherapy and counseling.

When we describe psychology as a "natural science," we mean that psychological events, like events in biology, chemistry, and physics, can be understood as variables with measurable relationships with other events. As such, psychological events can be understood, predicted, and controlled by applying the experimental method. The *natural science model* for psychology relies heavily on the assumptions of mechanism. This model has been most clearly articulated in the work of behaviorists like Watson and Skinner, but its basic assumptions have informed mainstream psychology from the very beginning.

In contrast to the natural science model, the *human science model* of psychology views human behavior as essentially different from events in the other natural sciences. The human science model is defined as a "series of assumptions about the definition and the methods of psychology, advocating recognition of the complexity of human motivation and dynamic activity and suggesting that human psychology is qualitatively different from other forms of life" (Brennan, 1982, p. 357). These ideas were evident in Gestalt psychology as well as in the humanistic-existential psychology movement.

The specifics of the argument between advocates of the natural science model and those of the human science model were articulated by the German philosopher Wilhelm Dilthey (1833–1911). Dilthey agreed that an empirical basis for understanding human behavior was necessary and that that understanding should not rely on revelation and pure reason (Polkinghorne, 1983, p. 24). But the methods of the natural sciences he viewed as too restrictive, too artificial. Human beings exist in time and place; each person's history gives his or her behavior a context. Moreover, humans give meaning to behavior. And human beings are creators, builders, institution makers (Polkinghorne, 1983, p. 32). Experimental methods and the assumptions that underlie them fail to do justice to these realities.

Historically, practitioners of psychology, depending on their education and training, have favored one or the other of these two models of science in their study of human behavior. The tension between the two models can be seen in the two traditions that inform contemporary counseling and psychotherapy: the **experimental research tradition** and the **clinical research tradition.**

Psychology's Two Traditions

Contemporary psychology, especially as applied in the therapeutic setting, is a hybrid: It has its roots in the experimental labs of physiologists and physicists and the examining rooms of physicians, as well as in the drawing rooms of philosophers. For the purpose of simplifying what is a rather complex study, we will look at psychology's history in relation to the research methods psychologists have used to study human behavior. As summarized in Figure 3.1, such research methods form two distinct traditions: One can be called the clinical research tradition, and the other, the experimental research tradition. Though this division represents a great simplification, it will provide a structure through which we can examine psychology's history as it relates to psychotherapy and counseling.

After our discussion of mechanism versus vitalism and natural science versus human science, it might be tempting to equate the clinical research tradition with vitalism and human science and the experimental research tradition with mechanism and natural science. There is some justification for doing so, especially with the experimental research tradition, but generally, these are not accurate divisions. Psychologists who define psychology as a human science are not necessarily vitalistic; further, defining psychology as a human science rather than a natural science does not preclude seeing experimentation as imperative. Most importantly, as we will see, it is quite possible for psychologists in the clinical research tradition to be mechanistic. (Remember who Brücke's student was!)

The Experimental Research Tradition

In Philadelphia in 1896, a declaration of some moment was made by James McKeen Cattell, the new president of the recently founded American Psychological Association: "The twilight of philosophy can be changed into its dawn only by the light of science, and psychology can contribute more light than any other science" (Hilgard, 1978, p. 23). This statement, made less than 25 years after the founding of Wundt's first psychological lab in Leipzig, presented a

Experimental Research Tradition	*Clinical Research Tradition*
Methodology: Experimental	*Methodology*: Clinical and survey
Major Topic: Learning	*Major Topic*: Personality
Other Topics: Sensation, perception, psycho-biology	*Other Topics*: Psychopathology, social psychology
Origin: Leipzig, Germany	*Origin*: Vienna, Austria
Founder: Wilhelm Wundt	*Founder*: Sigmund Freud
Dominant School: Behaviorism	*Dominant School*: Psychoanalysis
Period of Greatest Influence: 1920–1960	*Period of Greatest Influence*: 1920–1960

Major Contributions	*Major Contributions*
1. Advancements in the experimental method and statistical procedures	1. The development of interview, projective, psychometric, and other methods
2. Valuable data about the nature of human learning	2. Rich clinical and survey data on intrapsychic life and social behavior, with an emphasis on development
3. Insight into human behavior through comparative research	3. The development of social psychology

Influential Figures	*Influential Figures*
Edward Thorndike	Sigmund Freud
John Watson	Carl Jung
Clark Hull	Alfred Adler
Edward Tolman	Henry Murray
Neal Miller	Karen Horney
Harry Harlow	Gordon Allport
Kenneth Spence	Abraham Maslow
B. F. Skinner	Carl Rogers

Major Contributors to the Integration of the Two Traditions

Albert Bandura	Arnold Lazarus	Neal Miller
John Dollard	Kurt Lewin	Julian Rotter
Albert Ellis	Jules Masserman	Joseph Wolpe

Figure 3.1   *Psychology's two research traditions*

fundamental contention of psychologists in the experiment research tradition: Psychology could be an experimental science like physics and physiology, and it would tackle the ultimate issue: the human mind. In doing so, experimentalists believed, psychology would be capable of answering the great philosophical questions of all ages.

Wilhelm Wundt and Ganzheit Psychology

It is customary to date the beginning of the science of psychology from 1879, the year Wilhelm Wundt (1832–1920) founded the first experimental lab for the study of psychology, at Leipzig, Germany. Our understanding of Wundt's contribution to psychology has been enriched in recent years by scholarly attention to his life and works. We often associate Wundt with structuralism, a school of psychology founded by one of his students, Edward Titchener. But Wundt's psychology is best described using the term adopted by his German students, *Ganzheit,* or "holistic," psychology (Leahey, 1980). Wundt did study consciousness, or mind, and one of his techniques was *introspection.* Introspection involves asking experimental subjects about their immediate experiences and then pooling and comparing their reactions. In addition, beyond introspection, Wundt had a very broad notion of the potential sources for psychological information, including fields of study today called history, anthropology, and comparative psychology (Leahey, 1980). The two ideas that seem to have been emphasized by Wundt's students, however, at least by those who brought Wundt's psychology to the United States, were (1) reliance on the experimental method and (2) the use of introspective techniques to discover the nature of the human mind. The first of these ideas most certainly took hold in the U. S. The second idea, overemphasized and misrepresented by some of his students, simply did not appeal to the pragmatic Americans. It was, in the words of one writer, a "clash of two cultures" (Blumenthal, 1977, p. 13). American psychology accepted Wundt's emphasis on the experimental method as well as his laboratory experiments and apparatus, but much of the complexity and sophistication of his thinking were lost until recent scholarship unraveled it.[1]

Experimental Psychology in America

Anytime a new science emerges, conflicting schools of thought will vie for dominance. Psychology has been no different. Though psychology has matured beyond such factionalism and entered a "postschool" period in its history, its early years were dominated by various schools. A school consists of a group of practitioners of the science who share both common beliefs about what subject matter its scientists should study and how they should study it and a fundamental language for explaining the phenomena being studied. Schools generally have a leader and followers, and members usually live in the same region or come from similar cultures. As Figure 3.2 shows, psychology—specifically the experimental research tradition in American psychology—has had several schools.

When Wundt's students took Ganzheit psychology across the Atlantic, it became known, under the leadership of Edward Titchener, one of Wundt's most influential students, as structuralism. Early 20th-century psychology was

---

[1]Until relatively recently, Wundt's psychology was understood as very molecular—that is, concerned only with the bits and pieces of consciousness with little or no concern for how consciousness or cognition works as a whole and the higher mental processes governing these components. As more of Wundt's original work is being read and translated, however, it appears that Wundt was very much concerned with the principles that unify cognition, as well as deeply involved in the nonexperimental study of social behavior. Much of this material is in his 10-volume *Völkerpsychologie* [Social psychology]. Particularly interesting discussions of Wundt can be found in Blumenthal (1977) and Leahey (1980).

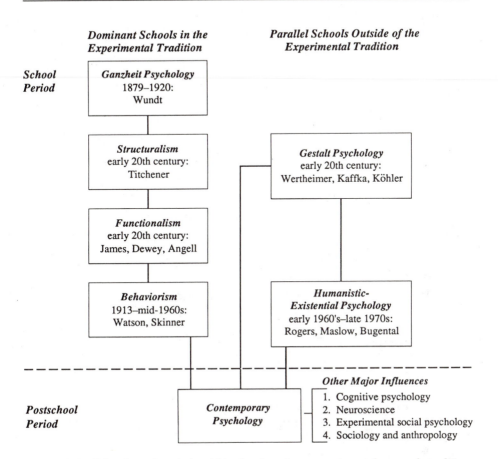

<table>
<tr><td></td><td>Dominant Schools in the
Experimental Tradition</td><td>Parallel Schools Outside of the
Experimental Tradition</td></tr>
</table>

Figure 3.2   *Schools and periods within the American experimental research tradition*

marked by confrontations between structuralists and their opponents, members of the functionalist school. Where structuralists advocated studying the mind directly, through experimentation that utilized introspection, functionalists advocated studying the mind inferentially, by observing and comparing actions and then inferring what took place in the mind. Functionalists considered introspection unreliable. Instead, they emphasized studying how people functioned—that is, how they acted, expressed feelings, expressed ideas, and so forth. Further, drawing on the ideas of Darwinism, functionalists argued that human behavior could be studied comparatively, by making inferences based on experimental research done with animals lower on the evolutionary scale. Functionalism and structuralism both had short lives as schools, although functionalism remains a strong influence in American psychology (Brennan, 1982). As Figure 3.2 shows, the school that would dominate the experimental research tradition in American psychology in the first half of the 20th century and beyond was behaviorism.

John Watson and Behaviorism

Until recently, John B. Watson (1878–1958) was known by most new students of psychology for two things: (1) conditioning an 11-month-old child named Little Albert to be so fearful that he would not go near a bunny rabbit and (2) promising, in a profoundly ominous statement, to turn a dozen infants into whatever he chose! This popular image is far from the complete truth. John Watson was educated as a comparative psychologist at the University of Chicago, a bastion of functionalism. But, in 1913, Watson wrote a paper entitled "Psychology as the Behaviorist Views It" in which he took functionalism one step further. Watson argued that all human behavior could be reduced to physical-chemical processes. Since respondent learning, as described by Ivan Pavlov and Vladimir Bekhterev, was involved in the acquisition of all nonreflexive behavior, careful study of an organism's environment and physiological reactions would show how behavior is produced and ultimately how to control it. Inferences about the "mind" or "consciousness" were unnecessary, he claimed, and, in fact, impeded psychologists' goal of establishing psychology as a natural science.

Beyond these ideas, Watson was a polemicist who took his ideas of a "Better World Through Behaviorism" beyond the confines of the scientific journals. Between 1913 and 1924, when Watson was doing his most serious writing, a scientific answer to the world's problems was not only hoped for but expected. Yet, time and textbook authors have failed to give a full account of Watson's importance, and at least some of his important ideas have been overlooked.

Recently, scholars have tried to unravel what really happened to the famous Little Albert, suggesting that the story as recorded is grossly simplified and improbable (Samelson, 1980, 1981). More importantly, a return to Watson's original documents has revealed some curious details. For example, below is the complete quote from Watson's *Behaviorism* (1924/1970). I have italicized the sentence not usually included in textbooks and other written sources.

> I should like to go one step further now and say, "Give me a dozen healthy infants, well-formed, and my own specified world to bring them up in and I'll guarantee to take any one at random and train him to become any type of specialist I might select—doctor, lawyer, artist, merchant-chief, and, yes, even beggar-man and thief, regardless of his talents, penchants, tendencies, abilities, vocations, and race of his ancestors." *I am going beyond my facts and I admit it, but so have the advocates of the contrary and they have been doing it for thousands of years.* (p. 104)

More directly related to counseling and psychotherapy is Watson's apparent interest in practical applications of psychology, evident in what appears to be a self-regulatory application of behaviorism. Long before the advent of the term *behavior modification,* Watson recounted spending a weekend with a demoralized colleague, predicting, through careful observation, events that would pose problems for his friend. By alerting the man and suggesting some alternative behaviors, he helped him avoid many potentially difficult situations. Watson commented:

> Being an unpsychological person, his relief was obvious and his next hour was his best. Without asking this man to introspect or psychologize or psycho-analyze himself, I could detect his weak spots, his strong points, where he went wrong with his children, where he went wrong with his wife. There can be little doubt but that the behaviorist, by training him both in principles and in particulars, could almost remake this very intelligent individual in a few weeks' time. . . .
> But you may say, "I am not a psychologist—I cannot go following people around telling them to go easy here and hard there." This is true, but has behaviorism nothing to teach you about your own life? . . . So with personal psychology you have to watch other people day by day—you have to systematize and classify your data—throw them into logical moulds—and verbalize your results. . . . This verbal formulation serves you as a stimulus. . . . It may lead to a changed response; for words whether spoken by others or spoken subvocally in your own throat are just as strong stimuli, lead just as swiftly to action, as hurtling stones, threatening clubs and sharp knives. Once you have acquired technical skill in watching the behavior of others, observation of your own behavior becomes much easier. (Watson, 1924/1970, pp. 46–47)

The claims Watson made in the above passage are clearly exaggerations of the facility with which behavioral techniques can be applied, and such overstatements are common in Watson's work. But because Watson's work was highly publicized and because it offered a relatively simple solution to the confusing state of psychology at that time, Watson's ideas gained wide acceptance. Was that of benefit to psychology as a science and as a profession? Many consider Watson's exclusion of the mind and his insistence on the experimental method to have unnecessarily narrowed the scope of psychology. Yet, with the advantage of hindsight, some say the opposite may in fact be true. As Hilgard (1980) has pointed out:

> Watson saw clearly that if consciousness was to be the only subject matter of psychology, with introspection its method, then the study of animals, infants, and mentally disturbed people would be excluded from an exact psychological science because they were either totally incapable of introspection or their introspections could not be trusted. Watson was not trying to narrow psychology; rather he was trying to broaden it. In his textbook, bearing a title similar to that of his paper announcing behaviorism, he stated in his preface that the instructor "should strive to get the beginner to view the organism as a whole as rapidly as possible and to see in the performance of each and all its acts the working of an integrated personality." He included a final chapter on personality and its disturbances in his book, at a time when other general textbooks had not gone that far beyond the laboratory. (pp. 3–4)

With Watson and those who espoused his science of behaviorism, the experimental research tradition became dominated by the following: (1) the exclusive use of the experimental method; (2) exploration of all behavior in terms of the interaction of biological mechanisms and automatic learning, or conditioning; (3) heavy reliance on comparative research (using rats, mice, monkeys, dogs, and cats); and (4) avoidance of any explanations of behavior that included internal concepts like cognition, mind, or consciousness. Clearly, American experimental psychologists, armed with a mechanist philosophy, set out to be natural scientists.

Edward Thorndike and a Science of Learning

Watson founded behaviorism, the philosophy of science and school of psychology. Though Edward Thorndike (1874–1949) may or may not have welcomed the *behaviorist* appellation (Leahey, 1980, p. 295), he founded a practical, experimental study of learning that is very much a part of behaviorism's legacy. Thorndike's doctoral research, written in 1898 and later expanded into his classic *Animal Intelligence* (1911), presented a reinforcement theory of learning that predated similar efforts by Pavlov, a fact acknowledged by Pavlov himself.[2]

Thorndike (1911) argued that though adult human beings may view themselves as "streams of consciousness" or "conscious selves with histories they report by word or deed," the same could certainly not be said for lower animals (pp. 3–4). Further, although consciousness cannot be studied in lower animals, behavior can, and important questions can be answered. When an animal learns a new behavior (for example, escape from a cage), is that instinctual? Does the animal "think the problem out," associating previous experiences with this current one? Thorndike's ingenious experiments provided a lawful explanation of animal learning, an explanation that depended on neither mentalistic concepts nor instinct theory. Although Thorndike recognized that critical differences exist between humans and other animals, he established that humans and infrahuman species share some common laws of learning. He also took his theory and research beyond the lab, applying it in education and other practical matters.

Watson and Thorndike inspired many researchers, and an extensive body of research on learning emerged. The work of Edwin Guthrie, Clark Hull, Edward Tolman, Neal Miller, Kenneth Spence, and others undeniably advanced the science of psychology. Yet, Watson's somewhat utopian applications of this knowledge were never actualized (at least beyond his advertising career), and even Thorndike's numerous educational applications did not spill over into counseling or psychotherapy in any major way. That would be left to Skinner.

B. F. Skinner: Practical Science, Radical Philosophy

B. F. Skinner (born 1904) has been called everything from genius to madman, visionary to dreamer, hero to fool. Indeed, the nature of some of his popular writings (in contrast to his scientific work)—for example, his utopian novel, *Walden II*—has sometimes distracted our attention from what Skinner has ac-

---

[2]According to Lundin (1985), Pavlov acknowledged that Thorndike's work on reinforcement, done independently, predated his own in his *Lectures on Conditioned Reflexes* (1928). Pavlov hailed *Animal Intelligence* (1911) as a classic. In the passage, however, he seemed surprised that in America the work was done by psychologists rather than physiologists.

tually done for most of his professional life. No better description of Skinner can be given than the one he gave himself:

> I have spent a good share of my professional life in the experimental analysis of the behavior of organisms. Almost all my subjects have been below the human level (most of them rats or pigeons). . . . My research has not been designed to test any theory of behavior, and the results cannot be evaluated in terms of the statistical significance of such proofs. The object has been to discover the functional relations which prevail between measurable aspects of behavior and various conditions and events in the life of the organism. The success of this venture is gauged by the extent to which behavior can, as a result of the relationships discovered, actually be predicted and controlled. (Skinner, 1972, pp. 257–258)

Skinner's most important contribution has been his methodical unraveling of the nature of *operant learning,* and the discovery and application of the relationships described above. Yet, he is also widely known for promulgating a brand of behaviorism usually referred to as *radical behaviorism,* a philosophy of science most clearly evident in Skinner's critique of Freud and others in the clinical research tradition.

Unlike some others from the experimental research tradition, Skinner was never comfortable with the concepts and research strategies of the clinical research tradition, and he has written a number of bold essays criticizing them. Freud, of course, has dominated the thinking of the clinical research tradition, and on no other psychologist has Skinner commented more than on Freud (Leahey, 1980). In an essay entitled "A Critique of Psychoanalytic Concepts and Theories," Skinner credited Freud with providing a view of human behavior based on cause and effect relationships and in which the individual's history provides the clue to understanding behavior. According to Skinner, Freud's achievement in this respect "appears all the more impressive when we recall that he was never able to appeal to the quantitative proofs characteristic to other sciences. He carried the day with sheer persuasion—with the massing of instances and the delineation of surprising parallels and analogies among seemingly diverse materials" (Skinner, 1972, p. 239). Skinner also contended, however, that Freud's thinking contained a causal chain: ENVIRONMENTAL EVENT > MENTAL STATE or PROCESS > BEHAVIORAL SYMPTOM (p. 241). Freud focused on that middle part, a state or process that is necessarily internal and about which little can be known directly. Skinner argued that Freud filled this space between environmental events and behavior with a "mental apparatus" comprising elements like id, ego, and superego in order to explain the relationship between past experience and present behavior. But is the apparatus real? Skinner wrote:

> To many followers of Freud the mental apparatus appears to be equally as real [as it was to Freud], and the exploration of such an apparatus is similarly accepted as the goal of a science of behavior. There is an alternative view, however, which holds that Freud did not discover the mental apparatus but rather invented it, borrowing part of its structure from a traditional philosophy of human conduct but adding many novel features of his own devising. (1972, p. 240)

For Skinner, Freud's explanation was an invention, a fabrication of an inner determiner (personality) that provides only a momentary explanation because it cannot be directly observed. The logical step, Skinner asserted, would have been for Freud to accept that conscious events, like unconscious ones, can only be inferred, not observed. Therefore, the science of human behavior should define behavior only in terms of those things that can be directly observed. For Freud to have done so, of course, would have put him in step with that approach "advocated a little later by the American movement called Behaviorism" (p. 242).

Skinner's differences with the dominant ideas of the clinical research tradition are thus fundamental ones. He disputes what clinical researchers study and how they study it, arguing that what should be studied is behavior and its consequences—experimentally, in research settings where all variables can be controlled, manipulated, and/or measured. It is clearly quite a distance from the couch to the bar press.

Though many contemporary practitioners find Skinner's views narrow and reductionistic, we owe Skinner a debt in several respects. First, our ability to modify human behavior through systematic application of the principles of operant learning rests heavily on the work of Skinner and his colleagues. All forms of behavior modification, behavior therapy, and other so-called performance-based therapies depend on Skinner's research and his applications of operant learning. Second, Skinner's goal of establishing "a science of the individual" led him away from the traditional psychological experiment with its use of large groups of subjects (Kazdin, 1978b). Rather, Skinner's experiments with individual animals over extended trials, an unacceptable method when he first introduced it, have provided practitioners with a model for evaluating changes in the behavior of individual clients. The practice of monitoring an individual client's behavior over a specified, extended period and the eventual development of single-case experimental design benefited from Skinner's work, although Skinner never did any clinical work himself.

Skinner represents the most extreme example of an experimental research psychologist. Still, he has helped demonstrate some of the limitations of the clinical research tradition and provided a technology valued in contemporary clinical practice.

Although mainstream American psychology in the experimental research tradition has gone through several schools, it has been essentially committed to the study of learning and its biological bases. Behaviorism appears to have been the dominant school for many years, although its philosophy of science has not always been as explicit as it is in Skinner's writings. Methodology in this tradition has been almost exclusively experimental, with comparative research commonplace. In the name of parsimony, psychologists within this tradition have generally avoided mentalistic concepts (cognition) and studied those overt actions of individuals that can be counted or measured. As we will see later, however, there have always been those within the tradition who sought to study internal processes like cognition and affect, and others who attempted to bring concepts from the clinical research tradition into the ken of experimental psychology. We will turn to that discussion after an examination of the clinical research tradition.

The Clinical Research Tradition

The same European intellectual climate that produced Wundt and the experimental research tradition also gave rise to the clinical research tradition and Freud. Freud's thinking emerged in an age that Robinson (1981) describes as "marvelously contradictory" (p. 378); that is, the major scientific and philosophical influences of the day were filled with apparent contradictions. Science's senior statesman was Helmholtz with his mechanistic, antivitalistic biology. Charles Darwin's theory of evolution was being espoused by many biologists, and with it came the idea that human progress is both inevitable and mechanistic. At the same time, Herbert Spencer was promoting a psychology of instincts. Science was thus deterministic, mechanistic, and reductionistic. On the other hand, philosophy was Hegelian, with psychology seen as concerned with consciousness, that most illusive and global of topics. Wundt's psychology took account of the science of his day and focused on the content of consciousness; yet, his work would not prosper beyond Europe's borders. Freud's psychology was also concerned with consciousness, with the added complexity of the important unconscious. For reasons that will be explained later, Freud's ideas survived numerous transplantings. We turn now to Freud and psychoanalysis.

Sigmund Freud and Psychoanalysis

In 1895, two Austrian physicians named Josef Breuer and Sigmund Freud published *Studies in Hysteria*. This book signaled the beginning of a new way of looking at human behavior, especially maladaptive behavior, and, of equal importance, a new way of changing that behavior: psychotherapy. It also marked the beginning of a new way of doing psychological research: collecting data through extended and probing conversations with clients—one at a time. Josef Breuer (1842–1925), the book's first author, made the initial contribution by developing what would later be called the "talking cure." Of course, it was the book's second author, Sigmund Freud (1856–1939), who introduced a revolutionary theory of behavior and form of psychotherapy, **psychoanalysis,** to the Western world. Chapter 6 presents the specifics of psychoanalysis as theory and therapy and can be referred to now as a preview. For our present purposes, after defining psychoanalysis, we will explore its historical and intellectual context.

Defining psychoanalysis   As Freud (1922/1963b) defined it, psychoanalysis is much more than a theory of behavior or a therapeutic technique. The term psychoanalysis refers to: (1) a philosophical position on the nature of human behavior, especially the human mind; (2) a theory about human personality and its development, especially the development of psychopathology; (3) a technique for therapeutic intervention in cases of psychopathology; and (4) a method of investigating human personality (Brenman-Gibson, 1984, p. 86). Psychoanalysis, has been more than that, however. It has changed Western humankind's view of itself and become one of the reference points against which Western intellectual life gauges itself.

A radical departure   One of the cases from *Studies in Hysteria* illustrates both the new understanding of maladaptive behavior brought about by psychoanalysis as well as its radical departure in the treatment of disorders. This is the case of Katharina, also referred to as "The Girl Who Couldn't Breathe" (Greenwald, 1959, p. 13).

When Freud was in his late 30s, he vacationed in the Alps for the purpose of forgetting medicine, "and more particularly the neuroses" (Breuer & Freud, 1895/1953, p. 125). As fate would have it, upon reaching a breathtaking viewpoint on a particular mountain, the physician was approached by a young woman of 18 who asked, "Are you a doctor, sir?" Katharina, as Freud called her, had seen the guest book at the inn where Freud was staying and wondered if the doctor would have time to discuss her "nervousness" with her. Katharina described numerous symptoms, but her chief complaints were readily identified by Freud as anxiety attacks, a central feature of which was a choking sensation and the inability to breathe. Freud pondered:

> Was I to make an attempt at an analysis? I could not venture to transplant hypnosis to these altitudes, but perhaps I might succeed with a simple talk. I should have to try a lucky guess. I had found often enough that in girls' anxiety was a consequence of the horror by which a virginal mind is overcome when it is faced for the first time with the world of sexuality. (p. 127)

An extended conversation ensued during which Katharina recounted a series of events that she only gradually recalled. The most recent event had taken place two years earlier, at the same time that her anxiety had begun. In brief, Katharina had discovered her uncle and cousin, Franziska, in a decidedly compromising position. Thanks to prompting from Freud, she recalled a series of even earlier events involving herself and the uncle as well as the uncle and Franziska. Freud wrote:

> At the end of these two sets of memories she came to a stop. She was like someone transformed. The sulky, unhappy face had grown lively, her eyes were bright, she was lightened and exalted. Meanwhile the understanding of her case had become clear to me. The later part of what she had told me, in an apparently aimless fashion, provided an admirable explanation of her behaviour at the scene of the discovery. (p. 131)

At this point Freud explained how past experiences and their associations accounted for the onset of Katharina's symptoms at the discovery of her uncle and cousin together. One by one, he explained each symptom, concluding, "I hope this girl, whose sexual sensibility had been injured at such an early age, derived some benefit from our conversation. I have not seen her since" (p. 133).

To be sure, Freud never considered this a complete case, and it took place early in the development of the theoretical foundations and therapeutic techniques of his psychoanalysis. The development of the techniques of **free association** and **dream analysis** would later enhance the psychotherapeutic process. At the same time, the case is illustrative of the origins of psychotherapy as we know it today. Consider the following points:

1. *Psychogenic origin of a "medical" disorder*: Katharina's nervousness is not medical in origin. Past experiences have interacted to cause the symptoms.
2. *Unconscious motivation*: Katharina does not readily remember her past experiences, and when she does remember them, she does not recognize how they interact with one another without the help of the analyst.
3. *The importance of insight*: Through insight based on experience, Freud does understand how the events interact.
4. *The clinician as skilled helper*: Freud helps Katharina by listening carefully, asking questions, and then revealing his understanding to her.
5. *Research by case history*: Katharina's case is like cases Freud has previously encountered, and he is able to apply information gathered from other young women suffering similar symptoms to Katharina. What he learned from this case he can generalize to other similar cases. And all cases contribute to his general theory of neurosis and ultimately his theory of human behavior.

During its early years, psychoanalysis clearly differed from both the medical establishment and the emerging social sciences, and the ideas listed above were radical departures from the current wisdom.[3] Freud established the practice of psychotherapy and the scientific study of personality as we know it today in the face of considerable opposition. He also founded a school of psychological thought and so established new criteria for what constitutes scientific knowledge. Eventually, his ideas came to dominate the clinical research tradition, prevailing until the middle of the 20th century. They continue to exercise great influence over both the process of psychotherapy and major theories of human behavior.

The social and intellectual movement Freud utilized the medical knowledge and language of his day. He also studied anthropology and was especially interested in archaeology, itself a metaphor for the "digging" that goes on in psychoanalysis. Still, Freud's thinking would go well beyond these other disciplines, and eventually, psychoanalysis would influence them. Psychoanalysis

---

[3]Freud's ideas emerged in the Victorian era. The medicine of that time differed from our own both in what passed for science and the role played by the physician. Much attention was given over to unraveling the mysteries of what was called "nervousness." Some of what was then called nervousness we now know to be medical disorders like epilepsy. Other cases we now call "neurosis" or "anxiety disorder." It is in this arena that Freud made his major contribution, and in doing so he changed both the criteria for science and the role of the physician. Yet, it is difficult to fairly evaluate Freud's contribution, as well as its limitations, without knowing the times from which and in which his ideas about neurosis emerged. A scholarly and readable book on the subject is *The Birth of Neurosis: Myth, Malady, and the Victorians* by George Drinka (1984).

was a uniquely independent movement. As Ellenberger wrote in *The Discovery of the Unconscious* (1970):

> With Sigmund Freud, a new feature is seen in the history of dynamic psychiatry. Whereas men such as Pierre Janet kept closely within established learned societies, wrote in journals open to any psychological or medical viewpoint, and never attempted to found a school, Freud openly broke with official medicine. With Freud begins the era of the newer dynamic schools, with their official doctrine, their rigid organization, their specialized journals, their closed membership, and the prolonged initiation imposed upon their members. The founding of this new type of dynamic psychiatry was linked with cultural revolution comparable in scope to that unleashed by Darwin. (p. 418)

Freud faced continuous opposition from colleagues and the public, and defections from among loyal followers were a constant source of pain (Adler and Jung were the most noteworthy). Orthodoxy became a prime concern, and those who deviated from Freud's teachings were often treated to a psychoanalytic explanation of their disloyalty. The letters between Freud and Carl Jung, published in 1974, are most telling in this regard. The letters are filled with mini-analyses that highlight the weaknesses of fellow and former analysts. Alfred Adler, once a promising disciple of Freud, received particular criticism. Consider these comments concerning Adler's editorship of the *Zentralblatt für Psychoanalyse,* an official publication on psychoanalysis. Freud wrote Jung on February 17, 1911:

> The last number of the *Zentralblatt* is a dreadful mess; it is Adler's doing—he and [Wilhelm] Stekel take turns as editor—and very interesting from a psychoanalytic point of view. I complained to Adler, and of course, instead of elucidating the secret motives behind his aberrations, he gave me nothing but lame excuses. (Freud & Jung, 1974, p. 396)

And in June of the same year:

> I have finally got rid of Adler. . . . The damage is not very great. Paranoid intelligences are not rare and are more dangerous than useful. As a paranoiac of course he is right about many things, though wrong about everything. A few rather useless members will probably follow his example. (p. 428)

By the end of 1912, however, the paternal Freud and the dutifully obedient Jung had come to a personal and professional impasse. Jung wrote Freud:

> May I have a few words to you in earnest? I admit the ambivalence of my feelings towards you, but am inclined to take an honest and absolutely straightforward view of the situation. If you doubt my word, so much the worse for you. I would, however, point out that your technique of treating your pupils like patients is a *blunder.* In that way you produce either slaving sons or impudent puppies (Adler-Stekel and the whole insolent gang now throwing their weight about in Vienna). . . . You see, my dear Professor, so long as you hand out this stuff I don't give a damn for my symptomatic actions; they shrink to nothing in comparison with the formidable beam in my brother Freud's eye. I am not in the least neurotic—touch wood! (p. 534)

The correspondence between Freud and Jung reveals both the genius and the limitations of the early psychoanalysts. It also highlights a unique feature of analysis: The theory can also be a weapon. In a 1925 essay entitled "The Resistance to Psychoanalysis," Freud used his theory to explain the failure of his colleagues and others to accept psychoanalysis. After explaining the slow acceptance of psychoanalysis by pointing to the narrowness of psychiatrists, the laziness of physicians, and the obtuseness of philosophers, Freud likened himself to Darwin, whose ideas had also upset the status quo. Freud wrote: "Thus the strongest resistances to psychoanalysis were not of an intellectual kind but arose from emotional sources. This explains their passionate character as well as their poverty in logic" (Freud, 1925/1963c, p. 261). In all of this, of course, is a curious double bind: In rejecting an idea of psychoanalysis we prove it, because our rejection can be explained as resistance covering up our vulnerability to that idea.

Psychoanalysis is a different kind of school than those of the experimental research tradition. Although the orthodoxy Freud initially sought did not prevent numerous variations of psychoanalysis from emerging, Freud left a unique grandness of scope and purpose to the adherents of psychoanalysis. As Fine (1979) has pointed out, recent documents, especially separate correspondences of Freud with Wilhelm Fliess and Jung, have brought to light goals for psychoanalysis well beyond Freud's public utterances:

> In his later writings [Freud] gives some hints about what he thought were the far-reaching effects of psychoanalysis. The strongest theoretical statement came in *The New Introductory Lectures* in 1932, when he said: "Strictly speaking there are only two sciences: psychology, pure and applied, and natural science." By implication he was asserting here that all social sciences represent applications of psychoanalysis. (p. 535)

Psychoanalysis gradually came to influence all practitioners of counseling and psychotherapy. In part, this is due to the quality of its concepts, the comprehensiveness of its scope, and the lack of an equally comprehensive alternative. In addition, the insularity and the mystique that characterized psychoanalysis during its development have aroused both awe and skepticism. Not surprisingly, the skepticism has come primarily from psychologists and other scientists trained in the experimental research tradition. Their question: Is psychoanalysis science?

Is psychoanalysis a science? In its broadest sense, the scientific method is the analysis of empirical data: "Complex events are analyzed into relevant variables, relationships among these variables are investigated, and theories consistent with the empirical results are created and critically evaluated" (Allen, 1984, p. 277). By this definition, psychoanalysis is a science. Psychoanalysts have observed behavior, identified variables, hypothesized relationships among the variables, developed a general theory, and set conditions for testing their hypotheses. Hypothesis testing, however, represents one of several problems with psychoanalysis as a science. The theory is tested clinically; thus, testing depends on verbal interaction between the analyst and the client and on the analyst's interpretation. This creates problems because, in the model, the processes that produce behavior are not observable and resist measurement. Thus, verification depends on the client's subjective report and the analyst's subjective translation of the report into the language of psychoanalysis. Further, when a client confirms an insight garnered through the therapy process and thus verifies some part of the theory, is that real scientific knowledge or an example of the client's susceptibility to the intentional and unintentional suggestions of the analyst? Could it be simply a matter of clients fitting their experiences to the expectations of the psychoanalyst and analysts listening selectively? Fortunately, many of the propositions of psychoanalysis can be and have been tested outside of the clinical setting, although how much practicing analysts use such information is unknown (Fisher & Greenberg, 1977; Luborsky & Spence, 1978). Nonetheless, the difficulties of clearly defining the relevant variables and providing adequate experimental conditions and realistic measures have been persistent problems in the clinical research tradition.

Freud, for his part, wanted to develop a science in the tradition of Helmholtz. Although Freud became a physician because of financial need and because there was a prejudice against Jews in university positions, his first love was clearly laboratory science. His mentor at the Physiological Institute at the University of Vienna had been Ernst von Brücke, who, as noted earlier, was one of those who vowed to overthrow vitalism. Freud's practice of medicine; his association with Breuer, the neurologist Jean-Martin Charcot, and others; and the development of psychoanalysis led him away from physical science, and until recently it was assumed that his early experiences with Brücke had little influence on him (Lowry, 1982). In 1950, however, the letters between Freud and Wilhelm Fliess were published, and they reveal an extended period of preoccupation with creating a neurological model of the human mind. His hope was to establish a neurological substructure for his psychological theory, but though he sent 100 pages of his "Project for a Scientific Psychology" (also called "Psychology for Neurologists") to his friend and fellow physician, Fliess, in 1895, Freud eventually abandoned the project (Fancher, 1973). Freud wrote the "Project for a Scientific Psychology" to "furnish us with a psychology which shall be a natural science: its aim, that is, is to represent psychical processes as quantitatively determined states of specifiable material particles and so to make them plain and void of contradictions" (Freud, 1895/1954, p. 355). As Fancher (1973) has pointed out:

> [Freud's] aim, in short, was to employ his knowledge of neurology in constructing a hypothetical "model of the mind" that could account for neurotic as well as normal mental functioning. His task was not unlike that facing an inventor who seeks to design a robot capable of thinking and behaving like a real human being, except that the inventor would probably design a robot composed of inanimate components instead of nerves and muscles. (p. 63)

Freud's "Project" complements his psychological writings as well as providing evidence of his strong orientation toward the physical science of his day

(Sirkin & Fleming, 1982). Why Freud abandoned the project is unknown; he eventually rejected the entire idea and moved away from articulating a neurophysiology to support his psychological theory.

Whether or not psychoanalysis is considered a science depends on one's definitions and perspective. Certainly its founder was keenly aware of the demands of a science in his own time and was also unafraid to seek truth where disposition and circumstance led him.

Two final thoughts on Freud from this historical perspective. Frankl (1973), quoting Wilhelm Stekel, likens those of us who follow Freud to dwarfs who stand on the shoulders of a giant. We see farther, but only because we stand on his shoulders (p. 3). That leads to truth, however, only if we are facing in the right direction. In the end, Freud demanded of all practitioners what he demanded of himself. As W. H. Auden expressed it in his poem "In Memory of Sigmund Freud": "All that he did was to remember like the old, and be honest like children" (Auden, 1945, p. 165).

The Clinical Research Tradition after Freud

Beginning with Freud, theories of personality and approaches to psychotherapy have often had the same sources. Not uncommonly, practitioners would implicitly or explicitly develop a theory of personality based on clinical observation, and theory and therapy would develop together. For the most part, these approaches were either reactions to Freudian psychoanalysis or developments of it. Figure 3.3 provides a selective listing of the major theories of personality and approaches to psychotherapy that have developed within the clinical research tradition. Though Figure 3.3 is a helpful guide, it is oversimplified. Thus, several very important factors related to this figure and to understanding post-Freudian developments must be noted.

Variants on the tradition Freudian psychoanalysis continues to develop as both a theory and a therapy. Much of this development remains true to the basic tenets of orthodox psychoanalysis. Some developments of psychoanalytic theory, however, have been so significant or so radically different that they have eclipsed the original analytic model, at least for adherents of the newer approaches. This is true of the theories and therapies listed in Figure 3.3. They are no longer included within mainstream psychoanalysis but represent major developments of or reactions to it.

Openness to nonclinical sources Theories and therapies developed after Freud, Adler, and Jung usually showed the influence of sources other than clinical research, as noted in Figure 3.3. Though Freud, Adler, and Jung also used research from other sources—Adler was especially concerned with social conditions, prevention, and other modern notions—adherents of later approaches were less concerned with orthodoxy and maintaining a school and, therefore, allowed themselves to be more influenced by movements outside of the traditional clinical setting. Each thus shows, to varying degrees, an integration of

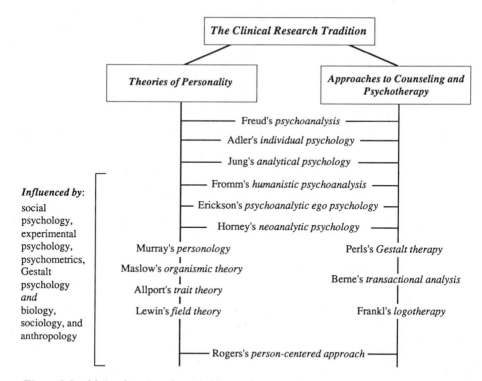

Figure 3.3   *Major theories of personality and approaches to counseling and psychother-apy in the clinical research tradition*

personality study and therapy development with research from experimental psychology, medicine, the social sciences, and/or the physical sciences.

Developments in the study of personality   Some of the major personality the-ories within the clinical research tradition were developed by people who were concerned more with research than with clinical practice. Notable among this group were Gordon Allport, Kurt Lewin, Abraham Maslow, and Henry Mur-ray, all of whom looked at personality from a social-psychological, rather than a psychopathological, point of view.

Gordon Allport (1879–1967) was one of the great social psychologists, and besides developing a major theory of personality based on traits, he also re-searched topics as diverse as rumor, radio, religion, and prejudice. He was crit-ical of both the strict experimentalists and the psychoanalysts, but he under-stood and appreciated their contributions. Kurt Lewin (1890–1947) brought the influence of Gestalt psychology to the study of personality and contributed many valuable insights into the nature of psychology as a science. Abraham Maslow (1908–1970), who began his career as a comparative psychologist, de-veloped a personality theory based on needs that stressed the development of the person beyond the mere absence of pathology. Like Allport, Maslow was equally at home and ill at ease in both the experimental and clinical traditions; though he is remembered as one of the major forces in the humanistic reaction to behaviorism and psychoanalysis, he saw himself as integrating them rather than overcoming them. Henry A. Murray (born 1893), physician, biochemist, and personality theorist, also developed a personality theory utilizing the concept of need and combined Freudian thinking with social research and humanistic concern.

In general, Allport, Lewin, Maslow, and Murray, as well as many others, differed from traditional contributors to the clinical research tradition in the following ways: (1) They placed greater emphasis on the social conditions that produce behavior and accepted many of the findings of experimental research on learning; (2) they developed a variety of new objective personality tests (and some projective tests) that could be used to survey the attitudes, values, and opinions of both clinical and nonclinical populations; (3) they relied increasingly on statistical analyses of results; and (4) they were open to research outside of their disciplines and emphasized integration rather than theoretical orthodoxy.

This period of personality studies and social-psychological research between the 1930s and the late 1960s (when an experimental social psychology emerged) was a very productive one. It was the beginning of the gradual rapprochement that would occur when the experimental method was applied in research that had been traditionally clinical and social.

Developments in psychotherapy   Each of the major therapeutic approaches that developed within the clinical research tradition will be examined later in this book, but a few historical comments might serve us well at this point. The internecine conflicts among Freud, Adler, Jung, and their followers often obscure the real contribution of each. At the risk of seriously understating their contributions, I submit that each advanced the study of personality and psychotherapy in the following ways. Freud gave us a comprehensive theory of human behavior that allowed us to see the role of the unconscious, the nature of intrapsychic conflict, and the importance of sexuality. He also gave us a working therapeutic approach that included both general procedures and specific techniques. Carl Jung (1875–1961) opened up the spiritual side of human experience and integrated it with psychotherapy, as well as introducing concepts of growth and potentiality to the study of personality. Alfred Adler (1870–1937), perhaps the most practical, gave us a view of human behavior as purposeful, socially significant, and reliant upon conscious decisions. His ideas about prevention, early intervention, therapy with children, and the psychology of women are so widely accepted today that we no longer bother to attribute them to Adler; transmitted through his lectures, books, and personal influence on others, much of Adler's thinking is now considered "common sense psychology."

The contributions of Eric Berne, Erik Erikson, Erich Fromm, Karen Horney, and Fritz Perls were clearly within the psychoanalytic tradition and represent a variety of modifications both of theory and therapy. In general, however, they all: (1) place less emphasis on the unconscious, (2) place more emphasis on the interpersonal, and (3) recommend more active approaches to psychotherapy. Viktor Frankl, William Glasser, and George Kelly represent even more distinct contributions. We will examine some of the above contributions in later chapters.

The unique contribution of Carl Rogers   The person-centered therapy of Carl Rogers (1902–1987), at first called *client-centered therapy,* will be treated extensively in later chapters. Yet, the historical importance of Rogers is noteworthy because he produced a radical shift in the philosophy, procedures, and techniques of large numbers of practitioners. As Figure 3.4 summarizes and Chapter 8 details, Rogers challenged the basic therapeutic model of Freud's psychoanalysis. He did so on both philosophical and scientific grounds. Instead of emphasizing unconscious determinants of behavior, Rogers understood motivation to be conscious and purposeful. He replaced insight coming from the therapist with self-understanding by the client that results in the client becoming a fully functioning individual. The client's changes are only facilitated by the therapist, specifically by a relationship between the therapist and client characterized by unconditional positive regard, genuineness, and empathy. Such a relationship promotes responsible behavior. Rogers's clear articulation of the central importance of this specific type of relationship remains one of the few widely accepted canons in contemporary counseling and psychotherapy. Whether practitioners acknowledge it or not, most use concepts and procedures drawn from Rogers's work as part of their day-to-day practice of counseling and psychotherapy.

Major Influences on the Two Traditions

Contemporary approaches to psychotherapy and counseling have grown out of the two traditions we have been looking at in this historical overview. As Figure 3.2 indicates, the two traditions gradually come together to inform contemporary psychotherapy. We will briefly discuss the history of their integration in the final section of this chapter.

Numerous intellectual and social forces have influenced both traditions. Some influences have come from other disciplines, while others have arisen from the professional application of psychology and its related fields. Advances in neuroscience, psychopharmacology, computer technology, and genetics have had a profound impact. The movement of psychologists out of the university setting and into business, industry, and the health services, as well as the emergence of new applications of psychology (for example, genetic counseling and marriage and family therapy), has spawned new expectations for specialists in human behavior.

Two intellectual influences require particular discussion: the critique of both traditions by humanistic psychologists and the emergence of an experimental psychology of cognition.

*Period of Greatest
Influence
on Practitioners*

Early 20th century
to the early 1950s

> ### *Psychoanalysis*
>
> Developed by Freud and others. Therapists' insights help clients understand the unconscious roots of their behavior. FREE ASSOCIATION AND DREAM ANALYSIS used with other techniques. Emphasis on past events. Traditionally, for part of the treatment, the client lies on a couch facing away from the therapist.

Early 1950s through
the 1960s

> ### *Client-Centered Psychotherapy*
>
> Developed by Rogers. The source of therapeutic change is within the client. Therapists facilitate that change by demonstrating UNCONDITIONAL POSITIVE REGARD, GENUINENESS, and EMPATHY. Treatment is conversational, with emphasis on the present and future rather than the past. The client and therapist sit facing each other. Later called person-centered therapy.

Mid-1960s through
the 1970s

> ### *Behavior Therapy*
>
> Based on the work of Skinner, Wolpe, Lazarus, and others. Less empasis on cognition, causes of symptoms, and the relationship between client and therapist. A variety of techniques, including SYSTEMATIC DESENSITIZATION and OPERANT LEARNING, are used to modify the client's biological reaction to environmental stimuli or increase or decrease the frequency or intensity of overt actions. Techniques derived and tested experimentally.

Figure 3.4 *Major shifts in approaches to psychotherapy*

The Humanistic Critique

I may agree with you that Freud was easily the greatest psychologist who ever lived, and yet a science is not made up of one leader and a lot of stooges or loyal devotees.

—A. H. Maslow

The behaviorists I know . . . are gentle people, deeply concerned with the problems facing us in the world today, who see a chance to bring the methods of science to bear on those problems, and who are fully aware of the dangers of the misuse of the power they are creating. . . . Behaviorism is humanism. It has the distinction of being effective humanism.

—B. F. Skinner

Behaviorism dominated American experimental psychology for much of the first half of the 20th century, while psychoanalysis dominated American clinical psychology. Often practitioners in one tradition knew little or nothing about the other. Experimental researchers studied learning, largely through comparative research, and clinical researchers developed theories of human personality and therapeutic techniques largely beyond the scope of experimental investigation. From their beginnings, however, both traditions had critics. Gestalt psychologists were uncomfortable with behaviorism, as were experts from disciplines like philosophy, biology, and sociology. On the other hand, scholars from many sides criticized orthodox psychoanalysts' heavy emphasis on the unconscious, sexuality, and deterministic developmental processes. Practitioners within both traditions tried to improve, correct, and unify their perspectives.

For academic psychology and related disciplines, such criticisms and common concerns coalesced at a 1964 conference in Old Saybrook, Connecticut. Among the participants were Allport, Kelly, Maslow, Rollo May, and Rogers, who like other clinical research psychologists were trying to expand the study of personality beyond the psychoanalytic model in an academic environment dominated by strict behaviorism. Rogers, Maslow, and May became the intellectual leaders of the movement called *humanistic psychology,* also known as the "third force"—behaviorism and psychoanalysis being the first two (M. B. Smith, 1984).

Since the beginning of humanistic psychology in the early 1960s, a core of scholars has sought to integrate the best of both research traditions, to expand the scope of scientific psychology, and to develop therapeutic strategies that do justice to human beings. For example, May introduced American psychology to *existentialism* and raised new psychotherapeutic issues. Rogers developed a major new psychotherapy, person-centered therapy, that was both humanistic and amenable to scientific scrutiny, and Maslow developed a theory of personality broad and deep enough to accommodate the full range of complexity.

Yet, humanistic psychology was more than a group of scholars trying to advance psychology by integrating and expanding two earlier traditions. Humanistic psychology, the social movement, was born in the expansive atmosphere of the 1960s and became for many an assault on behaviorism and psychoanalysis rather than an attempt to integrate them. Ironically, these two dominant schools were by that time clearly on the wane. Nonetheless, as the humanistic movement attracted people from diverse disciplines, backgrounds, and causes, there were times in the history of humanistic psychology when the science of psychology seemed to disappear and the *humanistic* label seemed simply a mask for manic self-indulgence, anti-intellectualism, antiscience, and a miscellany of "therapies" that were both whimsical and dangerous. Such was not the intent of the founders of the movement.

The social movement of the 1960s and 1970s aside, some practitioners still adhere to the views of humanistic psychology. Moreover, the movement, did influence contemporary psychology, especially in the area of psychotherapy and counseling. The significance of humanistic psychology is evident in how we view at least three issues in contemporary psychology: (1) human nature, (2) the role of the experimental method in a science of behavior, and (3) the nature of psychotherapy.

Human nature   The content and methodology of behaviorism and psychoanalysis are quite different. Behaviorism studies external behavior by means of experimentation; psychoanalysis explores internal behavior by means of interpersonal interaction. Yet, humanistic psychology argues that both are based on a philosophy of human nature that is deterministic, reductionistic, and mechanistic in regard to both content and methodology. The humanistic argument can be summarized as follows. In behaviorism, a person's behavior is viewed as absolutely determined by environmental conditioning without regard to choice or decision. Behaviorists recognize no factor in the science of psychology but the automatic, mechanical acquisition of behavior, despite our personal perceptions that we engage in elaborate decision-making processes with cognitive and affective components. Behaviorism thus reduces human behavior to habit formation, a convenient but grossly simplistic explanation of behavior. Behaviorists' exclusive reliance on the experimental method means that only small units of behavior can be studied; the result is a model of human nature that is incapable of explaining our own experience of ourselves. The psychoanalytic view of human behavior is equally bleak. Behavior is seen as the product of internal conflicts that are often not accessible to the conscious mind. In psychoanalysis, too, behavior happens without choice, and, in fact, much of one's life has been determined by a very early age. Behavior is produced automatically, unconsciously, instinctually.

The view of human nature provided by humanistic psychology has not been articulated as clearly as that of behaviorism or psychoanalysis but generally has emphasized: (1) the importance of choice, (2) the neutral or positive nature of human motives, and (3) the complexity of human behavior such that it defies ultimate quantification, classification, and control. This brings us to the second issue, the role of the experimental method in a science of behavior.

The role of the experimental method   This issue is related to humanistic psychology's critique of behaviorism, and the distinction made earlier between natural science and human science comes into play here. One source of light on this issue is Maslow, who, despite his role as a leader in humanistic psychology, was trained as an experimental psychologist and worked as a comparative psychologist under Harry Harlow studying primates and dogs at the University of Wisconsin. His interest in experimental psychology came from his youthful fascination with the ideas of Watson's behaviorism. In later years, he even presented a paper entitled "I Was a Teenage Mechanist," a play on the then-popular movie *I Was a Teenage Werewolf* (C. Wilson, 1972, p. 137). Maslow's thinking paralleled that of proponents of psychology as a human science, rather than a natural science, and he argued that, in psychology, the scientific method had become more important than science itself. Though science should be "problem-centered," he said, it had in fact become "means-centered," more concerned with the methodology than the unique demands of the problem being studied.

In general, Maslow's argument goes as follows. The experimental method was designed to meet the needs of the physical sciences in the 19th century. Applied to the study of human behavior, it has helped us understand some of behavior's more mechanistic aspects, but as a means of exploring the complexities of human thought, feeling, motivation, and so forth, it has been inadequate. Instead of focusing on the scientific means, psychologists should develop a variety of scientific strategies that center on the problem being studied rather than requiring the problem to fit the technique. Methods of scientific study appropriate to behavioral science may or may not be experimental, may or may not be objective. Further, they may or may not be able to demonstrate causal relationships; that is, they may be capable only of description. In essence, scientific orthodoxy should be replaced by scientific heterodoxy (Maslow, 1970a).

The methodologies used in at least some areas of contemporary psychology have broadened. In this postschool era, several changes have developed. The experimental method remains solidly in place but has become sophisticated enough to be applied in some form even to fairly complex social behaviors. The development of quasi-experimental design and single-subject experimentation and the inclusion of cognition within the ken of experimental science help counter the charge that psychology continues to require that the subject matter fit the method while excluding some topics completely. In recent years, psychologists have worked to fit the methodology to the subject matter, but efforts have varied from one psychological specialization to another. Clearly, the issue of natural science versus human science has not been resolved, but humanistic psychology has heightened our awareness of it.

The nature of psychotherapy   We have already touched on this topic in our discussion of Rogers and will refer to it again in later discussions. Humanistic psychologists emphasized two elements as essential to successful psychotherapy. The practitioner must: (1) believe in the ability of most clients to determine their own goals and effect their own changes in the psychotherapeutic process and (2) be a competent and caring person who is comfortable moving beyond the role of therapist or counselor. These ideas, largely based on the research of Rogers, Sidney Jourard, and their colleagues, are now part of most practitioners' basic understanding of their role.

It may be too early to determine the influence of the social movement that was humanistic psychology. Most certainly, many of its thinkers have profoundly changed the study of personality and the practice of psychotherapy and counseling.

The Emergence of Cognitive Psychology

Cognition is the activity of knowing: the acquisition, organization, and the use of knowledge. It is something that organisms do and in particular something that people do. For this reason the study of cognition is a part of psychology, and theories of cognition are psychological theories.

—Ulric Neisser

The title of this section is somewhat deceptive because it falsely implies that the topic of cognition is new to psychology. What has happened within the last 20 or so years is that cognition has emerged from the years of behaviorist dominance to become a major topic for experimental psychologists, and cognitive research derived from experimental psychology has become a necessary part of the theories, research, and therapies of the clinical research tradition. We will trace these developments here.

Historical overview Psychologists have studied cognition since the very beginning of the science of psychology, and there have always been advocates along the way for a holistic view of cognition and human behavior. Not only did Wundt and his students study aspects of cognition, but Wundt was also attacked by critics for dealing inadequately with cognitive-related topics. Though Wundt assumed that high mental processes like memory could not be studied experimentally, Hermann Ebbinghaus invented the nonsense syllable and, with himself as subject, published the first classic studies on memory in 1885. Oswald Külpe and his colleagues in the Würzburg school also took issue with Wundt and between 1901 and 1909 did numerous studies on the topic of imageless thoughts. Similar work was done by Alfred Binet in France and Robert Woodworth in the United States (Leahey, 1980, p. 199). One of the founding fathers of American psychology, William James, focused much of his attention on the topic of consciousness (he was far from an admirer of Wundt), and during structuralism's brief ascendancy in American psychology, cognition was a central focus. Even a traditional, behavioristic learning theorist like Edward Tolman, influenced by Gestalt psychology, did experiments with lab rats that demonstrated the cognitive in infrahuman learning. Developmental theorists like Jean Piaget and Jerome Bruner established theories of intellectual development with broad influence in psychology and education.

Paralleling all of this, and to a certain degree influencing it, was the development of Gestalt psychology, which made cognitive processes its main focus. Gestalt psychology came out of an intellectual tradition that opposed attempts to break psychological phenomena into small parts (atomism), an idea fundamental to Wundt's psychology as it was traditionally understood. The pioneering work in Gestalt psychology was done in the early part of this century by Max Wertheimer, Wolfgang Köhler, and Kurt Koffka. Some of Gestalt psychology's contributions took the form of research on cognitive processes

(Wertheimer and the phi phenomenon, Köhler and insight in apes); others were useful, demonstrable concepts (for example, closure).

Beginning at about the same time as behaviorism, Gestalt psychology was, like behaviorism, also a protest against traditional psychology. After behaviorism's broad acceptance, Gestalt psychology remained as a highly critical and vocal alternative to the philosophy and methodology of behaviorism, serving this role for much of the 20th century. Its ideas influenced psychologists like Tolman, Allport, and Maslow and it attained its greatest application in the social psychology and personality theory of Lewin. Though Gestalt psychology has never been embraced by American psychologists as a real alternative school or research modality, it has been a consistent source of valuable ideas and has influenced social psychology, developmental psychology, and other specialties (Murphy & Kovach, 1972).

Though the study of cognition has always been a part of psychology, it has usually lacked the scientific credibility granted the traditional, behavioristic study of classical and operant learning. In recent years, however, cognition has been investigated experimentally by an increasing number of behaviorists, and after 50 years of ascendancy, traditional learning theory has finally been granted its necessary complement: a science of cognition.

A science of cognition   By the 1960s, the research no longer adequately supported the behavioristic stimulus-response learning theories that formed the theoretical foundation of psychology (Leahey, 1980). Out of the experimental study of cognition (usually called *cognitive psychology*), and with input from other disciplines, came the study of the biochemical, anatomical, and technological concomitants of cognition (usually called *cognitive science*). Neisser (1976), after bemoaning the dominance of behaviorism and psychoanalysis between World War I and the 1960s, described the shift:

> This situation has changed radically in the last few years. Mental processes have again become a lively focus of interest. A new field called *cognitive psychology* has come into being. It studies perception, memory, attention, pattern recognition, problem solving, the psychology of language, cognitive development, and a host of other problems that had lain dormant for half a century. Technical journals once top heavy with articles on animal behavior are now filled with reports of cognitive experiments. (p. 5)

Although the above statement was made more than a decade ago, it reflects the early enthusiasm for what is now an accomplished fact: Not only are experimental researchers in psychology no longer afraid of studying cognitive processes, but most contemporary applications of psychology include cognitive variables in their explanations of behavior. Why did this shift take place? There were several causes, including: (1) the increasing inadequacies of traditional learning theories to explain complex human behaviors; (2) the development of the computer, which served both as a metaphor for a cognition and as a research tool; (3) the development of new strategies for studying mental processes that did not require introspection; (4) research advances in neuroanatomy and biochemistry; and (5) practical difficulties in applying behavioristic treatment strategies when working with normally intelligent adults.

Neisser (1982) argued that *ethology,* the scientific study of animal behavior, ended behavior theory's dominance of psychology. Ethologists, studying a variety of species in their natural environments, created a revolution by demonstrating that the "concepts and methods of learning theory were simply irrelevant to the understanding of natural behavior. Every species seems to have a different set of learning abilities, and to respond to different sorts of variables" (pp. 10–11). The variability made traditional learning explanations of little value. Since lab animals had been the primary source of traditional learning theory, and since the theory depended on generalization from these less complex animals to humans, the whole enterprise became questionable. Perhaps overstating the case, Neisser opined: "Today, learning theory has been almost completely swept away. Not entirely, perhaps: with the mainland of animal behavior lost to their foes, a behaviorist remnant is holding out on well-defended islands like 'behavior modification' or 'behavior therapy.' They still sound confident, but they are watching the straits with an anxious eye" (p. 10).

Merging the Traditions: Contemporary Clinical Practice

Figure 3.1 lists some of those who have contributed to the integration of the two traditions from which contemporary counseling and psychotherapy have come. In this section, I describe some of their contributions and identify some of the common ideas that are central to this merging.

The two influences just discussed, humanistic psychology and the emergence of cognitive psychology, have certainly played a part in the integration of the two traditions. In the present discussion, however, I focus on the more specific, intentional development of approaches to psychotherapy and counseling that benefit from both the richness and diversity of the clinical research tradition and the verification standards of the experimental research tradition. One caveat is in order. The events in the following discussion are relatively recent, and my vision may be distorted by proximity as well as inadvertent bias.

The Traditions Meet

The year is 1950. A book is published with the following dedication: "To Freud and Pavlov, and Their Students." The opening lines of the first chapter read:

> This book is an attempt to aid in the creation of a psychological base for a general science of human behavior. Three great traditions, heretofore followed separately, are brought together. One of these is psychoanalysis, initiated by the genius of Freud and carried on by his many able students in the art of psychotherapy. Another stems from the work of Pavlov, Thorndike, Hull, and a host of other experimentalists. They have applied the exactness of the natural-science method to the

study of the principles of learning. Finally, modern social science is crucial because it describes the social conditions under which human beings learn. The ultimate goal is to combine the vitality of psychoanalysis, the rigor of the natural-science laboratory, and the facts of culture. We believe that a psychology of this kind should occupy a fundamental position in the social sciences and humanities—making it unnecessary for each of them to invent its own special assumptions about human nature and personality. (Dollard & Miller, 1950, p. 3)

Although the next section of the book talks about psychotherapy as "the window to higher mental life," much of the text is filled with words like *reinforcement, discrimination,* and *cue.* References to *repression* and *free association* and the *unconscious* are mixed with illustrative graphs labeled "Average speed of bar pressing," "1/sec" and "Successive bar-pressing trials without shock." The book is entitled *Personality and Psychotherapy: An Analysis in Terms of Learning, Thinking, and Culture.* Its authors are John Dollard and Neal Miller, and almost 40 years later, it remains a landmark publication.

During the 1940s and 1950s, the Institute of Human Relations at Yale University was the site of a series of significant research efforts bringing together the study of personality and learning and making use of rich data from sociology and anthropology. The masterful and comprehensive learning theory of Clark Hull (1884–1952) was the major source of the learning component. Hull's theory of learning is essentially a reinforcement theory, one part of which is the concept of *drive reduction* central to Miller and Dollard's work. Freud's psychoanalytic theory was the source of the personality component, and what emerged was a major theory of personality based on two very different theoretical persuasions. Though a number of researchers were involved, the contributions of John Dollard and Neal Miller were of particular note.

John Dollard (1900–1980) was a sociologist with strong credentials in anthropology, psychology, and psychoanalysis. His partner in numerous publications was Neal Miller (born 1909). Miller's training was in experimental psychology, and his major contributions have been in the areas of learning, personality, and psychobiology. Miller had also trained in psychoanalysis, however, and, with Dollard, published two very important books. The first, *Social Learning and Imitation* (N. E. Miller & Dollard, 1941), presented a personality theory based on Hull's learning theory. *Imitation* was defined operationally in this theory, and reaction to the concept would eventually lead to Bandura's concept of *modeling,* of major importance today. In 1950, the publication of *Personality and Psychotherapy* (Dollard & Miller) brought the theory of personality into the applied area of clinical psychology. Although the drive theory on which these books were based is no longer a theoretical force, and the highly psychoanalytic cognitive components they translated into learning theory may hold less appeal now, Miller and Dollard's contribution is critical, because they did what others who tried to integrate the two traditions could not. They developed a workable, testable personality theory based on the sophisticated literature of learning theory while retaining concepts germane to the clinical tradition. Theirs may not be the final answer, but like the work of Freud and Skinner, little moves without reference to it.[4]

Miller and Dollard's approach is referred to as a "social/learning" approach, and its roots go back to the psychologies of James, Freud, and Piaget (Woodward, 1982). The term *social learning theory* is now generally associated with the work of Albert Bandura, Walter Mischel, and Julian Rotter, but Miller and Dollard were clearly the first to develop a systematic personality theory with all the essential elements: They formalized a theory of human behavior that accounted for the fundamental interaction of behavioral, cognitive, and social variables and comprehensively explained human conduct and its modification.

On a more practical level, the work of Miller and Dollard was also part of a larger set of developments that began to create for nonmedical practitioners a theoretical and technological base separate from psychiatry and medicine. In *Personality and Psychotherapy,* several chapters are given over to explaining the origins of neurotic behavior. Freud had argued that neurosis was learned and emerged in response to real and imagined internal conflicts caused by poorly recalled memories from childhood. No scientific explanation of such learning existed, however. Miller and Dollard were among a number of researchers who demonstrated experimentally how neurotic behavior could be acquired, helping to open the door for a learning-based method for changing human behavior: behavior therapy.

The Advent of Behavior Therapy

Neurosis is a term used to describe patterns of behavior that are characterized by anxiety and that fail to adapt an individual successfully to her or his environment. From Pavlov through Watson through Skinner, the assumption was that neurotic behavior, like all behavior, was acquired and maintained through some form of conditioning or learning (as opposed to being biological or ingrained in the personality through some early trauma). Pavlov had observed anxiety responses typical of neurosis early in the century in his lab (Wolpe, 1982), and Watson had elicited a generalized fear response in Little Albert around 1920. By 1924 Mary Cover Jones had become the first "behavior therapist" by removing similar fear responses from a less famous "little," Little Peter. But it would be in animal research labs that evidence would accrue to explain neurosis. Harry Harlow, Jules Masserman, Joseph Wolpe, and others would demonstrate neurotic responses in animals, preparing the way, along with Miller and Dollard for treatment strategies capable of removing neurotic symptoms.

What we today call behavior therapy has many sources, and we will investigate these sources thoroughly in the next two chapters. For now, it is worth

---

[4]See Wachtel (1977) for a detailed treatment of Dollard and Miller's integration of psychoanalysis and learning theory.

noting that the work of Skinner, Wolpe, Arnold Lazarus, and Hans Eysenck, among others, brought behavior therapy to prominence in the 1970s. As noted in Figure 3.4, behavior therapy dominated psychotherapeutic practice until recently, and it remains one of two main sources from which most practitioners choose their eclectic assembly of techniques.

Social Learning Theory

Explicitly or implicitly, one of the dominant theories of personality for the contemporary practitioner is social learning theory. Its fundamental view of human behavior informs this text, and its use of learning theory to explain personality development, its reliance on scientific research, and its integration of cognitive concepts make it a comprehensive and useful scientific model.

Miller and Dollard's social learning theory depended on Freudian concepts and on drive-reduction theory. Modern social learning theory, however, does not. There are really several social learning theories, each proposed by a different theorist and supported by his colleagues and students, but each is a theory of personality that uses concepts of reinforcement to explain behavior. Further, each shares a strong emphasis on cognitive processes, especially expectations and beliefs (Phares, 1984).

Julian Rotter's *Social Learning and Clinical Psychology,* published in 1954, represented an early and significant move toward a cognitively oriented personality theory and approach to therapy based on learning theory. In 1966, Rotter published a major theoretical paper in *Psychological Monographs* that since 1969 has been the most widely quoted single article in the social sciences (Sahakian & Lundin, 1984b). The paper, entitled "Generalized Expectancies for Internal Versus External Control of Reinforcement," presented both a useful construct (*locus of control*) and a measure for its evaluation.

Another version of social learning theory was proposed by Albert Bandura and articulated in his book *Social Learning Theory* (1977). Bandura's theory uses the concept of *self-efficacy* for which an appropriate measure has also been developed. Bandura has pursued some different theoretical avenues and applications than Rotter.

Rotter and Bandura are only two of the psychologists who can be called social learning theorists. As one might suspect, Rotter and Bandura disagree considerably, as the writings of their students and colleagues show. At the same time, there are more commonalities than differences among the various theorists, and all of the approaches have direct clinical applications and enjoy wide support among practitioners. Social learning theory is a highly influential offspring of the marriage of the two research traditions.

Common Ground

With the merging of the two traditions, a consensus appears to have been reached in regard to several important ideas. Though today these ideas may seem little more than common sense to some, their acceptance has not come easily. The first of these ideas is that a theory of human behavior capable of forming the basis of an approach to psychotherapy or counseling should be derived from and/or verified using scientifically sound research, preferably experimental or quasi-experimental. Second, such a theory should use terminology that can be defined operationally. Third, the theory-therapy should account for behavioral, cognitive, and social aspects of human conduct. Fourth, practitioners should continually measure treatment outcomes and identify which strategies have been effective. Fifth, research from other fields, especially the biological sciences and the social sciences, should be continually integrated into the theory.

Summary of Chapter 3

This chapter presents an overview of some of the intellectual trends and prominent thinkers that have contributed to counseling and clinical psychology. The major points covered are:

Science and Behavior: Basic Issues

1. Psychotherapy emerged in the 19th century, when many important changes in the thinking of Western humankind were taking place. Scientific investigation of the functioning of the human body was begun, for example, a venture that came to rely on the same assumptions about cause and effect that were increasingly evident in physics.

2. Two conflicting ideas that developed were vitalism and mechanism. Vitalism held that the human body functions as it does because of some nonphysical entity and that it is therefore ultimately beyond the realm of science. Mechanism, which eventually dominated science in the latter part of the 19th century, held that human physiology follows laws identical or similar to those that explain other physical phenomena and that no nonphysical reality is involved. Experimental psychology, as well as psychiatry, was greatly influenced by mechanistic ideas.

3. Another question to emerge as psychology was developing as a science concerns whether psychology, as the study of human behavior, is a natural science or a human science. Those who view psychology as a natural science break human behavior into smaller components, perform experiments, establish cause and effect relationships, and try to predict future behaviors. Those who view it as a human science argue that human behavior is too complex for the controls and manipulations necessary for a true experimental science. Rather, human science psychologists describe and explain events but do not limit themselves to the assumptions and methodologies of the natural sciences. Historically, some psychologists and

schools of psychology have viewed psychology as a natural science; others, as a human science.

Psychology's Two Traditions

4. Contemporary counseling and psychotherapy have come from two traditions that differ in their method of research, subject matter, and conclusions.
5. The experimental research tradition began with Wundt in Germany but, transported to America, quickly evolved into the philosophy of science called behaviorism. This school of psychology focused primarily on the study of human and animal learning and relied exclusively on the experimental method. The leading exponent of behaviorism in recent times has been Skinner, who consistently argues that for psychology to be a natural science psychologists must restrict themselves to studying overt behaviors while avoiding making inferences about internal processes.
6. The clinical research tradition began with Freud, who originated psychotherapy as we know it and proposed that clinical intervention could be a source of research data about psychological functioning. The major focus of this research tradition was personality. Freud's psychoanalysis and its offshoots and variations have dominated the tradition and have yielded many theories of personality, usually coupled with an appropriate type of psychotherapy. Social psychology also developed within this tradition as an attempt to bring academic psychology and clinical research into harmony and to study personality outside of a clinical setting.

Major Influences on the Two Traditions

7. Humanistic psychology greatly influenced the two traditions. Generally, humanistic psychology's most important contributors sought to integrate the rigor, precision, and emphasis on quantification of the experimental research tradition with the insights and broader view of the clinical research tradition. Humanist psychologists criticized both behaviorism and psychoanalysis, however, for promoting a view of human nature that was mechanistic, deterministic, and reductionistic. Humanistic psychologists further argued that psychology should be more of a human science than a natural one.
8. The emergence of the experimental study of cognition also greatly influenced the two traditions. Human cognition had taken a back seat in the experimental research tradition during the reign of behaviorism. Gradually, however, a new psychology of cognition developed and, capitalizing on the inadequacies of behaviorism, became increasingly important. Today, a theory of human behavior is incomplete unless it accounts for cognition as a major variable.

Merging the Traditions: Contemporary Clinical Practice

9. Beginning with the early social learning theory of Miller and Dollard in the experimental research tradition, as well as efforts in the clinical tradition by Allport, Maslow, and Rogers, active attempts began pulling the traditions together. The disappearance of the schools, along with a number of other social and intellectual changes, helped pull the two traditions closer together. Today, practitioners tend to integrate research from both traditions in an eclectic fashion.

10. This pulling together of the two traditions led to behavior therapy as a dominant approach to intervention. It also set the stage for modern social learning theory, a theory of personality, and more generally of human behavior, that combines the central elements of both traditions: the study of learning and the study of cognition.

11. Most practitioners now seem to agree on several issues. The points on which they agree support a scientific orientation in which therapeutic outcomes are continually evaluated. There is also greater emphasis on integrating various approaches than on orthodox adherence to one approach or another.

CHAPTER 4

Self-Regulation and Behavior Therapy: Theoretical and Practical Foundations

> *A*ny of my pupils could give you so much insight and understanding that you could treat yourself if you don't succumb to the prejudice that you receive healing through others. In the last resort every individual alone has to win his battle, nobody can do it for him.
>
> **Carl Gustav Jung**

Once upon a time, Cinderella Smith lived with her unpleasant mother, three distractingly ugly sisters, and a cat in a middle-class condo somewhere in the Midwest. Cindi was constantly put upon by the others and made to do all the family's cleaning, cooking, washing, and (ugh!) ironing. Unlike her sisters, she was not permitted to attend college, had no nice clothes, and did not even have her own hair dryer. The local mayor, a handsome bachelor looking for a wife, was giving a bash for prominent locals around the pool at the local Holiday Inn. The Smiths were invited, but Cindi was told by Mom that she would have to stay home; the ugly sisters would attend, of course, and each fantasized being first lady of the town by year's end.

Donning tight, new designer jeans and polka-dot halter tops, the three siblings and Mom headed for the party. Cindi, left alone to do the ironing, was sad, depressed, lonely, and dejected. "Why do I have to stay home? Why don't I just give Mom a piece of my mind, and get out of this place? What's stopping me from changing all this?" With that, she cast her eyes upward. All of a sudden, a flash of light and a puff of smoke came from the direction of the dishwasher, and there stood someone who claimed to be Cindi's Fairy Godperson.

"Listen, dear," the sequined figure announced, "I can make you a star! You've got problems, you're shy, unassertive, caught up in a lot of goofy stuff that keeps you from the goodies. Well, kid, that's all over. With one wave of this magic wand, you will have it all. Freedom from malice-Mom, your silly sisters, and no more Shysville! I'll even throw in a beautiful gown, a taxi to the party, two sure close dances with the mayor, and I wouldn't be surprised if you end up the mayor's wife! That's magic, dear, and that's what I'm here for."

"Gee, Fairy Godperson, a lot of that sounds pretty good, but I was planning to do that stuff myself. I'm getting out of this place as soon as I get my nerve up, and as for your mayor, he's a jerk. Can't you just help me get started without being so darn condescending? I don't want magic, I want help!"

At these words, Fairy Godperson yelled something mildly obscene about ingratitude and vanished between the wall and the dishwasher. Almost simultaneously, however, there was a knock at the door. When Cindi opened the door, she found a person dressed in rather common clothes. "Hi. Corny as it may sound, I'm your Fairly Good Person. I've got some ideas about how you can gain some control over your life. Nothing magical, but I think I can help. May I come in?" It was the beginning of a happy ending.

Fortunately for science, art, and the world of make-believe, this story is intended only to illustrate a few key points about counseling and psychotherapy. First, there are no "fairy godpractitioners" who can transform patterns of behavior with the wave of a wand or even something more high tech. Though some clients may fervently hope this will happen when they enter the practitioner's office, it simply never does. Second, psychotherapy and counseling are based on the assumption that clients are capable of controlling or regulating their own behavior. This being so, when an individual needs help in achieving or maintaining that self-regulation and believes that the practitioner has the resources to help him or her, then therapeutic change can occur (Strong & Claiborn, 1982).

Psychotherapy and counseling provide personnel and strategies through which clients can enhance their self-regulation. Many of the self-regulatory strategies used presently can be classified as behavior therapy, or behavior modification.

Self-Regulation and Behavior Therapy

Our present discussion counters two misconceptions. First, terms like self-regulation and self-control seem to be nothing more than updated versions of good old will power, that oft-prescribed cure for dietary and gonadal hyperactivity. Our own use of the terms will be quite different, although the ends may at times coincide. Second, the terms behavior therapy and behavior modification still have the power to conjure up images of middle-aged men in white lab coats manipulating the behavior of mentally retarded orphans by offering them colorful tokens in exchange for life-sustaining nourishment. Such a cynical caricature of early attempts to apply learning research to humans greatly misrepresents the intent, sophistication, and philosophy of behavior therapy today.

The fundamental contentions of this chapter are: (1) that control over one's own thoughts, feelings, and actions (self-regulation) is a major goal of psychotherapy and counseling; (2) that a variety of therapeutic approaches grouped under the umbrella of behavior therapy are among the most effective means of accomplishing self-regulation; (3) that most approaches to behavior therapy fall within the theoretical framework of social learning theory.

Self-Regulation

The current literature uses the terms self-regulation, self-control, and self-management to describe a host of client- and client-practitioner-initiated strategies for attaining and maintaining control over thoughts, feelings, and actions. Underlying each term are different theoretical explanations and supporting research. Although we will mention some of this research, we will use the term **self-regulation** to include all variations of this concept.

Over the past 20 or so years, anecdotal evidence from Eastern cultures about the potential of self-regulatory processes has been supported by experimental research that suggests that individuals can control even so-called autonomic biological functions. Further, dissatisfaction with pharmacological solutions to stress-related problems has led practitioners to develop effective self-initiated and self-sustained strategies (Shapiro, 1984). Behavior therapists have also explored self-management strategies, because they found that environmental control programs were not always sustained in the absence of the therapist (Kanfer, 1975). Still, the problem facing the science of human behavior from the beginning remained: free will. If individuals choose, then how are scientific prediction and control possible? As we have seen, earlier explanations of human behavior, **behaviorism** and **psychoanalysis,** opted for a pandeterminism that solved the problem posed by concepts like free will, volition, and choice, by simply eliminating them. The problem has not gone away, however, because we continue to experience ourselves as making choices and acting on them.

The determinism necessary for a science of human behavior does not preclude choice or self-regulatory processes if we operate within the following framework. First, determinism is not passivity. Thoresen and Mahoney (1974) point out that many of the conditions that influence an individual's behavior can be changed by the actions of that individual; that is, the individual's behavior and the conditions that influence the behavior determine each other. Second, we must separate self-regulation from the concept of will power because of the misleading implications associated with that term. Though self-regulation is a voluntary process, it is not simply an act of will. Rather, self-regulation involves systematically evaluating the internal and external conditions that have led or could lead to a particular goal, and changing those conditions so that the goal is attained. Self-regulation, therefore, requires that an individual decide to change. It is assumed, following Goldfried and Merbaum (1973), that self-regulation "does not emerge from any innate potential within the individual, but is acquired through experience, whether it be trial-and-error or more systematic learning" (p. 13).

Without fully resolving the philosophical issue of individual choice and freedom, it is possible to study how individuals set goals, identify the conditions that will direct them toward those goals, and choose to act within the limits imposed by genetics, previous learning, and the immediate environment. Further, it is possible through psychotherapy and counseling to improve how people make these changes.

Behavior Therapy

In the opening section of this chapter, I mentioned the misconceptions surrounding behavior therapy and behavior modification. A number of studies have demonstrated that people often react negatively to the label *behavior modification* because it connotes manipulation, an association fostered by the media and, possibly, the exaggerated claims of early researchers and practitioners (see Barling & Wainstein, 1979; Woolfolk & Woolfolk, 1979; Woolfolk, Woolfolk & Wilson, 1977). Though giving behavior therapy a new name (for example, social learning therapy) has been suggested, this would not solve the problem; the solution lies in educating the public so that people correctly understand and appreciate what behavior therapy is (Kazdin & Cole, 1981). Readers of this text, as future practitioners, consumers, or both, are key participants in this educational attempt. The following discussion of behavior therapy in its various forms is therefore aimed at clarifying the true nature of behavior therapy.

Such misconceptions exist in part because of the dramatic changes that have occurred over the past 20 years, especially in what therapeutic strategies are defined as behavior therapy. Kanfer (1977) described the problem:

> If a practitioner of behavior therapy had decided to take a long leave of absence in 1965 and returned today [1977], he would be astonished and confused. The multitude of books and articles on behavior modification contains contradictions and complexities that represent many of the positions which the systematic approach of the conditioning therapies had attempted to avoid. For example, use of self-reports for assessment and treatment, methods designed to alter thinking and imagery, concern with the client's attitudes toward himself and motivation to change, and stress on the patient's self-management of the treatment program are new ingredients of behavior therapy. These techniques seem to be flourishing and gaining wide acceptance by clinicians of all orientations. While the precariously thin theoretical and research base has made many psychologists uneasy, many contemporary behavior therapists seem all too eager to absorb, compromise, integrate or incorporate all the concepts and methods of traditional systems, which focused on the "processes-in-the-head" (and perhaps in the heart and hormones) as the primary determinants of action. (p. 1)

What changes have occurred since the beginnings of behavior therapy up to the present day, and why did they take place? We begin to answer these questions by defining behavior therapy.

Defining behavior therapy   Following one trend (Kazdin, 1978b; Kazdin & Wilson, 1978), the terms behavior therapy and behavior modification will be used synonymously, although behavior modification is sometimes used as a more general term for the application of learning principles in a variety of settings, while behavior therapy is used to refer to the application of those principles in changing maladaptive behavior (Kalish, 1981). In the beginning, behavior therapy was "the use of experimentally established principles of learning for the purpose of changing unadaptive behavior. Unadaptive habits are weakened and eliminated; adaptive habits are initiated and strengthened" (Wolpe, 1969, p. vii). Today, there are many definitions, but most are broader (and perhaps more tentative) than the one above. For our purposes, behavior therapy is defined as "(1) the use of a broadly defined set of clinical procedures whose description and rationale *often* [italics added] rely on the experimental findings of psychological research, and (2) an experimental and functionally analytic approach to clinical data, relying on an objective and measurable outcome" (Craighead, Kazdin, & Mahoney, 1981, p. 24).

Historical overview   Whether the change is viewed as beneficial or deleterious, the more restricted and rigorous notion of behavior therapy has given way to a broader, less well-established one. The brief history that follows draws on Kazdin's comprehensive treatment of the subject, *History of Behavior Modification* (1978b).

Behavior therapy developed in several different places at about the same time. The term behavior therapy was first used in 1953 by Skinner and his colleagues while applying operant conditioning techniques to psychotic patients for the U.S. Navy's Office of Naval Research (A. A. Lazarus, 1971). The application of Skinner's "experimental analysis of behavior" was later taken beyond the initial work by others (Skinner, 1978), and numerous applications of operant learning, usually called behavior modification, were born.

In South Africa in the 1940s and 1950s, Joseph Wolpe (born 1915), a physician, developed *systematic desensitization* (explained in Chapter 5). Among those working with him toward the end of that period were Stanley Rachman and Arnold Lazarus. As noted earlier, Wolpe's work concerned the study of neurotic reactions in animals and led him to both a theory and a therapy for the treatment of neurosis. In 1958, Lazarus used the term behavior therapy to describe the work of his teacher, Wolpe. Then, in the 1960s, both Wolpe and Lazarus brought systematic desensitization to the United States and began training others in its use. Although they worked together for a period in the United States, their current views on behavior therapy are as widely divergent as opinions can get, as we will see in some detail later.

In England during the 1950s, Hans Eysenck (born 1916), an experimental psychologist, revolutionized clinical psychology in his country by demonstrating to the satisfaction of many that traditional psychotherapy (largely psychoanalytic) was no more effective as a treatment than spontaneous remission and urging that clinical psychologists rely on their research in learning to find effective treatments. In 1959, Eysenck published a paper introducing the term behavior therapy to England. Eysenck has been credited by Wolpe (1969) with popularizing behavior therapy throughout the world.

Advocates of the behavior therapy that swept psychology in the 1960s had a very narrow but secure view of their approach. Although some variations existed, Wolpe's (1982) definition clearly stated the limits: "the use of experimentally established principles and paradigms of learning to overcome unadaptive habits" (p. 2). To this day, Wolpe remains among those who would maintain this narrow yet effective definition, and he regrets that behavior therapy was not named "conditioning therapy" so that "travesties" like "cognitive behavior therapy" could not have occurred (p. 3).

Why was behavior therapy so popular despite the predilection practitioners had for neopsychoanalytic and, later, Rogerian forms of treatment? Behavior therapy was more than the application of learning research to broader conceptions of human behavior as we saw in the work of Miller and Dollard. It was part of a social movement by counselors and psychologists who, dissatisfied with the control psychiatry had over mental health, delighted in using a distinctive technology (Yates, 1970). It was also effective, and researchers were constantly expanding the possibilities for its application. Initially, behavior therapists stayed away from anything that would even appear mentalistic, and their early applications were most successful. Pioneers in behavior therapy were convinced that applying experimentally established research with both humans and infrahumans would provide effective, broadly applicable treatment. While that belief is still widely held, behavior therapists have broadened both their research and clinical strategies as well as incorporating within their theoretical framework explanations of behavior that involve cognitive processes.

What happened between 1960 and the present has already been mentioned. The generalizability of learning research done with animal subjects was seriously questioned, as was its applicability to humans. Its practicality was also questioned: Did behavior therapists really use those experimental data? Such questions remain open (Kazdin, 1979). Some of the most virulent and effective criticism came from sources within the behavior therapy establishment. Consider these comments by A. A. Lazarus in *Behavior Therapy and Beyond* (1971):

> Some approaches to behavior therapy may be said to constitute a game. The name of the game could be: "Let us never lose sight of the fact that man is an animal." A more detailed title would be: "Let us deny that human beings have a cerebral cortex and let us reduce man to a hypothalamic, subcortical creature dominated by a primitive autonomic nervous system". . . . When confronted by people intent upon self-destruction, torn asunder by conflicting loyalties, crippled by too high a level of aspiration, unhappily married because of false romantic ideals, or beset by feelings of guilt and inferiority on the basis of complex theological beliefs, I fail to appreciate the clinical significance of Wolpe's neurotic cats and sometimes wish that life and therapy were really as simple as he would have us believe. . . . But in my estimation, the twenty or so behavioral techniques described by Wolpe represent a useful *starting point* for increased clinical effectiveness rather than a complete system which can put an end to 90 percent of the world's neurotic suffering. (pp. 6–7)

Lazarus's critique was hardly a tame one, and some have argued that Lazarus has gone so far "beyond" that he no longer fits under even a broad behavior therapy umbrella (Krasner, 1984). Still, Lazarus has stated a basic criticism of traditional behavior therapy, and his comments set the stage for discussion of the key issue: the place of cognition in behavior therapy.

The issue is not whether or not human cognition exists. Rather, the controversy concerns the utility of the concept of cognition as a variable in research (Skinner, 1978) and clinical practice (Wolpe, 1982). Throughout their work, Skinner and Wolpe independently explain cognitive activity in terms of overt behaviors. Their argument is that such explanations avoid obtuse mentalistic concepts and explanations and thus permit experimental research. The above quotation from Lazarus clearly expresses the opposite opinion: The scientific study of human behavior cannot avoid cognitive processes; they are central to all other activities. At the moment, the broader perspective dominates, though it includes the therapeutic strategies of the narrower perspective. Yet, debate over the role of cognition, the scientific foundations of behavior therapy, and its integration with other approaches continues to fill the journals (for example,

Goldfried, 1982; Kazdin, 1979; Kendall 1982; Kendall, Plous, & Kratochwill, 1981; Tryon, 1981b; Ullmann, 1981; Wachtel, 1982b; G. T. Wilson, 1982; Wolpe, 1977).

Common features   The changes mentioned above make it difficult to establish what features the various behavior therapies share. Kazdin (1982a) has pointed out that one common feature is that behavior therapy still rejects the disease model of mental disorders and the intrapsychic approach to their treatment. More positively, Kazdin lists five characteristics of behavior therapy (p. 27). Behavior therapy tends to: (1) focus on current rather than historical determinants of behavior, (2) emphasize overt behavior change as the main criterion in evaluating treatment, (3) rely on basic psychological research to generate hypotheses about treatment and specific techniques, (4) specify treatment in objective and operational terms so that the procedures can be replicated, and (5) specify very carefully the target behavior and the techniques for measuring outcome.

In addition, some authors have argued that all behavior therapy can be seen as an application of social learning theory, viewing social learning theory not just as a specific application of behavior therapy but as a broad theory of human personality (Craighead et al., 1981). We will return to this topic later in the chapter, after examining some basic learning processes, as well as some therapeutic tools commonly used in behavior therapy.

Theoretical Foundations: Learning Theory

Human beings learn. Within our biological, psychological, and social limits, we acquire and integrate new ideas, actions, and feelings. When psychologists examine the topic of learning, they seek to explain the phenomenon as parsimoniously and comprehensively as possible. Learning is not directly observable. It is possible to see the effects of learning in specific behavioral responses (for example, riding a bike, reciting the alphabet, or becoming fearful in the presence of a snake), but the actual learning cannot be observed. In this regard, therefore, learning is an *intervening variable*; that is, it cannot be directly observed, but its existence can be inferred to explain relationships among those events that can be observed.

Two general theories have been developed to explain learning: **behavior theory** and **cognitive theory** (see Figure 4.1, page 95).[1] Behavior theorists argue

[1]Behavior in this context is used in its narrow sense (overt, observable activity) rather than in the broader one used in the first chapter (including affect and cognition). Since psychology is defined as the scientific study of human behavior, advocates of various approaches have found it necessary to redefine the term behavior to include or exclude different parts of the total package. When behavior theories of learning were dominant, the term excluded cognition and most internal processes. Theorists who wanted to include cognition, affect, or social behavior had to add these as though they were not actually part of human behavior. Modern psychologists, including behavior therapists, tend to use the word more encompassingly to include both internal and external events.

for parsimony; cognitive theorists argue for comprehensiveness. Behavior theorists assert that inferences about intervening variables are unnecessary if the events can be explained without making such inferences; cognitive theorists see those intervening variables as the true heart of the matter. At issue in this matter of differences is how thoroughly and precisely each theory explains the phenomenon in question.

As Figure 4.1 illustrates, the focus of behavior theory is overt behavior, specifically, the relationship between stimulus (S) and response (R). Cognitive theory focuses on what goes on inside the organism (O). As described in the previous chapter, a behavior theory formed the basis for the study of learning in the **experimental research tradition.** Behavior theory has been generally associated with the philosophy of science and school of psychology called behaviorism, often in the form of *methodological behaviorism*; that is, behavior theorists have relied on the research strategies of the behaviorism without accepting its philosophical assumptions. Cognitive theory has its roots in Gestalt psychology and eventually contributed to the development of contemporary cognitive psychology.

Behavior Theory

A learning theory describes or explains what takes place between two potentially observable events: some sort of input of energy to an organism, a *stimulus,* and some sort of output from that organism, a *response.* These events are only potentially observable because in everyday life we generally see the effects of learning (in a response like reciting a prayer, climbing a rope, or laughing at a joke) without seeing either the remote external conditions through which the response was acquired or the precise set of immediate stimuli that triggered the response, let alone the internal process of learning. One way to solve this problem is by creating an artificial situation in which the researcher can control all external conditions. Behavior theorists argue that by setting up controlled experiments in which the stimulus conditions can be varied (manipulated) and the responses measured, it is possible to identify the basic mechanisms of learning without regard to unobservable factors. Further, because humans are exposed to so many extraneous factors that may or may not play a part in learning, behavior theorists have relied heavily on animal research (mostly with rats) where breeding procedures can control genetic factors and the environment from birth on can be kept relatively constant. In the basic research paradigm the *independent variable* is manipulated, and the *dependent variable* is measured. By holding all other variables constant and changing the independent variable, researchers can assume that changes in the intensity or frequency of the dependent variable are causally connected to the independent variable.

In behavior theory, learning is generally explained in terms of a connection between the stimulus and response; theories that do so are referred to under

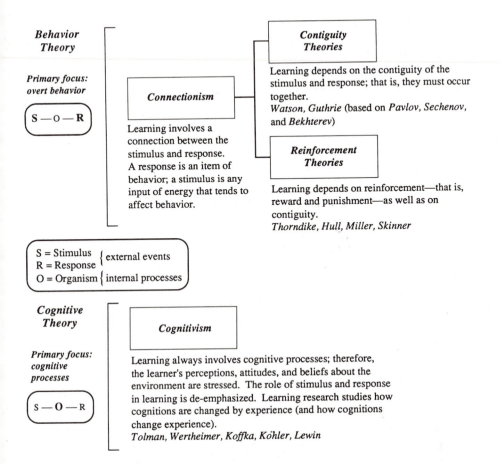

Figure 4.1 *Major theories of learning*

the general heading of *connectionism*. All connectionistic theories are either *contiguity theories* or *reinforcement theories*. Contiguity theories explain learning by the coesixtence in time and space of the stimulus and the response. Such learning is usually described as *classical conditioning*. Reinforcement theories explain learning in relation to reward and punishment—that is, the presence or absence of reinforcers—as well as through contiguity. The most thoroughly developed and widely accepted reinforcement theory of learning today is *operant conditioning* or *operant learning*. Figure 4.1 provides a handy summary for reviewing these concepts.

It is important to note that some behavior theories of learning, for example, Hull's learning theory, use intervening variables extensively. Yet, in such cases, the intervening variables are assumed to be functionally related to the stimulus and response, and the focus remains on external events.

Cognitive Theory

Cognitive explanations of learning focus on the internal events mediating between the stimulus and the response. Cognitive explanations of learning, from Gestalt psychology through Piaget to contemporary cognitive psychology, assert that input into the human organism must be attended to, given meaning, and integrated with previous learning for the response to take place. Though to assume that this is a passive process would be parsimonious (what goes in is what comes out), such is not the case with human beings, and such a mechanical notion is a gross oversimplification. The true focus of the study of learning, say cognitive theorists, should be that active mediational process called cognition.

In the previous chapter, several points about the study of cognition were made: (1) Though the study of cognition per se has always been part of psychology, the dominance of behaviorism among experimental psychologists gave it a secondary place until two decades or so ago; (2) advances in research methodology, as well as growing reservations about the applicability of behavioral explanations to humans, have boosted the status of cognitive psychology; and (3) though contemporary behavior therapy still relies heavily on research findings based on behavior theory, broader limits now usually include cognitive theories and research.

How Firm the Foundation?

Behavior therapists set out to apply experimentally derived principles of learning to the modification of human behavior. Following in the best traditions of behavior theory, behavior therapists would disregard nonobservable events, apply infrahuman research to humans, and permanently arrest a myriad of "mental disorders" and other inappropriate responses. Though behavior therapy techniques have become prominent among practitioners' tools, the process did not happen as planned. Rather, as we have seen previously, the modus operandi and the philosophy underlying it have been largely abandoned by both contemporary learning theory and behavior therapy in favor of models that emphasize cognitive, personality, and social factors (Murray & Jacobson, 1978). Kanfer and Karoly (1973, p. 396) called this an "excursion into the lion's den," but behavior therapy has emerged live and whole and, if anything, healthier. The passive model of human learning, in which cognition was ignored, has been replaced by a model emphasizing active, problem-solving, information-processing cognition as central to explaining human learning and behavior. This shift toward cognitivism reflected a crisis. The reason appears clear: Though behavior theory's explanations of human learning were parsimonious, they were not comprehensive enough to accommodate the complexity of human activities. Still, the contributions of behavior theory have been notable: (1) Many of the principles of learning derived from infrahuman research can be applied to humans; (2) behavior theory represents an advance over nonbehavioral approaches because of its specific identification of variables and emphasis on experimental verification; and (3) because behavioral assessment provides a means by which the effectiveness of treatment can be measured, as well as serving as a source for theory development, it enables psychotherapy to justify its value to society (Levis, 1982).

Contemporary Approaches to Behavior Therapy

The various behavior therapies in use today can be grouped in several ways. Table 4.1 follows the classifications provided by Kazdin and Wilson (1978), and G. T. Wilson and Franks (1982): (1) the neobehavioristic mediational S-R model, (2) applied behavior analysis, (3) social learning theory, and (4) cognitive behavior modification. The classifications represent four different approaches to behavior therapy. We will use these classifications to organize the theoretical material that will serve as background for the next chapter.

The Neobehavioristic Mediational S-R Model

> *T*hought obeys the same *"mechanistic"* laws as other behavior. There is no need for the invocation of an entity or a realm of activity independent of the mechanism-controlled organism.
>
> **—Joseph Wolpe**

The name given to this category of behavior therapy may appear confusing. It refers to a type of approach in which the principles of conditioning, particularly classical conditioning and counterconditioning, are used to change maladaptive behavior (Kazdin & Wilson, 1978). This model borrows the stimulus-response (S-R) concept from behavior theory, primarily (but not exclusively) from contiguity theory, to explain learning. It is called *neobehavioristic* because it is based on the work of psychologists who moved beyond Watson's basic theory and philosophy of behaviorism and abandoned his sole reliance on classical conditioning. It is called *mediational* because, in moving beyond Watson's reliance on classical conditioning, neobehaviorists introduced nonobservable, intervening variables that mediate between the stimulus and the response. The theoretical foundation for these explanations of learning was classical conditioning as described by Pavlov, but the model also shows the influence of the instrumental conditioning described by Thorndike, Hull, and many others.

In its most basic form, classical conditioning concerns the process whereby a new stimulus acquires the capacity to elicit a given behavioral response. In 1904, Pavlov began his well-known conditioning experiments, in which animals learned to salivate in the absence of food but in the presence of stimuli that had appeared contiguously with food. The working assumption underlying

Table 4.1 *Four Contemporary Approaches to Behavior Therapy*

	Neo-behavioristic Mediational S-R Model	*Applied Behavior Analysis*	*Social Learning Theory*	*Cognitive Behavior Modification*
Theoretical Perspective	Neo-behaviorism*	Radical Behaviorism*	Social Learning Theory	Social Learning Theory
Description of Human Behavior	based primarily on classical conditioning and countercondi-tioning, also some instrumental conditioning; allows for intervening variables, but views covert processes as following overt processes	based on the principles of operant learning; explanations of human behavior restricted to observable events	behavior is the product of external stimuli (classical conditioning), reinforcement (operant conditioning), and, especially cognitive mediation	integrates behavioral and cognitive explanations of behavior; behavior therapy viewed by some (Beck) as a division of cognitive therapy
Applications to Therapy	numerous techniques, especially systematic desensitization, implosive therapy	techniques use reinforcement, punishment, extinction, and stimulus control	intervention at level of stimulus, reinforcement, and cognition; expectancy, attribution, and modeling emphasized	variety of techniques including stress inoculation, self-instruction, and problem solving
Major Pioneers	Wolpe Eysenck	Skinner	Rotter Bandura	Ellis Meichenbaum Mahoney Beck

*The techniques associated with this approach also fit under the umbrella of social learning theory, but each approach's understanding of human behavior differs fundamentally.

such experiments, accepted by Watson and early behaviorists, was that the acquisition of all human behavior beyond that which is biologically determined can be explained in terms of the continual elaboration and refinement of conditioned responses.

As noted in Chapter 3, behavior therapy was able to develop because of psychologists' attempts to explain neurosis through infrahuman research. Neurotic behavior in humans is self-defeating behavior characterized principally by *anxiety*. Though there are numerous ways to define and explain anxiety, it is most fundamentally a biological event of the autonomic nervous system. Anxiety is often expressed as a pattern of avoidance or escape, sometimes taking the form of phobias, compulsions, or obsessions. By the turn of the century, Pavlov had demonstrated *experimental neurosis* in dogs by changing experiments in which the animals were conditioned to salivate in the presence of conditioned stimuli that led to a reward of food (CS^+). Conditioned stimuli that did not lead to food (CS^-) but that were similar to the CS^+ were presented. In the end, the animal could be conditioned to discriminate between the two similar stimuli, salivating only in the presence of the CS^+ despite its similarity to the CS^-. But what would happen if one reversed this conditioning in an animal that has already learned that the CS^+ leads to reward and the CS^- does not? Consider this description by B. Schwartz (1978) of a Pavlovian strategy:

> A dog has been trained in a Pavlovian discrimination procedure. The CS^+, a circle, is followed by food. The CS^-, an ellipse, is not followed by food. The dog learns the discrimination and at the end of the training salivates only to the CS^+. Now the procedure is changed. The CS^+ becomes an ellipse, but one that looks almost like a circle. The CS^- is also an ellipse, but one that looks more like a circle than the old CS^-. Despite the greater similarity between CS^+ and CS^- than before, the dog once again learns the discrimination. The procedure is changed again. CS^+ and CS^- are both ellipses, but even more like each other than before. Again, with greater difficulty, the discrimination is learned. Finally, a new pair of ellipses is chosen, and now the dog finds it impossible to make the discrimination. However, the dog does not simply salivate to both stimuli, nor does it simply stop salivating. It shows tremendous agitation. It barks and howls and attempts to escape the harness. It shows signs of distress that have not been observed before. If the dog is returned to the original discrimination between circle and ellipse, it fails to master the discrimination. The dog seems to have broken down. (p. 101)

Findings like these, along with more casual demonstrations by Watson, established the idea that learning theory held the key to explaining and possibly curing maladaptive behaviors. If conditioning could produce these symptoms, then some form of *counterconditioning* could alleviate them. Mary Cover Jones, with the help of Watson, had demonstrated this possibility by eliminating fear responses in a boy referred to as Little Peter. But the pioneers who provided the technological and theoretical bases for behavior therapy were Wolpe, Jules Masserman, Miller, O. H. Mowrer, and others. As psychologists applied these findings to humans, they recognized that humans mediate stimulus events through cognition and have the capacity to evoke anxiety by verbalizing or imagining the anxiety-producing stimuli. Mediational processes like language and imagination have therefore become part of the neobehavioristic model but not the primary focus nor in any manner separate from the stimulus response. Exponents of this model continue to reject cognitive explanations of behavior (Kazdin & Wilson, 1978).

The behavior therapies that correspond to the neobehavioristic model share the following features: (1) Principles of learning derived from the study of classical conditioning and counterconditioning form much of the basis for techniques currently in use; (2) mediational (for example, verbal or imaginal) processes often play a role in treatment procedures, although cognitive explanations of this mediation are avoided; and (3) the maladaptive behaviors most commonly treated are neurotic disorders where anxiety is seen as underlying the expression of phobias and obsessive compulsions. Examples of techniques corresponding to this model are systematic desensitization and flooding.

Applied Behavior Analysis

The field of psychotherapy is rich in explanatory fictions. Behavior itself has not been accepted as a subject matter in its own right, but only as an indication of something wrong somewhere else [Skinner's emphasis]. The task of therapy is said to be to remedy an inner illness of which the behavioral manifestations are merely "symptoms."

—B. F. Skinner

Applied behavior analysis involves the application of the principles of operant learning to changing human behavior. Adherents of this approach view behavior as a function of its consequences and avoid cognitive processes and internal events in explaining human behavior (Kazdin & Wilson, 1978). The approach focuses on socially important behaviors that are part of everyday life: mental illness and mental retardation, education, child rearing, and crime. Change is usually undertaken in the client's natural setting (Kazdin, 1978b). Although in this text I am using the term behavior modification more broadly, that term is often used, as in Eysenck's (1982) distinction between behavior therapy and behavior modification, to refer to what we are here calling applied behavior analysis.

Applied behavior analysis is a direct outgrowth of the experimental analysis of behavior undertaken by B. F. Skinner and his colleagues, and the technology that has come from the study of operant learning often seems inseparable from Skinner's radical behaviorist philosophy of science and human behavior. An example of Skinner's views on self-regulation can be found in *Science and Human Behavior* (1953) in a chapter entitled " 'Self-Control.' " In this chapter, Skinner argued against more traditional notions of internal control by the self. Giving practical examples of changes in external conditions that can effectively modify unwanted behavior, he argued that attempts to change behavior internally, through will power or self-control, fail in comparison to systematically changing the consequences of that behavior. For Skinner, self-controlling behavior is a function of identifiable variables. It is psychology's task to identify these variables and society's role to use this technology for the common good.

Skinner's experimental analysis of behavior, developed through years of research with laboratory animals, has been successfully applied in many ways, and practitioners need not be radical behaviorists to use Skinner's techniques. However, because Skinner's philosophy of radical behaviorism often deters practitioners from using his techniques, a clarification of the philosophy is in order.

Radical behaviorism's pragmatic viewpoint   The misconceptions that exist concerning behavior therapy are in no small part a result of the philosophy of radical behaviorism promulgated by Skinner in his writings and lectures. Several points can be made here. Operant techniques will either work or not work regardless of the philosophical assumptions of the practitioner (although the same may not be true in regard to the client's assumptions). Research indicates that operant techniques do work with certain populations in certain settings, and no therapeutic approach can claim more. All the same, many practitioners who use the techniques of applied behavior analysis clearly do accept the underlying philosophy. But what exactly is it? Is it as restrictive as many of us have been led to believe? Baer's chapter on applied behavior analysis in G. T. Wilson and Frank's *Contemporary Behavior Therapy* (1982) contains an enlightening (and lengthy) footnote. In part it reads:

> Radical behaviorists do not ignore, escape from, or avoid descriptions of private behaviors observable only to their possessor; they do, however, strenuously avoid any implication that such private events are different in kind or function from observable behaviors. Thus, they assume that private events are behaviors subject to environmental control, which is what they assume about observable behaviors. . . . For the radical behaviorists, private events are certainly possible; probably all radical behaviorists observe those events operating in their own individual behavior, and, as an act of probability (or at least charity), will suppose that similar events operate unobservably in the behavior of others, too. The question is not whether they operate, but how they operate. The assumption of radical behaviorism is that they operate as elements in chains that begin with observable environmental events and end with observable responses by the organism; thus, their thorough analysis is environmental and empirical, as in the analysis of observable behavior. For this reason, I have ensconced this special tolerance for private events by the radical behaviorists (of whom I consider myself one, except for occasional lapses) in a footnote. (p. 279)

Though some argue that such a position simply ignores the complexity of human behavior, its underlying assumptions fit its techniques, and the techniques work with certain populations with certain types of problems.

Operant technology as psychotherapy   The therapeutic tools of applied behavior analysis are widely used by practitioners of every persuasion, some formally, with various reward methods, others with less formal strategies that could be described as unsystematic reward/punishment schemes.

Skinner rejects traditional explanations of both the etiology of mental disorders and their remediation, and although his position was radical when he first stated it, in the 30 years since, many practitioners have implicitly or explicitly accepted his logic, albeit in less restrictive forms. According to Skinner, individuals seek psychotherapy in response to the ubiquitous controls placed on them by government, religion, family, employment, and so forth. Often the controls rely heavily on punishment and are excessive or inconsistent. As a by-product of such controls, individuals react emotionally with fear, anxiety, anger, or depression, or behaviorally with excessive or deficient behavior, addiction, defective discrimination of stimuli, defective self-knowledge, or aversive self-stimulation (Hilgard & Bower, 1966; Skinner, 1953).

The fundamental ideas of operant learning as applied to psychotherapy and counseling can be summarized as follows:

1. The consequences of most of an individual's behavior are either satisfying and pleasant or unsatisfying and aversive. When the behaviors an individual has learned have consequences that consistently fail to satisfy or are aversive, then an individual may seek or be sent for counseling or psychotherapy.
2. This failure to successfully adapt to the demands of the environment exists because of some *behavioral deficit* or *behavioral excess*. A behavioral deficit exists when a necessary behavior does not exist or is inadequate in its present form (too weak, too infrequent, too slow, and so forth). A behavior excess exists when an existing behavior is entirely ineffective or ineffective in its present form (too intense, too frequent, too exaggerated, and so forth).
3. The effects of this inadequate adjustment intensify emotional responses like fear, anxiety, or depression, and increase behavioral reactions like escape, avoidance, or withdrawal.
4. The individual's behavior has been acquired largely through learning. Some is learned by responding to stimuli in the environment (respondent or classical conditioning), but most is acquired as a function of its consequences (operant conditioning).
5. Human beings operate on the environment; that is, we manifest behaviors, some of which come under the control of stimuli. To come under control of stimuli means that the behaviors increase or decrease in frequency, intensity, magnitude, or speed in accordance with their consequences.
6. A *contingent* relationship is established between the *operant behavior* and the consequences of that behavior such that the consequence depends on the performance of the operant behavior. This means that the consequence occurs only when the operant behavior is performed.
7. The consequences of an operant behavior are *positive reinforcement, negative reinforcement,* or *punishment.* An operant behavior can be changed by controlling its consequences. Figure 4.2 illustrates the principles involved in changing behavior.
8. The probability that a behavior will become more frequent, more intense, more elaborate, or faster will increase if its performance results in the presentation of a positive event (positive reinforcement) or the removal of an aversive or noxious event (negative reinforcement). Behavior followed by the presentation of an aversive event or the removal of a positive event (punishment) may also change.

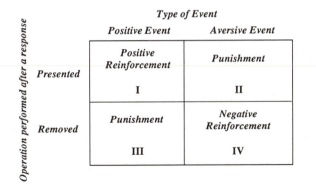

Figure 4.2   *The principles of operant conditioning* (from: Kazdin, 1975a)

9. Everyday behavior is under operant control, but human beings often learn patterns of behavior that fail to achieve maximum reward. Responses to this failure include emotional distress and increased patterns of self-defeating behavior.

10. Applied behavior analysis emphasizes thorough behavioral assessment of the contingencies of reinforcement existing in a client's life and initiates new schedules of reinforcement designed to extinguish or modify maladaptive patterns of behavior and initiate or increase adaptive patterns.

Techniques for measuring changes in individual clients come largely from applied behavior analysis, but since these techniques can be used in all forms of behavior therapy, a summary of them is included in the Assessment and Accountability section later in this chapter.

Social Learning Theory

*I*s *a holistic view of psychology better than an atomistic view? Is a perceptual explanation better than a learning approach? Is a cognitive explanation better than a behavioral one? I have learned to regard such questions as silly.*

—Julian Rotter

Social learning theory is the third of the four classifications of behavior therapy outlined by Kazdin and Wilson (1978) and G. T. Wilson and Franks (1982). Typically, descriptions of behavior therapy using these categories equate social learning theory with the work of Albert Bandura (for example, Rosenthal, 1982; S. M. Turner, Calhoun, & Adams, 1981). In fact, however, another major social learning theory was developed by Julian Rotter and deserves inclusion here, although Rotter's approach is anything but a traditional behavior therapy.

Defining social learning theory The term social learning theory can be used in both a general and a specific way. Specifically, it refers to the distinct but similar theoretical and empirical contributions of Bandura and Rotter. Their separate theories form the cornerstones of a more general perspective that includes contributions by Mischel (1973, 1979), E. R. Patterson (1982), Lefcourt (1976, 1981), Levenson (1974), and numerous other researchers who work with concepts, assumptions, measures, and a view of human behavior common to the work of Rotter or Bandura. How broadly the term social learning theory should be applied is, in fact, controversial. Some restrict its reference to one or the other of Rotter's or Bandura's theory; others use it to include all or most approaches to behavior therapy and some nonbehavioral approaches. Further, social learning theory has so much in common with the next approach we will examine, cognitive behavior therapy, that it is difficult to determine whether therapies based on social learning theory are part of a broadly defined cognitive behavior therapy, or whether cognitive behavior therapy belongs with social learning theory. Perhaps both alternatives are true. Nevertheless, I shall use the term social learning theory to refer to the more general perspective.

Social learning theory as a more general theory of human behavior is really a loose collection of theories and research that, pulled together, provides a remarkably comprehensive view of human behavior. It incorporates both behavior and cognitive theories of learning. It represents a major theoretical perspective in personality psychology, developmental psychology, and social psychology and has contributed much to community psychology (Rappaport, 1977). As noted earlier, the scope of social learning theory has allowed it to be used in counseling and psychotherapy as an umbrella term, and it is in this sense that all behavior therapy can be viewed as an application of social learning theory (Craighead et al., 1981) (review Table 4.1).

The development of social learning theory Chapter 3 provided an historical overview of the merging of psychology's two research traditions, and a theoretical perspective emphasizing both social behavior and learning was clearly part of that merger. Although Miller and Dollard (1941) were the first to use the term social learning, the first fully developed social learning theory was presented by Julian Rotter (born 1916) in 1954, with the publication of *Social Learning and Clinical Psychology*. Rotter has consistently seen his theory as one possible social learning theory rather than as the social learning theory (Phares, 1984), but neither he nor his students have been afraid to criticize other social learning theories (for example, see Bandura, 1983; Kirsch, 1982). Reflecting more recently on the development of his theory, Rotter (1982a) wrote:

> Social learning theory in its earliest formulations was an attempt to integrate the two modern trends in American psychology—the stimulus-response or reinforcement theories on the one hand, and the cognitive or field theories on the other. Social learning theory includes both behavioral constructs and internal or subjective constructs; but it requires the performance of objective, indirect operations to measure the subjective constructs. Consequently, the development of social learning theory has been concerned from the beginning with problems of measurement. (pp. 2–3)

Miller and Dollard had based their social learning model on the work of Hull and thus postulated that a behavior must reduce some acquired drive for reinforcement, and therefore learning, to take place. They took cognitive concepts from Freudian theory (for example, defense mechanisms) and defined them operationally in drive-reduction terms, but their explanation of behavior was not truly cognitive. Rotter's approach was quite different. As Rotter has noted, "The name *social learning theory* derives from the principles that (1) reinforcement is not tied to physiological drives or drive stimulus reduction, and (2) in complex postinfancy human behavior, it is the behavior of other humans—that is, social reinforcement—that becomes the more important determinant of behavior" (Rotter, 1982a, p. 4).

Rotter's theory of personality places great emphasis on the cognitive phenomena of expectancy and attribution and focuses on the conditions under which acquired behaviors will be performed as opposed to the actual process by which they are acquired. As Phares (1984) has pointed out, this contrasts with Bandura's approach to social learning theory, which centers on the ways in which individuals acquire complex patterns of behavior in social settings. In this sense, the work of Rotter and Bandura complement each other.

As noted earlier, in the behavior therapy literature, the term social learning theory is usually used to refer to the contribution of Bandura; often the work of Rotter is ignored or mentioned only in passing as a contribution to cognitive therapy (Kazdin, 1978b). At least two factors explain this omission of Rotter and emphasis on Bandura. First, given the early, restrictive model of behavior therapy, the clearly cognitive thrust of Rotter's approach would have kept it outside the realm of behavior therapy; despite its emphasis on reinforcement, Rotter's work has generally been viewed as a personality theory within the clinical research tradition. Second, Bandura's contributions to behavior therapy have been continuous and voluminous, and his own development toward a cognitive emphasis occurred in tandem with behavior therapy's development toward the same. His development, of course, helped bring about the changes in behavior therapy while in turn being influenced by them.

Albert Bandura (born 1925) has contributed significantly to several areas of psychology, and some of his experimental findings, especially those concerning modeling, can be found in a broad range of psychological and educational journals and textbooks. For our present purposes, we will trace his contributions to behavior therapy and describe his social learning theory in broad terms. In a 1961 issue of *Psychological Bulletin,* Bandura wrote an important article entitled "Psychotherapy as a Learning Process." Like many of Bandura's most influential papers, it was both informative and a call for change. The article began:

> While it is customary to conceptualize psychotherapy as a learning process, few therapists accept the full implications of this position. Indeed, this is best illustrated by the writings of the learning theorists themselves. Most of our current methods of psychotherapy represent an accumulation of more or less uncontrolled clinical experiences and, in many instances, those who have written about psychotherapy in terms of learning theory have merely substituted a new language. (p. 143)

In his article, Bandura provided a list of psychological processes by which behavior can be changed. Though he indicated that the list was not exhaustive, it included counterconditioning, extinction, discrimination learning, methods of reward, punishment, and social imitation. In this article, Bandura used the term social learning theory broadly to include the behavior therapies, but with the 1969 publication of his *Principles of Behavior Modification,* he had clearly integrated the various processes noted above into a theoretical framework with clinical and experimental support. His book served to demonstrate that diverse learning theories and techniques could be synthesized. More importantly, it presented a vision of human behavior characterized by *reciprocal determinism* and gave greater importance to cognition. Not until the 1977 publication of *Social Learning Theory,* however, did Bandura present his full theory. The evolution of Bandura's thinking, as well as the change that had occurred in the field of psychology, is evident in the opening line of the preface: "In this book I have attempted to provide a unified theoretical framework for analyzing human *thought* [italics added] and behavior" (1977b, p. vi). Bandura thus advanced cognition from a secondary role in his theory to a central role as he developed an information-processing model of cognition (Rosenthal, 1982).

As mentioned above, Bandura proposed reciprocal determinism as an explanation of the causes of human behavior. As summarized in Figure 4.3, in the social learning view, human behavior is explained in terms of continuous reciprocal interaction among the person (internal processes of thought and feeling), the person's behavior (external action), and influences in the environment (rewards and penalties associated with the behavior). These three determinants interact continually; no single factor causes another without being influenced itself. As Bandura (1977b) has pointed out, "This conception of human functioning then neither casts people into the role of powerless objects controlled by environmental forces nor free agents who can become whatever they choose" (p. vii).

Bandura's social learning theory provides an explanation of human behavior that gives a central role to cognitive processes as well as identifying determinants of human behavior that translate readily into a variety of intervention techniques. In summary, social learning theory, with its emphasis on integrating behavioral and cognitive processes with the social environment, is more than one of four approaches to behavior therapy. It is also a broad and comprehensive theory that supports many therapeutic strategies.

Cognitive Behavior Modification

Because cognitive phenomena are easily identified through introspection, they may be readily investigated.

—Aaron T. Beck

Cognitive therapy, cognitive-learning therapy, cognitive behavior therapy, and *self-control therapy* are all alternative names for all or part of the approach

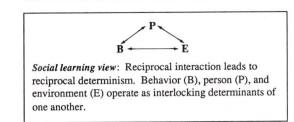

B = *f* (**P, E**)

Unidirectional. The person and situation are independent. Behavior (B) is a function of the person (P) and the environment (E).

B = *f* (**P ⇌ E**)

Personal and environmental influences are bidirectional, but behavior is unidirectional. Behavior (B) is a function of the interaction between the person (P) and the environment (E).

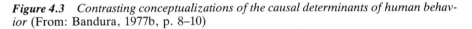

Social learning view: Reciprocal interaction leads to reciprocal determinism. Behavior (B), person (P), and environment (E) operate as interlocking determinants of one another.

Figure 4.3 *Contrasting conceptualizations of the causal determinants of human behavior* (From: Bandura, 1977b, p. 8–10)

called *cognitive behavior modification.* The confusing diversity of teims has come about as contributors have given their approaches slightly different names to distinguish them from the work of others. Ultimately, the similarities among the approaches are more pronounced than the differences, but the different terms live on.

The place of the study of cognition in the science of psychology is one of this book's recurring themes. Chapter 3, for example, traced the history of cognitive processes as a topic among researchers and practitioners and discussed the emergence of cognitive psychology as an experimental science. Though the present chapter shows that the role of cognition is still being debated, there is no question that a great many contemporary practitioners of behavior therapy view cognitive processes as a necessary part of both theory and therapy. Again, the issue is not whether cognition exists and is important but whether or not a scientific psychology can deal with what is not observable, and further, whether in the long run that involvement, to paraphrase Ullmann (1981), will prove to be more of a hindrance or a help.[2]

[2]Ullman's (1981) article "Cognitions: Help or Hindrance?" clearly stated the problems many see in introducing cognitive concepts into the practice of behavior therapy. Of particular interest is Ullmann's "glossary of cognitive terms for the behaviorally oriented." He gave behavioral (see footnote 1) definitions to such cognitive terms as *expectation, attitude, feeling, meaningful, feelings about self, ideal, self-actualization, self-control, wish,* and so forth. For example, he defined "personality/personality trait" as "the relative frequency, latency, duration, and intensity of a person's behavior. People who are aggressive aggress sooner or more frequently or longer or stronger than some hypothetically average person" (p. 22).

To add to the confusion, in the last section we saw the central role given to cognitive processes in social learning theory. What distinguishes cognitive behavior modification from social learning theory? The basic distinction is the degree to which advocates of each emphasize cognition in therapy. Social learning theorists typically prefer performance-based approaches, while cognitive therapists emphasize changing thought processes as a means of changing performance (G. T. Wilson, 1978).

The development of cognitive behavior modification   Kazdin and Wilson (1978), noting that cognitive behavior modification is the most recent development within behavior therapy, described it as follows:

> The unifying characteristic of cognitive behavior modification techniques is the emphasis on the importance of cognitive processes and private events as mediators of behavior change. Implicit assumptions about the world, interpretations and attributions of one's own behavior, thoughts, images, self-statements, sets, strategies of responding, and similar processes are considered the source of a client's problem and the determinants of therapeutic change. (pp. 5–6)

A number of authors have identified the sources of cognitive behavior therapy (Kazdin, 1978b; Mahoney & Arnkoff, 1978; Meichenbaum & Cameron, 1982). The reasons behavior therapists shifted toward including cognitive processes in therapy were described earlier. Of special historical importance was the development of Bandura's thinking outlined in the last section. The publication of Bandura's *Principles of Behavior Modification* in 1969 set the stage for cognitive behavior modification, as the central role of cognition and the notion of reciprocal determinism were important components in its development (Mahoney & Arnkoff, 1978). Parallel changes had occurred in personality theory and nonbehavioral therapy, especially with the 1954 publication of Rotter's *Social Learning and Clinical Psychology,* which emphasized cognitive phenomena like expectancies, but this and other personality research appear to have had little direct influence on behavior therapy (Kazdin, 1978b).

Most descriptions of cognitive behavior modification credit Albert Ellis (born 1913) with its formal beginning. Despite the clear connection between behavior therapy and cognitive behavior modification, Ellis developed much of his *rational-emotive therapy* (RET) outside of the confines of traditional behavior therapy. Ellis's work is fully described in Chapter 10, but a few comments are necessary here. Ellis developed his particular brand of cognitive behavior modification, RET, after several disillusioning years as a practitioner of psychoanalysis. His intent was to blend behaviorism with his philosophical interests: pragmatism, phenomenology, humanism, and existentialism (Sahakian & Lundin, 1984a). He began RET in 1955, and although it was slow to catch on, by 1976 it claimed a larger following among practitioners than did Rogers's person-centered therapy (Mahoney & Arnkoff, 1978, citing Garfield & Kurtz, 1976). The popularity of Ellis's approach is due in part to the enthusiasm of Ellis himself, but a commonsense quality to the therapy also makes it attractive. Ellis asserted that changing behavior means changing the self-verbalizations in which we humans continuously engage, and changing those self-verbalizations is a relatively straightforward matter. As Rimm and Masters (1979) have pointed out, practitioners and laypeople alike have found such an approach logical and easy to apply.

More recent developments in cognitive behavior modification have paralleled, rather than grown out of, Ellis's work. Ellis (1980) has outlined the similarities and differences between his work and other cognitive behavior therapies. Meichenbaum's (1977) cognitive-behavior modification, Beck's (1976) cognitive therapy, and Thoresen and Mahoney's (1974) work on self-control all fit in this category. In general, cognitive behavior modification approaches can be grouped into the following categories: cognitive restructuring, coping skills therapies, and problem-solving therapies. Figure 4.4, reprinted from Mahoney and Arnkoff (1978), provides an overview.

Cognitive Restructuring	Coping Skills Therapies	Problem-Solving Therapies
Rational-emotive therapy (RET) (Ellis, 1962)	Covert modeling (Cautela, 1971; Kazdin, 1973)	Behavioral problem solving (D'Zurilla and Goldfried, 1971)
Self-instruction (Meichenbaum, 1974)	Coping skills training (Goldfried, 1971)	Problem-solving therapy (Spivack and Shure, 1974; Spivack, Platt, and Shure, 1976)
Cognitive therapy (Beck, 1970, 1976)	Anxiety management training (Suinn and Richardson, 1971)	
	Stress inoculation (Meichenbaum, 1975)	Personal science (Mahoney, 1974, 1977)

Figure 4.4 Contemporary approaches to cognitive behavior therapy. (From: Mahoney & Arnkoff, 1978, p. 703. [Original title of table: "Contemporary Cognitive Learning Therapies"])

In summary, cognitive behavior modification is the most recent development in behavior therapy, and it parallels the shift toward the study of cognition within the discipline of experimental psychology. Along with social learning theory, cognitive-behavioral therapies are well-grounded in experimental psychology (Foreyt & Rathjen, 1978), and there appears to be serious commerce between experimental cognitive psychologists and those applying cognitive theory in cognitive behavior modification (Bower, 1978). We appear to have arrived at a new treatment paradigm, and social learning theory, cognitive behavior modification, and probably the multimodal therapy of A. A. Lazarus

(1976) together seem to constitute a trend in which the differences among the various approaches are less striking than their similarities.[3]

Assessment and Accountability in Behavior Therapy

When behavior therapy restricted its focus to overt actions and avoided cognition, it was clear what distinguished it from more traditional therapies. But as both the subject matter and the methods of behavior therapy have broadened, its boundaries have blurred, so that, today, some may see little or no difference between, for example, cognitive behavior modification and some Rogerian or neo-Freudian approaches. Behavioral and nonbehavioral approaches to therapy differ fundamentally, however, in regard to the concept of personality.

Most nonbehavioral approaches to therapy depend on a personality theory of some sort. In such approaches, personality is viewed in terms of structural components (traits, drives, needs, and so forth) that express themselves in behavior. Behavior is often seen as the product of some form of conflict or other type of internal activity. Changing behavior means changing some internal set of events, and preparation for therapy includes doing a personality assessment (if any assessment is considered important). As outlined in Chapter 2, numerous projective and psychometric tests were developed for that purpose.

Behavior therapy has generally avoided personality constructs in favor of measuring responses. These responses may be verbal, emotional, mental, physiological, or physical, but treatment deals directly with the various expressions of personality. The general term used for this type of evaluation is *behavioral assessment,* and the literature on the subject is growing (for example, see Ciminero, Calhoun, & Adams, 1977; Cone & Hawkins, 1977). Behavioral assessment and personality assessment differ in their subject matter, method, and purpose. The difference in subject matter is obvious. Methodologically, behavioral assessment procedures are more direct, although not necessarily less sophisticated, than those used in personality assessment. In regard to purpose, assessment is for behavior therapists a sine qua non rather than a potential shortcut in the therapeutic process. As discussed earlier, assessment enables behavior therapists to identify the client's complaint as specifically and operationally as possible, quantify it, and then monitor changes. Whether those changes are in the frequency and intensity of an upsetting thought, the amount of muscle tension in the forehead, or the number of cigarettes smoked on a given morning, assessment continues throughout the process of therapy rather than being a prelude.

---

[3]Despite differences among the work of Bandura, Beck, Ellis, Mahoney, Meichenbaum, and Rotter, one journal—*Cognitive Therapy and Research*—presents much research based on their theories and therapies.

Behavioral Assessment

Cautela (1977) explained the role of assessment (calling it "behavioral analysis") in the practice of behavior therapy using what he called his *ABC* paradigm. In this paradigm, *A* represents the antecedent events (stimuli) that elicit the behavior (*B*) targeted for change, which must be defined operationally and appropriately measured. *C* refers to the consequences of the behavior, which influence the probability of its occurring. The purpose of behavioral analysis, or assessment, is to discover and show the relationships among *A, B,* and *C.* Thorough behavioral assessment provides: (1) the client's description of the problem or problems, (2) the historical events that have contributed to the development of the problem, (3) current situations that maintain the problem, and (4) any biological factors.

To assess behavior, practitioners may use one or more of the following: (1) interviews, (2) direct behavioral observation in natural settings, (3) written checklists or questionnaires, and (4) physiological measures. The focus of these procedures is always on obtaining specific information about the problem behavior.

Interviews   Interviews are a regular part of assessment in most approaches to counseling and psychotherapy. In behavior therapy, however, although practitioners use the traditional rapport-building skills of unconditional positive regard, empathy, and genuineness in interviewing, they do not assume that either assessment or therapy works simply because of those skills (Rimm & Masters, 1979). Meyer, Liddell, and Lyons (1977) have pointed out that the behavioral interview is important because it enables the therapist to gather information about the problem from the client's unique perspective, thus making the client the center of therapy as well as providing time for the necessary client-therapist relationship to develop. The important questions in behavioral interviews are not why but what, where, when, and how (Meyer et al., 1977, citing Ullmann & Krasner, 1969; Rimm & Masters, 1979, citing A. A. Lazarus, 1971). In other words, the interview solicits specific information about *what* the problem is (the actual response), *where* and *when* the problem occurs (the stimulus conditions eliciting the response), and *how* the problem developed and *how* it is maintained (the circumstances surrounding its appearance and the consequences maintaining the response).

Direct observation in natural settings   The social and biological sciences have a tradition of naturalistic observation, in which a trained observer studies an organism in its natural context. In anthropology and sociology, this technique of careful observation of behavior in its cultural context is known as *ethnography.* Naturalistic observation has a special appeal for behavior therapists because of behavior therapy's emphasis on the environment's role in the development and maintenance of the problem behavior. Practitioners can set up both assessment and treatment to be done in the natural setting where the client's problem behavior occurs. Though institutional settings like hospitals, schools, correctional institutions, and so forth are ideal for complete observation, behavior therapists have done assessment and treatment in the home or workplace as well (Kazdin, 1975a, 1978b; G.R. Patterson, Reid, Jones, & Conger, 1975). Assessment in the natural setting may involve having the client or a significant other person in the client's life monitor the frequency, duration, or intensity of a target behavior or, in an institutional setting, having a trained observer do so (Goldfried & Davison, 1976).

Checklists and questionnaires There are numerous checklists, schedules, questionnaires and other self-monitoring techniques that can be grouped under the heading of "paper-and-pencil techniques" (Ciminero, Nelson, & Lipinski, 1977). Some forms are general questionnaires. For example, Cautela's (1977) Behavioral Analysis History Questionnaire (BAHQ) provides the client with an opportunity to describe his or her problem, personality, and so forth, as well as asking direct questions about marital, family, sexual, employment, educational, religious, and health histories. Other forms are more specific. For example, Cautela's (1977) Psychiatric Reinforcement Survey Schedule (PRSS) may be used to identify what activities a client would find reinforcing, so that appropriate rewards can be used to shape behaviors. Figures 4.5 and 4.6 show sample items from some of the useful surveys developed by Cautela.

One of the most comprehensive and useful paper-and-pencil assessment tools is the Life History Questionnaire developed by A. A. Lazarus (1976). For a discussion of Lazarus's multimodal therapy and his questionnaire, the reader may skip ahead to Chapter 10.

Physiological measures Changes in action, feeling, and thought are biological events. Measures of physiological changes often provide the most solid data for determining changes in the client's behavior, and, increasingly, behavior therapists are taking advantage of the considerable technology now available for measuring and monitoring biological changes. This assessment strategy is discussed more fully in the Biofeedback section later in this chapter.

Thorough methods of assessment provide information about the development and maintenance of problem behaviors. Generally, though, such assessment tools do not generate data that can be generalized to other clients or incorporated into the scientific literature. Until recently, the difficulty of doing serious scientific investigation with single clients created a formidable gap between the work of researchers and the work of practitioners. With the development of single-case experimental design, this appears to be changing.

Single-Case Experimental Design

One of the most promising developments in the quest to bring research and clinical work together has been the *single-case experimental design,* also called

---

Sexual History

When and how did you first learn about sex? _____ _____
_____

Was sex ever discussed at home?

        not at all _____ occasionally _____ a fair amount of time _____ frequently _____

What was the attitude of your parents concerning sex?

        It was considered shameful to discuss _____

        Not exactly shameful, but not discussed much_____

        A natural function to be discussed without embarrassment _____

Describe your first sexual experience _____ _____
_____

If you masturbate, when did you first start? _____

When did you have your first sexual intercourse? _____

Have you ever had any homosexual experience? _____

	Times per week	*Times per month*
What is your sexual activity at the present time?		
a. Masturbation	_____	_____
What do you imagine when you masturbate?		
_____		
_____		
b. Light petting (kissing and hugging)	_____	_____
c. Heavy petting (touching sexual organs)	_____	_____
d. Homosexual contacts	_____	_____
e. Intercourse	_____	_____

(for female clients)

When did you have your first period? _____

How comfortable are your periods?

____ very uncomfortable   ____ uncomfortable   ____ fairly comfortable   ____comfortable

Do you often feel depressed just before your period? _____

Do you use birth control devices or pills? Yes _____ No _____ If so, what type? _____

Figure 4.5 *Sexual History section of the Behavioral Analysis History Questionnaire (BAHQ)* (From: Cautela, 1977, p. 11)

intrasubject experimental design (Craighead et al., 1981). Although it has primarily been applied in behavior modification, it can be readily used in all forms of counseling and psychotherapy (Kazdin, 1982b). In *The Scientist Practitioner,*

A: The Self-Rating Behavioral Scale (SRBS) (Cautela, 1977, p. 17)

Directions: The behaviors which a person learns determine to a large extent how well he gets along in life. Below is a list of behaviors which can be learned. Check the ones which you think you need to learn in order to function more effectively or to be more comfortable.

I need to learn:

_____ 1. to stop drinking too much.
_____ 2. to stop smoking too much.
_____ 3. to stop eating too much.
_____ 4. to control my feelings of attraction to members of my same sex.
_____ 5. to control my feelings of attraction to members of the opposite sex.
_____ 6. to overcome my feelings of nausea when I'm nervous.
_____ 7. to stop thinking about things that depress me.
_____ 8. to stop thinking about things that make me anxious.

...

_____ 24. to feel less afraid of the darkness.
_____ 25. to feel less afraid of certain animals.
_____ 26. to stop thinking the same thoughts over and over.
_____ 27. to stop counting heartbeats.
_____ 28. to stop hearing voices.
_____ 29. to stop thinking people are against me or out to get me.
_____ 30. to stop seeing strange things.
_____ 31. to stop wetting the bed at night.

...

B: The Assertive Behavior Survey Schedule (ABSS) (Cautela & Upper, 1976, pp. 97–98)

1. What would you do in the following situations? Indicate by circling number 1, 2, or 3.
   A. In a restaurant, you have ordered your favorite meal. When it comes, it is not cooked to your liking.
      1. You tell the waitress that it is not cooked to your taste or liking and have her take it back to be cooked to your taste or liking.
      2. You complain that it is not cooked to your taste or liking, but you say you will eat it anyway.
      3. You say nothing.
   B. You have been waiting in line to buy a ticket. Someone gets in front of you.
      1. You say it is your turn, and you get in front of him.
      2. You say it is your turn, but you let the person go before you.
      3. You say nothing.
   C. In a supermarket, you are waiting in line at the checkout counter. Someone gets in front of you.
      1. You say, "I'm sorry, but I was here first," and you take your turn.
      2. You say, "I'm sorry, but I was here first," but you let the person go ahead of you.
      3. You say nothing.

Figure 4.6   Excerpts from two behavior analysis forms

an important book for practitioners of all persuasions, Barlow et al. (1984) presented a rationale for quantifying and monitoring client behavior by means of single-case experimentation. Their three principal reasons were that these practices: (1) improve treatment, (2) enhance clinical science, and (3) provide accountability.

In general terms, single-case experimental design involves monitoring problem behaviors continually over a period of time during which treatment procedures are introduced. The practitioner identifies and quantifies the targeted behaviors (thoughts, feelings, actions, physiological activities) and selects a treatment procedure that directly addresses those behaviors. Logically, changes in the independent variables (treatment) should be reflected in changes in the dependent variables (the targeted behavior) if the treatment is indeed effective.

A number of designs exist for measuring therapeutic change and assessing the effectiveness of specific treatments with specific clients. The actual strategies of single-case experimentation can become rather involved, and most are beyond the scope of this text. For our present purposes, we will look at three of four general strategies identified by Craighead et al. (1981): ABAB design, multiple-baseline design, and changing-criterion design.[4]

ABAB design   After identifying a targeted behavior, the practitioner records its frequency or collects similar data for a period of time. This period is referred to as the "A phase," or baseline phase. After the behavior has stabilized, a treatment phase begins, the "B phase." If the treatment results in some modification of the target behavior, and once that change has stabilized, the practitioner initiates a "reversal phase." In this second A phase, the practitioner restores the baseline conditions—that is, withdraws treatment. If the treatment has indeed been the factor effecting the change, the client's behavior should revert to its baseline pattern. Initiating a second B phase should then cause the client to resume the modified pattern of behavior. While the ABAB design vividly demonstrates the effectiveness of a treatment because a clear causal relationship exists, a number of problems are associated with it, not the least of which is the issue of the ethics of withholding an effective treatment.

Although this strategy is regularly applied to serious, complex problems, a simplified and somewhat whimsical example may serve to illustrate its use. You, the reader, are a practitioner, and your client is a balding, moderately rotund, 40-year-old university professor who is trying to write a textbook. He complains of being easily distracted, and he simply is not producing as much as he would like. Assuming that his semicompulsive nature will keep the quality of his writing adequate, you decide on the ABAB design for treatment with the hope of increasing his productivity. As part of Phase A, you have the client collect baseline data (the number of pages he completes each day) for a 2-week period. You then begin Phase B treatment. You decide on a positive reinforcement strategy, and the professor agrees to restrict his daily "playtime" on his personal computer to 15 minutes for every three pages he manages to write

---

[4]The present discussion of these three designs is drawn primarily from Craighead et al. (1981) and Kazdin (1975a, 1982). Craighead et al. (1981) presents a clear, comprehensive description of intrasubject experimental design (pp. 63–71).

that same day. He keeps an accurate measure of his productivity and, for several weeks, restricts his use of the personal computer to the formula agreed on with you, the practitioner. Within several weeks, his productivity has improved significantly. Following the ABAB design, you now discontinue the agreement to determine whether the reward system the two of you established is the cause of the change or whether the change is due to some other factor. A drop in productivity would indicate the treatment did cause the outcome; no decrease in productivity would suggest another cause. If the professor's productivity does drop, you eventually resume treatment. Should it not, you may have to examine your interpretation: He may simply have learned, in the best Skinnerian tradition, to produce more, even in the absence of reinforcement! This example also illustrates the ethical problem of the ABAB design: If the professor's productivity does improve, and it appears that he will meet his editor's deadline, does the practitioner have the right to suspend treatment?

Multiple-baseline design   This strategy for single-case experimentation measures the effectiveness of a treatment without treatment having to be withdrawn. There are three principal variations on this strategy: multiple-baseline design across *behaviors,* across *individuals,* and across *situations.* In each variation, the practitioner obtains baseline data on several items. In the first variation, the practitioner, working with one client, collects baseline data on several different behaviors but treats only one of them. If the targeted behavior changes, but the untreated ones do not, the treatment can be regarded as effective, and it can then be applied to the untreated behaviors. In the second variation, applying this strategy across individuals, the practitioner first obtains baseline data on a specific behavior for two or more persons. The practitioner then starts treating each client at a different time and, by comparing the results, determines whether or not the treatment has been effective. The third criteria, multiple-baseline design across situations, is used with individuals and groups when the targeted behavior exists in more than one situation. Following the same logic as in the other variations, after obtaining baseline data on each situation, the practitioner initiates treatment first in one situation and, later, in the other situations. Although in real life, changes in the baseline of the treated behavior, individual, or situation can affect the baseline of nontreated ones, multiple-baseline design has generally been an effective way of determining effectiveness without having to withdraw treatment (Kazdin, 1982b).

As another example, let us assume that you have chosen this strategy rather than the ABAB design for curing our poor professor. In addition to lacking productivity in writing his book (a deficit), our professor is also overindulging in food intake (excess par excellence). Initially, you have him monitor both behaviors, recording the number of pages he completes each day and the number of calories he consumes each day. Using the same treatment strategy as before (having him reward himself with time on the computer according to a formula related to the targeted behavior), you then apply it to his writing behavior only. Assuming that he eats just as much while writing more, after he has established his new level of productivity, you can apply the same strategy to his eating behavior; that is, you can relate his caloric intake to his computer time. If his first targeted behavior (the number of pages written) remains increased, and his second behavior (food intake) decreases, then you can assume that your reinforcement strategy works with clients like our professor and in similar situations.

Changing-criterion design Using this strategy, the practitioner identifies the behavior to be changed and establishes a baseline for it. A treatment procedure is introduced, typically a reward. Initially, the practitioner rewards the client liberally, but gradually, he or she changes the criterion for the reward. If changes in the client's behavior accord with the changes in the reward conditions, then one can be assumed to have caused the other. (As ersatz practitioner, the reader should be able to save our professor using this strategy without the help of the author, who is scheduled for computer time and some celery.)

Though the above discussion and examples may have at times suggested otherwise, single-case experimental design has become quite elaborate and is no longer viewed as useful only in simple applications of behavior modification. More importantly, such strategies allow practitioners to ask the right questions about treatment so that we will be better able to identify the real agents of change.

Basic Tools for Self-Regulation

Self-regulation is the goal of all of the behavior therapies. At the end of treatment, after formal treatment procedures have stopped, the client must still be able to maintain the changes achieved in therapy. There are other means to achieving self-regulation besides formal treatment, some of which have been integrated into contemporary behavior therapy and serve as basic tools. We will examine four such self-regulation tools, which can be used alone or as part of behavior therapy. Two of them, **meditation** and **hypnosis,** have existed in some form for many centuries. The other two, **progressive relaxation** and **biofeedback,** are products of our own century. In some interventions, practitioners will use one or more of these as a treatment without the benefit of other techniques. In other situations, they will use one or more of them during and after treatment to help the client stay free from symptoms.

The strategies to be outlined in this section benefit human beings by preventing or short-circuiting a potentially dangerous biological reaction: the stress reaction or stress response. Figure 4.7 presents a simplified model of the stress response that will help in understanding the discussion that follows.

The Stress Response

What we are calling the stress response is part of a defensive system first described by physiologist Walter B. Cannon (1929). Environmental demands

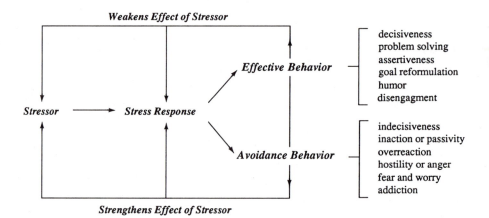

1. At times, the demands of life are so great, even catastrophic, that no behavior can effectively prevent a severe stress response.
2. Generally, though, an individual develops a repertoire of behaviors that he or she typically uses when physical, social, interpersonal, and psychological demands present themselves.
3. Effective behavior is realistic. The individual evaluates and acts when appropriate to reduce the demands. When that is not possible, the person recognizes that no solution is possible and disengages. When no solution or disengagement is possible, the stress reaction must be reduced directly through exercise, meditation, hypnosis, or some other means of short-circuiting the stress reaction.
4. Avoidance behavior is unrealistic. The individual may misevaluate the situation (underestimate or exaggerate the demands) or act inappropriately. In the end, the stressor is intensified. An extended pattern of this sort of behavior constitutes neurosis. Psychotherapy can help to change the pattern of behavior. Stress-reduction methods may also be used.

Figure 4.7   Stress response model

activate the sympathetic division of the autonomic nervous system. Through complex hormonal activity we prepare to meet the demands either by "fight" or "flight." This emergency reaction causes changes in the distribution and pressure of blood, heart rate, muscle activity, digestion, excretion—in other words, to the degree that there is real or anticipated threat, our entire body is affected. Pioneering research by Hans Selye (1956/1978), however, has demonstrated that, as important as this reaction is as part of our survival armament and as a source of motivating us to act, constant activation of this defense can eventually cause damage to one or more of the body's systems (constantly elevated blood pressure, for example, can lead to hypertension in the cardiovascular system). For men and women in the last half of our own century, everyday demands are not usually as dramatic as meeting a famished lion in the wild. Rather, a variety of demands from family, job, and social relationships activate the same system. The difference, of course, is that neither flight nor fight is an effective way of dealing with the everyday demands we face. Further, because the environmental demand is less dramatic and the activation milder, we often fail to notice that our defense system is being activated.

Stressor is a general term for those environmental demands. Stressors may be *physical* (pushing your car to the side of the road), *social* (completing a report for your boss), *interpersonal* (telling your spouse about your lost wedding band), or *psychological* (worrying about what might happen if a unicorn eats your okra plants). This last example is more important than it might appear, because highly improbable, and even impossible, events can trigger stress responses. Stress responses can come from real, anticipated, or imagined environmental demands.

Describing stress in terms of stimulus and response is one way of looking at it. Another view is provided by R. S. Lazarus and Folkman (1984), who view psychological stress as "a relationship between the person and the environment that is appraised by the person as taxing or exceeding his or her resources and endangering his or her well-being" (p. 21). This perspective is less mechanical and acknowledges the importance of cognitive appraisal.

Stress has been implicated in many medical and psychological disorders either as a cause or as an exacerbating factor. In fact, in the revised third edition of the *Diagnostic and Statistical Manual of Mental Disorders,* DSM–III–R (1987), each case receives a "multiaxial evaluation"; that is, it is evaluated along five separate diagnostic axes. One of the evaluation axes (IV) is Severity of Psychosocial Stressors. A variety of possible sources of stress are described, and the practitioner is asked to assess the severity of the stressors along a continuum from *none* to *catastrophic*. This development is an important recognition of the role of stress in maladaptive behavior.

The four basic tools described below are means of preventing or lessening the effects of stress in our lives. Each technique has the potential of producing in our bodies an effect opposite to that of the stress response: what Benson (1975) has called the *relaxation response*. In essence, these techniques activate the parasympathetic division of the autonomic nervous system. Activation of the parasympathetic division of the autonomic nervous system inhibits the sympathetic division. Thus, by teaching the body to relax—that is, to activate the parasympathetic system—the stress response can be prevented or interrupted.

Until recently, it was assumed in the West that functions controlled through the autonomic nervous system (for example, digestion) were beyond our control because they happened automatically. Still, Eastern cultures had always asserted that such control was possible through meditation, and some evidence of the truth of this existed in Western cultures in the practice of hypnosis. Serious scientific research on meditation and hypnosis, as well as Jacobson's (1929, 1934/1962) influential work on relaxation, now suggests that we can learn to relax, we can learn to activate the parasympathetic division of the autonomic nervous system. Further, biofeedback now permits accurate monitoring of body signals, while providing a new technology for controlling them. We turn now to the tools themselves.

Meditation

Meditation is the most basic and oldest form of purposeful self-regulation. Though meditation procedures of various sorts have existed for millennia, only within the last 50 years or so have Western scientists sought to explain the self-regulation achieved through these procedures. Western scientists' interest in meditation comes from an increasing awareness of a by-product of meditation: relaxation. Fascinating as watching someone walk on hot coals may be, modern-day scientists appear to be more fascinated with meditators' lowered blood pressures and heart rates.

Herbert Benson, a physician specializing in hypertension, summarized his research in the popular book *The Relaxation Response* (1975). According to Benson, despite a variety of differing descriptions of meditation, all include four basic elements: (1) a quiet environment, (2) an object to dwell on, (3) a passive attitude, and (4) a comfortable position. Benson also provides a straightforward meditation procedure free of philosophical and religious explanations. His and others' research confirms that meditation does produce relaxation (Benson & Wallace, 1972; R. K. Wallace, 1970) and can be readily integrated into a comprehensive program of psychotherapy or counseling (Kutz, Borysenko, & Benson, 1985).

Hypnosis

For the contemporary practitioner, hypnosis is one of the most useful tools available. It can be used to induce relaxation, reduce physical or psychological distress, enhance motivation, modify moods, and promote changes in behavior. Unfortunately, mention of hypnosis often conjures up images of entertainers (usually magicians) performing stage versions of hypnosis or, in the cinematic stereotype, of a deep-voiced man with dark-circled eyes who puts a damsel into a trance by swinging a gold watch while informing her that she is "under his power." Popular images like these bear little resemblance to modern hypnosis, although the popular images and the therapeutic tool have a common history. The use and abuse of hypnosis are intertwined with the beginning of psychotherapy, and we will examine that relationship in a later chapter. For our present purposes, we will outline hypnosis as currently understood by scientists, based on the work of Barber (1969, 1970, 1972), Hilgard (1965, 1973), Orne (1966, 1971, 1972), and others. Unanimity does not exist, but the brief description of hypnosis in a clinical setting that follows benefits from their research.

Hypnosis is a waking state characterized by increased relaxation and a heightened capacity for being influenced (suggestibility). The desired effects of hypnosis are put in the form of suggestions, the wording of which emerges from the discussion between the practitioner and the client. Achievement of these desired effects (for example, enhanced relaxation, reduced pain, improved memory, controlled emotions) is not unique to hypnosis, although hypnosis can be an efficacious way of tapping those potentials. Hypnosis is an interpersonal process characterized by trust that takes place because the client has learned what to expect and how to behave. The techniques used by the practitioner to elicit hypnosis can, therefore, take many forms, as long as the client knows what to expect. To undergo hypnosis, the client generally assumes a comfortable position and restricts his or her attention to a visual stimulus (real or imagined), a verbal stimulus, or both. Hypnosis is a social and cognitive skill that is learned over a period of time. As in other forms of learning, the readiness and motivation of the client as a learner, the persuasiveness and skillfulness of the practitioner as a teacher, and the characteristics of the environment influence the outcome. The client's imaginative capacity is one of the most important factors in the successful use of hypnosis. The client must also perceive the practitioner as knowledgeable, skilled, and trustworthy. The power rests with the client, however; the process is only facilitated by the practitioner. Hypnosis is used as a treatment by itself or with other techniques in all areas of psychotherapy and counseling and increasingly with behavior therapy.

The power of hypnosis has often been misunderstood and exaggerated. Like all forms of interpersonal influence, hypnosis has the potential for abuse. Therefore, like all techniques used in counseling and psychotherapy, hypnosis is best learned from an experienced practitioner in a supervised environment. Because hypnosis depends heavily on the expectations of the person being hypnotized, popular how-to books can be particularly misleading and dangerous. These books tend to emphasize outmoded techniques that reinforce the worst stereotypes the subject of the hypnosis may have. This can lead to outcomes that run the gamut from disappointing to tragic.

Progressive Relaxation

In 1929, Jacobson published *Progressive Relaxation,* and a few years later, he published a popular version of his ideas entitled *You Must Relax* (1934/1962). Jacobson, trained in psychology, physiology, and medicine, was convinced that stress, or tension, was a primary factor in heart disease and many other illnesses, and long before such ideas became popular, he developed techniques for counteracting the effects of stress. These techniques, described in the two books mentioned above and known as progressive relaxation, were based on numerous studies conducted by Jacobson and his colleagues. His basic technique involves systematically tensing then relaxing one muscle group after another. The effect of this progressive relaxation of the voluntary muscles is a generalized relaxation of the body that counteracts anxiety: In a short excerpt from *You Must Relax,* Jacobson (1934/1962) detailed his procedure. After telling the reader to lie on his or her back with arms unfolded and legs uncrossed, Jacobson instructed:

Under the condition stated, lie quietly on your back for about three or four minutes with eyes gradually closing. Delay in closing the eyes permits a more gradual letdown. You should neither speak nor be spoken to. After this preliminary rest, bend your left hand back at the wrist. While so doing, do not raise the left forearm, including the left elbow, from the couch, where it should rest throughout the period. . . . While this bending is maintained and your eyes remain closed, you should observe carefully a certain faint sensation in the upper portion of the left forearm. To give yourself time to become acquainted with this faint sensation, continue to bend back steadily for several minutes. This sensation is the signal mark of tension everywhere in your body. It deserves your interest, for it can prove a daily help to you. Vague as it is, you can learn to recognize and to distinguish it from other sensations. This will enable you to know at any moment when and where you are tense. (p. 100)

Throughout his relaxation exercises, Jacobson emphasized awareness of tension and awareness of relaxation as keys to self-regulation. Jacobson's contribution is particularly important because it provided a systematic way for an individual to influence autonomic functioning long before biofeedback made it possible to demonstrate that influence. Jacobson's techniques have been modified and developed by others and form an important part of Wolpe's reciprocal inhibition techniques described in the next chapter. In addition, progressive relaxation can be used with other forms of therapy or in combination with biofeedback.

Biofeedback

Feedback mechanisms are a vital part of the human body's natural means of self-regulation. Examine Figure 4.8 carefully. This diagram was created by G. E. Schwartz (1978), and it provides a simplified view of the ways in which the environment, the brain, and the organs of the body interact. A built-in feedback loop informs the brain of difficulties in the organs of the body, and the brain automatically regulates the total system. At certain levels of distress, of course, we become conscious of the process: Physical or psychological symptoms appear. We may experience dizziness, a headache, severe stomach pain, or some other indication of trouble. Unfortunately, by the time such an indication appears, serious damage may have already occurred. Biofeedback provides an artificial source of feedback that allows us to be aware of much less dramatic changes in biological functioning. This information can then be applied to self-regulation.

Numerous involuntary changes in our body take place without our awareness. Gradual changes in the distribution of blood, heart rate, blood pressure, gastric secretions, and muscle contractions mostly go unnoticed yet may eventually become a source of distress. Biofeedback, a general term for a collection of electronic instruments and clinical procedures, allows individuals to directly and indirectly monitor and change these underlying biological events. It does so by providing the client with continuous information about the *bioelectric* activity of specific physiological functions (Budzynski, Stoyva, & Peffer, 1980). Such information, or feedback, is usually relayed through visual or auditory

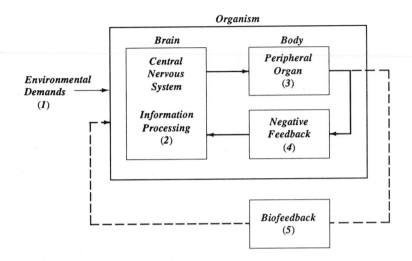

Simplified block diagram depicting (1) environmental demands influencing (2) the brain's regulation of its (3) peripheral organs, and (4) negative feedback from the periphery back to the brain. Disregulation can be initiated at each of these stages. Biofeedback (Stage 5) is a parallel feedback loop to Stage 4, detecting the activity of the peripheral organ (Stage 3) and converting it into environmental (Stage 1) input that can be used by the brain (Stage 2) to increase self-regulation.

Figure 4.8 *Simplified block diagram of the biofeedback process* (From: Schwartz, 1978, p. 75)

signals; therefore, what the client actually attempts to change is usually the frequency or intensity of a tone or light. The client thus changes the biosignal indirectly, by learning to change the visual or auditory stimulus that represents the biosignal. Although this type of new learning can clearly occur, how the laws of learning operate in this regard remains controversial (Kazdin, 1978b).

Biofeedback has been used alone to induce relaxation, in conjunction with systematic desensitization and other therapies to treat maladaptive behaviors, and as an adjunct or substitute for the medical treatment of numerous stress-related biological disorders, including migraine headaches, tension headaches, impotence, hypertension, stuttering, asthma, heart disease, muscle damage, and ulcers (for examples, see Benson, Shapiro, Tursky, & Schwartz, 1971; Budzynski, Stoyva, & Adler, 1970; Friar & Beatty, 1976; Lanyon, Barrington, & Newman, 1977).

A number of different biofeedback instruments have been devised, and some are rather specialized (for example, PERFS, the penile erection feedback system for the treatment of impotence).[5] The more commonly used biofeedback instruments are designed to monitor the relaxation response, since gaining control over the autonomic nervous system benefits a large number of phys-

[5]Your curiosity only merits the information that the penile erection feedback unit was developed by Biofeedback Systems, Inc., Boulder, Colorado.

ical and psychological disorders. Typically, the functions monitored are: brain wave activity (through an electroencephalograph, or EEG), muscle activity (through an electromyograph, or EMG), skin temperature (as a measure of blood flow), and sweating (the electrodermal response, or EDR, commonly called the galvanic skin response, or GSR) (Budzynski, Stoyva, & Peffer, 1980).

Unlike the other approaches mentioned above, biofeedback provides the practitioner with precise measures of changes in biological functioning. Given the present emphasis on accurate assessment and accountability, biofeedback is an important advance.

Meditation, hypnosis, progressive relaxation, and biofeedback are powerful tools for the eclectic practitioner. To attain self-regulation, clients often must reduce the body's stress response to real or anticipated threat. Apart from the use of chemicals, no more useful strategies exist for achieving that end than the tools described above.

Final Comments

My intention in this chapter was to set the stage for presenting some specific behavior therapy techniques, each of which aims, in one way or another, at some form of self-regulation. The last two chapters have described a number of major historical shifts. First, psychotherapy as a process became increasingly technical, increasingly dependent on research findings; second, behavior therapy, once a narrow perspective confined to the changing of overt behaviors, broadened its perspective to include cognitive processes as well as social behavior. What has emerged is a technology-based approach to changing every aspect of human behavior. Is this broadened and increasingly refined approach to psychotherapy enough? Is it capable of addressing more personal, existential questions that are major sources of conflict in people's lives?

To try to answer these questions, a look at an article by R. L. Woolfolk and Richardson (1984) might be helpful. Woolfolk and Richardson have pointed out that behavior therapy is much more than an approach to treatment; it is "an intellectual movement, a set of social practices, and a system of thought" (p. 778). As such, it promotes a worldview with all the strengths and weaknesses of a viewpoint based on science and technology. Behavior therapy, they said, is a product of a culture that has been transformed by scientific technology ("modernity"), and the worldview of such a culture is "rooted in the ideal of progress, a faith in the power of human abilities to be equal to any problem, the quest of certitude, and a devaluation of the traditional past" (p. 778). Behavior therapy is essentially amoral and humanistic, excluding from consideration all that cannot be brought under scientific scrutiny.[6] This being

---

[6]After the earlier discussions of humanistic psychology and its opposition to behaviorism, this description of behavior therapy may be confusing. Woolfolk and Richardson asserted that there are at least two kinds of humanism. The humanistic psychology of Maslow, Perls, and Rogers they term "romantic humanism"; behavior therapy, "classical humanism." Of this they wrote: "This

so, issues presented by the client that deal with values, meaning, and ultimate concerns fall outside the ken of behavior therapy. Woolfolk and Richardson wrote:

> But not all existential quandaries can be explained away. And those that cannot do not admit of technical answers. About all behavior therapy can offer here is some technique to control the emotional and behavioral impact of and absence of meaning. And although such palliatives have their place, one doubts that the simple elimination or control of the negative affect and cognitions emanating from our modern existential predicament is either an effective or a worthy solution. (p. 784)

It is with concerns like these in mind that I propose a model that joins self-regulation with maturity. In the lives of individuals faced with befuddled identities, social injustices, shifting values, nuclear threat, and ultimate death, effective psychotherapy and counseling require more resources than those provided by behavior therapy. At the same time, effective psychotherapy or counseling cannot tackle those questions until adequate levels of self-regulation are achieved.

Summary of Chapter 4

Chapter 4 addresses the topic of self-regulation by examining the theoretical and practical foundations of behavior therapy, a principal means of attaining self-regulation in therapy. The major points covered in this chapter are:

Self-Regulation and Behavior Therapy

1. The term self-regulation is used to refer to an individual's capacity to selectively monitor and modify his or her thoughts, feelings, and actions. Improved self-regulation is a common motivation for deciding to begin counseling or psychotherapy.
2. Self-regulation differs from will power and other traditional concepts. It involves systematically evaluating the internal and external conditions that have led or could lead to a particular goal and changing those conditions so that the goal is attained.
3. Behavior therapy is a term used for a broad group of behavioral, cognitive, and cognitive-behavioral treatment strategies, all aimed at enhancing the client's self-regulation.
4. Behavior therapy and behavior modification are used synonymously to refer to a set of clinical procedures in which practitioners: (1) define the client's behavioral, cognitive, and affective complaints in terms of specific,

---

is the tradition that, without reservation, commits its allegiance to the primacy of science and reason in intellectual affairs, opposes all irrational authority and arbitrary privilege, and dedicates itself to the active enhancement of human liberty . . ." (p. 781).

measurable operational variables; (2) use change strategies based upon experimental psychological research, principally research on human learning; and (3) measure outcomes to gauge their success.

Theoretical Foundations: Learning Theory

5. Behavior therapy is an application of the experimental research done on human and animal learning. As such, it emerged from the experimental research tradition rather than the clinical research tradition.

6. Two major theoretical perspectives exist in regard to human learning: behavior theory and cognitive theory. Behavior theory focuses on the study of overt behaviors with little regard to internal processes. Rather, the behavior theory of learning emphasizes the connection between the stimulus and the response (connectionism). Behavior theory may also emphasize either the contiguous relationship between the stimulus and the response (contiguity theory) or the role of the consequences of the learning (reinforcement theory). Cognitive theory focuses on the various internal processes that mediate between the stimulus and the response. Topics of concern in cognitive theory include attention and perception, the development of learning ability, attitudes, knowledge acquisition and storage, and so forth.

7. Though behavior therapy has traditionally been based on behavior theory, serious reservations have arisen concerning the applicability of much of experimental research on learning to human behavior. Learning research based on behavior theory has relied heavily on infrahuman subjects, and though some treatment strategies have been successfully developed for use with humans based on this work, it now appears to provide only part of the treatment picture. Therefore, contemporary behavior therapy uses research from other sources, including cognitive psychology and social psychology, while maintaining its emphasis on specifying behaviors, measuring outcomes, and the value of experimental data.

Contemporary Approaches to Behavior Therapy

8. Contemporary behavior therapy can be grouped into the following categories: (1) the neobehavioristic mediational S-R model; (2) applied behavior analysis; (3) social learning theory; and (4) cognitive behavior modification.

9. The neobehavioristic mediational S-R model represents a group of behavior therapies that rely heavily on classical conditioning and counterconditioning as a means of changing behavior. In this approach, mediational factors (for example, imagination) are recognized but are assumed to follow stimulus-response laws. Therapies in this approach avoid cognitive interventions, and treatment often focuses on anxiety-based disorders.

10. Behavior therapies within the applied behavior analysis approach are based on the principles of operant learning. Treatment is aimed at correct-

ing behavioral deficits or behavioral excesses by systematically changing the consequences of the targeted behavior. The techniques used in this approach include but are not limited to those described as behavior modification techniques.

11. The term social learning theory is used in a number of different ways. As an approach to behavior therapy, it emphasizes the roles of the external environment (classical conditioning), reinforcement (operant conditioning), and cognitive mediation. Importance is given to expectancies, attribution, and modeling in the process of therapy.

12. In cognitive behavior modification, behavior is changed through intervention at the level of cognition. Rational processes, problem solving, attitude changing, and the like are emphasized.

Assessment and Accountability in Behavior Therapy

13. Unlike more traditional therapies, which begin with some form of personality assessment, behavior therapy emphasizes behavioral assessment. Behavioral assessment is used to determine the relationships among antecedent events (stimuli), the behavior targeted to be changed, and the consequences influencing the probability that that behavior will be performed (rewards and punishments).

14. A variety of behavioral assessment techniques exists, including the interview, direct behavioral observation in natural settings, written checklists and questionnaires, and physiological measures.

15. Single-case experimental design allows practitioners to assess behavior and treatment on an ongoing basis. This should eventually enrich the literature of the field, as well as providing accountability. Three single-case experimental designs were discussed: ABAB design, multiple-baseline design, and changing-criterion design.

Basic Tools for Self-Regulation

16. To enhance self-regulation, behavior therapists often use four basic tools: meditation, hypnosis, progressive relaxation, and biofeedback. Each of these techniques can be used apart from psychotherapy to counteract the stress response by producing the relaxation response. Each of these techniques in some way affects the autonomic nervous system.

17. Meditation is the oldest of these relaxation tools. Meditators require a quiet environment, an object to dwell on, a passive attitude, and a comfortable position. Beyond these elements, a number of systematic approaches for relaxation through meditation exist.

18. Hypnosis, often confused with stage hypnosis and other forms of magic, is a waking state characterized by relaxation and enhanced suggestibility. Understood and applied systematically, hypnosis is a powerful adjunct to many approaches to therapy, because in addition to providing relaxation,

it can be used to change a client's mood, awareness of pain, and performance.

19. Progressive relaxation works by systematically tensing muscles and then relaxing them. This causes a general relaxation and a reduced level of stress. Progressive relaxation techniques are a central part of systematic desensitization therapy and can be used with biofeedback training.

20. Biofeedback makes use of the body's own feedback loops to indicate changes in biosignals. The electrical activity of specific parts of the body is translated electronically into a visual or auditory signal. The client learns to control that signal, thereby regulating the biological events it represents.

Final Comments

21. Despite the technological and theoretical advances made in behavior therapy, serious questions remain about whether it can address humankind's existential questions. Questions related to values, morals, and ultimate realities are commonplace in psychotherapy, but behavior therapy is inherently ill-equipped to handle them. Self-regulatory strategies must thus be combined with approaches that address these wider concerns. The self-regulation and maturity synthesis is offered to address this issue.

CHAPTER 5

Contemporary Behavior Therapy Techniques

Happiness or misery is determined after the child is born. . . . Heredity provides the phonograph, but environment builds the record collection of the brain.

Andrew Salter

In organizing this chapter, I have departed from the usual way in which textbooks present the various approaches to counseling and psychotherapy. Typically, each therapy is presented as a system or school unto itself, identified with a particular practitioner and his or her followers. Accordingly, an author might talk about Rogers's person-centered therapy or Freud's psychoanalysis or Ellis's rational-emotive therapy, emphasizing the differences between them, both in theory and in practice. Indeed, they are different. Though the various approaches to behavior therapy are less sharply defined because there is so much commerce among them, they too can be, and usually are, organized in the same way. In this chapter, however, I emphasize the commonalities among the approaches to behavior therapy rather than their differences and so have organized my discussion according to the specific techniques used by behavior therapists of whatever approach. In essence, my organization acknowledges that the philosophical, methodological, and practical similarities among the various leading practitioners are more pronounced than their differences. The growing consensus is no more evident than in the diverse backgrounds of the over 3500 practitioners who belong to the Association for the Advancement of Behavior Therapy. Despite the many differences, the practitioners would appear to share the view K. Daniel O'Leary (1984) expressed in his Presidential Address to that body: "I believe that behavioral conceptualizations and theories have provided us with views of human behavior that are unrivaled except for psychodynamic theory. I believe that behavior therapy has had an influence in the mental health field throughout the world that is unprecedented since Freud's contribution in the early 1900's" (p. 219). Despite occasional quarrels, practitioners of behavior therapy share a concern for determining the best technique for modifying a specific behavior in a specific client population, and this has meant much borrowing, integrating, and reformulating of techniques. Although social learning theory appears to provide behavior therapy with a common theoretical framework, practical rather than theoretical or philosophical concerns dominate the relevant literature.

This chapter presents over a dozen specific behavior therapy techniques and uses two fictitious cases, designed to aid the reader in understanding the techniques rather than to instruct the reader how to use them.

Behavior Therapy Techniques: An Overview

Sample Case: Benny B. Bashful

A combination of utter misery and the prodding of a professor finally forced Benny Bashful (not his real name) to go to the university's counseling center in the second semester of his senior year. For almost four years, he had avoided taking part in even the most banal banter and spent most of his time on campus avoiding places where he might accidentally meet people who could recognize him from classes. This meant avoiding the cafeteria during peak hours, passing up recreational opportunities, and studying in the Classical Languages section of the library. Although on occasion Benny had spoken to professors, he felt anxious in the presence of his peers, because he believed that he was not as good-looking, articulate, or intelligent as they were. He never initiated conversation and avoided eye contact or even facial expressions that might suggest he was open to dialogue. This problem was especially pronounced when Benny was among women students. He was deeply in love with Celeste, a student in one of his classes, but while he would go to some lengths to observe her from a distance, approaching her and speaking to her were unthinkable. Benny recognized that the energy he put into avoiding other people was misdirected and that in the end he was only hurting himself; yet, this realization only depressed him further.

Objectively, Benny was average in appearance and intelligence, with a good sense of humor that he usually used to mock himself. His grades were below average, reflecting the amount of time Benny gave over to worry and depression. Benny's venture to the counseling center was part of a "deal" made with his history professor. The professor's class was a seminar requiring considerable interaction, a particularly difficult setting for Benny. Benny's unique brand of inertia and nervousness had earned him the nickname of "Mousy" among the other seminar students, and this alarmed the professor. She confronted him on his reticence one day after class and began to unravel the complex motivations behind the silence. A combination of persuasion, promises, and threats took Benny to the counseling center.

By way of introduction to the techniques of behavior therapy, let us consider Benny's case. Benny acts fearfully in a wide range of social situations, avoiding most interpersonal encounters. Why is he like this, and what type of therapeutic help will benefit him most? Pretending, for the moment, to be practitioners of behavior therapy, we have at least three ways of viewing and treating Benny's problem. First, we can see Benny as a person whose past social experiences have been difficult and anxious and whose anxiety has intensified and become generalized to a wide range of situations. Benny minimizes his anxiety by avoiding social situations. Therapy or counseling should overcome the anxiety, thereby enabling Benny to successfully challenge social situations. Alternatively, we can focus on Benny's lack of social skills. Once Benny learns successful coping skills and finds the use of those skills rewarding or satisfying, his anxiety will be overcome. Third, we can see Benny's problem as due to faulty thinking. He interprets events in self-deprecating ways, attributing positive qualities to others and negative ones to himself. No wonder he becomes anxious! The goal of counseling or psychotherapy must be to repair how Benny thinks. Which of the three explanations represents contemporary behavior therapy? Which best represents the techniques commonly used?

These are trick questions because these explanations and treatment descriptions are not mutually exclusive. This brings us to several fundamental points about the use of behavior therapy techniques today.[1] Each of the techniques of behavior therapy grows out of one of the four approaches outlined in Chapter 4: the neobehavioristic mediational S-R model, applied behavioral analysis, social learning theory, and cognitive behavior modification (see again Table 4.1). The four classifications are convenient ways of identifying the sources and theoretical foundations of the various behavior therapy approaches, but they can be misleading in terms of actual clinical practice. As noted early, considerable technical and theoretical commerce takes place among behavior therapy practitioners, and one technique may be found within several approaches, modified and given different causal explanations. In particular, techniques developed early in the history of behavior therapy (for example, assertiveness training, systematic desensitization, or modeling) have been incorporated across a full range of behavior therapies, sometimes with slightly different names, explanations, or both. For example, many behavior therapists would recommend some form of **assertiveness training** (also known as *assertion training or assertive training*) for Benny, but at least three basic models and many associated techniques exist for this training. Developed within the neobehavioristic approach and based on classical conditioning, it has been modified and adopted by each of the other approaches and today accords more closely with social learning theory (Fodor, 1980). Further, practitioners rarely use one technique alone. Rather, they select various techniques, working them into specific strategies for specific clients approaching problems from several angles.

In the present chapter, I assume a working knowledge of the previous one but focus on the specific techniques used by behavior therapists. For our present purposes, the techniques used in behavior therapy can be grouped as follows: (1) reciprocal-inhibition techniques, (2) anxiety-evoking techniques, (3) operant techniques, (4) modeling techniques, and (5) cognitive techniques. Table 5.1 relates these techniques to the four approaches to behavior therapy, providing an important overview of the chapter and complementing Table 4.1.

---

[1]The term *technique* is used as before to refer to a systematic procedure for completing a complex task. An individual approach to counseling or psychotherapy may use any number of techniques. The term *strategy* is really a military word referring to the planning of combat! Although these terms appear interchangeably in some of the literature, we will restrict the term strategy to an individualized plan, tailored to a specific client, that may incorporate a number of different techniques.

Table 5.1   *Types of Behavior Therapy Techniques and Their Theoretical Approaches*

Type	Specific Techniques	Theoretical Approach
Reciprocal-Inhibition Techniques	Thought-Stopping Assertiveness Training Systematic Desensitization	Neobehavioristic Mediational S-R Model
Anxiety-Evoking Techniques	Flooding Paradoxical Intention	Neobehavioristic Mediational S-R Model
Operant Techniques	Reinforcement Punishment Extinction	Applied Behavior Analysis
Modeling Techniques	Overt Modeling Symbolic Modeling Covert Modeling Participatory Modeling	Social Learning Theory
Cognitive Techniques	Covert Conditioning Cognitive Restructuring Stress-Inoculation Training	Cognitive Behavior Modification

Reciprocal-Inhibition Techniques

Practitioners of all forms of counseling and psychotherapy attempt to provide clients with the skills, information, awareness, and/or reassurance they need to confront the situations distressing them. Reciprocal-inhibition techniques, as well as anxiety-evoking techniques, involve identifying each situation that produces anxiety and leads to unadaptive behavior as a conditioned stimulus and systematically exposing the client directly to the evoking stimulus until it no longer produces the distressing anxiety (Eysenck, 1982). The difference between reciprocal-inhibition techniques and anxiety-evoking techniques has to do with how the client is exposed to the anxiety-evoking stimulus. Both types of techniques fit the neobehavioristic theoretical approach (see Table 5.1), and for both, the principles of classical conditioning are of central importance. In the neobehavioristic approach, cognition is viewed as a part of human behavior that follows the same mechanistic laws of biology and learning that apply to actions, but the approach neither ignores cognitions nor views them as falling outside the therapeutic process (see Wolpe, 1978).

    The first comprehensive application of the law of learning to psychotherapy without reliance on psychoanalytic concepts came with the publication of Andrew Salter's *Conditioned Reflex Therapy* in 1949.[2] Salter used Pavlovian

---

[2]Salter developed the first comprehensive approach to therapy based upon Pavlovian conditioning. His outspoken rejection of psychoanalysis contrasts his work sharply with other important contributions of the time, especially that of Dollard and Miller (described in Chapter 3). Salter's work has generally been acknowledged (Kazdin, 1978b; Wolpe, 1958, 1982), but his

conditioning to "recondition" and "disinhibit" client behavior. Our contemporary understanding of reciprocal-inhibition techniques relies more heavily on the work of Wolpe, however, beginning with the publication of *Psychotherapy by Reciprocal Inhibition* in 1958. Since that time, Wolpe has developed a comprehensive approach to behavior therapy that uses a wide range of techniques based principally on classical and operant learning. Wolpe's *The Practice of Behavior Therapy* (1982), now in its third edition, is the most complete presentation of his ideas.

Reciprocal-inhibition techniques, as well as anxiety-evoking techniques, are designed to help the client overcome unadaptive habits—that is, ways of thinking, acting, and feeling that limit or distress the client. Although other disorders are treated, these techniques are applied primarily to neurotic disorders. Wolpe (1982) defines neuroses as "persistent unadaptive learned habits whose foremost feature is anxiety" (p. 23). Anxiety is a person's characteristic pattern of autonomic response to a stimulus so noxious or painful that it prompts escape behavior (Wolpe, 1958, 1982). *Fear,* a synonym for the anxious response to the noxious stimulus, is described by Wolpe (1982) as the "centerpoint of the neuroses" (p. 1); in other words, fear is the manifestation of this neurotic reaction in the client. Neurotic fear, like everyday fears, has two forms: *classically conditioned* neurotic fears and *cognitively based* neurotic fears (Wolpe, 1981). Classically conditioned neurotic fears are learned through conditioning, just like other behaviors, as described in Chapter 4. Cognitively based neurotic fears, on the other hand, come from misinformation rather than conditioning. In some cases, the client has been told that something is painful, evil, or dangerous. In others, the fear comes from having observed the responses of others to a stimulus rather than having encountered it directly. Conditioned and cognitive neurotic fears can both be acquired through a single intense event or through a series of related experiences.

Drawing on several years of his own research on fear responses in cats, as well as on Sherrington's (1906) description of the operation of the nervous system, Wolpe (1958) articulated the principle of *reciprocal inhibition*: "If a response antagonistic to anxiety can be made to occur in the presence of anxiety-evoking stimuli so that it is accompanied by a complete or partial suppression of the anxiety responses, the bond between these stimuli and the anxiety responses will be weakened" (p. 71). At the level of autonomic functioning, what sorts of responses can be shown to be antagonistic to anxiety? Wolpe identified three such responses: *assertive* responses, *relaxation* responses, and *sexual* re-

techniques and ideas are less well known among practitioners than they might be. This is probably because Salter is neither a psychiatrist nor a Ph.D. psychologist. He is a practicing bachelor-level psychotherapist whose enthusiastic writing style is accurately described by Wolpe (1958, p. 119) as "flamboyant." Although his views on psychoanalysis are not very different from those of Wolpe, Lazarus, or Ellis, his scathing attacks on psychoanalysis often lack the more restrained rhetoric characteristic of the criticisms of others. Consider this comment: "It is high time that psychoanalysis, like the elephant of fable, dragged itself off to some distant jungle graveyard and died. Psychoanalysis has outlived its usefulness. Its methods are vague, its treatment is long drawn out, and more often than not, its results are insipid and unimpressive" (Salter, 1949, p. 1).

sponses. Assertiveness training makes use of the first of these types of responses, systematic desensitization makes use of the second, and sexual responses used in combination with relaxation training, biofeedback, or both are a part of behavioral sex therapy (see LoPiccolo & LoPiccolo, 1978, for a review of behavioral techniques used in sex therapy). The objective of reciprocal-inhibition techniques is thus to teach the client responses (assertive, relaxation, or sexual) that are strong enough to displace anxiety's attachment to the evoking stimuli. The specific techniques designed for doing this include thought-stopping, assertiveness training, and systematic desensitization. We will look at them in the order of their complexity, which is also the order in which they are likely to be introduced in counseling or psychotherapy.

Thought-Stopping

Thought-stopping is one of several cognitive therapeutic procedures identified by Wolpe (1958, 1982) and is based on the work of Taylor (1955, cited in Wolpe, 1982) and others. Thought-stopping inhibits anxiety by stopping the thoughts that produce it. Consider the following dialogue between Benny and a practitioner at his university's counseling center:

Benny (B): I know, I know. It does me no good to keep thinking about all that, and I know it just makes me madder and more depressed, but I really have trouble stopping.

Practitioner (P): You mean that no matter how you try to distract yourself, you simply cannot stop the negative thinking?

B: That's right. It's pretty hopeless. I'll be sitting there trying to read about Luther and the Diet of Worms or something, and, boom, I'm thinking about Celeste, feeling really wimpy, you know, and I keep going over the same things: the time I sat next to her, and didn't say a word! And the time she asked about the homework and I froze! And the time I really screwed things up by—

P [*yelling forcefully*]: STOP!

B: Wow! What's up? You scared me.

P: What happened to your thoughts?

B: They stopped—you startled me!

P: Exactly. The thoughts stopped. Let's practice it again, and later you will learn to do it. First, out loud and, gradually, to yourself. We'll stop those thoughts.

B [*optimistically*]: Watch out, Diet of Worms!

This imaginary dialogue demonstrates the use of thought-stopping as a technique. Through thought-stopping, the practitioner and client attempt to confront one of the central features of neuroses—"unrealistic, unproductive, and anxiety-arousing, perseverating trains of thought" (Wolpe, 1982, p. 112). The client practices saying "Stop" in front of the practitioner and then does so subvocally. The key to success is practice—the more the client interrupts the thought, the more she or he interrupts the anxiety that accompanies it. A number of variations on the technique exist, including one in which the thought-stopping is coupled with a mild electric shock.

Assertiveness Training

We use some curious words to describe passive, unassertive individuals: *push-over, Milquetoast, wimp,* and a few unprintable anatomical analogues. We seem equally uncomfortable with people who are hostile and inappropriately aggressive (*hotheads, hammers,* and assorted animal analogues); we avoid them, fear them, and often patronize them. Assertiveness training includes techniques designed to teach people that balance between passivity and aggressivity that enables us to attain what we want without violating the rights of others.

Assertiveness training, first described by Salter (1949) and further developed by Wolpe (1958) and Wolpe and Lazarus (1966), has actually become several different therapeutic techniques. As alluded to earlier, the question of how to teach clients assertiveness depends on whether the unassertiveness is viewed primarily as the result of: (1) anxiety-based inhibitions, (2) insufficient social skills, or (3) faulty cognitions. At least three distinct approaches to teaching assertiveness exist, each based on one of these three views of the cause of unassertiveness. We will use the term *assertiveness training* for the approach espoused by Wolpe (1982), which attributes unassertiveness to anxiety and relies primarily on reciprocal inhibition to foster assertive behavior. That approach is described in this section. Approaches that emphasize a lack of skills will be examined later, in the section on modeling techniques. Approaches that attribute the problem to faulty cognition use cognitive restructuring techniques, also covered later in this chapter, as well as Ellis's rational-emotive therapy and Lazarus's multimodal therapy (see Chapter 10), to enhance assertiveness. Assertion training, the most general term for this type of technique, includes all of the various behavioral and cognitive techniques used to enhance assertiveness (see Lange & Jakubowski, 1978, for a practical description of the various techniques).

Wolpe (1982) defined assertive behavior as "the appropriate expression of any emotion other than anxiety toward another person" (p. 118). Typically, the emotions to be expressed to another are *affectionate* or *oppositional*; Figure 5.1 illustrates the difference between appropriate and inappropriate expressions of those emotions. Elsewhere assertiveness has been defined as the refusal to comply with unreasonable requests (Fiedler & Beach, 1978) and as a human right to act without anxiety in one's own right without denying the rights of others (Alberti & Emmons, 1979). For our present purposes, assertiveness is defined as the ability to act on one's needs and wants with a minimum of personal anxiety and distress to others. Assertiveness usually involves the expression of negative and/or positive thoughts and feelings free from the self-defeating manipulations of false compliance or excessive anger.

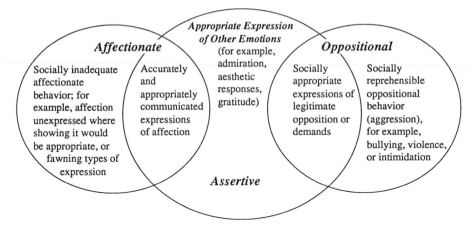

Figure 5.1   *Assertive and unassertive expression of affectionate and oppositional emotions* (From: Wolpe, 1982, p. 121).

The historical causes of unassertiveness, as well as the degree of difficulty the client experiences in being assertive, vary from client to client. Additionally, some clients may be capable of being assertive when expressing affectionate feelings but not oppositional feelings, and vice versa. Let us look at an example from Benny's life. After 10 minutes at the reference desk of the library, Benny feels invisible when Mr. Dewey passes over him to help another student who arrived later than Benny. Benny waits another 6 minutes for a begrudging acknowledgment from the librarian. Benny's fear of saying anything to either Mr. Dewey or the student served before him triggers an anxiety response: racing heart, cold and clammy hands, soggy armpits, and so forth. Through some series of past events, Benny has become conditioned to respond to this and similar situations with anxiety. Over time, his fear has become generalized to even more situations, and his physical symptoms have intensified. Consider the stipulation that assertiveness be socially acceptable. This, too, is part of Benny's dilemma. Sufficiently frustrated, Benny could pound his shoe on the desk while stringing together angry expletives for Librarian Dewey; yet, if he does so, he will find himself rebuked, embarrassed, and even further from the library materials he wants than before. Although reinforcement principles as well as faulty cognitions appear to be at work in Benny's situation, assertiveness training is designed to interrupt the biological response of anxiety directly, through reciprocal inhibition, rather than attending to these other factors.

Systematic desensitization is the most widely used method of combating classically conditioned anxiety responses, but assertiveness training is generally introduced first and may be reintroduced after the anxiety has been controlled through systematic desensitization. Though in other approaches to counseling, assertiveness is a desired by-product of treatment, assertiveness training is aimed at unblocking that skill directly (Wolpe, 1958). The approach is fairly straightforward and can be tailored to the needs of the individual. In assertiveness training the client is assumed to have the necessary interpersonal skills to be assertive but to be too inhibited by fear to use these skills. When such is not the case, Wolpe has used operant conditioning to help the person acquire the appropriate skills.

Assertiveness training, like all forms of behavior therapy, begins with behavioral assessment. For assessment, Wolpe (1982) has suggested that the practitioner start with the personal narratives provided by the client. Additionally, a number of questionnaires, checklists, and inventories exist for making the initial assessment and for measuring effectiveness. Sample items from two such scales are shown in Figure 5.2.

The actual training in assertiveness takes place in conversations between the practitioner and the client. Although there is no rigid format, the process usually proceeds as follows: (1) The client identifies situations in which she or he is typically passive or aggressive instead of assertive; (2) the practitioner encourages the client to express the feelings accompanying the unassertiveness (for example, longing, anger, hurt); (3) the client identifies future situations in which he or she could act more assertively; (4) the practitioner uses "pressure and encouragement" (Wolpe, 1982, p. 128) to convince the client to practice assertiveness and teaches the client to use *assertive statements* (see below); (5) the client attempts assertiveness in the situations; (6) the client reports back to the practitioner so that progress can be monitored; and (7) training continues until the client displays adequate assertiveness. Wolpe (1982, p. 127) has listed a number of oppositional and commendatory assertive statements that can serve as examples to clients. Our own client, Benny, finding himself in a situation similar to the one in the library, may want to try something like, "Pardon me, I was here first." Celeste he may eventually delight (or amuse) with, "Hi, Celeste. You look terrific today." That Benny can be encouraged to actually speak up is critical to inhibiting his anxiety. In selecting assertive actions and statements to use in specific situations, the client and the practitioner must remember Wolpe's one rule: Never instigate an assertive act that is likely to have punishing consequences [italics omitted] (p. 128). We would not, for example, encourage Benny to assert himself by initiating a conversation with something like "Celeste, I must have you!" even though at times he may feel compelled to.

Assertiveness training is augmented by a technique called *behavior rehearsal* designed to help the client better express assertive statements (Wolpe, 1958, 1982). In behavior rehearsal, the practitioner role-plays a person from the client's life. Typically, this person is one with whom the client feels anxious or fearful. The practitioner opens up the improvised session with an oppositional statement. By going over the dialogue a number of times, the client can refine both the form and the content of her or his responses. Audio tapes, as well as videotapes, can be used to enhance this procedure. Behavior rehearsal is widely used in conjunction with other behavior therapy techniques as well.

Name	Summary of Directions	Sample Items		

Gambrill & Richey Assertion Inventory

(Gambrill & Richey, 1975)

Clients rate each situation twice: first, for the degree of discomfort or anxiety it arouses and, second, for the probability or likelihood that they would display the behavior if the situation presented itself. Both measures use a 5-point numerical scale.

Clients are instructed to first complete each item for discomfort and then to cover their responses before answering for response probability.

(40 items total)

Degree of Discomfort	Situation	Response Probability
____	1. Turn down a request to borrow your car	____
____	2. Compliment a friend	____
____	3. Ask a favor of someone	____
____	4. Resist sales pressure	____
____	5. Apologize when you are at fault	____
____	6. Turn down a request for a meeting or date	____
____	7. Admit fear and request consideration	____
...		
____	17. Request a meeting or a date with a person	____
____	18. Your initial request for a meeting is turned down, ask the person again at a later time	____
____	19. Admit confusion about a point under discussion and ask for clarification	____
____	20. Apply for a job	____
____	21. Ask whether you have offended someone	____
____	22. Tell someone you like him/her	____
...		
____	37. Receive compliments	____
____	38. Continue to converse with someone who disagrees with you	____

Willoughby Personality Schedule

(Wolpe, 1982)

Instructions state that the schedule is intended to indicate various "emotional personality traits" and that there are no right or wrong answers. The schedule uses a 5-point scale, from 0 to 4, where 0 means "No" or "Never" and 4 means "Practically always" or "Entirely."

(25 items total)

1. Do you get stage fright?	0 1 2 3 4
2. Do you worry over humiliating experiences?	0 1 2 3 4
3. Are you afraid of falling when you're on a high place?	0 1 2 3 4
4. Are your feelings easily hurt?	0 1 2 3 4
5. Do you keep in the background on social occasions?	0 1 2 3 4
6. Are you happy and sad by turns without knowing why?	0 1 2 3 4
7. Are you shy?	0 1 2 3 4
8. Do you daydream frequently?	0 1 2 3 4
9. Do you get discouraged easily?	0 1 2 3 4
10. Do you say things on the spur of the moment and then regret them?	0 1 2 3 4
11. Do you like to be alone?	0 1 2 3 4
12. Do you cry easily?	0 1 2 3 4
...	
24. Do you feel inferior?	0 1 2 3 4
25. Is it hard to make up your mind until the time for action is past?	0 1 2 3 4

Figure 5.2 *Excerpts from* Assertiveness Inventories: the Gambrill and Richey Assertion Inventory (From: Gambrill & Richey, 1975, pp. 552–553) and the Willoughby Personality Schedule (From: Wolpe, 1982, p. 337)

Systematic Desensitization

Our friend Benny is shy and unassertive. Lydia rarely leaves her house and avoids "crowds" of more than five people. Bill, who makes his living as a house-painter, has become extremely fearful of heights following a brush with disaster. The minute Roberto's new wife begins to get enthusiastic during romantic moments, Roberto's penis becomes flaccid. Most of Pamela's life has been spent avoiding situations in which she would have to speak to a group.

Each person mentioned above is a potential candidate for *systematic desensitization,* a technique developed primarily by Wolpe (1958, 1982) and designed to overcome habitually fearful responses by applying the principle of reciprocal inhibition to interrupt the connection between the anxiety and the situation that evokes it. Systematic desensitization is among the most widely used behavior therapy techniques and has been demonstrated to be an effective treatment for a variety of maladaptive behaviors, especially specific phobias, agoraphobia, social anxiety, psychophysiological disorders, and sexual dysfunction (Foa, Steketee, & Ascher, 1980; Goldfried & Davison, 1976; S. M. Turner et al., 1981; Wolpe, 1982). There is long-standing disagreement, however, about its adequacy as an exclusive treatment for many problem behaviors (A. A. Lazarus & Serber, 1968), and about whether systematic desensitization is effective because of reciprocal inhibition or is best explained by social and cognitive factors (Bandura, 1969; Ellis, 1983; Kazdin & Wilcoxon, 1976; A. A. Lazarus, 1971; Murray & Jacobson, 1978; Yates, 1975). Wolpe has consistently responded to his critics, often citing the methodological inadequacies of their studies to explain contradictory findings (for example, see Wolpe, 1982, pp. 176–180).

The steps of systematic desensitization include: (1) introduction to the subjective anxiety scale, (2) training in deep muscle relaxation, (3) construction of the anxiety hierarchies, and (4) pairing relaxation and anxiety-evoking stimuli from the hierarchies (Wolpe, 1982, p. 141).

First, the client learns how to subjectively quantify anxiety using imagination. Though the client's ability to imagine must be adequate for systematic desensitization to succeed, to imagine simply means to create a mental picture of a real or potentially real event. It does not require any special creativity as the word *imaginative* suggests. The client is directed to think about the most anxiety-producing event she or he has either experienced or can imagine and to assign that event the number 100, on a scale from 0 to 100. The client then imagines complete calm and assigns that the number 0. Working down in *subjective units of disturbance* (abbreviated *suds*), the client develops a personal scale of anxiety-producing events. For example, in the case of a simple phobia, a fear of snakes, a client may assign 100 *suds* to "walking into a pit of pythons with a boa constrictor around each arm." For 80 *suds,* the client may recall actually stepping barefooted on a garden snake in the middle of the night. Somewhere around 20 *suds* might be "sitting in a room with a feather boa imagining it's a real snake." In the case of a simple phobia like this one, the objective is not to make the client capable of scampering through snake pits; rather, it is to eliminate an *irrational fear* of snakes so that the client takes fewer unnecessary actions to avoid snakes. Clearly the actions of a herpetologist and a bank teller after treatment will differ, but eliminating the irrational component of their fearfulness is the objective of treatment for both individuals. Another client may list a variety of anxiety-producing situations: 100 *suds* for being left all alone in an open field at night; 60 *suds* for being around a large animal; 40 *suds* for being asked to give a spontaneous talk; 25 *suds* for meeting new people. The actual hierarchy that will be used in the systematic desensitization will be more comprehensive than this initial listing by the client, but from the beginning, the client is taught to evaluate the intensity of his or her reactions to different anxiety-evoking situations.

Second, the practitioner teaches the client to relax, usually using the **progressive relaxation** discussed in the previous chapter. This procedure, often augmented with **biofeedback** and **hypnosis,** or both, provides the client with the essential component of reciprocal inhibition: a readily produced response that counteracts anxiety and that can become attached to the anxiety-evoking stimulus. Jacobson's basic procedure, originally designed for working with psychophysiological disorders, is cut from 50 sessions to about 6 sessions in systematic desensitization (Wolpe, 1982). Most practitioners of systematic desensitization require *homework* of the client—in this case, daily practice of the relaxation skill (Wolpe, for example, recommends 10 to 15 minutes twice a day).

The third step in systematic desensitization is construction of the anxiety hierarchies. In its finished form, the hierarchy is a list of scenes ranked in order of the intensity of the anxiety produced by imagining these scenes. Later, these scenes will be presented to the client while she or he is relaxed. One obvious source of these scenes is the first step, in which the client learned about *suds*. The scenes and assigned values generated by the client are important input. Wolpe (1982) has recommended a number of sources for the basic data necessary to construct a hierarchy. In addition to a careful history of the client's problem taken early in the intervention, as well as the inquiries made throughout treatment by the practitioner, he suggested two measures. The first is the Willoughby Questionnaire; sample items from that measure appear in Figure 5.2. The other is the Fear Survey Schedule (Wolpe, 1982; Wolpe & Lang, 1969). This survey lists 108 things and experiences that a client might fear. The client places a check for each item along a 5-point scale ranging from *not at all* to *very much*. Sample items include: noise of vacuum cleaners, dead people, flying insects, ugly people, being in an elevator, airplanes, losing control, becoming mentally ill, a lull in conversation, and worms. Pooling the information from the various sources usually yields several interrelated hierarchies to which *suds* values can be assigned. Wolpe (1982) has pointed out that certain *themes* can usually be observed, around which the hierarchies can be organized. For example, some of Benny's social anxieties could be organized as follows:

A. Evaluation by others at the university
    1. Being asked an opinion by the professor during the seminar course (90)

2. Being watched during class by another student (80)
3. Being looked at encouragingly by the professor during class (70)
4. Being watched by another student while walking into class (55)
5. Walking down the school hallways, where others may notice him (50)
6. Thinking about getting out of bed to get ready for classes (20)

B. Expression of differences with others
1. Confronting his mother about her excessive drinking (95)
2. Disagreeing with his father about his choosing history as a college major (90)
3. Arguing with his mother and father over something petty (80)
4. Being ignored by a staff person at the library (60)
5. Being cut in front of in the cafeteria line (50)
6. Hearing two strangers criticize the history department (20)

The actual hierarchies are products of the client's experience and imagination and are subject to ongoing revision. Benny's hierarchies are typical of individuals with social anxieties; clients with other problems will generate different hierarchies. The following hierarchy, for example, was developed for a survivor of rape (Becker & Abel, 1981, p. 363). The hierarchy progresses in reverse order from the example given above, from the least-anxiety-evoking situation to the most.

1. You think about having to deal with your fears of therapy.
2. You are walking to a building from the parking lot.
3. You are lying on the couch at home with your eyes closed at night.
4. You enter your apartment and make only a minimal check of the rooms.
5. You enter your apartment and do not check to see if someone is hiding in it.
6. You receive an obscene phone call.
7. You are walking around your apartment in the dark.
8. You enter your apartment, alone, at night, and the lights are out.
9. A customer at work tells you he is going to follow you home.
10. You are walking to your car, alone, at night, and you do not see anyone along your path.
11. You are at home, alone, at night, in a part of the apartment where you cannot see either entrance.
12. You are in your old apartment the night of the attempted rape, just before anything happened.
13. You are alone in your current apartment, at night, taking a bath.
14. You think about the woman's body that was found in the car near your apartment.
15. You are walking to your car, alone, at night, and see a man along your path.
16. You are driving alone when you see a car that appears to be following you.

17. You are lying in bed at night with your eyes closed.
18. A male stranger knocks on your door when you are at home, alone, at night.
19. You are at home alone, and it sounds like someone is in the house.
20. You think about your friend's recent rape.
21. You approach your car and see that someone is in the back seat.

Note that actual or attempted rape is not included in the hierarchy, because the goal of systematic desensitization with rape survivors is to reduce the number and kind of events that produce anxiety following the rape. Fear of rape itself is not an irrational fear and not a subject for desensitization.

The final step in systematic desensitization is the actual counterposing of the anxiety-evoking stimuli from the hierarchies with the relaxation that the client has learned. By this step in the process, the client regularly begins the session with relaxation. This may be done seated or reclining. Once the client has gone through the relaxation procedure, the practitioner asks the client to imagine a particular scene. The first scene presented is a *control scene*—that is, one that does not evoke anxiety. Subsequent scenes are drawn from one of the client's anxiety hierarchies, beginning with the scene with the lowest *suds* value. Throughout the process of pairing relaxation with the anxiety-evoking images, the same basic pattern is followed. The practitioner describes the scene to the relaxed client, and the client signals when the scene is clear in his or her mind by raising the left index finger. After the image has been held for a time (5 to 7 seconds), the client is instructed to stop and to assign a *suds* value to the image. The client is then instructed to relax for a time (for example, 30 seconds), then the practitioner either reintroduces the same scene or presents a new scene one step higher on the anxiety hierarchy. A scene is reintroduced if its *suds* value is above zero, although in practice, Wolpe (1982) has indicated that progress through the hierarchy may make proceeding with a value as high as 25 *suds* necessary. Once the anxiety evoked by a scene falls within this acceptable range, then the next highest scene is presented. This continues until even the highest ranked situations produce only minimal anxiety.

The actual systematic desensitization procedure may take less than half of a typical counseling session. The remaining time is used to discuss the client's day-to-day success at decreasing the number and kind of episodes in which he or she experiences irrational fear and avoidance behavior. The practitioner encourages the client to gradually risk exposure to fearful situations. This in vivo exposure is the critical test of both the sufficiency of the relaxation training and the utility of the scenes in the hierarchy. There is a certain improvisational quality to this aspect of systematic desensitization that is illustrated by a case presented by Goldfried and Davison (1976). A client who had begun treatment for cynophobia (fear of dogs) received a telephone call from a friend who jokingly asked the client if he would like to have a brand new puppy. Recalling the practitioner's emphasis on gradual exposure to anxiety-producing stimuli, the client answered affirmatively. As the therapy progressed, the gentle puppy grew up, providing an almost perfectly graduated in vivo exposure. The intervention succeeded.

Though practitioners continue to disagree on the relative utility of systematic desensitization in treating certain disorders, as well on what variables are crucial to its effectiveness, systematic desensitization remains one of the most successfully and widely used behavior therapy techniques.

Anxiety-Evoking Techniques

Imagine a radical solution to Benny's problem. If we could somehow arrange to lock Benny in a room with Celeste (or 50 Celestes!) for several hours, what might be the result? Though on a daytime soap opera, murder or marriage might ensue, in real life, one of two outcomes is more likely. The radical exposure to this anxiety-evoking situation might so exacerbate Benny's anxiety that he would not only behave self-defeatingly during the confinement but would avoid any situation in the future where this painful event might reoccur. On the other hand, the extended exposure might reduce his anxiety; as the situation and its social requirements become more familiar, his actions might become more adaptive. He would, in that case, probably continue to grow more and more comfortable in such situations. The laws of learning, as well as a variety of research studies and clinical opinions, support both possibilities, depending on the individual client, the individual problem, and the length of exposure. Though the reciprocal-inhibition techniques we have just examined expose the client to anxiety-evoking stimuli, they do so gradually and after some sort of preparatory training. Anxiety-evoking techniques, on the other hand, expose the client fully and directly to feared stimuli without any graduation or preparation. We will examine two behavior therapy techniques of this sort: flooding and paradoxical intention.

Flooding

When a client successfully avoids an aversive stimulus, the resulting reduction in anxiety serves as a negative reinforcement, thus increasing the frequency of the avoidance behavior, as well as promoting generalization to similar situations. Flooding techniques expose the client directly to the aversive stimulus without the possibility of escape and without any injurious consequences apart from anxiety itself. The client may be exposed to the stimulus through imagination (*imaginal flooding*) or directly, usually in the natural environment where the stimulus occurs (*in vivo flooding*). Without the reinforcement that comes with escape, the client discovers that the only aversive consequence of being in the presence of the stimulus is the anxiety itself. With no other aversive consequences to worry about, the client gradually relaxes, and the anxiety response is extinguished. Permanent extinction of the anxiety response to that stimulus, however, takes place only when the client remains in the real or imagined presence of the stimulus until her or his anxiety actually abates. This may take a few minutes or several hours.

Some flooding techniques are referred to as *implosion* techniques; these are derived from Stampfl's *implosive therapy* (Stampfl, 1970; Stampfl & Levis, 1967). Implosion techniques are based partly on psychoanalytical concepts and emphasize exposing the client to stimuli representative of unconscious conflicts. Otherwise, they are applied in essentially the same manner as flooding. Flooding and implosion techniques have been successfully applied to a variety of phobias, especially agoraphobia, and with considerable success to obsessive-compulsive behavior (Boudewyns & Shipley, 1983; Emmelkamp, 1982; Rimm & Lefebvre, 1981).

Despite the success practitioners have had using flooding techniques, debate exists about why it works (Eysenck, 1982), the potential dangers (Eysenck, 1968; Wolpe, 1982), and whether or not it is significantly more effective than less dramatic and less distressing techniques (for example, systematic desensitization). This last concern is important: Confronting, without the possibility of escape, frightening situations, whether real or imagined, causes considerable distress. Research continues on the relative merits of flooding techniques.

Paradoxical Intention

In moments of great stress, some good soul will always tell you to "try to relax." Anyone who has actually tried to relax knows the principle underlying paradoxical intention: Direct, intense efforts to transform anxiety often have the opposite effect. To try to relax is to increase one's anxiety. Fortunately, the reverse, trying to become anxious, can lead paradoxically to reduced anxiety. In paradoxical intention, anxiety is purposely evoked; when the technique works, the anxiety is forestalled by the very act of trying to create it.

The term *paradoxical intention* was first introduced by existential psychiatrist Viktor Frankl (1960, 1967, 1973, 1975a, 1985) who also described many examples of its clinical use. In addition, a number of practitioners, operating, at times, from very different perspectives (for example, Fay, 1973; A. A. Lazarus, 1971; Weeks & L'Abate, 1982), have developed paradoxical approaches. Most recently, Ascher (1980) has identified the behavioral components of paradoxical intention, prompting its integration into the repertoire of behavioral techniques. Paradoxical intention has been applied as a behavioral technique to the treatment of anxiety (Ascher, 1980), insomnia (R. M. Turner & Ascher, 1979, 1982), urinary retention (Ascher, 1980), and agoraphobia (Ascher, 1981). Broader applications of paradoxical techniques can be found in Seltzer (1986) and Weeks (1985).

Paradoxical intention involves encouraging the client to exaggerate the performance of the maladaptive behavior. Following Frankl's lead, the technique is applied in a humorous context when that is possible.[3] Benny, for example, may be encouraged to perfect those feelings of panic he experiences by practicing them in front of a mirror before leaving for classes. He should do so with great intensity, observing himself carefully. Nothing should stop him from making his symptoms the best possible! Clearly, the hope is that in trying to feel anxious, Benny will (1) fail to evoke anxiety and (2) see some of the essential humor in his preoccupation with his inability to perform socially. In a sense, the technique short-circuits the anxiety response.

Experimental support for the technique of paradoxical intention, as practiced within the context of behavior therapy, is still being developed. Within the context of existential therapy, however, the technique is supported by a considerable body of clinical literature, which we will review in Chapter 8.

Operant Techniques

As Table 5.1 reminds us, operant techniques, which apply the principles of operant conditioning described in the previous chapter, accord with the approach known as applied behavior analysis. The term *contingency management* is also used to describe the application of operant techniques (Rimm & Masters, 1979). Operant techniques are unique in several ways. First, they are applied broadly in settings other than that of individual counseling or psychotherapy, for example, in psychiatric hospitals, schools, child care facilities, nursing homes, drug treatment facilities, weight management centers, and medical and dental facilities, as well as the home. In these various settings, the behaviors targeted for change run the gamut from poor study habits to psychotic withdrawal (see Kazdin, 1975a, 1978a). Second, operant techniques are unique in the degree to which they have been integrated into other techniques, behavioral or otherwise. All of the other behavior therapy techniques make use of operant techniques in some way, and formally or informally, operant techniques have found their way into strategies designed by practitioners from quite nonbehavioral backgrounds.

Operant techniques require the practitioner to identify specific, overt behaviors that can be modified. The client begins therapy with a complaint that centers on some problem. The goal of the practitioner is to translate that problem into specific behavioral excesses and deficits and to identify the contingent relationships between those behaviors and their consequences. The practitioner then works with the client to establish new contingencies that reduce or eliminate the undesirable responses or produce or increase desirable responses.

---

[3]Numerous practitioners have described the importance of humor as a therapeutic tool, including Ellis (1973), Frankl (1973), and Greenwald (1975). The use (and possible abuse) of humor in various systems of psychotherapy has been reviewed by Kuhlman (1984) in *Humor and Psychotherapy.*

Operant techniques can be classified as follows. *Reinforcement* techniques use a desirable consequence—a reward (positive reinforcement) or the removal of an aversive condition (negative reinforcement)—to increase the frequency of a specific behavior. *Punishment* techniques use either an aversive consequence or the removal of a rewarding consequence to decrease the frequency of a behavior. *Extinction* techniques involve withholding reinforcement previously attached to a behavior to decrease its frequency. Unlike other sets of techniques that can be applied separately in practice, reinforcement, punishment, and extinction techniques are usually used together. We will look at these techniques first as a central feature of the therapeutic relationship itself and then as contingency management tools in the client's day-to-day life. A glance back at Figure 4.2 before reading on may be helpful.

Operant Techniques in the Therapeutic Relationship

Whether used systematically or occurring willy-nilly, reinforcement, punishment, and extinction are parts of the therapeutic relationship. The practitioner's attention, posture, gestures, and words serve as feedback to the client about events taking place during sessions. Further, as Goldfried and Davison (1976) have pointed out, the uniquely human capacity to symbolize means that events occurring between sessions are also presented during sessions—symbolically, through verbal descriptions. The practitioner thus responds to—and thereby affects—both behaviors performed by the client in the therapeutic setting and those performed outside it and described by the client.

The practitioner's attention, posture, gestures, and words can be used to positively reinforce constructive behaviors or to punish—as with a mild rebuke or frown—self-defeating behaviors. Nonresponse can begin the extinction of a behavior (or at least the practice of describing it). Ideally, the practitioner and client can openly discuss the ways in which reinforcement, punishment, and extinction are used, so the client can initiate *self-reinforcement.* For example, the client can be trained to make positive *self-statements* when performing a particular behavior between sessions or to use more tangible reinforcers (like food or entertainment) (Goldfried & Davison, 1976). The process requires that the practitioner be what Goldfried and Davison call a *Menschenkenner,* "someone who understands people" (p. 212). This means that the practitioner must be a skilled and sensitive observer capable of determining what consequences will be rewarding or aversive to each particular client in each particular situation.

Operant Techniques in the Client's Life

As indicated above, the practitioner's objective is to teach the client operant techniques so that the client can identify and regulate the day-to-day contingencies operating in his or her life. In the most frequently cited examples of operant techniques, some undesirable behavior (for example, smoking or overeating) is identified and carefully monitored; a set of rewards (for example, watching television for an hour) is established, to be obtained when the frequency of the behavior is reduced; and some noxious event (for example, housecleaning for an hour) is introduced when the undesirable behavior is performed. The example that follows is an attempt to show some ways in which reinforcement, punishment, and extinction interact in more complex situations, although the same basics are at work.

Our example comes from Baer (1982), who summarized a study he completed several years before in which complaints of "loneliness" among three residents of a retirement home were successfully ameliorated by means of an operant strategy (R. S. Goldstein & Baer, 1976). In that case, the practitioner listened to the residents' complaints about being "unhappy" and "lonely." On fuller investigation, it became apparent that the issue was not visits from relatives who lived far away, but the paucity of letters received from significant others. After questioning the three residents and examining the letters they were writing, the practitioner discovered a pattern in their letter-writing habits. Typically, the residents wrote only in response to letters received, and their replies to these letters generally contained a complaint about the quality or quantity of the letters received. In other words, their correspondents were punished for writing! A contingency had been established: To write to these people was to be punished; to not write had no consequence. Thus, a functional relationship appeared to exist between the behavior of the residents and the behavior of their correspondents. Baer (1982) explained:

> Was it functional? To find out, the [applied behavior] analyst had only to change the letter-writing behavior of the elderly complainers, so that their letters would be neither reproachful nor accusatory. That change was a very easy one, requiring only the slightest application of any behavioral technology—a nonreproachful letter that asked at least one question meriting an answer was modeled, and the next several letters written by the elderly complainers were read and commented on, approvingly or disapprovingly according to their content, before they were mailed. A few early ones needed rewriting; the complainers always agreed readily to do so. The analyst then prompted the complainers to write to relatives or old friends who rarely or never wrote to them. Within a very few tries, the complainers were now writing totally unreproachful, nonaccusatory letters to everyone. Perhaps to fill the space formerly occupied by the reproachful kind of content, they now wrote about their daily lives, happenings of interest, and memories of their past experiences with their correspondents, which probably made it easy for their correspondents to reply responsively and may well have reinforced rather than punished the correspondents' letter writing. (pp. 285–286)

The residents were further taught to include self-addressed, stamped envelopes to ease replies. The results were fascinating. Not only did the three residents receive prompt replies, but their input of letters tripled. They received letters from new correspondents, and much of their time was filled with activities related to letter writing. A by-product of this activity was that three residents, by their own report, were now happy and no longer lonely.

Recounted here in such an abbreviated form, this story has a certain deus ex machina quality to it, but it illustrates how operant techniques can be used comprehensively. In the barest terms, the manner in which the clients were punishing friends and relatives was identified and changed. A specific type of letter-writing behavior was shaped gradually through verbal reinforcement from the practitioner, and that verbal reinforcement was replaced by the reinforcement that came with the incoming mail. In the end, the clients' complaining behavior was extinguished because it was not reinforced and because another behavior (writing letters) was being rewarded.

Operant techniques have been most broadly and successfully applied in institutional settings where contingencies can be readily controlled and in the elimination of readily identified maladaptive or unhealthy habits (for example, smoking or overeating). As I hope is clear from the preceding discussion, however, clients living in the real world can also benefit from operant techniques, as part of an eclectic strategy tailored to the individual client's objectives.

Sample Case: Barbara Bellicose

At 38 years of age, Barbara Bellicose was an assembly-line supervisor at Plowshare Munitions Factory. Barbara's hair-trigger temper and constant invectiveness made her extremely unpopular with subordinates, who referred to her by several unprintable epithets. Her immediate superiors avoided disagreeing with her because of her fiery reactions, and peers who occasionally enjoyed her sarcasm were careful not to say anything that might direct it toward them. All in all, Barb was someone to be avoided if possible and patronized when confronted.

Apart from her work at the factory, Barb had few sources of happiness. A teenage marriage had lasted only 3 years, and a decade of fighting with her parents and younger brother had finally ended in estrangement. Barb's private life was lonely, and she fought depression with a popular depressant: alcohol. When she drank excessively, she also ate excessively, and she was at least 30 pounds overweight. Her fantasy life centered around television shows, and her occasional male companion, Butch, was described even by her as "low life." He had struck her on several occasions, and their time together was spent fighting. At times, Barbara admitted to herself that much of her unhappiness came from her combativeness, but she had seen this same rage and hostility in her parents and was convinced that she was destined to act this way. At other times, of course, she reasoned that her vitriolic temperament was just what others deserved.

Eventually, Barb's way of working with her subordinates was reflected in production output, and Barb found herself confronting a manager as interested in personnel as he was in productivity. Barb ended up seeing a counselor in the personnel services program at Plowshare.

Modeling Techniques

Who has not been chided with the adage "Monkey see, monkey do"? We are all aware of the human propensity to mirror or copy the actions of others. Human beings are capable of more than mere mimicry when it comes to imitating the behavior of others, however. Through observation, with or without immediate practice, we are capable of integrating those observed behaviors (actions and expressions of thought or emotion) into our own behavioral repertoires. The term *modeling* is used to describe the vicarious acquisition of new behaviors through observation of another person's behavior and its consequences. The role of modeling in the acquisition and modification of patterns of behavior has been extensively researched, within the framework of social learning theory, by Bandura and his colleagues (Bandura 1969, 1971, 1973, 1977a, 1977b; Rosenthal & Bandura, 1978). The discussion that follows is drawn primarily from that literature.

The Effects of Modeling

Rosenthal and Bandura (1978) described four separate effects of modeling on the observer. First, the observer of the model may acquire a new behavior or coping strategy not previously in her or his behavioral repertoire. For example, through watching a model, an individual may learn to successfully dial a phone, wrestle a tiger, respond to criticism, or initiate a conversation. This is known as *observational learning*. Second, the observer's inhibitions against performing a particular action may be either strengthened or weakened through exposure to the model. For example, frustrated by a professor's outlandish reading assignment, a student may fume internally but say nothing. If a respected fellow student politely challenges the professor on the assignment, the first student's inhibition about speaking will be weakened if the professor accepts the second student's comments and strengthened if the professor or other students deride the comments. This is the *inhibitory and disinhibitory effect*. Third, the observer may perform an already known behavior not constrained by inhibition, just because another person has performed the activity first. Examples abound: In a group of friends, is there ever just one joke told, one trivia question asked, one person clapping, or one escapade recounted? This is *response facilitation*. Fourth, when changes in his or her life make judging the adequacy or appropriateness of a behavior difficult, the observer may use the model as a *cognitive standard for self-regulation*. The model helps to resolve the observer's ambiguity by providing specific behaviors that can be imitated. Consider an individual who has just been promoted to a vice presidency in a firm. How much does a vice president contribute to the "Coffee Club"? With whom should a vice president not be seen at lunch? How appropriate is it to kid the firm's president about midriff bulge? These as well as more substantive questions can be answered by observing models.

Processes Involved in Modeling

Modeling can be broken down into four district processes: *attentional* processes, *retention* processes, *motor reproduction* processes, and *motivational* processes. All of these processes must take place for an individual to learn a behavior through modeling. To try to understand modeling, we can examine these processes in relation to Barbara Bellicose's aggressivity. Barbara believes that her truculence is immutable since she believes she has inherited it from her combative parents. More probably, however, Barbara has acquired her behavior through exposure to her parents as aggressive models rather than through chromosomal aberration.

Modeling begins with attention—that is, selectively focusing one's consciousness on one stimulus over competing stimuli. Many behaviors, including nonaggressive ones, were part of Barbara's developmental experiences at home and school. Why did she regularly attend to aggressive ones? The answer rests in both the nature of aggressive actions and the salience of parents as models. Because of the intensity and abruptness of acts of verbal or physical aggression, such acts attract attention readily. Parental models command attention because parents control reward and punishment.[4]

Retention of an experience depends on how the individual cognitively organizes, rehearses, and reorganizes the observed behavior. Retention begins with the *symbolic coding* of the experience, either as an imaginal representation, a verbal representation, or both. The observed behavior may then be rehearsed covertly (in the mind) and reorganized. For example, Barbara continually observed her parents in stressful situations where a conflict was "resolved" when one individual became more abusive than the other. Since she never saw conflict resolved nonabusively, the image she retained as a model for imitation was aggressive.

Motor reproduction processes put the stored and covertly rehearsed behavior into practice. This is the point at which an individual tries out the behavior, refining the skills needed to perform the behavior.

Motivational processes come into play as the individual performs the modeled behavior in anticipation of reinforcement. If the behavior is reinforced, the probability of that behavior being performed in that and similar situations eventually increases.

Through continual exposure to aggressive models, Barbara has acquired a collection of angry and abusive responses to situations where there is disagreement, and since these behaviors serve to extricate her from conflict by silencing the opposition, the probability of her continuing to behave aggressively is high. Though these responses in fact alienate others and in the long

---

[4]Ironically, a child's aggression is often punished with verbal or physical abuse, and teaching a child to "do as I say, not as I do" only changes the locus of the aggression without eliminating or diminishing its existence. A child will learn aggressive responses from the parents, using them when the parents are not present. Chapter 2 ("Origins of Aggression") of Bandura's *Aggression: A Social Learning Analysis* (1973) provides an enlightening discussion of this topic.

run have led to her unhappiness, these are the responses that have been most consistently reinforced and so most carefully learned.

Self-Efficacy

Let us assume that Barbara realizes that her petulance at work is a source of her unhappiness. Let us also assume that, from an objective point of view, she is capable of learning interpersonal skills that are less abrasive to others. How can we account for the fact that she does not change? The missing part of our explanation of Barbara's resistance to change comes from the theory of *self-efficacy*. Considerable research now exists on the concept of self-efficacy, introduced by Bandura and his colleagues (for example, Bandura, 1977a, 1981, 1982, 1983; Bandura, Adams, Hardy, & Howells, 1980; Bandura, Taylor, Williams, Mefford, & Barchas, 1985; Davis & Yates, 1982; Lee, 1983; Telch, Bandura, Vinciguerra, Agras, & Stout, 1982).[5]

Self-efficacy is the "common cognitive mechanism of operation" at issue in the maintenance and modification of human behavior; it determines an individual's actions, the intensity of his or her strivings, and the level of his or her endurance in the face of adversity (Rosenthal & Bandura, 1978). Figure 5.3 shows Bandura's diagram of the interaction between the person (internal processes of thought and feeling), behavior (what is done), and outcome (reinforcement). An *outcome expectation* is "a person's estimate that a given behavior will lead to certain outcomes" (Bandura, 1977a, p. 193). Barbara, for example, believes that "calm, gentle encouragement of her subordinates" is a behavior that could have positive outcomes, performed in her workplace. This cognition is of little value, however, if Barbara does not believe that she is capable of successfully performing that behavior and thus attaining the outcome. This belief in or expectation of one's ability to actually perform the behavior is the *efficacy expectation*. No matter how clearly Barbara understands the potential a new behavior has for gaining desirable outcomes, the behavior will not take place if she doubts her ability to actually perform it. As shown in Bandura's diagram, the efficacy expectation enters into the interaction between the person and the behavior, while the outcome expectation affects that between behavior and outcome.

Self-efficacy comes from direct experience of one's own performance, vicarious experiences (models), and verbal information from other sources. Bandura (1977a) has pointed out that different types of counseling and psychotherapy change clients' efficacy expectations by providing different kinds

---

[5]Self-efficacy theory has become an object of intense research, as well as critical comment. Sources for some of the controversy include Bandura, 1983, 1984; Eastman and Marzillier, 1984; Kirsch, 1980, 1982; and Tryon, 1981a. There is little doubt, however, that social-psychological constructs like *expectancy* and *attribution*, first systematically explored in relationship to psychotherapy by Rotter (1954), have become important to contemporary practitioners. They will be examined in more detail in Chapter 10.

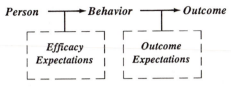

Figure 5.3 *Efficacy expectations and outcome expectations* (From: Bandura, 1977a, p. 193)

of information. Some approaches use *verbal persuasion* to modify the client's efficacy expectation. Others attempt to change the emotional arousal caused by the anticipated situation, as in biofeedback or relaxation training. Modeling techniques are means of changing efficacy expectations by exposing the client to live, symbolic, or imaginary models who engage rewardingly in behavior that the client does not presently perform, either because of fear or because of lack of skill.

Types of Modeling Techniques

Overt modeling techniques use living models to change the client's behavior; *symbolic modeling* techniques use filmed or videotaped models. In both cases, the client observes another person perform the desired behavior. The model may either perform with mastery from the beginning of the client's observation or acquire mastery gradually, as the client observes. Typically, the client then attempts to produce the behavior and is appropriately reinforced. Overt and symbolic modeling techniques have been successfully used in numerous studies where some new behavior was desired or where an existing behavior was to be inhibited. At the moment, however, *participant modeling* and *covert modeling* appear to be more popular in treating the types of problems typically presented by noninstitutionalized clients of normal intelligence.

The relationship between client and practitioner is a natural place to apply modeling techniques, because of the practitioner's status and control over reinforcement. In all approaches to counseling and psychotherapy, the client observes the practitioner's capacity for dealing with stress as well as how she or he expresses affection, disagreement, and anger. Participant modeling procedures formalize this process, making it specific to the needs and concerns of the client. This type of modeling is most frequently used in eliminating phobias, with living organisms like dogs, cats, rats, and snakes heading the list of feared objects. As Rimm and Masters (1979) have pointed out, this is really a form of *vicarious extinction* of the fearful response: The practitioner performs the action without experiencing punishing consequences, thereby encouraging the client to expect the same consequences when he or she is exposed to the feared stimulus. This technique can be used in a number of ways but generally involves developing a hierarchy of anxiety-evoking activities related to the fear stimulus.

For a simple example, let us look at a client who fears white laboratory rats.[6] The practitioner explains the modeling procedure and then gradually performs a series of actions leading up to direct contact with the lab rat. The client observes the practitioner put on gloves, move toward the rat's cage, touch the rat, and then hold the lab rat. Then the practitioner does the same procedure without gloves. Throughout the entire event, the practitioner is reassuring and encouraging, and if at any time the client experiences more than minimal anxiety at observing the practitioner's activities, the procedure is ended for the time being. Eventually, the client dons the gloves, moves toward the lab rat, and slowly pets and then holds the fearsome creature. Finally, the client does this without gloves. (This example is modeled after one in Rimm & Masters, 1979, where a fuller description can be found; for examples of research on participant modeling see Bandura, Blanchard, & Ritter, 1969; Bandura, Jeffery, & Gajdos, 1974; Etringer, Cash, & Rimm, 1982; Ladouceur, 1983.)

The modeling techniques we have considered thus far require the existence of a live, filmed, or videotaped model whose behavior the client can observe. Not only is that sometimes impractical, it may also be unnecessary. If covert (imagined) events obey the same laws as overt (in vivo) events, then clients should be able to change their behavior by modeling it on behavior observed only in imagination. This idea of covert modeling was proposed and initially researched by Cautela (1971) as part of *covert conditioning* (examined in the next section). Research has generally supported its usefulness with various avoidance reactions (Cautela, 1971, 1976; Cautela, Flannery, & Hanley, 1974; Kazdin, 1973, 1974a, 1974b), and Kazdin and others have successfully demonstrated the potential uses of covert conditioning in improving assertiveness skills (Kazdin, 1974c, 1975b; Kazdin & Mascitelli, 1982; Pentz & Kazdin, 1982; Rosenthal & Reese, 1976).

Although several variations of covert modeling exist, the basic technique is fairly direct. The practitioner develops a list of imaginable scenes in which an individual models appropriate behavior in a situation that would be problematic for the client. The number of scenes will depend on the nature of the client's problem. With eyes closed, the client listens as the practitioner describes the least potentially problematic scene. The client signals when the scene is clear in his or her mind and continues to imagine it. In some uses of the procedure, both the client and practitioner repeat the description of the scene aloud several times, and the client is instructed to practice the covert modeling of the scene on a daily basis at home. In the sessions that follow, the

---

[6]The literature on behavior therapy includes a surprisingly large number of studies on the treatment of animal and reptile phobias—and not just to provide companionship in the history books for Little Hans, Albert, and Peter. Even the most straightforward phobic reaction can be terribly limiting and can affect the individual's personal sense of worth. Also, phobias of one sort or another are ubiquitous. The choice of a white lab rat for the example in the text was not gratuitous. The author had chaired a psychology department for close to 10 years and would have been a wealthy man if he had had a dime for each time a prospective psychology major pointed to a caged white rat and said: "If I become a psych major, I won't have to touch that, will I?"

client proceeds through the list of scenes. Two sample scenes for our old friend Benny might be:

> Imagine that a young man about your age is waiting in line to fill his glass at the orange-juice machine in the school cafeteria. A taller man, casually talking with a friend, edges in front of the first man. The first man says, "Excuse me, there's a line to use this machine." The taller man says, "Sorry, buddy. I wasn't paying attention," and then moves to the end of the line.

> Imagine that a young man about your age is entering a classroom after the bell has rung. As he opens the door, two of his books slip from his arms and fall onto the floor. An attractive woman student seated near the door picks up the books and hands them to the young man. The professor continues teaching. The young man chuckles to himself about the incident and after class approaches the student who helped him, saying, "Thanks for your help with the books. My name is Tom." She says, "Hi. I'm Nancy."

Note that in these scenes the model is rewarded for practicing a social skill that the client does not presently perform. The practitioner constantly encourages the client to think about the modeled behavior and to gradually try out what she or he has covertly observed. Following the processes described earlier, the covert modeling technique, carefully practiced by the client, activates the attention and retention processes. Encouraged by the practitioner to rehearse the modeled behavior (motor reproduction) and motivated by anticipation of the reinforcement observed in the model, the client is gradually led to perform the behavior when occasions present themselves. In the end, covert modeling, like all modeling procedures, demonstrates to the client that (1) certain specific behaviors are likely to be reinforced (outcome expectation) and that (2) the client, like the model, can also perform those specific behaviors (efficacy expectation).

Modeling Techniques in Context

In clinical practice, modeling techniques are applied within the context of a larger therapeutic strategy. A common context for modeling techniques is referred to as *social-skills training*. The assumption underlying social-skills training is that the client lacks certain necessary interpersonal skills. Social-skills training may include: (1) presenting the rationale behind the training, (2) modeling, (3) role-playing, (4) feedback, and (5) homework (Sprafkin, 1984). After explaining the procedure to the client, the practitioner exposes the client to models practicing the required skill. This may take the form of overt, symbolic, covert, or participant modeling. Following exposure to the models, the client engages in role-playing or behavior rehearsal to practice the skill that she or he has observed. The practitioner typically take an active part in improvising and rehearsing appropriate scenes. Encouragement and corrections from the practitioner serve as feedback as the client shapes the new skill. Eventually, homework in the form of in vivo demonstrations of the new skill shifts the locus of reinforcement (see, for example, Curran, 1981). Modeling techniques in the context of social-skills training can be part of even larger therapeutic strategies. They are used, for example, in conjunction with cognitive techniques in assertion training (Lange & Jakubowski, 1978) and as an important part of Lazarus's multimodal therapy (see Chapter 10). Even Wolpe (1982) has suggested that modeling techniques be used in the treatment of phobias (presumably as adjuncts to reciprocal-inhibition techniques), although he finds the theoretical context of self-efficacy theory "untenable" (p. 203).

Modeling techniques are popular and practical for two reasons: First, because modeling motivates the client by showing him or her the possibilities of success, it can serve as a necessary first step within a larger therapeutic strategy; second, modeling techniques are amenable to improvisation and can be creatively tailored to meet individual client needs. In addition, the theory of self-efficacy is generating a growing body of related research and promises to be a major theoretical focal point of counseling in the future. Some of the relevant research, however, has been criticized for its heavy focus on the treatment of animal phobias and for its reliance on analogy rather than on actual clinical populations for its subjects (see Bandura, 1978; Emmelkamp, 1982; R. L. Woolfolk & Lazarus, 1979).

Cognitive Techniques

In a very real sense, all of the techniques we have examined thus far are cognitive techniques; that is, their effectiveness cannot be explained without direct or indirect reference to cognitive processes. In the techniques that follow, however, intentional and direct modifications in cognitive processing itself are assumed to lead to changes in feelings and actions. That said, though, the reader should realize that throughout the relevant literature the inclusion of cognitive techniques within the larger framework of behavior therapy is somewhat arbitrary, as is true of our present grouping. It can be argued, for example, that techniques like thought-stopping and covert modeling are cognitive and that covert conditioning, described below, is really an operant technique. Referring back to Table 5.1, the reader will see that cognitive techniques are associated with the theoretical approach known as cognitive behavior modification.

Covert Conditioning

As the name suggests, covert conditioning techniques apply the principles of operant and classical learning to imagined events to change behavior. The client is instructed to imagine the targeted behavior and its consequences. As with the covert modeling discussed earlier, in vivo changes in behavior result from changes in imaginal scenes. The major proponent and leading researcher of covert techniques, as noted earlier, is Cautela (Cautela & Kearney, 1984; Upper & Cautela, 1977). In addition to covert modeling, Cautela has identified the following types of covert conditioning: covert sensitization, covert positive reinforcement, covert negative reinforcement, covert extinction, and covert response cost. Since each of these covert techniques depends for theoretical support on research done with its overt counterpart, certain underlying assumptions deserve mention. As Cautela has pointed out, the same laws are assumed to govern overt and covert processes (the *homogeneity assumption*), overt and covert processes are assumed to interact with and influence each other (the *interaction assumption*), and laws of learning that affect overt processes are assumed to affect covert processes in the same way and vice versa (the *learning assumption*) (Upper & Cautela, 1977).

Covert sensitization, unlike systematic desensitization, is directed at changing *approach* behavior rather than avoidance behavior. In other words, the targeted behavior is one that the client regularly performs but that is maladaptive or undesirable (for example, excessive drinking). Covert sensitization has been successfully applied to a variety of problems, including "obesity, drug abuse, self-injurious behavior, alcoholism, sexual disorders, smoking, and compulsive stealing" (Cautela & Kearney, 1984, p. 305). The technique involves teaching the client progressive relaxation and, while the client is relaxed, having him or her imagine the pleasurable but inappropriate behavior. The practitioner pairs the pleasurable activity in the client's imagination with becoming physically ill and vomiting, and the client is required to practice the technique regularly as a homework assignment. As the reader undoubtedly is now imagining, the practitioner systematically presents the client with highly evocative images of both the pleasurable behavior and the physical sickness. Detailed clinical examples of covert sensitization applied to exhibitionism, pedophilia, homosexuality, nail-biting, and eating and drinking disorders can be found in Upper and Cautela (1977).

In *covert positive reinforcement,* the client imagines, first, performing the desired behavior and then a pleasant scene. In *covert negative reinforcement,* after imagining the desired behavior, the client imagines the removal of a noxious stimulus. In *covert extinction,* the client repeatedly imagines an unwanted behavior without receiving the reinforcement she or he might have had the behavior actually been performed. In *covert response cost,* the client imagines that a positive reinforcer is removed following the performance of an unwanted behavior. In a sense, this is imagining punishment.

More recently, Cautela (1983) has described a combination of procedures that he calls the *self-control triad* (SCT). The triad consists of thought-stopping, relaxed breathing exercises, and covert positive reinforcement and is aimed at teaching clients self-regulation. To illustrate, we can see how our friend Barbara might use the SCT.

Barbara's mind is filled with thoughts of verbal abuse and possible dismemberment as she barrels down the hall toward her boss's office. "Imagine that two-bit jerk thinking he can up my quotas," she mumbles irately. Suddenly, Barbara remembers what she has learned in her counseling sessions and practiced regularly at home: the SCT. She yells, "Stop!" and, leaning against the wall, closes her eyes, takes a deep, long breath, holds it, and then lets it out. Barbara continues the breathing exercise while imagining a beautiful day at the beach, complete with sand, waves, and gliding gulls. After a few minutes, Barbara is planning a less volatile and potentially more productive interaction with her boss.

In this fanciful example, we see the basics of the SCT. Thoughts are interrupted, the physical reaction is defused, and a distracting positive image allows rationality to return. The SCT has been applied to undesirable avoidance and approach behaviors, depression, pain responses, and other organic problems and has been successfully taught to children as young as 6 years of age (Cautela, 1983).

Although the SCT is a promising application of covert conditioning techniques, considerably more research is needed. Covert modeling has received more attention than the other techniques, and the evidence on the effectiveness of covert conditioning techniques is inconclusive (Craighead et al., 1981; Mahoney & Arnkoff, 1978).

Cognitive Restructuring

Ellis (1962), with the development of his rational-emotive therapy, was the first to identify irrational ideas as the root cause of emotional disturbances. His approach to counseling and psychotherapy, which will be examined in some detail in Chapter 10, was the first of several approaches aimed at helping the client develop more adaptive thought patterns by altering her or his beliefs or self-verbalizations (Mahoney & Arnkoff, 1978). For our present purposes, we will look at two other prominent techniques for modifying or restructuring an individual's cognition: Beck's cognitive therapy and Meichenbaum's self-instructional training.

Independent of the work of Ellis, psychiatrist Aaron Beck developed his own techniques for restructuring cognitions, calling his approach **cognitive therapy.**[7] Beck and his colleagues have applied cognitive therapy to a full range of emotional disorders, including depression, suicide, anxiety, phobias, obsessions, and psychosomatic disorders (Beck, 1967, 1976; Beck & Emery, 1979; Beck & Lester, 1973; Bedrosian & Beck, 1980; Burns, 1980; Burns & Beck, 1978; Holroyd & Andrasik, 1982; Lester, Beck, & Mitchell, 1979). The logic underlying cognitive therapy is simple; a quotation from Maslow that Beck (1976) uses to introduce one chapter sums it up: "The neurotic is not only emotionally sick—he is cognitively wrong" (p. 76). Maladaptive actions are the product of illogical, irrational, and negative thoughts. Though an individual may only be aware of the emotions caused by his or her thoughts, the process of cognitive therapy uncovers those underlying irrational thoughts, demon-

---

[7]Obviously, Beck's cognitive therapy is really one cognitive therapy, much the same way that Wolpe's behavior therapy is really one behavior therapy. Beck (1976) views behavior therapy as a subset of cognitive therapy; Wolpe does not afford Beck a similar status. In the view taken in this text, Beck has developed a set of techniques and strategies that accords well with the broader conception of behavior therapy we are using.

strating their inaccuracy and deleterious effects to the client and, in doing so, changing the emotions and actions that accompany them.

Understanding the development of Beck's thinking is helpful to understanding his technique. Beck began his career as a psychoanalyst, and despite the distance he has now come from psychoanalytic therapy, through it, he came to understand the relationship between emotional distress, maladaptive actions, and what Beck calls *automatic thoughts* (1967, 1976). Beck (1976) recounted an experience with a patient that is illustrative. During the psychoanalytic session, a client was experiencing considerable anxiety as she described various sexual conflicts. Following some hunches based on earlier cases, Beck asked her to focus on the internal, personal dialogue that accompanied her external description. "She then reported the following sequence [of thoughts]: 'I am not expressing myself clearly . . . He is bored with me . . . He probably can't follow what I'm saying . . . This probably sounds foolish to him . . . He will probably try to get rid of me' " (p. 32). The "he" was clearly Beck; thus, the client's anxiety was coming not from describing her sexual conflicts but from this internal monologue. Although Beck initially thought that these anxiety-producing thoughts were an expression of **transference,** he soon discovered that this stream of automatic thoughts extended well beyond the confines of the therapeutic relationship.

Automatic thoughts are part of our moment-to-moment consciousness. They are short, often judgmental messages about our performance. The thoughts occur in response to our immediate situation, and they produce a corresponding emotion and influence our actions. We cannot always fully attend to these automatic thoughts, however, and it is often necessary to "tune them in." The content of these automatic thoughts varies from disorder to disorder, as summarized in Table 5.2. The thoughts also differ in how readily a client can attend to them. In some disorders, for example, obsessions, the automatic thoughts are, predictably, quite pronounced, but in anxiety disorders, the obvious emotional component may make the automatic thoughts more difficult to uncover.

Table 5.2   The Cognitive Content of Various Disorders (From: Mahoney & Arnkoff, 1978, p. 706.)

Disorder	Cognitive Content
Depression	Thoughts center on the experience of loss along with the "cognitive triad": (1) a devaluation of the self, (2) a negative view of life experiences, and (3) a pessimistic view of the future
Anxiety	Thoughts of danger predominate
Paranoia	Thoughts focus on interference from and intrusion by other people
Obsession	Thoughts generally focus on doubts (for example, about a past performance or a future capacity)

Whether rational or irrational, positive or negative, automatic thoughts represent the content of cognition. In contrast, that fact that one thought rather than another is present in consciousness at any given moment is due to the process of cognition—that is, the idiosyncratic manner in which an individual selects, interprets, and catalogues everyday events. If an individual's processing of environmental information is accurate, then the thoughts, emotions, and actions that follow will be adaptive. If, on the other hand, this processing is distorted or skewed in some way, then the subsequent thoughts, emotions, and actions will not be adaptive, because they will be either excessive or inadequate. Burns (1980, pp. 49–50) has identified 10 of these cognitive distortions:

1. *All-or-nothing thinking:* You see things in black-and-white categories. If your performance falls short of perfect, you see yourself as a total failure.
2. *Overgeneralization:* You see a single negative event as a never-ending pattern of defeat.
3. *Mental filter:* You pick out a single negative detail and dwell on it exclusively so that your vision of all reality becomes darkened, like the drop of ink that discolors the entire beaker of water.
4. *Disqualifying the positive:* You reject positive experiences by insisting they "don't count" for some reason or other. In this way you can maintain a negative belief that is contradicted by your everyday experience.
5. *Jumping to conclusions:* You make a negative interpretation even though there are no definite facts that convincingly support your conclusion.
   a. *Mind reading:* You arbitrarily conclude that someone is reacting negatively to you, and you don't bother to check this out.
   b. *The Fortune Teller Error:* You anticipate that things will turn out badly, and you feel convinced that your prediction is an already-established fact.
6. *Magnification (catastrophizing) or minimization:* You exaggerate the importance of things (such as your goof-up or someone else's achievement), or you inappropriately shrink things until they appear tiny (your own desirable qualities or the other fellow's imperfections). This is also called the "binocular trick."
7. *Emotional reasoning:* You assume that your negative emotions necessarily reflect the way things really are: "I feel it, therefore it must be true."
8. *Should statements:* You try to motivate yourself with "shoulds" and "shouldn'ts," as if you had to be whipped and punished before you could be expected to do anything. "Musts" and "oughts" are also offenders. The emotional consequence is guilt. When you direct should statements toward others, you feel anger, frustration, and resentment.
9. *Labeling and mislabeling:* This is an extreme form of overgeneralization. Instead of describing your error, you attach a negative label to yourself: "I'm a *loser.*" When someone else's behavior rubs you the wrong way, you attach a negative label to him: "He's a goddamn louse." Mislabeling involves describing an event with language that is highly colored and emotionally loaded.

10. *Personalization:* You see yourself as the cause of some negative external event which in fact you were not primarily responsible for.

Cognitive distortions color the meaning of everyday events, produce negative automatic thoughts, and lead to maladaptive emotions and actions. In turn, the existence of the maladaptive emotions and actions serves to intensify the entire process.

Cognitive therapy changes maladaptive behavior by restructuring cognition—that is, by altering the assumptions and premises that underlie the distortions. The process begins with the client learning what maladaptive automatic thoughts are, how to monitor them, and their relationship to maladaptive emotions and actions. Then, through a series of Socratic dialogues, the client tests the accuracy of the irrational automatic thoughts and develops rational responses to them. This process takes place both during the therapy sessions and in homework assignments. Consider the following dialogue between a cognitive therapist and our old friend Benny. Earlier explanations of Benny's lack of assertiveness centered on the role played by anxiety as an inhibitor and on Benny's lack of social skills. Now we look at a cognitive explanation and treatment. In this case, the focus is on the depressed mood that is part of Benny's problem.

Benny (B): Yeah, I know I went up after class and asked her for a date, but I felt nervous even when it was over and kind of depressed even though she said she'd go out with me!

Practitioner (P): But you did what you had wanted to do. What thoughts made you feel nervous and depressed?

B: My thought was that most of the time I can't do things like that, and that this was just kind of a fluke, you know. So I still felt pretty bad about myself. And now I'm worried about the date. I'll probably make a fool of myself.

P: Slow down. How do you know this positive action was a fluke? What proof do you have?

B: Well, I don't. But lots of times when I do something that's really OK, I get that rotten feeling anyway. It's not fair.

P: But there's the distortion in your thinking. Is there another thought, a more rational thought you can put in its place?

B: Well, yeah. I could say, "This is not a fluke. I've done things well before, and I can continue to do them that way!"

P: Good. There's something you can say that is true and will dispute the irrational thought. What have you learned from this, Benny?

B: I almost hate to say it, Doc, but I learned you'll get screwed, if your thinking's skewed!

P: Oh.

In this dialogue, we can see several of the cognitive distortions from Burns's list (for example, disqualifying the positive), as well as how a client can be taught to replace irrational thoughts with realistic, positive ones. The client is often instructed to keep a daily record of stimulus situations, emotional reactions, underlying automatic thoughts, disputing rational responses, and outcomes (see Burns & Persons, 1982, and Burns, 1980, for examples). These records then become grist for the therapeutic session.

Cognitive therapy has become a major treatment procedure for depression, and the Beck Depression Inventory (1967) is a widely used research and clinical tool. Unfortunately, the necessary brevity of our present discussion of cognitive restructuring as practiced in cognitive therapy does not permit us to do justice to the sophistication that characterizes the work of Beck and his colleagues.[8]

Donald Meichenbaum has proposed *self-instructional training* as a means of cognitive restructuring (Meichenbaum, 1975, 1977, 1985a, 1985b; Meichenbaum & Cameron, 1973).[9] Meichenbaum's work has two theoretical sources: Ellis's (1962) rational-emotive therapy, and Luria's (1961) research on the central role of language in the acquisition of behavior. Meichenbaum's theoretical ideas were bolstered by research with schizophrenic adults and hyperactive and impulsive children.

In acquiring a new behavior, whether as a child or an adult, we often instruct ourselves vocally or subvocally until we have the new behavior firmly learned. When we go to change a pattern of behavior, we do the same thing. We use self-instructions in learning such diverse behaviors as typing, not yelling at the referee, or meeting the Queen of England for the first time. Whether our acquaintance with the behavior to be mastered has come from verbal instructions from others or from observing models, fully acquiring it often involves this self-instructive verbalization. Self-instructional training formalizes this distinctly human way of cementing behaviors into our repertoires. After the client learns to identify maladaptive self-statements, the practitioner models the appropriate behaviors and the self-instructions that ideally accompany the appropriate behavior. The self-instructions are verbalized overtly and include detailed evaluation of the performance requirements, potential obstacles, and ways of successfully overcoming the obstacles. The client performs the behavior while reciting the corresponding self-instructions, with the practitioner providing ongoing feedback (G. T. Wilson, 1978). The process thus includes modeling, reinforcement, and problem-solving procedures. The objective, of course, is to have the client perform the behavior without overt self-

---

[8]In the day-to-day practice of cognitive therapy, Beck and his colleagues use a variety of behavioral and medical techniques, and Beck's Center for Cognitive Therapy in Philadelphia is an important training and research center. One of the most clinically useful publications about cognitive therapy is Burns's *Feeling Good: The New Mood Therapy* (1980). Reading it is a good way for a beginning student, a motivated client, or even an experienced practitioner to understand depression and its treatment by cognitive therapy.

[9]Meichenbaum (1985a) uses the term *cognitive behavior therapies,* as distinct from behavior therapies, for the various attempts that have been made to integrate the techniques and theories of cognitive therapists and behavior therapists. His distinction in terms reflects an ongoing controversy, a taste of which can be found in Ledwidge (1979), Mahoney and Kazdin (1979), and Meichenbaum (1979). R. C. Miller and Berman (1983) have evaluated the effectiveness of these therapies, and Turk and Salovey (1985a, 1985b) have provided a helpful discussion of related theoretical
issues.

instruction in the absence of the practitioner. We can see how self-instructional training works in Meichenbaum's summary of a training regimen intended to teach impulsive children to think before they act (Meichenbaum, 1985a, p. 281).

1. An adult model performs a task while talking out loud (cognitive modeling);
2. The child performs the same task under the direction of the model's instructions (overt external guidance);
3. The child performs the task while instructing [her- or] himself aloud (overt self-guidance);
4. The child whispers the self-instructions as [she or] he goes through the task (faded, overt self-guidance); and finally,
5. The child performs the task while guiding [her or] his performance via inaudible or private speech or nonverbal self-direction (covert self-instruction).

Cognitive restructuring by means of self-instructional training has been widely applied and plays an important role in an increasingly important cognitive technique called stress-inoculation training.

Stress-Inoculation Training

From a practical point of view, the idea of being able to inoculate individuals against the ravages of stress much as we inoculate against measles is an appealing one. In a sense, *stress-inoculation training* attempts to do just that, by teaching clients specific coping skills that can improve their capacities to endure stressful situations. Stress-inoculation training is a self-instructional method originally developed by Meichenbaum (1977) for the purpose of teaching clients to deal with anxiety disorders. It has also been applied to improving pain tolerance (Girodo & Wood, 1979; Hackett & Horan, 1980; Jaremko, 1979; Meichenbaum & Jaremko, 1983; Meichenbaum, Turk, & Burnstein, 1975; Vallis, 1984; Worthington, 1978). Paralleling this work, Raymond Novaco has applied stress-inoculation techniques in the treatment of maladaptive anger (Meichenbaum & Novaco, 1978; Novaco, 1976, 1977, 1978; Novaco, Cook, & Sarason, 1983).

Stress-inoculation training has a three-phase structure: (1) educating the client in the nature of stress reactions and the need to adequately prepare for them, (2) training in specific coping skills, and (3) practice of the skills in the clinical setting and in vivo through graduated exposure to the stressor. Typically, self-statements like those used in self-instructional training are tailored to the client's needs. In addition, the client learns a variation of systematic desensitization in which the client is allowed to experience his or her anxiety gradually while practicing constructive self-statements.[10] Since the stressors move

---

[10]This variation of systematic desensitization is part of the *coping skills training* developed by Goldfried (1971). Reviews of the literature often identify it as a separate technique. Coping skills training uses covert modeling techniques and pairs scenes of successful self-statements with graduated presentations of anxiety-evoking stimuli within the context of relaxation training.

from imagination to real situations gradually and the resulting anxiety is controlled by the self-instructions, the client becomes increasingly tolerant of the stressors. In theory and practice, the procedure provides a preventive measure against the targeted and similar stressors. There are, of course, a number of variations and applications of these techniques; one of the most interesting applications is to problems of chronic anger.

Anger is a human emotion, a reaction to a provocation from the environment, either immediate or remembered. Anger can lead us to actions that are either constructive or destructive. Anger sustained over time can affect our psychological and biological well-being, and inappropriate expressions of anger as verbal or physical aggression can lead to embarrassment, alienation, or incarceration. As mentioned earlier, Novaco has developed a procedure for treating what he calls "chronic anger problems" and "proneness to provocation" (Novaco, 1983). His treatment, generally referred to as *stress-inoculation therapy for anger control,* uses the cognitive techniques introduced by Meichenbaum. In addition to publishing several articles describing the treatment, Novaco has developed a training manual for therapists (1983) and a manual for clients (1985).

The goals of stress-inoculation therapy are "to prevent anger from occurring when it is maladaptive, to enable the client to regulate arousal when it occurs, and to provide the performance skills necessary to manage the provocation experience" (Novaco, 1983, p. 14). Because of the thoroughness with which Novaco's procedures address the problems associated with anger, it is only possible to provide a brief sketch. We will do so by again returning to our friend Barbara.

After explaining the rationale behind stress-inoculation therapy, the practitioner carefully interviews Barbara and has her complete various behavioral measures to get a picture of her problems with anger. Early in the intervention, the practitioner needs to know: (1) what external events arouse Barbara's anger, (2) what she thinks and feels when she is angry (cognitive and affective factors), and (3) specifically how she behaves and what the consequences are. In Barbara's case, the practitioner might determine that one of the external events that evokes her anger is disagreement from one of her subordinates about how a task is to be performed. Cognitive and affective factors might include the feelings of tension that the event creates, and negative self-statements like "He thinks I'm a fool," "I've got to be right," or "I'm going to lose control." Behavioral factors might include Barbara's verbal abuse of the workers and their sneering and avoidance of her. From the beginning of therapy, the practitioner instructs Barbara to maintain a very specific diary of anger experiences, complete with successes and failures at coping with her anger. Those experiences form the basis for developing a hierarchy of anger-evoking scenarios. At the same time, Barbara receives training in progressive relaxation and learns how to monitor the internal dialogues that go on, being especially attentive to irrational beliefs and expectations. Relaxation and breathing procedures are used as Barbara is covertly presented with the scenarios. In the imagined scenes, Barbara copes successfully, using new, more adaptive self-statements as well as adaptive actions, to interrupt her anger. Gradually, events that evoke anger when imagined are short-circuited cognitively by changing the internal dialogue, and this learning is transferred to the real world. Events recorded in the diary chart the progress of treatment. The process as described by Novaco (1983, 1985) is far from a mechanical training procedure. It is an educational experience in which specific information about how human emotion and cognition operate leads to success.

Final Comment

Behavior therapy, with its increasing emphasis on cognition, promises to generate many effective, scientifically derived techniques for changing maladaptive behavior. Yet, utopia is nowhere in sight. At the moment, no single approach to psychotherapy or counseling is universally more successful than any other. At the same time, behavior therapy's present attempts to do justice to both the complexity of the individual and the standards of scientific research show an unusually high level of vitality and openness, necessary ingredients for progress.[11] In a very real sense, behavior therapy has become a reservoir of ideas and techniques for enhancing self-regulation that are increasingly being integrated into approaches with decidedly different theoretical and philosophical views.

Summary of Chapter 5

In Chapter 5, we have examined specific techniques commonly in use among practitioners of behavior therapy. The techniques are classified into five types, around which the chapter is organized: reciprocal inhibition techniques, anxiety-evoking techniques, operant techniques, modeling techniques, and cognitive techniques. The types and techniques are listed with the theoretical approaches to which they correspond in Table 5.1. In the treatment of individual clients, more than one of these techniques is often used, and treatment is always initiated after behavioral assessment.

Reciprocal-Inhibition Techniques

1. Reciprocal-inhibition techniques aim at breaking the connection between maladaptive anxiety and the conditions that produce it. The anxiety is assumed to have been acquired following the laws of classical conditioning;

---

[11]Typifying behavior therapy's vitality and openness is a book entitled *Failures in Behavior Therapy* (Foa & Emmelkamp, 1983). Within its pages, over 40 practitioners of behavior therapy describe failures and relapses.

recpirocal-inhibition techniques apply those same laws to counter the anxiety. Change occurs when the anxiety-evoking condition has been associated with a response other than anxiety. Three specific responses are incompatible with anxiety: relaxation, assertiveness, and a sexual response.

2. Thought-stopping is a reciprocal-inhibition technique that emphasizes the role of cognition in producing the anxious response. In thought-stopping, the client is taught to interrupt the connection between the evoking stimulus and the anxiety by yelling "Stop" when thoughts are producing anxiety. With practice, and usually in connection with other techniques, the client eventually does the "yelling" mentally.

3. Some individuals fail to act as they would like to because anxiety prevents them from doing so. Assertiveness training teaches the client to perform actions that have been inhibited. This is done largely through practicing oppositional and commendatory assertive statements and rehearsing behavior during the therapy session. Constant encouragement and pressure from the practitioner helps the client transfer his or her assertiveness to the real world.

4. Systematic desensitization is one of the most widely used and thoroughly researched behavior therapy techniques. After thorough evaluation, the client and practitioner develop a graduated list of anxiety-producing events called an anxiety hierarchy. The client assigns each event value indicating its relative ability to distress. The client is also taught how to relax using Jacobson's progressive relaxation. Treatment consists of having the client imagine the anxiety-provoking events in a graduated sequence while relaxed. The client proceeds through the hierarchy until she or he can stay relaxed in the imagined presence of the most evocative stimulus. The client is encouraged to use the new learning in vivo—that is, in real-life situations.

Anxiety-Evoking Techniques

5. Anxiety-evoking techniques place the client in the very situations that produce anxiety. In the first of these techniques, flooding, carefully orchestrated exposure of the client to anxiety-producing events, first in imagination and then in real life, extinguishes the anxiety.

6. Paradoxical intention is based on the fact that intentional efforts to control autonomic functions often have the opposite effect. The client is instructed to perfect the symptomatic behavior with the paradoxical effect of reducing or eliminating it.

Operant Techniques

7. Operant techniques, sometimes referred to as contingency management, rely on the elements of operant learning, primarily reinforcement, punishment, and extinction, to effect changes in behavior.

8. Operant learning takes place in all therapeutic relationships, albeit perhaps unsystematically. Operant techniques can be applied systematically in many practical ways, both in individual counseling or in institutional settings.

Modeling Techniques

9. Modeling techniques capitalize on the capacity of humans to learn vicariously, through observing the behavior of others and its consequences. Modeling is viewed as a cognitively mediated learning process in which the individual's belief in his or her ability to actually perform the modeled behavior (self-efficacy) is important in determining whether or not it will be performed.
10. Therapeutic applications of modeling include overt modeling (with a live model), symbolic modeling (on film or videotape), covert modeling (in imagination), and participant modeling (the practitioner first performs the desired behavior).
11. Modeling techniques are widely used to help clients acquire skills they are lacking, often assertive skills.

Cognitive Techniques

12. Covert conditioning is a cognitive technique that applies the principles of classical and operant learning through imagination. Several types of covert conditioning are described in the chapter.
13. Cognitive restructuring involves replacing irrational, negative thoughts and reasoning with more realistic ones. In cognitive therapy, this is done by examining and changing the content of the client's automatic thoughts as well as eliminating faulty reasoning patterns. In self-instructional training, this is done by having the client observe a model perform appropriate behaviors while verbalizing constructive self-statements. The client then practices the behavior together with the restructured cognitions.
14. Stress-inoculation training uses training in social skills along with graduated clinical and in vivo exposure to stressors to build up a client's tolerance for stressful situations. In the treatment of chronic anger, stress-inoculation training uses relaxation training and constructive self-statements to short-circuit anger.

CHAPTER 6

Maturity and Insight Therapy: Theoretical and Practical Foundations

> *Personality is a process, not an onion.*
>
> **Paul Wachtel**

The Metaphor of Matthew May

In his private thoughts, where the merit of his metaphor could not be questioned, Matthew May liked to think of his impending fiftieth birthday as another tollgate along life's highway: a forced stop, exacting tariff from the heart by its very suddenness. A bookstore manager and would-be poet, Matthew May had smiled and bantered his way through four jobs and two marriages, all of which had ended, to use his own debasement of Eliot, "not with a bang but a whine." The divorces had been stolid affairs with love and hate hoarded between the lines of his all too private poems. The death of his only son some eleven years before still gnawed at him, but his only tears were Budweiser trickles having less to do with memories than emptiness. When he was younger, he had believed in God. These days he sat in the back of the church, ogling young girls, flirting with guilt, and feeling somewhat chastened by that very fact. And now, turning fifty, at another tollgate, the many whys and why nots of his life, answered over the years in couplets and half-truths, came back to him exacting tribute for a life only figuratively lived.

Matthew May's life is fiction, but his experience of himself and the value and meaning of his life strike familiar chords in all of us. Emotionally, we understand his sense of alienation, his self-deceit, his loneliness, his need for love, and his questioning of his very existence. Intellectually, we want to understand what makes him tick, to find out what past event, concealed desire, anguished decision, or buried urge has brought him to this point. The quest to understand the inner person is an enduring concern for the philosopher, and an endlessly fascinating topic for the artist. Likewise, for many who have pursued careers in the helping professions, it is fascination with the inner workings of human beings, coupled with the hope of relieving the pain some individuals suffer, that has led us to choose this kind of work. As the reader will recall from Chapter 3, the questions being addressed here are part of the study of personality, a study pursued, for the most part, within the clinical research tradition that began in the 19th century with the work of Freud. But is any of this really relevant to today's practitioner? Are insight-oriented approaches to counseling and psychotherapy of any practical value? Have not advances in medicine, especially chemotherapy, coupled with the increasing efficacy of behavior therapy, all but obviated the need for what is now often called "traditional therapy"?

The twin technologies of chemotherapy and behavior therapy have made and will continue to make significant advances in providing clients means for self-regulation. Medication will control panic attacks and anxiety, certain types of depression, psychotic symptomatology, and perhaps other types of disorders; behavior therapy will help individuals control excesses and deficits of action, thought, and feeling. Yet, for many individuals, self-regulation is just a starting point for a more distinctly human quest for self-understanding, meaning, fulfillment, or happiness—elements of what we are calling maturity. This chapter presents a selective overview of the major theoretical perspectives and practical concerns of therapeutic approaches that aim at enhancing maturation by inducing insight in or from the client. In doing so, I hope to demonstrate that the insight therapies are not only relevant to the work of the contemporary practitioner but provide an essential context for the application of self-regulatory approaches.

Maturity and the Role of Insight

What are the qualities of a mature person? Most cultures establish different criteria for maturity depending on the age of the individual. Within our culture, for example, we expect different abilities, knowledge, mannerisms, and responses to stressful situations from mature 10-year-olds than we do from mature 17- or 39-year-olds. Thus, we are not surprised when a 14-year-old responds to parental divorce with anger, resentment, and periods of melancholy, nor are we surprised to see 19-year-olds at a sports event be highly animated or even boisterous. We do, however, begin to question the maturity of a 27-year-old who becomes permanently morose and socially withdrawn over the separation of his or her parents, or a 50-year-old who customarily becomes drunk and rowdy at church picnics and PTA meetings. Our commonsense assumption is that immature individuals lack some fundamental knowledge or experience typical of others in the same age group and culture. This knowledge or experience is another name for insight. In this sense, insight means the knowledge or experience necessary to discern the real nature and demands of a situation. We assume that were immature individuals to arrive at some insight that would allow them to recognize their real motivations, their true feelings, or the effects of their actions on others, their immature behavior would end. Indeed, since the beginning of human cultures, every culture has designated certain individuals to induce insight in or elicit insight from those who stray outside of the culture's rules and expectations. The one designated to make these changes may be the head of the family or tribe, the religious leader, the physician, or the educator—a person with the authority and the skills to engage, inform, interpret, and, when necessary, inspire.

Psychotherapy and counseling, beginning with Freud and the clinical research tradition, have operated under these same cultural assumptions. The practitioner has become the culturally sanctioned source of insight for individuals behaving outside of the culture's norms. Each approach to therapy or counseling within the clinical research tradition has sought to explain the normal as well as the abnormal development of personality and to unravel the complexities of human behavior. Each approach has also attempted to modify behavior by means of some kind of insight. Typically, this insight has taken the form of some parcel of knowledge, experience, or both with the power to either gradually or radically alter maladaptive patterns of behavior.

Two important factors related to insight deserve mention before we proceed. The first factor is *time* — the past, present, and future. The various insight therapies tend to focus on one period more than another. Psychoanalytic approaches, for example, obviously emphasize the past; cognitive approaches tend to emphasize the present and, sometimes, the future as well. As can be seen in Table 6.1, the temporal focus of the therapy affects the nature of the insight that will be engendered.

Table 6.1   *Temporal Focus and the Nature of Intellectual and Emotional Insight*

Temporal Focus	*Nature of Intellectual Insight*	*Nature of Emotional Insight*
Past	Recalling past events; recognizing the role of past events in current behavior; reinterpreting past events based on new information	Experiencing and expressing emotions associated with past events; accepting the past
Present	Learning alternative ways of behaving; understanding the dynamics involved in current behavior patterns; reinterpreting the meaning of behavior	Experiencing one's true feelings about events; expressing one's true feelings appropriately; accepting the full range of one's feelings
Future	Identifying future events that may be problematic and determining the most effective behavioral response	Accepting one's inability to change some future events, especially sickness, aging, and death

The second factor is the distinction between *intellectual insight* and *emotional insight*. Some approaches to counseling or psychotherapy emphasize intellectual insight — that is, the acquisition of information about some event, person, or relationship, whether in the past, present, or future. Other approaches emphasize emotional insight — that is, the experience of conditions and changes in the individual's emotional life. In Table 6.1, the nature of intellectual insight is contrasted with that of emotional insight in relation to the temporal focus of therapy. Bear in mind as we continue through this chapter that, although specific approaches often emphasize one type of insight or another, no approach to counseling or psychotherapy works exclusively with the past, present, or future, nor does any approach avoid either the intellectual or the emotional.

Three Perspectives on Personality and Behavior Change

The clinical research tradition has spawned a variety of seemingly different approaches to counseling and psychotherapy. While there are several ways to group these approaches, I have organized them according to three perspectives on personality and behavior change: the *psychoanalytic,* the *neopsychoanalytic,* and the *humanistic-existential.* These three perspectives differ without being totally discrete; absolute lines of separation are impossible because the perspectives are linked, historically, theoretically, and methodologically. My objective in this section is to highlight both their distinctiveness and their interrelatedness by examining them in relation to the following conceptual benchmarks: (1) the self, (2) anxiety, and (3) insight. In other words, the three perspectives differ from each other in: (1) their descriptions of the nature and development of the self, especially the mature self; (2) their identification of the sources and role of anxiety in adaptive and maladaptive behavior; and (3) their descriptions of the nature and role of insight in counseling and psychotherapy, especially as insight relates to time (past, present, or future) and intellect and emotion.

The Psychoanalytic Perspective

During his last two years of college, Matthew May had fancied himself possessed by the ghost of Sigmund Freud. Following a particularly provocative course entitled "Freud, Marx, Darwin, and the Beatles: An Introduction to Modern Thought," convinced that Freud's spirit and his were sympatico, *Matthew determined to read all of Freud's works. To that end, he purchased several paperback volumes of Freud's most important (sex-laden) work, and procured from the library a German edition of* Beyond the Pleasure Principle, *which he left open in his dormitory room with notes penciled in the margins. His dreams began to brim with trains, tunnels, breasts, and imaginary nannies. He became preoccupied with his childhood and berated his mother for not remembering the specifics of his toilet training. He went through a "period of impotence" (recognizing the bisexual mix inherent in the expression) and was convinced he was becoming gay (he told his girlfriend he had "dislodged libido"). In the end he wrote a poem, and all of his problems disappeared. The poem was nothing more than a convoluted, self-deprecating exposé of his "true" inner feelings, conflicts, desires, hopes, dreads—the psychoanalytic waterworks. The poem was tedious beyond measure, and the few friends who read it recognized little of Matthew May in it. He had missed Freud's message about the secrets we keep from ourselves, the lies we spread even in our deepest heart. He had mistaken truth for a litany of uncommitted urges. At the same time, the self-consciously clever title of his poem quite by accident caught a meaning of Freud even analysts repress; he called his poem "The Illusion of a Future."*

————

The above excerpt illustrates how readily psychoanalytic thinking can be simplified and trivialized. At its core, though, the message of psychoanalysis remains a profound and disturbing one. Locked within each of us are secrets we keep from others and, often, from ourselves. Deception and distortion are the tools of this sham, and the worst lies are those we save for ourselves. While the content of the self-deception of Freud's patients may seem Victorian to us today, only the content—if even that—has changed, not the practice of self-deception. Theories of and approaches to counseling and psychotherapy that remain within the psychoanalytic perspective emphasize the development, maintenance, and uncovering of the internal, or *intrapsychic,* dynamics of deception, of oneself and of others.[1]

Overview

The scientific study of personality and the development of counseling and psychotherapy began with Freud's **psychoanalysis.** Psychoanalytic thinking is sometimes viewed as a monolithic structure that varied little during Freud's lifetime and, since his death, has undergone little change or development. In fact, this is far from the truth. Throughout Freud's long career, he continuously revised his thinking in response to clinical experience as well as changes in society. These were neither peripheral nor cosmetic changes. Even an idea as central as the number and nature of instincts went through several major revisions, as did many other important ideas. Those who have continued Freud's work have extended his ideas in several different directions. Baker (1985), for example, lists four distinct psychoanalytic traditions, each with different conceptual frameworks and clinical applications. For our own purposes, we will include within the psychoanalytic perspective those theories and therapies that continue to emphasize the primacy of intrapsychic events in the development of personality and the modification of human behavior (as opposed to the neopsychoanalytic perspective's greater emphasis on interpersonal events). In addition to Freud, many individuals have contributed to the psychoanalytic perspective, including Franz Alexander, Erik Erikson, Anna Freud, Heinz Hartmann, Melanie Klein, Heinz Kohut, and David Rapaport.

The Self

"Who am I?" "Why am I doing this?" "Is this the 'real' me speaking?" How very strange that human beings from the Greek philosophers to the most recent

---

[1] A recent book by Daniel Goleman (1985), *Vital Lies, Simple Truths,* presents a fascinating overview of the psychology of self-deception. Drawing on the work of Freud, Sullivan, and cognitive psychology, as well as contemporary events, Goleman has provided an informed and readable introduction to our skills of mendacity.

songsters have uttered and reuttered these same questions in one form or the other! Embedded in these seemingly self-evident questions are several profound issues: (1) the nature of one's development as an individual different and distinct from others; (2) the degree to which one is consciously in control of one's thoughts, feelings, and actions; (3) the disparity between one's perception of self and the perceptions of others; and (4) the unexplained discomfort, conflict, or anxiety one feels in certain situations. These issues are not only substantive but an integral part of the therapeutic process. From the psychoanalytic perspective, the answers to these questions come from understanding the nature, structure, and function of the mind.

The nature of the mind   Inherent within Freud's conception of the mind is the assumption that the mind is a closed energy system. Our lives are spent distributing and redistributing energy within the mind itself and in exchanges with the external world. The energy that can be seen in our behavior is called *libido,* a psychic, sexual, and aggressive energy that is a given in our lives, because it is instinctual. The process of investing that energy in some object, person, or idea is called *cathexis.*[2] The laws that Freud used to describe the regulation of this flow of energy are drawn from biology and physics.

Freud was keenly aware of the link between the biological and the psychological, and, as described in an earlier chapter, he unsuccessfully tried to anchor his psychological theory to a biological one. Though at times this link between the biological and the psychological is hidden from view in Freud's writing, in a very fundamental way, psychoanalysis depends on biological concepts.[3] Two principles from the realms of biology and physics that Freud incorporated into his explanation of the nature of mental life were the *principle of stability* and the *principle of economy* (Alexander, 1948). Both of these principles relate to a fundamental fact of our biology: We use and expend energy.

Our biological lives are part of the continuous exchange of energy. Eating, moving, sleeping, hearing, sweating—all these regular human behaviors are part of the ongoing cycle of energy consumption and replacement. One principle that explains the physiological aspect of this process is *homeostasis.* Our bodies are designed to maintain certain temperatures, blood levels, levels of muscle excitation, and so forth, and when these levels change because of external demands, our bodies automatically return them to a state of equilibrium,

[2]As Bettelheim has documented in a fascinating and readable book, *Freud and Man's Soul* (1983), translations of Freud's work into English have often obscured the true meaning of the words he chose to use. No better example exists than the term cathexis. Freud's original German word was *Besetzung,* a common German word meaning "filling" or "occupation." Translators "improved" Freud's work by using the Greek word meaning "to occupy" to make it sound more sophisticated and scientific (Fancher, 1973). This is just one instance of how Freud's interpreters made Freud less accessible and more mysterious.

[3]Freud abandoned the project described in Chapter 3, but in a very real sense, he remained a "cryptobiologist"—that is, a hidden or secret biologist—as Sulloway (1979) has argued. Sulloway pointed out that Freud spent considerable energy arguing against the wholesale incorporation of biological concepts into psychology, while doing that very same thing himself. Sulloway's book, *Freud: Biologist of the Mind,* makes stimulating reading.

following the principle of homeostasis. Homeostasis thus enhances our bodies' ability to endure and therefore has survival value. The psychoanalytic principle of stability is the psychological equivalent of homeostasis. We experience internal tension in the form of unfulfilled desires, wishes, or needs. To reduce this psychic tension, to return to stability or equilibrium, we are driven to experiment with different patterns of behavior capable of reducing this tension. When these behaviors succeed—that is, when they reduce the tension and return us to psychological equilibrium—then the principle of economy takes over. We acquire this new behavior so thoroughly that it becomes automatic and requires less and less expending of energy. We thus are constantly learning ways in which to reduce internal tension (by fulfilling those needs, wishes, and desires) while expending the least amount of energy (Alexander, 1948).

The structure and function of the mind   The above description of how new behavior is acquired resembles operant learning, and a basic learning theory can be identified in psychoanalysis (Hilgard & Bower, 1966; Murray & Jacobson, 1978). Yet, psychoanalysis is unique in its explanation of how the mind is structured and how these structures function. Freud's final description of the structure of the mind included three components: the *id,* the *ego,* and the *superego.* Because these structures of the mind interact with each other, it is tempting to turn this triad into three little persons perched in different recesses of the brain battling for control of our behavior. The problem of personifying the elements of personality was not unknown to Freud himself, who wrote of the ego: "The poor ego has things even worse: it serves three masters and does what it can to bring their claims and demands into harmony with one another" (1933/1964b, p. 77). The tendency to reify aspects of personality comes from the emphasis placed by Freud and some psychoanalysts on structure, yet as Alexander (1948) has suggested, discussions of the structure of the mind are less enlightening than those that focus on how the mind functions. In the descriptions that follow, therefore, maps and models of the structure of the mind have been avoided, and emphasis has been placed on understanding how each aspect of personality operates.

The id is that aspect of personality that reflects our biological inheritance, the "it" (which is what "id" means in Latin) is often talked about metaphorically as a reservoir of psychic energy that directs us instinctually toward unbridled sex and aggression.[4] Viewed functionally, the id is our inborn propensity toward tension reduction. This reduction of tension is what we call

---

[4]Because Freud viewed the id as the "dark, inaccessible part of our personality" (1933/1964b, p. 73), his descriptions of the id have not always been illuminating from a functional point of view. As he wrote in *New Introductory Lectures on Psychoanalysis*: "We approach the id with analogies: we call it a chaos, a cauldron full of seething excitations" (p. 73). The philosophical implications of Freud's description of the id have always provoked criticism. The idea that human beings are by nature best directed toward rape and pillage is a notion as unpopular with priests as with politicians, and contemporary psychoanalysis de-emphasizes this aspect of Freud's description of the id.

"pleasure," and the id operates according to the *pleasure principle.* Whether by eating an apple, punching a playmate, or achieving orgasm, some psychological tension rooted in our biology is reduced. The id is wholly unconscious; in other words, our behavior reflects the existence of the id, but the id does not select the apple, decide to punish, or choose the sexual partner.

It is the ego that "chooses" the appropriate behaviors for reducing the tension; in other words, the ego directs the cathexis. The ego operates according to the *reality principle,* and it functions consciously and preconsciously to a greater extent than the id—which brings us to another aspect of the mind.

When an individual makes a decision, she or he is aware of a reasoning process; that is, the process is conscious. At times, however, an individual may retrospectively realize that the behavior was not motivated by the factors considered in making the decision but by some fact, wish, desire, or urge only belatedly recalled. This information can be made conscious, but for reasons we will discuss later, it is not always readily available. Some of this less accessible information is said to be *preconscious*; that is, it can be recalled with minimal anxiety by means of introspection. Other bits of information about a person's desires, wishes, or urges are *unconscious*; that is, they can be made conscious only with great anxiety, if at all.[5]

The aspect of personality called the superego accounts for why some of our thoughts, feelings, and actions are kept from consciousness and why they cause anxiety when they become conscious. Anxiety occurs when consciousness is invaded by the impulses of the id (real, imagined, remembered, or intended) and contradictory dictates from the superego. The superego's function is to promote moral behavior—that is, behavior that conforms to the values, rules, and expectations of society. We typically learn society's directives through parental rewards and punishments during childhood. In forming our idea of what is wrong—the *conscience*—as well as a picture of how we "should" behave—the *ego ideal*—the superego sets us up for inevitable conflict with the amoral, hedonistic impulses of the id. Because much of the superego's psychic input is unconscious, we may not recall the proscription, but we will feel the anxiety and guilt.

As the influence of the id on the ego is evident in the forces of cathexis, so the influence of the superego is evident in the forces of anticathexis. In the

---

[5]Freud argued that the purpose of psychoanalysis is the strengthening of the ego, to make it more independent of the superego. As he wrote in *New Introductory Lectures on Psychoanalysis* (1933/1964b): "Its intention is, indeed, to strengthen the ego, to make it more independent of the superego, to widen its field of perception and enlarge its organization, so that it can appropriate fresh portions of the id. Where id was, there ego shall be. It is a work of culture—not unlike the draining of the Zuider Zee" (p. 80). The Zuider Zee was a shallow inlet in the North Sea that was being drained by the Dutch so that its land could be reclaimed, and it gave Freud a curiously apt image for this unseen process. However, Freud is referring to more than some simple psychic reclamation project within an individual. The ego is the most rational, most evolved aspect of personality. In Darwinian terms, the enhanced power of the ego over the strictures of the superego secured by the reclaiming of psychic territory formerly in the chaotic claws of the id, represents a step forward both for the individual and for the species.

end, it is the ego's function to direct psychic energy into behaviors that reduce tension (to gratify the id). Ideally, this is done without provoking anxiety and guilt from the superego—in other words, without producing *conflict.* At the same time, the ego is not without its defenses.[6]

Ego-defense mechanisms A few years before his death in 1939, Freud wrote an open letter to honor the 70th birthday of the French novelist and playwright, Romain Rolland. In it, he discussed defense mechanisms:

> There are an extraordinarily large number of methods (or mechanisms, as we say) used by our ego in the discharge of its defensive functions. . . . Between repression and what may be termed the normal method of fending off what is distressing or unbearable, by means of recognizing it, considering it, making a judgment upon it and taking appropriate action about it, there lies a whole series of more or less clearly pathological methods of behaviour on the part of the ego. (Freud, 1936/1964a, pp. 245–246)

This passage brings out several important points. First, the most fundamental means of ego-defense is *repression,* the automatic, involuntary removal from consciousness of some potentially anxiety-evoking impulse, memory, idea, or wish. Second, in "normal" functioning, the individual does not repress the potentially disturbing thought but, rather, confronts and acts upon it. Third, since Freud's letter is really about his own experiences (a trip to Greece with his brother in 1904), it is apparent that repression and the other defenses are not the sole province of the pathological but are part of all of our lives to a greater or lesser degree. In fact, as Rychlak (1981) has suggested, since Freud extended his theory to "normals" by examining the "psychopathology in everyday life," the defense mechanisms may best be called by the less pejorative *"adjustment* or *mental mechanisms"* (p. 60).

As noted above, the central ego-defense mechanism is repression. Repression occurs when the force of anticathexis dominates the force of cathexis by preventing ideas that would propel the individual toward unacceptable behavior from becoming conscious. The conscious counterpart of repression is *suppression.* An individual suppresses an undesirable thought by willfully replacing it with another thought. Suppression is an intentional distraction that prevents greater anxiety, worry, anger, sexual excitation, or the like. Some of the more important defense mechanisms described by the psychoanalytic perspective are listed and explained in Table 6.2; the discussions that follow depend on the reader's understanding this table.

The development of personality On the surface, personality development appears to be a smooth and continuous process that extends throughout our lives.

---

[6]It is difficult not to lapse into personification in describing the ego's role. As even Freud (1933/1964b) reminded us: "No wonder that ego so often fails its task. Its three tyrannical masters are the external world, the super-ego and the id. . . . It feels hemmed in on three sides, threatened by three kinds of danger, to which, if it is hard pressed, it reacts by generating anxiety" (p. 77).

However, in the psychoanalytic view, an individual's personality is largely determined during the first 6 years of life. Further, personality develops in certain steps or stages that are related to the locus of tension reduction. These *psychosexual* stages are age-related, and though they are biologically determined their successful completion depends on social interaction. In each of these

Table 6.2   *Definitions and Examples of Ego-Defense Mechanisms*

Defense Mechanism	Definition	Example
Denial	The refusal to acknowledge the existence and impact of a painful event happening in the present	An individual is extremely unhappy in a marriage but continues to deny the marriage's limitations and the unhappiness it causes.
Displacement	The unconscious redirection of energy from one person or object to another when the latter is less threatening or more readily available	Energy in the form of anger and hostility toward a spouse is stifled, then redirected toward the family dog in the form of a kick.
Intellectualization	The isolation of intellect from emotion for the purpose of avoiding emotional pain resulting from events in the person's life	Rejected by a member of the opposite sex, a psychiatrist explains the reasons for the rejection in elaborate psychoanalytic jargon while denying any personal anguish.
Projection	The attribution to others of motives, traits, or behaviors that are in reality characteristic of oneself	A person whose feelings and behavior bespeak racism accuses members of another racial group of being racist.
Rationalization	The use of a rational and well-reasoned explanation for a behavior that was actually motivated by an unacceptable emotion	An individual leaves a good position in a firm claiming that it is not sufficiently challenging when in fact the real motive is a fear of failing in the difficult job.
Reaction Formation	The conversion of undesirable impulses in oneself to overt demonstrations of behaviors that are diametric to those impulses	An adolescent with strong and confusing feelings toward members of the same sex becomes an outspoken leader in the harassment of another student who is suspected of being a homosexual.

Repression	The automatic and unintentional removal from awareness of unacceptable impulses in the form of ideas	Thoughts involving sexual contact with a sibling are prevented from reaching consciousness.
Undoing	The performance of behaviors that an individual falsely believes will in some way correct undesirable thoughts or actions. Typically, the "undoing" behaviors are ritualistic, exaggerated, and/or irrational.	A person who frequents pornographic films despite strong religious convictions about their evilness, begins bathing four or five times a day, attending daily religious services, and watching televised religious shows late into the night.

stages, some area of the body is the primary focus of tension reduction. These areas of the body are called the *erotogenic zones*. Movement through the psychosexual stages depends on successful tension reduction. If tension reduction is in some way impeded or confused, a person can become stuck in that stage; that is, *fixation* can occur. Pathological *character types* can result from fixation in one of the three stages before the age of 6. A summary of the stages of psychosexual development and the character types that may result from fixation in them can be found in Table 6.3; again, the discussions that follow assume familiarity with the table's contents.

The success each individual has had in moving through these stages in part distinguishes one individual's personality from another's. This is not an all-or-nothing proposition, and to some extent, each of us reduces tension in ways typical of earlier developmental stages. In certain intellectual (and pseudo-intellectual) circles, individuals may be described as "oral," "anal," or "phallic," as if every unnecessary dish of ice cream, spit-polished shoe, or randy remark were symptoms of fixation. In fact, a review of the descriptions of the character types in Table 6.3 should make clear that most of us have moments of immaturity in which we exhibit some of these behaviors. However, when excessive energy is diverted from the activities of the mature adult (at the genital stage) into tension reduction typical of earlier developmental stages, then *regression* to an earlier stage has taken place. Following the definitions established earlier, such an individual is immature, since he or she directs energy in ways that are essentially narcissistic and unproductive. An immature individual squanders the energies that could lead to intimacy and social benefit on the continual pursuit of infantile pleasures that fail to satisfy.

The mature self From the perspective of psychoanalysis vis-à-vis development, the mature person (the genital character type) is one who funnels libido into two endeavors: First, the mature person develops a sexually and psychologically intimate relationship with a partner of the opposite sex; second, the mature person redirects libidinal energy into socially sanctioned activities like

Table 6.3 *Freud's Psychosexual Stages and Their Corresponding Fixated Character Types*

Stage	Erotogenic Zone	Ages	Description	Character Type
Oral	mouth	birth until about 2	Psychosexual gratification comes primarily from sucking, eating, biting, and other oral activities. This stage is characterized by narcissism. Fixation can result from overindulgence and overprotectiveness as well as inadequate meeting of physical and emotional needs.	If the parent was overindulgent, the oral character type is dependent, usually optimistic and trusting, and may display gullibility and patterns of overeating. If the parent was inadequate, the adult may be manipulative and demanding of others.
Anal	anus	2–3	The child begins to gain independence, and toilet training is the focus of attention. Elimination of fecal matter is a major source of psychosexual pleasure.	Having learned to retain feces as a means of independence, the anal character type is selfish, narrow, and suspicious, with an unnecessary concern for order and cleanliness.
Phallic	genitalia	4–5	Manipulation of the genitals becomes the primary source of tension reduction. The male child, fearing castration (castration anxiety), competes with his father for the affection of his mother (male Oedipus complex) until he learns to identify with the more powerful father. The female child, believing herself deficient without a penis (penis envy), competes with the more powerful mother.*	Fixated at this stage, the male phallic character type displays behavior indicative of castration anxiety. He is typically self-centered and self-indulgent and often exaggeratedly seductive, constantly seeking a substitute for his mother. The female phallic character type displays behavior indicative of penis envy. She is excessively aggressive and domineering and typically attempts to dominate men.

Latency		Between the age of 6 and puberty, the child sublimates sexual energy into socially accepted pursuits. This is a period of dormancy: the calm before the storm.		
Genital	genitalia	puberty through adulthood	During puberty, both males and females become capable of reproduction. Ideally, the individual moves from the narcissism of the earlier stages toward discovering the potential role of sexuality in loving intimacy with others.	Capable of redirecting energy into work and creativity that benefit society (sublimation), the genital character type is also capable of loving intimacy with others and competent parenting. This represents ideal character development.

*Although some of Freud's followers called the female Oedipus complex the "Electra" complex, Freud did not.

work, parenting, creativity, and so forth.[7] The latter process is called *sublimation*. Essentially, ego is increasingly capable of cathexis (to gratify the id) within the limits set by society and the strictures of the superego. Yet, is the ego really a vassal of the id, an ever-conflicted part of the psyche moving from cathexis to cathexis? What, if anything, does the ego have to do with what I call my "self"?

Since Freud's death, one of the areas of psychoanalysis that has received the most attention has to do with the role and nature of the ego. Several developments are noteworthy. One of the most important contributions has come from Heinz Hartmann (1939), who described the *autonomous ego*.[8] Hartmann argued that the ego's central role is to adapt the individual to the environment. The ego is in constant, conscious interaction with environmental demands and can act independently of the pleasure (tension-reduction) priorities of id. Further, the ego's involvement in many aspects of cognition (for example, language development and abstract thinking) is not motivated by tension reduc-

[7]The reader may be surprised by reference to a "partner of the opposite sex," given our current awareness of same-sex sexual partnerships, not to mention Freud's contention that we are all essentially bisexual. However, Freud believed that sexual energy is correctly directed (toward the opposite sex) during the phallic stage, and that homosexuality represents an unfortunate arresting of that development. Therefore, in psychoanalysis, homosexuality is tolerated as an understandable developmental problem, but it is not viewed as part of the mature person's behavior.

[8]It can be argued that Freud's own description of personality shifted from an id psychology to an ego psychology, but that the ego's complete role was not fully described. Hartmann's *Ego Psychology and the Problem of Adaptation* (1939) was an attempt to complete Freud's own ego psychology rather than to replace it, and it is viewed within the psychoanalytic perspective as a major contribution. Adler also made important contributions to an ego psychology, but Freud's personal antipathy toward Adler prevented him from fully recognizing that contribution. For a thorough description of the development of ego psychology and the various contributors to it, see Fine's *History of Psychoanalysis* (1979).

tion, and these processes, as well as other human behaviors, do not necessarily involve conflict. Hartmann (1939, 1964) argued that there is a "unit" of the ego that engages in cognitive activities completely devoid of conflict and the need to reduce tension. Hartmann calls this part of the ego the *conflict-free* or *nonconflictual sphere.* Hartmann's contribution began moving the psychoanalytic perspective away from its tendency to explain normal personality development by theories and research that depend on models of pathological development.

Though Hartmann is credited with completing the shift of psychoanalysis from an *id psychology* to an *ego psychology,* the work of Heinz Kohut is currently promoting a shift to a *self psychology.* Personality theories that use the concept of self are not new, and within the neopsychoanalytic and humanistic-existential perspectives, they are commonplace. Kohut (1971, 1977, 1984), however, has proposed a self psychology developed within rather strict psychoanalytic thinking, and that constitutes a major shift. Kohut's work is presently receiving considerable attention within the psychoanalytic community and has recently been integrated into counseling-outcomes research (Patton, Connor, & Scott, 1982).

For Kohut, the ego, id, and superego constitute the structural apparatus of the mind, but not its content. *Self* is the content of the mind. In regard to development, Kohut argued that we begin life with a nuclear self that contains our inherent talents, skills, and other abilities, along with the *grandiose self* and the *idealized parental image.* The former represents our essential narcissism, the latter our dependence on and idealization of powerful others. Ideally, these two parts of the self develop in parallel, becoming integrated into an adult self who is capable of using the talents, skills, and other abilities without conflict, self-centeredness, or dependency on others on a day-to-day basis. Kohut's conception of the mature self is evident in the following statement:

> Within the framework of the psychology of the self, we define mental health not only as freedom from the neurotic symptoms and inhibitions that interfere with the functions of a "mental apparatus" involved in loving and working, but also as the capacity of a firm love to avail itself of the talents and skills at an individual's disposal, enabling him [or her] to love and work successfully. (Kohut, 1977, p. 284)

The descriptions of the contributions of Hartmann and Kohut are not intended to suggest that most psychoanalysts agree with their positions. In fact, there is considerable diversity of opinion. Further, despite the contributions of Hartmann, Kohut, and others, the psychoanalytic perspective's description of the mature individual depends heavily on descriptions of pathological ones.

Anxiety

Freud described anxiety as a "specific state of unpleasure accompanied by motor discharge along definite pathways" (1926/1959, p. 133). Intrinsic to this definition is awareness of anxiety as a biological event (activation of the autonomic nervous system) that an individual experiences as discomfort, nervousness, or tension. At times, an individual may call it fear, at other times, worry, but inherent in both of these experiences is anxiety.[9] Freud wrestled with the role of anxiety in psychopathology for some years and developed several models of how it operates. In Freud's initial formulation, anxiety was the product of repression; in his final version of psychoanalysis, repression was the product of anxiety. Much of what concerns us presently in relation to psychoanalysis's view of anxiety is raised in the following passage from Freud's *New Introductory Lectures* (1933/1964b).

> With the thesis that ego is the sole seat of anxiety—that the ego alone can produce and feel anxiety—we have established a new and stable position from which a number of things take on a new aspect. And indeed it is difficult to see what sense there would be in speaking of an "anxiety of the id" or in attributing a capacity for apprehensiveness to the superego. On the other hand, we have welcomed a desirable element of correspondence in the fact that the three main species of anxiety, realistic, neurotic, and moral, can be so easily connected with the ego's three dependent relations—to the external world, to the id and to the superego. Along with this new view, moreover, the function of anxiety as a signal announcing a situation of danger . . . comes into prominence. (p. 85)

The psychoanalytic position described above by Freud can be summarized as follows:

1. Anxiety is a psychobiological response to real or anticipated threats to the physical and/or psychological well-being of a person. Anxiety is a capacity of the ego that serves as an indicator or signal to the ego that some danger, real or imagined, present or anticipated, threatens the person. The term *signal anxiety* is used to describe this function of anxiety.

2. *Realistic anxiety* is the result of accurate appraisal of real events in the external world. An individual anticipating an important job interview will experience a certain amount of realistic anxiety; she or he may, for example, have difficulty sleeping the night before the interview. The interviewee's thoughts, however, are realistic: the interview is important, much depends on it, but there will be other interviews if this one does not work out. In short, realistic anxiety involves: (1) an accurate perception of the demands of a specific situation in the external world, (2) a realistic appraisal of the individual's ability to handle those demands, and (3) an acceptance of the outcome of the situation that is neither defeatist nor compensatory.

3. *Neurotic anxiety* is the result of unconscious distortions of the demands of the external world. These distortions express themselves as powerful yet vague fears that emerge from unconscious intrapsychic conflict. This conflict is the result of repressed impulses that threaten to be acted out in the real world and that would result in punishing consequences. The individual is "protected"

---

[9]Although he did not do so consistently throughout his writings, Freud did distinguish between fear (*Furcht*) and anxiety (*Angst*). When the object of the feeling of anxiety was known, he called the feeling fear. When the object of the feeling of anxiety was unknown, he called it anxiety (Freud, 1926/1959, p. 165).

by patterns of self-defeating behavior—specifically by misevaluation of the demands of the environment—from situations that might invite these impulses into consciousness. In anticipating an important interview, an individual suffering neurotic anxiety replaces well-organized preparation with agitated worry, pacing, sleeplessness, and chronic bouts of self-doubt. The interview is all but ruined by the anxiety, and future interviews are imperiled by emerging phobias. In short, neurotic anxiety involves unconscious intrapsychic conflict that results in: (1) an inaccurate perception of the demands of a specific situation in the external world, (2) an unrealistic appraisal of the individual's ability to handle those demands, and (3) a string of ego-defensive maneuvers that usually result in unsuccessful resolution of the real-life situation.

4. *Moral anxiety* takes the form of guilt and is the result of the demands of the superego. In its more benevolent forms, moral anxiety prevents us from performing socially unacceptable destructive or sexual acts. In its more extreme, neurotic forms, it produces self-defeating, self-punishing behavior. While preparing for an interview, for example, an individual might begin to fantasize about deceiving the interviewer or even using sexual favors to improve rapport in the interview. Crippling anxiety in the form of guilt ends these fantasies, as well as whatever confidence the person may have had. In short, moral anxiety involves conscious and unconscious intrapsychic conflict that results in: (1) strong feelings of guilt in response to real or imagined behavior, (2) the establishing of self-defeating behaviors (for example, compulsions or phobias) that temporarily eliminate the guilt but punish the person, and (3) a decreasing capacity to cope successfully with real-life demands.

From the psychoanalytic perspective, anxiety is the indicator of conflict, the gauge of both psychological sickness and psychological wellness. Though anxiety can be transformed into other symptoms (hysteria, phobias, obsessions, or compulsions), it remains the underlying feature of the group of maladaptive behaviors we call the neuroses. If anxiety and its related symptoms are caused by conflicting ideas largely outside of consciousness, then the role of therapy is to discover and understand the link between the anxiety as a symptom and the ideas as a cause. The process of discovering and understanding that link is called insight.

Insight

Anxiety and other symptoms signal that all is not well, that a conflict exists between the demands of the external world and the demands of the internal world. Most of the "action," however, is intrapsychic and hidden from consciousness by the deceptions of the ego-defense mechanisms, especially repression. The working assumptions of psychoanalysis are that present events trigger and maintain anxiety and related symptoms in the analysand (the psychoanalytic client) because these events are emotionally and intellectually connected with unconscious past experiences and emotions and that the anxiety can only be eliminated when the meaningful connections between the present events and the repressed past experience are brought into consciousness. Because this information (ideas and feelings) is unacceptable to the conscious mind and will cause even greater distress, the analysand consciously and unconsciously delays the discovery. This process of delaying the identification of the causal links between the past and the present is called *resistance.*[10]

Resistance, insight, and the therapeutic process Freud described the task of the psychoanalyst as "to bring to the patient's knowledge the unconscious, repressed impulses existing in him, and, for that purpose, to uncover the resistances that oppose this extension of his knowledge about himself" (1919/1955, p. 159). Thus, in psychoanalysis, the focus of therapy is breaking through resistances with insight—identifying resistance as resistance and gradually discovering the links between the present behavior and repressed past experiences. Resistance can take many forms: arriving late to appointments, posing seductively, telling elaborate but unrelated stories, telling jokes, having emotional outbursts, presenting false symptoms, and even pretending that symptoms have disappeared when they have not. The unmasking of resistances, though painful, is really a process of mending rather than rending. As Freud wrote: "In actual fact, indeed, the neurotic patient presents us with a torn mind, divided by resistances. As we analyse it and remove the resistances, it grows together, the great unity which we call his ego fits into itself all of the instinctual impulses which before had been split off and held apart from it" (1919/1955, p. 161).

Understandably, the removal of resistances will produce distress in the form of anxiety, and defensive maneuvers by the analysand may make the relationship between the analysand and analyst quite uncomfortable. Freud cautioned against resolving this discomfort prematurely, arguing that complete recovery requires complete disclosure of the causal links. He warned against saying and doing things that may merely palliate—temporarily reduce—the analysand's distress:

> But this instinctual force is indispensible; reduction of it endangers our aim—the patient's restoration to health. What, then, is the conclusion that forces itself inevitably upon us? Cruel though it may sound, we must see to it that the patient's suffering, to a degree that is in some way or other effective, does not come to an end prematurely. If, owing to the symptoms having been taken apart and having lost their value, his suffering becomes mitigated, we must re-instate it elsewhere in the form of some appreciable privation; otherwise we run the danger of never achieving any improvements except quite insignificant and transitory ones. (p. 163)

To understand the importance of Freud's statement, it is helpful to discuss the relationships among *insight, abreaction,* and *working through* (Alexander,

---

[10] The concept of resistance has traditionally been associated with psychoanalysis and related approaches to therapy, but recently considerable commerce has occurred between psychoanalytic and behavioral approaches on this topic. An important collection of writings on this sharing of views is Wachtel's *Resistance: Psychodynamic and Behavioral Approaches* (1982a). The book provides thought-provoking debate and discussion.

1948). In psychoanalysis, insight is focused on the past and is fundamentally intellectual; the analysand comes to know and understand the link between past and present. However, recalling events without experiencing the repressed emotions that accompany them does not lead to real healing. The expression of the repressed emotions is called abreaction. Working through the various thoughts and feelings is also necessary for complete healing. Gradually, by repeating the experiences, examining the resistances, and gaining new insights into the complete process, the analysand reduces the ego's defenses and can give up the protective symptoms. Thus, in psychoanalysis, insight is focused on the past and requires both intellectual and emotional activity (see again Table 6.1).

Freud's psychoanalytic language reveals a view of therapy as a deep exploration into the mind, a sort of psychic archeological dig.[11] Layers of complex associations of repressed ideas and emotions must be uncovered for healing to take place. Access to this hidden world comes from three sources: (1) free association, (2) the analysis and interpretation of dreams, and (3) the analysis and interpretation of transference.

Free association Freud came to realize that when his patients were allowed to move at will from one topic to another, to practice what is called *free association,* useful information came to light, and insights into the patient's unconscious became possible. Typically, in the practice of psychoanalysis, the analysand is allowed or encouraged to speak freely of issues of concern. By listening for the connections being made among certain words, events, ideas, and emotions, as well as for the connections that seem to be avoided, the analyst comes to understand some of the probable unconscious associations of the analysand. The analyst may ask the analysand to do further free association on specific words or ideas that have emerged in his or her initial comments. Free association is used liberally throughout psychoanalytic sessions, and the ongoing process helps to crystallize the analyst's hunches about the true dynamics of the analysand's problems. This is a slow and painstaking way of unraveling the hidden meanings, but it can be augmented by **dream analysis.**

Dream analysis Freud called dream analysis and interpretation the "royal road to the unconscious," and in his classic *Interpretation of Dreams* (1931/ 1972; original German work published in 1901), he set down his views on the role of dreams in understanding human behavior. Unlike many other aspects of his work, Freud's views on dreams underwent very little later modification. For Freud, dreams reveal our most elemental unconscious wishes. Dreams tell

[11]Freud's use of archeological metaphors comes from his lifelong hobby of collecting artifacts from earlier cultures. There is no better way to see this fascination than to examine the photographs of Freud's home and offices taken by Edmund Engleman (1976) in 1938 just before Freud escaped to London. These photos, and the accompanying commentary, are most enlightening. The book is entitled *Berggasse 19:Sigmund Freud's Home and Offices, Vienna, 1938.*

us who we really are, what secret tendencies, desires, and hostilities lurk beneath the censorship of the ego. On the surface, a remembered dream has *manifest content,* specific, identifiable images and feelings that may or may not correspond to day-to-day life. From the moment an individual awakens, however, and with each recounting of the dream, the details of the dream gradually blur and fade, becoming less specific and further obscured. Freud called this phenomenon *secondary revision,* suggesting that even the surface meaning of the dream could distress a person, requiring it to be further obscured.

Secondary revision is the most obvious example of what Freud called *dream work,* the masking of the real, primal meaning of the dream. The more elemental content of the dream, the *latent content,* remains outside of consciousness. In addition to secondary revision, dream work operates through *condensation, displacement,* and *symbolization.* In condensation, diverse elements of a dream are put together: Grandmother's chartreuse coat appears (appropriately fitted) on Aunt Mary's cat. In displacement, elements of a dream that have great latent significance are minimized in the manifest content of the remembered dream, while elements that have minimal latent significance are maximized. Thus, the remembered dream may feature a hearse containing the remains of Aunt Mary's cat passing among a row of brightly colored automobiles containing family members (including Grandmother and Aunt Mary). In recalling the dream, the analysand focuses on the automobiles and the persons within rather than on the images of death. Latent within the dream is apprehension (over the possibility of Grandmother's death) or hostility (toward Grandmother, Aunt Mary, or both). Displacement sometimes takes the form of symbolization. The hearse may become a recurring symbol for death, with a menagerie of different occupants representing various relatives and friends.

In keeping with Freud's larger theory of human behavior, much of the symbolization in dreams is considered to mask sexual and aggressive wishes, and Freud argued that certain symbols are common in all dreams. The shapes of objects that appear in dreams often suggest symbolic representation of either the penis or the vagina, allowing for meaningful interpretation. Not all such symbols are as unambiguous as a water tower, pencil, tunnel, or oven. Consider the following dream and its interpretation from Freud's *Interpretation of Dreams* (1931/1972). The dream is from a woman who had become agoraphobic because of her fear of being seduced:

> "*I was walking in the street in the summer, wearing a straw hat of peculiar shape; its middle-piece was bent upwards and its side-pieces hung downwards*" (the description became hesitant at this point) "*in such a way that one side was lower than the other. I was cheerful and in a self-confident frame of mind; and, as I passed a group of young officers, I thought: 'None of you can do me any harm!'*" [Freud's emphasis]. Since nothing occurred to her in connection with the hat in the dream, I said: "No doubt the hat was a male genital organ, with its middle-piece sticking up and its two side-pieces hanging down. It may seem strange, perhaps, that a hat should be a man, but you will remember the phrase '*Unter die Habe kommen*' " ("to find a

husband" [literally "to come under the cap"]). I intentionally gave her no interpretation of the detail about the two side-pieces hanging down unevenly; though
it is precisely details of this kind that must point the way in determining an interpretation. I went on to say that as she had a husband with such fine genitals there
was no need for her to be afraid of the officers—no need, that is, for her to wish
for anything from them, since as a rule she was prevented from going for a walk
unprotected and unaccompanied owing to her phantasies of being seduced. I had
already been able to give her this last explanation of her anxiety on several occasions upon the basis of dream material.

The way in which the dreamer reacted to this material was most remarkable.
She withdrew her description of the hat and maintained that she had never said
that the two side-pieces hung down. I was too certain of what I had heard to be
led astray, and stuck to my guns. She was silent for a while and then found enough
courage to ask what was meant by one of her husband's testes hanging down lower
than the other and whether it was the same in all men. In this way the remarkable
detail of the hat was explained and the interpretation accepted by her. . . . Other,
less transparent cases had led me to suppose that a hat can also stand for female
genitals.[12] (pp. 395–397)

In the case recounted above, albeit a rather straightforward one, Freud's
interpretation implies that repressed wishes and curiosity in the form of fantasies unacceptable to the conscious mind are provoking the dreams. This
points to a fundamental assumption underlying Freud's view of dreams: There
is *discontinuity* between the latent content of dreams and the priorities, concerns, and conscious motives of waking life. What are revealed in examining
the latent content of dreams are assumed to be wishes, fears, and aspects of
the self that are not really part of day-to-day living. An alternate view of the
relationship between dreams and waking has been presented by Calvin Hall
and his colleagues (Hall, 1953/1966; Hall & Nordby, 1972; Hall & Van de Castle,
1966). Hall, using the techniques of *content analysis,* has demonstrated that
there is considerable *continuity* between our waking state and the latent content of our dreams. From this point of view, the analysis and interpretation of
the dreams reveal more about the worries, concerns, affections, and hostilities
of day-to-day living than they do about unconscious realities. For Hall, "the
truth revealed in dreams is the same truth we have to face and deal with in waking life" (Hall & Nordby, 1972, p. 155).

Whether a psychoanalyst emphasizes the continuity or the discontinuity
between our waking and sleeping lives, the method of gaining insight from the
dream is the same. The elements of the dream are taken apart and their relationship analyzed. Then the analysand is asked to free associate with each

[12]The observant reader may have noticed that Freud said "I stuck to my guns." Since a gun
is about as phallic as one can get, it might be interesting to know whether or not Freud actually
used that expression. A more literal translation of the original German (Freud, 1901/1977) would
be: "What is very remarkable is the way in which the dreamer conducts herself after this interpretation. She withdraws the description of the hat and denies having said that the two side parts
were hanging downward. But I am too certain of what I heard to allow myself to grow confused,
so I persist [italics added]." Alas, it was the translator, James Strachey, who used the expression
"I stuck to my guns." Whether he did so consciously or unconsciously is not known. (The author
is indebted to Professor Vincent Kling of La Salle University for the translation.)

of the various elements of the dream. In the end, each dream, in relationship to other dreams, is interpreted according to the relationships that appear in the free association.

Transference Successful psychoanalytic treatment requires that the analysand remember key emotional relationships from the past, especially those with parents. One manifestation of resistance to recalling the past is the unconscious process of transference. In transference, the analysand does not recall the past; rather, she or he "*repeats* [Freud's italics] attitudes and emotional impulses from his early life which can be used as a resistance against the doctor and the treatment" (Freud, 1917/1963a, p. 290). Transference is an interpersonal process in which the analysand repeats early emotional patterns based on parent-child interaction with the analyst for the purpose of resistance. The analysis of transference is a rich source of information about the analysand's psychic life, as well as a vehicle for emotional maturity.

As we grow up, we repress impulses and emotions that our parents disapprove. The defense mechanisms that help contain the repressed material may be seen in our adult lives in the form of symptoms, but the primitive impulses and emotions themselves cannot. Transference depends on the establishment of a close, parental type of relationship between the analyst and analysand that will evoke reactions mirroring the analysand's early parent-child interactions, thus offering clues to the repressed psychic content. Transference is resolved through careful identification of the interpersonal dynamic, together with continual probing into the repressed impulses and emotions that eventually allows the repressed materials to emerge. Once in the conscious mind, these impulses and emotions can be transformed through information about the real demands of present life. The establishment and resolution of transference in the relationship between the analyst and analysand is fraught with resistances. First, the analysand resists the awareness of transference; that is, she or he denies having strong feelings of affection, hostility or both toward the analyst, then denies the parallels between this relationship and her or his parental relationships. Once the analysand recognizes the phenomenon of transference, he or she resists its resolution, repressing early experiences and emotions to avoid anxiety (see Gill, 1982).

The establishment and resolution of transference is key to successful psychoanalysis, but how do these take place? Is the resolution of transference facilitated by a warm, supportive analyst or a neutral, disquieting one? What techniques promote and resolve transference? What factors apart from insight are required for change to take place? Are the aims of analysis best served by the posture dictated by the couch or by a chair? These issues remain, active and unresolved, within the psychoanalytic perspective.

Insight and the practice of psychoanalysis Freud (1919/1955) anticipated, early on, a question that would be continually debated regarding the actual practice of psychoanalysis:

> It is very probable, too, that the large-scale application of our therapy will compel us to alloy the pure gold of analysis freely with the copper of direct suggestion; and hypnotic influence, too, might find a place in it again, as it has in the treatment of war neurosis. But, whatever form this psychotherapy for the people may take, whatever the elements out of which it is compounded, its most effective and important ingredients will assuredly remain those borrowed from strict and untendentious psycho-analysis. (p. 168)

Indeed, more recently, Nemiah (1984) has used the same metaphor of "pure" analysis "contaminated" by the "baser metal" of other forms of psychotherapy in describing the current conflict between the modifiers of psychoanalysis and its purists. Inherent within Freud's statement is a call for orthodoxy—that is, for loyalty to the fundamental techniques of psychoanalysis (free association, dream analysis, and transference analysis) without resort to more direct, seemingly more facile methods. The techniques developed by Freud are both time-consuming and painful, because they allow pertinent psychic information to surface in a largely neutral, nonsupportive, and therefore distressing relationship rather than directing the client within a supportive and caring relationship. Yet, Freud's statement also reveals his practicality; he recognized that combining psychoanalytic techniques with other methods may sometimes be necessary.

The battle between orthodox analysts and less orthodox ones continues to this day. Advocates of orthodoxy eschew involvement in the practical, day-to-day concerns of the analysand. Orthodox analysts facilitate transference by maintaining an attentive but passive attitude that neither directs nor supports the analysand, avoiding nontraditional methods. Traditional psychoanalysis necessarily takes a long time and, indeed, may never really end, given the complexity of the analysand's intrapsychic life and the nondirective methods of analysis.

An alternative view has emerged following the work of Franz Alexander and Thomas French. Alexander and French (1946) argued that traditional psychoanalysis fits the analysand's problem to the techniques of analysis rather than fitting the techniques to the problem. They called for a blending of the "real psychoanalyst" and the "practical psychotherapist," and they encouraged greater flexibility in the therapeutic relationship, in the use of nonanalytic techniques, and in the duration of treatment. Alexander and French used a classic distinction between the two types of psychotherapy: "uncovering therapy" and "supportive therapy." Uncovering therapy, also called insight therapy, is aimed at permanently changing the ego through the insight gained in the emotional resolution of transference. Supportive therapy is not aimed at changing the ego; rather, the therapist, by expressing the caring and persuasion possible in the therapeutic relationship, encourages the analysand's ego to respond maturely to life's demands. Alexander and French argued that the practice of contemporary psychoanalysis calls for both uncovering and supportive methods and that, in fact, in all forms of therapy, these methods necessarily overlap. From this alternative psychoanalytic viewpoint, long treatment is not necessarily better than short treatment, supportive and caring interpersonal relationships are no less effective than passive ones, and knowledge and techniques from other sources are appropriately integrated into treatment as long as the fundamental concepts and techniques of the psychoanalytic perspective are maintained.

Summary

Contemporary psychoanalysts remain divided on the issues discussed above. We have followed the lead of Alexander and French in arguing that there is no such thing as a true insight therapy without both uncovering and supportive methods. Throughout the remainder of this chapter we will see the varying degree to which these two sets of methods are used. In the next chapter, psychoanalysis will be represented by time-limited dynamic psychotherapy, a descendant of Alexander and French's alternative to orthodox psychoanalysis that allows for the temporal and fiscal demands of contemporary living and that has benefited from contemporary psychological research.

The reader may wonder why, compared with the neopsychoanalytic and humanistic-existential perspectives that follow, Freud's psychoanalytic perspective has been given so much space in this chapter. The words of Rollo May (1977) suggest why: "Whether we are 'Freudians' or not, as I am not, we are surely all post-Freudians" (p. 132).

The Neopsychoanalytic Perspective

Matthew May met the woman who was to be his second wife when he was thirty-nine. She was twenty-nine (and a half). Matthew May was surely in love this time, he was certain of that, and he knew it the very first time he saw her in her waitress costume at the Merry Mermaid Bar at the Fisherman's Wharf Holiday Inn. He knew instantly that the right woman had come along. He was just above thigh level when she asked him what he wanted to drink.

The romance did not always go smoothly. Linda was more put off by Matthew's incessant questions and promises of gifts that never materialized than by the balding head that most concerned him. She fancied it a novelty; he fancied it a liability. She abided his "interest" in hats, some bizarre, some very bizarre. (She secretly decided to draw the line if he ever showed up in a babushka.) He could be sullen, sometimes angry, sometimes worrisome. He kept his feelings to himself, but he was ("Really!") a poet. In the end, Linda was charmed by his quiet ways, his deference, and his many promises, those endless promises. She convinced herself that he was a man of promise rather than a man of promises, and that his unassuming ways would lead to happiness. (Also, as her Aunt Kate said, she wasn't getting any younger.)

Matthew treated her like the shoe of a one-legged man who had once lost both shoe and foot through his own stupidity. He was careful of himself— nothing ventured, nothing lost. He said only what he fancied she wanted to hear. He was careful of her—nothing ventured, nothing lost. A watchful eye. A former cocktail waitress, even one married to a part-time poet, cannot be left to chance. . . . The relationship ended as it had begun: in a dark, dank bar with two people who did not know each other.

———————

Human beings are cultural animals. Like our fictional character, Matthew May, we exist within a certain culture at a certain time. The beliefs, institutions, and rituals of that culture shape us and are shaped by us. As cultural animals, we view our behavior and its merits according to the criteria established by the culture in which our behavior developed. We are also social animals. Within the context of culture, we form, maintain, and alter a variety of interpersonal relationships. Other human beings, because of their affection, attractiveness, authority, or status, are capable of modifying our behavior and influencing the way in which we view ourselves. The neopsychoanalytic perspective is essentially a *sociocultural* perspective, focused on the cultural and social aspects of personality and behavior change. Unlike the psychoanalytic perspective, which emphasizes inner experience, the neopsychoanalytic perspective focuses on the interplay between inner experience and outer experience as it is embodied in culture and social relationships.

Overview

Unlike the psychoanalytic perspective, the neopsychoanalytic perspective on personality and behavior change has neither one singular figure of central importance nor one principal theory or model accepted by all those included in this perspective. Rather, the neopsychoanalytic perspective is a weave of diverse insights, theories, and therapeutic techniques inspired by the psychoanalytic perspective but differing from it in some essential way. As described in Chapter 3, a number of Freud's followers broke with him over personal, professional, and theoretical issues. Generally, the following individuals are listed as the major contributors to the neopsychoanalytic perspective: Alfred Adler, Erik Erikson, Erich Fromm, Karen Horney, Carl Jung, and Harry Stack Sullivan. Half of them—Erikson, Horney, and Sullivan—can also legitimately be viewed as major contributors to the psychoanalytic perspective; the others—Adler, Jung, and Fromm—provided important groundwork for the humanistic-existential perspective. Further, each of the six had tremendous influence on a large number of other practitioners; Adler and Jung, in particular, have considerable followings among practitioners today.

To allow comparison of the three perspectives described in this chapter, I present a synthesis in this section of the major points on which most of the six main contributors to the neopsychoanalytic perspective agree.[13] The discussion that follows cannot do justice to the richness of their work, however. I, therefore, urge readers to explore the work of these six contributors more fully on their own.

The Self

Erich Fromm (1941/1965) wrote: "Contrary to Freud's viewpoint, . . . the key problem of psychology is that of the specific kind of relatedness of the individual towards the world and not that of the satisfaction or frustration of this or that instinctual need *per se*" (p. 27). From the psychoanalytic perspective, the key to understanding the self is understanding the mental apparatus involved in successful instinctual gratification. From the neopsychoanalytic perspective, the key to understanding the self is understanding the influence of sociocultural factors on the development of the self and on the maintenance of behavior. Table 6.4 contains a brief, nontechnical summary of the various views of the self within the neopsychoanalytic perspective.

The development of the self From the neopsychoanalytic perspective, our behavior is not the product of largely unconscious conflicts, nor is the self a passive victim of sexual drives. Rather, the self develops through interaction with significant others within the context of various cultural institutions, especially the family. The developmental process is a lifelong one, although early interpersonal experiences in the family, especially with parents, can be crucial in establishing later patterns of interaction. Life is viewed as a series of challenges to the maturation of the self, sometimes conceived of as crises or stages, during which we either do or do not acquire the capacity to live life in a rewarding way.

Although the neopsychoanalytic perspective generally accepts the importance of unconscious motivation, as well as the operation of defense mechanisms, the self is largely viewed in terms of its capacity to make constructive, conscious choices based on what is uncovered in exploring the unconscious and identifying ego-defensive maneuvers.

The mature self First, the mature individual realistically appraises his or her strengths and is willing and able to challenge his or her limitations, setting and striving for goals. Second, the mature person is successful at interpersonal relationships, giving and receiving love and trust comfortably and honestly. Third, a mature individual directs energy toward the social good; the culture

---

[13]Jung's perspective differs considerably from that of the others on a number of major issues, especially on the nature and function of the unconscious and the role of the interpersonal. Yet, the Jungian literature is so rich and has been developed over such a long period of time that much of what is being described as part of the neopsychoanalytic perspective is in some way part of Jung's views, if not among his core concepts. His work is especially noteworthy in viewing human development as a lifelong process characterized by crises. Samuels has explored the current status of Jung's work in *Jung and the Post-Jungians* (1985).

benefits from his or her contributions. In sum, maturity is reflected in successful interpersonal relationships and social productivity based increasingly on conscious choices rather than on the redirection of psychosexual energies.

Table 6.4 *Neopsychoanalytic Views of the Self*

	Self
Adler	>People are not victims of heredity or environment. People determine their actions by setting and striving toward goals. >Behavior cannot be isolated from its social context. >Conscious decisions, especially those directed toward improving society, are characteristic of humans and bespeak the mature self.
Jung	>Individuals engage in a lifelong process of psychological and spiritual development requiring the integration of complex unconscious experience with conscious experience. >Movement through life involves confronting various crises and integrating past experience with aspirations for the future. >The realization of the mature self is an ideal toward which we strive but which we do not attain.
Fromm	>In the present age, alienated from nature and perceiving themselves as powerless, individuals often choose blind conformity to culture, acquiesence to authority, or destructiveness. >The mature self is one who loves others, treating them as individuals, not as means to some selfish end. >The individual can only become a mature, loving person in a society that is humanistic rather than authoritarian—that is, one that emphasizes the common good, not profit.
Horney	>The interpersonal coping strategies of the adult originate in the person's childhood relationship with her or his parents. >Approving, affectionate, and supportive parenting allows the individual's real self to emerge, and he or she is capable of successful loving relationships and actualization of potentials. >Parenting that engenders anxiety and hostility leads to self-defeating interpersonal patterns. A person becomes distanced from the real self and may try to become perfect (the ideal self) by succumbing to the "tyranny of the shoulds," unattainable achievements that dominate thinking and prevent real success.

Erikson	>The self is conceived of primarily in terms of the ego, which serves to adapt the individual to the environment. The ego integrates inner experience with cultural experience to promote satisfying interpersonal relationships and careers. >The development of the self proceeds through a series of eight universal, unvarying stages that confront the individual at various points between birth and late adulthood. >Each stage is characterized by a psychosocial crisis that the individual must actively overcome to mature.
Sullivan	>The self is viewed entirely within the context of interpersonal life. >The self is the process through which one evaluates and controls one's relationships with others, whether real or imagined. >The self seeks to provide security—that is, to avoid anxiety—by living up to the expectations of others.

Anxiety

Within the neopsychoanalytic perspective, anxiety is viewed in two ways. First, anxiety is a sign of danger or threat (Freud's signal anxiety). Second, anxiety functions as a tool of interpersonal manipulation that restricts relationships and limits human potential. Table 6.5 contains a brief, nontechnical summary of the various views of anxiety within the neopsychoanalytic perspective.

Anxiety as a signal From the psychoanalytic perspective, the early experiences that cause anxiety are largely sexual in nature; from the neopsychoanalytic perspective, they are interpersonal. Early relationships, especially with parents, may be hostile, unloving, or inadequate. These early experiences color the rest of the person's developmental process. As life presents challenges and crises, a basic or pervasive anxiety, experienced as feelings of inadequacy or insecurity, reemerges, signaling the existence of unresolved conflicts or unmet needs. The presence of anxiety distorts the person's ability to make realistic decisions, so relationships and contributions to society are unnecessarily limited. This pattern of restricted and self-defeating behavior underlain by anxiety constitutes neurotic behavior.

Anxiety as interpersonal manipulation Neurotic behavior is also characterized within the neopsychoanalytic position as involving anxiety used as manipulation. In reference to people whose insecurities promote maladaptive behaviors, Adler (1927/1969) wrote: "Anxiety helps them evade the demands of life, and enslaves all those about them. Finally it worms itself into every relationship in their daily lives, and becomes their most important instrument to effect their

Table 6.5 *Neopsychoanalytic Views of Anxiety*

	Anxiety
Adler	>A variety of neurotic symptoms serve to protect individuals who have come to believe that they are inferior but who secretly seek superiority from actually assuming responsibility for life. >These symptoms are often accompanied by anxiety, which intensifies the safeguards against being responsible and actually attaining superiority.
Jung	>Anxiety and other symptoms are signs of inadequate integration of daily life and unconscious experience, whether repressed intrapsychic material (as in Freudian theory) or repressed racial history (the collective unconscious). >The reduction of anxiety and other symptoms calls for an inner journey in order to establish a balance between the conscious and the unconscious realities.
Fromm	>Our anxiety is an existential; that is, it arises from our awareness of our freedom coupled with our fear of assuming that freedom in the form of love and constructive change of the social order.
Horney	>Basic anxiety is at the core of the self-defeating interpersonal strategies that characterize neurotic behavior. >Basic anxiety is a profound feeling of insecurity, isolation, loneliness, and hostility that is caused by overprotective, neglectful, hostile, abusive, overindulgent, or overdomineering parenting. >In adult life, basic anxiety takes the form of neurotic interpersonal needs (for example, a neurotic need for affection or a neurotic need to exploit others) that are inherently self-defeating and that intensify anxiety in day-to-day life while restricting the person's ability to find real security and to actualize his or her true potentials (self-realization).
Erikson	>Anxiety is expressed in some form as a person moves through the various stages of crisis. >Inadequate parenting during the first year of life can result in basic mistrust that can express itself in a full range of problems from anxiety to psychosis. >During adolescence, the challenge is to establish a clear identity (the identity crisis), a task that can occasion considerable anxiety.

Sullivan	>Interpersonal relationships can be characterized by anxiety from the initial mother-child relationship on. >Anxiety arises from insecurity about interpersonal relationships and can be reduced by living up to the expectations that others have of one, whether real or imagined. >One can reduce anxiety by distorting the way one thinks about interpersonal relationships, but these distortions lead to a full range of mental disorders.

domination" (p. 216). Anxiety makes an individual uncertain and insecure, and despite the objective presence of personal qualities, the anxious individual's subjective feelings cause her or him to pursue an inordinate amount of attention, affection, or success. Relationships become confused and distorted, and ultimately unsatisfying. Additionally, the individual's awareness of the fundamental inauthenticity of this manipulative behavior becomes a further source of anxiety.

The descriptions of anxiety as interpersonal manipulation vary considerably within the neopsychoanalytic perspective, and little common language exists. At the same time, most contributors to the neopsychoanalytic perspective agree that: (1) interpersonal relationships during early stages of development determine the degree to which anxiety characterizes later life, and (2) this anxiety can produce patterns of self-defeating, manipulative behavior that distort relationships and limit human potential.

Insight

The shift from a psychoanalytic to a neopsychoanalytic perspective necessarily involved changes in theory, and changes in theory necessarily led to changes in the practices based on that theory. As Karen Horney (1939) put it, "Psychoanalytic therapy, in so far as it is not intuitive or directed by plain common sense, is influenced by theoretical concepts. . . . New ways in theory necessarily condition new ways in therapy" (p. 276). The neopsychoanalysts challenged three key assumptions of psychoanalytic theory: (1) the essential unreliability of the client's subjective experience, (2) the paramount importance of uncovering the past, and (3) the necessity of the practitioner maintaining interpersonal neutrality in the therapeutic process. Table 6.6 contains a brief, nontechnical summary of the various views of insight within the neopsychoanalytic perspective.

Though recognizing the importance of understanding unconscious motivational factors, neopsychoanalysts place greater emphasis than psychoanalysts on the conscious, subjective experience of the client. Further, the focus is more on the present than on the past. As Horney (1939) explained it, "I differ from Freud in that, after recognition of the neurotic trends, while he primarily investigates their genesis I primarily investigate their actual functions and their consequences" (p. 282). The unraveling and interpreting of past events is not

Table 6.6   *Neopsychoanalytic Views of Insight*

	Insight
Adler	>The subjective experience of the client is central to the process of providing helpful insight, and the practitioner works within its framework. >Insight must help the client see and understand the logic directing or misdirecting behavior, as well as revealing hidden motives and assumptions. >Insight directly promotes positive social feelings.
Jung	>The focus of insight is typically the client's internal world, especially images, symbols, dreams, and other experiences that reflect the content of the unconscious and the racial content of the collective unconscious. >The analysis of dreams provides a major source for understanding the unconscious aspects of life. >The final aim of insight is the integration of the client's conscious life with the unconscious life.
Fromm	>Insight involves promoting increased awareness in the client in regard to development conditions in the family and in society that are part of the maladaptivity. >The client's values are a focus of the intervention. >Changes in the client are not enough; individual behavior depends on the society being "sane."
Horney	>The objective of intervention is the emergence of the client's real self. >Through dream analysis and free association, the practitioner can glimpse the client's essential conflicts; through developing an interpersonal relationship with the client, the practitioner can sample the self-defeating characteristics of the client's relationships. >Insight in the form of knowledge about the conflicts and relationships is necessary for the emergence of the client's real self, but the change is incomplete without an accompanying emotional experience.
Erikson	>Insight that is of value emerges from a direct, conscious, and highly motivated partnership between the client and practitioner. >The insight the practitioner is able to provide the client will depend on the insight the practitioner has into him- or herself. >The focus of the insight is the unique life cycle of the client. The client is helped to move beyond the developmental stage in which he or she is caught.

Sullivan	>Individuals dominated by strong needs for security can have very distorted perceptions of their interpersonal relationships. >Insight involves uncovering these distortions and the anxiety underlying them. >The only real source of insight that the practitioner has in regard to the client is the interpersonal relationship between the client and practitioner.

an end in itself from the neopsychoanalytic perspective. Rather, though exploring the past is seen as contributing to the understanding of the total developmental process, the focus of insight is present ways of thinking, feeling, and acting within specific cultural institutions and specific relationships. The relationship between the practitioner and client is not only a forum for understanding transference phenomena. It is also a microcosm of the client's contemporary life in which both successful and unsuccessful interpersonal strategies can be observed. Therefore, though the therapeutic process is aimed at understanding and integrating the past with the present, insight is primarily focused, through concrete observations and directive challenges, on the present. This occurs within the context of a therapeutic relationship that is supportive and encouraging rather than neutral or distant. To use the terms established earlier in the chapter, within the neopsychoanalytic perspective, supportive methods are at least equal in importance to uncovering methods.

Summary

Jung (1931/1971) observed that "the psyche, as a reflection of the world and man, is a thing of such infinite complexity that it can be observed and studied from a great many sides" (p. 23). The contributors to the neopsychoanalytic perspective shed light on aspects of our lives left unexplored within the mainstream of the psychoanalytic perspective. Yet, for all the differences that exist between the psychoanalytic and the neopsychoanalytic perspectives, they share some key similarities: (1) Past events are held to be largely responsible for shaping behavior, and the exploring of those events and their meaning, especially their unconscious meaning, is considered crucial, if not sufficient, for therapeutic change to occur, (2) therapeutic change is regarded as the product primarily of one-on-one interaction during which the practitioner provides insight to or elicits insight from the client in the form of new information that produces emotional change, and (3) knowledge about human personality is generated largely from clinical work done with individuals whose behavior is maladaptive.

The neopsychoanalytic perspective is represented in Chapter 7 by Adlerian psychotherapy and counseling and, to a lesser extent, by time-limited dynamic psychotherapy.

The Humanistic-Existential Perspective

"God, forgive me. To life, adieu!!" With these bellowed words, Matthew May stepped from the ladder. His feet hit the ground, and though he bobbed his knees to hasten death's approach, the rope around his neck snapped and failed to halt his fall. He was not dead. He was not injured. Suicide (especially "attempted suicide") can be a humiliating task.

Matthew's venture into creating his own destiny (he considered it a form of poetic license) promised to make his fiftieth birthday unique. Perhaps, for all its stupidity and indignity, his failure signaled a beginning. As he sat there on the floor, he almost gained the courage to laugh, almost gained the courage to cry. In the humiliation, in the humility, in the silliness of it all, he thought (he hoped) that he had found the peace he needed to be someone other than someone else.

As Matthew May found, there are times in each of our lives when experience mirrors both our absurdity and our promise. We recognize that no matter how many meaningful relationships we develop, no matter how many significant things we do during our lifetimes, each of us contends with suffering, loneliness, aging, and death. Yet, at special moments at life's mirror, we also espy an even more frightening reality: Despite all of life's ambiguity and tenuousness, we alone are responsible for our lives, we alone are capable of making the fact of our existence an evolutionary plus. The humanistic-existential perspective, though acknowledging the primacy of personal and shared experiences as a source of knowledge, is focused primarily on individual responsibility for personal and cultural progress. Additionally, unlike the psychoanalytic and neopsychoanalytic perspectives, where philosophical assumptions are crucial but largely unarticulated, the humanistic-existential perspective is, to a great extent, an articulated philosophy that expresses at once faith in human beings and a warning about the vagaries of life itself.

Overview

The humanistic-existential perspective on personality and behavior change represents an amalgam of what is usually called humanistic psychology and existential psychotherapy. As described briefly in Chapter 3, humanistic psychology was a social movement in American psychology during the 1960s and 1970s whose critique of behaviorism and psychoanalysis revealed their philosophical and methodological limitations. Among the principal contributors to humanistic psychology were Gordon Allport, Sidney Jourard, Abraham Maslow, Rollo May, and Carl Rogers. As a contemporary psychotherapeutic perspective, humanistic psychology can be linked with existential psychotherapy. Existential psychotherapy represented a movement within European psychiatry, and later within American psychology, to integrate the insights of the philosophical movement known as *existentialism* into the practice of counseling and psychotherapy. The principal contributors to the movement within European psychiatry were Medard Boss, Ludwig Binswanger, Viktor Frankl, R. D. Laing, and Fritz Perls. Although a number of American psychologists helped to introduce existentialism to American practitioners, Rollo May remains the chief American proponent.

The humanistic-existential perspective does not have a single central figure or a unified theory of human behavior, nor are its contributors inspired by or working from such a single theory. Further, the humanistic-existential perspective can be viewed either as a reaction against psychoanalysis and behaviorism or as an attempt to synthesize them. Both viewpoints are valid. Whichever view is taken, however, the humanistic-existential perspective does represent a reorientation of psychology and other helping professions on several core issues that behaviorism and psychoanalysis appear to ignore or deny. In sum, those issues are: (1) the centrality of individual or personal experience in the science and practice of psychology, (2) the potential in each person for lifelong psychological growth, (3) the essential place of responsible self-determination in human existence, and (4) the characterization of the effective therapeutic relationship as authentically caring and self-disclosing. We will see these issues embodied in the discussions of the self, anxiety, and insight that follow.

As in the previous section, the following discussion cannot do justice to the work of the contributors to this perspective. The reader is again urged to explore their work independently.

The Self

In an elegant statement applying humanistic and existential principles to psychology, Hubert Bonner (1965) wrote:

> A psychology that defines health and "normality" in terms of the degree of happiness and social adjustment which we display in our daily lives, not only encourages self-deception but destroys or weakens the basis of our moral strengths. Wise men have always known what many adjustment psychologists cannot understand, that a life built by an individual's own efforts is attained only by means of individual strife and torment. The search for tranquility characterizes those individuals who have stopped living and are waiting to die. (p. 184)

Contrasted with the ideas of two previously discussed perspectives, these statements seem paradoxical. Bonner's assertions suggest that what we have viewed as normal—freedom from anxiety and concern, the attainment of homeostasis—is far from the goal of human development. Rather, human beings are at their natural best when engaged in the day-to-day fray that leads to fuller utilization of their potential. Following Bonner's lead, we will concern ourselves with two fundamental concepts about the self within the humanistic-existential perspective: (1) Human beings are potentially *proactive* rather than simply reactive, and (2) the goal of life is *self-actualization,* the individual attainment of one's unique potential.

Proactivity   A fundamental question asked by the psychoanalytic and neopsychoanalytic perspectives is: How does the damaged pathological self interact with the environment? The question asked by the humanistic-existential perspective is: How does an undamaged or repaired normal self interact with the environment? These questions point up a basic difference in how the perspective regard the self and its interaction with the environment. The issue: reactivity versus proactivity.

One of the important lessons of the psychoanalytic and neopsychoanalytic perspectives concerns the elaborate array of defense mechanisms that human beings are capable of using to defend the self. In the face of external threats and internal demands, human beings are *reactive*; that is, we act simply to restore or maintain homeostasis by protecting the self through repression and other defense mechanisms. Once properly defended, the self is vigilant but passive. The humanistic-existential perspective describes the self's proactive capabilities. In the absence of pathology, human beings act upon the world: planning, creating, building, and problem solving. We purposefully engage ourselves in new relationships, projects, hobbies, challenges, and so forth. This full engagement with life is much more than a product of homeostasis. Our personal happiness is, rather, a product of proactivity, a form of self-inflicted disequilibrium that stretches us, matures us, and makes us more constructive contributors to humanity.

Proactivity implies an emphasis on the present and the future rather than the past. Allport (1955) expressed a humanistic-existential perspective when he said, "People, it seems, are busy leading their lives into the future, whereas psychology, for the most part is busy tracing them into the past" (p. 51). Ideally, a person lives neither in the past nor in the future. The humanistic-existential perspective challenges us, rather, to accept the past and to live in the present in such a manner that the future, both personal and societal, will be better. This is what it means to live humanistically; this is what it means to live for the existential moment.

Actualizing the self   Humanistic-existential psychology views each individual as potentially engaged in a continual process of becoming all that he or she can become. Although different authors use different terms to talk about this process, Maslow has articulated the most widely accepted position.

For Maslow, human beings are motivated by a number of *basic* or *deficiency needs* that are species-wide and unchanging: physiological needs, safety and security needs, love and belongingness needs, esteem and self-esteem needs. (These are described briefly in Chapter 2.) Beyond the satisfaction of these needs, however, Maslow saw a need for what he called **self-actualization.** Maslow (1968) defined self-actualization as the "ongoing actualization of potentials, capacities and talents, as fulfillment of mission (or call, fate, destiny, or vocation), as a fuller knowledge of and acceptance of, the person's own intrinsic nature, as an unceasing trend toward unity, integration, or synergy with the person" (p. 25).

For Maslow and others within the humanistic-existential perspective, life is a matter of choices. Some choices are *progressive*; that is, they move an individual away from the mere meeting of basic needs and toward fulfilling unique, more meaningful goals. Other decisions are *regressive*; that is, they maintain the status quo or move the individual backwards. Some of these choices are major ones; for example, a physician may decide to remain in a difficult and lower paying position because of the good she is accomplishing and the meaning her work provides. Some of these choices are small, day-to-day decisions that shape the future; for example, a student may regularly avoid his studies, thereby reducing the probability that he will contribute meaningfully to the world later on, as well as reducing the satisfaction he will later feel. For each of us, however, life provides a personalized set of opportunities and challenges that allow us to find meaning, to become increasingly self-actualizing, to become increasingly mature. Though the psychoanalytic and neopsychoanalytic perspectives generally describe the mature self in terms of an absence of pathology, the humanistic-existential perspective describes the self-actualizing or mature individual more fully.

The mature self Maturity from the humanistic-existential perspective can be defined using Maslow's list of the characteristics of self-actualizing persons.[14] First, mature persons possess a more accurate perception of reality and are comfortable in relating to the real world. Mature individuals live more in the real world of nature rather than in the "man-made conceptions, abstractions, expectations, beliefs, and stereotypes that most people confuse with the real world" (Maslow, 1970a, p. 154). Second, mature individuals accept themselves, others, and nature without chagrin or complaint; that is, they see human nature "as it *is* and not as they would prefer it to be" (p. 155). Third, mature individuals are spontaneous. Although externally the mature person may be quite conventional, what goes on internally is quite unconventional. An inner naturalness allows thoughts, feelings, and actions to occur without rehearsal, phoniness, or artificiality. Behavior is determined according to personal values rather than primarily in response to the opinions and directives of others.

Other characteristics of the mature person include: problem-centeredness rather than ego-centeredness; a quality of detachment and a need for privacy; relative freedom from culture and environment so that one is an active agent rather than a reactor; a continued freshness of perception; an intense feeling of identification with humanity; deep and profound interpersonal relationships

---

[14]Self-actualization or maturity is never a finished product. One is always in the process of self-actualizing, becoming increasingly mature, becoming increasingly capable of living meaningfully and effectively. To talk about a self-actualiz*ed* person, therefore, is inaccurate unless, of course, he or she is dead.

with a few special friends; a democratic character structure; an ability to discriminate between ends and means and between good and evil; a philosophical and nonhostile sense of humor; creativity of a special caliber; and a familiarity with peak experiences—special, transient moments of intense personal awareness, integration, and ecstasy.[15]

As might be expected from this list of characteristics, exceptionally mature or self-actualizing people are relatively rare. Paradoxically, we cannot strive to become more mature, to become more self-actualizing (Frankl, 1967). Maturity is not a goal; it is a by-product. In our day-to-day lives, we confront both challenges and opportunities that can make our lives meaningful and therefore enhance our maturity. We either accept or fail to accept these challenges and opportunities. Decisions that intensify our meaningful involvement with day-to-day life lead us toward increasing maturity. Decisions that avoid or abandon that involvement fail to enhance our maturity.

Defining the nature of maladaptive behavior, specifically neurotic behavior, from the humanistic-existential perspective is easy: Neurosis is immaturity; it is the failure to move beyond the mere satisfaction of basic or deficiency needs, the failure to respond to our natural impetus toward self-actualization. In practice, it involves behaving in ways that are both selfish and self-defeating. Neurotic life is painful and self-conscious, anxious, devoid of meaning, and socially unproductive.

Anxiety

In the psychoanalytic and neopsychoanalytic perspectives, we have seen the role played by developmental experiences in the creation of anxiety. The humanistic-existential perspective focuses our attention on the source of a more widespread form of anxiety: the times in which we live. It was the poet W. H. Auden who first called our times the "age of anxiety," a period in human history in which a parade of human tragedies, rapid social change, and the ominousness of the nuclear age have fostered anxiety in each of us. It is more than the nature and the swiftness of the changes that threaten us, however. As May (1977) has pointed out, the underlying values and standards of our culture have been shaken. Culture, through its various political, religious, and social organizations, provides answers to why what happens in the world and in an individual's life happens. Cultural assumptions about the meaning of life, the value of the person, and the nature of ultimate realities provide a structure for understanding and accepting even the most horrendous events and personal strife. We in the 20th century have witnessed the gradual erosion of the power of all but the most insular of cultures to answer such questions. The individual

---

[15]Although Maslow was trained as an experimental psychologist, the theory of self-actualization is based largely on interviews and questionnaires, and Maslow left the development of objective measures of self-actualization to others. Shostrom developed the Personal Orientation Inventory (1964) and Personal Orientation Dimensions (1974) as means of measuring levels of self-actualization. The measures have been used extensively, especially during the 1970s. Shostrom has also developed an approach to therapy based partly on Maslow's theory called "actualizing therapy" (Shostrom, 1976).

is thus left to face the uncertainties of immediate and ultimate realities alone.

Though recognizing that some forms of anxiety are crippling, the humanistic-existential perspective also points to the anxiety that comes from facing the ambiguities and uncertainties of modern life. This anxiety is not a symptom of pathology but rather a sign of aliveness, of a willingness to look at the real world and to seek a meaningful understanding. Understanding is not to be found in the pat answers provided by our culture, however, but is attained personally and interpersonally through responsible commitment to the human community.

Insight

A key assumption of the humanistic-existential perspective is that human beings are naturally directed toward self-actualization. Tapped by whatever challenges life might provide, the insights and other resources necessary for growth reside within the individual. The role of counseling or psychotherapy is to provide a climate in which that growth can occur more quickly, more efficiently. Professional psychological intervention is directed toward those who have for one reason or another slowed or stopped their natural tendency toward growth.

Typically, humanistic-existential approaches to psychotherapy and counseling de-emphasize techniques in favor of development of a facilitative relationship between the client and practitioner. This does not mean to suggest, however, that the practitioner's role is a passive one. On the contrary, many of the humanistic-existential approaches to treatment are very active, and several are confrontative. At the same time, these approaches show an essential trust in the resources of the client and a reliance on the client-practitioner relationship as the means of tapping those resources.

Rather than viewing the relationship between the client and the practitioner as transference phenomenon, humanistic-existential practitioners work to establish a trusting, genuinely caring relationship in the here and now with little hearkening back to the past. A distinction made by Jourard (1971) between authentic *dialogue* and *manipulation* is helpful in understanding how humanistic-existential approaches differ from more psychoanalytically oriented ones. The essence of this distinction comes through in the following comments:

> Surely, our patients come to us because they have become so estranged from their real selves that they are incapable of making these [facts about themselves] known to their associates in life. I don't see how we can reacquaint our patients with their real selves by striving to subject them to subtle manipulations and thus to withhold our real selves from them. It reminds me of the sick leading the sick. In point of fact, if my experience means anything, it has shown me that I can come *closest to eliciting and reinforcing authentic behavior in my patient by manifesting it myself* [Jourard's italics]. (p. 141)

In humanistic-existential approaches, insight is thus a product of the dialogue between the client and practitioner. The client, alienated from his or her capacity to interact honestly and spontaneously with others, learns through experiencing his or her relationship with the practitioner what authentic sharing is. The honesty and spontaneity of the practitioner both facilitates and serves as a model for client change.

Summary

The beliefs, values, and priorities included within the humanistic-existential perspective are considerably more diverse than our discussion has suggested; as noted earlier, no single theory or set of techniques is espoused by practitioners who identify with this perspective. As Jourard (1968) has pointed out, however, since the humanistic-existential perspective represents a goal rather than a doctrine, this does not matter. Because it acknowledges the realities of the human condition, as well as describing human potential, it provides a broad philosophical and ethical framework within which a variety of therapeutic techniques can be applied.

Though some may argue that changes in both behavior therapy and psychoanalysis have made the promulgation of humanistic-existential views unnecessary, others would argue that such a position is premature. As M. B. Smith (1984) has pointed out, "As psychotherapy becomes more technological and the new cognitive psychology occupies itself with flow charts of information processing, the need continues for close attention to human experience in psychological studies" (p. 159).

The humanistic-existential perspective is represented by all three of the therapies presented in Chapter 8: Gestalt therapy, person-centered therapy, and logotherapy.

Beyond the Three Perspectives

Although the three perspectives on personality and behavior change considered here are linked historically, theoretically, and methodologically, many contemporary practitioners view themselves as exclusively part of one—or at least their work expresses the assumptions and techniques of one. Still, it is possible to look beyond the differences and recognize several important points of convergence:

1. *The self as growth-oriented:* Developments within each of the perspectives suggest an increasingly common view of the self as capable of functioning autonomously, beyond the dictates of unconscious conflict resolution and sociocultural determinants. For example, in a recent comparison of the work of Kohut (associated with the psychoanalytic perspective) and Rogers (associated with the humanistic-existential perspective), Kahn (1985) demonstrated that the concept of the self that emerges from the work of both is of a self that is capable of moving beyond self-centeredness, is directed naturally toward maturity or fulfillment, thrives on intra- and interpersonal empathy, and is capable of making choices that control personal destiny.

2. *The importance of emotional insight:* The three perspectives also converge in regard to the nature of insight. Insight that is simply new knowledge unaccompanied by an emotional experience does not lead to a permanent change of behavior. Each of the perspectives describe insight as a process that must be both intellectual and emotional (see Ellis, 1963).

3. *The importance of the present:* Each of the three perspectives has increasingly come to focus on the client's here and now. The past is understood as relevant to therapy to the degree that affects present behavior. The future is understood as relevant to therapy to the degree that it can be realized.

4. *The centrality of the therapeutic relationship in therapeutic change:* Although the three perspectives's descriptions of the effective therapeutic relationship differ, they also show striking conceptual and practical similarities. The genuine caring shared by the practitioner interacts with the trust invested by the client to produce the basic rapport (climate) necessary for insight to occur and lead to behavior change.

In Chapters 7 and 8, we will examine a number of contemporary approaches to insight therapy in which we will be able to see the commonalities identified above, as well as the considerable differences that remain.

Summary of Chapter 6

In Chapter 6, we have addressed the topic of maturity and insight therapy by examining the three major perspectives on personality and behavior change that have developed within the clinical research tradition. The major points covered are:

Maturity and the Role of Insight

1. Maturity is defined by each culture in terms of the expectations it holds for differing age groups, sexes, and social groups. Immature people are assumed to lack some fundamental knowledge or experience that would make their behavior more appropriate and acceptable.
2. Counseling and psychotherapy are contemporary means of enhancing a client's maturity by bringing her or his behavior more within the expectations of society, thus potentially adding to the individual's satisfaction in life.
3. This is accomplished by providing the client with insight, new information and experience that promote increasingly mature behavior.

Three Perspectives on Personality and Behavior Change

4. Three basic perspectives on personality and behavior change have developed with the clinical research tradition: the psychoanalytic, the neopsychoanalytic, and the humanistic-existential perspectives.

5. The three perspectives are linked historically, theoretically, and methodologically but can be distinguished by their positions vis-à-vis three conceptual benchmarks: the nature of the self, especially the mature self; the sources and role of anxiety in adaptive and maladaptive behavior; and the nature and role of insight in therapy and counseling.

The Psychoanalytic Perspective

6. Freud, the founder of psychoanalysis and the clinical research tradition, was the key contributor to this perspective. What follows in this and the other two perspectives is either a development of or a reaction to Freud's pioneering work.
7. Freud viewed the mind as a closed energy system powered by libido, a psychic energy that can be invested in any person, object, or idea. Psychologically, as well as biologically, we are directed toward tension reduction—that is, toward a state of homeostasis.
8. Freud's description of the mind emphasized the structural components of the id, ego, and superego. These structures can be described functionally as constituting a tension-reduction process directed by the ego in which energy from the id is invested in persons, objects, or ideas in such a manner that the social dictates of the superego do not produce guilt and anxiety. Much psychic activity is unconscious.
9. A variety of defense mechanisms exist to help the ego function successfully, the most important of which is repression, the automatic, involuntary removal from consciousness of some potentially anxiety-producing impulse, memory, idea, or wish.
10. Personality development is viewed as a passage through age-related psychosexual stages. Psychopathology results from unsuccessful passage through one of these stages.
11. Within the psychoanalytic perspective, conceptions of the mature self or ego have been developed largely by those who followed Freud. What has emerged is a view of the self as potentially free of conflict and capable of functioning in an increasingly conscious manner.
12. Freud described anxiety as a signal of intrapsychic conflict existing below the level of consciousness. By means of dream analysis, free association, and the analysis of transference, the client's resistance to insight can be broken through and the conflict can be resolved.

The Neopsychoanalytic Perspective

13. The neopsychoanalytic perspective is sociocultural; that is, it emphasizes the role of cultural institutions and interpersonal relationships in the development of normal and pathological behavior.
14. From the neopsychoanalytic perspective, the self develops through interaction with persons and institutions. When that interaction is successful, the mature self emerges.

15. Anxiety is considered to function as more than a signal; it also serves as a manipulative tool that an individual can use to avoid the demands of life.
16. In regard to insight, the developing relationship between the practitioner and client is considered a microcosm of interpersonal patterns that have limited the client in the past. The therapeutic relationship is therefore an important source of insight.

The Humanistic-Existential Perspective

17. The humanistic-existential perspective complements the other two perspectives by providing a view of human beings as capable of psychological growth beyond the simple absence of pathology.
18. The self is viewed as proactive, purposefully and consciously engaging in activities that do not produce homeostasis. The self is potentially engaged in the actualization of unique, highly personal potentials that depend on a person's full and active involvement in the world.
19. Anxiety, as part of the reality of modern life, is viewed as a sign of alive engagement rather than merely of psychic conflict.
20. Therapeutic insight results from dialogue between a trusting client and an authentically caring practitioner.

Beyond the Three Perspectives

21. Although considerable differences remain among the three perspectives, four points of convergence can be identified: (1) the self as growth-oriented, (2) the importance of emotional insight, (3) the importance of the present, and (4) the centrality of the therapeutic relationship in therapeutic change.

Contemporary Insight Therapy: Psychoanalytic Approaches

Psychotherapy, assuredly, cannot be all things to all people, but if it can be some things to some people, there is no need for its proponents to feel defensive or ashamed. The task for the future is precisely to find out what it can do and for whom.

Hans H. Strupp

Chapter 7 is the first of two chapters presenting *insight therapies*—a total of six important approaches to psychotherapy and counseling developed within the **clinical research tradition.** As **insight** therapies, each approach is aimed at promoting the **maturity** of clients by providing new information and experience. Each of the six approaches described in these two chapters partakes in some way of one or more of the three perspectives described in Chapter 6, and each shares the four points of convergence identified there: (1) the self as growth-oriented, (2) the importance of emotional as well as intellectual insight, (3) an emphasis on the present rather than the past, and (4) the centrality of the therapeutic relationship in therapeutic change. The three approaches described in this chapter are: (1) time-limited dynamic psychotherapy, (2) Adlerian psychotherapy and counseling, and (3) transactional analysis. These approaches share at least one commonality: Each in some way depends on psychoanalysis as its theoretical and therapeutic starting point.

The six approaches we will consider in these chapters are individual therapies; that is, the focus of the intervention is an individual client. In some of these approaches, however, intervention may take place in a group setting. Chapter 9 will consider family approaches that focus on treating social units (typically a family).

We will examine each of the approaches in relation to: (1) its historical and theoretical foundations, (2) the process of intervention, (3) a sample session, and (4) evaluation. An ongoing sample case will be presented in the chapter to serve as the basis for the sample sessions.

The reader is reminded that the descriptions that follow are distillations of rich bodies of theory, research, and clinical experience. If what follows encourages the reader to explore primary sources, it has achieved one of its goals.

Sample Case: Dexter Drudge

At 34, Dexter Drudge's professional life was a success. After attaining an outstanding undergraduate record, Dex attended a prestigious law school, graduated near the top of his class, and landed a position in one of the city's more important law firms. Much of his success came from methodical attention to detail rather than creative bursts, and though his colleagues viewed him as competent, they also saw him as outwardly cooperative but highly critical of subordinates. Socially, Dexter was aloof.

Dex's personal life was generally dull. The few attempts Dex had made at establishing long-term relationships with women had ended badly, as had most extended friendships with other males. Dex tended to attach himself to one other person at a time, typically becoming preoccupied with the relationship. If the relationship was with a woman, he would continually send her flowers and gifts. He further primed himself with crash diets, workout programs, expensive clothing, and overwhelmingly sumptuous dates including fancy dinners and esoteric concerts. If the relationship was with a man, he would develop a mutual interest, for example, playing handball or attending sports events. While Dex acknowledged no sexual interest in other men, he desperately sought their approval. In his relationships with both women and men, Dex would eventually smother the relationship and return to a life restricted to work and loneliness.

His most recent relationship had finally brought Dex to therapy. At a meeting of apartment building tenants, Dex had met Frank Noon, M.D. Frank Noon was a recently widowed man at least 10 years older than Dex. Dex and Frank were members of a committee to work on one of the building problems, and it became apparent to both that the loneliness that had characterized their lives was being in some way answered by their common interests. As Dex learned of Frank's interest in art, he, too, became a devotee and took considerable pains to learn about Frank's favorite artists. Frank, for his part, enjoyed Dex's company, although he did find that Dex was consuming too much of his time. Gradually, Frank got involved in a relationship with a physician at the hospital and, through her, moved into a new social circle. He avoided Dex and only rarely returned Dex's calls and notes. In the end, Frank received an extremely hostile letter from Dex, one that ended with a plea to reestablish the relationship "or else." Frank was amazed at the letter and assumed that Dex was suffering from a serious psychosexual problem. In a well-intentioned phone call, Frank suggested that Dex was consciously or unconsciously trying to seduce him and recommended that he seek professional help immediately. Frank's accusation infuriated and confused Dex, and as an act of self-vindication and hostility, he made an appointment with a practitioner.

Time-Limited Dynamic Psychotherapy

It was the summer of 1910 in the city of Leyden in the Netherlands. Two men, both in their early 50s, strolled the streets of the city engaged in conversation. One man was Gustav Mahler, a world-famous composer and conductor. The other man was Sigmund Freud, an increasingly important physician on a long-overdue family vacation. Mahler's problem was sexual impotence in his relationship with an adoring but considerably younger wife. Freud's goal was to effect a quick cure. At the end of the conversation, Mahler was so enlightened and encouraged that his impotence ceased (Jones, 1955, pp. 88–89).[1]

[1]Ernest Jones recounted the story of Freud's meeting with Mahler in his classic, three-volume biography of Freud. He reported that Freud credited Mahler with an incredibly swift understanding of psychoanalysis, and Mahler, for his part, was amazed at Freud's ability to gain insight into his marital relationship based on a few facts about Mahler and his wife. The long-term effect of this intervention cannot be evaluated, however, since "Mahler recovered his potency and the marriage was a happy one until his death, which unfortunately took place only a year later" (Jones, 1955, p. 89). Jones's description of the event is supported by Mahler's wife, Alma, in her memoirs. She wrote: "[Mahler] realized that he had lived the life of a neurotic and suddenly decided to con-

The story of Freud and Mahler seems too good to be true: an effective and brief intervention exploiting the richness of psychoanalytic theory and therapy! Certainly it flies in the face of our image of psychoanalytic treatment, which we typically think of as taking many years and often involving several sessions a week. Indeed, the story of Freud and Mahler is one of several rare exceptions in the history of psychoanalysis to the common practice of allowing as much time as necessary to effect significant changes in personality and behavior through complete sounding of the psychic depths.

The preference for long-term treatment goes back to the development of psychoanalysis by Freud himself (Flegenheimer, 1982, pp. 2–36). In his early work, Freud emphasized the removal of symptoms through catharsis, strong emotional experiences resulting from the recollection of repressed memories. The practitioner's role was an active one, often confrontative as well as supportive. With the development of the technique of free association, however, treatment became longer, and the role of the practitioner, more passive. Gradually, the focus of treatment shifted toward recognizing and resolving **transference** (see Chapter 6). This required still more time and made it necessary for the analyst to be passive in order to resist the transference phenomenon. During Freud's lifetime, Ferenczi and Rank (1925) tried to hasten and enhance the process of psychoanalysis by increasing the activity of the analyst and by directing the focus of treatment toward more immediate, emotion-ladened events in the client's life. Freud strongly resisted these attempts. Later, after Freud's death, Franz Alexander (Alexander & French, 1946) continued the work of Ferenczi and Rank by again challenging the necessity of universal long-term, in-depth analysis. Alexander promoted experimentation with a variety of aspects of treatment, and the manner in which transference phenomena are resolved (Flegenheimer, 1982). Since that time, considerable effort has been directed at making psychoanalysis a more efficient therapy, and the professional literature abounds with books and articles about "time-limited," "brief," or "short-term" psychoanalytic treatment (Budman, 1981; Flegenheimer, 1982; Gelso & Johnson, 1983; Malan, 1963; Marmor, 1979; Sifneos, 1979; Strupp & Binder, 1984; Wells, 1982; Wolberg, 1980).[2]

The goal of this movement within psychoanalysis is to develop a form of therapy that: (1) utilizes and advances psychoanalytic thinking, (2) is amenable to scientific scrutiny, and (3) is economical and temporally efficient. Time-limited dynamic psychotherapy, developed by Hans H. Strupp, is a significant step toward attaining that goal.

---

sult Sigmund Freud. . . . He gave [Freud] an account of his strange states of mind and his anxieties, and Freud apparently calmed him down" (Mahler, 1964, p. 175). Both Jones's biography and Alma Mahler's memoirs offer more interesting reading on the topic.

[2]It would be misleading to suggest that time-limited approaches to psychoanalysis are the most common. Rather, mainstream psychoanalytic thinking remains committed to long-term intervention (Strupp & Binder, 1984). Also, a distinction is sometimes made between psychoanalysis and psychoanalytically oriented therapy. The first is the standard technique of orthodox Freudian psychoanalysis. The second refers to those approaches that vary from the orthodox position by incorporating changes recommended by Alexander and others (Flegenheimer, 1982).

Historical and Theoretical Foundations

For contemporary practitioners of psychotherapy, especially psychoanalytically oriented psychotherapy, the name of Hans H. Strupp is a familiar one. Born in Germany in 1921, Strupp was trained in the United States, receiving his Ph.D. from George Washington University in 1954. Unlike most psychologists, however, Strupp had an opportunity to train in psychoanalysis among psychiatrists at the Washington School of Psychiatry, where he received the Certificate in Applied Psychiatry. Presently, Strupp is Distinguished Professor of Psychology at Vanderbilt University and director of Vanderbilt's Center for Psychotherapy Research. Much of Strupp's research has focused on determining what specific elements make psychotherapy effective. As part of that search, he and his colleagues undertook the "Vanderbilt studies," which will be described later; these studies form the foundation of time-limited dynamic psychotherapy (TLDP). In 1984, Strupp published *Psychotherapy in a New Key: A Guide to Time-Limited Dynamic Psychotherapy* with Jeffrey L. Binder, a senior member of the Center for Psychotherapy Research. The respect with which Strupp is regarded by his colleagues is best understood from these comments about Strupp's contribution from the *Encyclopedia of Psychology:* "Reliance on empirical data, systematic research, and conceptual clarification of basic issues is seen as the best hope of advancing knowledge in this increasingly important area. Strupp's research has been guided by a commitment to open and nondogmatic inquiry, and excellence in training and practice" (Sahakian & Lundin, 1984c, p. 379).

Psychoanalytic and neopsychoanalytic roots As noted earlier, Strupp was thoroughly trained in psychoanalysis, and all of his contributions to psychotherapy have psychoanalysis as a starting point. Strupp's essential modification of psychoanalysis is related to what he identifies as one of the basic ingredients of all psychotherapy: "a helping relationship patterned after the parent-child relationship" (Strupp, 1973, p. 1). For Strupp, one of Freud's principal contributions was his recognition of the centrality of the parent-child relationship in normal and neurotic development. In normal development, memories of our early dependent experiences are positive; therefore, relationships later in life have the potential to be therapeutic. Neurotic individuals, on the other hand, suffer negative parent-child relationships, reproducing these relationships in therapy as well as in their day-to-day lives. As discussed in Chapter 6, this phenomenon is called transference, which can be defined as "the expression of impulses, feelings, fantasies, attitudes and defenses with respect to a person in the present which do not appropriately fit that person but are a repetition of responses originating in regard to significant persons of early childhood, unconsciously displaced on to persons in the present" (Greenson & Wexler, 1969, cited in Strupp & Binder, 1984, p. 22).

Though traditional psychoanalysis attempts to resolve present conflicts by reconstructing past events, Strupp follows the lead of Alexander and the neopsychoanalytic work of Sullivan, Horney, Erikson, and Kohut in shifting the focus from the past to analysis of the present manifestations of those past events in the client's present interpersonal relationships. Further, Strupp accepts the emphasis proposed by Rogers and others on the elemental (if not singular) importance of a good human relationship as a basic ingredient in psychotherapy (Strupp, 1973; Strupp & Binder, 1984). Theoretically, therefore, Strupp's TLDP is a psychoanalytic and neopsychoanalytic therapy incorporating elements from the humanistic-existential perspective.

Research orientation   If Strupp's psychoanalytic theory puts TLDP in the clinical research tradition, his methodological rigor makes his therapy part of the experimental research tradition. Strupp (1982) has pointed out the false dichotomy between research and practice, noting that Freud, unlike many present-day analysts, made systematic use of the research tools available to him. For us today, the ideal is to bring the precision of experimental methodology to the therapeutic session. Strupp (1971) has identified the dilemma this involves: "The greater the realism of the situation, the less it is possible to isolate variables and subject them to experimental manipulation. Contrariwise, the greater the experimental control over single variables, the greater the artificiality of the situation and the more questionable the validity of the results obtained under those conditions [italics omitted]" (p. 150).

Strupp's efforts to bridge the methodological gaps can be seen in his work at the Vanderbilt University Center for Psychotherapy Research and the studies generated from that center since 1970.

The Vanderbilt studies   One of the most persistent issues in the study of psychotherapy and counseling has to do with the roles that *specific* and *nonspecific* factors play in changing maladaptive behavior (Strupp & Binder, 1984). One way to view therapeutic change is in relation to specific techniques or procedures identified with specific approaches to therapy. In behavior therapy, an array of specific techniques are said to produce change (for example, systematic desensitization), while in psychoanalysis, any cure is attributed to the practitioner's interpretation of the client's resistances and transferences. Another view, following the work of Frank (1973), emphasizes nonspecific interpersonal factors, for example, understanding, acceptance, encouragement, or the practitioner's enthusiastic commitment to a belief system or rationale. These basic human qualities combat a client's demoralization but are not the exclusive province of practitioners. Therefore, an essential question in research on psychological intervention has to do with the relative contributions of specific and nonspecific factors. The Vanderbilt studies, funded by the National Institute of Mental Health as part of the Vanderbilt Psychotherapy Project, are the direct result of Strupp's efforts to shed light on this and other important issues surrounding therapy.

The working assumption underlying the designs of the first set of Vanderbilt studies (referred to as Vanderbilt I) was rather straightforward. Successful therapeutic change occurs because of the contributions of both specific and nonspecific factors. Therefore, if two experimental treatment groups could be established in which nonspecific (interpersonal) factors played an equal role, with one group also relying on specific (technical) factors, then the contribution made by the specific factors could be gauged. In one study undertaken as part of Vanderbilt I, Strupp and his colleagues set out to clarify the specific versus nonspecific issue within the context of time-limited treatment (Strupp, 1980a; Strupp & Hadley, 1979).[3] In the study, 18 clients were assigned to individual therapy with one of five highly experienced psychotherapists operating in a time-limited fashion—that is, restricted to 25 sessions on a twice-weekly basis. The subjects were all single male college students ranging in age from 18 to 25. They were selected on the basis of their scores on several scales of the Minnesota Multiphasic Personality Inventory (MMPI) and were judged to be suffering from relational problems, anxiety, and depression. In addition to the group of trained professional psychotherapists, a comparison group of approachable, caring, helpful, but untrained college professors was also assigned clients. Two control groups were also established to compare treatment with nontreatment.

A number of measures were utilized to assess the degree of therapeutic change that occurred for each treatment group, and the evaluation procedures produced some interesting results. Though clients in both sets of treatment groups showed greater improvement than those in the control groups, on the average, clients assigned to college professors showed as much improvement as those assigned to professional therapists. Though these preliminary results may seem to suggest that specific training in psychotherapy is of little value and that only interpersonal variables are critical, closer examinations of the cases revealed additional factors. Strupp and his colleagues undertook a careful examination of specific clients, comparing "high changers," who had had positive outcomes, with "low changers," who had had negative or no treatment outcomes. They found that though both professional therapists and college professors had success with highly motivated clients who were able to form a working relationship, neither had much success in treating individuals with more severe personality problems or those who for some reason resisted the establishment of a working relationship early in treatment. In other words, in time-limited interventions like those undertaken in the study, individuals with more than minor difficulties were not capable of being helped. Further, when the professional therapists and college professors failed with difficult clients, they failed for different reasons. Typically, the college professors got caught up in **countertransference** by falling into detrimental interpersonal patterns from the client's developmental years. The professional therapists in the Vanderbilt I study were largely analytically trained, however, and adopted an interpersonal

---

[3] The Vanderbilt studies are models of comprehensive clinical research and are described here only in part. An article by Strupp and Hadley (1979) has best explained the study; three articles by Strupp have provided illustrative case material (1980a, 1980b, 1980c).

pattern that was passive, nonsupportive, and restricted interaction to the interpretation of important aspects of the client's intrapsychic life. Such strategies are designed to avoid countertransference, but when faced with client resistance in the form of negativity and hostility, this neutrality prevented the formation of a working therapeutic alliance. Thus, the technical skill of the professional therapists proved of little value, and the psychoanalytically oriented, time-limited treatment used in the study proved ineffective.

TLDP was developed as a means of enabling clients with more difficult problems to benefit from psychoanalytically oriented, time-limited treatment. This is accomplished by training practitioners how to establilsh therapeutic relationships that use countertransference to benefit the client. Although TLDP was an outgrowth of the Vanderbilt I study, it continues to be refined as part of the Vanderbilt II studies currently under way.

The Process of Intervention

As described in Strupp and Binder (1984), time-limited dynamic psychotherapy (TLDP) , though unique, shares several similarities with other psychodynamically oriented, time-limited therapies. First, of course, the number of sessions is limited (25 to 30), and termination of the treatment is a continual topic. Second, as in all time-limited approaches, *patient selection* is crucial. Typically in TLDP, the nature of the client's pathology is secondary to the degree to which the client is judged capable of forming a collaborative relationship. The judgment is based on trial interventions conducted during the first few sessions. Third, in TLDP, treatment revolves around a *dynamic focus* in the client's life—that is, a central theme, conflict, dilemma, or behavioral pattern identified by the practitioner. In TLDP, however, the dynamic focus does not serve as a rigid explanation of the client's behavior but is used *heuristically,* as a guide to inquiry, a hypothetical way of explaining what is not readily understood otherwise. In identifying the dynamic focus, the TLDP practitioner depends less on exploration of the client's early experiences and more on the client's descriptive narratives of present interpersonal relationships. These narratives are obtained through a careful assessment process consisting of interviews early in the therapeutic process that allow the practitioner to set the interpersonal tone, as well as gather the information necessary to determine the dynamic focus. Fourth, though the analysis of resistance and the analysis of transference are part of all dynamically oriented therapies, TLDP take a unique approach to resistance and transference by making the practitioner an active participant in the process.

The analysis of resistance   In keeping with traditional psychoanalysis, TLDP views the analysis of resistance as a continual activity in therapy. Resistance in TLDP includes anything that disturbs communication between the practitioner and the client—that is, any attempt to halt the analysis of transference. Underlying the client's defensive behavior are unconscious beliefs, conflicts, or fantasies that set the interpersonal pattern. The practitioner continually examines the therapeutic relationship to see what unknown factors may be preventing the development of transference. The working assumption here is that once the early resistances are revealed, the practitioner can make interpersonal adjustments that will allow transference to develop. Of course, the analysis of resistance on the part of both the client and practitioner continues throughout therapy.

The analysis of transference   The fundamental role of the analysis of transference in TLDP is evident in the following statement from Strupp and Binder (1984):

> We posit that psychotherapy is basically a set of interpersonal transactions. It is a process which may become therapeutic because of the patient's unwitting tendency (which he or she shares with all human beings) to cast the therapist in the role of a significant other and to enact with him or her unconscious conflicts. Through participant observation, the therapist provides a new model for identification. He or she attempts then to grasp latent meanings in the patient's interpersonal behavior and communicates this understanding to the patient, thereby helping the latter to assimilate aspects of his or her experience that were hitherto unrecognized or disowned (repressed). To this end, the patient's experiences with significant others in his or her current and past life represent important sources of information which aid the therapist's understanding; however, they are secondary to the contemporary transactions between patient and therapist. (p. 29)

TLDP views the client's presenting problems as evidence of immaturity caused by the emotional inadequacies or traumas of childhood. However, the dynamic focus of the therapy is how those deficiencies are expressed in *cyclical maladaptive patterns*.[4] Though the events of childhood are considered to set the pattern of behavior in action, the client's present defensive behavior is seen as self-perpetuating. Typically, an individual sets out on a pattern of behavior that ensures rejection by others. Dexter Drudge, for example, destroys interpersonal relationships by acting alternately obsequious and hostile depending on how much self-doubt he is feeling. His insecurities may have originated in his relationship with highly critical parents, but they are played out and reaffirmed in his unsuccessful everyday relationships. In TLDP, the self-defeating patterns of the client are changed in two interrelated ways: (1) *interpretation* and (2) *corrective interpersonal experience*.

Insight into the client's recurring behavior patterns comes from the interpretations provided by the practitioner in therapy. In a sense, the practitioner continually *renarrates* the client's own stories to bring out themes and patterns to which the client has been resistant. This process helps in establishing and refining the dynamic focus. Through interpretation, change in the client's be-

---

[4]In Strupp and Binder (1984), cyclical maladaptive patterns are called *cyclical psychodynamic patterns*. The author uses the former expression based on a workshop by Strupp conducted in 1985. Strupp's description of the role of the feedback mechanism in both adaptive and maladaptive behavior draws on a fascinating paper by Wender (1968) in *Psychiatry*.

havior takes place in a three-part process: (1) becoming aware of the self-defeating interpersonal patterns, (2) understanding the meaning and purpose of the patterns, and (3) trying out alternative ways of acting. Throughout this process, the practitioner's relationship with the client increasingly serves as a corrective emotional experience; that is, rather than overreacting or underreacting to the client's transference behavior, the therapist acts to provide new interpersonal experiences that break the pattern. This is really an example of using countertransference in a positive way. For example, the practitioner meets the client's pattern of anger and resentment with nurturance, empathy, patience, and persistence rather than annoyance or rejection. The client's pattern of childlike charm neither seduces nor alienates the practitioner, who remains supportive and challenging. Here, the relationship between the client and practitioner becomes a trusting therapeutic alliance that the client can see as a microcosm of other relationships and in which the client can try out patterns of interpersonal activity that are not self-defeating. Further, the client is given the support necessary to do so outside of treatment.

TLDP is in constant refinement through the ongoing Vanderbilt studies. In those detailed investigations, researchers are examining the interventions of experienced psychiatrists and clinical psychologists to discover the process through which significant change takes place. Such reliance on careful research is all too novel within the psychoanalytic and neopsychoanalytic perspectives.

Sample Session

Below is an exchange from an imaginary session with Dexter Drudge. The reader should be alert for: (1) the client's defense mechanisms, (2) interpersonal ploys on the part of the client, and (3) efforts by the practitioner to identify patterns that form the dynamic focus. This is Dexter's sixth TLDP session with Dr. Rita Merelove. For the most part, Dexter has spoken of the inexplicable but irritating rejection he has experienced from various friends, while asserting the reasonableness of his demands on them. Dr. Merelove has listened to several long monologues, one tearful, one angry. She has just asked Dexter to narrate again what happened in his relationship with Dr. Frank Noon:

> *Dexter (D):* I'm not sure why you want to hear about that so much. You know, he just thought he was too good for me, I guess. Typical doctor, with the attitude that they're so much better than everybody else. I went to a lot of trouble to get to know the guy, only to have him accuse me of sexual perversion. Imagine. But this is a real reverse for me. Usually my relationships don't work because other people, especially the ladies, don't think they're good enough for me. Fact is, you're about the first woman I've met in some time who struck me as having real brains. [*Pause, with sustained eye contact.*] You don't mind a compliment, do you?

Practitioner (P): No, Dexter, I don't, I appreciate it. Tell me, though, in your relationship with Frank Noon, what sorts of things did you do to get to know him better?

    D (after recounting a litany of things he did to ingratiate himself to Dr. Noon): . . . Frank just turned out to be a loser, I guess. I certainly was the most caring, helpful friend he'd ever had. I felt sorry for him—you know, his wife had just died and all. He said I was pressing him too much, you know, spending too much time with him. That's stupid. I just tried to fit him into my busy schedule. Maybe he was just afraid of friendship. Who knows?

    P: You talk about the efforts you took in Dr. Noon's case as if they were exceptional for you. Yet, if I remember correctly, you did similar things for Sally Bates and Joanne Hook.

    D: Noon was different. He could have helped me in my career. He's an important guy, you know. [*Annoyed.*] Don't you see the difference, Doc? With the gals, it was hormones. [*He laughs nervously.*] With Noon, it was kind of like business.

    P: What I mean, Dex, is that you talked about the letdown you felt when Dr. Noon ended your relationship, and it sounded to me as though you felt the same way when Sally broke up with you. There seems to be a certain loneliness that's at work here.

    D: You know, I get sick to my stomach thinking about all this. I don't feel real good right now. Maybe you're right. Maybe I'm just too sensitive, too caring. It just makes a wreck of me. Did I tell you about the headaches?

    P: No, and we'll certainly talk about them. I'm willing to wait until you feel better, Dex. [*Pause.*] I feel badly that this all has upset you. However, I think there is a pattern here that we can begin to explore. It's one that seems to hurt you a great deal.

    D: Don't worry, Doc. I won't fold. You've got to have guts, as the old man would say.

    P: I'm not sure what you mean by that, Dex.

    D: Well, if I got one thing from my father, it was the ability to stand on my own two feet. Sometimes I lose control, but . . .

Evaluation

Time-limited dynamic psychotherapy is an answer to a rather challenging question. Can an effective therapy be developed that is: (1) true to the insights of Freud and psychoanalytic theory; (2) capable of doing justice to the complexities of intrapsychic and interpersonal life; (3) parsimonious in relation to time, money, and personnel; and (4) based on and continually refined through solid research?

TLDP, Freud, and psychoanalysis   TLDP is clearly a form of psychoanalysis. And, certainly, psychoanalysis provides an intriguing picture of the human psyche. Yet, is psychoanalysis a profound expression of the whys of human behavior, or an imaginative but dated critique of Victorian mores? Strupp accepts much of Freud's description of human personality as timeless and accurate, but at the same time, he views it as dynamic—that is, alive and in constant development. One of TLDP's key developments is its new understanding of transference and countertransference, as well as of the role the practitioner can play in using these phenomena as vehicles for insight and behavior change. For some, this may appear to be a distortion of a basic psychoanalytic tenet. For others, it is a necessary and useful refinement.

The complexities of intrapsychic and interpersonal life TLDP is not a "cookbook" approach that offers a few techniques to which all human problems must be fitted. Rather, a reading of Strupp's work suggests that he is keenly aware of the uniqueness and resourcefulness of each individual. In TLDP, techniques are secondary to the practitioner's ability to develop a therapeutic alliance by maintaining empathy and promoting insight. Technical skills are tailored to the individual client and fine-tuned through careful supervision.

Still, it is surprising that TLDP uses none of the many behavior therapy techniques. Strupp and Binder (1984, p. 170n) acknowledge some similarities between TLDP and some of the more cognitive behavior therapy techniques, but none of the techniques are formally used. (This contrasts sharply with Wachtel's integrative psychodynamic therapy, a psychoanalytically oriented approach that has several striking similarities to TLDP, but that uses behavior therapy.)

Parsimonious use of time, money, and personnel At a time when only the well-heeled and the well-insured can begin to pay for long-term psychological services, it is more than idealism that has led many to try to shorten the typical intervention. Within the psychoanalytic framework, this is a particular challenge. Strupp and his colleagues appear to have identified at least some of the critical obstacles to making psychoanalysis both more accessible and more economical. It is worth noting, however, that Strupp does not suggest that TLDP is appropriate for everyone or that long-term therapy is no longer viable. Rather, the goal of TLDP is to make short-term therapy available to as many people as possible through careful research into those factors that make therapy effective.

Reliance on research Strupp (1981) has suggested that there are two basic research questions in psychotherapy: "Does it work?" and "Why does it work?" The first question is of the most practical and immediate importance and is often answered by comparing one technique with others in the treatment of a particular problem. The second question is more fundamental but more difficult to answer. The Vanderbilt studies are focused on identifying the factors that make all psychotherapeutic interventions work. TLDP has taken the preliminary answers to those research questions and given them expression in a time-limited format. Assuming that TLDP continues to reflect this ongoing research project and that the research continues to chip away at the second question, TLDP would seem to be one of the most promising developments in psychotherapy in the past several decades.

Adlerian Psychotherapy and Counseling

If you were an enthusiastic follower of the emerging discipline of psychoanalysis in the summer of 1911, you might have opened your copy of the official "newspaper" of the field, *Zentralblatt für Psychoanalyse,* only to find the following announcement from one of its editors: "I wish to bring to the attention of the readers of this periodical that I am resigning from the editorial staff. The publisher, Professor Freud, was of the opinion that such diverging views exist between him and me that a common publication of this periodical does not appear feasible. I have therefore decided to resign voluntarily (Orgler, 1972, p. 21).[5]

These were the words of Alfred Adler, one of the original group of physicians invited by Freud to investigate with him the mysteries of neurosis and the potential of psychoanalysis. Between 1902 and 1911, Adler was a regular member of Freud's "Wednesday evening" meetings, which eventually became the Vienna Psychoanalytic Society. By 1910, Adler was president of that society, but by 1911, he was out of the group, having formed one for *Individualpsychologie,* "individual psychology." Although the exact nature of Adler's role in the early days of psychoanalysis has been argued, Adler was clearly not a follower of Freud in the manner of other early analysts. Adler never submitted to psychoanalysis with Freud, something required of most in the circle. Further, though Adler apparently found Freud's ideas both exciting and challenging, he never absorbed them totally as his own. Rather, even during the meetings that centered on Freud, Adler focuses on his own ideas about neurosis and its treatment. At the end of their relationship, the two men shared little more than a fondness for cigars.

Although Adler's ideas have never been as revered or as vilified as Freud's, several of Adler's basic concepts now appear to be supported by research (Watkins, 1982), and some now consider Adler the "true father of modern psychotherapy" (Ellis, 1970). Adler was the first true psychologist of the ego or self and has therefore been a major neopsychoanalytic force (Marmor, 1972; Strephansky, 1983), as well as a strong influence on humanistic-existential psychology (Frankl, 1970; Maslow, 1970b). The cognitive approaches to behavior therapy, as described in Chapters 4 and 5, also acknowledge a debt to Adler's pioneering work (Ellis, 1970, 1971).

[5]Freud's biographer, Ernest Jones (1955), spent considerable time painting Freud as a man uninterested in making himself the center of the psychoanalytic world and exceptionally patient with Adler's differences with Freud's thinking (pp. 145–151). The letters between Freud and Jung suggest considerably more self-interest and less patience on Freud's part, however (Freud & Jung, 1974). The reader may recall a sampling of this in the section on Freud in Chapter 3. The Adlerian perspective on Adler's relationship to Freud is presented in Ansbacher's (1962) article, "Was Adler a Disciple of Freud?"

Historical and Theoretical Foundations

Historically and theoretically, the Adlerian approach to psychological intervention is neopsychoanalytic. Unlike many of the other neopsychoanalytic approaches, however, it has maintained a following beyond the death of its originator, and its influence on later approaches is acknowledged more and more.

The theory of personality that undergirds Adler's psychotherapeutic approach represents a confluence of developmental, social, and professional sources.[6]

Sources   Adler's childhood was an important source of his ideas. Few children come to know the frailty of life as directly as young Adler did. Born near Vienna in 1870, Adler was a sickly and awkward child who had numerous bouts with disease and injury. Compared to his older brother, he was inept and unattractive; compared to his younger brother, who had "dethroned" him from his position as favored child, he was less lovable. His personal feelings of inadequacy and jealousy led him to understand the role of *striving for superiority* and the influence of birth order in personality development. His physical vulnerability, along with the death of his older brother and his own near death, prompted his determination to conquer death and disease by becoming a physician. He received his medical degree from the University of Vienna in 1895 and began a private practice in ophthalmology. However, discouraged by his sense of helplessness in treating the then often fatal disease of diabetes, he switched his attention to neurology and, eventually, psychiatry (Orgler, 1972).[7]

A second source of Adler's theory and therapy was social, specifically, Marxist socialism. Although he was not involved in the economic and political aspects of the Marxist movement, he accepted the social and psychological mandates that argued for improved working conditions, prevention of medical and social problems, aid to the poor, and the emergence of a new social order (Ansbacher in Adler, 1964). Out of this social involvement came Adler's notion of *social interest,* to be described later, as well as a strong sense of the potential role of the practitioner in preventing rather than simply remediating psychological problems. To this end, Adler was instrumental in founding child guidance centers throughout Vienna, and he later influenced the establishment of similar centers throughout the world, including the United States, where he frequently visited and eventually settled in 1934 (Orgler, 1972).

---

[6]Omitted here is a discussion of the philosophical sources of Adler's ideas. Clearly, Adler was influenced by Nietzsche's thinking, but ultimately, Nietzsche's "superman" idea and Adler's less ambitious notions of superiority strivings differ dramatically. (Critics of Adler are happy to overlook the differences.) Linden (1984) has drawn several parallels between Adler's work and that of Epictetus and Spinoza (ideas as a source of emotional and behavioral problems), as well as that of Kant (the role of common sense). In the end, Linden concluded that Adler's ideas were well-grounded in the "profound thought of the past" (p. 267). Adler might have suggested that the more important thing is that they make sense and they work.

[7]Mosak and Kopp (1973) have applied Adler's approach to analyzing early recollections to the published recollections of Adler, Freud, and Jung. The results are fascinating.

A third source of Adler's thinking was Sigmund Freud. As noted earlier, Adler was part of Freud's circle for 8 years, gradually developing his own unique perspective on human personality. Despite the differences, Freud's thinking significantly influenced Adler and gave him a context for the development of his own perspective. On some issues, like the analysis of dreams, Adler suggested that he simply profited from Freud's mistakes (Ansbacher & Ansbacher, 1956, p. 358). On others, like the role of sexuality, he differed considerably. In the end, how essential was Freud's thinking to the development of Adler's thought? Was it merely coincidental to it? Such questions remain to be further debated by Freud's and Adler's followers.

In 1931, 6 years before his own death and 8 before Freud's, Adler published a paper on the differences between individual psychology and psychoanalysis (Ansbacher & Ansbacher, 1956, pp. 205–223). Though the fundamental intrapsychic dynamism at the heart of psychoanalysis remains intact within Adler's system, some essential differences exist: (1) The ego's role shifts from that of a skittish id gratifier to that of a purposeful and creative director of a person's strivings for significance in the real world, (2) the sexual nature of the Oedipus conflict is reframed in terms of striving for equal power with the parent, (3) the self-love of narcissism becomes the self-centeredness that accompanies feelings of inferiority, (4) intrapsychic dynamics are not held to be directed merely at tension reduction but at the accomplishment of some personal or social goal, and (5) dreams are considered to reveal more about a person's hopes for the future than about traumas of the past.

Indivisibility of purpose   Adler's view of personality is frequently described as holistic. At the risk of offending some, I suggest that this word has been so widely and imprecisely applied that it is now moribund. Adler's own choice of the term individual psychology was meant to express the *indivisibility of purpose* toward which all expressions of personality are directed (Adler, 1917). This formulation suggests some important and influential Adlerian convictions: (1) An individual's behavior is inseparable from its social context; (2) although it may be possible to talk about structures within an individual's personality (for example, the ego), personality is most accurately viewed as a *lifestyle* that always moves an individual toward some conscious or as yet unconscious goal, ideal, or purpose; and (3) awareness of an individual's subjective experience is the key to understanding and changing human behavior. One clarification is necessary concerning the expression "as yet unconscious." For Adler, the unconscious was not a cranny in the mind into which repressed material was stuffed; in fact, it was not a thing at all. Rather, Adler argued that unconscious ideas or feelings simply have not been clearly formulated in the person's conscious awareness. Unconscious ideas or feelings are not alien or opposed to what is conscious; they are simply unrealized or unarticulated (Ansbacher, 1982).

Inferiority and compensation   In *The Neurotic Constitution* (1917), one of Adler's earliest and most important works, he identified the role that *organ in-*

feriority, physical abnormalities or deficits, plays in the development of neurosis. Consider Adler's definition of psychology:

> Psychology is the understanding of an individual's attitude towards the impressions of his body. We can begin to see how the great differences between human minds come to arise. A body which is ill-suited to the environment and has difficulty in fulfilling the demands of the environment will usually be felt by the mind as a burden. For this reason children who have suffered from imperfect organs meet with greater hindrances than usual for their mental development. . . . Imperfect organs offer many handicaps but these handicaps are by no means an inescapable fate. If the mind is active on its own part and trains hard to overcome the difficulties, the individual may well succeed in being as successful as those who were originally less burdened. (Adler, 1931, pp. 34–35)

The *feelings of inferiority* that result from organ inferiority can also come from economic and social deprivations—in fact, "every life is fraught with a more or less deep feeling of inferiority when one sees the weakness and helplessness of every child" (Adler, 1927/1969, p. 65). An individual's feelings of inferiority can result in *compensation,* a biologically based striving for superiority, either in the area in which inferiority is felt or in some other area. For example, an individual who feels inferior because of an underdeveloped physique might engage in diligent bodybuilding and athletics. On the other hand, the same individual might throw all of his or her efforts into running a business. People may also combine various compensatory behaviors. Developmentally, the self we accept and present to the world is the product of numerous compensatory actions, personal strivings for superiority in the face of inferiority. Ideally, once the self is established and secure, we can turn from egocentric activities to the needs of society.

Social interest Following the lead of Rudolf Dreikurs (1953), an articulate proponent of Adler's thinking, we can identify both subjective and objective elements in the expression of social interest. First, "social interest is expressed subjectively in the consciousness of having something in common with other people and of being one of them" (p. 5). Second, expressed objectively, social interest produces the "good comrade," characterized by a "readiness to demand less than he offers" (p. 6). This consciousness and the behaviors that flow from it may begin as a commitment to a club, neighborhood, or nation, but ideally they grow to encompass all humanity, with the individual partaking in an awareness of "co-humanness" and participation in humankind's striving for perfection (Adler, 1964, pp. 39–40).

Adler viewed social interest as an innate potential that must be consciously developed (Ansbacher, 1968). Further, he saw all psychopathological conditions as manifestations of conflicts between the individual and the social obligations of day-to-day living (Dreikurs, 1963).

Neurosis and its treatment Although Adler and his followers have applied their therapy to most forms of maladaptive behavior, as with most psychoanalytic and neopsychoanalytic work, most theoretical and therapeutic efforts have focused on neurotic behavior. The negative feelings that predispose an individual to a neurotic life-style can come from three developmental factors: (1) actual organ inferiority, (2) childhood neglect or rejection, or (3) childhood pampering. The idea that neglect or rejection can provide fertile ground for neurosis was (and is) widely accepted. However, the further Adler lived into the 20th century, the more he emphasized childhood pampering as a source of neurotic adulthood. One of Adler's more succinct definitions describes neurosis as "the natural, logical development of an individual who is comparatively inactive, filled with a personal, egocentric striving for superiority, and is therefore retarded in the development of his social interest, as we find regularly among the more passive pampered styles of life" (Ansbacher & Ansbacher, 1956, p. 241).[8]

While the behavioral manifestations of neurosis may be quite varied, at the core is a fundamental disparity between self-centered strivings for superiority and actual accomplishments. As Dreikurs (1953) put it, "The lives of neurotics are full of contradictions between wishes and actions" (p. 60). Adler argued that the neurotic's withdrawal from the true problems of life is the product of vanity. Such an individual follows a private logic, eschewing the benefits that come from sharing one's view with others. The common view shared by those who live more normally in the world would be at great odds with the neurotic's private logic and would force her or him to reconsider and adjust (Adler, 1964, pp. 110–111). Put another way, the neurotic lacks what for Adler is one of the most critical human qualities: *common sense.* For Adler, common sense is the greatest expression of human reason, and he defined it "as all those forms of expression and as the content of all behavior which we find beneficial to the community" (Ansbacher & Ansbacher, 1956, p. 149). The vanity of the neurotic prevents him or her from behaving in accordance with common sense, and this, in turn, discourages the neurotic. The purpose of psychological intervention is to dispel the neurotic's discouragement and promote common sense.

The Process of Intervention

Successful Adlerian intervention changes behavior by focusing on the client's thinking; changes in behavior result from changes in the goals the client sets (Dreikurs, 1963). The client is assumed to be capable of creative thinking, of making and remaking decisions, and, faced with the truth about the limited ways in which he or she reasons, of changing his or her behavior. When the objective of the intervention is to change inappropriate goals in the immediate situation, it is called counseling; when the objective is to change the client's life-style and personality, it is called psychotherapy (Nikelly, 1971, p. 27).

The process of Adlerian intervention includes the following stages: (1) establishing rapport between the client and the practitioner, (2) assessing the cli-

[8]Ansbacher, Ansbacher, Shiverick, and Shiverick (1966) have done a fascinating Adlerian interpretation of the pampered development of Lee Harvey Oswald, the alleged assassin of President Kennedy. It is interesting to contrast it with Freudian interpretations.

ent's life-style, (3) generating insight into the client's mistaken cognitions and the resulting maladaptive behaviors, and (4) effecting changes in the behavior by encouraging the client to act on alternative ways of thinking.[9]

Establishing rapport The key to effective Adlerian counseling and psychotherapy is the establishment of a caring and trusting partnership between the client and practitioner. Establishing rapport is a process characterized by mutually determined goals, confidentiality, and respect for the client's ability to ultimately direct his or her own life (Dinkmeyer, Pew, & Dinkmeyer, 1979).

The most essential component of Adlerian interventions, especially of establishing rapport, is *encouragement.* Practitioners of Adlerian counseling and psychotherapy begin with the assumption that the client is experiencing a fundamental discouragement, a sense of personal powerlessness akin to the demoralization described earlier (see Chapter 2). Encouragement involves accepting the client as is and focusing on the client's assets rather than on liabilities. Behavior change is a by-product of changes in the client's opinion of him- or herself; the practitioner therefore acts as a continual, consistent source of increasingly vigorous (but not vehement) encouragement. The ultimate aim of the encouragement is to get the client to accept responsibility for living, to share and analyze his or her private logic, and to decide to change self-defeating behaviors (see Nikelly & Dinkmeyer, 1972).

Assessment Understanding the client's life-style is the key to engendering insight that leads to behavior change. The client's life-style is her or his basic orientation toward life, a cognitive framework or plan within which specific behaviors are selected to deal with the demands of living (Mosak, 1972). Understanding this life-style entails examining the client's past, present, and future.

The major factors to be assessed in relation to the client's past are: (1) the family constellation, (2) birth order, (3) the family atmosphere, and (4) early recollections. *Family constellation* refers to the "socio-psychological configuration of a family group" (Shulman & Nikelly, 1972, p. 35). The family constellation includes descriptions of each person in the family, their respective personalities, their relationships with each other, and the dynamics of interpersonal power and influence. *Birth order* is part of the family constellation. Adlerians argue that children in the same family are born into very different psychological environments depending on the order in which they are born (ordinal position), the interval between siblings, and the strengths and weaknesses of fellow siblings (Shulman & Mosak, 1977). An individual's birth order is an important determinant of later behavior. Adler identified five basic positions:

---

[9]Although Adler never developed a road map for the process of intervention, Dreikurs (1956) described four overlapping stages typically involved in all interventions, and Dinkmeyer, Pew, and Dinkmeyer (1979) have suggested four goals or objectives with corresponding stages. Despite some rhetorical differences, these two descriptions are basically the same. The stages presented here have been distilled from those sources.

firstborn, second child, middle child, youngest child, and only child. Different personality characteristics and interpersonal behaviors are attributable to each of these positions (Perlin & Grater, 1984). The *family atmosphere* is the general tone or theme that colors all family activities. Some of the possible family atmospheres are: rejecting, authoritarian, overprotective, materialistic, disparaging, disorderly, or overly orderly (Dewey, 1972; Dinkmeyer, Pew, & Dinkmeyer, 1979). The eliciting of *early recollections* in the assessment process is really a conversational projective test (Nikelly & Verger, 1972) that can be used in conjunction with other, more traditional measures (Barrett, 1983). In asking the client to recall early events as completely as possible, the practitioner is looking for themes that reveal the client's inner life. Early memories are not sole determinants of behavior but rather provide glimpses into the events that helped shape the client's beliefs about life and its demands.

The major assessment issues in the client's life-style from the present and the future life are linked: private logic and goal recognition. As noted earlier, based on family and other social interactions, each individual develops a personal way of perceiving the world complete with personal goals for the future and the means for achieving them. Normally, one's private logic is continually revised through interaction with others, so common sense interrupts any irrationality that may exist in one's private logic. Therefore, one's goals are realistic and one attains personal satisfaction. However, when an individual's goals are the product of completely private logic, largely unchecked by the common sense of others, attaining those goals is an impossible and painful process. The client experiences the pain of the struggle but is unaware of the private logic and misguided goals underlying it. The practitioner generates insight into these unconscious thoughts.

Insight   Dewey (1984) described Adlerian counseling and psychotherapy as a cognitive therapy in which emotions and actions are assumed to be under the control of thoughts. Thus, in Adlerian interventions, the client comes to recognize that faulty ways of thinking have resulted in unrealistic goals and that the behaviors directed at attaining those goals are self-defeating (Dinkmeyer, Pew, & Dinkmeyer, 1979). Insight is an interpersonal achievement involving both encouragement and confrontation. The general tone of encouragement set during the rapport-building early sessions allows the practitioner to confront the client about her or his goals and behavior. The process of confrontation may be quite argumentative, but the practitioner maintains a fundamental respect for the client's own value and resources (Dreyfus & Nikelly, 1972). The insight that comes from encouragement and confrontation must always lead to changes in behavior.

Behavior change   Adlerian interventions are fundamentally action-oriented. In early stages of the intervention, the practitioner reveals failed patterns of thinking, feeling, and acting. Changing these patterns begins with the client establishing new, more realistic goals. With the help of the practitioner, the client then decides what behaviors will help him or her attain those goals. In one situation, the client may be encouraged to overcome patterns of interpersonal avoidance and to develop new social skills to be practiced immediately in real situations (Nikelly & O'Connell, 1972). In another situation, the client may be taught to overcome disabling emotions by replacing self-defeating cognitive statements with more adaptive ones (for example, replacing "I can't help the way I feel" with "I can decide the way I feel") (Dewey, 1984).

As the client gradually sets and attains goals that have been shaped with the help of commonsense feedback from the practitioner and others, social interest becomes possible. The client not only functions in a self-satisfying manner but becomes a force for good in the human community.

Sample Session

Below is an exchange from an imaginary session with our current client, Dexter Drudge. The reader should be alert for: (1) the self-centeredness of the client, (2) encouragement and confrontation from the practitioner, (3) the focus on action, and (4) the push for social interest. For the sake of our discussion, let us assume that Dexter ended up seeing Dr. Jerry Glück, an Adlerian practitioner, instead of Dr. Merelove. Dr. Glück has listened to Dexter's stories of rejection and spent several sessions finding out about Dexter's family and early recollections. He has learned that Dexter was the second of four children, with a brother just 2 years his senior. Dexter's mother spoiled him terribly, clearly favoring him over his older brother. Dexter recalled how he would set up situations in which his older brother would get punished for what Dexter had done. Dexter's father could be very strict and demanding and generously rewarded achievement in school. Dex's brother was a top student and often did better than Dex. Dexter has admitted to Dr. Glück that at work he feels like he is "always running but never catching up," a fact that Dr. Glück has related to Dexter's position as second child. His possessiveness of others, Dr. Glück feels, has something to do with the total control Dexter once enjoyed over his mother's affections. We join an early therapy session already in progress:

> *Dexter (D):* It just doesn't make any sense, Dr. Glück. I mean, I'm smart, attractive, make a good salary, you know, and all the women ever say is that I'm smothering them. I'm just trying to be a gentleman, you know. The days of chivalry are gone, I guess.
>
> *Practitioner (P):* It occurs to me, Dex, that you're being very unrealistic about this. You seem to believe that everyone else can see your sincerity, generosity, and gentleness, but some others may see you as pushy or overbearing. It may simply be a case of "too much, too soon" in those relationships.
>
> *D:* It's real hard for me to see that. I work very hard at those relationships when they come along. You know, I don't just jump into relationships. There have been months when I've avoided them altogether, waiting for the perfect one to come along.

P: You seem to think of yourself as a sort of Grand Prize—a gift of incredible value that others should want on whatever terms you decide.

D: I've never thought of it quite that way, Dr. Glück, but maybe that is part of the way I think about it.

P: What I mean, Dex, is that you think about yourself in grandiose terms at times, seeing yourself as superior to others. In terms of your feelings, though, you're afraid. You work very hard so you can overcome these feelings of inferiority, but the feelings are still there. You're still running hard but never catching up. Tell me, Dex, is that what you really feel at times: inadequate, inferior?

D [*uncomfortable silence*]: You're right, I guess. Sometimes all my drive is just a front. There are times when I can't seem to stop thinking about me. Then, when I go to do something—ask someone for a date or something—I kill the whole thing. Something's screwed up in me, that's for sure.

P: Dex, that's a terribly difficult admission to make, I know, and I feel honored to be trusted with that. I am confident you can get beyond the self-defeating ways you have been thinking. I think you can begin to move in several important directions, doing things that will make your life much happier.

D: You mean asking more women out for dates? You know, to get over my fears. Maybe I'll get one relationship to work.

P: Yes, that will certainly be a first step, but there are also some challenges I would like to present you with. I'd like you to give some serious thought to using some of your enormous talent in some volunteer work at the Youth Center, and . . .

Evaluation

Adler's approach to counseling and psychotherapy is as old as psychoanalysis and remains as alive today as ever. Despite a recent resurgence in interest in Adler's work, however, the vitality of Adlerian counseling and psychotherapy is not presently evident in the number of exclusive adherents among practitioners. In fact, of the over 400 clinical and counseling psychologists who responded to D. Smith's (1982) survey of practitioners, less than 3% described themselves as "Adlerians." Rather, Adler's approach lives on in two additional and quite substantive ways: (1) through intentional and accidental integration of his ideas and techniques into other approaches to counseling and psychotherapy (for example, in rational-emotive therapy), and (2) through the application of his ideas and techniques in the work of eclectic practitioners.

Several of Adler's ideas appear to be almost ubiquitous among a large number of practitioners. These ideas include: (1) the primacy of cognition, (2) the role of social interest in countering self-centeredness, and (3) the role of encouragement in restoring a client's sense of power.

The primacy of cognition For Adlerians, cognition is the primary behavioral process. Maladaptive behavior is the product of faulty thinking. The deliberate and purposeful change of conscious thought is at the core of all effective interventions. Historically, practitioners have been tied to one of two quite different ideas: (1) that conscious cognition matters much less than unconscious cognition, as proposed by psychoanalysis, or (2) that cognition per se is relatively unimportant when it comes to changing human behavior, as proposed by behaviorism. Curiously enough, various forms of psychoanalysis are now preoccupied with the conscious mind, and contemporary behavior therapy could be called cognitive therapy with few eyes batted.

Social interest and self-centeredness   One of Adler's most important insights has to do with the self-centeredness inherent in neurosis. Of course, he shares the stage with Freud in this regard, since Freud also understood the role of narcissism in neurosis. The critical difference, however, is Adler's challenge to the client to battle self-centeredness by choosing to do something for society, choosing to display social interest. In this regard, contributions to the well-being of society are not unconscious redirections of libido but conscious choices made by a reforming neurotic. The key importance of the client's becoming absorbed in things other than the self is recognized in more than a few contemporary approaches to counseling and psychotherapy.

The role of encouragement   Powerlessness is at the heart of all psychological problems, regardless of what other symptoms might be present. The Adlerian emphasis on overcoming powerlessness through encouragement is almost universally accepted by contemporary practitioners.

Perhaps there are so few Adlerians because we are all adlerians.

Transactional Analysis

Consider the following stories:

> An eight-year-old boy, vacationing at a ranch in his cowboy suit, helped the hired man unsaddle a horse. When they were finished, the hired man said, "Thanks, cowpoke!" To which his assistant answered: "I'm not really a cowpoke, I'm just a little boy." (Berne, 1957, p. 611)

> A 38-year-old man, practicing law in a three-piece suit, spoke convincingly to the jury for his client. When the trial was finished, his client said to him, "Thanks, Mr. Defense Attorney!" To which the lawyer answered: "I'm not really an attorney, I'm just a little boy."

The first version of the story was told to psychiatrist Eric Berne by a lawyer he was treating for a gambling addiction. The second version of the story is an imaginary exchange expressing how that lawyer really experienced himself when he was practicing law. He saw himself as a little boy, someone simply playing the role of lawyer. Is the little girl or boy you once were still living in you, shaping your choices, coloring your emotions, and speaking for you so you can get life's goodies? And after all those years of being "raised" and "razed" by your parents, do you still hear their voices forbidding those goodies, insisting on hygiene, planting guilt, and making promises? Even today, if you listen carefully to yourself, can you hear the child in you delight, manipulate, baffle, or anger other people? Do you sometimes hear your parents speaking through you as you comfort, cajole, placate, and admonish others? How you answer such questions will determine whether you find *transactional analysis* self-evident or far-fetched. Certainly, its ideas are fascinating. They are part of the legacy of a creative and influential practitioner, Eric Berne, and they are largely built on the contributions of two giants: Freud and Adler.

Historical and Theoretical Foundations

In 1964, a relatively unknown California psychiatrist by the name of Eric Berne published a book entitled *Games People Play*. It was intended as a follow-up to an earlier book directed at practitioners, but it became a smashing best-seller. The cognoscenti of the day became conversant in the jargon of transactional analysis, or "TA," as it became known. People began talking about their "Child," "Parent," "Adult," "games," "rackets," and "scripts." The diagrams, made up of circles and arrows, that Berne used to explain interactions between people became increasingly commonplace in practitioners' offices, classrooms, management seminars, and Sunday School classes (see Figure 7.1 for a sampling). A popular song even bore the same name as Berne's book. The whole phenomenon became even more widespread with the publication of Thomas Harris's *I'm OK–You're OK: A Practical Guide to Transactional Analysis* in 1967. Harris, who had worked with Berne since 1960, was an experienced psychiatrist who was able to translate some of TA's more difficult concepts into popular language. Harris also introduced TA's four *life positions*: I'm OK–You're OK, I'm not OK–You're OK, I'm OK–You're not OK, and I'm not OK–You're not OK. The four life positions were added to the other terminology and diagrams of a uniquely American "pop psychology."[10]

Unlike other casualties of the 1960s and 1970s, TA survived popularity and is generally listed with the other major approaches to counseling and psychotherapy. It is unique among the other approaches, since it is generally viewed as a group treatment rather than an individual one. However, many of TA's ideas and techniques are used eclectically in individual intervention, and TA can be used on an individual basis as preparation for or follow-up to group treatment.

Eric Berne   As noted, transactional analysis was developed by Eric Berne (1910–1970). Berne was Canadian by birth and education (born in Montreal;

[10]Harris's book was social and political as well as psychological. It was published during the years of the heaviest U.S. bombing of Vietnam, and the dust jacket of the hardback edition of the book bears the three circles that stand for TA's Parent, Adult, and Child, with a most curious addition to the center, Adult circle—the international peace symbol. At the time, that symbol was usually intended as a protest against American policies in Vietnam.

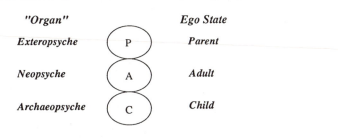

A: The Three Ego States and their Corresponding "Organs"

"Organ"		Ego State
Exteropsyche	P	Parent
Neopsyche	A	Adult
Archaeopsyche	C	Child

B: Descriptive Aspects of the Personality

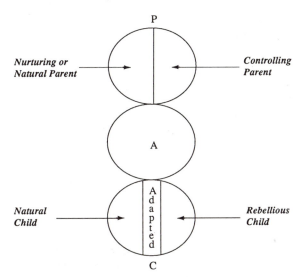

P

Nurturing or
Natural Parent — Controlling
Parent

A

Natural
Child — Adapted — Rebellious
Child

C

Figure 7.1 *TA's ego states; Phase 1 developments* (A: From Berne, 1961; B: From Berne, 1972, p. 13)

M.D. from McGill University) but became an American citizen in 1941 following his psychiatric residency at Yale. He worked as a clinical assistant in psychiatry at Mt. Zion Hospital in New York, trained at the New York Psychoanalytic Institute, and later served in the military during the war. In 1946, he established a private practice in San Francisco, where he trained further in psychoanalysis under Erik Erikson at the San Francisco Psychoanalytic Institute. His unorthodox views cost him full recognition in psychoanalytic circles, however, and he maintained a nonhostile distance from the analytic establishment. Berne was a prolific writer and a man of considerable influence among his peers. He began promoting his theory and procedures at seminars in the 1950s and published his early work on TA in a number of journal articles and in a book called *Transactional Analysis in Psychotherapy* (1961). Following *Games People Play* in 1964, he wrote *Group Treatment* (1966) and *What Do You Say*

After You Say Hello? (1972), a posthumously published work that shows the full scope of his thinking. By the time of his death in 1970, he had founded the *Transactional Analysis Journal* and the International Transactional Analysis Association, a group of professionals and nonprofessionals with membership in the thousands. Both the journal and the organization continue to exist today (Peyser, 1984).

Although TA depended largely on the clinical experience of its practitioners for its development, it did not emerge in a theoretical vacuum. Not only does TA owe an enormous debt to Freud and, to a lesser extent, Adler, but Berne integrated many ideas from his extensive reading in communications theory, systems theory, and cybernetics, as well as neurophysiology, especially from the work of neurosurgeon Wilder Penfield (1952). Otherwise, TA's theoretical development has been straightforward and can be divided into historical phases. Dusay (1977) has described four such phases: Phase 1, Ego States (1955–1962); Phase 2, Transactions and Games (1962–1966); Phase 3, Script Analysis (1966–1970); and Phase 4, Action (1970–1977).

Phase 1: ego states   The Nevada lawyer who felt like a little boy even when he was successfully practicing law and whose story was quoted earlier was one of Berne's early cases, and the treatment of his gambling problem helped Berne develop his understanding of ego states (Berne, 1957, 1977). Berne observed that the lawyer was at once a rational person and an irrational one, at once confident and insecure. This duality exhibited itself in a number of ways. For example, if the lawyer was winning in one casino, he would take a shower before going to another as a means of washing away the guilt he felt about gambling. He avoided getting depressed about losses by using an unusual form of reasoning: If he set out with $100 and lost $50, he would tell himself, "I was prepared to lose $100 tonight and I've only lost $50, so I'm really $50 ahead and I needn't be upset" (Berne, 1977, p. 99). Berne suggested that two distinct types of reasoning were going on here, two different, conscious ways of assessing the world. At times, the lawyer viewed the world rationally and confidently. At other times, he was a child again, caught up in self-centeredness and insecurity. Berne argued that these were both conscious states, aspects of the ego, and that psychological conflict must exist in and its treatment must address these differing and real aspects of ego rather than unconscious conflicts among the id, ego, and superego.

Berne described the structure of the human personality in relation to three "organs": the *exteropsyche,* the *archaeopsyche,* and the *neopsyche.* These structural components manifest themselves as three corresponding conscious *ego states* (see Figure 7.1.A). Unlike the id, ego, and superego of psychoanalysis, which only give rise to conscious states and which are known only inferentially, an ego state is a "consistent pattern of feeling and experience directly related to a corresponding pattern of behavior" (Berne, 1972, p. 444). At any given moment, each individual has three such ego states available to consciousness, the Parent, the Child, and the Adult.

The Parent, or the exteropsychic ego state, is "borrowed from parental figures" and reproduces the thoughts, feelings, attitudes, and actions of those figures. Depending on the actual parenting the child received during the first 6 years of life, the Parent that expresses itself may be either a *Nurturing* or *Natural Parent* or a *Controlling Parent*. These terms are self-descriptive, but it is important to recognize that the type of Parent that a child internalizes (or more technically, *introjects*) comes from the complete constellation of encouragement, prohibitions, nurturance, restrictions, and so forth, she or he received. The Parent that emerges from this experience, whether nurturing or controlling, is always with us, always capable of being heard in the conscious mind (see Figure 7.1.B).

The Child, or the archaeopsychic ego state, manifests the thoughts, feelings, attitudes, and actions of the individual as she or he was as a child. The Child is considered an "archaic" ego state; that is, the behaviors it produces are "relics" of childhood. The Child is not the libidinal "cauldron" represented by the id, nor is it "infantile" or "childish" in the usual senses of those words. Rather, the Child is another way each of us has of experiencing the world, another way of acting in relationship to the world, based on our developmental experiences. The Child expresses itself in one of three ways: (1) as the Natural or Free Child, (2) as the Adapted Child, or (3) as the Rebellious Child. The *Natural* or *Free Child* is the expressive, spontaneous, and creative ego state that has not been overly corrupted by parental admonitions. The *Adapted Child* is the child who has learned how to conform to the demands of parental figures. Berne observed that children can misunderstand the intention of their parents' communication because children are more likely to speak "Martian" than "Earthian." Martian represents the nativistic frame of mind—understanding the world without the preconceptions culture provides during childhood. Earthian is the type of communication parents eventually teach us, complete with preconceived ways of viewing the world. Before children replace Martian with Earthian, they may misassess the intent of some parental messages. For example, a man with a serious drinking problem recalled being given the following Earthian message from Mom when caught sniffing, as a 6-year-old boy, at an open bottle of whiskey: "You're too young to be drinking whiskey." His Martian interpretation, available for later use, was: "When the time comes to prove you're a man, you'll have to drink whiskey" (Berne, 1972, p. 100). Clearly, the intent of the parent matters little in comparison with the child's Martian interpretation during the "plastic years" between birth and 6. The *Rebellious Child* does not conform to the parent but resists restrictions and prohibitions. To each adult at any given time, one of these versions of the Child ego state is available.

The Adult ego state is likened to a computer that directs behavior on the basis of realistically calculated possibilities and probabilities. It is the objective executive, assessing environmental demands and, when necessary, mediating between the Child and the Parent. The Adult, however, can be caught in conflict between the Child and the Parent, and either can *contaminate* its boundaries. Psychopathology involves a loss of control on the part of the Adult to an irrational Parent, Child, or both.

Phase 2: transactions and games   As its name states, transactional analysis involves the observation and evaluation of *transactions,* the most basic units of social intercourse. A transaction consists of stimuli and responses, and every dialogue between people can be examined as to the type and qualities of its transactions. All human social interaction is motivated by the need for *strokes,* attention or recognition that is essential for healthy functioning. In TA, any transaction or pattern of transaction between two individuals is assumed to involve the Parent, Child, or Adult of each. Transactions are typically visualized and graphically represented using circles, lines, and arrows. Many kinds of transactions and parallel graphics are described in the TA literature, but some of the basic ones described by Berne are presented in Figure 7.2.

When the stimulus and response of a transaction parallel each other and thus do not distress either individual, a *complementary transaction* has taken place. As illustrated in Figure 7.2.A, the lines representing the stimulus and the response do not cross. This type of transaction can last for a long time, whether as a single conversation between two individuals or as an enduring pattern of transaction. There are 9 types of complementary transactions, and in each, the transaction can endure as long as neither of the parties changes the nature of the transaction.

Crossed transactions occur when the stimulus and the response are not parallel. This causes distress, and communication in this transaction is not likely to endure. There are 72 separate types of crossed transactions, but 4 basic crossed types are worth noting (Berne, 1972). As illustrated in Figure 7.2.B, a Type I (Adult-Adult–Child-Parent) transaction involves an Adult-to-Adult stimulus and a Child-to-Parent response. In therapy, this is a transference reaction, in which the practitioner's Adult-Adult transaction ("Tell me about your week") is met with a Child-Parent reaction ("You're always prying into my personal stuff"). A Type II (Adult-Adult–Parent-Child) involves an Adult-to-Adult stimulus and a Parent-to-Child response. In therapy, this is a countertransference reaction, in which the client's Adult-Adult stimulus ("I got fired from my job") is met with a Parent-Child response ("You must have done something to upset your boss"). A Type III (Child-Parent–Adult-Adult) transaction (not shown in Figure 7.2.B), referred to as the "exasperating response," occurs when a person who seeks sympathy or understanding is met with facts. In this case, a plea for a nurturing parent ("I feel really awful today, and I think I've got a fever") is met with a matter-of-fact adult statement ("One out of every four people in this office had a cold last week"). A Type IV (Parent-Child–Adult-Adult) transaction, called the "impudence response," occurs when a person makes a Parent-Child statement expecting compliance ("No doubt, you'll want to accompany me to the ballet next Saturday") but gets a factual (Adult-Adult) response ("I'll be out of town for the weekend") that is interpreted as flippant.

A: Complementary Transactions, AA-AA and PC-CP

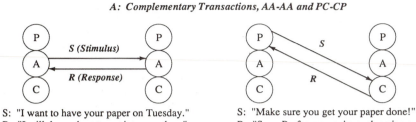

S: "I want to have your paper on Tuesday."
R: "I will do my best to get it to you then."

S: "Make sure you get your paper done!"
R: "Sure, Professor, you're such a nice guy."

B: Crossed Transactions, Type I (AA-CP) and Type II (AA-PC)

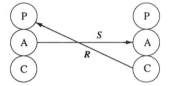
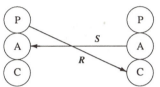

S: "I want to have your paper on Tuesday."
R: "Gee, don't you like our class, Dr. Smith?"

S: "Dr. Smith, I'll have my paper done by Monday."
R: "An early paper isn't going to impress me."

C: Duplex Transaction: A Game

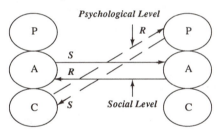

Social Level
S: "You can turn in your paper as late as Wednesday."
R: "I'll do my best to get it there on Wednesday."

Psychological Level
S: "Idiot. Later than Wednesday and you fail."
R: "You wouldn't flunk me, would you?"

Figure 7.2 *Transactions and games between a professor and student; Phase 2 development*

Thus far, we have been discussing specific isolated transactions between individuals, but in day-to-day living, most transactions take place in series and represent different forms of social activity with different ways of structuring time. Berne (1964, 1972) has identified six forms of social activity, ways of structuring time: (1) withdrawal, (2) intimacy, (3) rituals, (4) activities, (5) pastimes, and (6) games. *Withdrawal* and *intimacy* are at the two extremes of the social interaction continuum. Withdrawal involves breaking off the transaction; intimacy, the most rewarding form of interaction, involves the honest sharing of feelings, thoughts, and mutual experience. Life is directed toward the attainment of intimacy. A *ritual* is a highly stylized complementary transaction that may be either formal (as in a ceremony) or informal (the exchange of greetings and brief conversation between two people meeting on the street). The exchange of important information is not key in rituals. Rather, rituals serve to provide each participant with strokes in the form of mutual attention and recognition. *Activities* are forms of Adult-Adult social interaction commonly known as work. Activities are dictated by external reality and follow a prescribed social structure. *Pastimes* are less structured and controlled by social realities. The banter that typifies parties is a pastime activity in which individuals who do not know each other question each other in appropriate ways to become better acquainted. Pastimes, however, can turn into *games* when the transactions take on an ulterior level of transaction.

A game is a series of *duplex* transactions that lead to negative consequences for one or both of the participants. When people communicate at more than one level at a time and when that communication leads to a *payoff* of bad feelings, then a game is taking place (Berne, 1972). People do not purposefully engage in games but are largely unaware of the other level of meaning. In Figure 7.2.C, we can see the disparity between the social level of communication, which appears to be at the Adult level, and the psychological level, which ends in an offended student and a frustrated professor. Games help us occupy our social time with minimum discomfort, but they eventually cause distress and do not lead to intimacy, because they are fundamentally lacking in honesty. One purpose of TA is to identify and change the games we have learned to play over the years. Berne and his colleagues have identified numerous games, giving them all descriptive names. A partial listing of the over 100 games in Berne's *Games People Play* (1964) includes: "Kick Me"; "Now I've Got You, You Son of a Bitch"; "Frigid Woman"; "Ain't It Awful"; "Why Don't You— Yes But"; "Rapo"; "Cops and Robbers"; and "Let's Pull a Fast One on Joey."

Phase 3: script analysis and life positions   During the 4 years before Berne's death, he and his colleagues began to ask where games come from and why people engage in them. Berne used the concept of the *script,* an idea strikingly similar to Adler's life-style, although Berne's notion is less encompassing. A script is an "ongoing program, developed in early childhood under parental influence, which directs the individual's behavior in the most important aspects of his life" (Berne, 1972, p. 418). A game is only part of a more comprehensive script, a "transference drama" split into acts (Berne, 1977, p. 156). Various "acts" may be repeated again and again, or the drama may take a lifetime. Without much attention to it, each of us lives out a variety of scripts, some of which inherently contradict one other. The living out of conflicting scripts can lead to psychological distress, as illustrated in Figure 7.3.

While Berne and other colleagues were working on script theory, Thomas Harris identified and described four basic life positions in *I'm OK—You're OK.* The scripts that people live out are expressions of life positions taken during the early years of life. The four basic positions are (Harris, 1969, p. 37–53):[11]

[11]In the recent *Staying OK.* (1986) Harris and Harris described only two life positions as critical: I'm Not OK–You're OK and I'm OK–You're OK. These two are emphasized because the critical decision about life position is made during the first or second year of life in a "world of

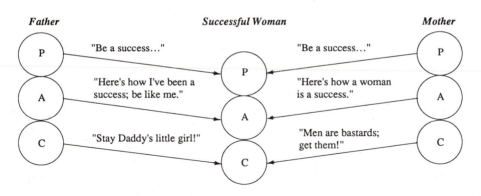

Figure 7.3 *Sample of script analysis. A successful businesswoman is troubled by doubts, guilt, and resentment. An evaluation of the scripts by which she has been operating in her career reveals that though she is motivated to succeed and expects rewards for it, she has learned two conflicting ways of behaving. From her father, she has learned a "dog-eat-dog" style. When she acts out that script, however, she feels guilty because it conflicts with her mother's script for success, which stereotypes successful women as guileful and manipulative. At the same time, the mother's Child-Child script, based on resentment about her own failure to succeed, contains a hostile antimale message. The father, despite encouraging her to succeed, and suggesting formidable strategies by which to succeed, still wants "Daddy's little girl." The woman's doubts, guilt, and resentment are thus the product of conflicting scripts that cannot successfully be played out at the same time.*

1. *I'm Not OK—You're OK:* Because each of us enters the world dependent, this is the universal position of early childhood. At the same time, because our physical and emotional needs are being met to some degree (through stroking), there is also "OK-ness" during this time. If this position continues and dominates, then the unconsciously written life script will confirm this position.

2. *I'm Not OK—You're Not OK:* In the absence of stroking from parents and significant others, the child may live out a script that is hostile and possibly self-destructive, destructive to others, or both.

3. *I'm OK—You're Not OK:* A child who is ill-treated or brutalized may come to see the parent or parents as not OK and, in an act of psychological defensiveness, may take the position "I'm OK by myself but not with them." Such an individual may act out a script characterized by distrust, suspiciousness, or even greater hostility to others.

4. *I'm OK—You're OK:* The first three positions are based on emotions and are unconscious. One of the three positions is firmly established in each of us by the age of 3. The final position, I'm OK–You're OK, is conscious, based on "thought, faith, and the wager of action" (p. 50). We choose this position in spite of the not-OK recordings from childhood. Living from this life

giants" (p. 4). The other two life positions, I'm Not OK–You're Not OK and I'm OK–You're Not OK, are seen as only variations on the two other positions.

position means rewriting other, less adaptive scripts. It means engaging in continual *redecision* about life's choices to reconcile the conflicting conscious life position and the programming left from early childhood.

The relative importance of scripts, script analysis, and life positions differs among practitioners of TA. Different schools of TA evaluate the utility of the concepts differently (Barnes, 1977).

Phase 4: action Dusay (1977) ended his tracing of TA's development with his own development of the *egogram*. We can bring our examination even more up to date following the lead of Corey (1986) in his discussion of Goulding and Goulding's (1979) version of TA, called *redecision therapy.*

The egogram is concerned with function rather than structure. Examples of egograms are shown in Figure 7.4. Egograms depict the amount of time and energy expended in each ego state. Since the egogram represents a closed system, changes in the amount of time and energy expended in one ego state will be reflected in changes in other ego states. The various techniques of TA are designed to get the client to expend more energy in psychologically productive combinations of ego states than in others. The ideal distribution of time and

A: The basic grid showing ego states that operate in all individuals at all times. Each ego state is understood as a psychological force influencing behavior.

Critical Parent (CP)	*Nurturing Parent* (NP)	*Adult* (A)	*Free Child* (FC)	*Adapted Child* (AC)

B: Four sample egograms built on the basic grid. A person with a "bell-shaped curve" egogram is well-balanced. A person with a "Don Juan" egogram has fun (high FC), tells people off (high CP), and doesn't care about their feelings (low NP). The "depressed" person's high CP and AC overcome resources that would help, and the "wallflower" worries about what others think (high AC).

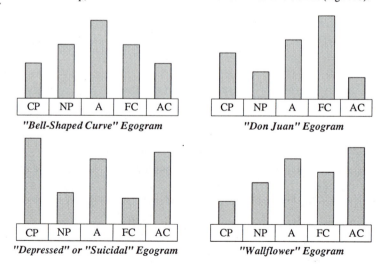

"Bell-Shaped Curve" Egogram

"Don Juan" Egogram

"Depressed" or "Suicidal" Egogram

"Wallflower" Egogram

Figure 7.4 *Egograms* (B: From Dusay & Dusay, 1984, p. 378)

energy in the ego states is represented by the bell-shaped curve egogram (Figure 7.4.B). An individual with such an egogram is continually capable of Adult-to-Adult transactions, is more likely to become a Nurturing Parent to another person than a Critical Parent, and exhibits the acceptance and aliveness of the Free Child more than the passivity and resentment of the Adapted Child.

One of the major schools in contemporary TA is known as the "redecision school" of Mary McClure Goulding and Robert L. Goulding (Barnes, 1977). In "classical" TA, which follows Berne's teachings, practitioners work largely at an intellectual level with the Parent and play a key role in identifying and changing scripts. The Gouldings believe that individuals make and can change their own scripts through redecision, an emotional, intellectual, and behavioral process that takes place in the Child with the support of the Adult and Parent. Because of its emphasis on self-direction, the redecision school of TA incorporates concepts and techniques from Gestalt therapy and other approaches. One of the most oft-cited contributions of the Gouldings (1979, pp. 34–36) is a list of injunctions beginning with "don't." These are messages to a child communicated by the Child ego state of an unhappy, angry, or frustrated parent. The basic list includes: don't, don't be, don't be close, don't be important, don't be a child, don't grow, don't succeed, don't be you, don't be sane, don't be well, don't belong. These injunctions can result in patterns of maladaptive behavior if the child decides to accept them. They can be changed later by identifying them and rejecting them.

. TA as it is practiced today takes advantage of the post-Berne contributions of many practitioners, especially Dusay and the Gouldings. The discussions that follow include some of their ideas and techniques.

The Process of Intervention

Although transactional analysis was designed to be used in small groups (seven to eight members), it is presently used with individuals, groups, and families, as well as in marathon sessions and as part of training programs in business, industry, and education. Its application may change in different settings; there are no rigid rules about how TA is to proceed. In fact, experimentation and integration with other approaches are encouraged (Dusay & Dusay, 1984).

Despite diversity in how TA is implemented, the practice of TA includes some universal elements. By design, TA is: (1) interactional, (2) didactic, (3) contractual, and (4) decisional. It is *interactional* because the client's growth develops out of a facilitative relationship with the practitioner, although the practitioner is not the cause of change but rather a "catalyzer of change" (Dusay & Dusay, 1984). In TA, the client is assumed capable of growing toward intimacy by identifying and changing patterns of self-defeating game playing, and the practitioner is assumed to facilitate that change by interacting with the client in ways that will help the client identify and change games. The interaction is frequently *didactic,* using learning tools such as various diagrams (for example, egograms) and a nontechnical vocabulary (for example, the Parent). The language of TA is easy to learn and use, and though it may appear simplistic, practitioners of TA contend that underlying that apparent simplicity are essential truths about human behavior. Practitioners of TA use the vocabulary and the various diagrams extensively and may communicate with clients by actually drawing the lines, circles, and grids on conveniently available blackboards. TA is also *contractual.* Early in the process, the client and practitioner meet "Adult to Adult" to establish mutual responsibilities and form a therapeutic alliance. Contracts with specific objectives are drawn up and reviewed on a regular basis. Contemporary TA is founded on the belief that bad decisions have brought the client to therapy and that good decisions will move the client toward well-being. This essential *decisional* quality to TA means that at each step of the treatment, the client is encouraged to change, to act in the face of what had appeared to be set patterns of game playing and script enactment.

Beyond these basic elements, TA's therapeutic process consists of: (1) *structural analysis,* (2) *transactional analysis,* and (3) *script analysis and redecision.* There is a natural progression through these stages of the process, although as stages, they are not entirely discrete.

Structural analysis   TA begins with teaching the client the language, concepts, and diagrams of TA. This is done very directly. Depending on the clinical setting, the client can learn through reading, lectures, workshops, or more casual interaction with the practitioner. The objective is to get the client to think in terms of the Parent, Child, and Adult, and to come to understand that present behavior is a product of patterns of stroke attainment established during childhood. TA is, therefore, especially attentive to how clients seek and receive strokes.

Transactional analysis   The actual analysis of transactions is at the core of TA, and after the client learns TA's basic language and theory, she or he is taught how to identify the various kinds of transactions. The transactions between client and practitioner become a microcosm for studying the client's transactions in everyday life, and when TA is used in a group setting, the variety of transactions that take place in the group provide a constant source of information about clients' transactions outside of treatment. Whether in group or individual therapy, a practitioner may interrupt an ongoing conversation and draw the client in to an Adult-Adult conversation so that they can talk about what has been happening and the client can understand the games being played. This technique is known as *crystallization.*

Of special interest in relation to the analysis of transactions is *game analysis.* Again, actual therapeutic sessions are an arena for understanding the games the client plays. In essence, game analysis involves recognizing *ulterior transactions,* in which overt messages conceal covert ones. For example, a male client may act in an arrogant, know-it-all manner that appears on the social level to suggest excessive self-confidence. In fact, however, the psychological message may be quite self-destructive; and the name of the game may really be "Kick Me." His hidden communication may be, "I'm a real pain in the extremity. Go ahead, kick me. Avoid me, call me arrogant. Go ahead, I've been a bad boy!" The practitioner's job is to help the client identify these games and rework them. The client may be asked to role-play a conversation using the Adult rather than the Child, to write and direct a psychodrama with members of the group in which the transactions are free of this game, or speak to an empty chair containing his or her highly critical parent. Several techniques are used by practitioners of TA to accomplish this end, but typically they involve confronting the client with the game and having her or him practice alternative patterns of transacting.

In TA, the client is assumed to be facing two major problems. First, the client is living out parental scripts that are self-defeating and that contain negative injunctions (for example, "don't succeed"). Second, the client is expending energy and time in ego states that are creating self-defeat and, thus, misery. The didactic component of TA has two sets of tools for understanding the effects scripts: circles-and-line diagrams (Figure 7.3) and egograms (Figure 7.4). Once the client has identified his or her scripts and misdirected energy through interaction with the practitioner and, possibly, with group members, change becomes a matter of relearning, rescripting specific decisions. TA has a number of techniques for enhancing the decision process, including:

1. *Counterinjunctions:* The client lives out a script with numerous behaviors and injunctions. For example, a young man was obsessed with the belief that he must kill himself because he had failed to pass the bar exam for the third time. The suicidal script came from childhood tauntings from his alcoholic father's Child that conveyed the message "better dead than a failure." The practitioner, after listening attentively, may forcefully present the following injunction: "You want to kill yourself but you may not! It is not permitted to do so!" This counterinjunction interrupts the script, presenting the client with a new imperative and possibly relieving the conflict.

2. *Egogram Energy Transfers:* Once the client and practitioner have graphed the client's typical behavior patterns in an egogram, the practitioner encourages the client to direct energy in new, more productive patterns. For example, Dusay and Dusay (1984) described a client named Fanny who was a "naughty little pest." She needed to develop her Free Child and her Nurturing Parent. In a group setting, Fanny was encouraged to engage in hugging exercises and exercises in which group members shared authentic positive statements.

3. *Redecision Scenes:* Goulding and Goulding (1979) use redecision scenes to change life scripts. The client and practitioner select a present, recent, long-past, or imaginary scene as a vehicle for freeing up the client's Child. As the scene is acted out, the client makes or remakes decisions about which scripts to live out and which to abandon. For example, a young woman who has internalized the messages "Don't grow up" and "Be a good little girl" may still

behave like a proper little girl with little or no enjoyment of life. She may imagine scenes between her mother and herself, engaging in a new dialogue in which she liberates her Free Child and rescripts her life so that Free-Child behaviors rather than Adapted-Child behaviors get the strokes.

Sample Session

Below is an exchange from an imaginary session with Dexter Drudge. Dexter is now in his fourth individual session with TA practitioner Dr. Frieda Freikinder, a psychiatrist. She is preparing Dexter to become part of a TA group. The reader should be alert for: (1) the use of the analysis of transactions within the therapy, (2) the use of the egogram, (3) the use of script analysis, and (4) the initiation of a redecision scene. We enter in the middle of the session.

> *Dexter (D):* Dr. Freikinder, those drawings are very helpful in getting me to see what is going on, but I just feel so lost when I think of them. I just can't seem to know what to do. If I didn't have you to help me, I think I'd be really lost.
>
> *Practitioner (P):* You can do it, Dexter, you know. You can change the way you communicate with other people. I'm sure you can. I've got confidence in you, Dex.
>
> *D:* Gee, I don't know. I always seem to be OK if people tell me what to do, but inside of me, I just feel like a hurt and angry little child.
>
> *P:* Let my Adult talk to your Adult, OK? In what you have been saying to me so far this session, your Child has been speaking, and my Parent has been answering. You tell me you are lost and hurt, and I try to help you. But when we keep this up for a long time, I get tired of being your Parent, and you get tired of being the Child. I get annoyed but can't seem to change it, and you get hurt and angry. This is the same pattern as in many of your other relationships.
>
> *D:* I see. On the surface, we're like a child and his parent, but underneath that, there's another set of messages that aren't nearly as friendly.
>
> *P:* Sure. You don't always want to be the Adapted Child, but you can't get out of that script because when you've been that way people have responded with strokes. Other people don't always want to be the Nurturing Parent, and when that begins to annoy them, their Critical Parent may take over.
>
> *D:* Yeah. And what goes on inside of me is also a battle. Remember my egogram—the worried Adapted Child and the Critical Parent both taking over parts of me. I remember, when I would talk to Dr. Frank Noon, I would be kind of coy, looking for attention from him. Then when he would disappoint me, I could almost hear my father's voice come out of my throat as I got angry at him for not paying enough attention.
>
> *P:* You've developed a script that says: "I can only get attention if I'm a nice little boy, doing everything exactly right, and staying

quiet. No one can love me, and if they love me it will only be because I am so nice, so quiet."

D: That's my Adapted Child saying what my father used to tell me.

P: Well, at least what you remember of what your father told you.

D: Right.

P: Let's try to enact an imaginary scene in which you and your father talk about this. Let's imagine that your father has just criticized you for not doing something he told you to do. Can you answer him and deal with him not as your Adapted Child but as your Free Child?

D: Yes. Father, I'm not perfect. I am going to make mistakes, and I'm going to have weaknesses. I want to be loved with those weaknesses, not in spite of them. There are lots of reasons why people can love me with my weaknesses, and I . . .

Evaluation

Transactional analysis was developed by a master practitioner, Eric Berne, and his writings evidence a comprehensive knowledge about and insight into the process of successful therapeutic intervention and the theories that underlie it. He created a system designed to be both simple and profound, accessible to all but fully understood and utilized only by the thoroughly trained practitioner. The TA that Berne developed has changed in many ways, and it is a matter of opinion whether those changes have been for good or ill. Regardless, TA is now clearly past its heyday. Has it outlived its usefulness? Is there anything about TA that deserves inclusion in the repertoire of the eclective practitioner?

It is difficult to assess the importance of transactional analysis at the present time. In D.Smith's (1982) survey of over 400 clinical and counseling psychologists, less than 1% identified TA as their basic theoretical orientation, and a survey of major American psychological and psychiatric journals between 1980 and 1986 indicates that what research is being done using TA is being published almost exclusively in a journal and newsletter dedicated entirely to TA. At the same time, TA continues to be included in all major textbooks in counseling psychology and in most in clinical psychology, and the International Transactional Analysis Association continues to have membership in the thousands. Three attributes of TA make it both appealing and a target of criticism: (1) its grounding in the psychoanalytic tradition, (2) the simplicity of its language and methods, and (3) its intuitive attractiveness.

Grounding in the psychoanalytic tradition Berne never denied his indebtedness to psychoanalysis. Berne was accused, however, of doing nothing more than giving the id the ego, and the superego new names—Child, Adult, and Parent—and of corrupting the sophistication of psychoanalytic theory. Berne tried to do what many other neopsychoanalytic practitioners did, namely, make psychoanalysis more interpersonal and less mysterious and inaccessible.

In doing so, Berne created a new therapy that looked for a new understanding and explanation of the psychological impact of the developmental years and, more specifically, of transference phenomena. In this regard, he is like many other psychoanalysts and neopsychoanalysts. However, Berne, and perhaps more cogently, his followers, never took up the task of generating scientific support for TA. The systematic and controlled studies that support Strupp's work, for example, are absent from the literature of TA. There now appears to be little interest in doing so.

Simplicity of language and methods   TA is relatively easy to use. A client can be taught about TA very directly and can learn its language and diagrams readily. Within a very short time, the client and the practitioner can be speaking a common language. Applied in a group, TA is able to bridge the awkwardness that exists when clients have different levels of sophistication regarding psychological terms and concepts. At the same time, the language of TA is heavily metaphorical. An individual does not in fact carry around a Critical Parent and a Free Child. Individuals are capable of remembering messages from their childhood, but no little persons dwell inside the human brain. In this respect, TA presents an enormous temptation to the practitioner. TA's very ease of use, coupled with the seemingly endless complexity of human behavior, could make it a vehicle for projection on the part of the practitioner. Rather than reflect what clients are experiencing in life, TA's language and concepts can become a template to which clients must fix their experience. This peril exists in all therapies, but when the language of the therapy relies on metaphor and lacks scientific support, the danger is especially real.

Intuitive attractiveness   What makes TA attractive to practitioners and clients alike is more than its apparent simplicity. We seem to relate intuitively to the idea that conflicting voices contribute to producing our behavior. TA emerged at a time when psychoanalysis was trying to convince us that what we were experiencing was unrelated to the real reasons for our behavior. TA, on the other hand, explained behavior in terms of conflicting messages and explained the ambiguity and anxiety many experience in understanding their behavior. Further, we seem to understand that we do play games, that some people do seem to live out personal scripts, and that some people do seem to see themselves and others as OK, while others do not. Because there is so little empirical support for TA, it is difficult to know whether the credit for this fit between TA and human intuition should go to TA or to the marvelous inventiveness and complexity of human cognition. One also wonders what TA would be like if it were reformulated in relation to contemporary cognitive psychology.

Summary of Chapter 7

Chapter 7 is the first of two chapters presenting approaches to psychotherapy and counseling that are considered insight therapies. The three approaches described in this chapter are: time-limited dynamic psychotherapy, Adlerian psychotherapy and counseling, and transactional analysis.

Time-Limited Dynamic Psychotherapy

1. Time-Limited dynamic psychotherapy (TLDP) is being developed by psychologist Hans Strupp and his colleagues at Vanderbilt University, who are trying to apply the richness of psychoanalysis in a more economical, short-term format and to provide scientific procedures to evaluate its effectiveness and continually refine it.
2. Unlike traditional psychoanalysis, which requires the reconstruction of past events, TLDP focuses on the present manifestations of past events in the client's current life. More specifically, TLDP focuses on transference and countertransference phenomena in the actual therapy session.
3. As in traditional psychoanalysis, in TLDP, the practitioner continually analyzes the client's resistances, viewing resistance as an attempt to halt the therapy's most essential process, the analysis of transference. Clients are seen as entrenched in cyclical maladaptive patterns, recurring and self-perpetuating patterns of interpersonal behavior that ensure rejection. These patterns become evident in the client's interactions with the practitioner.
5. Therapy consists of interpreting the client's narration and renarration of life experiences through a process that involves: (1) awareness of self-defeating behavior patterns, (2) understanding of the meaning and purpose of those patterns, and (3) the trying out of alternative ways of acting. Throughout this process, the client's attempts to pull the practitioner into countertransference responses are resisted, and the practitioner provides corrective emotional experiences—that is, experiences that are growth-enhancing rather than supportive of the cyclical maladaptive patterns.
6. TLDP views human behavior in a way that is true to the essentials of psychoanalysis, while emphasizing interpersonal phenomena, the importance of conscious decisions, and the centrality of the present over the past. It is continually being refined through active research.

Adlerian Psychotherapy and Counseling

7. Alfred Adler, an early colleague, collaborator, and, eventually, competitor of Freud, developed an alternative and influential theory of human behavior and therapy. It emphasizes the central role of the ego in human motivation, the importance of the conscious over the unconscious, and the superiority of prevention over remediation.
8. Adler argued that human beings are directed toward a lifelong process of growth, but that real or imagined feelings of inferiority can interrupt that natural process. The biologically based process of compensation leads a person to counter that inferiority either directly or indirectly by constantly striving for superiority.

9. Neurosis results from a misdirection of the striving for superiority toward egocentric aims rather than toward the benefit of society. Ideally, the striving for superiority should be an expression of social interest, a person's natural inclination toward benefiting humankind.

10. Neurosis is viewed as a cognitive disorder, an excursion into private logic, a self-centered and distorted way of reasoning that is contrary to the logical reasoning of which all human beings are capable: common sense.

11. The process of Adlerian intervention includes four components: (1) the establishment and continual enhancement of rapport through encouragement; (2) assessment of the client's life-style through an examination of the family constellation, birth order, the family atmosphere, and early recollections; (3) insight into the client's private logic, confused goals, and maladaptive behavior patterns; and (4) moving the client toward specific changes of behavior by establishing new goals and encouraging the client to move in directions that benefit both the client and society.

12. Despite the recent resurgence of interest in Adler's approach, its power lies in its influence on other approaches, especially those described as cognitive and those within the humanistic-existential perspective.

Transactional Analysis

13. Transactional analysis (TA) was developed by psychiatrist Eric Berne. Although drawing heavily on psychoanalysis, TA features an easy-to-learn vocabulary and uses diagrams to explain psychological processes. Although TA was designed primarily as a form of group treatment, it has been used extensively with individuals.

14. Human personality is composed of three "organs" or ego states: the exteropsyche or Parent, the archaeopsyche or Child, and the neopsyche or Adult. At any given time, an individual has each of these ego states available to consciousness. The Parent reproduces the thoughts, feelings, and attitudes of parental figures in an individual's life; the Child reproduces the thoughts, feelings, and attitudes of the individual during early childhood. The Adult functions like a computer, directing behavior realistically by calculating possibilities and probabilities.

15. The Adult can become contaminated by the intrusion of either the Child or the Parent. Psychopathology involves the loss of control on the part of the Adult to an irrational Parent, Child, or both.

16. Human beings are directed toward the acquisition of strokes, attention and recognition provided by others. Strokes come to us through interpersonal transactions. Some transactions are really games; that is, they are unconscious manipulations of the social transaction that have negative consequences. In part, TA consists in identifying and controlling game playing.

17. Games are part of a larger phenomenon called scripts. Based on the messages we receive during childhood, human beings live out scripts, some of which involve the heavy use of games and are therefore self-defeating.

Analysis of and redecision in regard to these scripts are an important part of TA.

18. In practice, TA emphasizes the learning of a specialized but simple vocabulary and a set of diagrams that enhance communication between the client and the practitioner. Beyond that, practitioners of TA use a wide variety of techniques for changing game-playing behavior and rewriting scripts.

19. TA experienced a period of immense popularity during the 1960s and 1970s but presently attracts only a small number of practitioners. Its future appears uncertain.

CHAPTER 8

Contemporary Insight Therapy: Self-Actualization Approaches

What matters is never a technique per se but rather the spirit in which the technique is used.

Viktor Frankl

This chapter presents three additional approaches to psychotherapy and counseling developed within the **clinical research tradition** that can be considered **insight** therapies. Like the three approaches in Chapter 7, each aims at promoting the **maturity** of clients by providing new information and experience. The three approaches in this chapter have at least one important commonality. Each approach acknowledges or makes use of the concept of **self-actualization.** The three approaches to counseling and psychotherapy described in this chapter are: (1) Gestalt therapy, (2) person-centered therapy, and (3) logotherapy.

As in Chapter 7, we will examine each of the approaches according to (1) its historical and theoretical background, (2) the process of intervention, (3) a sample session, and (4) evaluation. A sample case will be presented to serve as a basis for the sample sessions.

The reader is again reminded that the descriptions that follow are mere distillations of rich bodies of theory, research, and clinical experience. If what follows inspires the reader to explore the primary sources, it has achieved one of its goals.

Sample Case: Constance Craver

After 35 years of marriage to Carl Craver, Constance Craver felt she was on the verge of either homicide or suicide. She saw him as nothing more than a large, self-centered, insensitive, loudmouthed jerk, destined to ruin her life. She alternated between feeling hostile toward Carl, then feeling guilty about feeling hostile, then feeling angry about feeling guilty. Each day, she became more deeply aware of her own isolation, her loneliness, her depression. Hers was a private hell, masked by obsessive dedication to her housework, quiet sufferance of his stories, and stoic submission to their once-a-week sex. Her resentment surfaced only in "little things"— accidentally overstarching his shirts or misplacing his most recent issue of Indoor Sportsman.

Carl was the owner of a fairly successful neighborhood hardware store, and his home life with Constance consisted of a painfully predictable routine. In fact, it had been the same for 35 years: work at 7:00, lunch at noon, dinner at 6:00, and bed at 10:00—except on Saturdays, when bed was at 10:20, following sex. All he ever seemed to talk about was the hardware store: nuts, bolts, plywood, and screws! When the kids were still at home, Constance had had occasional relief from the monotony, an occasional break in Carl's monologue. But now it seemed endless, hopeless.

One of Carl's strengths, as he saw it, was that he left the running of the household to Constance. She took care of the children, the finances, cleaning, cooking, and the repairs—everything but the business, Carl's responsibility. Over 30 years earlier, Carl and Constance had agreed to this arrangement. It had made sense to Constance then, but it overwhelmed her now.

Some day, she said, she was going to leave him. Now, thanks to her sister, she was seriously thinking about getting professional help.

Gestalt Therapy

It is the late 1960s, and you are one of the lucky ones to attend a "human potential" seminar at the Esalen Institute, a center for workshops and training programs nestled between the mountains and the Pacific Ocean at Big Sur, California. You walk into a large room jammed with people, some seated on chairs, some sitting cross-legged on the floor, some standing along the sides. Every type of person imaginable appears to be here. There are young people, denim-clad, some a bit seedy. There are professorial types, casually dressed, engaging in lively debate. There is even a psychoanalyst in the group, bearded, smoking a pipe, and looking more than a trifle uncomfortable in these environs. As a grandfatherly man walks into the room, the hum of conversations becomes a hush punctuated by cries of "Fritz, Fritz." Fritz is wearing a dashiki, and his round, smiling face peers out from an abundant white beard. What follows is a miracle to behold. One by one, like children before a Santa, members of the group volunteer to join Fritz at one end of the room on a "stage" set with three chairs, one for Fritz, one for the volunteer, and one empty. Fritz seems to know each person's soul, if not their names. One by one, he cajoles them, picks on them, intimidates them, surprises them. In response, they cry, laugh, scream, hug, and, from most reports, heal.

Almost 20 years later, this may seem an unlikely forum for training in psychotherapy, but scenes like this were repeated often during the 1960s. The "Fritz" of our story was Frederick J. Perls, M. D., from 1964 until 1969 resident associate psychiatrist at the Esalen Institute. To many at the time, Perls was a sort of guru, a one-man liberator of human potential. Many bright and articulate practitioners were drawn to him, and his particular brand of therapy, *Gestalt therapy,* became a major approach to counseling and psychotherapy. Today, the enormous public and professional popularity of Perls's unique style of psychotherapy has largely passed. Only a small minority of contemporary practitioners describe themselves as exclusively Gestalt therapists, although noteworthy research on Gestalt therapy is still being conducted, and numerous Gestalt therapy training centers still exist. In fact, Perls's ideas and techniques appear to have become part of the practice of many eclectic practitioners. We turn now to that legacy.

Historical and Theoretical Foundations

Frederick "Fritz" Perls (1893–1970) was born in Berlin and received his medical degree in 1920.[1] Perls received training in **psychoanalysis** at both the Vienna and Berlin Institutes for Psychoanalysis. His principal training analyst was Wilhelm Reich, who became fairly well-known later for his attempts to treat

---

[1] Perls's publications usually list him as an "M.D., Ph.D.," but the Ph.D. was an honorary degree from an unaccredited college of psychoanalysis. This tidbit is from C. H. Patterson (1980) who provides an exceptionally thorough treatment of Perls's ideas and techniques.

neurosis by regulating clients' orgasms. Perls worked with, knew, or at least had met many of the luminaries of the world of psychoanalysis and related therapies, including Adler, Otto Fenichel, Freud, Horney, and Jung (C. H. Patterson, 1980). Perls's concept of the Gestalt apparently came from neurologist-psychiatrist Kurt Goldstein, in whose Institute for Brain-Injured Soldiers Perls began working in 1926. Goldstein argued that human beings, no matter what physical or psychological limitations face them, strive for completion, strive to form a whole, a Gestalt. While at Goldstein's lab, Perls met, and later married, Laura Posner, now Laura Perls. Laura Perls is generally recognized as an important contributor to Fritz Perls's work; some descriptions of Gestalt therapy identify her as a co-founder of the therapy (for example, Simkin & Yontef, 1984).

At the outbreak of Nazism in Germany, Perls went to Holland, eventually moving to South Africa, where he founded the South African Institute for Psychoanalysis in 1935. In 1946, Perls moved to New York and, in 1952, along with Laura Perls and American psychologist Paul Goodman, founded the New York Institute for Gestalt Therapy. After several other moves within the United States, Perls accepted his appointment at Esalen and settled in California from 1964 to 1969. He died in 1970 on Vancouver Island while helping to form a Gestalt commune.

Unlike Freud and Adler, Perls did not develop a formal personality theory and made no definitive and final statement either of his theory or on the practice of his therapy. This fact is in keeping with Perls's basic belief that his approach to therapy, like all living things, was in continual evolution, necessarily never reaching final form (Passons, 1975). Perls's *Ego, Hunger and Aggression* (1947/1969a) is his most complete presentation of the theoretical foundation of Gestalt therapy. As for the practice of therapy, Perls believed that the techniques of Gestalt therapy could be learned only through direct experience. One of his books, however, *Gestalt Therapy Verbatim* (1969b), does give an engaging firsthand taste of how his therapy operates. His part-prose, part-poetry autobiography, *In and Out of the Garbage Pail* (1969c), provides a glimpse into Perls's life, as well as into his unique way of perceiving.[2] Not long before his

---

[2]Perls's *In and Out of the Garbage Pail* (1969c) provides a curious glimpse into Perls the man. The autobiography is seemingly casual, natural, spontaneous, and self-effacing, but that may not be entirely the case. After mentioning that in the 1920s he had met Albert Einstein, Jung, Adler, Freud, and Marlene Dietrich, Perls wrote: "They were casual encounters, mostly resulting in nothing but providing some material for boasting and indirectly impressing my audience with my own importance—glamor often overshadowing vision and judgement" (the Real People Press edition of the book has no page numbers, thus adding to its naturalness and spontaneity). Yet, he also noted: "I spent one afternoon with Albert Einstein: unpretentiousness, warmth, some false political predictions. I soon lost my self-consciousness, a rare treat for me at that time. I still love to quote a statement of his: 'Two things are infinite, the universe and human stupidity, and I am not yet completely sure about the universe.' " Perls then went on to describe his meeting with Freud. Or consider this following passage about changes in his sex life: "I used to enjoy screwing for hours, but now, at my age, I enjoy mostly being turned on without having to deliver the goods. I like my reputation as being both a dirty old man and a guru. Unfortunately the first is on the wane and the second ascending."

death, convinced that his earlier writings were dated, Perls began writing two books, one on theory and one on practice. Although he never completed the books, they have been published in their incomplete form in one volume as *The Gestalt Approach* and *Eye Witness to Therapy* (1973).

Several aspects of the theoretical basis of Gestalt therapy are key to understanding it: (1) the Gestalt, (2) self-actualization and responsibility, (3) the role of the intellect, and (4) the nature of neurosis.

The Gestalt   The theoretical basis of Gestalt therapy is a unique blend of psychoanalysis, humanistic psychology, existentialism, Eastern religions, and Gestalt psychology. Because of their names, Perls's therapy might be assumed to derive directly from Gestalt psychology, but such is not the case. The idea of a Gestalt as an inseparable unit of perception does come from Gestalt psychology, as developed by Wertheimer, Koffka, and Köhler. Perls had met these pioneers of Gestalt psychology in the 1920s (Shilling, 1984) and even dedicated one of his early books to Wertheimer (Perls, 1947/1969a). As noted earlier, Perls's basic idea of the Gestalt came from Goldstein, generally considered a contributor to Gestalt psychology, and also from his later reading of Gestalt psychologist Kurt Lewin, especially Lewin's field theory. Nevertheless, Perls appears to have made relatively modest use of Gestalt psychology in the theoretical development of Gestalt therapy (Henle, 1978; Wertheimer, 1978).

Perls did borrow Gestalt psychology's concept of the Gestalt. For Perls, a fundamental lawfulness directs each living organism to completeness, to wholeness, to formation into a Gestalt. This Gestalt is the elementary *experiential unit*—that is, that form in which a living organism can be experienced as itself; nothing can be added to or subtracted from a Gestalt without changing its nature (Perls, 1969b). Perls's favorite example of a Gestalt is water, H_2O. Broken down into hydrogen and oxygen, it ceases to be experienced as water. This lawfulness applies to human beings as well.

In Gestalt therapy, the psychologically healthy person is a whole person, a person in whom all parts interact to form one, irreducible, and complete Gestalt that changes from moment to moment without breaking down into its component parts. In Gestalt therapy, this reality is understood in terms of the relationship between figure and ground, as illustrated in Figure 8.1 using these common distinctions regarding human experience: (1) self, others, and environment; (2) thinking, feeling, and acting; (3) psychological and biological; and (4) past, present, and future. These distinctions mislead us about our nature. A person can never be experienced apart from the environment and the others who populate it. To abstract oneself from the environment and others is a meaningless mental exercise. To distinguish among thoughts, feelings, and actions is artificial; in practice, all are part of an integrated process. Likewise, for the distinction between the biological and the psychological: A person is mind and body and always operates psychologically and biologically. Nor can the past, present, and future be separated. Time, like a river, is always flowing, always moving. Here, though, the present is primary, since one exists, knows,

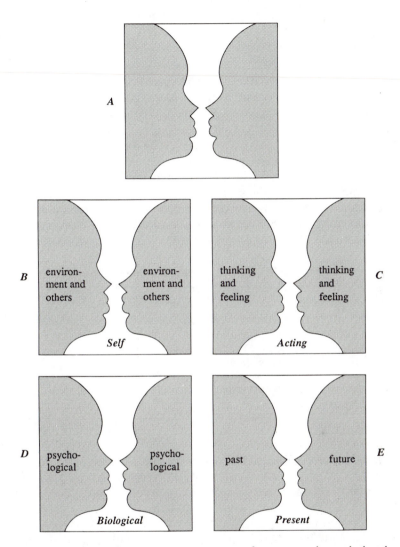

A: Basic Gestalt. At any given moment, one can see two faces or a vase but not both at the same time. Although they can be perceived as separate, to remove one changes the other: together they are complete and form a Gestalt.

B–D: Various aspects of human behavior that can be separated in theory but that are always experienced as one, as a single Gestalt. Separating these aspects of experience is artificial.

E: The centrality of the present in relation to the past and future.

Figure 8.1 *The concept of "figure and ground" in Gestalt therapy*
Note. The idea for presenting material in this manner came from Shostrom (1976, p. 70).

and is known only in the here and now. The key to psychological well-being is allowing oneself to live in the now, fully aware. In Perls's (1970) words: "Now = experience = awareness = reality" (p. 4).

Self-actualization and responsibility   Awareness of one's ever-changing experience, living in the here and now, is essentially the process of self-actualization. The development of one's unique potentials is a by-product of total awareness. Responsibility for succeeding or failing in this awareness rests solely with the individual. In a very real sense, the message of Gestalt therapy is "Take responsibility." Responsibility means, literally, being able to respond to one's own needs, desires, fantasies, and opportunities for growth. Nothing that one has done, felt, or thought belongs to anyone else. The environment cannot be blamed or credited; the past cannot be blamed or credited. Responsibility also means being able to "shed responsibility" for ideas, values, and actions that actually belong to others (Van De Riet, Korb, & Gorrell, 1980, p. 57).

This view of responsibility applies in interpersonal relationships, including the one between the client and practitioner. Nowhere is the nature of that responsibility more tellingly expressed than in Perls's controversial "Gestalt Prayer" at the end of the introduction to his *Gestalt Therapy Verbatim* (1969b, p. 4):

> I do my thing, and you do your thing.
> I am not in this world to live up to your expectations
> And you are not in this world to live up to mine.
> You are you and I am I,
> And if by chance we find each other, it's beautiful.
> If not, it can't be helped.

The role of the intellect   Kogan (1976) uses the following metaphor to describe Perls's mission: "Fritz Perls was like a Moses, eschewing false gods, leading the children of Israel out of the wilderness to a promised land. The wilderness was unawareness. The children were his students. The false gods were those constructed from abstract philosophic rationalism" (p. 244).

The "false god" Perls warned us about was the traditionally esteemed rational intellect itself, the "computer," as Perls unflatteringly called it. Perls described intellect as "the whore of intelligence," arguing that intuition, not rational intellect, constitutes real intelligence (Perls, 1969b, p. 22). Intellect in the form of abstract ideas keeps us from experiencing the here and now, prevents us from meeting our needs directly and without mental roadblocks. Put another way, the Gestalt directive is thus "Don't tell me what you *think,* tell me what you are experiencing at this moment. That is the most important thing. All else is distraction." The locus of this moment-to-moment experience is necessarily the body. The experience may take the form of feelings of anger, a knot in the stomach, goose bumps, flashing images of violence, a pleasing fantasy, or a strong impulse to scream. The truth about oneself rests in experiencing these momentary events, not in thinking about them.

The nature of neurosis   In one of his last writings, Perls (1973) set the scene for a chapter entitled "Here Comes the Neurotic": "And now here comes the neurotic—tied to the past and to outmoded ways of acting, fuzzy about the present because he sees it only through a glass darkly, tortured about the future because the present is out of his hands" (p. 44). This anxious state of temporal insecurity originates when the self is unable to determine the boundaries between the individual and the environment. In Perls's thinking, the self (the ego) is not a part of personality but a function of it (Perls, 1947/1969a). The self determines the boundaries between the organism and the environment. When all is going properly, there is a constant flow or exchange between the self and the environment. Behavior is a function of the accuracy of the self's continual assessment of the demands of the environment and its potential for meeting the organism's needs. When that continual, moment-to-moment exchange with the environment breaks down, when the process of self-actualization ceases, the result is what Perls (1969b) preferred to call a "growth disorder" but which he commonly called neurosis. As in all neuroses, the symptom of this disjointedness between the individual and the environment is anxiety. Perls defined anxiety as simply the "gap between the now and later" (p. 30).

Disruption of the boundaries between the self and the environment takes the form of **resistance** to awareness. Perls (1970) identified four *neurotic mechanisms,* or "resistances": (1) confluence, (2) introjection, (3) projection, and (4) retroflection. *Confluence* involves a loss of boundaries between the person and the environment: "I" and "they" become indistinguishable. Though the inability to distinguish between the self and the environment is developmentally a part of infancy and is a temporary characteristic of ritualistic behavior, as a permanent characteristic, it results from continual and intentional denial of an individual's needs, emotions, and desired actions. In time, this pattern of self-repudiation becomes habitual, and the individual can no longer determine what is a personal need, emotion, or desire. Such a person may become demanding and intolerant, unable to accept that others have different wants and needs. *Introjection* is a disruption of the normal process by which we assimilate information from our environment. It involves the wholesale, uncritical acceptance of all ideas, norms, and standards that come from the environment, despite incongruities among them: "I" really means "they." An individual who interjects may not develop a very distinguishable personality and, as life goes on, may have major periods of emotional conflict in which differing ideas, initially accepted without evaluation, come to conflict with each other. *Projection* is the reverse of introjection. Unacceptable needs, emotions, and desires are attributed to others in the environment: "they" really means "I." *Retroflection* is a combination of introjection and projection. Initially, a person may blame, reject, or punish others for behaviors that she or he has actually projected on to them. When this projection fails, however, the person redirects the blame, rejection, or punishment toward her- or himself: "I" and "they" merge to become "we." Typical of retroflection are statements like "I am ashamed of myself" or "I have to force myself to do this job" (Perls, 1970, p. 41).

The Process of Intervention

Perls (1973) wrote that "the idea of Gestalt therapy is to change paper people to real people" (p. 118). In somewhat less metaphorical terms, the objective of Gestalt therapy is to get clients to "reown" themselves, to become self-supportive, to move from stagnation to growth. The client is assumed to be unable to live satisfactorily in the present because of *unfinished business*— experiences from the past that continue to cause anger and resentment (Perls, 1973). By identifying and resolving the unfinished business, the client becomes aware of self-defeating patterns and real needs, desires, and goals and lives life without anxiety, guilt, and depression. Identifying and resolving unfinished business does not mean simply knowing about it; it means *reexperiencing* in the present the past events and the emotions that accompanied them.

Gestalt therapy depends on a specific kind of client-practitioner relationship, as well as on a collection of techniques. As what follows will highlight, Gestalt therapy is unique in both regards.

The therapeutic relationship   The objective of Gestalt therapy is to make the client capable of *self-support,* a by-product of increased awareness on the part of the client. The relationship between the practitioner and client is central to awakening this awareness. Although the practitioner does provide some support to the client, the practitioner's primary role is to confront, frustrate, and challenge the client so that through his or her growing awareness, the client comes to accept responsibility and becomes self-reliant. The practitioner does not *interpret* the client's behavior. Interpretations are verbal explanations that cannot substitute for the understanding that comes with reexperiencing events and emotions. As Perls (1973) pointed out, as long as clients are "fed with interpretations, especially if they are emotionally blocked, they'll snuggle happily back in the cocoon of their neurosis and stay there, purring peacefully" (p. 77). Rather, the practitioner uses direct statements and questions concerning the client's experience in the present to force the client to be aware of his or her behavior patterns. Typically, a client must complete the statement "Now I am aware . . ." throughout the therapeutic process and is challenged with questions like "What are you doing?" "What do you avoid?" and "What do you want?" (p. 74). According to Perls, the least valuable questions begin with why. Looking for the cause of behavior is considered a misguided and doomed undertaking. Perls put the whole business of questions and their role in Gestalt therapy in unique perspective:

> If we spend our time looking for causes instead of structure we may well give up the idea of therapy and join the worrying grandmothers who attack their prey with such pointless questions as "Why did you catch that cold?" "Why have you been so naughty?" . . . Of course, all of the therapist's questions are interruptions of some on-going process in the patient. They are intrusions, very often miniature shocks. They lead to an apparently unfair situation. If the therapist has to frustrate the demands of the patient but feels [her- or] himself free to fire questions, is this not an unfair situation, an authoritarian procedure, completely antithetical to our

effort to elevate the therapist from the position of a power figure to a human being? Admittedly, it is not easy to find the way through this inconsistency, but once the therapist has resolved the psychotherapeutic paradox of working with *support* and *frustration* both, his [or her] procedures will fall correctly into place. (pp. 76–77)

Gestalt therapy clearly operates by both supporting and frustrating the client, and the practitioner clearly takes a fairly authoritarian role. The balance between support and frustration, as well as how the practitioner expresses his or her authority, differs considerably depending on the personalities of the practitioner and client.

Gestalt therapy techniques All of the techniques of Gestalt therapy are designed to promote awareness in the client. In keeping with the philosophy of the approach, there are no hard and fast rules about how specific techniques are to be implemented. Rather, the emphasis is on spontaneity and improvisation. Although Perls came to favor using Gestalt therapy in group settings (Rosenfeld, 1978), it is practiced equally with individuals. Most of the rules and techniques that follow can be applied in both settings (see Feder & Ronall, 1980, for an overview of group techniques).

Before looking at the techniques of Gestalt therapy, we must examine some elementary Gestalt rules. In a sense, these rules are also techniques, a distinction not easy to make in practice. The rules prescribe: (1) present-centeredness, (2) personalizing pronouns, (3) avoiding questions, (4) no "shoulds," and (5) the awareness continuum. The rule of *present-centeredness,* or "the principle of the now" (Levitsky & Perls, 1970), is applied in two techniques. First, at any time during the therapy, the practitioner can request that the client return to the now, expressing her or his immediate experience rather than talking about the past or future. A second technique is called *presentification,* a form of fantasy in which the client is asked to experience a past or future event as vividly and emotionally as possible in the present, talking about it in the present tense (Naranjo, 1970). Both of these techniques prevent the client from skirting awareness by keeping him or her in contact with the now.

Personalizing pronouns, avoiding questions, and *no "shoulds"* are three examples of Gestalt therapy's many *language rules.* Personalizing pronouns — turning all sentences into "I" statements — forces the client to take responsibility for her or his thoughts and feelings. For example, the practitioner might direct the client to replace the sentence "It would be nice if Mary called me" with "I want Mary to call me." The second rule, avoiding questions, also prevents the client from disowning thoughts and feelings. If the client vaguely and manipulatively says, "Doesn't anybody care about me?" the practitioner may tell the client to turn that into a statement. Possible results include "I want someone to care about me" or, even more direct, "I want you [the practitioner] to care about me." This last statement is the most direct, the most risky, and potentially the most growth-producing. The third rule, concerning use of the word *should,* is drawn from the work of Karen Horney. Shoulds, especially those directed at oneself, skip the step of accurately assessing what one truly wants. By not using should, one is forced to assess one's real needs and desires. This philosophy has resulted in some curious catch phrases like "Don't 'should' on yourself" or "Don't 'should' on me." Of course, built into these aphorisms is a should: "You should not 'should' on yourself."

The *awareness continuum* (Levitsky & Perls, 1970) concerns the how of experience rather than the why. Typically, the client is asked a question like "What are you aware of right now?" The client answers, usually identifying some emotion, for example, "I'm aware of listening to you, wondering why you are making me do this again, and also getting annoyed at you for doing it again." The practitioner's response: "How do you experience that annoyance?" Ideally, the client learns to experience the moment immediately by answering in terms of the senses, for example, "Well, I notice that my hand is shaking a little and that I'm clenching my teeth a bit and that my heart just started racing."

Four key Gestalt therapy techniques merit special attention: (1) the shuttle technique, (2) the top dog–underdog dialogue, (3) the empty-chair technique, and (4) dreamwork. In the *shuttle technique,* the practitioner directs the client's attention back and forth from one experience to another. The client may be asked to shuttle between the past and the present, the past and the future, or the present and future. Or the client may be asked to shuttle between saying something and listening to it being said. Many other Gestalt therapy techniques use the basic shuttle technique.

The *top dog–underdog dialogue* is a very specific kind of shuttle technique. In essence, neurotic conflict is an unproductive dialogue between two belligerent voices. One voice is that of the "top dog," the perfectionist in each of us that follows the rules, strives for more than is possible, and is miserable with less than the ideal. The top dog, roughly an updated equivalent of Freud's superego, is not realistic. The underdog, which roughly parallels Freud's id, is weak, evasive, and indecisive. In the internal dialogue, the underdog is always making excuses, avoiding action, and short-circuiting the efforts of the top dog. In Gestalt therapy, the client is asked to bring this dialogue out into the open. The client shuttles back and forth between voicing the dialogue and listening critically to it. In doing so, the client is encouraged to find realistic solutions to the situations being debated, solutions represented by neither the top dog nor the underdog. Suppose, for example, that the top dog makes mental comments like "I must finish writing this section on Gestalt therapy before April, or my book will never get published." The underdog's responses may include "Don't worry, there are 25 more minutes left in March" or "Even if you finish by April, it's going to be rotten." After shuttling back and forth between voicing these voices and being aware of them, the client may be instructed to say, "I want to finish this section on Gestalt therapy by April, and I am going to do it!"

The *empty-chair technique* is one of the most widely borrowed Gestalt techniques. It, too, is essentially a shuttle technique, as well as a dialogue technique, in which the client is asked to voice an internal, historical, or imaginary dialogue. It can be used in conjunction with the top dog–underdog dialogue. In the empty-chair technique, the client actually moves back and forth between two chairs while speaking the parts of the dialogue. Each chair is seen as being occupied by a different (usually conflicting) person, feeling, or idea. The practitioner is particularly directive during this technique, signaling the client when to move between chairs and how to respond and forcing the client to experience the dialogue.

Dreamwork—not to be confused with Freud's term—is Gestalt therapy's term for its special way of using the client's dreams to promote growth. In psychoanalysis, dreams are interpreted as expressions of the unconscious. In Gestalt therapy, dreams are reexperienced as projections of different, conflicting sides of oneself (Perls, 1970). Dreams are assumed to represent things that are missing in our lives, things we avoid doing but that need to be integrated into our daily lives if we are to be whole (Perls, 1969b). In dreamwork, the client is asked to actually act out or relive each element of the dream, whether person or object, as a means of pulling the diverse and conflicted elements together into the here and now of therapy.

Gestalt therapists have developed a good number of techniques built on the basic rules and methods described above; a selection of these is described, with examples, in Table 8.1.

Table 8.1 Additional Gestalt Therapy Techniques (Sources: Passons, 1975; Levitsky & Perls, 1970; Van De Riet, Korb, & Gorrell, 1980).

Technique	Description	Example
Being the Elements	The client is instructed to become the various elements of a story, dream, fantasy, or the like.	Annette, recounting a past argument with family members, is asked to play each of the characters in her story, exploring their views, feelings, and so forth.
Exaggeration	The client is asked to exaggerate a feeling or action to better experience it.	A young man, describing feelings of anger toward his father, is told to give exaggerated expression to the anger as a way of getting in touch with it.
Exposing the Obvious	Obvious behaviors of the client are often important. The practitioner points out the obvious to expose its meaning.	The practitioner asks George if he is aware that upon mention of his job, George's back becomes rigid.

(continued)

(Table 8.1 continued)

Technique	Description	Example
Feeding Sentences	The practitioner gives the client sentences to say that pull together the diverse elements of the client's experience in a way that reveals previously hidden elements.	Betty talks about how unsatisfied she is at home. The practitioner says, "May I feed you a sentence?" The practitioner exposes her should by having her repeat, "I *should* be happy at home."
Rehearsal	By voicing his or her concerns, fears, needs, desires, or fantasies out loud, the client comes to understand and express them more satisfactorily.	A middle-aged woman is tired of living with her unattentive husband. She is instructed to rehearse sentences that clearly express to him her dissatisfaction and anger.
Reversal	The client is asked to experiment with the reverse feeling, need, desire, or fantasy.	Juan proclaims his sincere love for Meg but has been unable to commit himself to marriage. Juan is asked to give expression to his negative feeling toward Meg as a means of understanding his behavior.
Stop Trying to Be Sane	Human beings are conditioned to act rationally no matter how they really feel. The practitioner undercuts this tendency by telling the client, "Stop trying to be sane."	Confused by Juan's rejection, Meg has become hostile and she feels guilty about that. She is told to "stop trying to be sane," allowing her to experience her true feelings.

Sample Session

Below is an exchange from an imaginary session with our new client, Constance Craver. Thanks to the efforts of her sister, Constance has begun working with Dr. Gloria Asserti, an experienced Gestalt therapist. The reader should be alert for: (1) the practitioner's attempts to keep the client in the here and now, (2) the practitioner's application of the awareness continuum, (3) the use of the empty-chair technique, and (4) the nature of the relationship between the client and practitioner. We join Constance and Dr. Asserti in the middle of an early session:

> *Constance (C):* I'm still not sure if I should leave him, you know. I feel so terribly guilty all the time.

Practitioner (P): Constance, remember what we say; "Guilt is nothing but unexpressed resentment." Tell me how you feel right now.

C: He is such a nothing, I guess, but how will he manage by himself? Still, he's only getting what he deserved, right? Isn't that what you said to me? If only I had told him off years ago, you know, and now I'm just so upset, not knowing what I'm going to do, you know—

P [*gently breaking into Constance's sentence*]: Hold on a minute, Constance, let's look at a few of these things one at a time. Try something for me, will you? Put the word "now" in every sentence that you say. It will help you focus on the only important thing: what's going on in you here and now.

C: OK. I'll try. What did I see—no. What *do* I see in him *now*? Should I go back to him?

P: "Should"?

C: Huh?

P: You said "should," as if there were some clear-cut right or wrong thing you *should* do that is more important than what you *want* to do. Say what you want. Say, "I want him," or "I don't want him." Say, "I love him," or "I hate that jerk." Say what you want now, not what you should want.

C: [*hesitating*]: I don't know what to say. You want me to use the word "now" when I say things, but what I really feel now is very, very confused.

P: *How* does that feel? Where does that hit you? Remember: NOW!

C: Right now. You mean my body? Now my stomach hurts a little, and I feel dizzy. I feel all pulled in, all hurting. It's hard to tell you. I feel like two people are fighting over me, like a sweater on sale at a discount store. Does that make sense?

P: It doesn't have to make sense. It's how you feel right now, and that feeling is part of the pull you feel both toward Carl and away from him. Let's see if we can get more in touch with that. I want you to try something. Pretend that you are sitting in that chair over there. It's the you who loves Carl, who has stayed with Carl all these years. Tell her what you feel *now*.

C: Are you sure that's a good idea, I mean, it seems kind of silly to—

P: Go ahead. Tell her. Remember that the anger that you feel now is bottled-up resentment for all those years. Tell her.

C [*mildly*]: Carl hurt me—no, *now* he is hurting me. Sometimes I'm not sure I can go on. All those years, wasted. He never seemed to care [*beginning to cry*], never noticed me, probably doesn't even care that I'm gone now. But I don't know that—he never told me anything about love or even hate! [*Pause. She resumes, increasingly angry.*] He's really a bastard, you know. He only cared about himself, never even mentioned all the years I'd given him, all the things I've sacrificed. I'm furious at him, and I'm very hurt. Why have you stayed with him? Why have you done what he wanted all these years? You are such a fool!

P: Good, Constance. Stay with that feeling for a bit. [*She pauses as Constance collects herself.*] Now, let's work a bit. What did you hear when you listened to yourself talk about him?

C: Wow. I heard so much anger, so much resentment, so much that I should have said—I mean, *could* have said—years ago. But it makes me feel bad to have to say that. [*Pause.*] I also feel love. I do still love him, I guess, and I don't like hearing so much anger. People would never understand if they heard that, and—

P [*interrupting*]: It doesn't matter what others would understand. What you mean is "*I* don't understand these feelings." Say that. Say, "*I* don't understand these feelings."

C: *I* don't understand these feelings.

P: Again.

C: *I* don't understand these feelings!

P: Good. Well, let's see the other side of this, the love you feel also tearing at you. What would that love look like? Go to the other chair and be the loving Constance and talk to the one that hates Carl. Go ahead.

C [*going to the other chair*]: Oh, I love Carl, don't you see why? I loved him so much years ago, but maybe it's done. [*Pause.*] No, I love him now, I guess. I want him to change. I want you to change, to stop hating him, but you say you can't and I don't understand. It makes me very distressed. I want him to care for me, love me more than that damn store, and . . .

Evaluation

Although some institutes and workshops regularly offer training in Gestalt therapy, the enormous popularity Gestalt therapy once had has now waned. Only a small minority of practitioners describe themselves as Gestalt therapists (7% in D. Smith's 1982 study of clinical and counseling psychologists). Unlike Strupp's TLDP, Gestalt therapy has no serious ongoing research to support it, nor has it been the influential precursor of more contemporary approaches that Adler's approach has. Almost 20 years after Perls's death, what place does Gestalt therapy have in contemporary eclectic practice?

Gestalt therapy has offered a variety of useful concepts and techniques that deserve integration into contemporary practice. We will examine some of these before discussing Gestalt therapy.

Concepts and techniques Psychotherapy can become nothing more than a "mind game." It can dwell on the past, get mired in vague and unexpressed feelings, and ignore the client's fundamental responsibility for his or her own life. Perls systematically (although not single-handedly) assaulted this type of passive, indirect, intellectualized, and retrospective treatment, and the field is probably better off for it.

Although difficult to demonstrate, practitioners probably use many of Perls's techniques in their day-to-day practice. For example, requesting first-person pronouns, staying in the here and now, bringing out internal dialogues, feeding the client sentences—these and many other Gestalt techniques are common practice. Some techniques, like the empty-chair technique, have enormous versatility and can be modified to meet a variety of client needs and practitioner preferences. Thus, many of Gestalt therapy's concepts and techniques have value in contemporary practice.

Limitations Gestalt therapy's inventive and eclectic approach to therapy fit comfortably into a turbulent period of American history, the 1960s. Perhaps in keeping with its times, Gestalt therapy, with its charismatic leader and no want for followers, pushed a philosophy that now seems devoid of concern for social value and social action. Perls and his followers have been criticized as promoting what Cadwallader (1981) has called "half-truths" by accepting emotion and intuition while denigrating intellect. In Gestalt therapy, responsibility to self eclipsed responsibility to others, and some vague sense of self-actualization replaced engagement with the needs and values of humanity. The actualization of self became a goal in itself—something it never was in the work of Maslow, who developed the concept of self-actualization. In the end, Gestalt therapy seems to have missed the point that Maslow took from his exposure to Adler and Frankl: Self-actualization is not a goal but a by-product, the by-product of interpersonal, social, aesthetic, and spiritual involvement rather than self-involvement (see Dolliver, 1981, for a fuller critique of Gestalt therapy's limitations).

Gestalt therapy is an unsystematic, conceptually rigid approach to intervention that depends on the improvisational and spontaneous use of a collection of inventive techniques. Gestalt therapy is intended to be a growth experience that emerges from a certain amount of discomfort or disquiet in the client. The client gains insight at the experiential level by being confronted by an authoritarian practitioner. Ideally, this experience is neither overly distressful nor manipulative. However, it is difficult to observe or read Perls's interventions without discovering elements in them that are both unnecessarily distressful and outright manipulative. Although such may not generally be the case among Gestalt therapists, the design of Gestalt therapy seems to invite manipulative and distress-producing behavior from the practitioner. Were there solid outcome studies to support the contention that this is the best way to help clients, the risk could perhaps be justified. Unfortunately, no such research justification exists.

Person-Centered Therapy

In Chicago, in 1956, two men in their early 50s presented papers at a symposium on the "control of human behavior" at the annual convention of the American Psychological Association. One of the men was Harvard professor B. F. Skinner, then an increasingly influential comparative psychologist and proponent of the philosophy of science known as **behaviorism** (see Chapters

3 and 4). In his remarks, he described the inevitability of various forms of personal and social control, and, noting the dangers inherent in some forms of control, called for the systematic implementation of benign controls based on scientific knowledge about human behavior. An article in *Science* included some of Skinner's comments:

> If the advent of a powerful science of behavior causes trouble, it will not be because science itself is inimical to human welfare but because older conceptions have not yielded easily or gracefully. . . . What is needed is a new conception of human behavior which is compatible with the implications of a scientific analysis. All men control and are controlled. The question of government in the broadest possible sense is not how freedom is to be preserved but what kinds of controls are to be used and to what ends. (Rogers & Skinner, 1956, p. 1060)

The man who responded to Skinner's comments was Carl Rogers, a professor of clinical psychology at the University of Chicago. If at that time Skinner was becoming a force in the **experimental research tradition,** Rogers was becoming the same in the clinical research tradition. His recently published book, *Client-Centered Therapy* (1951), had offered a fresh and appealing alternative to psychoanalytic therapies, and his integration of scientific rigor and clinical practice held the promise of a new way of doing and evaluating counseling and psychotherapy. In his response to Skinner's remarks, Rogers noted a key point of agreement: "that the whole question of the scientific control of human behavior is a matter with which psychologists and the general public should concern themselves" (p. 1060). For Rogers, however, the point at issue concerned the actual locus of behavioral control. Is human behavior under the exclusive control of external forces that should be formalized according to the findings of science, as Skinner suggested, or are the essential behavioral controls individualized within each of us and determined by choice? Relating this issue to his practice of client-centered therapy (the early name for person-centered therapy), Rogers remarked:

> In client-centered therapy, we are deeply engaged in the prediction and influencing of behavior, or even the control of behavior. As therapists, we institute certain attitudinal conditions, and the client has relatively little voice in the establishment of these conditions. We predict that if these conditions are instituted, certain behavioral consequences will ensue to the client. Up to this point this is largely external control, no different from what Skinner has described. . . . But here any similarity ceases. . . . [We] have established by external control conditions which we predict will be followed by internal control by the individual, in pursuit of internally chosen goals. . . . To me this has the encouraging meaning that the human person, with his [or her] capacity of subjective choice, can and will always exist, separate from and prior to any of his [or her] scientific undertakings. Unless as individuals and groups we choose to relinquish our capacity of subjective choice, we will always remain persons, not simply pawns of a self-created science. (p. 1064)

If Skinner's proposal for a science-based society made him a revolutionary of sorts, Rogers's assertions about human behavior and its modification made him, in Farson's (1975) words, "a quiet revolutionary." Rogers's fundamental contention that each human being is essentially capable of self-directed behavior change may appear nothing more than mildly optimistic common sense. Nevertheless, in its day, it was profoundly at odds with the prevailing professional assumptions about people who came for therapy, and it had dramatic implications for the practice of psychotherapy and counseling.

Historical and Theoretical Foundations

In 1973, after 46 years as a practitioner of psychology, Carl Rogers was honored by the American Psychological Association with the Distinguished Professional Contribution Award. In his remarks on that occasion, he said that the major element in his reaction to looking back at his great impact on the profession over those years was astonishment and surprise (Rogers, 1975b). Certainly his beginnings did not portend anything so dramatic. Carl Ransom Rogers was born in 1902. He was one of six children raised in a "narrowly fundamentalist religious home" that was tolerant of but aloof from people who did not abide by the same strictures (Rogers, 1980b, p. 28).[3] Although he attended grade school in Oak Park, Illinois, an affluent suburb of Chicago, the family later moved to a rural estate, where his engineer father applied the principles of experimental science to farming. Rogers worked on the farm and eventually majored in agriculture at the University of Wisconsin. He later changed his major to history to prepare for the ministry, enrolling in Union Theological Seminary in New York. After 2 years of study, however, he transferred to Columbia University, where he completed a Ph.D. in clinical and educational psychology in 1931.

Between 1928 and 1940, Rogers worked as a clinical psychologist at a child guidance clinic in Rochester, New York. During this period, Rogers encountered the work of Otto Rank. Rank was a psychoanalyst who had been expelled from Freud's inner circle because of his unorthodox ideas about birth trauma as the primary source of neurosis. Rogers was not taken by Rank's psychoanalytic theories but by the emphasis he placed on *will* in therapy—that is, the role that personal decisions could play in behavior change. After teaching, counseling, and serving as an administrator at Ohio State University, the USO, the University of Chicago, and the University of Wisconsin between 1940 and 1962, Rogers became a fellow at the Center for Advanced Study in the Behavioral Sciences and later a resident fellow at the Western Behavioral Sciences Institute in California. In 1968, Rogers helped found the Center for Studies of the Person, an experimental "psychological community" in which social and behavioral scientists and others undertake a variety of training, research, and

[3]Most approaches to therapy reflect some of the needs and concerns of their developers. This is true also of person-centered therapy. In an autobiographical essay entitled "My Philosophy of Interpersonal Relationships," Rogers traced his personal development from being a young man with no close friends, through the mistakes and misperceptions of his early years as a therapist, to his (then) current experience of himself and society. The essay is included in *A Way of Being* (1980b).

social projects (Meador & Rogers, 1984). Rogers remained a resident fellow at the center in La Jolla, California, until his death in 1987.

Rogers shares with Skinner, Freud, Piaget, and a few other psychologists the dubious distinction of having his name turned into an eponym, as in "a Rogerian" or "Rogerian counselors." Rogers, for his part, proclaimed, "I am no Rogerian." More on that later.

The development of Rogers's approach A review of Rogers's major publications provides an avenue for examining the development of his thinking. In 1942, Rogers published *Counseling and Psychotherapy: Newer Concepts in Practice.* In this work, Rogers argued for several positions that are widely accepted today but that represented major shifts at the time. He described counseling or psychotherapy as a "knowable, predictable, understandable process, a process which can be learned, tested, refined, and improved" (p. ix)—in other words, a process that is amenable to scientific scrutiny. This new psychotherapy had a different goal, the integration of the individual, and it placed greater emphasis on emotions and on immediate situations in the client's life. In the new psychotherapy, change was held to take place during therapy and not after it, an approach that "lays stress upon the therapeutic relationship itself as a growth experience" (p. 30). Lastly, the new approach was *nondirective* rather than directive; Rogers argued that a nondirective approach that facilitates an individual's self-directed maturing is more appropriate for the overwhelming majority of clients.

By 1951, with the publication of *Client-Centered Therapy,* Rogers's movement toward a nondirective therapy had crystallized into a clearly articulated approach to therapy including a personality theory and specific techniques. In the years following the publication of *Client-Centered Therapy,* Rogers and his associates produced a continual flow of studies on the entire process of therapy and its outcomes. Rogers and his colleagues pioneered the use of recording equipment in the evaluation of therapy and the training of practitioners and made use of a wide range of methodologies and measures in developing and evaluating client-centered therapy.[4] An important collection of research studies on client-centered therapy was published in 1954 under the title *Psychotherapy and Personality Change: Coordinated Studies in the Client-Centered Approach* (Rogers & Dymond, 1954). In 1961, Rogers published *On Becoming a Person: A Therapist's View of Psychotherapy.* This work, addressed to the professional and nonprofessional alike, presented Rogers's approach to therapy and the research supporting it, his personality theory, and his philosophy of science.

---

[4]Raskin (1985) recently summarized the various studies undertaken by Rogers and his associates. Though audio and videotape recordings are now commonplace in the evaluation of counseling and psychotherapy, as well as in the training of practitioners, such was hardly the case when Rogers set out to see what really takes place in the therapeutic process. Raskin recounted how, in 1939, a doctoral student of Rogers at Ohio State University who was also a ham radio operator improvised a 78-rpm disc-recording system so that cases could be recorded.

In 1974, Rogers and his associates changed the name of client-centered therapy to **person-centered therapy,** making it part of the larger *person-centered approach* or *person-centered way of being.* In a sense, this change was emblematic of a shift in focus that had begun when Rogers moved to California in 1964 (Raskin, 1984). As Rogers wrote in *A Way of Being* (1980b):

> The old concept of "client-centered therapy" has been transformed into the "person-centered approach." In other words, I am no longer talking simply about psychotherapy, but about a point of view, a philosophy, an approach to life, a way of being, which fits any situation in which *growth*—of a person, a group, or a community—is part of the goal. (p. ix)

This new scope took Rogers and his colleagues into a variety of social, educational, and political arenas where the person-centered approach is used to reduce conflict and promote necessary change. The quiet revolution that began in the 1940s has thus become a cultural movement.

The person-centered approach The theoretical base undergirding Rogers's approach to psychological and social intervention is a personality theory within the humanistic-existential perspective discussed in Chapter 6. The following tenets and assumptions from Rogers's personality theory are germane to our understanding of person-centered therapy:

1. Human beings have a propensity for developing all of their capacities. This *actualizing tendency* is a natural tendency in every organism toward "constructive fulfillment of its inherent possibilities" (Rogers, 1980b, p. 117). By nature, human beings are directed toward becoming *fully functioning persons.* Fully functioning persons are: (1) increasingly open to experience, (2) increasingly accepting of their own feelings, (3) increasingly capable of living in the present from moment to moment, (4) increasingly free to make choices and to act on them spontaneously, (5) increasingly trusting of self and of human nature, (6) increasingly capable of balanced and realistic expressions of affection and aggression, and (7) increasingly creative and nonconformist (Rogers, 1961). As Rogers put it, "Such a person would, I believe, be recognized by the student of evolution as the type most likely to adapt and survive under changing environmental conditions" (p. 194).

2. Human reality is essentially subjective, and subjective *experience* is responsible for behavior. This subjectivity constitutes an ever-changing private world, some of which is in conscious awareness and some of which is only available to consciousness (Rogers, 1959).

3. The *self-concept* is an "organized configuration of perceptions of the self which is admissible to awareness" (Rogers, 1951, p. 136). It is a collection of perceptions about and conceptions of: (1) one's abilities and characteristics; (2) one's relationships with others and the environment; (3) the value one places on experiences, objects, and persons; and (4) one's personal goals and ideals (Rogers, 1951, 1959).

4. The *ideal self* is the self-concept an individual would like to have. It includes the components of the self-concept listed above but is at any given moment not yet attained by the individual (Rogers, 1959).

5. Ideally, a person's experience, self-concept, and ideal self are *congruent.* In other words, one's day-to-day living experience should largely support one's self-concept, and the discrepancy between one's self-concept and ideal self should allow one to remain engaged in the process of actualizing the ideal self rather than becoming disheartened by the gap between the real and the ideal.

6. *Psychological maladjustment* results when one denies or distorts an experience, causing *incongruence* between the experience and one's self-concept. If conscious of this incongruence, the individual becomes tense and confused in trying to adjust to two conflicting sets of goals. Such a person acts in ways that are not consistent with his or her internal realities (thoughts and feelings). Such a person is described as *vulnerable,* because this state can result in increasing psychological disorganization.

7. If the individual is unaware of the incongruence, anxiety results. *Anxiety* is a "state of uneasiness or tensions whose cause is unknown" (Rogers, 1959, p. 204). *Threat* is the state that exists when an individual anticipates that an experience will be incongruent with her or his self-concept. *Defensiveness* is the behavioral response to threat.

8. The resources needed to bring an experience and one's self-concept into congruence exist within each individual. In the person-centered approach, however, certain interpersonal qualities in the practitioner help activate the client's resources. The qualities the practitioner must have are: *genuineness, unconditional positive regard,* and *empathic understanding* (Rogers, 1980b).

The Process of Intervention

Person-centered therapy is an interpersonal relationship in which the attitude and orientation of the practitioner allow the client to experience that relationship in such a way that the client is able to move through a series of internal and interpersonal stages that result in beneficial changes in personality and behavior. Following an organization set out by Rogers (1951), we will look at the three basic components of the intervention process in person-centered therapy: (1) the philosophical orientation and qualities of the practitioner, (2) the relationship as experienced by the client, and (3) the process of therapy.

The philosophical orientation and qualities of the practitioner In many approaches to counseling and psychotherapy, the emphasis is on technique, on what the practitioner actually does during the sessions. In person-centered therapy, techniques are spontaneous verbal and nonverbal *implementations* of the practitioner's philosophical orientation and personal qualities and are important only to the degree that they accurately portray those inner realities (Rogers, 1951).

Rogers has articulated the philosophical orientation required in person-centered therapy in many different ways, but essentially it comes down to the practitioner's *faith in* and *respect for*: (1) the client, (2) the practitioner's own abilities, and (3) the potential of the relationship. The following quotation captures the basic gist:

> I launch myself into the therapeutic relationship having a hypothesis, or a faith, that my liking, my confidence, and my understanding of the other person's inner world, will lead to a significant process of becoming. I enter the relationship not as a scientist, not as a physician who can accurately diagnose and cure, but as a person, entering into a personal relationship. (Rogers, 1951, p. 267)

The practitioner enters the relationship as a "midwife" of change rather than its originator; the authority for change always remains with the client, since the client is essentially trustworthy (Rogers, 1977). Besides this basic philosophical orientation, however, are certain personal qualities or characteristics that the practitioner must exhibit if the necessary conditions of change are to be established.

In 1957, Rogers wrote a now-famous paper entitled "The Necessary and Sufficient Conditions of Therapeutic Change." In that article, Rogers identified six conditions for constructive personality change, arguing that the degree to which these conditions are present is the degree to which significant personality change will occur. According to Rogers, no other conditions or techniques apart from these conditions need be present for significant change to occur, but for change to occur they must be at least minimally present. Figure 8.2 both lists those conditions and graphically represents the process. Take a few minutes to review that figure before going on.

The key to appreciating Rogers's description of successful intervention is understanding the three qualities or characteristics that the practitioner must both personally experience and successfully communicate to the client: genuineness, unconditional positive regard, and empathic understanding. Genuineness is related to the term congruence, used earlier to describe the relationship between the self-concept and experience; congruence is sometimes used synonymously with genuineness. The practitioner's genuineness is an inner experience, an experience of congruence, of actually being comfortably and confidently oneself. Genuineness is expressed in the ability to enter the relationship with the client without facade, without sham, without a professional persona. Such a practitioner is wholly with the client, spontaneously sharing feelings and experiences. However, the successful practitioner never becomes so spontaneous that the client becomes burdened with impulsively shared experiences that do not directly relate to creating the necessary conditions of change (Rogers, 1980a).

Unconditional positive regard goes by many names: warmth, caring, prizing. While recognizing the client's limits, the practitioner experiences the client as worthy of love, especially prized, valuable as she or he is, and capable of expressing that value in more constructive behaviors. Though the practitioner

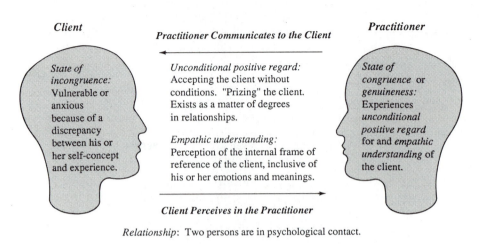

Relationship: Two persons are in psychological contact.

Figure 8.2 *The "necessary and sufficient conditions of therapeutic personality change"* (Rogers, 1957, p. 96). *The six conditions necessary for constructive personality change to occur are: (1) Two persons are in psychological contact; (2) the first person, the client, is in a state of incongruence, and is vulnerable or anxious; (3) the second person, the practitioner, is congruent or integrated in the relationship; (4) the practitioner experiences unconditional positive regard for the client; (5) the practitioner experiences an empathic understanding of the client's internal frame of reference and endeavors to communicate that experience to the client; and (6) the practitioners success in communicating her or his empathic understanding and unconditional positive regard for the client to at least a minimal degree.*

may accept some of the client's present behaviors only conditionally, he or she assents to the client's essential humanness wholeheartedly. The practitioner's experience of wholehearted faith in the client spills over into specific words and actions that express that positive regard in the therapeutic session. Unconditional positive regard becomes an environment that the client comes to expect and in which the client can explore without fear of criticism or rejection.

Sympathy is feeling for someone else; it is an expressed acknowledgement of another person's suffering, given with the hope that one's support will reduce the distress. Empathy is being with someone else; it involves a relationship in which one has the capacity to almost experience with the other person. In counseling and psychotherapy, empathic understanding is the ability to see from the client's frame of reference, to share in the client's experience. At any given moment, the client's experience of him- or herself and the world is more than an idea; it includes emotions, special meanings, expectations, and the like. The practitioner listens carefully, searching for verbal and nonverbal ways to alert the client to the practitioner's growing appreciation of the client's total experience.

Genuineness, unconditional positive regard, and empathic understanding are qualities of the practitioner as a person. Assuming that the practitioner has these qualities, her or his challenge is to behave in such a way that the client will experience these qualities in the relationship.

The relationship as experienced by the client   Clients come to psychotherapy and counseling with a variety of expectations, often expecting to be given strong direction, sagacious advice, or parental exhortation. In person-centered therapy, what they find is a person "simply" exhibiting genuineness, unconditional positive regard, and empathy. This shattering of expectations can be disconcerting to the client, but it can also promote insight. For example, Rogers (1951) quoted a college student undergoing therapy as saying: "You make me think for myself and I don't like it. I want advice. I've been going to everyone for advice. You can't lose when you get it. If the person gives you advice you like, that makes you feel fine; if they give you advice you don't like, they're fools, and *that* makes you feel fine" (p. 68).

Eventually, the environment of "constancy and safety" created by the practitioner's unfailing support and appreciation leads to a number of important experiences for the client: (1) the experience of responsibility, (2) the experience of exploration, (3) the discovery of denied attitudes, (4) the experience of reorganizing the self, (5) the experience of progress, and (6) the experience of ending (Rogers, 1951). Although the client may come to therapy expecting the practitioner to provide a "cure," it becomes apparent rather quickly in person-centered therapy that change is the product of work by the client. The frustration that comes from trying to read the practitioner may lead to confusion or anger, but ultimately, the client's *experience of responsibility* leads her or him to search within for answers. This search, engaged in with both fear and desire, often uncovers inconsistencies within the self as the client freely shares his or her attitudes in this supportive environment. Gradually, the modus operandi of the sessions becomes one of self-discovery, and the *experience of exploration* further encourages the client to freely express her or his attitudes and feelings. As the client allows thoughts and feelings to surface that had previously been kept out of awareness, he or she encounters distress caused by his or her *discovery of denied attitudes*. Consciousness of previously denied attitudes, thoughts, and feelings necessarily creates inconsistencies, and consciousness of those inconsistencies can cause considerable distress. Eventually, however, fresh insights into her or his behavior allow the client to move away from interpersonal facades and phoniness toward the emergence of a new, more whole and integrated person. This process is necessarily a slow and difficult one, but in time this *experience of reorganizing the self* gives rise to an *experience of progress,* an awareness that the struggles of self-exploration are actually moving in a positive direction. The client moves closer and closer to his or her self-concept and experience. In time, the client's *experience of ending* brings him or her to the realization that true integration means moving beyond even this most facilitative and caring relationship to a new independence outside of the client-practitioner relationship.

From the client's perspective, at any given moment in the process of person-centered therapy, one of these experiences predominates. For the client, these are very personal, almost indescribable experiences. In the end, we can only grasp those experiences through metaphors, understanding the process as the gradual "unmasking of the true self" or as a difficult but satisfying "journey into self."

The process of therapy   Rogers and his associates spent an incalculable number of hours reviewing therapy sessions, and they gradually determined that the experiences expressed by clients during therapy followed a pattern and that gradually a very specific process of therapy was emerging (Rogers, 1961). The process consists of seven stages arranged along a continuum through which each client moves. Although a client may occasionally slip back, typically clients move forward gradually. A client moves to the next stage after being *received* in the previous one. Being received means that regardless of the client's emotions (for example, fear, anger, insecurity, or despair) and actions (for example, silence, tears, words, gestures), the practitioner expresses empathic understanding and acceptance of the client as he or she is and thus allows and challenges the client to move forward (Rogers, 1961). The seven stages are described below (pp. 133–155):

1. *Stage 1*: Clients in this stage are unwilling to enter into relationships that require revelation; they neither want to change nor acknowledge that change is necessary. Such individuals react to experiences in the present only in terms of the past and in a fixed and rigid manner. Such a person is unlikely to come voluntarily to therapy. Individuals who complete the first stage may do so in group therapy or play therapy (a variation designed for children) where a receiving climate is established but where no initiative is required.

2. *Stage 2*: Clients in this stage are able to talk about topics unrelated to themselves, but accept little personal responsibility and do not acknowledge or express any consistent appreciation of themselves.

3. *Stage 3*: Clients in this stage are able to talk about events, people, and themselves and may express strong emotions, especially negative ones about past events. Such individuals speak of themselves *objectively*—that is, as disowned or remote. Stage 3 clients do begin to see inconsistencies and contradictions in their experiences, however, and begin to realize that some patterns of behavior are ineffective. Many clients enter therapy at this stage.

4. *Stage 4*: Clients in this stage are able to acknowledge and own intense feelings from the past and are increasingly able to express present feelings. This is sometimes done by objectifying the feelings, as in the sentence "It really makes me feel discouraged and unhappy, and that makes me angry." These clients begin to question the typically rigid manner in which they have understood and described their experiences and begin to view the relationship with the practitioner as an interpersonal one with all the risks and opportunities inherent in that relationship.

5. *Stage 5*: Clients in this stage live more directly in the present, with unexpected and intense feelings "bubbling up." Although these clients greet the feelings that "seep through" with "surprise and fright," they increasingly accept the feelings in particular and themselves as a whole (p. 141).

6. *Stage 6*: Stage 6 is dramatic, critical, and probably irreversible. Clients begin to live at one with themselves, subjectively living through problems rather than objectifying the self or their feelings as a means of surviving them. Important feelings that have been blocked are expressed without inhibition and are greeted with delight rather than fear. The expression of intense emotions may bring with it biological changes, such as tears, laughter, or relaxation, and Rogers has suggested that some even greater benefit to physical well-being may occur as a result of this emotional release.

7. *Stage 7*: Clients in stage 7 no longer need to be received by the practitioner, although this may still be helpful. These clients are able to transfer what they have learned in therapy to real situations outside of therapy. Stage 7 clients experience life with openness, making real choices based on clear perception of their personal needs and opportunities in the environment. Communication within these clients happens freely and easily without inhibition or fear. Interpersonal communication likewise flows freely and spontaneously.

Although the process of person-centered therapy can be broken down into these common stages, the process will appear different for each client, because each client has different personal issues, experiences, and needs. Likewise, the diverse personalities and skills of practitioners will make each intervention technically different. At the same time, there is consistency and unity at the experiential level. Person-centered therapists assert that: (1) regardless of differences among clients, each client experiences the therapeutic relationship in a similar way and journeys through a predictable therapeutic process; and (2) regardless of differences among practitioners, the ability to communicate empathic understanding and acceptance sparks and sustains that process.

Sample Session

Dr. Freddie Gentler, schooled in person-centered therapy, usually describes himself as an eclectic counseling psychologist. Although he occasionally borrows a behavioral technique, his essential approach to therapy is person-centered. Our client, Constance Craver, has come to Dr. Gentler on the recommendation of a friend. The reader should be alert for: (1) the client's entry into therapy at Stage 3; (2) the client's gradual acceptance of inconsistencies in her feelings; (3) the practitioner's use of genuineness, unconditional positive regard, and empathic understanding; (4) the practitioner's attempts at crystallizing the client's thoughts and feelings, then checking them out with the client; and (5) the practitioner's acceptance and encouragement when the client acknowledges her feelings. The reader is reminded that person-centered therapy depends on the practitioner's total demeanor, and the exchange given below cannot capture that. What follows is a fragment of a very early session between Constance and Dr. Gentler:

Constance (C): It's been so difficult, Doctor, keeping my mouth shut around Carl, trying to make a home for the children and all, and not causing any trouble. I get so angry at times, and then I just cry. Like the time he forgot my birthday—didn't even remember it until one of the kids reminded him. There are lots of things like that, but there's no point mentioning them to him. It just gets me feeling uptight.

Practitioner (P): You've felt angry, kind of bottled up all these years . . .

C: Yes, bottled up. That's it . . .

P: And no one was there to listen, and you feel angry and at times very sad. I can see that, Connie, and you feel you've had enough now.

C: Yes, and plenty of times in the past I would be ready to say something, almost ready to scream, and then I'd stop it. You know, worried about how it might hurt the children.

P: Mm-hm. In other words, there were times when you were ready to tell him what you thought, but because of what might happen, you held back. [*Pause.*] I'm not too clear on how you feel now that the children are gone, Connie.

C: Well, I guess it's just like a habit, you know. I take care of him and all that, but I don't think I could love him now, not with all that has gone on, all the trouble he's caused me. At times he seems OK, but most of the time I just resent him.

P: You seem somewhat uncertain about your feelings about Carl—almost unsure whether you care for him or not.

C: I don't . . . [*She stares off, silent for a long moment.*] It's not easy to say . . . if I love him still; it's only a habit, you know. What else could it be? After all he's done to me, and after all I've done for him. It's just not natural.

P: Sure, I understand that. You feel some affection, but you don't know whether or not you should, whether or not it's OK, given what he's done to you.

C: I guess that's it. You know, Doctor, you seem to really understand, and I feel so silly telling you all this. It seems so trivial and such a burden to make someone else take . . . [*She begins to choke up and diverts her eyes*]

P [*leaning forward*]: Mm-hm.

C [*after a long pause*]: It's so rare that someone really listens to me, really pays any attention, and . . . [*Pause.*]

P: I can feel, Connie, how very much it hurts you to not have anyone to share your feelings with, and yet even as little a time as I have known you, it's easy to listen to you, and I am especially honored that you are willing to make me part of your life. And you should know, I think, that it's possible for you to go beyond the sadness that you now feel; it's possible for you to make your life a happier one. I want to be able to be part of that change, if you will let me.

C [*looking up*]: Oh, yes, I want you to; I do. I feel that you *do* understand me and that there's some hope. But I just don't know what to do, and part of me really wants you to just tell me what to do, and part of me knows that I have to do that myself.

P: Sure. And that's it, Connie. You have to do it, and you can.

C: Yeah. I guess I can.

P: Sure. And part of getting going again, getting unstuck, means getting a sense of just what your feelings toward Carl are.

C: Oh, Doctor, that's so difficult, you know. He's been such a jerk and hurt me so much.

P: It sounds as if you *could* express some love for him, could even tell him that you care for him but find him very difficult, but that something holds you back, something stops you . . .

C: Something does hold me back. [*Pause.*] I feel like I've been a fool all these years, like I've been a dupe. Now I even feel I love him, that I want to make it all still work, but I don't know how. But feeling that way is stupid. I *should* just hate him, I *should* leave him. To stay with him, no matter how much he's changed, would be dumb.

P: You feel torn between what your heart says—"Make the relationship work. Tell him how you feel, what has been happening"—and what you think you ought to feel, what your head says—"Get the bastard. Make him suffer."

C [*tearfully*]: That's it, Doctor. I don't like the feelings of affection to come out, they're weakness, and yet I've been so weak all these years, I just don't know why it's so rough to admit all this.

P: Ah. And now you're ready to accept some of your positive feelings about him as well as the negative ones, and . . .

C: And I want to, and I want to tell him . . .

Evaluation

Next to Freud, no single psychologist has influenced the actual practice of counseling and psychotherapy more than Carl Rogers. Some of the assumptions and strategies of person-centered therapy are explicitly or implicitly integrated into the work of almost all contemporary practitioners. One of person-centered therapy's clear strengths has been its reliance on research. From the beginning, the development and refinement of person-centered therapy have been linked with ongoing research, and those studies have largely supported the ideas and strategies proposed by Rogers (see Raskin, 1985, for a recent review).

For our present purposes, two issues concerning person-centered therapy must be addressed: (1) the validity of the contention that genuineness, unconditional positive regard, and empathic understanding are *necessary and sufficient* conditions for personality change; and (2) the tendency for the practice of person-centered therapy to become stylized through imitation.

The conditions of change   No aspect of person-centered therapy has been more scrutinized than the contention that the triad of genuineness, unconditional positive regard, and empathic understanding are necessary and sufficient conditions for therapeutic change. Historically, the research has largely supported the essentialness of the triad in all types of interpersonal relationships, including those established in counseling and psychotherapy (Truax & Carkhuff, 1967), and there seems to be little disagreement with the hypothesis that some minimal expression of the triad is a *necessary* condition for change. However, regarding the stronger assertion — genuineness, unconditional positive regard, and empathic understanding as necessary *and sufficient* conditions for therapeutic change — there is both skepticism and conflicting evidence. The skepticism surfaced fairly early, and some of it is striking. Ellis (1962), for example, presented a small catalogue of exceptions to the requisite conditions as outlined by Rogers and argued that Rogers had confused the *desired* characteristics of the practitioner with the necessary ones. Further, the most recent comprehensive review of the literature on therapist variables described the evidence supporting "necessary and sufficient" as "increasingly clouded," adding that Rogers's original formulation now appears too simplistic (Parloff et al., 1978). Lack of clear support for Rogers's full contention does not suggest, however, that the variables he identified are not important ones. Indeed, a wide range of practitioners and researchers affirm the necessity of the triad in some form for successful intervention. Ultimately, it is difficult to dispute the statement made by Parloff et al.:

> We share with Rogers the conviction that the importance of his hypothesis lies not simply in whether it is supported or disconformed, but rather in the possibililty that it might stimulate research that would produce new and more refined understanding of the therapist's role in relation to the process and outcome of psychotherapy. In this endeavor Rogers' efforts have been rewarded. (p. 252)

The stylization of person-centered therapy   Several generations of practitioners have watched Carl Rogers actually do person-centered therapy. The many live, filmed, and videotaped demonstrations of his personal expression of genuineness, unconditional positive regard, and empathic understanding have led to an understandable but unfortunate confusion of style with substance. Students and practitioners of person-centered therapy not uncommonly become little versions of Carl Rogers rather than themselves. They get stuck in what Jourard (1968) called the "impersonation stage," an "experimentally induced character disorder" in which precise imitation replaces genuine development (p. 77). Rogers's style of doing therapy, which, to an untrained eye, can seem paternalistic, passive, and artificial, often replaces the practitioner's own traits. For example, Rogers used short vocalizings like "Mm-hm" and "Un-huh" to acknowledge the client's experience without interrupting it. Taken to an extreme by imitators, however, these utterings have become more the grist for parody than therapy. A similar fate has befallen many of the more specific skills identified and used by Rogers.

The effectiveness of person-centered therapy does not depend on the creation of little "Rogerians"; in fact, if such things can be, Rogers claimed even he was not one! The challenge of person-centered therapy is, rather, to develop within one's own personality the personal congruence and therapeutic skills that will enable one to become as therapeutically effective as Carl Rogers was. From all the evidence, that is no small accomplishment.

Logotherapy

In 1942, Viktor Frankl (born 1905) was a physician in his late 30s, trained in psychiatry and neurology. He had published his first paper at the invitation of Freud, had been a student and colleague of Adler, and was considered by many the up-and-coming successor to those two giants of Viennese psychiatry. His career had seemed assured, and he was hard at work on a manuscript that would present his own approach to psychotherapy, an approach built on the insights of the philosophy of existentialism. Now he was huddled in a shed with other prisoners, preparing to begin what would turn out to be 3 years in Nazi concentration camps, including Auschwitz and Dachau. Frankl continued to cling to his manuscript, sharing with the others the utter disbelief that even the SS troops would take absolutely everything from them. Later, Frankl (1962) would write of this moment:

> I tried to take one of the old prisoners into my confidence. Approaching him furtively, I pointed to the roll of paper in the inner pocket of my coat and said, "Look, this is the manuscript of a scientific book. I know what you will say; that I should be grateful to escape with my life, that that should be all I can expect of fate. But I cannot help myself. I must keep this manuscript at all costs; it contains my life's work. Do you understand that?"
>
> Yes, he was beginning to understand. A grin spread slowly over his face, first piteous, then more amused, mocking, insulting, until he bellowed one word at me in answer to my question, a word that was ever present in the vocabulary of the camp inmates: "Shit!" At that moment I saw the plain truth and did what marked the culminating point of the first phase of my psychological reaction: I struck out my whole former life. (pp. 20–21)

Within minutes of this conversation, Frankl would not only be without his manuscript, he would be standing naked in a herd of other men, thankful that what was coming from the showers above them was only water rather than the gas that killed millions. This was the beginning of 3 years of hell, 3 years during which he would cling to the image of his wife, 3 years during which he would try to reconstruct his manuscript. In the end, his wife and other family members would not survive the camps. In the end, the philosophical tenets that had been the basis of his manuscript would be put to the most severe test a human being can endure: humankind's capacity for inhumanity.

Historical and Theoretical Foundations

Logotherapy, developed by Frankl, has been described as the "Third Viennese School of Psychotherapy," after those of Freud and Adler. When he was a young man, Frankl had corresponded with Freud and, at Freud's invitation, published his first article in 1924. Later, however, Frankl became a follower of Adler until he was expelled from that circle for his increasingly divergent views. Frankl obtained his M.D. at the University of Vienna in 1930 and, after World War II, a Ph.D. in philosophy from that same institution. Like Freud and Adler, Frankl is Jewish, but unlike the others, he did not leave Austria, even when Nazism was at its most threatening. Despite a visa for immigration to the United States, Frankl remained in Austria hoping that through his position, he would be able to save the lives of his parents. (He was unable to do so.)[5] As noted earlier, the manuscript that Frankl took with him into the concentration camps was lost forever. However, during and after his imprisonment, Frankl reconstructed the book, published in German in 1946 and in English in 1955 with the title *The Doctor and the Soul*. This book is generally considered Frankl's most comprehensive presentation of the tenets of logotherapy. In 1946, Frankl also wrote an account of his experiences in the concentration camps that was published in English in 1959 under the title *From Death Camp to Existentialism* and revised and reissued with a section on logotherapy in 1962 as *Man's Search for Meaning*. This book has provided millions of people with a unique glimpse of the perniciousness, suffering, and occasional heroism that occurred in the camps. Frankl has published many other works in German on psychiatry, neurology, and logotherapy. His other major works in English include *Psychotherapy and Existentialism* (1967), *The Will to Meaning* (1969), *The Unconscious God* (1975b), and *The Unheard Cry for Meaning* (1978).

Frankl is professor of neurology and psychiatry at the University of Vienna Medical School, and a distinguished professor of logotherapy at the United States International University in San Diego. He has held visiting professorships at Harvard University, Southern Methodist University, Duquesne University, and Stanford University Medical School. He has also served for many years as head of the Department of Neurology at the Poliklinik Hospital of Vienna. Various logotherapy institutes exist throughout the world, and the World Congress of Logotherapy is held regularly.

Logotherapy is a philosophically oriented psychotherapy within the humanistic-existential perspective. Saying that it is philosophical does not mean that it is ethereal or unrelated to day-to-day struggles—quite the contrary. Logotherapy begins with a specific ontology, a view on what it means to be human, that challenges the client to choose certain attitudes and actions that benefit both the client and humankind. The ontological position inherent

---

[5]Frankl's writings are sprinkled with stories about his experiences before, during, and after his concentration camp experience. His reasons for remaining in Austria were complex, but his description of his sense of responsibility to his parents is particularly telling. It can be found in *The Will to Meaning* (1969), pp. 58–59.

in logotherapy rests on three basic concepts: (1) freedom of will, (2) the will to meaning, and (3) the meaning of life.

Freedom of will Practitioners from the humanistic-existential perspective have commonly criticized psychoanalysis and behaviorism for their deterministic views of human behavior, views that leave little place for individual conscious choice. In response to this apparent determinism, *freedom* has become a watchword of the humanistic-existential perspective. Frankl is very much concerned with freedom but reminds us that human beings are not free from physical, social, and psychological determinants. At any given moment in each of our lives, we are limited by our health; our genetic endowments; and social, political, and economic conditions, as well as the many psychological vulnerabilities engendered during our developmental years and exacerbated by the stresses of daily living. At the same time, Frankl has argued, human beings possess a freedom of will—not freedom from determinants but rather freedom to take a stand in the face of those determinants. At times, this freedom prompts us to act; at other times, in the face of unavoidable and unchangeable determinants, it is expressed only as an attitude.

This unique capacity to take a stand in the face of determinants is a product of the *spiritual* or *noölogical* dimension of human behavior. Although the physical and psychological dimensions of human behavior are the most apparent, it is a tenet of logotherapy that human beings also possess a spiritual or existential dimension that allows us to go beyond our physical and psychological limitations, to transcend whatever instincts link us with other animal species. This spiritual dimension is not a religious dimension, although it can lead us to God and religious practice. Rather, it is our ability to realize personal happiness through our discovery of meaning in love, suffering, and the accomplishment of personal missions.

More specifically, freedom of will can be seen in two uniquely human capacities: self-detachment and self-transcendence. *Self-detachment* is the ability to view oneself as if from a distance, to momentarily detach from self-consciousness and observe oneself and the requirements of the situation on their own merits. Self-detachment expresses itself in heroism and humor. In *heroism,* we assess the demands of a situation and assume a "selfless" attitude toward meeting those demands. Although most of our lives provide us with few opportunities for newsworthy acts of heroism, we have ample chances to be heroes. Heroism can take many everyday forms: uncritical acceptance of an aging parent's idiosyncrasies, uncomplaining and enthusiastic day-to-day attention to the needs of one's students, or steadfast attention to a dying friend. Put in those terms, no one lacks for opportunities for heroism. *Humor,* too, involves the ability to see our own behavior from a bird's-eye view, to see the lighter and, at times, absurd side of life's follies and foibles. Such humor is not hostile or self-deprecating. Rather, it both acknowledges and accepts the limitations of being human. Subjects for humor abound: our unfounded fears, endless primping, exaggerated story telling, and inflated self-importance.

Self-transcendence refers to our ability to choose to move beyond our own needs and priorities to love another person or fulfill a unique task or mission. To love another person is to reach beyond oneself, to forget oneself, to revel in the experience of encountering the uniqueness of another person. While sex per se is tension reduction, the sexual expression that comes with self-transcendent love is humanizing, liberating, and spiritual. Self-transcendence is also apparent in our ability to respond to our consciences in accepting tasks or missions that we have a unique capacity to fulfill. Though pursuing other tasks may yield more money or other rewards, we are capable of choosing instead to do things that stretch ourselves and benefit others.

What directs us to use our freedom of will to go beyond the merely physical and psychological? What motivates us to express self-detachment and self-transcendence? The answers rest in our will to meaning.

The will to meaning For Freud, behavior is motivated by a "will to pleasure." For Adler, behavior is motivated by a "will to power." For Frankl, the *will to meaning* ultimately directs our behavior. To seek pleasure, power, or happiness for its own sake necessarily leads to disillusionment and dissatisfaction. With apologies to Thomas Jefferson, Frankl has suggested that the "pursuit of happiness" is misguided. So, too, is the pursuit of any desirable outcome, including self-actualization. Pleasure, power, happiness, success, self-actualization—these are by-products of being meaningfully engaged in life. When we go beyond ourselves in self-detachment and self-transcendence, we discover meanings unique to ourselves, meanings that yield happiness and self-actualization for each of us individually. This paradox is illustrated and described more fully in Figure 8.3.

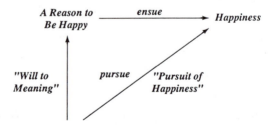

Figure 8.3 *The will to meaning* (From: Frankl, 1969, p. 34). *Ironically, when we pursue happiness, pleasure, power, or even self-actualization, our absorption in the goal precludes our discovery of those people and activities with which we can meaningfully engage—thus precluding the happiness, pleasure, power, or self-actualization that is a by-product of meaningful engagement. In expressing our freedom of will in attitudes and actions that are self-detached and self-transcendent, we discover meaning, receive both pleasure and power, and become increasingly self-actualizing.*

Self-actualization is a by-product of fulfilling the will to meaning. In practice, meaning comes from the realization of specific human values. Frankl described three kinds of values: creative values, experiential values, and attitudinal values. *Creative values* are those that are actualized by performing tasks or completing missions. A young physician's choice to stay in a lower paying position because she "likes the work," for example, suggests that the meaningfulness of the work provides satisfaction greater than the value of monetary or status gains and thus reflects an actualization of creative values. *Experiential values* are realized through involvement in "the Good, the True, and the Beautiful." Much meaning can be found in allowing oneself to fully experience the world of ideas, science, the arts, nature, and interpersonal relationships. Lastly, *attitudinal values* allow us to find meaning in the face of limits, especially those of guilt, suffering, and death. Each of us is capable of assuming an attitude that endows such limits with meaning. Each of us is under a biological death sentence. As we grow older or face grave sickness, our ultimate end can depress and disable us. Yet, we can make the remaining time meaningful by choosing an attitude that acknowledges the past and charts a productive future, no matter how fleeting that future may be! Remember: Frankl formed and tested these ideas in the futureless void of concentration camps.

So life provides each of us with opportunities to discover meaning by realizing creative, experiential, and attitudinal values. Actualizing any of these values requires that we use our unique human capacities of self-transcendence and self-detachment. Discovering meaning, realizing values, and detaching from and transcending the self are thus uniquely human, characteristically spiritual activities.

The will to meaning is the most distinctly human source of motivation. Frustration of the will to meaning leads to noögenic neurosis, a neurotic condition that results from a failure to discover meaning through the actualization of values. Noögenic neurosis is specifically exhibited in a symptomatic triad: depression, aggression, and addiction.

The meaning of life The will to meaning directs a person to discover meaning in life. The age in which we live, however, does not provide ready-made meaning; no absolute certainties automatically provide meaning. Nor are we left merely to invent or fabricate meaning, as some existential philosophers suggest. Rather, meaning is unique to each individual and can be found only in the context of that person's life. Asked, "What is the meaning of life?" Frankl might answer as life itself does: "What will you make of your life?" As human beings, we are in the continual process of answering that question through the realization of creative, experiential, and attitudinal values. If a person is bereft of a meaningful purpose in life, however, logotherapy is designed to provide an *existential analysis*—that is, a careful and very specific evaluation of the potential sources of meaning in the client's life. We look now at how that intervention works.

The Process of Intervention

In a very real sense, all good practitioners are logotherapists, whether they formalize the process or not. Counseling and psychotherapy continually involve challenging the client to become more fully, more uncomplainingly involved in life. Practitioners often find themselves helping clients determine possible sources of meaning, encouraging them to pursue those ends. Logotherapy is a full and formal articulation of this process that complements traditional therapeutic techniques but remains distinct from them.

As an article in the *New York Times* put it, "If 'shrink' is the slang for the Freudian analyst, then the logotherapist ought to be called 'stretch' " (Frankl, 1978, p. 30). Clearly, the analysis that takes place in psychoanalysis is different from what must transpire in the existential analysis of logotherapy. What specifically are the differences? When Frankl is asked this question, he typically answers with something like this: Psychoanalysis involves lying on a couch saying things you don't want to say; logotherapy involves sitting in a chair hearing things you don't want to hear.

As in other forms of counseling and therapy, the client-practitioner relationship is considered basic to logotherapy, but the logotherapist's role is neither passive nor nondirective. Essentially, logotherapy is nondidactic, nonconformative "education toward responsibility." Logotherapy consists of a chain of improvisations by the logotherapist that honestly and forthrightly motivate the client to assume responsibility for finding meaning in life. At times, the ongoing dialogue may focus on the beliefs or aspirations of the client; at other times, it may address philosophical or religious concerns, interpersonal conflicts, suffering, or even death. The logotherapist accepts the value system of the client unless that value system is itself reductionistic or nihilistic. If the client expresses beliefs about human nature that view human beings as helpless victims of genetics, environment, or both, then the logotherapist shares a different value system with the client, a value system that encompasses the potential for change (Lukas, 1979). Logotherapy is always compassionate, but it also always moves the client to take an attitudinal stand in the face of difficulties and to act in ways that will endow life with purpose.

Logotherapy as a nonspecific therapy Logotherapy can be applied as a *nonspecific therapy* in the treatment of physical and psychological suffering of all kinds. While the client's source of suffering is being directly treated through a specific medical or psychological intervention, for example, logotherapy can be applied to help the client understand and deal with the suffering. In doing this, logotherapists do not usually use the specialized language of logotherapy. Rather, the dialogues happen in the language of the client, without reliance on technical terms.[6] With medical problems, logotherapy helps the client be-

---

[6]Clearly, practitioners of logotherapy, as well as other approaches, can also use Frankl's writings when working with clients. *Man's Search for Meaning,* for example, is so readily available and so directly addresses many key issues in clients' lives that it can be a valuable therapeutic adjunct.

come responsible for choosing attitudes toward suffering, confinement, and the possibility of death that result in ennobling and constructive behavior. In the treatment of psychological problems (for example, neuroses and psychoses), logotherapy can provide a context for other forms of intervention. Logotherapy directs the client to focus on the future rather than the past and encourages the client to use her or his human capacity for self-detachment and self-transcendence. The client is made to feel capable of change and worthy of the good that the changes will produce. Logotherapy thus becomes a context of concepts, attitudes, and interpersonal challenges that can facilitate the use of other more specific techniques.

Logotherapy as a specific therapy   Logotherapy can also be applied as a *specific therapy* in the treatment of noögenic neuroses. Frankl (1967) described the noögenic neuroses in this way:

> Every age has its neuroses, and every age needs its own psychotherapy. Existential frustration seems to me today to play at least as great a part in the formation of neuroses as formerly the sexual one did. I call such neuroses noögenic neuroses. When a neurosis is noögenic, that is, when it has its roots not in psychological traumata but in spiritual problems, moral conflicts, and existential crises, then such a spiritually rooted neurosis requires a psychotherapy focusing on the spirit; that is what I call logotherapy—in contrast to psychotherapy in the narrower sense of the word. (p. 122)

Frankl (1978) has pointed to a number of studies that support the existence of this separate neurosis, especially the work of Crumbaugh (1964, 1968).[7] Depression, anxiety, and addiction, what Frankl calls the "neurotic triad," can be symptomatic of a noögenic neurosis, as well as of the more traditional neuroses. Noögenic neuroses are rooted in the frustration of the will to meaning, in conflicts of conscience, in conflicts that are essentially spiritual. Again, spiritual is not meant to imply religious. An individual's depression, anxiety, or escape to addiction may reflect a failure to accept responsibility, a failure to become what she or he is capable of becoming.

A few examples of noögenic neuroses and their treatment may help. A man faces the terminal illness of his wife, to whom he has been happily married for 20 years. He becomes depressed and helpless and begins to disengage from her. Logotherapy helps him accept his own "response-ability" to her and to himself, challenging him to recognize that he can endow their years together with ultimate meaning by being with his wife, fully, completely, and uncomplainingly, now. A bright and talented college student drifts into using drugs as a means of dealing with the boredom and loneliness she feels. She looks to her future without hope and escapes her sense of futility through drugs. Logotherapy shows her that she need not be a victim of either boredom or loneliness by helping her identify the people and situations in which she can find meaning. She comes to see her dependence on drugs as an escape from her own ability

---

[7]James Crumbaugh's Purpose in Life Test was one of several measures designed to measure the noögenic neurosis and related phenomena. The test is published by Psychometric Affiliates.

to make her life more meaningful. In the end, she chooses to get involved in a campus project to help the homeless, reestablishes her failing relationship with her sister, and takes the risk of changing her major to the field she would really like to pursue rather than staying with the one that seemed easier.

Logotherapy is described as a "height" psychology rather than a "depth" psychology. In other words, logotherapy directs the client to ask, "What can I become?" rather than "What has made me the way I am?" Logotherapy helps the client replace pursuits that lead to only momentary satisfaction with ones that by their very difficulty or riskiness provide the more lasting satisfaction that comes from meaningful engagement in life.

Paradoxical intention Logotherapy is unique among existential approaches to therapy in its development of a specialized technique with broad applicability. In 1929, Frankl developed a specific technique for the treatment of neurotic symptoms called paradoxical intention, which he detailed in German in a Swiss psychiatric journal (Frankl, 1939) and later in a book (Frankl, 1947). Subsequently, Frankl (1960, 1967, 1973, 1975a, 1985) described paradoxical intention for English-speaking practitioners, and as described in Chapter 5, paradoxical intention has been widely integrated into behavior therapy. As we will see in Chapter 9, paradoxical intention is also an important part of family therapy.

Long before behavior therapy came into prominence, Frankl had argued that a conditioned reflex was at the heart of neurotic symptoms and that although psychoanalysis sought the primary conditions that caused the conditioned reflex, an equally valuable goal would be to change the secondary conditions that reinforce and maintain the neurosis. Paradoxical intention is designed to change those secondary conditions. Frankl (1985) has defined paradoxical intention as a "procedure in whose framework patients are encouraged to do, or wish for, the very things they fear—albeit with tongue in cheek" (p. 102). An example will illustrate its use. A young manager is in his first weeks at his first important job. On his way to lunch one day, he meets a senior manager from his own division, and she invites him to join her for lunch to discuss a project on which she might include him. Although this could be an opportunity for advancement, he becomes anxious, and without much thought, he says that he has other plans but would like to go with her to lunch some other time. Now as he heads to lunch each day, he experiences increasing *anticipatory anxiety,* a fear that he will meet her again under the same circumstances and that she will invite him again. He begins staying in his office during lunchtime and going out of his way to avoid her. Complex intrapsychic factors may explain why he became fearful of her, but what has been established here is a vicious cycle in which the anticipation and fear of the symptoms (anxiety and avoidance) intensifies the anxiety and avoidance pattern. Paradoxical intention is designed to break this cycle by making the feared symptomatic behavior the client's goal. The client may be instructed to actually try to find her and to become as anxious as possible in front of her. He may be told to practice becoming anxious in a mirror, exaggerating his symptoms as much as possible. In other words, the very thing that causes the anticipatory anxiety is used to make the anticipatory anxiety disappear. Humor is clearly at work here as the client exaggerates his symptoms and recognizes their absurdity. A person's ability to break free of symptoms with exaggeration and humor is an illustration of self-detachment at work.

Paradoxical intention has been broadly applied by logotherapists, behavior therapists, and other, eclectic practitioners.[8] It is effective with a wide range of neurotic symptoms and other types of problems but is inappropriate and dangerous when used with endogenous (biological) depression.

Sample Session

At the recommendation of her pastor, Constance Craver has begun visiting Dr. Vic Solomon, a logotherapist who often works with members of Constance's church. Dr. Solomon is particularly sensitive to the problems that arise over value conflicts and religious issues. The reader should be alert for: (1) the accepting but challenging tone of the logotherapist, (2) the practitioner's openness to discussions of values and beliefs, and (3) the use of paradoxical intention as a way of revealing possible sources of meaning. What follows is a fragment of an early session between Constance and Dr. Solomon:

Constance (C): I have nothing to live for, Dr. Solomon. I'm so lost and depressed.

Practitioner (P): If being with him is causing the depression and you have no real meaningful reason to stay, you might as well leave him.

C: I really want to get away from him, you know, but I know that other people will think poorly of me. They'll think I'm breaking up the marriage, but they haven't seen the hell he's put me through.

P: Do you think it would be wrong for you to leave him?

C: I guess I do. I've never approved of divorce, and for many years I didn't leave him because I thought it was wrong. I had spoken with the pastor a number of years ago, and he told me to try to stick it out, you know. He told me to pray over it and to try to tell Carl what I was feeling. The praying came easy, but I have always been afraid of talking with Carl about it.

P: I really think you ought to leave him tonight. As soon as you leave here, go home and pack your bags.

C: Oh, I couldn't just go and do that. There are so many things to take care of.

P: No, Constance. That's the only alternative. You have talked about it for years, and there is no reason not to.

C: But how will he take care of himself? What will our children think?

P: Those things are not important. You have no reason to stay with him.

C: I don't want to leave him.

---

[8]A comprehensive review of paradoxical strategies can be found in Seltzer's (1986) *Paradoxical Strategies in Psychotherapy.*

P: I thought that's what you wanted most? I thought that you could only find happiness by getting away from him.

C: Sometmes I love him, but most of the time I don't because he ignores me. And then I hate myself for not telling him how much I resent him. I'm just so afraid of him.

P: He would hurt you?

C: No. No. I'm just afraid he won't pay attention.

P: You don't want to leave him because so much of the purpose of your life is wrapped up in him. But you can't continue to make yourself miserable by staying with him. I think you must begin to talk with him about it, let him in on the decision you have to make. You have suffered over the past years for nothing! You've lived with and for this man for years, and now you seem to want to throw it away without a fight by just staying there and suffering more or leaving him without resolving anything with him.

C: I know you're right, Doctor, but I'm afraid.

P: You know, I imagine Carl as a great big monster—covered with scales and likely to swallow you.

C [*laughing*]: Don't be silly. He's not that bad. It's funny. I guess it is pretty silly for me to be so afraid of him. I do act like he's a monster.

P: You are going to need courage to face him, and then after facing him, you're going to need courage to stay with him or you're going to need courage to leave him. Your faith will help you, I think.

C: You're right, Doctor Solomon, it will. And you are willing to help me through it, aren't you?

P: Most certainly.

Evaluation

Logotherapy is unique because it does not compete with other systems but rather complements them. The issues that logotherapy addresses are certainly real and important ones, but intellectually, logotherapy can be rather abstract and philosophical. In practice, however, logotherapy is very practical, and freed of some of its terminology, it has an essential quality to it. In addition, paradoxical intention is now quite prominent as a precursor of a whole repertoire of paradoxical therapeutic strategies.

In the end, the value of Frankl's work lies in its confrontation of the most fundamental human experiences. Perhaps the reader of this book, like its author, has led a relatively happy life, one free from most of life's more harrowing experiences. Yet, each of us faces suffering and death and, in our present age, an ambiguous future. We can get a taste of the impact of Frankl's work from a letter written to Frankl by a prisoner at a maximum-security prison in Florida:

> Dear Dr. Frankl,
> During the past several months a group of inmates have been sharing your books and tapes. Yes, one of the greatest meanings we can be privileged to experience is suffering. I have just begun to live, and what a glorious feeling it is. I am constantly humbled by the tears of my brothers in our group when they can see

that they are even now achieving meanings they never thought possible. The changes are truly miraculous. Lives which heretofore have been hopeless now have meaning. Here in Florida's maximum security prison, some 500 yards from the electric chair, we are actualizing our dreams. It is near Christmas, but logotherapy was my Easter Morning. Out of the Calvary of Auschwitz has come our Easter Sunrise. From the barbed wire and chimney of Auschwitz rises the sun. . . . My, what a new day must be in store. (Frankl, 1978, p. 42–43)

Summary of Chapter 8

Chapter 8 is the second of two chapters presenting major approaches to psychotherapy and counseling that are considered insight therapies. The three approaches described in this chapter are: Gestalt therapy, person-centered therapy, and logotherapy. These three approaches all utilize the concept of self-actualization in some way, and all can be grouped within the humanistic-existential perspective.

Gestalt Therapy

1. Gestalt therapy was developed by psychiatrist Fritz Perls. Although it has borrowed some concepts from Gestalt psychology, its roots are in psychoanalysis. Perls described Gestalt therapy as "existential," but its connection with existentialism is not clear.
2. Unlike psychoanalysis, Gestalt therapy emphasizes the here and now. Gestalt therapy stresses each individual's unique potential for self-actualization and the importance of assuming responsibility for oneself. Intuition is favored over intellect as a source of knowledge.
3. Individuals who come for therapy are unable to live happily in the here and now. They are still living out unfinished business—that is, experiences from the past that still cause anger and resentment.
4. Gestalt therapy is improvisational in nature, and the practitioner ideally both supports and frustrates the client. The focus of therapy is on the client's immediate experience, especially feelings, and questions of why are discouraged.
5. Gestalt therapy pays special attention to the role that dreams play as projections of conflicting sides of the patient's psyche. Many Gestalt techniques exist for group and individual work.
6. Some ideas and techniques from Gestalt therapy appear to be commonplace among contemporary practitioners, but partly because of the unsystematic and improvisational nature of Gestalt therapy, it lacks solid research support.

Person-Centered Therapy

7. Person-centered therapy was developed by psychologist Carl Rogers as an alternative to psychoanalysis. Rogers believes that psychotherapy is a

knowable and predictable process that is amenable to scientific research. Much of his life has been spent trying to identify the elements common to all successful therapy.

8. Person-centered therapy, originally called client-centered therapy, is a nondirective approach that emphasizes the intrinsically healing nature of the therapeutic relationship itself. An individual's development as a fully functioning person is facilitated by the practitioner's genuineness, unconditional positive regard, and empathic understanding. Rogers has argued that these three characteristics of the relationship are "necessary and sufficient conditions of therapeutic change."

9. Therapy takes place in stages during which the client becomes increasingly independent from the practitioner. In the end, the client lives without pretense, clearly perceiving her or his needs and opportunities in the environment.

10. Rogers's person-centered therapy has had enormous impact on contemporary practitioners, both philosophically and practically. Rogers is credited with discovering some of the basic elements in successful therapy. Though the three conditions noted by Rogers appear to be necessary conditions of change, current research suggests that they are not typically sufficient.

Logotherapy

11. Logotherapy was developed by psychiatrist and neurologist Viktor Frankl as a complement to traditional psychotherapy. Logotherapy directly addresses spiritual rather than psychological conflict.

12. The concepts undergirding logotherapy are drawn from existentialism. Human beings are viewed as possessing a freedom of will that is expressed both in action and attitude. Rather than being motivated primarily by a will to pleasure (Freud) or a will to power (Adler), Frankl sees human beings as motivated by a will to meaning, an inborn desire of all human beings to be meaningfully engaged in life. A unique meaning in life exists for each person, but that meaning must be discovered individually. Happiness is a by-product of a meaningful life.

13. Human beings find meaning in life through the completion of special tasks or missions; the experience of love, art, science, and nature; and the choosing of productive attitudes toward suffering and death.

14. As a nonspecific therapy, logotherapy is used as a complement to medical treatment and psychotherapy. As a specific therapy, logotherapy is a treatment for the noögenic neuroses resulting from frustration of the will to meaning by the ambiguities of life in our age.

15. Paradoxical intention is a specialized technique developed by Frankl that short-circuits anticipatory anxiety by having the client approach or perform that which is most feared.

CHAPTER 9

Family Therapy

The family may be regarded as a kind of barter unit. The values exchanged are love, food, protection, material good, and information. Within the group the parents are in the beginning the prime givers. The children are at first mainly receivers, but, across time, they also make significant returns in kind.

Nathan W. Ackerman

Sample Case: Jason Flowers

The parents of Jason Flowers contacted the Uptown Family Institute when he was 18 years old, just 2 weeks after his high school graduation. Three days after his graduation, Jason locked himself in his room, refusing to eat meals with his family or to communicate with them. From all indications, he listened to music through earphones and, late at night, sneaked into the kitchen for food. When his father or brother would come to the door, Jason would insult them, often using obscenities. He continually told them to leave him alone. When his mother pleaded with him at the door, Jason said he was afraid to come out because his father and brother would beat him up. Promises from both his brother and father that they would not hurt him were to no avail. A variety of strategies were tried to get him out of the room, including promising him his favorite meal, arranging a visit from their church's pastor, and threatening to block his access to the bathroom and to keep him from getting into the refrigerator. None of the threats was carried out.

Jason's expressed fears had an ironic quality. At over 6 feet tall and 210 pounds, Jason was taller and significantly heavier than his parents and his 20-year-old brother, Michael. Further, Jason had taken boxing lessons and worked out on a regular basis. As a child, Jason had been fearful and shy, but throughout later childhood and adolescence, he had often verbally and angrily attacked family members and close friends. Household members, which included Jason's parents, brother, and maternal grandmother, had learned to be very careful when speaking to Jason. They tried very carefully not to upset him. Although he never physically hurt others, he had injured himself at least a half-dozen times by punching or kicking a wall or door. Of course, this also occasioned some damage to the family's property.

The family's call to the Uptown Family Institute brought a visit from Nancy Bond. Ms. Bond's background in both social work and anthropology made her a keen observer of family life; the following comments are excerpted from her notes:

> *The Flowers family lives in a row house in a middle-class, blue-collar neighborhood [in a large East Coast city]. I was greeted at the door by Mr. Flowers, who showed me into the living room (he referred to it as the "front room," while his wife called it the "parlor"). My visit was in the late afternoon, and Mr. Flowers, who works an 11 P.M.-to-7 A.M. shift as a warehouse supervisor, appeared freshly shaved and showered. He was dressed in slacks and a dress shirt, open at the collar. While we waited for Mrs. Flowers to arrive home from her job, Mr. Flowers briefed me on Jason's "terrible problem," as he referred to it.*

> *The living room of the Flowerses' home is small but comfortable. The two chairs and sofa are arranged around a large color television. The television is clearly the central focus of the room. On the television is an 8″ × 10″ color photograph of Michael Flowers in a gold frame. It appears to be a high school graduation picture. On an end table near one of the chairs is another set of pictures, both 5″ × 7″ black-*

and-white prints in plastic frames. One photo is of Jason, one photo is of Michael; both photos appear to be several years old. . . .

Mr. Flowers recounted the problems they have had with "Poor Jason." He explained that Michael had tried very hard to help Jason and that Michael had been very patient. The image of Michael that emerges from the conversation with Mr. Flowers is of a powerful giant, patient but surely capable of inflicting the beating that Jason reportedly fears. In speaking of Michael, Mr. Flowers referred to him usually as "our son, Michael," a habit that his wife also evidenced at a later time.

Mrs. Flowers returned home from her job as a department-store sales clerk about 40 minutes after I began speaking with Mr. Flowers. She was very warm and friendly and repeated with uncanny similarity the stories her husband had just told me. She, too, spoke of Michael as a powerful but patient older brother, but she warned me that his patience was probably "wearing thin" and that Jason might well find himself "taken care of" by Michael if he continued to "taunt" Michael. In her conversations about Jason, Mrs. Flowers did not refer to him as "poor Jason." Rather, she called him "Jassie," a "pet name" she admitted greatly displeased him. Later, when Mr. Flowers left the room, she whispered to me that she thought Mr. Flowers had been too strict with Jason. She said that since Michael had been such a "doll" when young, Mr. Flowers had overreacted to Jason when he started to cause trouble. She indicated that for her own part, she had been too easy on Jason, but Michael had been such an "easy child" that she was unprepared for all the "personal problems" Jason was going to develop. . . .

When I finally met Michael later that afternoon he turned out to be a good-looking, very friendly, somewhat shy young man with a winning smile and considerable charm. He expressed little anger about Jason's behavior, and indicated that he had long ago developed the ability to ignore Jason's taunts. He appeared genuinely concerned about his brother. Further (as I would notice the next day), Michael was easily 40 pounds lighter than Jason and almost 2 inches shorter.

Ms. Bond was able to speak through the door to Jason, and after some conversation, he agreed to come with his family to the institute. He emerged the next day at the appropriate time, and drove silently with his family to the institute.

Earlier, in Chapter 2, I discussed the inherent limitations of individual psychotherapy and counseling given the importance of culture in determining and maintaining our behavior. In the present chapter, I explore *family therapy,* a group of approaches to counseling and psychotherapy that treat the culture rather than the individual. By focusing on the family, family therapy looks at the most intimate culture, a culture made up of our most important interpersonal relationships and our most meaningful rituals, beliefs, myths, and artifacts. The clients of family therapy are all the individuals in the family, listened to and understood not as soloists, but as inseparable, interacting members of the family chorus. In the case of the Flowers family, individual therapists would traditionally view Jason as disturbed or sick. For family therapists, Jason Flowers is the *identified patient* or "IP." From this point of view, Jason is the person that the family identifies as sick, but that sickness is neither separable nor understandable apart from the familial context. Jason is part of a system, a culture that needs to be corrected, to be reharmonized.

The difference between family therapy and the more traditional individual approach is more than theoretical; family therapy differs in practice. Consider the following description of family therapy from Jay Haley (1976):

> Not long ago, it was expected that a therapist would be closeted along with one person who would talk at length about himself and his fantasies. Today, a therapy session may involve a whole family gathered together talking in a one-way mirror room with video cameras going and a supervisor watching and telephoning from behind the mirror. The room is full of action and emotion as the therapist shifts people from chair to chair and guides the action among the participants. When therapy takes this form, it becomes a human drama of action rather than a conversation about matters happening elsewhere. Husbands and wives negotiate and fight with each other, adolescents rebel against parents, children may be beaten on camera, and affection and tenderness appear in many forms and guises. The therapist is participant, guide, director, activator, and reflector as the important actions of life are recorded by video cameras. (p. 223)

One further comment by way of preamble. In the story of Jason Flowers, the reader may have been surprised by the social worker's attention to commonplace things: the use of particular expressions, the arrangement of the room, the description of a child, the placement of pictures, or the manner of dress. Yet, for the student of the family, whether from the perspective of anthropology, sociology, social work, psychology, or family therapy, nothing is commonplace. Everything is part of that complex system we call culture, in this case, the most intimate and formative culture, family. Culture, with all of its commonplaces, is the key to understanding the individual and the individual's difficulties. Perhaps anthropologist Jules Henry (1971) put it best when he wrote:

> I do not believe in the "commonplace." If a woman peels an onion; if a man reads a newspaper or watches television; if there is dust or no dust on the furniture; if a parent kisses or does not kiss his child when he comes home; if the family has eggs or cereal for breakfast, orange juice or no orange juice, and so on through all the "trivia" of everyday life—this is significant to me, if for no other reason than that commonplaceness proves the family sane. (p. xix)

Historical and Theoretical Foundations

The practice of psychotherapy began with Freud's **psychoanalysis** and its emphasis on the primacy of the individual's intrapsychic events. With the advent of neopsychoanalysts like Adler, Erikson, Horney, Jung, and Sullivan, there was a new emphasis on social and interpersonal development, and Adler in particular considered the family enormously important. This newer *social psychiatry,* as it has been called, certainly took account of the importance of interpersonal development in the family context, but like psychoanalysis, it was wedded to intrapsychic constructs, the identification of individual pathology, and one-on-one treatment. In practice, most contemporary family therapy is quite different. In family therapy, the intrapsychic is de-emphasized or ignored, individual pathology made secondary, and one-on-one treatment routinely abandoned in favor of treating the family per se. Nevertheless, family therapy developed largely in the world of the psychoanalytic and neopsychoanalytic perspectives and was strongly influenced by their ideas.

The other force that has shaped family therapy is **systems theory**.[1] Systems theory, like psychoanalysis, is really a model for explaining human behavior, but in systems theory, the focus is the *interactional process* between and among individuals rather than individual behaviors in themselves. In the systems model, individual behavior is always viewed in the context of interactions taking place within a structured, dynamic system. Systems theory is very different from psychoanalytic theory in two important ways. First, in systems theory, individual behavior is an inseparable product of the system; therefore, the basic objective of psychotherapy must be to change the system rather than the individual behavior. Thus, following the systems theory model, one speaks of a *dysfunctional family* rather than a pathological individual. Second, according to systems theory, systems exist independent of the conditions that set them in motion. This is known as the quality of *equifinality* and implies that there is little or no need to look at historical causes of present behaviors. This, too, is quite different from the assumptions that guide psychoanalysis.

Full transition from an individualistic view to an interactional one requires understanding the difference between linear and circular causality. Typically within the behavioral sciences, we have understood phenomena in terms of *linear causality*. Observing an event, we assume a causal link between that event and some prior, concurrent, or anticipated event, as if we could draw a line between events A and B and pronounce A the cause of B. This is a convenient way to operate, but in doing so, we assume that causation in nature actually occurs that way. An alternative view is to see an event in terms of *circular causality*—that is, as part of a series of other events that are interrelated in cycles maintained over time by their mutual interaction with one other. A linear explanation of Jason Flowers's behavior may focus on some early traumatic experience, the inadequacy of reinforcement for social behavior, a poor self-concept, or his anticipation that he will not be punished for the behavior. The assumption in each of these explanations is that some single event or series of events in the past, present, or future is causing Jason's behavior. Viewed in terms of circular causation, the complex interaction among Jason and the other members of his family means that no single event, intrapsychic state, or person can be "blamed" for Jason's present behavior. His behavior exists as one of

---

[1]Systems theory as applied to family therapy is part of a larger movement in the philosophy of science called *general systems theory*, a "science of science" pioneered by Ludwig von Bertalanffy (1968, 1977). Systems thinking came into psychology through the work of Kurt Lewin (1936).

many expressions of the unique interaction of these individuals within their cultural context. Jason's behavior is caused and maintained not by a series of historical events but by a complex of people, cultural institutions, and situations.

All approaches to family therapy evidence the influence of both the individual emphasis of the psychoanalytic model and the interactional emphasis of the systems model. In the sections that follow, we will see how these two potent theories have rivaled each other, and the diversity of family therapies that are their offspring.

Family Therapy Beginnings[2]

Family therapy has no undisputed founder and developed in several different quarters during the 1940s and 1950s. By the end of the 1950s, however, family therapy was a single movement within the mental health arena. Because of its varied sources, the family therapy movement that emerged was composed of diverse schools, but by the end of the 1950s a common understanding of what distinguished family therapy existed: "The whole family works with the same therapist in the same room at the same time [italics omitted]" (Bodin, 1984).[3] An important first step toward understanding the development of family therapy is understanding the world into which family therapy emerged.

The state of psychotherapy   In the 1940s and 1950s, during the long nascency of family therapy, the mental health establishment was dominated by psychiatry, and the therapy of preference was psychoanalysis. During much of this time, **behavior therapy** was at best in a germinal stage, and even Rogers's **person-centered therapy** was barely formed. In addition to the largely psychoanalytic therapy available to the affluent from psychiatrists in private practice, mental health services gradually became more widely available in psychiatric departments of hospitals and in specialized psychiatric hospitals.

An important part of this broadening was the nationwide establishment of *child guidance clinics.* A unique feature of the child guidance clinics was the development of an interdisciplinary team composed of a psychiatrist, a social worker, and a psychologist (Bierman, 1984). Typically at the time of family therapy's beginnings, the psychiatrist was the main service provider and worked with the patient in one-on-one psychoanalytic therapy. The psychiatrist did not meet with the family of the patient lest that interfere with the requisite transference phenomenon. A psychiatric social worker would take care of the practical matters associated with the family, while the psychologist's role was primarily to provide psychological assessment.[4] Given this sort of arrange-

[2]There are relatively few comprehensive histories of family therapy. Information in this section has been drawn from or checked against Guerin (1976) and Broderick and Schrader (1981).

[3]Bodin is citing Don Jackson's (1959) description of *conjoint family therapy*. Especially in the early days of family therapy, this procedural matter, more than any particular theory or technique, linked the various schools.

[4]The reader may recall two earlier discussions about the enormous appeal of both person-centered therapy and behavior therapy among psychologists and counselors when they appeared. If

ment, it is not surprising that the early family therapists, who dared to suggest that patient and family sit down together as a treatment unit, were considered mad or heretical.

Guerin (1976) identified the frustrations of working with schizophrenic patients and troubled children as the issues that opened the door to the experimentation that led to family therapy. Traditional psychoanalytic methods simply did not work effectively in these cases. At a number of centers throughout the United States, practitioners treating these two populations began to experiment with variations on the traditional approach. Some of the major contributors to that experimentation are described below.

John Elderkin Bell In 1953, John Elderkin Bell, a professor of psychology at Clark University, reported at a meeting of the Eastern Psychological Association that over the past 2 years, he had successfully treated 10 youngsters using a new "family group therapy" in which the clients were seen with their entire immediate family. Bell's decision to treat his clients in this manner was triggered, or at least influenced, by a misunderstanding that had occurred 2 years earlier, when Bell was visiting England. The medical director of the famed Tavistock Clinic in London was describing to Bell the work of the prominent Tavistock psychiatrist John Bowlby and indicated that Bowlby was seeing the entire family of his patients. Because their conversation was interrupted, Bell never found out that Bowlby was seeing each of the family members individually rather than as a group. This (mis)information prompted Bell to develop the radical new approach he reported in 1953 (Bell, 1975). In 1961, Bell published a monograph entitled *Family Group Therapy* that became one of the family therapy's first two handbooks; the other was by Nathan Ackerman (Broderick & Schrader, 1981).

Nathan W. Ackerman Nathan W. Ackerman, a charismatic, grandfatherly child psychiatrist and psychoanalyst, was for many years the dominant figure in family therapy. Following his psychiatric training, Ackerman had spent some time during the Great Depression studying the families of unemployed coal miners in western Pennsylvania. What he discovered among these families led him in 1937 to write a seminal paper on family therapy: "The family as a Social and Emotional Unit" (Ackerman, 1937). Between 1937 and 1955, Ackerman served as chief psychiatrist at the Child Guidance Clinic in Topeka, Kansas; during these years, Ackerman and some of his colleagues gradually began to incorporate the entire family into therapy.[5] In 1960, Ackerman founded the Family Institute in New York, which was renamed the Ackerman

you consider the clearly secondary role played by nonpsychiatrists in these settings, it is not difficult to appreciate why.

[5]Ackerman has contended that the real start of family therapy was not in the work with schizophrenics that received so much notoriety. Rather, he credited the child guidance movement with representing the true beginning of family therapy (Guerin, 1976).

Institute for Family Therapy after his death in 1971. The Ackerman Institute continues to be a major center for family therapy. As noted above, Ackerman's (1958) *Psychodynamics of Family Life,* like Bell's work, was one of the early handbooks of family therapy.

Ackerman never abandoned the psychoanalytic model, incorporating social-psychological theories and systems theory into it. Ackerman was an insider to the largely psychoanalytic psychiatric establishment, as well as one of its critics, and he served as a critical link between family therapy and that establishment. In the actual practice of family therapy, Ackerman has been described as working with families like a "bullfighter does with a bull," a characterization that suggests that his level of activity and innovation were far beyond a mere translation of psychoanalytic principles into a family setting (Hoffman, 1981).[6] Ackerman was enormously influential both because of his pioneering efforts and because of his personal gifts as a practitioner. With his death in 1971, the center of the field of family therapy shifted away from psychoanalysis and toward systems theory (Guerin, 1976).

Lyman C. Wynne   Lyman Wynne received his M.D. from Harvard in 1948, and then completed a Ph.D. in the Department of Social Relations at the same university. During these latter studies, he encountered the sociological theories of Talcott Parsons, particularly his view that personality is a subsystem of the family system. In 1942, Wynne began working at the National Institute of Mental Health (NIMH), and in 1957, he became head of the Family Studies Section after the departure of Murray Bowen (see below). Gradually, Wynne and his colleagues began to incorporate family members into the therapeutic process, and working from a psychoanalytic foundation and the sociological ideas of Parsons and the developmental model of Erik Erikson, Wynne developed his own theory and approach to family structure in schizophrenic patients. Wynne moved to the University of Rochester in 1971 to continue his work with schizophrenics.

Most striking among the contributions of Wynne and his colleagues is the concept of *family boundaries.* Within families are boundaries that separate the identities and needs of each member of the family. In the families of schizophrenics, according to Wynne and his colleagues, boundaries become confused because of excessive rigidity or inadequate definition. Each individual within the family seeks self-identity and meaningful relationships, and four ways of relating to the family either foster or impede meeting those needs. The first is *mutuality,* the ideal way of relating, in which the different self-interests of family members are harmonized, and the individual's needs and the family's needs are balanced. With mutuality, the family boundaries are permeable

---

[6]Lynn Hoffman's splendid *Foundations of Family Therapy* (1981) provided a telling description of Ackerman as a practitioner. Noteworthy among her contentions is that, in practice, Ackerman used a structural approach, a type of family therapy pioneered by a colleague to whom he introduced family therapy, Salvador Minuchin.

enough to allow individual members to try out different roles but defined enough so that appropriate roles do not become ambiguous. The second is *non-mutuality*, in which the individual and the family share no common interest, and relationships are superficial. The third is *pseudomutuality*, in which the pretense of mutuality covers the loss of personal identity by one or more members of the family. Pseudomutuality is characteristic of the families of schizophrenics (Wynne, Ryckoff, Day, & Hirsch, 1958). The fourth is *pseudohostility*, where alienation among family members serves to obscure the real needs of the members for intimacy. These and other ideas from Wynne have helped to clarify some of the less apparent dynamics of family structures.

Murray Bowen   Wynne's efforts were augmented for a few years by those of psychiatrist Murray Bowen, who joined NIMH in 1954 after working at the Menninger Clinic in Topeka, Kansas. As head of the Family Studies Section at NIMH, Bowen undertook an extended project that involved having the families of hospitalized and schizophrenic youngsters actually live in the hospital for periods of up to 2 years. By the middle of 1956, however, it had become apparent to Bowen that NIMH was less than enthusiastic about his experimental approach, and he moved on to Georgetown University, where he continued his research. Bowen began to use this new family approach in his private practice and gradually developed a distinct school of family therapy. Bowen's approach to family therapy is a comprehensive one, with specific concepts, techniques, and terminology. Unlike Ackerman's approach to family therapy, Bowen's is not predominantly psychoanalytic in theory; rather, Bowen developed his own systems theory. In fact, he called his approach "family systems theory," a name he later changed to "Bowen theory" to avoid confusion with the "general systems theory" of the Palo Alto groups (Bowen, 1978).

Several of Bowen's ideas are used widely in family therapy. For Bowen, the family is a system of which each individual must become a part while remaining distinct from it. The process of maintaining one's own identity while remaining in relationship with the family is called *differentiation of self*. Differentiation depends on an individual's ability to separate intellect and emotion so that the emotion of the family does not supersede her or his ability to meet personal needs. *Fusion* is the opposite of differentiation. Fusion results when the boundaries between the needs of the individual and the emotions of the family blur so much that the individual reacts emotionally instead of responding rationally and productively. Bowen also introduced the concept of *triangulation*. When two members of a family are engaged in interpersonal conflict, a triangle is commonly formed in which a third party is pulled into the conflict. Not uncommonly, this third party is a child who then becomes the focus of the family's attention, thus diverting attention from the troubled relationship. As the conflict eases, the interpersonal dynamic of the triangle changes. Triangulation takes place in all families, but it produces its most telling changes in the behavior of the identified patient when the core problem is a serious one. Returning briefly to Jason Flowers, we might say that Jason has been pulled into an already existing, long-term, but unacknowledged conflict between his parents in such a manner that all of the family's energy goes to "helping" Jason, a young man whose behavior merely signals the real problem.

The Palo Alto groups   Palo Alto, California, was home to two groups of researchers—the Bateson project and the Mental Research Institute; it is largely through their research and publication that family therapy has been so influenced by systems theory. The first of these groups existed for 10 years, from 1952 to 1962, and the second began in 1958 and continues to this day. As we will see, the two groups are closely linked but distinct. The first group takes its name from Gregory Bateson (1904–1980), a British anthropologist and philosopher with expertise in general systems theory and human and animal communication. In 1952, Bateson was teaching at Stanford University and working at the Veterans Administration Hospital when he received a major grant from the Rockefeller Foundation to study paradoxical communication in humans and animals. He chose John H. Weakland, an anthropologist specializing in humor, and Jay Haley, a graduate student with a background in communication, as his first two research associates. The project's examination of communication included a wide range of topics: metaphor, humor, play, animal behavior, ventriloquism, popular films, and even the training of guide dogs for the blind (Bateson, Jackson, Haley, & Weakland, 1963). The two aspects of the research that were critical to the development of family therapy, however, had to do with paradoxical communication in psychotherapy and paradoxical communication in schizophrenia.

The first of these topics involved the Bateson project's study of the therapeutic techniques of a particular practitioner: psychiatrist Milton H. Erickson. At his own request, Haley was assigned to learn about Erickson, an extraordinary therapist whose use of paradox in hypnotherapy provided insight into communication as well as becoming a basic building block of contemporary family therapy (Haley, 1973). The second of the topics, paradoxical communication in schizophrenia, began in 1954. Don Jackson, a psychiatrist at the VA hospital, joined the project at this time and, with the other members of the team published a landmark paper, "Toward a Theory of Schizophrenia" (Bateson, Jackson, Haley, & Weakland, 1956). This article was an important addition to the literature on schizophrenia, but more importantly for our present discussion, it introduced a concept applicable beyond schizophrenia: double bind.

In 1958, Jackson, while remaining a consultant with the Bateson project, founded the Mental Research Institute (MRI) for the purpose of studying family therapy more directly. Jackson and Haley had been developing active intervention techniques that made the therapist an actual member of the family system rather than peripheral to it; MRI continued that research. On Jackson's original staff of MRI was Virginia Satir, a social worker who had joined Jackson at the recommendation of Murray Bowen (Jackson, 1968a). Satir was to become one of the most articulate and influential proponents of family therapy. The existence of family therapy as a single therapeutic perspective and movement might well be dated to around this time. In 1961, Jackson met Ackerman in New York, and together they planned *Family Process,* a journal dedicated to the study of family therapy published jointly by Jackson's MRI and Ackerman's Family Institute. *Family Process* began publishing in 1962, with Jay Haley as its first editor, and remains a major family therapy publication. Also in 1962, when the Bateson project ended, Haley and Weakland came to MRI, and Bateson began serving as a consultant. Haley remained at MRI until 1967, Satir stayed until the mid-1960s, and Jackson died in 1968. MRI has continued to study family therapy and related treatment approaches.

A few concepts from the Palo Alto groups are now universally accepted. The first is that of *family homeostasis* (see Jackson, 1968b). The patterns of communication that exist in a family serve to establish and maintain equilibrium, or homeostasis. When the system is threatened by conflict or negligence, patterns of communication develop that interrupt the change, returning the system to homeostasis. For example, continual fighting between parents that threatens the system may provoke *negative feedback* from a child; that is, the child may develop severe problems (for example, delinquency) that interrupt the conflict and return the system to homeostasis. *Positive feedback* affirms the need for changing the system, thus threatening the stability of the system. Of course, in a pathological system, this may be the goal of a therapeutic intervention.

A second major concept contributed by the Palo Alto groups is that of the *double bind.* In their original description of the double bind, the researchers identified a pattern of communication between schizophrenic youngsters and their parents in which contradictory messages so victimized the children that schizophrenia was the only escape. In later revisions of the theory, the notion of victimization was replaced with a view more in keeping with systems theory (Bateson et al., 1963). Double-bind communication, whether in schizophrenics or "normals," operates as follows: A person experiences subjective distress in response to receiving two contrary messages from one or more members of the same system. Both messages have implicitly or explicitly expressed consequences (reward or punishment), and the system is structured such that the distressed person cannot escape from the communication.

To illustrate, we return to Jason Flowers. As Jason was growing up, his parents communicated two messages, at times directly and at other times indirectly. The first message was a negative one with punitive consequences: "You don't confide in us, but you should. If you don't confide in us, we won't love you." When Jason tried to confide in his parents, they directly or indirectly communicated a second message: "Don't bother us now, we're busy," or "You are bad to be doing the things you're telling us about." For the young and dependent Jason, there was no escape from negative consequences, regardless of his behavior. The concept of double bind has generated a considerable amount of research and, along with other communications concepts, was critical to the development of family therapy.[7]

The Palo Alto groups, whose work is continued today through MRI, represent a major force in the development and continuance of family therapy.

The Philadelphia groups   Family therapy also developed and grew at two centers in Philadelphia. The first was the Eastern Pennsylvania Psychiatric Institute (EPPI), where Ivan Boszormenyi-Nagy, a psychoanalytic psychiatrist, began doing and researching family therapy in 1957. Many of the important contributors to family therapy passed through EPPI at one time or another, and Boszormenyi-Nagy, along with social worker Geraldine Spark and other colleagues, developed an intergenerational-contextual approach to family therapy that will be discussed later. EPPI has been a major training facility for family therapists, as has the Philadelphia Child Guidance Clinic, where psychiatrist Salvador Minuchin and his colleagues developed structural approaches to family therapy during the 1960s and 1970s. Minuchin was director of the Family Therapy Training Center at Philadelphia Child Guidance and was joined in the late 1960s by Jay Haley of Palo Alto fame. Both Minuchin and Haley have developed specific family therapies that will be discussed later.

Family therapy developed in a number of other places, and many important contributors have been omitted in our discussion. One thing appears certain though: Family therapy developed because of the apparent inadequacies of traditional therapies in dealing with all but the most simple problems. Of course, other efforts to address those same inadequacies parallel the development of family therapy, especially those in chemotherapy and behavior therapy.

Family Therapy Today

In the 1950s, family therapy was the unwanted offspring of the mental health establishment. Today, family therapy is more than legitimate; it flourishes. There are several dozen family therapy journals (Bodin, 1984), and it has been estimated that there are over 1,500 family therapy training programs and institutes in the world today (Grebstein, 1986). In 1987, the foremost professional organization for family therapists, the American Association of Marriage and Family Therapy (AAMFT), had over 13,000 full, associate, and student members.[8]

Family therapy emerged from psychoanalytic psychiatry but was influenced by the behavioral sciences, social work, sex therapy, and marriage counseling. Its developers and practitioners have included anthropologists, clergy, counselors, educators, nurses, social workers, psychiatrists, and psychologists.

---

[7]Particularly enlightening on communication patterns, including the therapeutic use of the double bind, is *Pragmatics of Human Communication* by Watzlawick, Beavin, and Jackson (1967).

[8]The membership of the AAMFT is quite diverse, with the majority of members holding master's degrees in a variety of disciplines. Fewer than 40% of the members hold doctoral-level degrees.

The unique success and interdisciplinary nature of family therapy have led to an unusual phenomenon: the emergence of "marriage and family therapy" as a separate profession. Today, many family therapy practitioners, although also allied with other professions, consider family therapy a distinct profession worthy of separate status and credentialing. In the United States, such decisions involve professional organizations, state legislatures, and some amount of politicking. Whether or not marriage and family therapy will emerge as a truly distinct profession remains in the hands of those forces, but its present vitality is unquestionable, as is evident in the diversity of approaches to family therapy to be found today.

Given a chance, even Solomon would abandon the task of sorting the approaches to family therapy! So much overlapping, borrowing, and combining of theories, techniques, and terminology have occurred that separating family therapies into discrete entities without distorting them is difficult. Family therapies can be grouped in several different ways, all legitimate; following a recent classification by Levant (1984), over 20 distinct schools of family therapy may be identified. For our own purposes, we will look at three established and fairly distinct approaches to family therapy that will give us only a sampling of the field: (1) the contextual approach, (2) the structural approach, and (3) the strategic approach. Though all of these approaches have been influenced by systems theory, they evidence it in very different ways. Similarly, the stances of the three approaches on the value of psychoanalysis range from contextual therapy's reliance on psychoanalysis to structural therapy's rejection of it.

One further point is worth noting here. The practice of working with the families of identified patients is not the exclusive province of marriage and family therapists. Historically, behavior therapists have often worked with families, although largely on pragmatic rather than on theoretical grounds. In recent years, the practice of family therapy and the practice of behavior therapy have overlapped considerably, and behavioral or social learning approaches are often included among listings of approaches to family therapy.[9]

The Contextual Approach

Contextual family therapy has developed gradually, primarily at the Eastern Pennsylvania Psychiatric Institute (EPPI) in Philadelphia, under the influence of psychiatrist Ivan Boszormenyi-Nagy. In 1973, Boszormenyi-Nagy and social worker Geraldine Spark published *Invisible Loyalties* (1973/1984), the first formal presentation of the approach that would later be called *contextual therapy*.

---

[9] The similarities are most striking in comparing the work of strategic family therapists like Haley and behavior therapists like Patterson and his colleagues (G. R. Patterson, 1982; G. R. Patterson, Reid, Jones, & Conger, 1975; Reid, 1978). The development of the behavioral approaches depended on neither systems theory nor, obviously, psychoanalysis. The social learning theory of Bandura (1977b), however, which is a powerful force in behavior therapy, is compatible with systems theory.

(It has also been known as *intergenerational family therapy*.) Since that publication, Boszormenyi-Nagy and colleagues Barbara Krasner and David Ulrich have continued to refine and explain the approach (Boszormenyi-Nagy, 1981; Boszormenyi-Nagy & Krasner, 1980; Boszormenyi-Nagy & Ulrich, 1981; Ulrich, 1983).

Theoretical Foundations

Contextual family therapy rests on three theoretical foundations: (1) systems theory, (2) psychoanalysis in the form of object-relations theory,[10] and (3) existential philosophy. The first two are readily apparent in a definition of family pathology from Boszormenyi-Nagy:

> . . . a specialized multiperson organization of shared fantasies and complementary need gratification patterns, maintained for the purpose of handling past object-loss experience. The very symbiotic or undifferentiated quality of transactions of certain families amounts to a multiperson bind, capable of preventing awareness of losses to any individual member. (Boszormenyi-Nagy & Spark, 1973/1984, pp. 199–200, quoting Boszormenyi-Nagy, 1965)

Although contextual therapy does not reflect systems theory thinking as formally or as completely as other approaches do, the above definition includes the basic systems contention that pathology emerges from the interaction among the individuals rather than from one person. However, contextual therapy differs from some more systems-oriented approaches by "never losing sight of the goal of benefiting persons, not systems" (Boszormenyi-Nagy & Ulrich, 1981, p. 159). In other words, contextual therapy begins by looking at individual or relational symptoms rather than at the system per se.

In keeping with its psychoanalytic roots, in contextual therapy, the pathology in the family is considered to be beyond the awareness of the family members, being embedded in their individual pasts, and to involve some object-loss. The term *object-loss* derives from the *object-relations theory* proposed by Melanie Klein and developed by Ronald Fairbairn. Object-relations theory replaces Freud's emphasis on instinctual gratification with one on early human relationships. The most fundamental human need is viewed as that for relationship with some "object"—that is, another person who is differentiated as "not subject," not oneself. This is a need for love, and the earliest relational object in a person's life is typically one's mother. When a child seeks to gratify relational needs, and the mother is for any reason not able to meet those needs, the child *introjects* or internalizes the characteristics of the lost object along

---

[10]A number of other approaches to family therapy are psychoanalytically oriented, including those of Ackerman (1966), Bowen (1978), and Skynner (1981). Despite family therapy's origins in psychoanalysis, more than a few family therapists reject psychoanalysis. Consider these comments from Jay Haley (1971), one of the leading shapers of family therapy: "The current attempt to save psychoanalysis by broadening its concepts to include a family view may have an effect on family therapy similar to that of the air pollution of a large city on a fresh breeze" (p. 8).

with hostility and resentment about the loss. This creates an essential, unconscious conflict that shapes adult behavior into self-defeating patterns.

The third influence, existential philosophy, comes from the work of Martin Buber (1958), specifically his description of the *I-Thou relationship*. According to Buber, human beings are capable of going beyond mere gratification of object-relations needs to engage in an "I-Thou dialogue," an interdependent relationship that affirms the identity of each participant based on an underlying trust. Contextual therapy accords in this regard with the humanistic-existential perspective, because its aim is to maximize human experience by engendering a higher form of interpersonal interaction.

Basic Constructs

The insight that separates contextual therapy from traditional therapies is its "discovery that the key dynamic of relationships is merited trust" (Boszormenyi-Nagy & Krasner, 1980, p. 767). In contextual therapy, as its name suggests, individuals within a family are always viewed *contextually*—that is, in terms of the relationships significant to each individual's life. The main therapeutic objective is to establish or reestablish *trustworthiness* and *fairness* among those family members and significant others. Contextual therapy operates according to a basic ethical premise that requires the "extension of equal concern to all those who may be affected by treatment, taking into account their basic welfare interests as perceived by themselves and by others" (Ulrich, 1983, p. 187). Contextual therapy is thus by its very design *intergenerational*; that is, it may extend beyond the *nuclear family*, which consists of the parent or parents and all children, to the *family of origin*, which consists of the families in which the parents were raised (grandparents). Because the effects of treatment go even beyond the family of origin, the therapy may expand to include the *extended family* of all blood relatives or even the *family network* of all significant other people with whom the family has contact.

Four dimensions Assessment and treatment in contextual family therapy proceed along four dimensions: (1) the dimension of fact, (2) the psychological dimension, (3) the transactional dimension, and (4) the ethical dimension. The *dimension of fact* consists of information about the family and its members. Examples of pertinent information include: a history of major family events across generations; the family's ethnic background and customs; birth order and family structure; the movement of members in and out of households; and changes in the composition of the family caused by births, death, illness, and separation. The *psychological dimension* concerns the intrapsychic life of each individual in the family. The individual is viewed as a subsystem of the family system whose conscious and unconscious perceptions of the impact of family events are as important as the facts themselves. Of particular concern in contextual therapy is *substitutive balancing*, an expansion of the traditional psychoanalytic concepts of displacement and projection. In this defensive process, one member of the family redirects attitudes and emotions about another toward a third, more accessible or approachable member. For example, the rage a man feels toward his mother may be directed toward his son, or the hurt and insecurity that a woman felt at the loss of her sister when she was a child may translate into hostility and distrust toward her husband and children. The *transactional dimension* is concerned with the interpersonal strategies members of the family use to meet their needs, especially as related to the formation of *power alignments*. Here, the contextual therapist may look at the establishment of various types of coalitions, triangulation, scapegoating, the creating of an identified patient, and other interpersonal changes that maintain or disrupt the family as a system.

The *ethical dimension* sets contextual therapy apart from other family approaches and is the focus of much of the therapeutic effort. *Relational ethics* concerns issues of fairness or *equitability* among individuals in the family rather than any established code of right and wrong. The fairness at issue here involves not who gets a bigger piece of pie or who gets to watch a favorite television program but the "long-term perseveration of an oscillating balance among family members, whereby the basic interests of each are taken into account by the others" (Boszormenyi-Nagy & Ulrich, 1981, p. 160). Each member of a family system contributes to it in affection, leadership, time, attentiveness, patience, nurturing, and the more mundane but essential matters of money, housework, meal preparation, planning, and so forth. Each individual in the family has a subjective opinion of his or her own contributions and those of the others, and each person has a sense of the reciprocity that exists among the family members. The balance is never perfect, and at any given moment in a family's life, one person may be giving much more or less than the others because of her or his relative position, age, skills, or personal qualities. The key here is for all family members to recognize and accept the differences in what each contributes. As the members of the family work at creating balance and fairness in the family, a sense of *trustworthiness of relationship* should emerge, expressed as mutual affection that assumes that eventually the respective contributions of family members will balance out. Actions that move the family toward trustworthiness are described as *rejunctive* actions; those that move the family away from trustworthiness are described as *disjunctive* actions.

Accountability and the family ledger   Each individual in a family is accountable to the other members for eventually balancing what each has given and received. Each child born into a family begins wholly dependent and, ideally, receives from the family what she or he needs to survive, develop psychologically, and join society. Gradually, that child begins to return some of the generosity of the family by attending to the needs of others, whether in the form of affection, achievement, emotional support, attentiveness, or otherwise. Eventually, the child reaches adulthood, prepared for individuation and independence.

Over those developmental years, what the child has received and given are registered in the family *ledger,* a collective mental record of the emotional and behavioral debts and assets of each family member, including what that child still "owes" the family in order to completely separate from the family while remaining loyal. If the child has been very attentive to the needs of others and has accumulated considerable merit beyond what is considered minimal to be accountable, then the child has achieved *entitlement.* Entitlement allows a person to complete individuation; it allows separation from the family without guilt or remorse. Each member of a family has an opinion about the state of balance of the family ledger, but "no family member can alone judge whether the ledger is in balance [italics omitted]" (Boszormenyi-Nagy & Ulrich, 1981, p. 164). The family ledger includes a record of entitlement and indebtedness for each member of the family, and an objective view of the ledger can only be arrived at through open communication of the subjective views of all family members in an environment of trust.

Individuals separate from the family system in many ways: A child becomes an adult and moves away or marries into another family; partners divorce or separate; a parent abandons the family; a child runs away; someone becomes severely ill or dies. In each of these situations, the balance in the family ledger dictates the amount of guilt and remorse individuals will experience. When an account has not been adequately settled in one generation, it can be passed along to another generation in the form of substitutive balancing, as noted earlier.

One particular form of substitutive balancing is found in the concept of the *revolving slate.* In a situation where a debt cannot be collected or paid because the other party is dead, absent, or unapproachable, a person may try to collect from or repay a third party. Of course, the new person cannot really settle the original debt but can, by participating in the revolving slate, pass along the unresolved indebtedness. This is a form of *substitutive blaming,* or *scapegoating,* and it is typically directed at a child or a partner. Take, for example, a woman who, as a child, was deprived of love and affection from her parents. Consequently, she feels they owe her love and affection, but one died when she was young, and the other abandoned her. The woman marries a man who cannot possibly give her the love she is owed by her parents, yet she demands it of him. After continually trying but failing to give her the affection she needs, he, in turn, becomes involved with another woman, who tries to give him the love he is owed by his wife. She, of course, cannot do so. All in all, no ledger is really settled, and no person is really satisfied.

Legacy and loyalty   Birth into a family brings with it a *legacy,* a set of cultural and familial expectations that the individual is bound to fulfill. These expectations are passed across generations and set the conditions for *loyalty* to the family. To be loyal to the family is to fulfill those expectations, regardless of the personal toll that fulfillment might exact. Ideally, the loyalty of the individual is a " 'reservoir of trust' that the child extends to its parents, siblings, grandparents, and others"; when there is familial conflict or sadness, the child can call upon that abundance of trust to help heal the problem (Ulrich, 1983, p. 192). At times, however, the legacy that binds a child is self-destructive or unattainable; nonetheless, abandoning that legacy is an act of disloyalty that causes enormous suffering for all concerned, particularly the disloyal child.

If a child is born into one family but raised by another, as in the case of an adopted child, or when the parents have split, the child has *split loyalties.* In the case of adoption, the child must find her or his biological family and fulfill that legacy as well as remaining loyal to her or his adoptive family. If the parents have split, the child's fulfillment of loyalty to one parent may be at odds with loyalty to the other.

Loyalty is sometimes expressed as *invisible loyalties,* in which a child's acts appear disloyal to the parent but are in fact loyal. For example, a daughter may marry a man of whom her mother disapproves while at the same time loyally developing a drinking problem just like her mother's. The self-destructive drinking behavior is a covert loyalty payment that partially nullifies the daughter's overt disloyalty.

Stagnation and exoneration   When the expectations of a family are too great, an individual may come up with solutions that are ethically invalid; this leads to *stagnation.* For example, in a family beset by conflict, a child may feel responsible for saving the parents' relationship. Some of the "solutions" the child develops may be clearly maladaptive, taking the form of psychosis, delinquency, outbursts of hostility, or compulsive cleanliness. These strategies do not work and are self-destructive, and the child must ultimately become autonomous from the situation.

Breaking away from the situation may leave a great deal of indebtedness unresolved in the child's relationships with each parent, some of which can be dealt with through exonerating one or both of the parents. *Exoneration* refers to the rebuilding of a relationship with a parent, usually after the child has become an adult and has gained the maturity to accept the parent's limitations without resentment. Through the new relationship, orchestrated by the child and based on a new trust and honesty, the child releases the parent from his or her emotional indebtedness.

The Process of Intervention

The basic guideline, methodology, and attitude of contextual therapy is *multidirectional partiality.* Boszormenyi-Nagy and Krasner (1980) described multidirectional partiality as follows:

> [Multidirectional partiality] assumes that sooner or later contextual therapists must be prepared to side with all family members, present or absent. It requires a therapist to hear and give courage to each family member as he or she struggles to bring to the surface his or her side. Each individual who is involved in contextual family therapy is viewed as part of the multigenerational pattern. It is a process of consecutive siding with now one and now the other relating partner in order to help

family members state their respective terms with some confidence that the opposing view can be heard and tolerated. (pp. 769–770)

Who and how long?   Because contextual family therapy is not merely a set of specialized techniques, it is not inherently limited to any particular type of problem or client population. Contextual therapy is, rather, a way of looking at and acting on all kinds of relational processes.

Ideally, contextual therapy begins with all members of a nuclear family, but in practice, it may start with an individual, a couple, or several members of a family. In addition, the number of individuals involved in the treatment process at any given time may vary depending on members' availability and the needs of the family. The fact that in a given session, some or even most family members might be missing does not mean that their interests should not be represented. When a member of the family is absent, the therapist attempts to speak for him or her. Since, ideally, two or more generations are involved in the therapy, the therapist may represent a number of absent or dead family members.

The duration of contextual therapy depends on the goals of the family; no set number of sessions is required. One or a few sessions may adequately help one family; in another case, therapy may extend for years. Despite the challenge that the contextual therapist faces in guiding individuals through complex and often turbulent interactions toward trustworthiness, however, the contextual approach is often short-term and direct.

The goals of treatment   The goal of contextual therapy is to enable the members of a family to take rejunctive action that will return trustworthiness to the family. This is done by helping the family bring to the surface and confront issues that have been fearfully avoided. An important by-product of the process is *relational multilaterality,* the gradual awareness on the part of each family member that every action or transaction entails at least two differing sides or opinions and that fairness dictates that all sides be heard and responded to.

The role of the practitioner   The practitioner acts as a guide and resource to the family rather than as one who explains family members to each other. The practitioner directs the family's inquiry into its problems, and when the family appears to be making serious efforts of its own, the practitioner may instruct, clarify, interpret, or confront. In early therapy sessions, the practitioner assesses the patterns of interaction and power alignments operating within the family. As quickly as possible, the practitioner then guides the family toward focusing on one issue at a time, inviting each participant to provide his or her side of the story. As each explains her or his position, other members are asked to respond. As family members describe the impact of the other members on their lives, the practitioner uses multidirectional partiality to increase the family's relational multilaterality. The practitioner sides with one member of the family, giving that person attention and empathy. The practitioner then does the same, in turn, for each of the adversaries of that member, whether present or not. All of the constructs described earlier are eventually incorporated into the intervention, with special emphasis on discussion of the family ledger and the gradual exposure of existing loyalties and legacies. The practitioner's aim in this regard is quite specific: "to loosen the chains of invisible loyalty and legacy, so each person can give up symptomatic behaviors and explore new options [italics omitted]" (Boszormenyi-Nagy & Ulrich, 1981, p. 174). Depending on how far family trustworthiness has been eroded, this process may be short or long.

Contextual therapists often work together as cotherapists. The intention behind cotherapy is not to boost the number of "cast members" available to play absent family members. Rather, cotherapy entails highly coordinated and creative teamwork, with one therapist actively interacting with the family while the other observes carefully to ensure the integrity of the process.

Sample Application[11]

Jason Flowers, his parents, and his brother have begun treatment with contextual cotherapists Dr. Jay Alexander and Dr. Beth Seadock. The early sessions were predictably filled with expressions of concern for Jason, with Jason remaining stolid. Dr. Seadock arranged an individual session with Jason, and Dr. Alexander did the same with his brother, Michael. Surprisingly, rapport was fairly easy to establish with Jason, but clearly he greatly resents the disparity with which he and his brother are treated. Jason says that his father always treats him as an incompetent. When he was younger, his father would get angry at him and strike him, but since Jason has become increasingly "crazy," that has stopped. Michael acknowledges that Jason has always gotten the "short end of the stick" from his father and admits that Jason is right in saying that his father treats Michael as if he can do no wrong and Jason as if he can do no right.

In the next session with the whole family, Mr. Flowers begins to provide some factual information about his background. Mr. Flowers was a second child and greatly admired his older brother (now deceased). His older brother had been "Mom and Dad's favorite, really everybody's favorite," and when the brother died in an accident just before Michael was born, Michael was named for him. Dr. Alexander asks Mr. Flowers about his father. Mr. Flowers describes him as a "good father" but a man he really never got to know because he was "quiet and kept to himself." Mr. Flowers says that he has raised his sons differently, always communicating with them. The copractitioners gradually realize that in fact Mr. Flowers acts toward Jason the same way his father acted toward him and that Michael has become idealized just as Mr. Flowers's brother had. The ledger between Mr. Flowers and his father has never been

---

[11]What follows is quite sketchy. However, most books by family therapists contain detailed case histories. Fascinating full-length case histories can be found in Papp's *Family Therapy* (1977).

settled, and Mr. Flowers has always blamed himself for not getting to know his father and not being as good as his brother. In an ironic act of invisible loyalty, Mr. Flowers has become the same sort of man his father was in regard to the second son: distant and critical. In another act of loyalty, Mr. Flowers has turned his first son into a surrogate for his dead brother, a brother whom he always secretly resented and is now guiltily repaying.

Mr. Flowers's way of treating Jason alarms Mrs. Flowers, but she was raised to believe that a woman must always obey her husband. She has become disloyal to him, however, by protecting Jason with lies and schemes. Over the years, this has led to periods of open conflict between the parents, forcing Jason into a triangulation with his parents in which his symptoms reduce their conflict temporarily by focusing the attention on him.

The copractitioners also come to realize that as the oldest child, Michael has become a victim of *parentification*. Like Jason, he is a victim of the family conflict, but unlike Jason, he has become a parent to his parents. In other words, he is the leader, the authority, the perfect one, the idol uniting his parents. For the copractitioners, the quiet, charming Michael is the child most at risk because he is responsible for the family in ways that he cannot possibly handle.

Over the course of 18 often painful sessions, each member of the family exposes previously unexpressed concerns, resentments, fears, and opinions about his or her and others' indebtedness, and the copractitioners represent various absent and dead family members involved in the past generation. This is especially helpful to Mr. Flowers, who needs to acknowledge the legacy he is still acting out on behalf of his father and brother. He comes to accept and forgive his father's limitations and his brother's untimely death and to free himself from guilt. Jason's symptoms gradually disappear, and Michael talks openly about how difficult it has been to never say anything that would betray weakness; his plastic smile disappears, and he begins palling around with Jason. Mr. and Mrs. Flowers begin to listen to each other and report a "freshness" in their relationship. Trust is established in the family, and various ledgers are settled. Within the next year, Michael gets a job in a nearby city and moves to his own apartment. Jason begins college and decides to live on campus. Mr. and Mrs. Flowers report enjoying visits from "our two sons."

The Structural Approach

"Psychotherapy has been handicapped by the nineteenth-century concept of man as a hero. . . . We have created a generation of sleuths who are looking for psychodynamic clues to the emotional crime" (Minuchin, 1981, pp. 129–130). These are the words of Salvador Minuchin, an influential family therapist and pioneer in the development of the structural approach to family therapy. As should be clear from this quotation, the structural approach to family therapy, unlike contextual therapy, has broken from the historical and intrapsychic concerns of traditional individual psychotherapy and counseling.

Salvador Minuchin received his medical education in Argentina and trained in child psychiatry at Bellevue Hospital in New York. Like most of his fellow psychiatrists, Minuchin was trained in psychoanalysis, studying at the prestigious William Alanson White Institute in the 1950s. Between 1962 and 1965, Minuchin served as the director of the Family Research Unit at the Wiltwyck School for Boys, a private residential treatment center for delinquent boys, most of whom were drawn from the disadvantaged black and Puerto Rican neighborhoods of New York City. Here, Minuchin saw young men and families for whom only the immediate concerns of survival held importance, and he and his colleagues developed approaches to family therapy designed to change the fundamental family structures that influence individual behavior rather than focusing solely on the psychodynamics of individuals. They geared their interventions to solving specific problems, publishing their work in *Families of the Slums* (Minuchin, Montalvo, Guerney, Rosman, & Schumer, 1967). In 1965, Minuchin and some of his Wiltwyck staff moved to the Philadelphia Child Guidance Clinic. Here, in cooperation with researchers at the Philadelphia Children's Hospital, Minuchin turned his attention to the treatment of psychosomatic disorders, particularly anorexia nervosa. This may seem like a far cry from the problems of inner-city delinquents, but from the structural point of view, the behavior of the delinquent and the behavior of the anorexic may be essentially the same: responses to dysfunctional family structures.

Between 1965 and 1975, Minuchin raised the Philadelphia Child Guidance Clinic to international prominence, especially with respect to the treatment of families. During Minuchin's tenure at the clinic, he benefited from the company and contributions of some of family therapy's brightest lights, including Harry Aponte, Jay Haley, Lynn Hoffman, and Braulio Montalvo. Minuchin's *Families and Family Therapy,* published in 1974, has become a classic of family therapy, and several more recent publications have further refined the techniques of structural therapy (specifically, Minuchin, 1984, and Minuchin & Fishman, 1981). For a number of years, Minuchin has held a professorship in child psychiatry and pediatrics at the University of Pennsylvania and more recently has added a research professorship at New York University's School of Medicine.

Unless noted otherwise, the description of structural family therapy that follows is based on Minuchin's (1974) *Families and Family Therapy* and has been updated according to the systematic overviews of structural family therapy done by Aponte and VanDeusen (1981) and Rosenberg (1983).

Theoretical Foundations

Levant (1984) has categorized Minuchin's structural approach with the "structure/process model" of family therapies (p. 122), which would also include the strategic approach, discussed next. Family therapies fitting the structure/process model focus on present, rather than past, patterns of inter-personal communication among family members. Concern for the intrapsychic life of the individual or the unconscious life of the family is replaced with an emphasis on changing current patterns of interaction. The approaches that fit the structure/process model have been influenced primarily by systems theory. The structural approach incorporates insights from the Palo Alto groups, as well as from the work of Ackerman, Wynne, Bowen, and others, emphasizing the underlying structures of the family system that regulate group and individual behavior.

Basic Constructs

Individuals in a family develop patterns of relatedness with each other, and these patterns constitute a structure that allows the family to respond to the needs of individual family members as well as to external environmental demands. Minuchin (1974) put it this way: "Family structure is the invisible set of functional demands that organizes the ways in which family members interact. A family is a system that operates through transactional patterns. Repeated transactions establish patterns of how, when, and to whom to relate, and these patterns underpin the system" (p. 51).

The structures of the family system consist of patterns of verbal and non-verbal communication (transactional patterns) that reflect the rules and regulations governing collective and individual behavior. These structures are shared experiences that establish and maintain organization and authority in the system. The system's structures also operate to establish and maintain the personal identity of each family member, whether she or he is acting inside or outside the family system. Structures are rarely made explicit and can only be observed when the family is in action—that is, when the family is responding to external and internal demands. Put another way, these structures are mutual expectations that change only when some institution or person inside or outside the family no longer abides by the structures. The most obvious examples involve children going through developmental changes. Because of influences outside the family, as well as the disquieting effects of hormonal upheaval, an adolescent, for example, may challenge the authority of his or her parents. If the structures are able to accommodate this demand by maintaining parental authority without alienating the youth, then the structures are said to work. Ideally, the structures in a family are dynamic, capable of changing while continuing to hold the system together.

Dominant and subordinate structures Family systems rest on two kinds of structures: dominant structures and subordinate structures (Aponte & Van-Deusen, 1981). *Dominant structures* are patterns of interaction that occur frequently and form the base for most family operations. *Subordinate structures* are patterns of interaction that occur less frequently but that undergird the dominant structures. For example, in one family, the father may express, through his demeanor and occasional instruction or reprimands, the rules governing group activities. Thus, the children may need to obtain the father's permission to leave the table after finishing their meals or check with him before making other plans on the family's bowling night. This is a dominant structure, since it regularly controls behavior. On the other hand, if the mother speaks privately with the father in support of one child's request to miss a family outing, this represents a subordinate structure, since the pattern supports his authority.

Subsystems   Each individual member of a family is a subsystem of the family system and may be part of other subsystems. Two individuals who make a public commitment to each other, typically through marriage, form a *spouse subsystem.* Through accommodation and acceptance, these individuals become sources of mutual pleasure, enlightenment, and maturity. Later, this same couple may form a *parental subsystem.* The objective of this subsystem is different: It cares for and socializes children. As a parental subsystem, therefore, the couple develops new structures, structures that clarify roles, responsibilities, and expectations so that their offspring will develop in a physically and emotionally secure environment. The child is also a subsystem, and if another child is born, they become a *sibling subsystem.* In a family consisting of a father, mother, and two children, each individual is a subsystem, and each different organization of two or three family members may also function as a subsystem. Subsystems, of course, have their own structures, structures that reflect the larger family system but that may also be unique.

Boundaries   To explain how communication happens in a family system, structural family therapists use the concept of boundaries. Ideally, clear boundaries separate the various family subsystems. In other words, the identities and responsibilities of the family subsystems are unambiguously differentiated; each subsystem knows what its proper role is, what responsibilities it must fulfill and which will be fulfilled by others, what it can expect from other subsystems, and what is expected of it by other subsystems. When the boundaries are clear, the balance between privacy and participation allows the family to respond to crises from within and from without with minimal stress to the system and its members. Indeed, according to the structural approach, the degree to which the boundaries between subsystems in the family are clear is the degree to which that family will be able to adjust to internal and external demands.

In reality, of course, there are no ideal systems, and in any given family at any given time, there are situations in which the boundaries are anything but clear. Figure 9.1 shows a continuum along which all boundaries between subsystems can be plotted. At one extreme is *enmeshment,* which results when boundaries are too easily penetrated. Enmeshment happens in all families. When a child is seriously ill, for example, the boundary that usually separates the child from the parents may become more permeable. Thus, typical transactional patterns that establish roles, responsibilities, and authority may be-

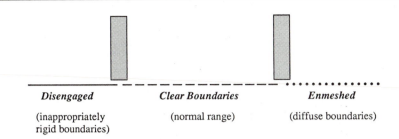

Figure 9.1 *Continuum of boundaries separating family subsystems. Family members who encounter rigid boundaries disengage from the family system. Family members who find the boundaries too easily penetrated become enmeshed in other subsystems. (From: Minuchin, 1974, p. 54)*

come temporarily diffused. At the other extreme is *disengagement.* When the boundaries are rigid and transactional styles allow for little variation or deviation, communication between subsystems becomes very difficult, and subsystems disengage from each other. Again, a certain degree of disengagement is normal in all families. The patterns of communication that worked in raising a child may prove alienating when the youngster reaches late adolescence, for example. Until the boundaries change and all parties can settle into a transactional style that is more flexible, the adolescent may disengage from the family.

A family is dysfunctional to the degree that patterns of enmeshment or disengagement have permanently replaced clear boundaries. In dysfunctional families, patterns of enmeshment or disengagement prevent the family system from successfully responding to internal or external demands. In a family or subsystem characterized by enmeshment, independent or idiosyncratic behavior is met with considerable resistance from others in the family or subsystem. Being oneself apart from the collective we is difficult, and efforts to differentiate one's subsystem may cause major conflict, because the structure of the family or subsystem does not permit it. In times of major change or crisis, the enmeshed family may respond so swiftly and emotionally that it is ineffective in meeting the challenge. In a family or subsystem characterized by disengagement, individuals can act independently or idiosyncratically but may lack the necessary loyalty and sense of belonging that a family needs to act decisively and effectively at times of major change or crisis.

Alignments and power   *Alignments* are interpersonal patterns based on mutual needs, interests, goals, and opinions (Aponte, 1976; Aponte & VanDeusen, 1981). Each member of a family system enters into many alignments, depending on the benefits to be derived. As the family structure changes, so do the alignments. Alignments are ubiquitous in families: A brother and sister align themselves to foil the dictates of an intolerably strict parent; a father and daughter share an interest and appreciation of music; a three-sibling subsystem works together to keep parents from engaging in open conflict.

Power, or force, refers to the real or perceived influence that individuals have over others in the family system that allows necessary tasks to get done (Aponte, 1976). The family is able to meet internal and external threat because some person or persons possess power. In regard to disciplining the children, one parent may have power, while the other parent supports that power through alignment. In matters of family finance, the other parent may actually have the power, but through alignment, the decision making may appear to be shared. As children mature, they normally gain power. Further, various alignments can challenge and shift power within a family.

At any point in a family's history, its structure determines the degree to which the family and its members will meet developmental and environmental demands. The components of that structure are boundaries, alignments, and power. Structural family therapy is designed to shift those structural components so that the family and its members can successfully meet intra- and extrafamilial demands.

The Process of Intervention

The focus of structural family therapy is the dysfunctional family system, not the identified patient sent for treatment. In the early days of the structural approach, that identified patient was typically a child; today, the approach is applied with all varieties of adult populations as well. The family is viewed as an "open sociocultural system" responding to "biopsychosocial" demands from its members, as well as demands from the larger social system (Minuchin, 1974, p. 110). The dysfunctional family is one whose structures permit only stereotyped and ineffective responses to internal and external demands. The purpose of therapy is thus to transform those structures.

Who and how long? The structural approach to family therapy was originally developed for use with poor families with delinquent children and was later applied with families of children with psychosomatic disorders. Over the years since its development, however, many of the practitioners of structural family therapy have applied it to a full range of problems among middle-class clients (Aponte & VanDeusen, 1981). Typically, sessions are held on a weekly basis, and the average duration of treatment may vary from less than 2 months in some settings to as long as 7 months with specific populations like psychosomatic families (Aponte & VanDeusen, 1981).

The goal of treatment The fundamental contention of this approach is that lasting changes in individual behavior are the result of changes in the structure of the system of which the individual is a part. Therefore, the primary goal of structural family therapy is to transform dysfunctional family structures. Structural transformation is defined as "changes in the position of family members vis-à-vis each other, with a consequent modification of their complementary demands" (Minuchin, 1974, p. 111). The therapist thus attempts to disrupt the homeostasis of the dysfunctional family so that the family will reorganize. Put another way, the therapist creates disequilibrium. The secondary goal of structural family therapy follows from the first: to change the experience of individual subsystems. Significant and lasting changes in individual behavior are a function of structural changes in the system to which the individual belongs.

The role of the practitioner   A family is a social group with established transactional patterns that have developed because of years of mutual *accommodation*. The practitioner begins by *joining* the family, a process of accommodation that requires actively learning about and participating in the transactional patterns of the family. While studying the system and trying to gain access to it, the practitioner uses three accommodation techniques: (1) maintenance, (2) tracking, and (3) mimesis. *Maintenance* means purposefully supporting the family structure as it is, reinforcing, for the time being, the existing structure. If, for example, the father is the clear authority in the family structure, the practitioner may speak to him deferentially. *Tracking* is following and fully encouraging typical family interaction during the sessions. The practitioner may use questions, statements, gestures, and nonverbal cues to help reveal the typical communication patterns. *Mimesis* literally means imitation or mimicry. Mimicry sometimes connotes mockery, but in this context, it refers to imitative behavior that complements or supports the behavior of another. The practitioner picks up the family tempo and selectively does and says things that in both form and content pull the practitioner into the family. Mimesis may mean slowing down or speeding up one's rate of talking or moving; it may require assuming an expansive, somber, or even giddy mood. At times, the practitioner may say things that connect to the family or one of its members: "I went to an all-girl school, too"; "My parents separated when I was young, too"; "I get nervous when I have to talk in front of a group." Mimetic processes are natural and often happen spontaneously even within therapy. The practitioner simply formalizes them to enhance kinship with the family (Minuchin, 1974).[12]

The real motive, of course, in joining the family system is to change it, to make of it a new system, a *therapeutic system* with the practitioner as its leader. To do this, the practitioner must make some educated guesses about what is wrong with the present system. This process of assessment or diagnosis is continuous in structural therapy and involves building hypotheses and then experimenting with them in the family sessions. Joining techniques, which bring the practitioner closer to the family, make restructuring possible. Minuchin's (1974) similes for the joining and restructuring processes are appropriately drawn from the theater. In joining the family, the practitioner is like an actor performing a part in a scripted production. In restructuring the family, the practitioner is like a director rehearsing and changing the scenes, scripts, and even the physical placement of the actors. Restructuring consists of "dramatic

---

[12]Minuchin's (1974) *Families and Family Therapy* contains a most readable and enlightening description of mimesis.

interventions" that so change the script that the family no longer comfortably fits into the old structures. In Minuchin's (1974) own words: "The therapist's job is to manipulate the family system toward planned change" (p. 140).

An abundance of techniques is available to the contemporary practitioner of structural family therapy, but Minuchin (1974, pp. 140–157) has identified seven basic categories of restructuring techniques:

1. *Actualizing family transactional patterns:* The practitioner, as leader of the therapeutic system, can easily become the center of attention, even when she or he is silent. In addition, the family can become accustomed to simply describing transactions instead of performing them. The practitioner can change this by having the family enact transactional patterns. For example, if a parent is talking about something a child does, the practitioner may direct him or her to talk directly to the child. Comments directed at the practitioner may be redirected with a word or gesture to another member of the system, thus creating communication channels not there before. This may even be done physically, by changing the proximity of various family members to each other. All of these strategies enable the practitioner to expose and modify real transactional patterns.

2. *Marking boundaries:* Through direct and indirect methods, the practitioner can help the family see the boundaries between subsystems. Where the family is enmeshed, the practitioner fights to strengthen or create boundaries. Where the family is disengaged, the practitioner attempts to break down rigid boundaries.

3. *Escalating stress:* The identified patient in the family is often the locus of stress in the system. Through a variety of maneuvers, the practitioner can actually increase the stress level so that family members can see how the identified patient is used by the system. The practitioner experiments with various means of increasing the stress. Some of those strategies may include: interrupting a typical transaction, not allowing it to take place; becoming part of an alliance with one family member that forces new structures on the rest; forcing out into the open an implicit conflict that never surfaces in typical sessions.

4. *Assigning tasks:* The practitioner can assign specific tasks to the family or family members. During sessions, for example, the practitioner may direct a child to turn her chair backwards so that she can no longer see her father's facial expressions. Homework assignments may cover all aspects of the family's life. In a family where a child is disengaged, each parent may be assigned a specific time to be with the child each day. In a family where everything depends on the mother, the practitioner may assign food shopping to the father. The tasks are designed specifically for each family.

5. *Utilizing symptoms:* For structural family therapists, the identified patient's symptoms are indicators of structural problems in the family, and the therapist may decide to de-emphasize or ignore them. At times, however, the best interests of the family are served by highlighting them. The family may thus be instructed to focus on the symptom. For example, the practitioner may have family members enact an argument over a child's self-injurious behavior,

believing that because of triangulation the symptom will continue until the hidden conflict among the members surfaces. The symptom thus becomes a means of uncovering the structural problem. The practitioner may also choose to exaggerate, de-emphasize, or relabel the symptom for the same purpose.

6. *Manipulating the mood:* Families in therapy will often exhibit a dominant mood pattern: morose, apathetic, jovial, or the like. These limited moods serve as indicators of what affective behavior is permissible in the system. To join the family, the practitioner has taken on the family's mood. Now, as part of the restructuring strategy, the practitioner may exaggerate the dominant mood to show its effect or assign to a family member an emotion that he or she does not seem able to express.

7. *Support, education, and guidance:* The structural family practitioner can offer care, knowledge, or skills to family members in many ways. At times, the practitioner may simply instruct parents in the art of parenting. At other times, the practitioner may bring in professionals or agencies for assistance or instruction. Where there are practical needs of any kind, the practitioner seeks to fill those gaps using all the resources possible.

The strategies identified above represent only a portion of the tools used by practitioners of structural family therapy, and their actual application depends on the personality, experience, and inventiveness of the practitioner. The reader may be struck by the apparent emphasis on manipulating the family rather than being openly empathic, honest, and direct. A fundamental assumption of family therapy is that participants in family systems are too close to truly observe the system. Even the practitioner, as a participant-observer, has to switch back and forth between the roles of participant and observer to understand the dysfunctional structures without becoming part of them. The apparent manipulations are thus therapeutic improvisations that are often very intuitive, creative, and effective.

Sample Application

Earlier in this chapter, we saw Jason Flowers's family being treated. Now we see how a structural family therapist, Dr. Annie Wilson, deals with the Flowerses. Dr. Wilson has begun seeing the entire Flowers family on a weekly basis. She finds joining the family fairly easy, with the exception of Jason, who remains sullen. She notes that authority in the family rests with the father, but that overt communication is minimal. When Mr. Flowers objects to something a family member says or does, he reacts nonverbally, by looking away and sighing. This is frequently his reaction when Mrs. Flowers speaks, but he never openly criticizes her. Mr. Flowers makes no overt signs of approval either, except on two occasions when Michael Flowers expresses the family's concern for Jason and Mr. Flowers says, "That's right," under his breath. Dr. Wilson hypothesizes that, despite the rhetoric of concern, rigid structures keep the family members emotionally disengaged from each other. They live out one-dimensional roles rather than integrated lives of true caring. Historically, the family has functioned adequately in meeting societal demands, but as developmental stresses have occurred in Jason's and Michael's lives, the weak relationship between the parents has not permitted real communication and problem resolution. Jason has become the scapegoat, and Michael is idealized. Both children are victims of the rigid structure and are similarly triangulated, albeit in different ways.

Early in the therapy, Dr. Wilson forms a coalition with the father, supporting his authority by asking his opinion about the family and its problems. On one occasion, he begins to speak about his own upbringing and various problems in his early life, but Dr. Wilson continues to bring him back to the current situation in the family. With a knowing and sympathetic look on her face, Mrs. Flowers whispers to Dr. Wilson, "Sometimes my husband needs an excuse, you know." Everyone hears the comment, though it was made quickly, *almost imperceptibly*. It would have passed, except that Dr. Wilson stops the conversation, turns toward Mrs. Flowers, and instructs her to direct her comment to Mr. Flowers. It is an awkward moment, but it creates a new structure, one absent for many years: direct critical communication from Mrs. Flowers to Mr. Flowers. As Mrs. Flowers timidly speaks to Mr. Flowers, Dr. Wilson notices that the otherwise inscrutable Jason is paying full attention. He tries to make eye contact with his mother as a means of support but catches instead the glance of Dr. Wilson. Her eyes encourage him to speak, but he looks away and hides his face.

Gradually, Mr. and Mrs. Flowers begin to talk more honestly about Jason's problems but never about each other. At various times, Dr. Wilson has them direct their comments to Jason, despite the fact that he remains uncommunicative. On several occasions, Dr. Wilson asks Michael to join in. Michael usually smiles and says that he is very worried about his brother. His eyes dart between his mother's wink and his father's nod, tokens of approval that seem to occur without cognizance. As Dr. Wilson becomes more certain about the family, she decides to demonstrate the structure to the family.

When the family members come to their sixth session, Dr. Wilson meets them outside the therapy room. She tells them to go into the room and sit in the seats that bear their names, without moving any of the chairs. The arrangement looks like this:

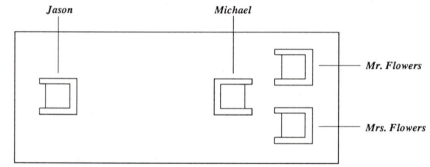

As the floor plan shows, Jason's chair faces away from his family, and the parents' chairs face only Michael's and not each other's. As the members of the family settle into their seats, Dr. Wilson notes a number of reactions. Clearly Michael is uncomfortable, and keeps his eyes turned away. Mr. Flowers appears annoyed but says nothing. Mrs. Flowers looks confused and a bit hurt. Suddenly, after 2 minutes of long silence, Jason begins to laugh. Dr. Wilson goes over to him quickly and crouches in front of him, saying, "Jason, tell us why you're laughing!" With bitter laughter, Jason explains that the chair arrangement is exactly how he feels: facing the wrong way, unable to make contact. His voice breaks, and he begins to cry privately. Dr. Wilson sees distressed looks on the faces of the parents, who turn to Michael for support. He looks away. As Dr.Wilson moves toward Michael, he looks up at his parents and says, "Stop pulling at me!"

Eventually, each speaks from his or her own perspective in the new chair arrangement. Each admits the uncomfortableness of the position, and each comes to see the chair experiment as a very real reflection of the structure of their family. At Dr. Wilson's direction, the Flowers family experiments with various other chair arrangements, and with each arrangement, new transactional patterns are rehearsed. First, the parents sit facing each other, communicating without reference to either child. Then, Jason and Michael do the same. Methodically, they experiment with every configuration of two, three, and then four, each time breaking old rules. Gradually, new family boundaries are established. The parents develop a relationship with each other, and Michael is liberated from his role. Jason begins to perceive his place in the family, and his symptoms disappear.

The Strategic Approach

"Therapy can be called strategic if the clinician initiates what happens during therapy and designs a particular approach for each problem" (Haley, 1973, p. 17). So Jay Haley, family therapy's guru and occasional gadfly, once part of both the Palo Alto and Philadelphia groups, described strategic family therapy. His definition readily betrays his emphasis on treatment as active, problem-specific, and essentially the responsibility of an active, directive practitioner. In these regards, strategic family therapy shares little kinship with psychoanalysis and, as noted earlier, unexpected commonality with **behavior therapy.**[13] Strategic family therapy is not aimed at providing insight except as a by-product of behavioral change. In the strategic approach, we encounter the most radical, practical, and increasingly influential form of family therapy practiced today.

[13]Haley's views on the passivity and ineffectiveness of psychoanalysis can be found in many sources, but one of the most amusing is a satire entitled "The Art of Psychoanalysis" in his *Strategies in Psychotherapy* (1963). Haley (1973) has identified *planning* as the characteristic that his brand of family therapy shares with behavior therapy.

Strategic family therapy's distinctiveness from other approaches developed very gradually, and it can be legitimately associated with the contributions of many family therapists, including Lynn Hoffman, Peggy Papp, Paul Watzlawick, John Weakland, and Gerald Zuk. Also related to strategic family therapy is the work of the "Milan associates," a team of four Italian psychiatrists headed by Mara Palazzoli-Selvini. Working at the Institute for Family Study in Milan, Palazzoli-Selvini and her colleagues have done pioneering work in applying systems-based strategies in the treatment of anorexia nervosa.[14] Although their work is often referred to as "systemic" rather than strategic, it bears important similarities to strategic family therapy. For our present purposes, however, we will look at the strategic family therapy of another important team of therapists: Jay Haley and his current professional colleague (and wife), Cloé Madanes. Together, they direct the Family Therapy Institute in Washington, D.C. Haley's continual contributions to family therapy justify our attention to his brand of strategic intervention over the others.

Theoretical Foundations

Strategic family therapy has two primary sources, one theoretical and one practical. Like all family therapies, the strategic approach can be traced to the theoretical wellspring of the two Palo Alto groups, the Bateson project and the Mental Research Institute. When those groups were both operating, Haley was a key contributor to the development of systems theory, and he later contributed to the development of the structural approach. In keeping with systems approaches, and like structural family therapy, the strategic approach emphasizes circular, mutually reinforcing patterns of interpersonal communication among family members in the present rather than in the past. Concern for the intrapsychic life of the individual or the unconscious life of the family is replaced with an emphasis on identifying strategies for changing the current patterns of interaction.

The more practical or technical source of strategic family therapy was psychiatrist Milton Erickson, a highly creative hypnotherapist and psychotherapist who initiated strategic approaches in individual therapy. What Haley learned from his extended studies of Erickson's therapeutic intervention was the use of very specific and often paradoxical strategies for changing maladaptive behavior. Although Erickson might know and appreciate the historical events that led to a client's symptomatic behavior, treatment often consisted of "encouraging the resistance"—that is, paradoxically instructing the client to continue the behavior, albeit with some unusual and distracting variations (Hoffman, 1981). In addition, Haley embraced Erickson's rejection of the notion that therapeutic change is the responsibility of the client. In Erickson's view,

---

[14]As always, Lynn Hoffman has written an excellent chapter in *Foundations of Family Therapy* (1981) on the "quiet revolution" taking place in Milan.

change is, rather, the responsibility of the practitioner, and covert forms of persuasion, direction, and manipulation can be legitimate ways of effecting change.[15]

Basic Constructs

Earlier in this section, strategic family therapy was referred to as radical. Practitioners of the strategic approach part company with the mental health establishment on the issue of psychiatric and psychological diagnosis and treatment, often considering mental health professionals as unwitting contributors to the problem. Further, following Hoffman's (1981) description, the strategic therapist is a "minimalist." This means that though a given problem may have a history, and though the practitioner may well see other problems unidentified by the clients, intervention is directed solely at the problems described by the family members. As Haley (1976) put it, "The first obligation of the therapist is to change the presenting problem offered. If that is not accomplished the therapy is a failure" (p. 129).

The dysfunctional family   The goal of strategic family therapy is not to teach a family about its dysfunctional ways but to change those ways (Haley, 1976). Dysfunctional families typically stand out when contrasted with cultural norms. The family is confused about hierarchies, and destructive coalitions may exist across generations. The dysfunctional quality of the family becomes apparent when it attempts to adjust to the transitions occurring in the *life cycles* of all families. Haley has identified six stages in the family life cycle: (1) courtship, (2) early marriage, (3) childbirth and parenting, (4) middle marriage, (5) the separation of parents and children, and (6) retirement and old age (Madanes, 1981). The dysfunctional family gets stuck at one of these stages, unable to move forward.

Control and communication   Control is at the heart of the dysfunctional family's inability to adjust to its life cycle, and interpersonal communication is the vehicle through which control is exercised. Messages between human beings typically have a *situational context* (where, when, and under what conditions), a *verbal component* (what is said), an *expressive component* (intonation, volume, and emotional tone), and a *physical component* (gestures and proximity). As described earlier in reference to the double bind, a message may be inherently contradictory or at least incongruent; for example, a parent's words may express affection while her or his physical distance, hostile inflection, and diverted eyes may send quite a different message.

In practice, communication is not a single exchange between two individuals; especially in the family, communication is highly complex, with multiple messages continually being sent and received at various intellectual, emotional, and physical levels. The patterns of interpersonal communication forge

---

[15]Haley's descriptions of Erickson's special genius can be found in his *Uncommon Therapy: The Psychiatric Techniques of Milton H. Erickson, M.D.* (1973).

what has been called "a family crucible," an arena of such forceful, encompassing, and intense interaction that no individual can pass through it without in some way becoming part of it, without in some way being a product of it (Napier & Whitaker, 1978).

Communication within the family defines the various familial relationships and reflects where real control or power exists. Some relationships are *symmetrical*: Individuals perform the same behaviors, thus establishing an equal give-and-take in the relationship that allows them to be peers. Some relationships are *complementary*: Individuals perform different behaviors, thus highlighting the "superior" position of one and the "secondary" position of the other (Haley, 1963). Whether the relationship between two individuals is symmetrical or complementary may vary from situation to situation. The shift may be abrupt and temporary, as when one spouse teaches the other how to prepare an omelet (symmetrical to complementary), or the shift may be gradual and permanent, as when a child's movement into adulthood changes how he or she interacts with his or her parents (complementary to symmetrical). According to Haley (1963), we engage in a variety of communication *maneuvers*— messages that at some level challenge the status quo—to shift the control in relationships. For example, an adolescent may wash the dishes as asked but sullenly and noisily to challenge her or his parents' control, or a spouse may become work-bound as a way of abdicating responsibility.

Problems as control maneuvers   What others call symptoms, Haley calls problems, viewing the problems of the identified patient as inseparable from the sequences of actions and communication that the patient is enacting with significant others. According to Haley (1976), problems really represent the crystallization of patterns of communication, and phobias or periods of depression are really tactics, interpersonal maneuvers that fit into the power or control patterns of the family. Usually, triangulation has occurred: The struggles or coalitions between two family members engulf or alienate a third party. The third party becomes the identified patient, the individual with the problem. The problem behavior, whether as simple as bed-wetting or as dramatic as schizophrenia, is an adaptive response, a tactic in the ongoing family maneuvering for control.

The identified patient's problem is viewed as part of a vicious cycle of control-related actions and communication: What others do to change the identified patient's behavior actually helps to maintain it. If we go back to the case of Jason, we recall that his outbursts occur because he was never lovingly integrated into the family and that he cannot become integrated into the family until his outbursts end. The family keeps him at a sympathetic but loveless distance for fear of his hostility, and his hostility has come out of his inability to bridge the gap between his parents and is maintained by their "helpful"disengagement from him. Jason's behavior is a strategy for control, an ineffective response to the life-cycle event of separation from his parents, in this case signaled by his graduation from high school.

Families move through the life cycle by means of established patterns of action and communication. When those patterns are inadequate to the developmental challenge, a crisis occurs, evidenced in the creation or exacerbation of the problems of one or more family members.

The Process of Intervention

The focus of strategic family therapy is neither the individual nor the family; it is the specific problem identified by the family. This problem is usually a behavior exhibited by one member of the family, the "identified patient," but the practitioner never forgets that it is the behavior that is to be changed.

Who and how long?   The strategic approach to family therapy has been applied to a broad range of problems. Haley's early work was with severely disturbed children, but in later years, he developed specific strategies for the disturbances associated with weaning children from parents (1980) and a host of interventions for particularly resistant problems like public masturbation (1984). As Madanes (1981) has pointed out, the problem-specific nature of strategic family therapy makes it readily applicable to a broad range of problems. That same specificity also makes it relatively short-term.

The goal of treatment   Strategic family therapy is a planned attack on specific problems exhibited by the identified patient. From the start, the practitioner's goal is to develop a specific plan that will prevent the reoccurrence of patterns of interaction that have created and maintained the problem. Although a family may come to understand the historical causes of a problem or the dynamics of familiar relationships, these are not the goals of therapy.

The role of the practitioner   To accomplish the goal of treatment, the practitioner must successfully join the family and gain control of it through whatever interpersonal maneuvers are necessary. The practitioner never argues with the family about causal factors, nor is there formal instruction in systems thinking. The practitioner may reframe the problem in a manner that reflects a systems orientation rather than an individual one, but the focus never shifts from the problem per se.[16]

Haley has asserted that effective strategic therapy takes place in identifiable stages, and the key to moving successfully through those stages is an effective *first interview*. As described by Haley (1976), the first interview with the family has four stages: (1) the social stage, (2) the problem stage, (3) the interaction stage, and (4) the goal-setting stage. During the *social stage,* the practitioner invites the family into the meeting room, exhibiting the same cordiality

---

[16]Haley (1976) eschewed the use of cotherapists as unnecessary and expensive additions to treatment. He pointed out that research does not suggest that cotherapy is more effective and suggested that only the security of the practitioner is served by having a companion.

that would be extended to company in one's home. The practitioner is attentive from the start to communication patterns and established hierarchies. Who appears to be in charge of the family? What overall emotion comes from the family? Who speaks first, and who is quiet? Who moves tentatively, and who moves with assurance? Who sits first, and who sits apart? In each new family situation, the practitioner begins to develop hypotheses about what sort of patterns of control exist.

After a few minutes of introduction and settling down, the practitioner asks why the family is there. This is the *problem stage* of the first interview, the period in which the family members identify what has brought them to therapy. To whom does the practitioner address questions about the problem? Although risky, the question is best directed at the person judged to possess the greatest power and influence in the family—in most cases, the person least involved in the problem. This question calls for a judgment based on experience and preinterview information. In one family, the question may best be addressed to the mother; in another, the father; in yet another, a grandparent. Gradually, everyone in the family has a chance to state the problem from his or her perspective. The practitioner remains neutral and avoids interpretation even when it is requested. In the practitioner's thinking about the problem, an important shift is taking place. Though the members of the family typically present the problems in terms of one family member's behavior (Robert steals; Madeleine cannot sleep; Mother is abusive; Father drinks too much), the practitioner listens for the links between the problem behavior and the actions and communications of other family members.

In the *interactional stage,* the practitioner initiates and directs direct interaction between and among family members. This interaction may encompass more than conversation, with family members acting out the problem while the others react as they would in real life. For example, the mother may act as if she has lost her temper, and the husband, child, and great aunt may respectively fume, cower, and explode. In a sense, the first interview serves as a laboratory for assessing the communication dynamics that produce and maintain the problem.

Lastly, in the *goal-setting stage,* each member of the family must agree on the problem, and a specific goal is set. Whether the family chooses to work on Mother's anger, Father's drinking, Robert's stealing, or Madeleine's insomnia, that person and that problem constitute the focus of the therapy. When the targeted behavior has changed, then all will know that the therapy has succeeded. Outcomes are unambiguous.

Once under way, strategic family therapy is *directive*: The practitioner determines a specific strategy and tells the family members what to do. The prescribed new behaviors interrupt the pattern of communication and the control that goes with it, and the problem disappears. The trick, of course, is finding the set of directives that fits the family. In this regard, the strategic approach is exceptionally improvisational. At times, the directives are straightforward, and the strategy, obvious. In the case of a disruptive and bed-wetting boy, for example, the boy's mother and grandmother disagreed on how to handle his problem. Rather than try to solve the conflict, Haley gave them each a chance to control the boy's behavior. The grandmother had a 2-week period to care for the boy, even to the point of washing the wet bed linen. The mother was instructed not to interfere or criticize. After 2 weeks that the grandmother found difficult, the mother was given the same responsibilities, also free from interference and criticism. Following the natural hierarchy of things, when the mother was free of the intrusions of the grandmother, the boy's problem abated. A new order of communication and power had been established, and the problem had disappeared (Haley, 1976, pp. 131–133).

At other times, paradoxical strategies are more effective than straightforward ones. We have seen paradoxical techniques in both behavioral and existential approaches, and they operate in a similar fashion here. Generally, the resistant behavior is encouraged rather than discouraged. An example from Cloé Madanes's *Strategic Family Therapy* (1981, pp. 80–84) is particularly enlightening. She recounted the case of a 7-year-old boy who suffered from frequent but nonspecific headaches. It became apparent in the treatment of the family that the parents of the identified patient had difficulty communicating about their own problems with each other, but on the issue of the son's headaches, they could communicate directly. Effectively, the son's headaches had become a metaphor for the father's "headache": fear that he would lose his job because of his status as a recovering alcoholic. One part of the early treatment is of particular interest here. The father was directed to complain of headaches every day upon returning from work and to describe make-believe problems from the office. The son was directed to try to cheer his father up and to find out whether the headaches and problems were real or not. After a number of weeks of doing this, the boy's headaches ended; the tie between the father's problems and the son's had been broken. At this point, the treatment moved on to deal with other specific problems in the family.

Strategic family therapy moves from specific problem to specific problem until no problem is reported by members of the family. The resolution of some problems, of course, creates new problems. At all times, however, the practitioner directs the family to actions that realign power by changing patterns of communication.

Sample Application

The Flowers family's time with strategic family therapist Dr. Timothy Monroe is anything but uneventful. Not long into the first session, all members of the family except Jason have agreed that the problem is Jason's self-imposed isolation in his room. It is apparent to Dr. Monroe that there are problems between the parents and that Michael is treated quite differently than Jason, but he decides to work on the specific problem of the conflict caused by Jason's isolation. Since Jason has not spoken in the group, Dr. Monroe asks him either to agree or disagree with the statement of the problem. When Jason does not respond, Dr. Monroe says that he must assume that since Jason is the one choosing and enjoying the isolation from the family, Jason could solve everyone's problem including his own, by moving out of the house. He directs Jason to do so as soon as possible, telling the parents that they should do their best to help Jason find another place to live. The practitioner tells them that at the next session, they will work out the details of the move. In the meantime, should he choose to, Jason is to be allowed to move around the house free of criticism, cajoling, or any attempts to interrupt his isolation. Family members are instructed to be friendly to him, especially since they will not be seeing very much of him in the near future. Dr. Monroe tells Michael that he will do well to loan Jason whatever money he has saved, since renting an apartment costs quite a bit, and assures him that having Jason move will make life in the house better, because the conflict over Jason's isolation will end. The parents and Michael object, but Dr. Monroe declares that he is certain that this is the best thing to do and asks that for at least 2 weeks they fully implement the change.

At first, no longer fearing that he will be caught outside his room and kept from reentering, Jason moves back and forth between the kitchen and bedroom but does not join in any family meals or activities. After a few days, he begins hanging out near the kitchen when meals are being served, and one morning, he says hello to his brother. Michael, for his part, has put about half of his savings in an envelope and left it outside of Jason's door. At the next session, Dr. Monroe asks Mr. and Mrs. Flowers if they have any plans for Jason's room once he moves out. Very tentatively, Mrs. Flowers mentions the possibility of a sewing room but then says she would rather have Jason there, even with his isolation. She says that she is sure that things are getting better and that Jason's isolation no longer really bothers her as it did. Dr. Monroe has her tell Jason this directly, and within minutes both Mr. Flowers and Michael chime in. Jason remains quiet, although he no longer diverts his eyes. The next evening, he comes down for supper, and not long after, he begins to talk about superficial topics with family members. The therapy sessions turn to other problems, specifically problems concerning the relationship between Mr. and Mrs. Flowers. Six months later, Jason moves into an apartment; the transition is smooth.

Evaluation

Serious research on the effectiveness of family therapy in general, and specific techniques and strategies in particular, has increased steadily over the past decade or so (see Gurman & Kniskern, 1978, 1981). That research, however, is inconclusive; the diversity of approach and the dynamism of the field tend to make concrete findings difficult. In the past, the people actually doing family therapy were often neither trained in nor inclined toward research. This has now begun to change, however, and research efforts are likely to increase and become more sophisticated. It is easy to see how formidable the challenge of studying family therapy is simply by contrasting contextual and strategic therapies, two extreme approaches to family therapy. If both are effective, as their proponents claim, what common element accounts for their mutual success?

For now, family therapy is, depending on one's perspective, a trendy diversion, an attractive adjunct to individual therapy, or the true alternative to traditional treatment.

Summary of Chapter 9

In Chapter 9, we have examined family therapy, a broad collection of approaches that address the problems of individual behavior in the social context in which those problems were born, nurtured, and can best be changed: the family. Family therapy shifts the focus of treatment from the identified client to the family members involved in the client's day-to-day life. In doing so, family therapy challenges traditional understandings of psychopathology, its prevention, and its remediation.

Historical and Theoretical Foundations

1. Family therapy emerged from several different quarters in the 1940s and 1950s, largely as a response to the inadequacies of individual therapy in treating more serious problems like schizophrenia and delinquency.
2. Family therapy has been influenced by two very different models of human behavior: psychoanalysis and systems theory. Systems theory emphasizes the circular rather than the linear nature of causality, viewing individual behavior as inseparable by nature from its context.
3. A number of practitioners working from one or both of these theoretical models began treating entire families. Although the psychoanalytic model dominated for some time, the systems model gradually came to prevail. Many approaches to family therapy still use concepts and language drawn from psychoanalysis, however.
4. Today, marriage and family therapy is enormously popular and considered by some to be a profession distinct from psychiatry, clinical psychology, or psychiatric social work, although its practitioners often come from these professions.
5. Three approaches to family therapy are described in this chapter, although over 20 distinct approaches may exist. The three approaches described are the contextual approach, the structural approach, and the strategic approach.

The Contextual Approach

6. The contextual approach was developed by psychiatrist Ivan Boszormenyi-Nagy at the Eastern Pennsylvania Psychiatric Institute in Philadelphia, although others have contributed to its development.

7. The contextual approach rests on three theoretical foundations: systems theory, psychoanalysis, and existential philosophy. Of the three approaches considered in this chapter, the contextual most clearly reflects psychoanalytic thinking.

8. The psychoanalytic roots of contextual family therapy are most evident in its use of object-relations theory, a neopsychoanalytic theory developed by Melanie Klein that connects the development of psychopathology with the real or perceived loss of a significant object (not subject, not oneself) during early childhood. This object-loss is played out within a family context where the loss prevents trusting relationships. The objective of contextual therapy is to establish trustworthiness and fairness in the family and, by doing so, to remedy the effects of the object-loss. The practitioner must establish fairness intergenerationally, since the effects of object-loss are often evident across generations.

9. Contextual assessment and treatment are concerned with facts about the family, the intrapsychic lives of the family members, the power alignments and transactions among family, and fundamental issues of equitability among family members.

10. Implicit within each family's interactions is the family ledger, a collective mental record of the psychological contributions and debts of each family member. A child does not fully individuate from the family until he or she has balanced his or her account. Each family member may have a different accounting of the respective contributions and debts of family members. Contextual family therapy involves having all members openly and directly reveal their perceptions of the family ledger to develop a mutually accepted understanding of it.

11. At times, a person cannot settle a debt with someone because he or she is dead, absent, or unavailable. By means of a revolving slate, the debt is settled through a third party, often a child, who becomes the victim of scapegoating.

12. The practitioner guides contextual therapy using multidirectional partiality, a process of consecutively siding with each family member so that all family members learn to see the problem from all possible vantage points.

13. The goal of contextual therapy is to return fairness and trustworthiness to the family. The practitioner serves as a guide and resource in this process, orchestrating the situation such that each family member's views are heard without rebuff.

The Structural Approach

14. The structural approach to family therapy was developed by psychiatrist Salvador Minuchin and his colleagues. Although Minuchin has worked at other places, the structural approach is generally associated with the Philadelphia Child Guidance Clinic, where Minuchin worked from 1965 to 1975.

15. The structural approach focuses on patterns of interpersonal communication among family members by emphasizing the structures that underlie the family system and determine that communication.

16. Family structure is the invisible set of functional demands that organizes how the family members interact. A family is a system that operates through transactional patterns; repeated transactions form the system by establishing the basic how, when, and with whom of behavior.

17. The family system is made up of various subsystems consisting of various combinations of family members. The parents themselves form a parental subsystem, and the children form a sibling subsystem. For structural therapists, understanding a family means understanding the boundaries between such subsystems. The degree to which the boundaries between subsystems are clear is the degree to which the family will be able to successfully adjust to internal and external demands. When the boundaries between subsystems are too easily penetrated, enmeshment can result, with an individual having no identity apart from the subsystem. When the boundaries are impenetrable, *disengagement* results, with an individual isolated, unable to move into a subsystem for support. Although both of these boundary phenomena happen in all families, they are chronic in maladaptive families.

18. The boundaries in a family demonstrate how power and alignments operate in that family. Alignments are patterns of interaction based on a common need, interest, goal, or opinion between two or more family members. Power is the real or perceived influence that individuals have in a family system. Changes in alignments can shift power in the system. Ideally, the family system is dynamic, with situational shifts in power and alignments being based on internal and external demands. The most common example of this is the gradual shift in alignments and power that takes place as children grow into adulthood.

19. The primary goal of structural therapy is the transformation of dysfunctional family structures. The therapist joins the family by using accommodation techniques, including: supporting the existing family structure (*maintenance*), encouraging typical family interaction (*tracking*), and imitating family moods and activities (*mimesis*).

20. Gradually, the practitioner begins restructuring the family, using dramatic interventions designed to force change. To this end, the structural therapist makes use of a variety of specialized techniques designed to disrupt the status quo. The practitioner may have the family act out behaviors that they usually only describe or may even intentionally escalate the stress level in the family. The various techniques are complemented by educational efforts.

The Strategic Approach

21. The strategic approach to family therapy draws chiefly on systems theory for its theoretical support and has little or no kinship with psychoanalysis.

Although widely practiced from Palo Alto to Milan, the most recognized representative of this approach is Jay Haley, who, together with Cloé Madanes, directs the Family Therapy Institute in Washington, D.C.

22. The strategic approach draws much of its clinical methodology from Milton Erickson, particularly his use of paradoxical instructions to clients.

23. The structural approach is essentially ahistorical and emphasizes direct and planned changes in the specific day-to-day problems identified by the members of the family.

24. The dysfunctional family is viewed as one in which confused hierarchies and destructive coalitions so disrupt the natural flow of communication, and therefore power, that the family is unable to successfully navigate through the stages of the family life cycle: (1) courtship, (2) early marriage, (3) childbirth and parenting, (4) middle marriage, (5) the separation of parents and children, (6) retirement and old age.

25. Problems of individual family members (for example, depression) are viewed as control maneuvers, tactics aimed at gaining control.

26. Regardless of whatever insight the practitioner might bring to a family's plight, treatment focuses on the specific problems identified by the family. During the first interview, the practitioner joins the family, quickly assessing the power structure, and establishes direct patterns of interaction between and among family members. By the end of the interview, the family has established specific goals for the treatment process.

27. Strategic family therapy is directive: The practitioner determines a specific strategy and tells the family members what to do. At times, these directives are straightforward. At other times, they are paradoxical; that is, the family member is instructed to actually perform the problem behavior, often with some variation or exaggeration that produces ironic outcomes. By its nature, the strategic approach is improvisational without being whimsical.

Evaluation

28. Although family therapy is enjoying increased popularity and is the subject of serious research efforts, its universal superiority to individual methods has not yet been established.

Comprehensive Approaches to Psychotherapy and Counseling

> *It is in the life situation, rather than the psychotherapy room, that the important insights and new experiences occur.*
>
> **Julian B. Rotter**

In the early chapters of this book, the **self-regulation** and **maturity** model was presented as a way of synthesizing or integrating the various approaches that reflect that model. In this chapter, I describe three approaches that reflect that model. They are labeled *comprehensive* because they go beyond simple eclecticism, integrating the two basic aims of psychological intervention. First, each in its own way draws from and contributes to the rich literature on self-regulation that comes from **behavior therapy,** as broadly conceived to encompass cognitive processes. Second, each in its own way sets self-regulatory procedures in a developmental context that recognizes the client's continuing potential for increased maturity through some form of **insight.** The three approaches presented in this chapter are theoretically rich and clinically and experimentally well-supported, and the practitioners of each are committed to the ongoing scientific investigation of outcomes.

The three approaches examined in this chapter are: (1) a *social learning approach,* Julian Rotter's early behavioral approach, which maintained an emphasis on cognitive processes at a time when it was unpopular to do so; (2) *rational-emotive therapy,* Albert Ellis's pioneering blend of cognitive therapy, behavior therapy, and common sense; and (3) *multimodal therapy,* the integrated and systematic approach of "reformed" behavior therapist Arnold Lazarus.[1]

Though Rotter, Ellis, and Lazarus have each dedicated much of their lifetimes to developing their approaches, each continues to benefit from the theoretical, clinical, and experimental efforts of numerous colleagues and former students. Each of these men has a certain charisma, albeit of very different styles, that has helped to build his following, but none is an ideologue or self-styled guru. Each in his own way has established an open and dynamic approach to psychological intervention that is designed to change and mature just like the clients who benefit from it.

Sample Case: Frank and Francine Perfetti

Francine: intelligent, statuesque, beautiful, and always precisely coiffured and attired. Frank: chiseled good looks, muscled torso, and a disarming boyish smile. When they married in their mid-20s, the quip among their peers was that the "perfect" man had found the "perfect" woman so they could have "a per-

---

[1]None of the three approaches selected for inclusion in this chapter is directly related to psychoanalysis. Despite the promising work of Strupp described in Chapter 7, most psychoanalytically oriented approaches continue to shun behavior therapy. One exception is Paul Wachtel's *integrative psychodynamic therapy,* which combines psychoanalysis with behavior therapy. As Wachtel's work becomes more widely recognized and utilized by practitioners, it is likely to be included in future editions of this book (see Wachtel, 1977, 1982a). Valuable reading in relation to the differences between and integration of behavior therapy and other approaches can be found in Kendall (1982) and Messer (1986).

fectly great time!" The marriage was in trouble within a month; the problem was sex.

Before they married, Francine and Frank had lived together for about 11 months. They had sex every evening—all evening—and regularly experimented with improbable locales and spine-stretching positions. With the exception of the heart-shaped bathtub, their honeymoon at the lodge on Lake Shazam was a bit of a letdown, but both Francine and Frank reveled privately in the admiring and envious glances from other newlywed couples. Honeymoon finished, the couple returned to their apartment and their respective careers. Frank was in "law enforcement," as he described his job as a security guard at the college campus. Frank had taken that job after dropping out of college 3 years before their wedding. Since their marriage, he had applied to several local police departments, but none had openings. Francine had a good job as an accountant with a small firm. She had been a good student through high school and college, although she had rarely missed a good time.

The early months of marriage were fine, except that Francine often claimed to be too tired to have sex, and when she did agree to it, Frank's performance was lackluster, to say the least. After one particularly unfulfilling sexual encounter, they discussed the matter openly. They agreed that it was a matter of fatigue and competition. Francine was working constantly at her job, and she was making a higher salary than Frank. Her disinterest was the result of tiredness, and his impotence was caused by her "putting me down all the time with all this talk about her job." It all made sense, at least until the day Francine came home early from work and found dear Frank in bed with one of the college's fine arts professors and her husband.

A Social Learning Approach

It is 1939, and the world is hurtling toward war, and you are a 35-year-old white male of average intelligence serving a 3-year term at the Indiana State Penal Farm. You have volunteered to be in an experiment being conducted by a young doctoral student from Indiana University, and you are surprised that he wants you to play a sort of game using an unusual apparatus—a 38-inch long board with a groove down the center of it. At one end of the board is a steel ball that can be shot down the groove using a miniature pool cue. At the other end of the board are numbers that correspond to depressions in the groove, which, depending on the speed of the ball, will stop its roll. The numbers, which are color coded, are arranged as shown.

After you practice a bit with the apparatus, you learn the rules of play. The aim of the game is to get a score of 10 each time you hit the ball. But there

is a twist. Before each hit of the ball, you are to tell the experimenter what score you expect to get. If you overestimate, you get no points. If you underestimate, you get your real score minus two points for each number you are away from your estimate. You, and over 200 other people from a variety of walks of life, are part of an early experiment by Julian Rotter that addresses a question central to his **social learning theory**: How do our expectations about our performance shape that performance, and where do those expectations come from? Almost 50 years after the "aspiration board" busied the inmates in Indiana, Rotter and his colleagues have systematic answers to those questions, answers with significant implications for the practice of psychotherapy and counseling.

Historical and Theoretical Foundations

Most of Julian B. Rotter's (born 1916) professional career has been spent at two institutions as a professor and director of training in clinical psychology: first, at Ohio State University and then for 20 years at the University of Connecticut. As the vignette above suggests, his life has been given over to experimental research, research undergirding the development of the social learning perspective in personality theory, personality assessment, developmental psychology, and community psychology. As the reader may recall from Chapter 4, social learning theory also represents one of the four major approaches to behavior therapy.

Although Rotter has been a pioneer in clinical psychology and the education of clinical psychologists in the U.S., he has never enjoyed the popular appeal of other prominent practitioners, for example, Carl Rogers or Albert Ellis. Until rather recently, Rotter's determination to integrate **behavior theory** with **cognitive theory** put him outside of the mainstream in clinical psychology, and the cognitive emphasis of his work did not fit with trends in experimental psychology. Further, Rotter has kept a relatively low public profile, and his approach has neither been translated into self-help books nor popularized by a following outside the academic community. Rotter's life has been that of the ideal scientist-practitioner. His clinical measures, most particularly his measure of locus of control, have been applied exceptionally broadly, and his former students are scattered throughout the nation's clinics and universities.[2] From our present perspective, Rotter's work was a precursor of

---

[2]As noted in Chapter 3, Rotter's 1966 paper on generalized expectancies has been the single most widely quoted article in the social sciences (Sahakian & Lundin, 1984b).

the theoretical integration and technical eclecticism that is now so highly valued. His unique blend of behavior theory and cognitive theory is a theoretical wellspring to contemporary psychologists, and his relentless integration of theory, research, and clinical practice has made him a model practitioner.

The basics of Rotter's theory of personality and approach to psychological intervention were set forth in *Social Learning and Clinical Psychology,* published in 1954. Many of the major papers on social learning theory can be found in *Applications of a Social Learning Theory of Personality* (Rotter, Chance, & Phares, 1972), and the research on the locus of control has been integrated in two works by Herbert Lefcourt (1976, 1981). More recently, Rotter compiled and edited some of his previously published and unpublished papers in *The Development and Application of Social Learning Theory* (1982a).

Great expectancies: Adler, Tolman, and Lewin   The theoretical foundations of Rotter's approach can be found in both the **clinical research tradition** and the **experimental research tradition.** In the clinical research tradition, Rotter's chief debt is to Adler; from the experimental research tradition, the influences of Tolman and Lewin are most apparent.

In an earlier chapter, I noted the often unheralded importance of Alfred Adler. Rotter is one person who has acknowledged his debt to Adler. Indeed, when Adler first came to the United States, Rotter, still an undergraduate, managed to meet him and attend both his clinical training seminars and the more private meetings held at Adler's home (Rotter, 1982a). Although Rotter did some early research on Adler's birth order hypotheses, three Adlerian principles influenced him more: (1) human behavior is goal directed, (2) subjective appraisal of reality determines behavior, and (3) human behavior is determined by and modified in social interaction (see Mosher, 1968).

Rotter derived similar conceptualizations of human behavior from the comparative experimental work of Edward Chance Tolman. Tolman, in his classic *Purposive Behavior in Animals and Men* (1949), argued for a behavioristic learning theory with a cognitive component drawn largely from Gestalt psychology. In explaining the behavior of his experimental rats, Tolman noted the goal-directed nature of their behavior and described the intervening variable of *expectancy* that Rotter would later modify to explain complex human behavior.

Kurt Lewin had perhaps the most profound effect on Rotter's work, however. Lewin is often described as one of the truly seminal minds in American psychology, and he was one of Rotter's graduate professors at the University of Iowa. Although Lewin's work as a social psychologist was quite varied, many of his more permanent contributions were highly mathematical theoretical schemata representing human personality and social interaction. Although Rotter has followed Lewin's tendency to express relationships among variables in formulas, it is Lewin's fundamental understanding of human behavior that is most apparent in Rotter's work. For Lewin, as well as Rotter, the study of human behavior is the study of the interaction between the individual and his or her meaningful environment. The individual is shaped by the environment following the various laws of learning, but the individual, through expectancies and attributions, endows that environment with the ability to change the individual's behavior. Human behavior, therefore, is learned and modified in an interactive process that is essentially cognitive.

Basic Constructs

Rotter's social learning approach to counseling and psychotherapy is an application of a larger personality theory that addresses the question of how rather stable patterns of behavior emerge and how differences between individuals develop. The fundamentals of Rotter's social learning theory are contained in nine key constructs: behavior potential, expectancy, reinforcement value, the psychological situation, need potential, freedom of movement, need value, minimal goal level, and locus of control.[3]

Behavior potential "Behavior potential may be defined as the potentiality of any behavior's occurring in any given situation or situations as calculated in relation to any single reinforcement or reinforcements [italics omitted]" (Rotter, 1982a, p. 49). As in other behavioral approaches, Rotter is talking about the probability that a given reinforcement or set of reinforcements will elicit specific behaviors. However, Rotter's conception of behavior is much broader than that underlying traditional behavioral models, including any "action of the organism that involves a response to a meaningful stimulus and that may be observed or measured directly or indirectly" (p. 30). In this view, less readily observed responses, like cognitions, are behaviors that follow the same laws as more overt actions.

A simple example may help here. A young woman, Annie, walks into a room and stands for the first time before the officers of Do Re Mi, a campus sorority she would like to join. The president of the sorority looks up and asks Annie if she is nervous. She reports that she is not. There are at least two specific behaviors we can look at here. First, Annie's hands are shaking, and her voice quavers. Second, Annie describes herself as not nervous. Each behavior had a given potential for occurring in this stimulus situation. Indeed, she could have reported that she was very nervous, or she could have in fact been very relaxed. She performed neither of those behaviors, however. One of the factors that shaped the behaviors Annie did perform is the meaning this situation has for her. This brings us to the concept of expectancy.

Expectancy If behavior is a response to a meaningful stimulus, *expectancy* provides the meaning. Rotter (1982a) defined expectancy as "the probability held by the individual that a particular reinforcement will occur as a function

---

[3]Following the lead of Lewin, Rotter expressed the relationships among these constructs using formulas. With one exception, I have avoided using them in the present discussion, but they are readily found in the original sources.

of a specific behavior on his [or her] part in a specific situation or situations. Expectancy is independent of the value or importance of the reinforcement" [italics omitted] (pp. 50–51). According to Rotter (1982b, p. 243) there are three kinds of expectancies. First, there are simple labelings of stimuli: "The president of the sorority is taller than I am," or "I am nervous." Second, there are expectancies regarding behavior reinforcement sequences: "If I act calm and cool, they will like me." Third, there are expectancies regarding reinforcement-reinforcement sequences: "If they like me, then I will get into the sorority and eventually become a college president just like I've always dreamed!" This last example highlights an important characteristic of expectancies: Expectancies are beliefs about what reinforcements will follow an action rather than necessarily accurate appraisals of the situation.

Reinforcement value Rotter (1982a) defined the *reinforcement value* of any external reinforcement as "the degree of preference for any reinforcement to occur if the possibilities of their occurring were all equal [italics omitted]" (p. 51). An individual moves from situation to situation. Some situations are quite familiar; others are novel. The culture and the individual's past experiences lead her or him to view some elements in the situation as rewarding and others as aversive. Let us return to the example of Annie. Not only was Annie offered an opportunity to interview before the officers of Do Re Mi sorority, but she was also invited to interview with another sorority, Fa So La. For the sake of our example, we will hold expectancy constant; that is, we will say that Annie was 100% convinced that she would be invited to join each group if she attended the interviews. Annie's experiences, along with the information available from the culture, indicate that being in a sorority can bring status, companionship, and personal networks that can make for a successful career. Based on her experiences with the women of the respective sororities and the campus culture's evaluation of the two groups, Annie has formed a judgment about the relative reinforcement value of each. Assuming that all other things are held constant, Annie's behavior—which interview she attends—will indicate the relative reinforcement value of each group. Of course, in real life, expectancy is rarely 100%, and people's expectancies in regard to two different reinforcements are rarely the same.

The psychological situation In traditional behavioral approaches to explaining human behavior, a great deal of emphasis is placed on the role of an individual's immediate environment. The assortment of stimuli in the immediate situation is considered to produce the behavioral response. Traditional insight therapists assume that more enduring internal characteristics (traits, dispositions, mechanisms, and so forth) produce the behavior. Rotter's approach strikes a balance between these two assumptions with the construct of the *psychological situation*. According to Rotter, the stimuli in a person's immediate situation produce behavioral responses when those stimuli are meaningful to the person because of previous experience. Meaningfulness is not to be equated with previous conditioning. Rather, based on our experiences within the culture, we classify a given situation in some way. Annie may classify her interviews with the sororities in several ways, depending on her past experience ("school-related," "important for career," "fun and games," or "demanding and stressful"), but how she ends up classifying them will largely determine her behavior in regard to the interviews.

Rotter (1982b) has described the relationships among the constructs presented above as follows:

1. "The potential for behavior *x* to occur, in situation 1, in relation to reinforcement *a,* is a function of the expectancy of the occurrence of reinforcement *a,* following behavior *x* in situation 1, and the value of reinforcement *a* in situation 1" (p. 242). Expressed in terms of our example, the potential for Annie to attend the sorority interview, a situation that is meaningful to her because it could get her into the sorority, is a function of her expectancy that she will get into the sorority after she attends the interview and the fact that she places specific value on getting into the sorority. In other words, whether or not Annie will attend the interview depends on whether or not she believes that attending will get her into the sorority and whether or not she wants to get into the sorority.

2. "The potentiality of functionally related behaviors *x* to *n* to occur, in specified situations 1 to *n* in relation to potential reinforcements *a* to *n,* is a function of the expectancies of these behaviors leading to these reinforcements in these situations, and the values of these reinforcements in these situations" (p. 242). In terms of our example, the potential for Annie to perform an assortment of related activities (attending meetings, introducing herself to new people, joining a club), in specific situations (belonging to a sorority, being among influential people, hearing about important clubs), leading to related reinforcements (being well liked, making important contacts, becoming an influential person) is a function of Annie's expectancies that performing those behaviors in those situations will lead to those reinforcements and the value she places on getting those reinforcements. Thus, if Annie believes that doing things like attending meetings, introducing herself to people, and joining clubs will help her be well liked, make important contacts, and become influential, and if she wants to be well liked, well connected, and influential, she is likely to do all those things when finding herself in the right situations.

The second of these two principles can be more succinctly understood in terms of the constructs of need potential, freedom of movement, and need value.

Need potential, freedom of movement, and need value   One of the main purposes of a psychological theory is to predict behavior. Accordingly, the first principle described above enables us to predict whether or not a person will perform a specific behavior, provided we know the situation, the potential outcome of the behavior, and how likely the person perceives the outcome to be. Now we turn to predicting more generalized patterns of behavior. To do so, Rotter introduced the construct of *need*. Needs are a common construct in personality theories, but they typically refer to an expression of a deficit state or disequilibrium in the organism. For Rotter, to talk about an individual's need is to refer to that individual's patterns of interaction with the environment, specifically, to behaviors that are functionally related because they direct that individual toward particular reinforcements (Rotter, 1954). This being so, we can talk about a group of functionally related behaviors occurring in a segment of a person's life having a certain *need potential*: a mean potentiality or likelihood of occurrence in the pursuit of certain obtainable reinforcements. Rotter used the following formula and statement to describe need potential:

NP = f (FM & NV)

Need potential is a function of freedom of movement and need value.

In this formulation, *freedom of movement* is a measure of expectancy, and it is defined as the mean expectancy an individual has regarding whether or not performing functionally related behaviors will lead to related reinforcements. *Need value,* an expansion of reinforcement value, is an individual's mean preference for a set of related reinforcements. Thus, the potential that an individual will perform a given set of functionally related behaviors (need potential) is a function of that individual's mean or *generalized expectancy* that those behaviors will lead to a set of related reinforcements (freedom of movement) and of that individual's relative desire for those reinforcements (need value).

Let us return briefly to Annie's case to illustrate this. Throughout Annie's childhood, she moved easily in and out of social situations; more often than not, she found that by talking with people in a particular manner she gained their attention and affection. Her sociability thus was reinforced. As a result, her generalized expectancy in regard to such behavior is high, as is the value she places on gaining the reinforcement. In terms of the formulation described above, both FM and NV are high, and the potential for Annie to behave in a similar manner at college is also high (NP). However, had Annie's experiences left her with a high need value—a strong desire for attention and affection—but a low freedom of movement—expressed in skepticism about her ability to act in such a way that she will get attention and affection—then we might have found her to be shy and defensive rather than outgoing. In other words, present behavior expresses an individual's experiences in two important ways: first, in terms of what situations the individual desires and finds reinforcing and, second, in terms of the expectancies the individual has in regard to actually performing the actions that may lead to reinforcements.

Minimal goal level   There is both consistency and individual variation in what human beings find satisfying or reinforcing. Each of us readily learns the cultural norms for satisfaction through the dictates and expectations of others. We also learn through our observation and imitation of others what may satisfy. Our experiences, however, in any aspect of life (for example, achievement, ethical behavior, expression of emotion) can alter what we accept as reinforcement. Each individual in each life situation has a continuum of reinforcements, expressed as goals, that she or he will perceive as satisfying. The lowest goal along that continuum of reinforcements is the *minimal goal level* (Rotter et al., 1972). This clearly affects the development of freedom of movement. If Annie's minimal requirements for satisfying her need for attention and affection include being elected president of the sorority, then failure to attain that reinforcement would greatly influence her freedom of movement.

Locus of control   Life is a series of ever-changing situations. Some situations, like illness or separation from loved ones, threaten us, filling us with feelings of dread and helplessness. Other situations, like receiving an award or escaping from prison, may fill us with excitement and anticipation. Most of the situations we confront are not so clear-cut, however, and how we interpret and categorize them depends on certain beliefs we have about our capacity to successfully cope with them—that is, our ability to control the reinforcement available in the situation. Consider more typical situations: meeting an attractive person, being offered a new job, or beginning graduate study. To each of these situations we bring beliefs about our ability to control the consequences of our actions in each. One person may shy away from the potential new relationship, while another may relish it. The offer of a new job may fill one person with anxiety and suspicion and another with excitement. One individual may face the trials and tribulations of graduate study confidently and with minimal discomfort, while another may live in dread of pending disaster. What these individuals bring to these situations are beliefs in their respective capacities to control the consequences of certain behaviors. In the language of social learning theory, this belief in our capacity to control reinforcement across a range of diverse situations is the generalized expectancy called *locus of control.*

Locus of control is a characteristic of personality and a predictor of behavior. It refers to a continuum of possible beliefs in one's ability to control reinforcement in a variety of external situations. At one end of the continuum is belief in an internal locus of control of reinforcement; at the other, an external. Individuals whose locus of control is more internal believe that they control reinforcement through their behavior. Individuals whose locus of control is more external do not believe that they control reinforcement. How then do such individuals account for their successes in securing reinforcement? They attribute successes either to chance or to the power of others.[4] Because such individuals attribute the power over actually gaining the reinforcement to powerful others ("My Mom's the president of the company") or to chance ("I'm lucky, not talented"), even those who experience success may be inhibited from further action.

---

[4]The distinction between attributing external control to chance and attributing it to powerful others is from the work of Hilda Levenson (1973a, 1973b, 1974). See also related studies in Lefcourt (1981).

The nine constructs outlined above thus serve as the foundation of Rotter's personality theory. They also form the basis for the approach to intervention to which we now turn our attention.

The Process of Intervention

For Rotter (1982a), the "problems of psychotherapy may be viewed as problems in how to effect changes in behavior through interaction of one person with another. That is, they are problems in human learning in a social situation or context" (p. 237). As one might suspect, Rotter's approach is neither highly stylized nor composed of elaborate techniques. Rather, the basic constructs described above constitute a conceptual framework based on which eclectically selected techniques are applied in the therapeutic relationship. The nature of that relationship will be revealed as we examine the goals of treatment.

The goals of treatment   Rotter (1982a) has pointed out that in relation to social values, a practitioner may have three possible goals in psychological treatment: (1) to help the client become more conforming and thus more "normal", (2) to improve the client's subjective feelings of happiness or well-being, or (3) to make the client's life more socially constructive, more beneficial to society (p. 240). In identifying the goals of the social learning approach, Rotter integrated the last two of these possible goals into four *value commitments* that both establish the treatment objectives and define the practitioner's behavior. In brief, they are: (1) The practitioner accepts *some* of the responsibility for the client's actions, goals, and ethical values, and he or she attempts to change them; (2) this change occurs as the practitioner tries to enhance the level of personal satisfaction the client receives from her or his actions by directing the client toward goals that accord with the client's ethical values; (3) in doing this, the practitioner aims at eliminating or preventing actions or goals that are clearly detrimental to others in society; (4) further, the practitioner believes that the client is responsible for contributing to the welfare of others in return for the satisfactions that others in society provide the client (p. 241). Rotter has pointed out that applying such a value-oriented approach is never simple and depends on the judgment of the practitioner. Rotter argued for careful exploration of the client's and practitioner's values rather than reliance on the false assumption that psychological intervention is value-free just because the values are unarticulated.

To accomplish the goals of the social learning approach, the practitioner must possess the "warmth, understanding, interest, and acceptance" necessary to facilitate the client's free expression and to set up conditions in which the practitioner can become a significant source of reinforcement (p. 247). More importantly, Rotter asserted, the practitioner must be a sort of mini-anthropologist, specifically, someone who encourages the client to describe her or his situation so the practitioner can understand the cultural and subcultural dimensions of the client's life.

The nature of the client's distress   Rather than rely on the usual classification system and jargon used in psychopathology, the social learning practitioner views the client's symptomatic distress as an expression of patterns of behavior that are inadequate for achieving personal satisfaction, responding to the legitimate needs of others, or both. Client distress is understood in terms of the formulation presented earlier: Need potential is a function of freedom of movement and need value. In the context of therapy, need potential refers to the probability that the client will perform a set of functionally related behaviors that can provide personal satisfaction or satisfy others. Clearly, the need potential will be lower if a client's freedom of movement is low—that is, if the client has little expectancy that her or his behavior will lead to satisfaction—or if the need value is low—that is, if the client does not value the satisfaction that will result from the behavior. More commonly in the therapeutic setting, however, the client's freedom of movement is low and his or her need value is high; in other words, the client values the potential satisfaction but does not believe that performing the behaviors will actually lead to that satisfaction. In such a case, potentially successful constructive behaviors are replaced with feelings of dissatisfaction, conflict, defensiveness, and/or "irreal" (avoidance) behavior (Rotter, 1982a).

Rotter (1970, 1982a) identified several causes of low freedom of movement. First, an individual may simply lack the skills or knowledge necessary to reach a particular goal. For example, a brand-new college graduate hoping to make new friends at her job on Madison Avenue may discover that she is unaware of, and unpracticed in, the rituals used to establish interpersonal contact in that environment. As a result, her general expectancy that her standard way of operating will lead to new friendships will be lowered.

Second, an individual may seek a goal that results in punishment in a given culture. As the reader may recall from the discussion of operant learning (Chapter 4), punishment decreases the likelihood that a behavior will be performed. Rotter might explain this as occurring because punishment lowers an individual's general expectancy that such behavior will lead to a desired outcome. For example, a newlywed husband, accustomed to a life of ease and independence and expecting his new wife to dote on and spoil him, may discover that the carefree, irresponsible behavior that used to charm her now irritates her. Consequently, his general expectancy that his old behavior patterns will bring him attention and affection will diminish.

Third, an individual may mistakenly expect failure as a result of other past or contemporaneous experiences. For example, a teenage girl may believe that the fragile health that restricted her physical activities in childhood also affects her present social and academic activities. Similarly, a man who fails at selling computers may generalize that experience and expect himself to fail as an illustrator as well.

As noted earlier, high minimal goal levels can and typically do cause low freedom of movement. If an individual's minimal goal level is very high, then even rewards that many others would find satisfying will fail to satisfy him or her. Thus, a woman honored by others as an accomplished musician but perpetually unsatisfied with her own performance may have set her minimal goal level so high that satisfaction is virtually impossible. The low freedom of movement that results may eventually be expressed in ritualistic behavior, depression, or bouts of anxiety.

Throughout the preceding discussion, we have been talking about low freedom of movement within a group of related situations, where interrelated expectancies and similar rewards result in functionally related behaviors and corresponding goals (for example, in the intellectual, athletic, or interpersonal realms). In discussing client distress, however, we must return to the broader concept of locus of control. Locus of control refers to a *generalized expectancy* that cuts across most of an individual's behaviors so that the individual habitually attributes control over reinforcement either to her- or himself (internal locus of control) or to something else (external locus of control).

Lefcourt (1976) has described some interesting issues related to locus of control. The more internal an individual's locus of control, the more likely that person is to attribute the responsibility for failure to him- or herself. Although this realization is distressful, the more internal individual typically works through the distress with the aid of defense mechanisms (for example, repression) and determination for renewed action. Thus, internal locus of control is generally associated with the successful resolution of distress through the assumption of responsibility and flexible behavioral responses. On the other hand, serious psychological problems generally correlate with external locus of control. Vicious circles of helplessness and defensiveness often characterize such persons' behavior. Although the presenting problems may range from anxiety and depression to histrionics or even aggression, a person trapped in such a vicious circle will generally continually fail to meet satisfying goals, attribute that failure to others, feel helpless, and repeat the maladaptive and unsatisfying behavior.

Changing behavior   In the social learning approach, behavioral change is considered to result from learning that begins in the therapeutic social interaction, then is tested and refined in real-life situations. In therapy, the client learns information and skills drawn from learning theory and research and insight generated in interpersonal exploration. Although insight gained during therapy can lead the client to change his or her behavior, the reverse is equally true: Changes in behavior promoted in therapy to relieve the client's symptoms can lead to changes in the client's attitudes and then to personal insight into the nature and causes of his or her problems. Thus, in the social learning view, insight can be both a spur to behavioral change and its by-product.

Although in practice the social learning approach varies from practitioner to practitioner, changing a client's behavior involves a dialogue between the client and practitioner that aims at one of the following cognitive changes (Rotter, 1954, 1978, 1982a):

1. *Changing expectancies*: Changing a client's expectancies involves two intertwined activities: (1) increasing the client's expectancy for positive rein-

forcement for adaptive behaviors and (2) lowering the client's expectancy for gratification from maladaptive behaviors. Rotter described a number of ways for changing the client's expectancies. First, the practitioner's systematic (but not mechanical) use of reinforcement during the sessions can be a subtle yet important source of expectancy change. When the client displays or describes adaptive behaviors, the practitioner responds with reinforcing words and actions. When the client displays or describes maladaptive behaviors, the practitioner avoids words or actions that might reinforce those behaviors. Second, in careful *verbal analysis* of the client's life, the practitioner can point out the role that patterns of avoidance behaviors have played in increasing the client's erroneous expectancies, as well as suggesting behaviors and situational opportunities that might have led to rewarding consequences. Third, within the confines of confidentiality, significant others from the client's life can be incorporated into the process of reinforcing adaptive behaviors and not reinforcing maladaptive ones. Fourth, the client can be assigned to participate in certain real-life or role-playing situations to challenge her or his assumptions about the rewards and punishments accompanying adaptive behaviors. At other times, the client may be assigned simply to observe the adaptive behaviors of others. These observations can become the topic of instructive discussions between the client and practitioner.

2. *Changing reinforcement values*: Because a client's expectancies are not always easily determined, the practitioner may spend considerable time examining the client's reinforcement values. Most typically, this involves verbally analyzing the client's past reinforcement values and reevaluating their current relevance. Take, for example, a client who, based on his or her early experiences, highly values independence. Even though the behaviors that protect his or her independence yield only marginal satisfaction, the client views dependence as the antithesis of independence and thus fails to value it. Through analyzing the client's assumptions, past experiences, and potential for future actions, the practitioner may help the client to see that his or her satisfaction depends on being both dependent and independent. Thus, the practitioner may raise the value of dependence for the client without lowering the value of independence. From there, the client can move to learning and practicing skills that evidence a healthy amount of dependence.

3. *Adjusting minimal goal levels*: As noted earlier, minimal goal levels that are very high can limit the amount of satisfaction an individual will experience and lower the individual's freedom of movement. On the other hand, if an individual's minimal goal levels are very low, he or she may engage only in activities that tap little of the individual's potential and thus yield only a fraction of the satisfaction he or she is capable of experiencing. To raise or lower a client's minimal goal levels appropriately, the practitioner again couples verbal analysis of the client's misinterpretation of past events with carefully applied reinforcement.

4. *Instilling generalized expectancies*: As noted earlier, in addition to expectancies that are specific to certain behaviors and their rewards, each client

carries generalized expectancies that influence a much wider range of activities. One of the practitioner's goals is to instill certain generalized expectancies in the client through verbal analysis, reasoning, and persuasion. Through research, Rotter (1978) has identified four generalized expectancies of particular value to clients: (1) One can control at least part of what happens to oneself (a more internal locus of control); (2) unless one has proof to the contrary, it is advantageous to trust other people;[5] (3) examining one's options and planning for the long-term are important; and (4) different situations have different behaviors appropriate to them.

Beyond the theoretical issues and general methods described above, the social learning approach encompasses a number of general and specialized techniques. Several of those techniques are described below:

1. *Structuring the therapy*: Structuring refers to discussions between the client and the practitioner about the therapeutic process itself. The purpose of structuring is to facilitate the process by establishing mutual goals, expectations, and patterns of interaction. The extent and timing of structuring will vary from client to client, but structuring is a touchstone to which the practitioner may intermittently return. Structuring is information: Through it, the practitioner establishes the client's expectation that therapy is an active, interpersonal process in which significant change requires full participation. Structuring fosters accountability: Through it, the practitioner and client establish mutual, verifiable short- and long-term goals. Structuring is persuasion: Through it, the client comes to expect that she or he can change and that the process will probably succeed; further, she or he learns that changing is valuable.

2. *The relationship*: Rotter (1954) described three aspects of the client-practitioner relationship: (1) acceptance, (2) reassurance, and (3) transference. *Acceptance* involves breaking with the ways in which the client's distress has typically been greeted by others by acknowledging its realness and demonstrating a willingness to engage with the client in changing the distress-producing behavior. *Reassurance* involves affirming that the client's problem is worth solving and that solutions to the problem can be found through the therapy. Acceptance and reassurance are both difficult but necessary skills to master, since their misuse can reinforce the client's negativity and defensiveness. **Transference** in the social learning approach refers to the reinforcement value of the therapist that results from his or her acceptance and reassurance of the client. A relationship characterized by trust, warmth, and affection endows the practitioner with a positive reinforcement value. Used effectively, that reinforcement value enables the practitioner to be persuasive. As therapy

---

[5] Trust is a key idea in Rotter's work. For example, stress may become a serious problem for an individual whose locus of control is strongly internal unless that person trusts other people enough to share responsibility. A more external person with high levels of trust may become dependent, and a more external person with low levels of trust may appear a touch paranoid. Worth reading is Rotter, 1980a (reprinted in Rotter, 1982a).

progresses, the practitioner relies less and less on direct reinforcement and more and more on the reinforcements the client secures outside of therapy.

3. *Insight and interpretation*: In the social learning approach, the client spends much time during therapy recounting past and present experiences. In the telling, the client may come to certain insights into the relationships between past patterns of reinforcement, her or his expectancies, and present behavior. More commonly, however, the practitioner engenders the client's new insights through his or her interpretations. After the practitioner has established trust and credibility, she or he often interprets for the client events and patterns in the client's past and present life, as well as promoting insight into what lies in the future if maladaptive patterns are maintained. Often the most important insights to be gained by the client are not into the client's reactions and motives but into the reactions and motives of others. The practitioner generally communicates her or his interpretations in an indirect and nonthreatening way so that the client is able to hear the new understanding and is free to accept it, reject it, or come to it later in therapy. The practitioner's interpretations and client's insights do not exist for their own sake. The focus is on changing maladaptive patterns of behavior, and interpretation need not continue beyond that point.

The social learning approach to therapy rests on a research-based theory of personality. In practice, practitioners rely on that theory for their understanding of client development and change while using both cognitive and behavioral strategies in the process of therapy.

Sample Session

Although practitioners of the social learning approach also work with couples and families, the approach has been most widely used with individuals. For our present purposes, we will take Frank to therapy with Dr. Frieda Formular, a psychologist who follows Rotter's social learning approach. In this scenario, we will assume that Frank has gone into therapy after a rather painful confrontation with Francine following his brief ménage à trois. We are several sessions into treatment, and Frank has begun to trust Dr. Formular. He has been recounting to her a personal history characterized by an inability to say no when others want him to do things. He recognizes that he is terribly insecure, despite his exceptional good looks and likable personality. The only thing that he knew he did well was sex, and for some reason, marriage has ended that also. His explanation of his involvement with the fine arts professor, Dr. O'Hare, and her husband is once again being discussed:

Practitioner (P): I think, Frank, that it's clear that you really enjoy the attention and admiration that people give you because of your appearance and your personality, yet you seem to distrust it—you want something different from them. Is that right?

Frank (F): You know, Dr. Formular, I think I've always assumed that when I got praise for something I did, it was really because I was good-looking and could throw some charm at them. Funny, but I always wanted to do something—anything—right. When somebody challenges me, I usually just throw some bull at them and disappear. To be honest, most of the time people really scare me, and I usually try to get away. I mean, that's really what threw me for a loop with Professor O'Hare. She started telling me about her husband and her being swingers, and I started throwing the bull, and she called my bluff. There just didn't seem to be any point in my saying no.

P: As in other situations we've talked about, you went along with what she suggested because you felt helpless, powerless.

F: Yeah. I mean, it was a turn on and all, but I thought it was wrong and I didn't want to do it. But Professor O'Hare had often talked to me about art and stuff like that, treated me like somebody who knew something, and then she went and showed what she was really interested in. She tricked me, trapped me with all of those good things she used to say.

P: I'm wondering if you're not going a bit too far in your understanding of that. It may well be that Professor O'Hare both respected your ideas *and* wanted to have you join her and her husband in bed! I mean, Frank, you are a fairly bright fellow—it's quite possible that Professor O'Hare didn't set out to "trap" you, as you put it.

F: Look, Doctor, I'm willing to say that I did the wrong thing in agreeing to do it with her and then getting caught and all, but she sure as hell trapped me.

P: You know, Frank, it occurs to me that if we piece together your history a bit, it has not been unusual for you to become seductive as a way out of a pressure situation. I'm just wondering what sort of signals you might have been sending. I don't think you feel very much in control of your life much of the time, and sex has been one way you have typically controlled others, only to feel guilty about it later. Is that right?

F: Yeah, I guess so, but I didn't make any serious moves like I typically would, although I might have flirted a bit.

P: Do a little role-playing, Frank. Show me how you might have acted toward Professor O'Hare.

Frank acts out conversations and actions that are characteristic of adolescent mating rituals. Frank, however, appears not to recognize how provocative his manner can be, and he continues to argue that it was not his intention to promote a tryst.

P: You know, Frank, your way of talking with Professor O'Hare might have seemed pretty tame if you were talking in a singles' bar or a health spa, but honestly, from what you've described, you don't have to be too good at reading between the lines to hear one clear message: ready, willing, and able. [*Pause.*] Frank, I think it's

important to recognize that different situations often require different behaviors. What you viewed as mere play was understood as
much more.

F: You may be right Doctor. You know, I really wanted her to like
me, to like me for myself. But what's that? Just some sexual ath-
lete who can't even make it with his wife!

P: Frank, I'm not convinced that the problem with Francine can't be
overcome. But first, you and Francine have to start talking, really
talking. You know I'm a fan of yours, and I can see beyond your
bull to the guy who worries and fears. I'd bet that the only person
Francine knows is the macho and arrogant one—the one who becomes defensive about his wife's success, who finds it very difficult
to express caring. That's the person who hasn't allowed himself to
surface, and I think that may have something to do with the problem. It's something we can work with, Frank, and I'm sure we can
succeed. But it's important that you begin to talk with her about
some of these things, perhaps even by bringing her with you to
therapy. If you aren't sure how to approach her, we can role-play
some of it here, but we've got to get moving. There are skills that
you can learn that will help you, but first, I think you've got to
take some steps on your own.

F: I know, I know. It's like you say: *Do* something.

P: You've got it.

Evaluation

Rotter's (1982a) own summary of his social learning theory serves as an apt
starting point for evaluating it:

> At present, social learning theory has demonstrated a strong heuristic potential.
> Both in its testing and in its application to a wide variety of problems, the theory
> has led to a substantial accumulation of research findings. . . . From its inception,
> the theory has proved useful as a way of *analyzing* problems. Constructs have been
> added only as satisfactory ways of measuring them as been developed, and the
> logical consistency of the operational definitions and ideal definitions has been
> strong. (p. 325)

Rotter's description points up the balance between comprehensiveness
and parsimony that has characterized his contribution. Unlike many of his colleagues in the clinical research tradition, Rotter has consistently striven to define his constructs operationally and quantify them, both in his theory and in
applying them in therapy. Unlike many of his colleagues in the experimental
research tradition, he has refused to abandon constructs and techniques that
are complex and difficult to work with scientifically or that are out of favor with
the research establishment. As a result, Rotter has given us a theory that is at
once scientific and interpersonal, cognitive and behavioral, theoretical and
practical, and an approach to therapy that is broad enough to include insight,
transference, behavior modification, and cognitive restructuring.

In these very qualities are also the approach's limitations. The theory that undergirds the approach is sophisticated and complex and requires considerable effort to master in full. For many practitioners, the heavy dose of theoretical terminology and research data required to really understand the social learning approach may simply be too much. Further, while the actual manner in which the therapy is conducted was in the past quite different from the practice of behavioral modification, **psychoanalysis,** or **person-centered therapy,** today many approaches to psychotherapy are quite similar in practice to the social learning approach, including the ones that follow in this chapter. Regardless of that fact, Rotter's contribution is a significant one; he has given us a theory of human behavior that is wholly contemporary and comprehensive and an approach to therapy that is both practical and effective.

Rational-Emotive Therapy

It is 1971, and you are one of nearly 100 graduate students crammed into a lecture hall to hear one of clinical psychology's hottest practitioners. He is a middle-aged man with a New York accent and a highly charged delivery peppered with expletives more suited to a barroom than a classroom. He invites a student to come to the front of the class and present a problem. He seems almost arrogantly confident about solving the problem. A young woman volunteers. She begins to explain a fairly complex situation involving the demands of caring for her aging mother. He interrupts her and seems almost to berate her for her stupidity. He tells her that she is a victim of her own irrational thinking, calling it nothing more than "horseshit." Some students in the class are embarrassed for the woman, some are offended, and others are delighted with the efficiency and cleverness of the approach. The man was Albert Ellis, and to this day, for over 30 years, his unique ebullience and genius have enlightened (and at times enraged) audiences in classrooms, church halls, boardrooms, and convention centers. If Albert Ellis is a consummate performer, though, he is also the creator and most celebrated practitioner of what may be the most widely practiced single approach to therapy today: *rational-emotive therapy,* usually called RET.

Historical and Theoretical Foundations

As Ellis has pointed out, an RET therapist could begin each therapeutic session by asking the client, "What problems have you been bothering yourself about?" Indeed, for the RET practitioner, the "fault" is not usually in the stars, genes, unconscious, or even conditioning; rather, it is in the way the client thinks about the effects of all of that. At first glance, such a view may seem self-evident, and indeed, the key concepts and terminology of RET are both straightforward and commonsensical. Although acceptance of the fundamental concepts underlying RET has been slow in a professional community that often prefers the theoretically elegant to the obvious, RET has managed to stand the tests of both scientific investigation and the vagaries of therapeutic trendiness in a way that few other approaches have. And it all began because a 19-year-old college guy was afraid to approach young women!

In recounting the beginnings of RET, Albert Ellis often talks about his own decision to cope with his profound fear of approaching women during his undergraduate days as a business major.[6] As Ellis tells it, he finally became comfortable in approaching women by making himself extremely uncomfortable. Indeed, he forced himself to approach and talk with 130 unfamiliar women until he could do so comfortably. As he has pointed out, his success at overcoming the fear was not a matter of reinforcement: He only got one date out of it, and she never showed up! Rather, he *acted* in the face of irrational doubts and fears.

This personal victory alone, of course, did not make RET happen. Ellis's professional clinical life began as a marriage, family, and sex therapist in the 1940s during and following his doctoral training in clinical psychology at Columbia University. Although pleased with his successes as a therapist, Ellis undertook psychoanalysis under supervision and practiced classical analysis until 1953. Ellis (1962) explained his reasons in this way:

> Although, from the very start, I had many reservations about Freud's theory of personality (since, even at the age of seventeen, it was not too difficult for me to see that the man was brilliantly *creating* clinical interpretations to make them fit the procrustean bed of his enormously one-sided Oedipal theories), I somehow, perhaps by sheer wishful thinking, retained my belief in the efficacy of orthodox psychoanalytic technique. (p. 3)

Ellis's faith in the psychoanalytic approach was short-lived, however. Although he knew himself to be a good practitioner of the art of psychoanalysis, he found it all an extremely prolonged form of "brain-picking" in which his interpretation and insight were often wrong, and even when they were not, the presenting maladaptive behavior did not change as a result of this analysis (Ellis, 1962). Gradually, Ellis slipped away from classical analysis and then from neopsychoanalytic approaches. Several other forces were at work in Ellis's thinking. Philosophically, Ellis was strongly attracted to both humanism and pragmatism, the latter a distinctly American philosophy that emphasizes the practical usefulness of ideas and practices over their more intellectual or emotional appeal. In keeping with pragmatism, Ellis was attracted to **behaviorism** and the approaches to learning being developed by first Pavlov and then Skinner. Although he was, for a time, one of those who hoped for a blending of the insights of behaviorism and psychoanalysis, Ellis soon realized that neither approach accounts for the unique intellectual and linguistic genius of human beings. Instead, Ellis turned to the cognitively oriented thinking of Alfred Adler and, finding that brilliant but incomplete and vague, began to develop

---

[6]No presentation by Ellis is really complete without his description of his shyness around women. Although every effort should be made to see and hear him in person, a number of excellent videotapes of Ellis are available through the Institute for Rational-Emotive Therapy in New York City. Several major American cities also have local chapters of RET organizations.

his own way of understanding human behavior. Ellis began with an idea as old as the Stoics: Human beings are not disturbed by things, but by the way they think of them. He realized that though human beings may experience the whole range of Freudian disturbances or be conditioned to some maladaptive behavior, what keeps people emotionally disturbed is how they view those disturbances. More specifically, it has to do with *self-talk,* the continual, cognitive rethinking of the individual's beliefs about the effects of the past and the demands of the future.

This basic insight into human behavior, now widely accepted among a fairly diverse body of practitioners, represented in its day a radical departure. When Ellis published his early papers on RET in 1962 in *Reason and Emotion in Psychotherapy,* he found no ready acceptance of his ideas in either the experimental or the clinical research tradition. In the more than 25 years since the publication of this first major work on RET, however, the importance of his approach has become widely acknowledged. Indeed, he is credited with founding cognitive behavior therapy, as noted in Chapter 4. The gradual recognition of RET can be explained in a number of ways. First, the spread of RET has been continually enhanced by the work of the Institute for Rational-Emotive Therapy, founded by Ellis in 1959 for both research and training. Second, Ellis's perspicuous and enthusiastic presentations on RET have for decades served to draw both clients and fellow practitioners who have grown dissatisfied with other approaches and who relish RET commonsense ideas. Third, RET itself has withstood continual scrutiny and has been successfully applied to a full range of problems. Although RET is now one of several similar approaches to cognitive behavior therapy, Ellis (1987b) has continued to argue that insights unique to RET are necessary to adequately explain in cognitive terms even the most commonplace psychological problems, depression and anxiety.

An enormous body of literature about RET exists, much of it written by Ellis himself, who has published several hundred articles and over 40 books. Some of the books are directed at the general public, for example, *How to Live with a "Neurotic"* (1957) or *The Intelligent Woman's Guide to Dating and Mating* (1979); others are directed at professionals, for example, *Overcoming Resistance* (1985). Research on RET can be found throughout the professional literature, and several comprehensive texts for practitioners exist, including Ellis and Grieger's *Handbook of Rational-Emotive Therapy* (1977) and Ellis and Bernard's *Clinical Applications of Rational-Emotive Therapy* (1985).

Basic Constructs

The practice of rational-emotive therapy is based on a theory of personality that in turn rests on a specific view of human nature. RET embodies a dynamic philosophy based on careful observation, refined by experience, relatively devoid of abstractions, and fundamentally practical. Statements about human nature and behavior are set forth as hypotheses to be tested in clinical practice and, ideally, through rigorous experimentation. As recently as 1987, Ellis (1987a) concluded an article in *American Psychologist,* provocatively titled "The Impossibility of Achieving Consistently Good Mental Health," by stating a series of working hypotheses about mental life and well-being. Several of these hypotheses, paraphrased and integrated with his earlier writings, will serve as our framework for understanding RET's theory of personality.

Hypothesis 1: Human nature   We human beings are separated from our phylogenetic ancestors by our capacity to bring our behavior under the control of *rational thinking.* We are capable of observing our world, logically thinking through its demands and our needs, and then behaving. Nevertheless, Ellis (1987b) also argued for the flip side: "I firmly hypothesize that virtually all people are born with very strong tendencies to think crookedly about their important desires and preferences and to self-defeatingly escalate them into dogmatic, absolutistic shoulds, musts, oughts, demands, and commands" (p. 373). Additionally, Ellis argued that families and social institutions often serve to directly and indirectly support these ideas. Fortunately, our natural and acquired tendencies toward self-defeating thinking are complemented by our potential for **self-actualization,** most importantly evident in our capacity to change our thinking and change our behavior. Put another way, we are capable of thinking in a clear, scientific, and flexible way that prolongs life and makes it happy (Ellis & Bernard, 1985). Ellis (1987a) has described himself as being optimistic without being Pollyannaish about human nature, and he sees RET as an important tool in an individual's potential shift to self-actualization from "self-sabotaging thoughts, feelings, and behaviors" (p. 374).

Hypothesis 2: Basic irrationality   Ellis described the human capacity for irrationality as well as its remediation in terms of the *ABC*s of rational-emotive therapy. The graphic representations that follow illustrate this process.

Our commonsense assumption is that an event in one's life causes one to feel distressed (angry, sad, lonely, and so forth) and makes one engage in self-defeating behavior (avoidance, aggression, and so forth). For example, not getting a promotion at work makes one sad and angry as well as withdrawn and tentative. This relationship between an event and its consequences can be represented as follows:

A activating event → *C* consequences: emotional and behavioral

---

According to RET, however, what shapes how one feels or acts in response to an event is a *belief* about the importance of the event, the nature of its consequences, or both rather than the event itself. It is not just that one would prefer to get the promotion. Rather, one believes that one must get it and that not getting it is awful, because in order to be a good or valuable person one must always get an available promotion. In this case, the event of not getting the promotion will make one miserable and self-defeating. This example illustrates two of RET's capital crimes: "*must*erbation" ("I must get the promotion") and "*awful*izing" ("It's awful if I don't get the promotion"). This process can be represented as follows:

> *A* activating event ← *B* belief → *C* consequences: emotional and behavioral

Feeling miserable about not getting the promotion is one of at least two possible ways of feeling. The belief that one must get promoted to be a good or valuable person is an *irrational belief* (*iB*). A more rational belief might be that getting a promotion is certainly good and admirable, and indeed one might strive to do so for any number of reasons, but not getting the promotion is not so awful and one will indeed survive and might well prosper in spite of the loss! Such an attitude enables one to feel satisfied with oneself and be ready to work for the next promotion if that is the rational thing to do. The following illustrates the different outcomes of irrational versus rational beliefs:

> *A* activating event
> ↙ *iB* irrational → *C* consequences: distress and self-
>   belief   defeating behaviors
> ↖ *rB* rational → *C* consequences: satisfaction and
>   belief   coping behaviors

One is able to shift from an irrational belief to a rational belief, either in everyday life or through RET, by *disputation* (*D*). Disputation involves applying the scientific method to the problem, working within a framework of logic and hypothesis-building and testing. One way to graphically represent this shift from an irrational belief to a rational one through disputation is:

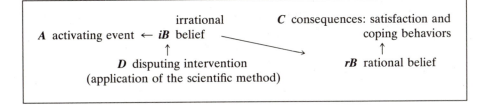

>   irrational   *C* consequences: satisfaction and
> *A* activating event ← *iB* belief   coping behaviors
>   ↑   →   ↑
>   *D* disputing intervention   *rB* rational belief
>   (application of the scientific method)

Hypothesis 3: Advanced irrationality   Ellis (1985, 1987a) has argued that the fundamental irrationality described above is only a small part of the picture. Rarely is changing behavior a straightforward matter of overturning simple bits of irrational thinking. Rather, human beings engage in elaborate forms of **resistance** designed to defend against positive change and maintain misery! Ellis (1987a) wrote:

> I also hypothesize that, in addition to holding these subtle irrational cognitions, vast numbers of people not only are talented at creating primary absolutistic musts that make them emotionally disturbed but that they also invent secondary musts about their primary disturbances, that they use their consequent disturbed feelings to exacerbate their irrational beliefs, that they unconsciously cognitively and behaviorally reinforce their crooked thinking, that they create thoughts that lead to disturbed feelings and behaviors as well as circularly use these feelings and actions to produce increased irrational thinking and that they falsely conclude, in many instances, that they are and must ever remain hopelessly aberrated. (p. 374)

Four of the major themes particularly susceptible to "irrationalizing" include: competence and success, love and approval, being treated fairly, and safety and comfort. Consider the following example on the theme of love and approval (based on Ellis, 1985, 1987a):

Blatant irrationality: Because I very strongly desire to be approved of by significant people in my life, I absolutely must have their total and unreserved approval at all times in order to be a good and valuable person.
Subtle irrationality: Because I strongly desire to be approved of by significant people in my life, *and because I have been so deprived of love in the past and must no longer be,* now I absolutely must have their total and unreserved approval at all times in order to be a good and valuable person;
or

because I strongly desire to be approved of by significant people in my life, and because if I am not loved in this way I will get very sick with depression and anxiety, I absolutely must have their total and unreserved approval at all times in order to be a good and valuable person;
or

because I strongly desire to be approved of by significant people in my life, and because I really try very hard to gain the love and approval of those significant people in my life, I absolutely must have their total and unreserved approval at all times in order to be a good and valuable person.

In the subtle irrationalities noted above, a personalized real, imaginary, or exaggerated fact, experience, or outcome seemingly justifies the irrationality and the inevitable anguish that results when not every significant other appears to love the person all the time.

The Process of Intervention

Rational-emotive therapy is at once humanistic in its philosophy and scientific in its method. We have seen the positive yet realistic philosophical view of human rationality and irrationality presented in RET. Additionally, in RET, the scientific method is applied to correcting the unrealistic philosophies of individuals so that they can live happy and fulfilling lives. Rational-emotive therapy is used with individuals, with couples, with families, and in groups. RET practitioners recognize and accept that the effectiveness of RET's cognitive techniques may be limited by the fact that psychotic, neurotic, and character disorders may involve biological causes or predispositions that are beyond psychological intervention.

Goals and Values

RET is a "system of psychotherapy designed to help people live longer, minimize their emotional disturbances and self-defeating behaviors, and actualize themselves so that they live a more fulfilling, happier existence" (Ellis & Bernard, 1985, p. 5). In practice, the RET practitioner strives to effect changes in three basic interacting modalities of human experience: (1) in *thought,* by helping the client think more rationally, more scientifically; (2) in *emotion,* by helping the client feel more appropriately in response to life events; and (3) in *action,* by helping the client act in more efficient and undefeating ways (Ellis & Bernard, 1985).[7]

To attain the therapeutic goals of a longer life, minimal emotional disturbance, minimal self-defeating behavior, and self-actualization, as well as the personal happiness that comes with attaining those goals, the client must internalize a set of specific values. These values (Ellis & Bernard, 1985, pp. 7–8) can be learned through the therapeutic process and include:

1. *Self-interest*: Recognizing that concern for the self is a necessary basis for other concerns, the individual looks out for and takes care of her- or himself.
2. *Social interest*: Recognizing that human life is social, the individual acts morally and protects the rights of others.
3. *Self-direction*: The individual assumes responsibility for him- or herself with minimal reliance on others.
4. *High tolerance for frustration*: The individual is able to patiently accept her or his own limits and those of others with minimal distress.
5. *Flexibility*: The individual is open to change and differences in others.
6. *Acceptance of uncertainty*: The individual can live with the fact that few things in life are definite and forever.
7. *Commitment to creative pursuits*: The individual maintains at least one creative avenue of expression.
8. *Scientific thinking*: The individual regulates his or her emotions through accurate rational evaluation.
9. *Self-acceptance*: The individual chooses to accept her- or himself unconditionally, with minimal comparison with others.

---

[7]Because RET practitioners work comprehensively with clients in the modalities of thought, feeling, and action, Ellis has argued that RET was the first truly "multimodal" therapy, not Lazarus's multimodal therapy, which follows in this chapter.

10. *Risk-taking*: The individual acts to attain goals while recognizing and accepting the possibility of failure.
11. *Long-range hedonism*: The individual seeks pleasure and avoids pain but is not obsessed with immediate gratification.
12. *Nonutopianism*: The individual accepts the fact that a perfect, pain-free life of pleasure is not possible.
13. *Self-responsibility*: The individual recognizes and accepts responsibility for his or her emotional disturbances without blaming him- or herself.

The RET Practitioner

In essence, RET is straightforward education: The practitioners teach clients to understand and change interactive patterns of thinking, feeling, and acting. Given this educational role, are there certain essential characteristics RET practitioners must possess? Ellis, in his introduction to *A Practitioner's Guide to Rational-Emotive Therapy* by Walen, DiGiuseppe, and Wessler (1980), identified some of the main characteristics of the effective RET practitioner. First, the effective RET practitioner possesses *intelligence*. Although intelligent people are just as capable as the less intelligent of disturbing themselves with irrational thinking, the RET practitioner must be able to solve problems systematically, and systematic problem solving requires intelligence. Second, the effective RET practitioner possesses *therapeutic knowledge*. Because RET incorporates a long list of proven behavioral, cognitive, and affective techniques, the practitioner must have a broad understanding of psychotherapy as well as a broad repertoire of specific therapeutic skills. Third, the effective RET practitioner possesses *empathy*. RET practitioners eschew the type of empathy associated with person-centered psychotherapy, because it tends to dwell upon the client's disturbed feelings and thus reinforces them. The RET practitioner truly understands the self-defeating strategies in which the client engages, however, and, in sharing that insight with the client, forges a bond of mutual understanding that enhances the therapeutic process. Fourth, the effective RET practitioner possesses *persistence*. The persistence with which the client returns to irrational thinking, disturbed feelings, and self-defeating behaviors must be met with persistent corrective instruction and techniques. Fifth, the effective RET practitioner possesses an *interest in helping others*. The effective practitioner of RET both likes and enjoys people. Though it may be easy to delight in a flashy new therapeutic approach, the type of interest and enjoyment Ellis believes is essential is able to endure the day-to-day persistent unmasking of faulty thinking and self-defeating behaviors. Sixth, the effective RET practitioner possesses a *scientific outlook*. The practitioner applies the scientific method in RET both in instructing the client and in refining the therapy. The client learns to specify variables, set up hypotheses, and test them in real life. The practitioner continually scrutinizes and tests the techniques she or he uses to continue the validation and expansion of the body of knowledge about RET.

Like Rogers's followers, neophyte practitioners of RET are tempted to adopt some of Ellis's personal feistiness and linguistic color. Fortunately, most learn that Ellis is an original beyond imitation. RET practitioners do typically emulate Ellis's directness, tenacity, avoidance of abstraction, and commitment to acting rather than talking about it, however.

Changing Behavior

Once some initial rapport has been established and the client has presented his or her problems, the RET practitioner begins to educate the client in the *ABC*s of irrational thinking. First, the client is made aware of how beliefs can shape emotional and behavioral consequences. In most cases, the client is actually instructed in the *ABC*s and may even be assigned appropriate reading on the subject. Second, the client is assisted in identifying and changing those patterns and consequences in his or her own life. Under the logical, persistent, and persuasive direction of the practitioner, the client progresses through several fundamental insights: (1) "People cause their own emotional pain and self-defeating behavior because of their irrationality"; (2) "*I* cause my own emotional pain and self-defeating behavior by allowing irrational beliefs, assumptions, and expectations to disturb my life"; and (3) "Knowing this about myself won't change it; I've got to *act!*"

To move the client beyond these fundamental insights, the practitioner applies a variety of cognitive, affective, and behavioral techniques. Although the techniques used in RET vary from client to client, certain basic activities are commonplace in RET (Ellis, 1973; Ellis & Bernard, 1985; Ellis & Whiteley, 1979):

1. Disputation and other cognitive techniques :[8]   Disputation involves the practitioner's continual challenge of the client's irrational beliefs, assumptions, and expectations. The practitioner instructs, cajoles, or directs the client to rely first of all on verifiable evidence and to reason logically from that evidence. Clients also learn to change their self-statements. Absolutist self-statements ("I must have a date with Sally, but I absolutely know that she will reject me, and that would be just awful!") are changed to nonabsolutist ones ("I would really prefer a date with Sally, and she may say no, and that may hurt me, but I would still be OK"). Changes in self-statements can be given as homework. In approaching dreaded tasks, clients can mentally repeat some realistic statement to counter the tendency to allow irrational ones to prevail ("Asking Sally for a date is difficult, but I can do it. If I screw it up, the world will not end, and I can try again later"). Quite naturally, humor is often a part of disputation. Purposeful exaggeration of the "awfulness" of an event can prompt new awareness in the client.

---

[8]The number of cognitive techniques that are commonly used by RET and other practitioners is growing. McMullin's *Handbook of Cognitive Therapy Techniques* (1986), with an introduction by Ellis, provides a highly useful overview of those techniques.

2. Experiential-emotive techniques: Because intellectual insight does not guarantee emotional insight (Ellis, 1963), RET also includes a number of techniques that use new experiences to evoke emotional reactions. Most of these techniques are RET variations on traditional therapeutic techniques. Role-playing, in either individual or group sessions, may help clients undertake feared tasks. Imagery exercises may help clients attach appropriate feelings to specific imagined situations so that the real situations eventually elicit the more appropriate feeling. Unique to RET are shame-attacking exercises. People often report that they would be "ashamed" or "embarrassed" to perform certain behaviors. In shame-attacking exercises, clients are assigned to work on their fear directly as homework. For example, a woman who is very concerned and fearful about what other people think of her may be assigned to approach strangers on the street and request money, or a man who is shy and fearful of crowds may be assigned to ride the subway during rush hour. The effect is the same: The shame or embarrassment is defused. In the emotive realm, humor again may play an important role in RET. The Institute for Rational-Emotive Therapy even produces an RET songbook and cassette recording entitled *A Garland of Rational Songs,* featuring songs actually sung by a spirited if not always bel canto Albert Ellis. The songs use familiar melodies, have clever titles and lyrics, and whether sung alone or with others, spark a whimsical understanding of irrational thinking. Imagine sitting in an individual or group session, singing "When I Am So Blue" to the tune of Strauss's "Beautiful Blue Danube":

> When I am so blue, so blue, so blue,
> I sit and I stew, I stew, I stew!
> I deem it so awfully horrible
> That my life is rough and scarable!
> Whenever my blues are verified
> I make myself doubly terrified,
> For I never choose to refuse
> To be blue about my blues![9]

3. Behavioral techniques: RET practitioners use the full range of formal behavioral techniques, especially operant conditioning, modeling, systematic desensitization, relaxation training, **biofeedback,** and **assertiveness training.** RET strongly emphasizes in vivo practice as homework assignments.

RET is fundamentally a cognitive approach to therapy that relies on direct, honest, and rational conversation between the practitioner and the client. Beyond that, RET uses a wide range of cognitive, experiential-emotive, and behavioral techniques that can be applied with individuals, couples, families, or groups.

[9]Copyright by Institute for Rational-Emotive Therapy, 45 E. 65th Street, New York, NY 10021. There are many more, including "Whine, Whine, Whine"; "I Love You Unduly"; and "I'm Just a Love Slob."

Sample Session

Returning to the distraught relationship between Francine and Frank, we recall Frank's tryst and its effect on their relationship. In this rewrite of their lives, Frank and Francine go their separate ways. Francine, feeling angry, depressed, and guilty about leaving Frank, seeks professional help from Dr. Rita Reasoner, an RET practitioner. We eavesdrop in the middle of the very first session:

Practitioner (P): You say you feel guilty and angry, but I'm not sure *why* you feel that way. Can you tell me what makes you angry?

Francine (F): Yes, I think I can, Dr. Reasoner. At first, right after I caught Frank with his little playmates, I was furious at him. Then, after I thought about it, I realized that it told me how bad our marriage was and how naive and stupid I had been. It may sound old-fashioned, but I believe a woman ought to be able to sense when things like this are going to happen. Like my mother, God rest her, used to say, "If you keep your head in the sand, all you'll get are a sore back and dry skin."

P: That's quite an expression!

F: Yeah. Well, if I'd have really listened to it, I would have been able to rescue our marriage, I'm sure.

P: Francine, let me see if I understand this. A "real" woman, a kind of superwoman, would have figured out that there were difficulties and then fixed them. To be good, you have to be that kind of woman, and if you are not, you are bad, you're a dud—as you said, "stupid" and "naive."

F: I know it doesn't make sense, but that's how I feel, and I think it's important to trust my feelings. Isn't that what you shrinks are always telling people?

P [*sotto voce*]: Not since the 60s!

F: What?

P: Never mind. About your feelings: Sure, Francine, your feelings are important, but at times, our feelings of distress are not appropriate or necessary—there's no particular value in suffering for its own sake. You seem to think that all the misery you've been through is because you failed to save your marriage—that you should have been able to do so if you were a good wife. When the event happened—finding Frank in bed with his companions—you saw this event through your beliefs about what you *should* do, what you should have done. In a sense, some of your negative feelings are the result of your should—you know, those things you believe in your own mind you should or should not do.

F: I guess so, but it's still pretty real, you know.

P: I know that. Listen to this: "Frank screwed around and, in doing so, broke his promises to me. That makes me really, really angry because he betrayed my trust. Still, even though I might have missed some signals of his unhappiness, I didn't make him do it.

No rule that I know of says I must figure out everything that's going to happen!"

F: But don't good wives stop things like that from happening?

P: Superwives? I don't know. Do you have any real proof for that? I don't, and I'm fairly well up on the serious studies in that area.

F: But my mother always said—

P: Look, Francine. Let's see if we can begin to deal with what is real, what we really know, rather than what beliefs and ideas you have gathered from other people. Something happened in your life, and it was a downer. It was important, but you're still in good health, beautiful, and worthy of happiness. Instead, you want to be miserable. That's your choice, but why should you be miserable—for your mother's sake? For Frank's sake? For the sake of living up to expectations that no one—not even Superwoman—could live up to?

F: You mean, just dealing with the facts as they come?

P [*animated*]: You've almost got it. Change the perception of the facts and the feelings will change. Let's talk about you calling Frank up on the phone! [*Whimsically*] Let's talk about you having his legs broken! Let's talk about you going out on a date with someone else! Let's do something. Let's decide on some homework for you to do for next week—something concrete.

F: Oh, but I'm not ready, really, am I?

P: Yes, sure you are. And you're super if not Superwife! Now, let's decide on some specific things you can do for next week . . .

Evaluation

RET is one of the most widely known and practiced cognitive—or, to be more accurate, "cognitive restructuring"—approaches to therapy (Mahoney & Arnkoff, 1978). As such, it rests on a sizable and growing body of clinical evidence, although the extent and adequacy of some of the research has been debated (see Ellis & Whiteley, 1979). RET however, can also be seen as much more than another approach to cognitive restructuring. The disputation techniques at RET's core, of course, are cognitive. At the same time, RET's fundamental pragmatism has allowed it to continually grow through eclecticism. As the body of effective behavioral and experiential techniques has grown, so too has the RET tendency toward eclecticism. Thus, RET today is a fairly comprehensive "multimodal" therapy that intervenes in the cognitive, affective, and behavioral modalities while allowing for the increasingly acknowledged role that biological (medical) factors play in mental disturbances.

One controversial characteristic distinguishes RET from other eclectic approaches: the consistent directiveness with which its techniques are applied. Indeed, given the evidence of the client's irrationalities, the practitioner may react with impatience that can intrude in the therapeutic process; thus, RET may not be designed for clients who require time to understand and accept themselves and the reasonableness of the directives. Put another way, RET's "obsession" with efficiency may not do justice to the needs of some clients. In practice, however, RET allows a certain amount of discursive and even self-indulgent talk from the client, especially early in treatment, and the pace of treatment is flexible enough to meet a variety of needs. At the same time, the RET practitioner does provoke, persuade, and direct until the client acknowledges and abandons irrational behaviors, distressful feelings, and self-defeating behaviors. Accordingly, it is designed to help practitioners avoid falling for the delay tactics often employed by clients.

On the issue of directiveness, RET can readily be contrasted with Rogers's person-centered therapy, which looks to the client rather than the practitioner for direction and which allows considerable time for self-discovery and self-disclosure. On this issue, the two approaches represent two extremes. From an historical point of view, both approaches have been exceptionally popular and influential, and both founders have been emulated by some and vilified by others. Both approaches have weathered over 30 years of critical observation by staying true to certain fundamental principles and techniques, albeit to quite different principles and techniques. Unlike person-centered therapy, however, RET has borrowed a broad range of other concepts and techniques, including several from person-centered therapy. This borrowing may be RET's key to continued contemporaniety. If its practitioners remain dedicated to building a strong empirical base, RET promises to be around for a long time. Given the vitality and charisma of Ellis, practitioners of RET face yet one large hurdle, one that psychoanalysts and person-centered practitioners understand: What happens when your energetic founder is no longer around? One can only hope that they have many years yet to find that out.

Multimodal Therapy

It is late in the 1980s, and you are in the last few weeks of a demanding course in counseling and psychotherapy at Everbroke University. Your professor has loaned you her copy of a videotape by Dr. Arnold Lazarus, the principal developer of *multimodal therapy*.[10] You pop in the tape and discover a trim, gray-haired, soft-spoken gentleman with just a hint of a British accent. After a brief introduction to his approach to therapy, you watch him engage in a simulation of an initial therapy session with a 45-year-old woman whose main symptom is depression. The session begins with Lazarus jotting down a few facts about the client: married (yes), children (two), occupation (secretary), and so forth. He then asks, "What brings you to me?" The client says that she has been depressed for about a year, that she was in treatment with a psychiatrist for about 9 months, and that he had told her she was depressed because she blamed herself for her mother's death. The psychiatrist had put her on an antidepressant

---

[10] The tape described here is actually one of three videotapes on multimodal therapy developed by Lazarus and available through Multimodal Publications, Inc., Kingston, NJ 08528.

medication for 3 months. Lazarus asks two questions: (1) Does she believe that she blames herself for her mother's death? (no) and (2) Did the medication help her? (no). Then, after all you have learned about therapy, you hear a statement from Lazarus's mouth that catches your attention. He says, without a hint of criticism or condescension, "Can I just mention two things right off the bat? You impress me as someone who is very acquiescent. You seem to give in very easily. This is just a feeling I have; I could be wrong. It's just a first impression. The second thing I want to say is this: Nobody knows you better than you know yourself! To say because the doctor said something he must know what he's talking about is not so. You know yourself best."

From here, he explores her acquiescence and timidity with her by describing it as a "lack of assertiveness." She tells him that she had once joined an assertiveness group but "failed." He carefully corrects her emphasis on her failure by restating that she joined the group but "didn't get anything out of it." He tells her that he has a theory that before people can change their behavior, they have to be able to picture themselves performing the behavior—he calls this "imagery." He asks her to imagine herself saying no, asking for something, or expressing a feeling. She cannot do so. They discuss where her inability to be assertive might have come from, and he asks her if she would like to work with him on improving her ability to imagine being assertive and then to change her behavior. She answers affirmatively. He then runs through a series of questions about her depression as it affects her sleeping, eating, living, and sexual patterns; you recognize these questions as the traditional psychiatric queries used to indicate whether or not a biological depression is present. Finally, Lazarus tells her about what will happen in the therapy, especially about learning how to use imagery. He tells the client that she is to complete a 12-page questionnaire that he will provide her with and mail it to him before the next session. She agrees. End of the abbreviated, simulated session.

What kind of approach joins the forthrightness of Ellis with the warmth and honesty of Rogers? Weds an emphasis on cognitive processes with the systematic concreteness of behavior therapy? Mingles the psychologist's world with a dose of medical diagnostics? The answer, of course, is multimodal therapy. But this is no hodgepodge of theories and techniques. Rather, multimodal therapy is a comprehensive approach to psychological intervention that systematically applies an integrated body of established techniques drawn from behavior therapy, cognitive therapy, insight therapy, and medical practice. All this from a New Jersey professor of South African descent: Arnold Lazarus.

Historical and Theoretical Foundations

Arnold Lazarus (born 1932) was educated in South Africa, receiving a Ph.D. in clinical psychology from the University of Witwaterstand, but he has taught and practiced in the United States since 1963. He has taught at Stanford University, Temple University Medical School, and Yale University, where he was director of clinical training. Presently, Lazarus is Professor II (a special distinction for outstanding full professors) at the Graduate School of Applied and Professional Psychology at Rutgers University. Additionally, he is the executive director of several multimodal therapy institutes.

Lazarus's name has been associated with behavior therapy in one form or another since its early days in the late 1950s and early 1960s, and during his time in South Africa, as well as his years at Temple University, Lazarus worked with psychiatrist Joseph Wolpe in the development of various behavioral techniques. Yet, Lazarus's association with "pure" behavior therapy was short-lived. His gradual shift away from traditional behavior therapy can be seen in the very titles of three of his most important books. In *Behavior Therapy and Beyond,* published in 1971, Lazarus reported on disappointing follow-up studies he had conducted on clients who had supposedly benefited from behavior therapy. In light of that evidence, he reiterated his 1967 espousal of *technical eclecticism*—integrating cognitive and other techniques into the behavior therapist's repertoire without necessarily accepting the theoretical bases of the techniques. He pointed out that the practitioner need not choose between producing either behavior change (as in behavior therapy) or insight (as in psychoanalysis and its variations). Indeed, Lazarus (1971) wrote, it "is fatuous to ask whether a change in cognition leads to a change in behavior or vice versa. 'Insight' may often *precede* an observable behavior change; at other times, insight clearly *follows* an individual's changed behavior" (p. 165). Gradually, Lazarus developed his own brand of behavior therapy, and in 1976, he published *Multimodal Behavior Therapy.* In this book, behavior—a person's overt actions—becomes one of seven modalities through which personality is expressed and changed. By 1981, with the publication of *The Practice of Multimodal Therapy,* the word "behavior" had been removed from the name of the therapy. In what ways is multimodal therapy similar to behavior therapy and in what ways is it different?

As pointed out in Chapter 4, behavior therapy refers to a set of clinical procedures that: (1) define clients' behavioral, cognitive, and affective complaints as specific, measurable, operational variables; (2) apply change strategies based on experimental psychological research, principally research on human learning; (3) use measured outcomes as a gauge of success; and (4) gather clinical information for feedback into the relevant therapeutic literature. Multimodal therapy is essentially true to this description; however, it transcends it. First, the client's behavioral, cognitive, and affective complaints are understood in terms of the interaction of seven modalities of human experience that constitute personality: behavior, affect, sensation, imagery, cognition, interpersonal relationships, and biological substratum. Second, therapeutic strategies are specifically designed for the client after a comprehensive evaluation of the specific manner in which the seven modalities interact. Third, more detailed analysis is given to the nonobservable and "non–operationally definable" experiences of the client (images, sensations, thoughts, feelings about the self and relationships) than is typical in behavior therapy. Fourth, greater attention is given to the relationship and mutuality of expectations between the client and practitioner than in more traditional behavior therapy. Fifth, multimodal therapy operates according to the principle of *technical eclecticism*; that is, it adapts and adopts techniques from other approaches to therapy into a cohesive theoretical framework that allows their effectiveness to be evaluated on the basis of how enduringly effective they are rather than how acceptable they are theoretically.[11]

Multimodal therapy's own theoretical foundation is drawn from two major theoretical wellsprings encountered earlier in this text: Bandura's **social learning theory** and **systems theory,** as well as *group and communications theory* (Lazarus, 1986). Much of the theoretical foundation of multimodal therapy remains implicit rather than explicit, however; the emphasis is on finding techniques and strategies that produce enduring change rather than on proposing an elegant theory.

Lazarus's openness to techniques drawn from different approaches to therapy should not be confused with attempts to integrate behavior therapy and psychoanalysis. Indeed, Lazarus is opposed to such efforts, since the two approaches are based on entirely different philosophical viewpoints. This statement sums up his view:

> Psychodynamic behaviorism makes about as much sense as democratic fascism! Isn't multimodal therapy a conglomeration of psychoanalysis, behavior therapy, and many other systems? Definitely not. While using effective techniques from many available sources, multimodal practitioners do not subscribe to any of their underlying theories. (Lazarus, 1981, p. 40)

Basic Constructs

Although multimodal therapy encompasses implicit theories of personality and psychopathology, it is free of abstractions and idiosyncratic constructs. Rather, multimodal therapy uses the terminology of everyday psychological and medical literature to describe how observable and inferable biological, psychological, and social processes interact with one other. Multimodal therapy is concerned with the essential modalities through which human beings experience and express themselves: We do things (Behavior); we have an array of feelings and moods (Affect); we are aware of sensory and other physiological changes (Sensation); we picture ourselves and others in real and fantastic situations (Imagery); we think, with differences in speed, knowledge, and logic (Cognition); we form bonds and antipathies with other human beings (Interpersonal relationships); and all of this takes place through biochemical and neurophysiological processes that form a biological substratum. If we refer to this biological substratum as D, for Drugs (which are often used to treat biological problems), we have a convenient acronym: BASIC I.D. (I.D. as in "identification," not as in "the id").

---

[11]See Lazarus, 1981, pp. 100–101, for a fuller description of similarities and differences.

The modalities in practice   All healthy human beings are biological entities capable of acting, feeling, thinking, sensing, imagining, and engaging in relationships with other human beings. These modalities exist in continual, reciprocal interaction with one other, although one modality may be more pronounced in the awareness of the individual at any given time. Initially, for example, clients often present their problem in terms of one modality: "I'm depressed" (affect), "I gamble" (behavior), "I hear voices" (sensation), "Nobody loves me" (interpersonal relations), "I can't stop thinking about Barney" (cognition), and so forth. On fuller examination, however, activity can generally be discerned in each of the modalities. A good example is the common problem of anxiety. Anxiety is generally thought of as involving affective processes. But are there such things as isolated affective processes? Lazarus (1986) has contended that "affect is the product of the reciprocal interaction of behavior, sensation, imagery, and cognitive factors, and biological inputs, usually within an interpersonal context [italics omitted]" (p. 68). In other words, the affective state we call anxiety is a biological event brought to awareness by physical sensations, preceded, accompanied, or followed by thoughts and images, and generally affected by or affecting relationships.

Figure 10.1 provides a graphic representation of the assertion that affect is a product of the other six modalities. We can examine this point by considering the following statement from a client whose presenting complaint is anxiety, a feeling, or affective, problem:

> I just feel so anxious and upset when I get to thinking about how my life is going (cognition). I get all nervous and my heart starts pounding and I get all sweaty (sensation). Then I just can't sleep at all! (behavior). The more I try to go to sleep, the more I think about all the mistakes I've made (cognition), and I can just see Cecilia and Barney having a good time making fun of me behind my back (imagery). No point trying to sleep, I say. So I just go downstairs, break my diet, and eat all the chocolate donuts and smoke cigarettes until morning! (behavior, biology). Life's just being so very unfair to me; God knows it's all my mother's fault! (cognition).

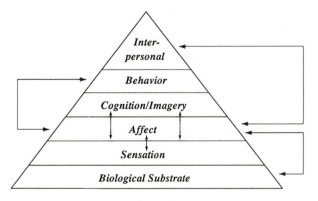

Figure 10.1   *Affect as the reciprocal product of the other six modalities*
(From: Lazarus, 1986, p. 69; graphic attributed to Clifford N. Lazarus)

In this example of an affective problem, all of the modalities are involved in some manner. In addition, a distinct *firing order* is evident: first cognition, then sensation, behavior, and imagery. Firing orders can vary significantly. Some may begin with imagery; others, with sensation. Determining the firing order is key to successful and enduring intervention.

The Process of Intervention

Multimodal therapy is used with individuals, couples, families, and groups, and benefits from a growing body of supportive case histories from practitioners (for example, see Lazarus, 1985). It is actively being applied in mental hospitals (Brunnell & Young, 1982) and has been adapted for working with children (Keats, 1979). Additionally, it has been proposed as a model for integration in the emerging field of behavioral medicine (Richard, 1978).

The client–practitioner relationship "Nobody knows you better than you know yourself." These words from the videotape described earlier highlight a fundamental characteristic of multimodal therapy in practice: an awareness and respect for the uniqueness of each individual client. This emphasis on the uniqueness of the individual is not to be confused with that of approaches to therapy emphasizing the emotional tie between the client and practitioner, however. The relationship between the client and practitioner in multimodal therapy is quite different from that in client-centered therapy, for example, which requires unconditional positive regard, or psychoanalytic approaches, which require transference. Lazarus (1981) has argued that therapies that require the client to deal with the practitioner along a love-hate continuum foster dependence and are quite different from multimodal therapy. He wrote:

> Since multimodal practitioners are largely task-oriented, so-called transference factors rarely intrude or erupt. Most of my clients regard me as a skillful professional who has the wherewithal to help them combat their negative emotions, maladaptive behaviors, interpersonal deficits, and so forth. They like and respect me and find they can relate to me, but they are not in love with me. They depend on me but are not dependent on me. (p. 134)

The principal task of the multimodal practitioner is to custom-make a treatment strategy for and with each client. This begins with assessing the client's unique expression of the modalities. The appropriate therapeutic techniques are then applied in the most effective order. Finally, the practitioner and client carefully determine the degree to which success has been achieved. Apart from positively affecting the client's life, there are no hard and fast rules about the relationship between the practitioner and client. In fact, multimodal therapy has only two "don'ts": "(1) Don't be rigid and (2) Don't humiliate a person or strip away his or her dignity" (Lazarus, 1981, p. 129).[12]

---

[12]The practitioner's role in multimodal therapy looks mechanical: applying scientifically derived treatments precisely. Actually, Lazarus (1981) has recognized that truly excellent therapy

Initial assessment In keeping with its link to behavior therapy, multimodal therapy places considerable emphasis on assessment, particularly on the initial interview and use of the Multimodal Life History Questionnaire. Although the multimodal practitioner seeks to establish rapport during the initial interview session, she or he is clearly focused on finding out specific information. In the initial interview, by means of questioning and several specialized interviewing techniques, the practitioner takes the client through four different phases, each focused on gathering different information (see Lazarus, 1981, Chapter 3). In Phase 1, the practitioner gathers specific information about the severity and duration of the client's problems, being especially attentive to *target behaviors*—that is, behaviors that can be measured and turned into specific attainable goals and to which homework assignments can be attached. As the client becomes familiar with the language of multimodal therapy, the client and practitioner talk about the client's problems in terms of the BASIC I.D. In Phase 2, the practitioner has the client describe the events antecedent to presenting problems, being especially attentive to discrepancies between the presymptomatic factors and the problem. This is especially important in determining whether a biological problem might be involved. In Phase 3, the practitioner's goal is to determine the conditions that are maintaining the problem—postsymptomatic factors. Determining what steps, professional and otherwise, have been taken to resolve the problem is especially important. In Phase 4, if the practitioner remains concerned about the mental competence of the client, a mental-status examination, similar to those used in the traditional psychiatric interview, may be used to determine whether brain damage or other medical conditions are involved.

Throughout the initial interview, the practitioner emphasizes specific attainable goals to inspire hope in the client, the counter to **demoralization.** Additionally, she or he relates these goals to the client's *modality profile,* charting the various problems and concerns in relation to the client's BASIC I.D. The client's BASIC I.D. is fleshed out using the Multimodal Life History Questionnaire, a 12-page questionnaire typically given as a homework assignment after the first session and to be mailed to the practitioner before the next session. In addition to eliciting descriptions of the client's problems and personal and social history, the Multimodal Life History Questionnaire provides the client an opportunity to elaborate on current problems by responding to specific questions and completing various checklists. It also allows the client to present a brief sequential history of his or her significant experiences.[13]

requires a special and very personal artistry expressed in "on-the-spot inventiveness" (p. 67). These artistic qualities that make for distinction as a practitioner are unevenly distributed across the profession, however, so multimodal therapy provides an effective, systematic starting point for those of us who are still developing our full artistic potential.

[13]A version of the Multimodal Life History Questionnaire can be found in Lazarus, 1981. It is copyrighted by Multimodal Publications, Inc., Kingston, NJ, and distributed by Research Press, Champaign, IL.

During the next sessions, the multimodal practitioner concentrates on translating the information generated in the initial interview and questionnaire into a more complete understanding of the client and on developing specific therapeutic objectives. This begins with the production of a *structural profile.* Through a series of questions and discussion, the practitioner and the client develop bar graph representations of the relative strengths of the different modalities. Two sample structural profiles are shown and described in Figure 10.2. (Structural profiles are considered particularly helpful in couples therapy, as we will see later in the chapter.)

The structural profile is complemented by a *modality profile,* as shown in Table 10.1. The client and the practitioner, or in some situations the client alone, draw up a list of specific problems to be addressed. The practitioner then discusses treatment possibilities, which are added to the profile. The order in which the potential treatment procedures will be used is determined largely through the essential multimodal techniques of bridging and tracking.

Bridging and tracking   Although early termination or failure to effect change in psychotherapy is generally attributed to client resistance, Lazarus believes that a form of practitioner resistance is often at work when the practitioner tries to fit the client to the techniques rather than the reverse. In such a case, the techniques are at odds with the client's goals or values, and the practitioner and client conflict. Though in some forms of treatment practitioners may relish this opportunity to work through the resistance, Lazarus has proposed two specialized techniques for avoiding it: bridging and tracking.

Bridging involves deliberately staying with the client's preferred modality rather than pursuing other modalities that the practitioner assumes will be more productive (Lazarus, 1985). For example, a practitioner's first temptation when confronted with an intellectualized discussion of a familial conflict may be to continually shift the client from the cognitive to the affective modalities because that appears to be where the "real" problem exists. In bridging, however, the practitioner initially remains with the client in the preferred modality, thus avoiding conflict that could short-circuit the intervention. Eventually, the practitioner may find an opportunity to ask what sensations the client is experiencing while talking about the conflict, thus creating a bridge to sensation and later to the affective modality. The shift is gradual and nondisruptive.[14]

Tracking refers to the tracing of the *firing order* of the various modalities — the sequence in which the client usually uses or experiences the modalities. For example, for one client, thinking catastrophically (cognition) may conjure up visual pictures (imagery) that lead to the bodily feelings (sensation) that the client calls anxiety and that prevent adequate action (behavior). For another client, certain unpleasant bodily feelings in a specific situation (sensation) may cause her or him to think about what could go wrong (cognition), thus evoking

---

[14]An example of this technique can be found on the tapes noted in footnote 10 (page 363).

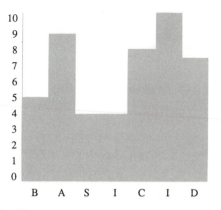

Francine's Structural Profile

Although Francine is a doer at work and can be gregarious at parties, she is often unable to confront others with whom she is angry or disagrees. Thus, she rates her *Behavior* fairly low. She is a "feeling person" with strong emotions. *Affect*, therefore, is high, although she realizes she is unable to express negative emotions. *Sensation*, especially as related to sexual expression, is less important than the emotional component, and she has difficulty with *Imagery*, especially images involving assertiveness. Francine also sees herself as fairly high in *Cognition*, largely because she is bright and articulate; however, cognition does not rule emotion. Interpersonal intimacy characterized by trust is very important to Francine; she rates the *Interpersonal* very high. In regard to *Drugs*, Francine is in good physical shape, exercises regularly, but has taken medically prescribed tranquilizers since her separation from Frank.

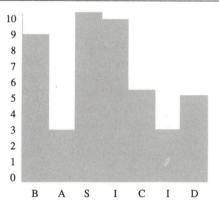

Frank's Structural Profile

Frank gets things done, although many of his actions are not very constructive. His impulsiveness, however, merits a high *Behavior* rating. His *Affect*, on the other hand, is not high, although he has learned to use emotions to get what he wants. Frank describes himself as a very *Sensation*-oriented person, especially in relation to sex, and a very active fantasy life keeps *Imagery* fairly high. Frank is also bothered by images of himself as a failure both personally and professionally. Frank admits that his head (*Cognition*) rarely rules his impulsiveness, although he can be reasoned with. Upon honest reflection, Frank rates the *Interpersonal* fairly low: Intimacy has almost exclusively sexual connotations for him. In regard to *Drugs*, Frank appears in excellent shape, but the prognosis is not good given his three addictions: excessive daily exercise, diet drugs, and beer by the gallon.

Figure 10.2 *Sample structural profiles. Multimodal practitioners work with the client to assess the various strengths of the different modalities. This can be represented using bar graphs, as shown above. These two samples are imaginary structural profiles for Francine and Frank Perfetti, the estranged couple described in this chapter's opening case history, following descriptions from Lazarus (1981).*

Table 10.1 *Sample Modality Profile. The client and practitioner (or the client alone) draw up a list of specific problems to be addressed initially. The practitioner discusses treatment possibilities, which are then added to the profile. This sample could have been drawn up by and for Francine. The techniques suggested here are drawn from Lazarus and Wolpe (systematic desensitization), Masters and Johnson (sensate focusing), and Ellis (disputation).*

Modality	Problem	Treatment
Behavior	Reticence in disagreeing with or expressing anger toward others	Assertiveness training
Affect	Anxiety and tension, strong negative feelings	Relaxation training and systematic desensitization
Sensation	Inadequate sensory awareness and enjoyment, particularly in sex	Sensate focus training
Imagery	Negative images of oneself	Coping imagery exercises
Cognition	Irrational thoughts about one's ability to overcome problems	Cognitive disputation techniques
Interpersonal	Avoidance of situations in which confrontation is likely, leading to anger and depression	Risk-taking exercises
Drugs/Biology	Dependence on tranquilizers	Renewal of fitness efforts, gradual replacement of tranquilizers with relaxation training

visual pictures of being unable to handle the situation (imagery), followed by withdrawal from that situation (behavior). What techniques the practitioner will use first depends on the firing order. For example, in the first sequence, CISB, the practitioner may begin with a cognitive disputation; in the second sequence, SCIB, relaxation and biofeedback training may be the preferred initial treatment (Lazarus, 1985). This does not mean, of course, that the other modalities will be ignored. On the contrary, multimodal therapy addresses as many modalities as are necessary to completely eliminate the problem.

Second-order BASIC I.D. assessment   During multimodal therapy, whenever a particular item from the initial modality profile does not readily yield to treatment, the practitioner undertakes a *second-order BASIC I.D. assessment.* Essentially, this involves developing a modality profile of the particular item. For example, Frank's initial modality profile suggests that he is a doer, a person who gets things done. Yet, Frank does not succeed, and attempts to get him to reapply to college are failing. He is filled with excuses and appears to be afraid of reapplying. Why, however, is uncertain. As Frank completes a new profile based on "fear of reapplying to college," he comes up with several competing images: "I see myself graduating and getting a better job," "I see myself getting praise from Francine," and "I see myself flunking out of school just like my older brother did." This last image, uncovered through the second-order profile, blocks treatment in the behavior modality until it is resolved.

An abundance of techniques Technical eclecticism allows the multimodal practitioner to use an abundance of techniques, although there is heavy reliance on behavioral and cognitive techniques. In *The Practice of Multimodal Therapy,* Lazarus (1981) identified 39 *principal* techniques in a descriptive glossary. To provide a sense of the breadth of the listing, a partial listing is provided below. Remember: Inclusion of a technique does not imply acceptance of the original explanation of why the technique works. The principal techniques include: anger expression, aversive imagery, behavior rehearsal, bibliotherapy, biofeedback, communication training, contingency contracting, Ellis's *A-B-C-D-E* paradigm, hypnosis, meditation, modeling, nonreinforcement, paradoxical strategies, positive imagery, positive reinforcement, relaxation training, social-skills and assertiveness training, the empty chair, and thought blocking.

Besides using a vast array of psychotherapeutic techniques, multimodal practitioners pay considerable attention to the biological substratum and do not avoid using drug therapy where appropriate (see Fay, 1976). Also notable is that Lazarus and his colleagues have made their most unique contributions in the use of imagery. Imagery refers to the ability to see in one's mind what is not physically present. The key principle involved can be stated in this way: You cannot do what you cannot picture yourself doing. Put another way, changing behavior often depends on changing images. Lazarus's work strongly suggests that for many clients changes in imagery are key to changes in the other modalities. No other approach to therapy addresses this issue as thoroughly as multimodal therapy (see Lazarus, 1977).

Sample Session

Fans of Frank and Francine will be happy to know that they eventually managed to visit a multimodal practitioner, Dr. Carl Cornucopia. Dr.Cornucopia first began seeing Francine. Later, Frank was able to join them. The couple seems determined to try to work things out. Francine and Frank have each completed the Multimodal Life History Questionnaire, and both have done structural profiles (see Figure 10.2). When working with intimate partners, multimodal therapists seek to establish a collaborative environment in which the partners can come to better understand their maladaptive patterns of interaction. In this session, Dr. Cornucopia is facilitating a discussion of those patterns based on Francine's and Frank's structural profiles. We pick it up in the middle of their discussion:

Practitioner (P): Francine. In your own structural profile, you rate yourself as very high on Affect and Interpersonal relationships. Is that right?

Francine: Yeah, that's right, Dr. Cornucopia. I really need to have someone to listen to me, someone to support me when I'm down. I think I'm pretty sensitive. I'm pretty easily hurt.

Frank: I'll say.

P: And, Frank, both your Affect and Interpersonal ratings are rather low. That would seem to make for some difficulties.

Frank: I think you're right, Dr. Cornucopia. I guess I've never realized it until now, but I just kind of assumed that all of Francine's sensitivity was a ploy to get something sexual out of me or to turn me off when I wanted sex. I've always said that all of her crying and all could be solved with a romp in the hay.

Francine: Yeah, you're right. That's always been your answer to everything. Even when I'd get angry at you for not doing something with your life, you'd always want to solve it in bed.

P: Let's look at a pattern here. Francine. As we've seen, you find it very difficult to be assertive, to let Frank know your negative feelings about something. And, of course, we're going to be working on that with some assertiveness training. But at times, when you get really frustrated, you blow up at Frank and hit him where he's most vulnerable: his career failures. Frank, for your part, you "macho" your way through all of that, but more than a few times, thinking about and imagining your failures have caused impotence. That's made you angry, and at times, because you're not able to share your real feelings, you've found other ways to express the anger. Maybe that's part of what happened in your affair with the professor. How's that sound?

Francine: I think that's pretty close to what happens, but I don't want him let off the hook for the affair that easy.

Frank: OK, OK. I was wrong. I've got no excuses. But you're right about why I had "performance problems," as you call them. I knew it wasn't my fault!

P: Don't miss the point here, Frank. There is a pattern of interaction at work here that is very complex. The "fault" for the sexual problems between you two doesn't rest solely on your doorstep or on Francine's.

Frank: I know that I've got to work on expressing and accepting emotional needs, but Francine's got to get with my physical needs without carping at me.

Francine: Frank, I love you, and I want us to have a really great sex life. But I find it difficult to move at your pace. I need more time. I need to know that it's me you love, not just my body.

Frank: But I do love you! Really.

P: You both love each other, but there must be more. Clearly, we need to initiate some strategies to bring greater sensory compatibility between the two of you, and I think we have some sensory awareness programs that will help here. I think it's time for us to work out a contract that will allow each of you to grow in directions that will give this relationship a chance to work. We'll work on specific issues for each of you—working through your various problems in each of the modalities—and then we'll look at some agreements we can reach about how you interact with each other day to day. Possibly we can agree that there's some time each day for uncritical conversation? A time to listen to each other's thoughts and feelings, a time to encourage each other. How's that sound as a starting point?

Frank: I'm game.

Francine: I would like that. And I'd also like a chance for us to play around with sensuality, I guess. All of this had me think I could be more in touch with my own body. I guess I've been trying to make it difficult for Frank.

Frank: Gee. I know I've been doing the same to you.

P: OK. Let's work out the specifics of a contract between you for the next week. First . . .

Evaluation

Multimodal therapy is vulnerable to criticism from two very different perspectives. From the viewpoint of traditional behavior therapy, multimodal therapy has contaminated "pure" behavior therapy by including cognitive processes and using therapeutic techniques not derived from experimental research. From the viewpoint of traditional insight therapy, multimodal therapy appears mechanistic, superficial, and overly concerned with complex assessment strategies. In reality, multimodal therapy is a comprehensive framework into which a wide range of therapeutic techniques can be eclectically integrated. It is a realization of an idea that has been in the psychotherapeutic literature for more than 50 years: the integration of various approaches to psychotherapy to encompass a comprehensive set of techniques supported by empirical findings and united by a common language and a common theoretical understanding of behavior change (Goldfried & Newman, 1986). With this in mind consider Lazarus's (1986) description of multimodal therapy:

> Multimodal therapy is an approach that endeavors to incorporate "state of the art" research and findings into its framework. It is not intended as yet another "system" to be added to the hundreds in existence. Rather it is an approach that attempts to be at the cutting edge of clinical effectiveness by continually scanning the field for better assessment and treatment methods. (p. 87)

Although the most commonly employed techniques of multimodal practitioners are well supported by research, on the relative effectiveness of multimodal therapy over other forms of treatment is still preliminary. As with the work of both Rotter and Ellis, however, there are numerous practitioners and scholars intent on thoroughly evaluating how effective the approach is with specific clients with specific problems. Like Rotter and Ellis, Lazarus has brought the concreteness and rigor of the experimental research tradition to bear on the priorities of the clinical research tradition without losing the best that the clinical tradition has to offer. What distinguishes multimodal therapy from social learning and RET, however, is its capacity to encompass the techniques of the others. Additionally, its emphasis on addressing the client's specific problems while enhancing the client's self-understanding makes it, along with the other two approaches in this chapter, an exemplary representative of the self-regulation and maturity model.

Summary of Chapter 10

Chapter 10 presents three approaches to counseling and psychotherapy that represent the self-regulation and maturity model in drawing on the rich self-regulatory literature of behavior therapy while acknowledging the value of insight in further maturity. The three approaches described in this chapter are: a social learning approach, rational-emotive therapy, and multimodal therapy.

A Social Learning Approach

1. Julian Rotter's social learning approach to psychotherapy, which includes a well-articulated personality theory, integrates both behavior theory and cognitive theory. Borrowing from both the clinical and experimental research traditions, it draws on the expectancies theories of Tolman and Lewin, as well as on the work of Adler.

2. For Rotter, the study of human behavior is the study of the interaction of the individual with his or her meaningful environment. Behavior is learned and modified in an interactive process that is essentially cognitive.

3. The social learning approach explains behavior and psychotherapeutic change in terms of nine key constructs, explained in detail in the chapter: behavior potential, expectancy, reinforcement value, the psychological situation, need potential, freedom of movement, need value, minimal goal level, and locus of control.

4. Locus of control is a characteristic of personality as well as a predictor of behavior. It refers to a continuum of possible beliefs in regard to one's ability to control reinforcement in various situations that exist in the environment. The two extremes of the continuum are internal locus of control and external locus of control.

5. The process of intervention involves interpersonal interaction that allows for the eclectic use of selected therapeutic techniques. The practitioner encourages the client to describe the life situations that prevent adaptive be-

havior. The approach is value-oriented, and the client is considered responsible for making a contribution to the well-being of others.

6. Client distress (resulting from failure to obtain the desired reinforcement) may come from a lack of skill or knowledge, seeking goals that are punished by the culture, or mistaken expectations of failure. Negative expectancies can become generalized from one area of competence to another. Generalized expectancies across many categories of activity explain so-called neurotic behavior.

7. The social learning approach to psychotherapy involves a dialogue between the client and the practitioner aimed at changing the client's expectancies, changing the value she or he places on certain reinforcements, adjusting her or his goals, and instilling generalized expectancies.

8. The successful practitioner structures the therapy—that is, establishes mutual goals and expectations by providing information, establishing accountability, and persuading the client that certain goals are within reach. The relationship between the client and practitioner is the key to successful intervention and involves a unique form of transference, in this case referring to a warm, trusting, and affectionate relationship through which the practitioner reinforces appropriate behavioral changes. Insight, often generated through the practitioner's interpretation of events in the client's life, is also an important part of the social learning approach.

9. Theoretically, Rotter's social learning approach is complex and requires considerable effort to master. In practice, however, it shares many characteristics with cognitive and cognitive-behavioral approaches to counseling and psychotherapy, including those that follow.

Rational-Emotive Therapy

10. Rational-emotive therapy (RET) was developed by Albert Ellis, who argued that most psychological distress is caused by irrational thinking. The way we think about events rather than events themselves causes our distress.

11. Human beings are capable of rational thinking and have a potential for self-actualization. However, a basic capacity for irrationality promotes self-defeating behavior. A rational belief about a specific activating event can have positive consequences: emotional satisfaction and adaptive behaviors. An irrational belief about a specific activating event can have negative consequences: emotional distress and self-defeating behaviors. Irrational beliefs can be overcome using disputation, which involves applying the scientific method to the problem.

12. RET is designed to help people live longer and become self-actualizing by freeing them of emotional disturbances and self-defeating behaviors.

13. The successful RET practitioner is intelligent, knowledgeable, empathic (without dwelling on the client's negative feelings), persistent, interested in helping others, and scientific in outlook.

14. Behavior is changed by educating the client in how irrational beliefs cause emotional and behavioral problems. Through persistent persuasion, the practitioner moves the client through various personal insights until the client both accepts responsibility and is determined to act.

15. RET uses a variety of techniques, including disputation and other cognitive techniques, experiential-emotive techniques (for example, imagery exercises and role-playing), and behavioral techniques. Humor plays an important role in RET.

16. RET is one of the major approaches to cognitive restructuring, and though it has been criticized for being overly directive, it is supported by considerable research.

Multimodal Therapy

17. Multimodal therapy was developed by Arnold Lazarus as a result of his dissatisfaction with the long-term effectiveness of behavior therapy. Though multimodal therapy remains true to behavior therapy's emphasis on defining clients' complaints operationally, applying strategies drawn from scientific research, measuring outcomes, and building up the scientific literature, it transcends traditional behavior therapy both theoretically and technically.

18. In keeping with Lazarus's promotion of technical eclecticism, multimodal therapy uses a wide array of therapeutic techniques without endorsing the systems or explanations that accompany them.

19. Human behavior is viewed within a framework of seven essential modalities: behavior, affect, sensation, imagery, cognition, interpersonal relationships, and the biological substratum, identified as D (for drugs, which may be used in treating biological problems) in the BASIC I.D. acronym.

20. Because how these modalities interact with each other will vary from person to person, multimodal therapy strongly emphasizes awareness and respect for the uniqueness of each client. Multimodal therapy is task-oriented, and the principal task of the practitioner is custom-making a treatment strategy with and for the individual client.

21. Multimodal therapy also emphasizes assessment, using, in addition to extensive interviewing, the Multimodal Life History Questionnaire. The client and practitioner construct a structural profile, a bar graph representation of the relative strength of the various modalities. The client and practitioner also construct a modality profile, a table listing specific modality problems and possible treatment procedures.

22. Although a number of techniques are unique to multimodal therapy, the multimodal practitioner uses an abundance of techniques drawn from various sources. The emphasis is on keeping multimodal therapy a state-of-the-art approach by continually refining the techniques through careful research.

Coda

This would-be behavioral scientist who knows nothing
of the basic structure of science and nothing of the 3000
years of careful philosophic and humanistic thought about
man—who cannot define either entropy or a sacrament—
had better hold his peace rather than add to the existing
jungle of half-baked hypotheses.

Gregory Bateson

At the beginning of this text, I defined counseling or psychotherapy as "the artful application of scientifically derived psychological knowledge and techniques for the purpose of changing human behavior." Nothing in that definition suggests immutability—quite the contrary. "Artful application" varies from artist to artist; "scientifically derived psychological knowledge" is ever expanding; and "human behavior," in continual adaptation to the political, economic, and social realities of culture, is anything but consistently predictable. Not surprisingly, therefore, over the past 10 chapters, we have examined a good number of vital and less vital approaches to counseling and psychotherapy, each draped with the mantle of science, each claiming considerable success, and each unable to wholly explain its failures and successes.

In order to make some sense of the numerous approaches to counseling and psychotherapy, this text presents them in relation to the **self-regulation** and **maturity** model. The basic argument is that most individuals who come for treatment are demoralized because they are powerless to control some thoughts, feelings, or actions. This need for self-regulation can be achieved either directly, through behavioral or medical techniques, or indirectly, through **insight.** In addition, many clients seek to understand themselves more fully, to become increasingly able to deal with life's stresses. Maturity is another name for the increasing capacity to successfully engage life's challenges and opportunities, and enhanced maturity can also be achieved as part of the therapeutic process. Although maturity is often directly related to insight, it does not occur unless minimal levels of self-regulation are present.

In this text, we have seen a full spectrum of approaches to psychotherapy and counseling. In earlier chapters, we looked at the considerable number of behavioral approaches to self-regulation; we then looked over the catalogue of insight approaches designed to foster maturity, or at least some internal change. In Chapter 10, we examined three approaches to psychotherapy that encompass both elements: a social learning approach, rational-emotive therapy, and multimodal therapy. These three approaches accord theoretically and technically with the self-regulation and maturity model because they break down a number of traditional barriers. All three begin by establishing self-regulation through behavioral means, but all three also promote insight. Further, all require both **cognitive theory** and **behavior theory** to explain human behavior, and all owe methodological allegiance to both the **experimental** and **clinical research traditions.** All share varying degrees of technical eclecticism, all are open to innovations and improvements from practitioners, and all are presently being subjected to serious scientific scrutiny. For these reasons, this text has shown a preference for them.

Since, however, nothing about counseling or psychotherapy is more certain than that it will change, it might be well to go beyond the last three approaches to look at one issue that just will not go away: Is psychology a science? Can counseling and psychotherapy really be scientific enterprises? Can counseling and psychotherapy contribute to science rather than merely consume it?

Psychologists have always had a rough time convincing some people that the discipline of psychology is truly a science. Certainly psychologists in the perception lab, rat lab, or physiological psych lab appear to be doing science (lab coats go a long way toward securing the image), but developmental, social, environmental, and especially counseling and clinical psychologists remain suspect. Indeed, one can question whether there is *a* science of psychology or a collection of different fields with differing and irreconcilable research paradigms, and methods.[1] Skinner (1987), in an article entitled "Whatever Happened to Psychology as a Science of Behavior," indicted psychotherapy, along with humanistic psychology and cognitive psychology, as the culprits keeping us from a true scientific analysis of behavior. His argument is straightforward: He asserts that many of the questions and issues of humanistic psychology, psychotherapy, and cognitive psychology should not be asked by a true science of psychology. As he put it, "Questions of that sort should never have been asked. Psychology should confine itself to its accessible subject matter and leave the rest of the story of human behavior to physiology" (p. 785).

Given cognitive psychology's current ascendancy and the present ubiquity of psychotherapy, it may be difficult to take Skinner's comments seriously. Certainly, cognitive psychology, despite its subject matter, appears to be scientific; further, practitioners of counseling and psychotherapy describe their efforts as scientific and appear to be making progress. Still, one wonders: Will all this lead to a unified science of behavior or will it simply further jumble a psychology that is now a patchwork of disparate and irreconcilable theories and findings? This is the concern underlying Skinner's seemingly narrow comments, and it should not be taken lightly. There is some comfort in the fact that the last three approaches to psychotherapy, all with decent behavioral and cognitive credentials, fit fairly comfortably into the metatheoretical framework called **social learning theory.** Optimists can take heart in the possibility that social learning theory, or some other metatheoretical perspective, will organize at least part of the patchwork into a unified theory of human behavior. The prospect is, at best a gamble, though.

Two final complementary pieces of advice on the attitude the contemporary practitioner, as artist and scientist, must take (the advice comes from no less a practitioner than Freud [1925/1963c]):

In scientific affairs there should be no place for recoiling from novelty. (p. 253)

Science, in her perpetual incompleteness and insufficiency, is driven by hope for her salvation in new discoveries and new ways of regarding things. She does well, in order not to be deceived, to arm herself with skepticism and examination. (p. 253)

Enough said.

---

[1]The nature of psychology as a science and the threat to its unity are lucidly explained in the last two chapters of Hilgard's *Psychology in America: A Historical Survey* (1987).

Glossary

*Terms listed in the Glossary are presented throughout the text in **bold** each time they are introduced into a new chapter. Some items were selected for entry in the Glossary because they are found throughout the book, while others were chosen simply because their first appearance in the text requires the aid of the Glossary. A term in bold within a Glossary entry means that that term is itself a Glossary entry. Each entry also identifies the chapter in which the term is explained more fully.*

assertiveness training: In a general sense, assertiveness training (also called assertion training) refers to a number of **behavior therapy** techniques aimed at improving clients' interpersonal relations by training them to express both positive and negative feelings with a minimum of personal anxiety and distress to others. More specifically, assertiveness training refers to the reciprocal-inhibition techniques developed by Wolpe and Lazarus. Chapter 5.

behavior theory: Behavior theory refers to one of the two general types of theories of human learning (the other is **cognitive theory**). The primary focus of behavior theory is overt (that is, observable) rather than covert (for example, mental) behavior. The research that supports behavior theory is experimental in nature and typically restricts its explanations to variables that can be observed and measured. Behavior theory describes learning in terms of the connection between a stimulus and a response. Chapter 4.

behavior therapy: Behavior therapy refers to a broad set of clinical procedures designed to enhance clients' self-regulation of thoughts, feelings, and actions. The procedures are typically based on experimental findings on human learning and contribute to the clinical literature by emphasizing the careful measurement of outcomes. Chapter 4.

behaviorism: Behaviorism is a philosophy of science that dominated American psychology for much of the first half of the 20th century. Originally promoted by John Watson and later associated with the research of B. F. Skinner, behaviorism holds that even the most complex human psychological activities can be explained in terms of a limited number of laws of learning and physiology. In its most extreme forms (radical behaviorism), behaviorism states that descriptions of human behavior in cognitive terms are useless because mental activity is not observable and is therefore scientifically unknowable. When the research methodology of behaviorism is used apart from the philosophy of science, it is referred to as *methodological behaviorism.* Chapters 3 and 4.

biofeedback: Biofeedback is a general term for a collection of electronic instruments and clinical procedures that allow an individual to monitor and change underlying biological events. It does so by providing the client with continuous information (usually auditory or visual) about the bioelectric activity of specific physiological functions. Through the equipment and procedures, the client learns to indirectly change the biosignal, thus moving from anxiety to relaxation. Biofeedback is often part of a larger program in **behavior therapy.** Chapter 4.

clinical research tradition: The clinical research tradition represents one of the two fundamental approaches to psychological investigation and theory building that inform contemporary clinical and counseling psychology (the other is the **experimental research tradition**). The clinical research tradition began with Freud's **psychoanalysis** and has relied on clinical evidence (descriptions of single cases) and survey methods for data gathering. Most of the major theories within this tradition have been personality theories, although some important contributions to psychopathology and social psychology are included. The clinical research tradition is no longer clearly distinct from the experimental research tradition. Chapter 3.

cognitive theory: Cognitive theory refers to one of the two general types of theories of human learning (the other is **behavior theory**). The primary focus of cognitive theory is mental activity (cognitive processes) rather than overt behavior. Contemporary cognitive theory relies on experimental methodology but emphasizes variables that are not readily observable (for example, perception, attitudes, beliefs, expectations). Chapter 4.

countertransference: In **psychoanalysis,** countertransference is an interpersonal process in which the practitioner's (analyst's) emotional attachment to the client (analysand) impedes therapeutic change. See also **transference.** Chapter 7.

demoralization: Demoralization refers to the feelings of personal failure and powerlessness that imbue the specific problems and concerns that clients bring to counseling and psychotherapy. Chapter 2.

dream analysis: Dream analysis is one of the principal methods in **psychoanalysis** for changing behavior through **insight.** Used in conjunction with **free association,** dream analysis involves the recollection and interpretation of series of dreams according to universal and personal symbols. Insight comes as the client (analysand) discovers the elemental unconscious wishes and meanings hidden in the dreams. Chapter 6.

experimental research tradition: The experimental research tradition is one of the two fundamental approaches to psychological investigation and theory building that inform contemporary clinical and counseling psychology (the other is the **clinical research tradition**). The experimental research tradition began with Wilhelm Wundt but has been dominated in America by the **behaviorism** of Watson and Skinner. Research within this tradition has been exclusively experimental and has relied partially on data from animal research. Major experimental contributions to psychology have been in the area of learning. The experimental research tradition is no longer clearly distinct from the clinical research tradition. Chapter 3.

free association: Free association is one of the principal methods in **psychoanalysis** for changing behavior through **insight.** It involves having the client (analysand) report what comes immediately to mind in connection with certain words, events, ideas, or emotions. Although the practitioner (analyst) is always attentive to associations that the client makes in conversation, the method can be used formally, with the practitioner introducing certain words to which the client must respond with the first thought or feeling that comes to consciousness. See also **dream analysis.** Chapter 6.

humanistic-existential therapies: Humanistic-existential therapies include a broad array of approaches to psychotherapy and counseling that fit within the *humanistic-existential perspective* on personality and behavior change. Although these therapies are methodologically varied, they share a view of human beings as capable of continual psychological maturation and an emphasis on the role of individual responsibility in accomplishing that growth. Chapter 6.

hypnosis: Hypnosis is a waking state of consciousness characterized by increased relaxation and a heightened capacity for suggestion. The desired effects of hypnosis are put in the form of suggestions that emerge from discussions between the practitioner and the client. The techniques used in hypnosis vary widely, but the beneficial effects of hypnosis (for example, enhanced relaxation, reduction of pain, improved memory, controlled emotions) are not unique to hypnosis. Hypnosis is an interpersonal process and a learned social and cognitive skill. Hypnosis is used as a treatment by itself or with other techniques in many areas of psychotherapy and counseling. Chapter 4.

insight: Generally, insight in psychotherapy and counseling refers to a personal illumination or awareness that changes a client's appreciation of self. As used in this text, insight refers to an affective and cognitive process that begins with a new understanding and acceptance of self and leads to a deliberate change in behavior. Theoretically, the change in behavior that results from insight moves the person toward psychological **maturity.** Chapters 1 and 6.

maturity: Maturity refers to the degree of psychological development a person exhibits at a particular age; as a person's chronological age advances so too should the person's capacity to successfully enjoy and contribute to human life. Most insight approaches to psychotherapy and counseling include an implicit or explicit description of the mature self. It is a working thesis of this book that **insight** leads to maturity, although the establishment of some minimal levels of control over thoughts, feelings, and actions (**self-regulation**) is a necessary condition for insight. Chapters 1 and 6.

meditation: Meditation is an age-old form of **self-regulation** through relaxation that involves focusing one's attention in a passive way on some object, sound, or image. Meditation takes many forms, some of which have explicit religious or spiritual components. Various forms of meditation are used in conjunction with counseling and psychotherapy. Chapter 4.

person-centered therapy: Person-centered therapy, developed by Carl Rogers, is a popular and influential approach to individual and group intervention that fits within the *humanistic-existential perspective* (see Chapter 6). It begins with the belief that the capacity for healing and maturity resides within the client rather than in some power of the practitioner. However, the client's ability to change can be facilitated by a relationship with the practitioner characterized by genuineness, empathy, and unconditional positive regard. Chapter 8.

progressive relaxation: Progressive relaxation, developed by Edmund Jacobson, is a technique for enhancing total body relaxation. It involves systematically tensing and releasing various muscle groups. Progressive relaxation has been shown to have beneficial medical and psychological effects and is used in conjunction with *systematic desensitization,* a **behavior therapy** technique. Chapter 4.

psychoanalysis: Psychoanalysis is a theory of human behavior and approach to research and psychotherapy developed by Sigmund Freud. Human behavior is viewed as being rooted in unconscious conflicts produced by the incompatibility of instinctual sexual and aggressive demands and the internalized dictates of society. Contemporary psychoanalytic psychotherapy takes a variety of forms, although all forms emphasize the importance of the client's gaining insight into the unconscious historical antecedents of present behavior. Chapters 3 and 6.

resistance: In general, resistance refers to the client's unwillingness or inability to progress in counseling or psychotherapy. The reasons may be conscious and purposeful or unconscious and unintentional. In **psychoanalysis,** resistance takes the forms of **transference** and repression, the automatic removal of anxiety-producing psychic material from consciousness. Chapter 2.

self-actualization: Generally, self-actualization refers to a philosophical tenet of the *humanistic-existential perspective* that emphasizes the unique, innate human capacity to realize or actualize a variety of inherent potentials. More specifically, self-actualization is a theory of motivation and personality based on the research of Abraham Maslow that argues that traditional personality theories emphasize pathology rather than the human capacity for increased maturity. Maslow's self-actualization theory provides a model for positive psychological development through various biological, social, and psychological stages. Chapter 6.

self-regulation: Self-regulation refers to an individual's ability to control his or her thoughts, feelings, and actions. Self-regulation is a voluntary process that requires systematic evaluation of the internal and external conditions that have led or could lead to a particular goal, and the changing of those conditions to attain the goal. In this text, some minimal attainment of self-regulation is seen as a precondition for **maturity.** Chapter 4.

single-case experimental design: Single-case experimental design provides procedures for engaging in experimental research where the number of subjects is below that which is traditionally required for true experimentation. The application of single-case experimental design involves the monitoring of target behaviors over a period of time during which treatment procedures are introduced, while maintaining control over variables affecting cause and effect relationships. Chapter 4.

social learning theory: Social learning theory is a major theoretical perspective in social, clinical, developmental, and personality psychology integrating social research and learning research that is based on both **cognitive theory** and **behavior theory.** The term is also used to refer to the theoretical underpinning of several approaches to **behavior therapy,** as well as to the respective work of Bandura and of Rotter. Chapters 2, 4, and 10.

synergy: Synergy, as described by Ruth Benedict, refers to the degree of mutuality existing within a culture or subculture between the individual and the culture. Cultures that are high in synergy are those in which the design of the culture promotes individual **self-actualization** without detriment to the culture. Cultures that are low in synergy are those in which the design of the culture makes individual and cultural attainment mutually exclusive. Chapter 2.

systems theory: Systems theory, as applied in *family therapy,* is a model for explaining human behavior that focuses on the interactional process between and among individuals rather than on individual behaviors themselves. In the systems model, individual behavior is always viewed in the context of interactions taking place within a structured, dynamic system. Chapter 10.

transference: In **psychoanalysis,** transference is an interpersonal process in which the client (analysand) repeats early patterns of parent-child hostility, attachment, or both with the practitioner (analyst) for the unconscious purpose of resisting change (**resistance**). The resolution of transference is key to successful psychoanalysis. See also **countertransference.** Chapter 6.

References

Ackerman, N. W. (1937). The family as a social and emotional unit. *Bulletin of the Kansas Mental Hygiene Society, 12,* 1–3, 7–8.

Ackerman, N. W. (1958). *The psychodynamics of family life.* New York: Basic Books.

Ackerman, N. W. (1966). *Treating the troubled family.* New York: Basic Books.

Adams, H. E., Doster, J. A., & Calhoun, K. S. (1977). A psychologically based system of response classification. In A. R. Ciminero, K. S. Calhoun, & H. E. Adams (Eds.), *Handbook of behavioral assessment* (pp. 47–78). New York: Wiley.

Adler, A. (1917). *The neurotic constitution* (B. Glueck & J. E. Lind, Trans.). New York: Moffat, Yard.

Adler, A. (1931). *What life should mean to you.* New York: Capricorn.

Adler, A. (1964). *Superiority and social interest: A collection of later writings* (H. L. Ansbacher & R. R. Ansbacher, Eds.). New York: Viking Press. (Original work published 1927–1937)

Adler, A. (1969). *Understanding human nature.* New York: Fawcett. (Original work published 1927)

Albee, G. W. (1969). Emerging concepts of mental illness and models of treatment: The psychological point of view. *American Journal of Psychiatry, 125,* 42–48.

Albee, G. W. (1979, May). Preventing prevention. *APA Monitor,* p. 2.

Albee, G. W. (1982). Preventing psychopathology and promoting human potential. *American Psychologist, 37,* 1043–1050.

Alberti, R. E., & Emmons, M. L. (1979). *Your perfect right* (rev. ed.). San Luis Obispo, CA: Impact.

Alexander, F. (1948). *Fundamentals of psychoanalysis.* New York: Norton.

Alexander, F., & French, T. M. (1946). *Psychoanalytic therapy.* New York: Ronald Press.

Allen, M. J. (1984). Scientific method. In R. J. Corsini (Ed.), *Encyclopedia of psychology* (Vol. 3, pp. 277–279). New York: Wiley.

Allport, G. W. (1955). *Becoming: Basic considerations for a psychology of personality.* New Haven, CT: Yale University Press.

Allport, G. W. (1960). *Personality and social encounter.* Boston: Beacon Press.

Allport, G. W. (1968). *The person in psychology.* Boston: Beacon Press.

American Psychiatric Association. (1987). *Diagnostic and statistical manual of mental disorders* (3rd, rev. ed.). Washington DC: Author.

Ansbacher, H. L. (1962). Was Adler a disciple of Freud? A reply. *Journal of Individual Psychology, 18,* 126–135.

Ansbacher, H. L. (1968). The concept of social interest. *Journal of Individual Psychology, 24,* 131–141.

Ansbacher, H. L. (1982). Alfred Adler's view of the unconscious. *Journal of Individual Psychology, 38,* 32–41.

Ansbacher, H. L., & Ansbacher, R. R. (Eds.). (1956). *The individual psychology of Alfred Adler: A systematic presentation in selections of his writings.* New York: Harper & Row.

Ansbacher, H. L., Ansbacher, R. R., Shiverick, D., & Shiverick, K. (1966). Lee Harvey Oswald: An Adlerian interpretation. *Psychoanalytic Review, 53,* 279–290.

Aponte, H. J. (1976). Underorganization in the poor family. In P. J. Guerin (Ed.), *Family therapy: Theory and practice* (pp. 432–448). New York: Gardner Press.

Aponte, H. J., & VanDeusen, J. M. (1981). Structural family therapy. In A. S. Gurman & D. P. Kniskern (Eds.), *Handbook of family therapy* (pp. 310–360). New York: Brunner/Mazel.

Ascher, L. M. (1980). Paradoxical intention. In A. Goldstein & E. B. Foa (Eds.), *Handbook of behavioral interventions: A clinical guide* (pp. 266–321). New York: Wiley.

Ascher, L. M. (1981). Employing paradoxical intention in the treatment of agoraphobia. *Behavioral Research and Therapy, 19,* 533–542.

Auden, W. H. (1945). *The collected poetry of W. H. Auden.* New York: Random House.

Baer, D. M. (1982). Applied behavior analysis. In G. T. Wilson & C. M. Franks (Eds.), *Contemporary behavior therapy* (pp. 277–309). New York: Guilford Press.

Baker, E. L. (1985). Psychoanalysis and psychoanalytic psychotherapy. In S. J. Lynn & J. P. Garske (Eds.), *Contemporary psychotherapies: Models and methods* (pp. 19–67). Columbus, OH: Merrill.

Bandura, A. (1961). Psychotherapy as a learning process. *Psychological Bulletin, 58,* 143–159.

Bandura, A. (1969). *Principles of behavior modification.* New York: Holt, Rinehart & Winston.

Bandura, A. (1971). *Psychological modeling: Conflicting theories.* Chicago: Aldine-Atherton.

Bandura, A. (1973). *Aggression: A social learning analysis.* Englewood Cliffs, NJ: Prentice-Hall.

Bandura, A. (1974). Behavior theory and the models of man. *American Psychologist, 29,* 859–869.

Bandura, A. (1977a). Self-efficacy: Toward a unifying theory of behavioral change. *Psychological Review, 84,* 191–215.

Bandura, A. (1977b). *Social learning theory.* Englewood Cliffs, NJ: Prentice-Hall.

Bandura, A. (1978). On paradigms and recycled ideologies. *Cognitive Therapy and Research, 2,* 79–103.

Bandura, A. (1981). Self-referent thought: A developmental analysis of self-efficacy. In J. H. Flavell & L. D. Ross (Eds.), *Cognitive social development: Frontiers and possible futures* (pp. 200–239). New York: Cambridge University Press.

Bandura, A. (1982). Self-efficacy mechanism in human agency. *American Psychologist, 37,* 122–147.

Bandura, A. (1983). Self-efficacy determinants of anticipated fears and calamaties. *Journal of Personality and Social Psychology, 45,* 464–469.

Bandura, A. (1984). Recycling misconceptions of perceived self-efficacy. *Cognitive Therapy and Research, 8,* 231–255.

Bandura, A., Adams, N. E., Hardy, A. B., & Howells, G. N. (1980). Tests of the generality of self-efficacy theory. *Cognitive Therapy and Research, 4,* 39–66.

Bandura, A., Blanchard, E. B., & Ritter, B. (1969). The relative efficacy of desensitization and modeling approaches for inducing behavioral, affective, and attitude change. *Journal of Personality and Social Psychology, 13,* 173–248.

Bandura, A., Jeffery, R. W., & Gajdos, E. (1974). Generalized change through participant modeling with self-directed mastery. *Behavior Research and Therapy 13,* 141–152.

Bandura, A., Taylor, C. B., Williams, S. L., Mefford, I. N., & Barchas, J. D. (1985). Catecholamine secretion as a function of perceived coping self-efficacy. *Journal of Consulting and Clinical Psychology, 53,* 406–414.

Barber, T. X. (1969). *Hypnosis: A scientific approach.* New York: Van Nostrand Reinhold.

Barber, T. X. (1970). *LSD, marihuana, yoga, and hypnosis.* Chicago: Aldine-Atherton.

Barber, T. X. (1972). Suggested ("hypnotic") behavior: The trance paradigm versus an alternative paradigm. In E. Fromm & R. E. Shor (Eds.), *Hypnosis: Research developments and perspectives* (pp. 115–182). Chicago: Aldine-Atherton.

Barling, J., & Wainstein, T. (1979). Attitudes, labeling bias, and behavior modification in work organizations. *Behavior Therapy, 10,* 129–136.

Barlow, D. H., Hayes, S. C., & Nelson, R. O. (1984). *The scientist practitioner.* New York: Pergamon Press.

Barnes, G. (1977). *Transactional analyis after Eric Berne: Teachings of three TA schools.* New York: Harper & Row.

Barrett, D. (1983). Early recollections as predictors of self-disclosure and interpersonal style. *Journal of Individual Psychology, 39,* 92–98.

Barron, F. (1972). *Artists in the making.* New York: Seminar Press.

Bateson, G. (1972). *Steps in an ecology of mind.* New York: Ballantine.

Bateson, G., Jackson, D. D., Haley, J., & Weakland, J. (1956). Toward a theory of schizophrenia. *Behavior Science, 1,* 251–264.

Bateson, G., Jackson, D. D., Haley, J., & Weakland, J. (1963). A note on the double bind. 1962. *Family Process, 2,* 154–161.

Beck, A. T. (1967). *Depression: Causes and treatment.* Philadelphia: University of Pennsylvania Press.

Beck, A. T. (1970). Cognitive therapy: Nature and relation to behavior therapy. *Behavior Therapy, 1,* 184–200.

Beck, A. T. (1976). *Cognitive therapy and the emotional disorders.* New York: New American Library.

Beck, A. T., & Emery, G. (1979). *Cognitive therapy of anxiety and phobic disorders.* Philadelphia: Center for Cognitive Therapy.

Beck, A. T., & Lester, D. (1973). Components of depression in attempted suicides. *Journal of Psychology, 85,* 257–260.

Becker, J. V., & Abel, G.G. (1981) Behavioral treatment of victims of sexual assault. In S. M. Turner, K. S. Calhoun, & H. E. Adams (Eds.), *Handbook of clinical behavior therapy* (pp. 347–379). New York: Wiley.

Bedrosian, R. C., & Beck, A. T. (1980). Principles of cognitive therapy. In M. Mahoney (Ed.), *Psychotherapy process* (pp. 127–154). New York: Plenum

Bell, J. E. (1961). Family group therapy. *Public Health Monograph No. 64.* Washington, DC: U.S. Government Printing Office.

Bell, J. E. (1975). *Family therapy.* New York: Aronson.

Benson, H. (1975). *The relaxation response.* New York: Avon.

Benson, H., Shapiro, D., Tursky, B., & Schwartz, G. E. (1971). Decreased systolic blood pressure through operant conditioning techniques in patients with essential hypertension. *Science, 173,* 740–742.

Benson, H., & Wallace, R. K. (1972). Decreased drug abuse with transcendental meditation: A study of 1,862 subjects. In C. J. D. Zarafonetis (Ed.), *Drug abuse: Proceedings of the International Congress* (pp. 369–376). Philadelphia: Lea & Febiger.

Berne, E. (1957). Intuition V: The ego image. *Psychiatric Quarterly, 31,* 611–627.

Berne, E. (1961). *Transactional analysis in psychotherapy.* New York: Grove Press.

Berne, E. (1964). *Games people play.* New York: Grove Press.
Berne, E. (1966). *Group treatment.* New York: Grove Press.
Berne, E. (1972). *What do you say after you say hello?* New York: Grove Press.
Berne, E. (1977). *Intuition and ego states: The origins of transactional analysis.* New York: Harper & Row.
Bertalanffy, L. von. (1968). *General systems theory.* New York: Braziller.
Bertalanffy, L. von. (1977). *Perspectives on general systems theory.* New York: Braziller.
Bettelheim, B. (1983). *Freud and man's soul.* New York: Knopf.
Bierman, K. L. (1984). Child guidance clinics. In R. J. Corsini (Ed.), *Encyclopedia of psychology* (Vol. 1, pp. 202–203). New York: Wiley.
Blumenthal, A. L. (1977). Wilhelm Wundt and early American psychology: A clash of two cultures. *Annals of the New York Academy of Science, 291,* 13–20.
Boaz, F. (1940). *Race, language, and culture.* New York: Macmillan.
Bodin, A. M. (1984). Family therapy. In T. B. Karasu (Ed.), *The psychiatric therapies* (pp. 439–481). Washington, DC: American Psychiatric Association.
Bonner, H. (1965). *On being mindful of man.* New York: Houghton Mifflin.
Borgen, F. H. (1984). Counseling psychology. *Annual Review of Psychology, 35,* 579–604.
Boring, E. G. (1950). *A history of experimental psychology* (2nd ed.). Englewood Cliffs, NJ: Prentice-Hall.
Boszormenyi-Nagy, I. (1965). The concept of change in conjoint family therapy. In A. Friedman, et al. (Eds.), *Psychotherapy for the whole family* (pp. 305–319). New York: Springer.
Boszormenyi-Nagy, I. (1981). Contextual therapy: Therapeutic leverages in mobilizing trust. In R. J. Green & J. L. Framo (Eds.), *Family therapy: Major contributions* (pp. 395–415). New York: International Universities Press.
Boszormenyi-Nagy, I., & Framo, J. L. (Eds.). (1965). *Intensive family therapy: Theoretical and practical aspects.* New York: Harper & Row.
Boszormenyi-Nagy, I., & Krasner, B. R. (1980). Trust-based therapy: A contextual approach. *American Journal of Psychiatry, 137,* 767–775.
Boszormenyi-Nagy, I., & Spark, G. M. (1984). *Invisible loyalties.* New York: Brunner/Mazel. (Original work published 1973)
Boszormenyi-Nagy, I., & Ulrich, D. N. (1981). Contextual family therapy. In A. S. Gurman & D. P. Kniskern (Eds.), *Handbook of family therapy* (pp. 159–186). New York: Brunner/Mazel.
Boudewyns, P. A., & Shipley, R. H. (1983). *Flooding and implosive therapy: Direct therapeutic exposure in clinical practice.* New York: Plenum.
Bowen, M. (1978). *Family therapy in clinical practice.* New York: Aronson.
Bower, G. H. (1978). Contacts of cognitive psychology with social learning theory. *Cognitive Therapy and Research, 2,* 123–146.
Bowers, K. S. (1976). *Hypnosis for the seriously curious.* Pacific Grove, CA: Brooks/Cole.
Brammer, L. M. (1979). *The helping relationship: Process and skills* (3rd ed.). Englewood Cliffs, NJ: Prentice-Hall.
Brammer, L. M., & Shostrom, E. L. (1982). *Therapeutic psychology* (4th ed.). Englewood Cliffs, NJ: Prentice-Hall.
Brenman-Gibson, M. (1984). Psychoanalysis. In R. J. Corsini (Ed.), *Encyclopedia of psychology* (Vol. 3, pp. 86–91). New York: Wiley.
Brennan, J. (1982). *History and systems of psychology.* Englewood Cliffs, NJ: Prentice-Hall.
Brenner, D. (1982). *The effective psychotherapist.* New York: Pergamon Press.
Breuer, J., & Freud, S. (1953). Studies in hysteria. In J. Strachey (Ed. and Trans.), *The standard edition of the complete psychological works of Sigmund Freud* (Vol. 2, pp. 1–305). London: Hogarth. (Original work published 1895)

Broderick, C. B., & Schrader, S. S. (1981). The history of professional marriage and family therapy. In A. S. Gurman & D. P. Kniskern (Eds.), *Handbook of family therapy* (pp. 5–35). New York: Brunner/Mazel.

Brunnell, L. F., & Young, W. T. (Eds.). (1982). *Multimodal handbook for a mental hospital: Designing specific treatments for specific problems.* New York: Springer.

Buber, M. (1958). *I and thou.* New York: Charles Scribner's Sons.

Budman, S. H. (Ed.). (1981). *Forms of brief therapy.* New York: Guilford Press.

Budzynski, T. H., Stoyva, J. M., & Adler, C. (1970). Feedback-induced muscle relaxation: Application to tension headache. *Journal of Behavior Therapy and Experimental Psychiatry, 1,* 205–211.

Budzynski, T. H. Stoyva, J. M., & Peffer, K. E. (1980). Biofeedback techniques in psychosomatic disorders. In A. Goldstein & E. B. Foa (Eds.), *Handbook of behavioral interventions: A clinical guide* (pp. 186–265). New York: Wiley.

Burns, D. D. (1980). *Feeling good: The new mood therapy.* New York: Morrow.

Burns, D. D., & Beck, A. T. (1978). Cognitive behavior modification of mood disorders. In J. P. Foreyt & D. P. Rathjen (Eds.), *Cognitive behavior therapy: Research and application* (pp. 109–134). New York: Plenum.

Burns, D. D., & Persons, J. (1982). Hope and hopelessness: A cognitive approach. In L. E. Abt & I. R. Stuart (Eds.), *The newer therapies: A sourcebook* (pp. 33–57). New York: Van Nostrand Reinhold.

Cadwallader, E. H. (1981). Values in Fritz Perls' Gestalt therapy: On the dangers of half-truths. *Counseling and Values, 28,* 192–201.

Cannon, W. B. (1929). *Bodily changes in pain, hunger, fear and rage* (rev. ed.). New York: Appleton-Century.

Cattell, R. B., Eber, H. W., & Tatsuoka, M. M. (1970). *Handbook of the Sixteen Personality Factors Questionnaire.* Champaign, IL: Institute for Personality and Ability Testing.

Cautela, J. R. (1971). Covert extinction. *Behavior Therapy, 2,* 192–200.

Cautela, J. R. (1976). The present status of covert modeling. *Journal of Behavior Therapy and Experimental Psychiatry, 7,* 323–326.

Cautela, J. R. (1977). *Behavioral analysis forms for clinical intervention.* Champaign, IL: Research Press.

Cautela, J. R. (1983). The self-control triad: Description and clinical applications. *Behavior Modification, 7,* 299–315.

Cautela, J. R., Flannery, R. B., & Hanley, S. (1974). Covert modeling: An experimental test. *Behavior Therapy, 5,* 495–502.

Cautela, J. R., & Kearney, A. J. (1984). Covert conditioning. In R. J. Corsini (Ed.), *Encyclopedia of psychology* (Vol. 1, pp. 305–306). New York: Wiley.

Cautela, J. R., & Upper, D. (1976). The behavioral inventory battery: The use of self-report measures in behavioral analysis and therapy. In M. Hersen & A. S. Bellack (Eds.), *Behavioral assessment* (pp. 77–109). Oxford: Pergamon Press.

Ciminero, A. R., Calhoun, K. S., & Adams, H. E. (Eds.). (1977). *Handbook of behavioral assessment.* New York: Wiley.

Ciminero, A. R., Nelson, R. O., & Lipinski, D. P. (1977). Self-monitoring procedures. In A. R. Ciminero, K. S. Calhoun, & H. E. Adams (Eds.), *Handbook of behavioral assessment* (pp. 195–232). New York: Wiley.

Coleman, J. C. (1980). *Abnormal psychology and modern life* (6th ed.). Glenview, IL: Scott, Foresman.

Cone, J. D., & Hawkins, R. P. (Eds.). (1977). *Behavioral assessment: New directions in clinical psychology.* New York: Brunner/Mazel.

Corey, G. (1986). *Theory and practice of counseling and psychotherapy* (3rd ed.). Pacific Grove, CA: Brooks/Cole.

Craighead, W. E., Kazdin, A. E., & Mahoney, M. J. (1981). *Behavior modification: Principles, issues, and applications* (2nd ed.). Boston: Houghton Mifflin.

Crumbaugh, J. C. (1964). An experimental study of existentialism: The psychometric approach to Frankl's concept of noögenic neurosis. *Journal of Clinical Psychology, 20,* 200–207.

Crumbaugh, J. C. (1968). Cross validation of Purpose-In-Life Test based on Frankl's concepts. *Journal of Individual Psychology, 24,* 74–81.

Curran, J. P. (1981). Social skills and assertion training. In W. E. Craighead, A. E. Kazdin, & M. J. Mahoney (Eds.). *Behavior modification: Principles, issues, and applications* (2nd ed.) (pp. 243–263). Boston: Houghton Mifflin.

Davis, F. W., & Yates, B. T. (1982). Self-efficacy expectancies versus outcome expectancies as determinants of performance deficits and depressive affect. *Cognitive Therapy and Research, 5,* 23–35.

Davison, G. C. (1980). Some views of effective principles of psychotherapy. *Cognitive Therapy and Research, 4,* 271–306.

Dewey, E. A. (1972). Family atmosphere. In A. G. Nikelly (Ed.), *Techniques for behavior change* (pp. 41–48). Springfield, IL: Charles C. Thomas.

Dewey, E. A. (1984). The use and misuse of emotion. *Journal of Individual Psychology, 40,* 184–195.

Dinkmeyer, D. C., Pew, W. L., & Dinkmeyer, D. C., Jr. (1979). *Adlerian counseling and psychotherapy.* Pacific Grove, CA: Brooks/Cole.

Dollard, J., & Miller, N. E. (1950). *Personality and psychotherapy.* New York: McGraw-Hill.

Dolliver, R. H. (1981). Some limitations of Perls' Gestalt therapy. *Psychotherapy: Theory, Research and Practice, 18,* 38–45.

Dreikurs, R. (1953). *Fundamentals of Adlerian psychology.* Chicago: Alfred Adler Institute.

Dreikurs, R. (1956). Adlerian psychotherapy. In F. Fromm-Reichmann & M. I. Stein (Eds.), *Progress in psychotherapy* (pp. 111–118). New York: Grune & Stratton.

Dreikurs, R. (1963). Psychodynamic diagnosis in psychiatry. *American Journal of Psychiatry, 119,* 1045–1048.

Dreyfus, E. A., & Nikelly, A. G. (1972). Existential-humanism in Adlerian psychotherapy. In A. G. Nikelly (Ed.), *Techniques for behavior change* (pp. 13–20). Springfield, IL: Charles C. Thomas.

Drinka, G. F. (1984). *The birth of neurosis: Myth, malady and the Victorians.* New York: Simon & Schuster.

Dusay, J. M. (1977). The evolution of transactional analysis. In G. Barnes (Ed.), *Transactional analysis after Eric Berne: Teachings of three TA schools* (pp. 32–52). New York: Harper & Row.

Dusay, J. M., & Dusay, K. M. (1984). Transactional analysis. In R. J. Corsini (Ed.), *Current psychotherapies* (3rd ed.) (pp. 392–446). Itasca, IL: F. E. Peacock.

D'Zurilla, T. J., & Goldfried, M. R. (1971). Problem solving and behavior modification. *Journal of Abnormal Psychology, 78,* 107–126.

Eastman, C., & Marzillier, J. S. (1984). Theoretical and methodological difficulties in Bandura's self-efficacy theory. *Cognitive Therapy and Research, 8,* 213–229.

Egan, G. (1982). *The skilled helper* (2nd ed.). Pacific Grove, CA: Brooks/Cole.

Ellenberger, H. F. (1970). *The discovery of the unconscious.* New York: Basic Books.

Ellis, A. (1957). *How to live with a "neurotic."* New York: Crown.

Ellis, A. (1962). *Reason and emotion in psychotherapy.* New York: Stuart.

Ellis, A. (1963). Toward a more precise definition of "emotional" and "intellectual" insight. *Psychological Reports, 13,* 125–126.

Ellis, A. (1970). Tribute to Alfred Adler. *Journal of Individual Psychology, 26,* 11–12.

Ellis, A. (1971). Reason and emotion in the individual psychology of Adler. *Journal of Individual Psychology, 27,* 50–64.

Ellis, A. (1973). *Humanistic psychotherapy: The rational-emotive approach.* New York: Julian Press.

Ellis, A. (1979). *The intelligent woman's guide to dating and mating.* Secaucus, NJ: Stuart.

Ellis, A. (1980). Rational-emotive therapy and cognitive behavior therapy: Similarities and differences. *Cognitive Therapy and Research, 4,* 325–340.

Ellis, A. (1983). The philosophic implications and dangers of some popular behavior therapy techniques. In M. Rosenbaum, C. M. Franks, & Y. Jaffe (Eds.), *Perspective on behavior therapy in the eighties* (pp. 138–151). New York: Springer.

Ellis, A. (1985). *Overcoming resistance: Rational-emotive therapy with difficult clients.* New York: Springer.

Ellis, A. (1987a). The impossibility of achieving consistently good mental health. *American Psychologist, 42,* 364–375.

Ellis, A. (1987b). A sadly neglected cognitive element in depression. *Cognitive Therapy and Research, 11,* 121–146.

Ellis, A., & Bernard, M. E. (Ed.). (1985). *Clinical applications of rational-emotive therapy.* New York: Plenum.

Ellis, A., & Grieger, R. (1977). *Handbook of rational-emotive therapy.* New York: Springer.

Ellis, A., & Whitely, J. (Eds.). (1979). *Theoretical and empirical foundations of rational-emotive therapy.* Pacific Grove, CA: Brooks/Cole.

Emmelkamp, P. M. G. (1982). Anxiety and fear. In A. S. Bellack, M. Hersen, & A. E. Kazdin (Eds.), *International handbook of behavior modification and therapy* (pp. 349–395). New York: Plenum.

Engelman, E. (1976). *Berggasse 19: Sigmund Freud's home and offices, Vienna, 1938.* New York: Basic Books.

Etringer, B. D., Cash, T. F., & Rimm, D. C. (1982). Behavioral, affective, and cognitive effects of participant modeling and an equally credible placebo. *Behavior Therapy, 13,* 476–485.

Eysenck, H. J. (1968). A theory of the incubation of anxiety/fear responses. *Psychotherapy: Theory, Research and Practice, 13,* 319–321.

Eysenck, H. J. (1982). Neobehavioristic (S-R) theory. In G. T. Wilson & C. M. Franks (Eds.), *Contemporary behavior therapy* (pp. 205–276). New York: Guilford Press.

Eysenck, H. J., Wakefield, J., & Friedman, A. (1983). Diagnostic and clinical assessment: The DSM-III. *Annual Review of Psychology, 34,* 167–193.

Fancher, R. E. (1973). *Psychoanalytic psychology: The development of Freud's thought.* New York: Norton.

Farson, R. (1975). Carl Rogers, quiet revolutionary. In R. I. Evans (Ed.), *Carl Rogers: The man and his ideas* (pp. xxviii–xliii). New York: Dutton.

Fay, A. (1973). Clinical notes on paradoxical therapy. *Psychotherapy: Theory, Research and Practice, 13,* 118–122.

Fay, A. (1976). The drug modality. In A. A. Lazarus (Ed.), *Multimodal behavior therapy* (pp. 65–85). New York: Springer.

Feder, B., & Ronall, R. (Eds.). (1980). *Beyond the hot seat.* New York: Brunner/Mazel.

Ferenczi, S., & Rank, O. (1925). *The development of psychoanalysis.* New York: Nervous and Mental Disease Publishing.

Fiedler, D., & Beach, L. R. (1978). On the decision to be assertive. *Journal of Consulting and Clinical Psychology, 46,* 537–546.

Fine, R. (1979). *A history of psychoanalysis.* New York: Columbia University Press.

Fisher, S., & Greenberg, R. (1977). *The scientific credibility of Freud's theories and therapy.* New York: Basic Books.

Flegenheimer, W. W. (1982). *Techniques of brief psychotherapy.* New York: Aronson.

Foa, E. B., & Emmelkamp, P. M. G. (Eds.). (1983). *Failures in behavior therapy.* New York: Wiley.

Foa, E. B., Steketee, G. S., & Ascher, L. M. (1980). Systematic desensitization. In A.

Goldstein & E. B. Foa (Eds.), *Handbook of behavioral interventions: A clinical guide* (pp. 38–91). New York: Wiley.

Fodor, I. G. (1980). The treatment of communication problems with assertiveness training. In A. Goldstein & E. B. Foa (Eds.), *Handbook of behavioral interventions: A clinical guide* (pp. 501–603). New York: Wiley.

Foreyt, J. P., & Rathjen, D. P. (Eds.). (1978). *Cognitive behavior therapy: Research and application.* New York: Plenum.

Frank, J. D. (1973). *Persuasion and healing* (rev. ed.). New York: Schocken.

Frank, J. D. (1978). *Psychotherapy and the human predicament.* New York: Schocken.

Frank, J. D. (1980). Some views on effective principles of psychotherapy. *Cognitive Therapy and Research, 4,* 271–306.

Frankl, V. E. (1939). Zur medikamentösen Unterstützung der Psychotherapie bei Neurosen. *Schweizer Archiv für Neurologie und Psychiatrie, 43.*

Frankl, V. E. (1946). *Ärztliche Seelsorge.* Vienna: Franz Deuticke.

Frankl, V. E. (1947). *Die Psychotherapie in der Praxis.* Vienna: Deuticke.

Frankl, V. E. (1955). *The doctor and the soul.* New York: Knopf.

Frankl, V. E. (1960). Paradoxical intention: A logotherapeutic technique. *American Journal of Psychotherapy, 14,* 520–535.

Frankl, V. E. (1962). *Man's search for meaning.* New York: Washington Square Press.

Frankl, V. E. (1967). *Psychotherapy and existentialism: Selected papers on logotherapy.* New York: Clarion.

Frankl, V. E. (1969). *The will to meaning.* New York: New American Library.

Frankl, V. E. (1970). Fore-runner of existential psychiatry. *Journal of Individual Psychology, 26,* 38.

Frankl, V. E. (1973). *The doctor and the soul* (2nd ed.). New York: Vintage.

Frankl, V. E. (1975a). Paradoxical intention and dereflection: Two logotherapy techniques. *Psychotherapy: Theory, Research and Practice, 12,* 226–237.

Frankl, V. E. (1975b). *The unconscious God.* New York: Simon & Schuster.

Frankl, V. E. (1978). *The unheard cry for meaning: Psychotherapy and humanism.* New York: Touchstone Books.

Frankl, V. E. (1985). Paradoxical intention. In G. R. Weeks (Ed.), *Promoting change through paradoxical therapy* (pp. 99–110). Homewood, IL: Dow Jones-Irwin.

Freud, S. (1954). Project for a scientific psychology. In S. Freud, *The origins of psychoanalysis.* New York: Basic Books. (Original written in 1895)

Freud, S. (1955). Lines of advance in psycho-analytic therapy. In J. Strachey (Ed. and Trans.), *The standard edition of the complete psychological works of Sigmund Freud* (Vol. 27, pp. 159–168). London: Hogarth. (Original work published 1919)

Freud, S. (1959). Inhibitions, symptoms, and anxiety. In J. Strachey (Ed. and Trans.), *The standard edition of the complete psychological works of Sigmund Freud* (Vol. 20, pp.77–175). London: Hogarth. (Original work published 1926)

Freud, S. (1963a). General theory of the neuroses. In J. Strachey (Ed. and Trans.), *The standard edition of the complete psychological works of Sigmund Freud* (Vol. 16, pp. 243–463). London: Hogarth. (Original work published 1917)

Freud, S. (1963b). Psychoanalysis. In S. Freud, *Character and culture.* New York: Collier. (Original work published 1922)

Freud, S. (1963c). The resistances to psychoanalysis. In S. Freud, *Character and culture.* New York: Collier. (Original work published 1925)

Freud, S. (1964a). A distance of memory on the Acropolis: An open letter to Romain Rolland on the occasion of his seventieth birthday. In J. Strachey (Ed. and Trans.), *The standard edition of the complete psychological works of Sigmund Freud* (Vol. 22, pp. 239–248). London: Hogarth. (Original work published 1936)

Freud, S. (1964b). New introductory lectures on psycho-analysis. In J. Strachey (Ed. and Trans.), *The standard edition of the complete psychological works of Sigmund Freud* (Vol. 22, pp. 5–182). London: Hogarth. (Original work published 1933)

Freud, S. (1972). *The interpretation of dreams* (J. Strachey, Ed. and Trans.). New York: Avon. (Original work published 1931)

Freud, S. (1977). *Die Traumdeutung.* Frankfurt am Main: Fischer Taschenbuch Verlag. (Original work published 1901)

Freud, S., & Jung, C. (1974). *The Freud/Jung letters.* Princeton, NJ: Princeton University Press.

Friar, L. R., & Beatty, J. (1976). Migraine: Management by trained control of vaso-constriction. *Journal of Clinical and Consulting Psychology, 44,* 46–53.

Fromm, E. (1965). *Escape from freedom.* New York: Avon Books. (Original work published in 1941)

Gambrill, E. D., & Richey, C. A. (1975). An assertion inventory for use in assessment and research. *Behavior Therapy, 6,* 550–561.

Garfield, S. L. (1980). *Psychotherapy: An eclectic approach.* New York: Wiley.

Garfield, S. L., & Kurtz, R. (1976). Clinical psychology in the 1970's. *American Psychologist, 31,* 1–9.

Gelso, C. J., & Johnson, D. H. (Eds.). (1983). *Explorations in time-limited counseling and psychotherapy.* New York: Teachers College Press.

Gill, M. M. (1982). *Analysis of transference: Theory and technique.* New York: International Universities Press.

Gilligan, C. (1982). *In a different voice: Psychological theory and women's development.* Cambridge, MA: Harvard University Press.

Girodo, M., & Wood, D. (1979). Talking yourself out of pain: The importance of believing that you can. *Cognitive Therapy and Research, 3,* 23–33.

Goldfried, M. R. (1971). Systematic desensitization as training in self-control. *Journal of Consulting and Clinical Psychology, 37,* 228–234.

Goldfried, M. R. (1982). On the history of therapeutic integration. *Behavior Therapy, 13,* 572–593.

Goldfried, M. R., & Davison, G. L. (1976). *Clinical behavior therapy.* New York: Holt, Rinehart & Winston.

Goldfried, M. R., & Lineham, M. M. (1977). Basic issues in behavioral assessment. In A. R. Ciminero, K. S. Calhoun, & H. E. Adams (Eds.), *Handbook of behavioral assessment* (pp. 15–46). New York: Wiley.

Goldfried, M. R., & Merbaum, M. (Eds.). (1973). *Behavior change through self-control.* New York: Holt, Rinehart & Winston.

Goldfried, M. R., & Newman, C. (1986). Psychotherapy integration: An historical perspective. In J. C. Norcross (Ed.), *Handbook of eclectic psychotherapy* (pp. 25–61). New York: Brunner/Mazel.

Goldstein, A. P. (1971). *Psychotherapeutic attraction.* New York: Pergamon Press.

Goldstein, R. S., & Baer, D. M. (1976). R.S.V.P.: A procedure to increase the personal mail and number of correspondents for nursing home residents. *Behavior Therapy, 7,* 348–354.

Goleman, D. (1985). *Vital lies, simple truths: The psychology of self-deception.* New York: Simon & Schuster.

Gottman, J., & Leiblum, S. (1974). *How to do psychotherapy and how to evaluate it: A manual for beginners.* New York: Holt, Rinehart & Winston.

Goulding, M., & Goulding, R. L. (1979). *Changing lives through redecision therapy.* New York: Brunner/Mazel.

Grebstein, L. C. (1986). An eclectic family therapy. In J. C. Norcross (Ed.), *Handbook of eclectic psychotherapy* (pp. 282–319). New York: Brunner/Mazel.

Greenson, R. R., & Wexler, M. (1969). The nontransformation relationship in the psychoanalytic situation. *International Journal of Psychoanalysis, 50,* 27–39.

Greenwald, H. (Ed.). (1959). *Great cases in psychoanalysis.* New York: Ballantine.

Greenwald, H. (1975). Humor in psychotherapy. *Journal of Contemporary Psychotherapy, 7,* 113–116.

Guerin, P. J. (1976). Family therapy: The first twenty-five years. In P. J. Guerin (Ed.), *Family therapy: Theory and practice* (pp. 2–22). New York: Gardner Press.

Gurman, A. S., & Kniskern, D. P. (1978). Research on marital and family therapy: Progress, perspective, and prospect. In S. L. Garfield & A. E. Bergin (Eds.), *Handbook of psychotherapy and behavior change* (2nd ed.) (pp. 817–901). New York: Wiley.

Gurman, A. S., & Kniskern, D. P. (1981). Family therapy outcome research: Knowns and unknowns. In A. S. Gurman & D. P. Kniskern (Eds.), *Handbook of family therapy* (pp. 742–775). New York: Brunner/Mazel.

Hackett, G., & Horan, J. (1980). Stress inoculation for pain: What's really going on? *Journal of Counseling Psychology, 27,* 107–116.

Haley, J. (1963). *Strategies in psychotherapy.* New York: Grune & Stratton.

Haley, J. (Ed.). (1971). *Changing families: A family therapy reader.* New York: McGraw-Hill.

Haley, J. (1973). *Uncommon therapy: The psychiatric techniques of Milton H. Erickson, M.D.* New York: Norton.

Haley, J. (1976). *Problem solving therapy.* San Francisco: Jossey-Bass.

Haley, J. (1980). *Leaving home: The therapy of disturbed young people.* New York: Grune & Stratton.

Haley, J. (1984). *Ordeal therapy: Unusual ways to change behavior.* San Francisco: Jossey-Bass.

Hall, C. S. (1966). *The meaning of dreams.* New York: McGraw-Hill. (Original work published 1953)

Hall, C. S., & Nordby, V. J. (1972). *The individual and his dreams.* New York: Signet.

Hall, C. S., & Van de Castle, R. L. (1966). *The content analysis of dreams.* New York: Appleton-Century-Crofts.

Harris, A. B., & Harris, T. A. (1986). *Staying OK.* New York: Avon.

Harris, M. (1968). *The rise of anthropological theory.* New York: Thomas Y. Crowell.

Harris, T. A. (1969). *I'm OK–You're OK: A practical guide to transactional analysis.* New York: Grove Press.

Hartmann, H. (1939). *Ego psychology and the problem of adaptation.* New York: International Universities Press.

Hartmann, H. (1964). *Essays on ego psychology: Selected problems in psychoanalytic theory.* New York: International Universities Press.

Hathaway, S., & McKinley, J. (1951). *MMPI manual.* New York: Psychological Corporation.

Hebb, D. O. (1972). *Textbook in psychology* (3rd ed.). Philadelphia: Saunders.

Henle, M. (1978). Gestalt psychology and Gestalt therapy. *Journal of the History of the Behavioral Sciences, 14,* 23–32.

Henry, J. (1971). *Pathways to madness.* New York: Random House.

Hersen, M., & Barlow, D. H. (1976). *Single-case experimental designs.* New York: Pergamon Press.

Hilgard, E. R. (1965). *Hypnotic susceptibility.* New York: Harcourt, Brace & World.

Hilgard, E. R. (1973). The domain of hypnosis. *American Psychologist, 28,* 972–982.

Hilgard, E. R. (Ed.). (1978). *American psychology in historical perspective.* Washington, DC: American Psychological Association.

Hilgard, E. R. (1980). Consciousness in contemporary psychology. *Annual Review of Psychology, 31,* 1–26.

Hilgard, E. R. (1984). Mesmer, Franz Anton. In R. J. Corsini (Ed.), *Encyclopedia of psychology* (Vol. 2, p. 369). New York: Wiley.

Hilgard, E. R. (1987). *Psychology in America: A historical survey.* San Diego: Harcourt Brace Jovanovich.

Hilgard, E. R., & Bower, G. H. (1966). *Theories of learning* (3rd ed.). New York: Appleton-Century-Crofts.

Hoffman, L. (1981). *Foundations of family therapy.* New York: Basic Books.

Holroyd, K. A., & Andrasik, F. (1982). Do the effects of cognitive therapy endure? A two-year follow-up of tension headache sufferers treated with cognitive therapy or biofeedback. *Cognitive Therapy and Research, 3,* 325–334.

Horney, K. (1939). *New ways in psychoanalysis.* New York: Norton.

Horwitz, L. (1974). *Clinical prediction in psychotherapy.* New York: Aronson.

Jackson, D. D. (1959). Family interaction, family homeostasis, and some implications for conjoint family psychotherapy, in J. H. Masserman (Ed.), *Science and Psychoanalysis, Vol. 2: Individual and Familial Dynamics.* New York: Grune and Stratton.

Jackson, D. D. (1968a). A forward to the MRI volumes. In D. D. Jackson (Ed.), *Communication, family, and marriage* (pp. v–vi). Palo Alto, CA: Science and Behavior Books.

Jackson, D. D. (1968b). The question of family homeostasis. In D. D. Jackson (Ed.), *Communication, family, and marriage* (pp. 1–11). PaloAlto, CA: Science and Behavior Books.

Jacobson, E. (1929). *Progressive relaxation.* Chicago: University of Chicago Press.

Jacobson, E. (1962). *You must relax.* New York: McGraw-Hill. (Original work published 1934)

Jakubowski, P., & Lange, A. J. (1978). *The assertive option: Your rights and responsibilities.* Champaign, IL: Research Press.

Jaremko, M. (1979). A component analysis of stress inoculation: Review and prospectus. *Cognitive Therapy and Research, 3,* 325–334.

Johnson, T. H. (Ed.). (1960). *The complete poems of Emily Dickinson.* Boston: Little, Brown.

Jones, E. (1955). *Sigmund Freud: Life and work* (Vol. 2). London: Hogarth.

Jones, R. (1977). *Self-fulfilling prophecies: Social, psychological, and physiological effects of expectancies.* Hillsdale, NJ: Erlbaum.

Jourard, S. M. (1968). *Disclosing man to himself.* New York: Van Nostrand Reinhold.

Jourard, S. M. (1971). *The transparent self.* New York: Van Nostrand Reinhold.

Jung, C. G. (1971). The structure of the psyche. In C. G. Jung, *The portable Jung* (pp. 23–46). New York: Viking Press. (Original work published 1931)

Jung, C. G. (1973). *Letters.* Princeton, NJ: Princeton University Press.

Kahn, E. (1985). Heinz Kohut and Carl Rogers: A timely comparison. *American Psychologist, 40,* 893–904.

Kalish, H. I. (1981). *From behavioral science to behavior modification.* New York: McGraw-Hill.

Kanfer, F. H. (1975). Self-management methods. In F. Kanfer & A. Goldstein (Eds.), *Helping people change* (pp. 309–353). New York: Pergamon Press.

Kanfer, F. H. (1977). The many faces of self-control, or behavior modification changes focus. In R. B. Stuart (Ed.), *Behavioral self-management* (pp. 1–48). New York: Brunner/Mazel.

Kanfer, F. H., & Karoly, P. (1973). Self-control: A behavioristic excursion into the lion's den. In C. M. Franks & G. T. Wilson (Eds.), *Annual review of behavior therapy: Theory and practice, 1973* (pp. 396–415). New York: Brunner/Mazel.

Kazdin, A. E. (1973). Covert modeling and the reduction of avoidance behavior. *Journal of Abnormal Psychology, 81,* 87–95.

Kazdin, A. E. (1974a). Covert modeling, model similarity, and the reduction of avoidance behavior. *Behavior Therapy, 5,* 325–340.

Kazdin, A. E. (1974b). The effect of model identity and fear-relevant similarity on covert modeling. *Behavior Therapy, 5,* 624–635.

Kazdin, A. E. (1974c). Effects of covert modeling and model reinforcement on assertive behavior. *Journal of Abnormal Psychology, 83,* 240–252.

Kazdin, A. E. (1975a). *Behavior modification in applied settings.* Homewood, IL: Dorsey Press.

Kazdin, A. E. (1975b). Covert modeling, imagery assessment, and assertive behavior. *Journal of Consulting and Clinical Psychology, 43,* 716–724.

Kazdin, A. E. (1978a). The application of operant techniques in treatment, rehabilitation and education. In S. L. Garfield & A. E. Bergin (Eds.), *Handbook of psychotherapy and behavior change* (2nd ed.) (pp. 549–589). New York: Wiley.

Kazdin, A. E. (1978b). *History of behavior modification.* Baltimore: University Park Press.

Kazdin, A. E. (1979). Fictions, factions, and functions of behavior therapy. *Behavior Therapy, 10,* 629–654.

Kazdin, A. E. (1982a). History of behavior modification. In A. S. Bellack, M. Hersen, & A. E. Kazdin (Eds.), *International handbook of behavior modification and therapy* (pp. 1–32). New York: Plenum.

Kazdin, A. E. (1982b). *Single-case research designs: Methods for clinical and applied settings.* New York: Oxford University Press.

Kazdin, A. E., & Cole, P. M. (1981). Attitudes and labeling biases toward behavior modification: The effects of labels, content, and jargon. *Behavior Therapy, 12,* 56–68.

Kazdin, A. E., & Mascitelli, S. (1982). Covert and overt rehearsal and homework practice in developing assertiveness. *Journal of Consulting and Clinical Psychology, 50,* 250–258.

Kazdin, A. E., & Wilcoxon, L. A. (1976). Systematic desensitization and nonspecific treatment effects: A methodological evaluation. *Psychological Bulletin, 83,* 729–758.

Kazdin, A. E., & Wilson, G. T. (1978). *Evaluation of behavior therapy.* Cambridge, MA: Ballinger.

Keats, D. B. (1979). *Multimodal therapy with children.* New York: Pergamon Press.

Kendall, P. C. (1982). Integration: Behavior therapy and other schools of thought. *Behavior Therapy, 13,* 559–571.

Kendall, P. C., Plous, S., & Kratochwill, T. R. (1981). Science and behavior therapy: A survey of research in the 1970's. *Behavioral Research and Therapy, 19,* 517–524.

Kirsch, I. (1980). "Microanalytic" analyses of efficacy expectations as predictors of performance. *Cognitive Therapy and Research, 4,* 258–262.

Kirsch, I. (1982). Efficacy expectations or response predictions: The meaning of efficacy ratings as a function of task characteristics. *Journal of Personality and Social Psychology, 42,* 132–136.

Kogan, J. (1976). The genesis of Gestalt therapy. In C. Hatcher & H. M. Higgins (Eds.), *Handbook of Gestalt therapy* (pp. 237–257). New York: Aronson.

Kohn, M. (1976). The interaction of social class and other factors in the etiology of schizophrenia. *American Journal of Psychiatry, 133,* 177–191.

Kohut, H. (1971). *The analysis of the self.* New York: International Universities Press.

Kohut, H. (1977). *The restoration of the self.* New York: International Universities Press.

Kohut, H. (1984). *How does analysis cure?* Chicago: University of Chicago Press.

Korchin, S. J. (1976). *Modern clinical psychology.* New York: Basic Books.

Korchin, S. J. (1980). Clinical psychology and minority problems. *American Psychologist, 35,* 262–269.

Krasner, L. (1984). Behavior therapy. In R. J. Corsini (Ed.), *Encyclopedia of psychology* (Vol. 1, pp. 137–139). New York: Wiley.

Kratochwill, R. T. (Ed.). (1978). *Single-subject research: Strategies for evaluating change.* New York: Academic Press.

Kroger, W. S., & Fezler, W. D. (1976). *Hypnosis and behavior modification: Imagery conditioning.* Philadelphia: Lippincott.

Kuhlman, T. L. (1984). *Human and psychotherapy.* Homewood, IL: Dow Jones-Irwin.

Kutz, I., Borysenko, J. Z., & Benson, H. (1985). Meditation and psychotherapy: A rational for the integration of dynamic psychotherapy, the relaxation response, and mindfulness meditation. *American Journal of Psychiatry, 142,* 1–8.

Ladouceur, R. (1983). Participant modeling with or without cognitive treatment of phobias. *Journal of Consulting and Clinical Psychology, 51,* 942–944.

Lange, A. J. & Jakubowski, P. (1976). *Responsible assertive behavior: Cognitive/ behavioral procedures for trainers.* Champaign, IL: Research Press.

Lanyon, R. I., Barrington, C. C., & Newman, A. C. (1977). Modification of stuttering through EMG biofeedback: A preliminary study. In J. Kamiya, T. X. Barber, N. E. Miller, D. Shapiro, & J. Stoyva (Eds.), *Biofeedback and self-control: 1976/77* (pp. 565–572). Chicago:Aldine.

Lazarus, A. A. (1967). In support of technical eclecticism. *Psychological Reports, 21,* 415–416.

Lazarus, A. A. (1971). *Behavior therapy and beyond.* New York: McGraw-Hill.

Lazarus, A. A. (1976). *Multimodal behavior therapy.* New York: Springer.

Lazarus, A. A. (1977). *In the mind's eye.* New York: Rawson.

Lazarus, A. A. (1981). *The practice of multimodal therapy.* New York: McGraw-Hill.

Lazarus, A. A. (Ed.). (1985). *Casebook of multimodal therapy.* New York: Guilford Press.

Lazarus, A. A. (1986). Multimodal therapy. In J. C. Norcross (Ed.), *Handbook of eclectic psychotherapy* (pp. 65–93). New York: Brunner/Mazel.

Lazarus, A. A., & Serber, M. (1968). Is systematic desensitization being misapplied? *Psychological Reports, 23,* 215–218.

Lazarus, R. S., & Folkman, S. (1984). *Stress, appraisal, and coping.* New York: Springer.

Leahey, T. H. (1980). *A history of psychology.* Englewood Cliffs, NJ: Prentice-Hall.

Ledwidge, B. (1979). Cognitive behavior modification or new ways to change minds: Reply to Mahoney and Kazdin. *Psychological Bulletin, 86,* 1050–1053.

Lee, C. (1983). Self-efficacy and behaviour as predictors of subsequent behaviour in an assertiveness training programme. *Behaviour Research and Therapy, 21,* 225–232.

Lefcourt, H. M. (1976). *Locus of control: Current trends in theory and research.* Hillsdale, NJ:Erlbaum.

Lefcourt, H. M. (1981). *Research with the locus of control construct.* New York: Academic Press.

Lester, D., Beck, A. T., & Mitchell, B. (1979). Extrapolation from attempted suicides to completed suicides: A test. *Journal of Abnormal Psychology, 88,* 78–80.

Levant, R. F. (1984). *Family therapy: A comprehensive overview.* Englewood Cliffs, NJ: Prentice-Hall.

Levenson, H. (1973a). Multidimensional locus of control in psychiatric patients. *Journal of Consulting and Clinical Psychology, 41,* 397–404.

Levenson, H. (1973b). Perceived parental antecedents of internal, powerful others and chance locus of control orientations. *Developmental Psychology, 9,* 781–786.

Levenson, H. (1974). Activism and powerful others: Distinctions within the concept of internal-external control. *Journal of Personality Assessment, 38,* 377–383.

Levis, D. J. (1982). Experimental and theoretical foundations of behavior modification. In A. S. Bellack, M. Hersen, & A. E. Kazdin (Eds.), *International handbook of behavior modification and therapy* (pp. 33–56). New York: Plenum.

Levi-Strauss, C. (1963). *Structural anthropology.* New York: Basic Books.

Levitsky, A., & Perls, F. S. (1970). The rules and games of Gestalt therapy. In J. Fagan & R. Rondall (Eds.), *Gestalt therapy now* (pp. 140–149). Palo Alto, CA: Science and Behavior Books.

Levy, L. H. (1984). The metamorphosis of clinical psychology. *American Psychologist, 39,* 486–494.

Lewin, K. (1935). *A dynamic theory of personality.* New York: McGraw-Hill.

Lewin, K. (1936). *Principles of topological and vectoral psychology.* New York: McGraw-Hill.

Lewis, W. (1972). *Why people change: The psychology of influence.* New York: Holt, Rinehart & Winston.

Linden, G. W. (1984). Some philosophical roots of Adlerian psychology. *Journal of Individual Psychology, 40,* 254–269.

LoPiccolo, J., & LoPiccolo, L. (Eds.). (1978). *Handbook of sex therapy.* New York: Plenum.

Lowie, R. (1937). History of ethnological theory. New York: Farrer & Rinehart.

Lowry, R. J. (1982). *The evolution of psychological theory* (2nd ed.). New York: Aldine de Gruyter.

Luborsky, L., & Spence, D. P. (1978). Quantitative research on psychoanalytic therapy. In S. L. Garfield & A. E. Bergin (Eds.), *Handbook of psychotherapy and behavior change* (2nd ed.) (pp. 331–368). New York: Wiley.

Lukas, E. (1979). The "ideal" logotherapist: Three contradictions. *International Forum for Logotherapy, 2,* 3–7.

Lundin, R. W. (1985). *Theories and systems of psychology* (3rd ed.). Lexington, MA: Heath.

Luria, A. (1961). *The role of speech in the regulation of normal and abnormal behavior.* New York: Liveright.

Madanes, C. (1981). *Strategic family therapy.* San Francisco: Jossey-Bass.

Mahler, A. (1969). *Gustav Mahler: Memories and letters* (Donald Mitchell, Ed.). New York: Viking Press.

Mahoney, M. J. (1974). *Cognition and behavior modification.* Cambridge, MA: Ballinger.

Mahoney, M. J. (1977). Reflections on the cognitive-learning trend in psychotherapy. *American Psychologist, 32,* 5–12.

Mahoney, M. J., & Arnkoff, D. (1978). Cognitive and self-control therapies. In S. L. Garfield & A. E. Bergin (Eds.), *Handbook of psychotherapy and behavior change* (2nd ed.) (pp. 689–722). New York: Wiley.

Mahoney, M. J., & Kazdin, A. E. (1979). Cognitive behavior modification: Misconceptions and premature evacuations. *Psychological Bulletin, 86,* 1044–1049.

Malan, D. H. (1963). *A study of brief psychotherapy.* New York: Plenum.

Mandler, G. (1975). *Mind and emotion.* New York: Wiley.

Marmor, J. (1972). Holistic conception, and points of mild issue. *Journal of Individual Psychology, 28,* 153–154.

Marmor, J. (1979). Short-term dynamic psychotherapy. *American Journal of Psychiatry, 136,* 149–155.

Marzillier, J., & Eastman, C. (1984). Continuing problems with self-efficacy theory: A reply to Bandura. *Cognitive Therapy and Research, 8,* 257–262.

Maslow, A. H. (1965). *Eupsychian management.* Homewood, IL: Irwin-Dorsey.

Maslow, A. H. (1968). *Toward a psychology of being* (2nd ed.). New York: Van Nostrand Reinhold.

Maslow, A. H. (1970a). *Motivation and personality* (rev. ed.). New York: Harper & Row.

Maslow, A. H. (1970b). Tribute to Alfred Adler. *Journal of Individual Psychology, 26,* 13.

Maslow, A. H., & Honigmann, J. (Eds.). (1970). Synergy: Some notes of Ruth Benedict. *American Anthropologist, 72,* 320–333.

Matson, F. K. (Ed.). (1973). *Without/within: Behaviorism and humanism.* Pacific Grove, CA: Brooks/Cole.

May, R. (1977). *The meaning of anxiety* (rev. ed.) New York: Norton.

McMullin, R. E. (1986). *Handbook of cognitive therapy techniques.* New York: Norton.

Meador, B. D., & Rogers, C. R. (1984). Person-centered therapy. In R. J. Corsini (Ed.), *Current psychotherapies* (3rd ed.) (pp. 142–195). Itasca, IL: F. E. Peacock.

Meeker, W. B., & Barber, T. X. (1971). Toward an explanation of stage hypnosis. *Journal of Abnormal Psychology, 77,* 61–70.

Meichenbaum, D. (1974). *Cognitive behavior modification.* Morristown, NJ: General Learning Press.

Meichenbaum, D. (1975). A self-instructional approach to stress management: A proposal for stress inoculation training. In I. G. Sarason and C. D. Spielberger (Eds.), *Stress and anxiety.* (Vol. 2., pp. 227–263). New York: Wiley.

Meichenbaum, D. (1977). *Cognitive-behavior modification: An integrative approach.* New York: Plenum.

Meichenbaum, D. (1985a). Cognitive-behavioral therapies. In S. J. Lynn & J. P. Garske (Eds.) (pp. 261–286). Columbus, OH: Merrill.

Meichenbaum, D. (1985b). *Stress inoculation training.* New York: Pergamon Press.

Meichenbaum, D., & Cameron, R. (1973). Training schizophrenics to talk to themselves: A means of developing attentional controls. *Behavior Therapy, 4,* 515–534.

Meichenbaum, D., & Cameron, R. (1982). Cognitive-behavior therapy. In G. T. Wilson & C. M. Franks (Eds.), *Cognitive behavior therapy: Conceptual and empirical foundations* (pp. 310–338). New York: Guilford Press.

Meichenbaum, D., & Jaremko, M. (1983). *Stress prevention and reduction.* New York: Plenum.

Meichenbaum, D., & Novaco, R. (1978). Stress inoculation: A preventative approach. In C. D. Spielberger & I. G. Sarason (Eds.), *Stress and anxiety* (Vol. 5, pp. 3127–3129). New York: Wiley.

Meichenbaum, D., Turk, D., & Burnstein, S. (1975). The nature of coping and stress. In I. G. Sarason & C. D. Spielberger (Eds.), *Stress and anxiety* (Vol. 2, pp. 337–360). New York: Wiley.

Messer, S. B. (1986). Behavioral and psychoanalytic perspectives at therapeutic choice points. *American Psychologist, 41,* 1261–1271.

Meyer, R. (1983). *The clinician's handbook: The psychopathology of adulthood and late adolescence.* Boston: Allyn & Bacon.

Meyer, V., Liddell, A., & Lyons, M. (1977). Behavioral interviews. In A. R. Ciminero, K. S. Calhoun, & H. E. Adams (Eds.), *Handbook of behavioral assessment* (pp. 117–152). New York: Wiley.

Miller, N. E., & Dollard, J. (1941). *Social learning and imitation.* New Haven, CT: Yale University Press.

Miller, R. C., & Berman, J. S. (1983). The efficacy of cognitive behavior therapies: A quantitative review of the research evidence. *Psychological Bulletin, 94,* 39–53.

Minuchin, S. (1974). *Families and family therapy.* Cambridge, MA: Harvard University Press.

Minuchin, S. (1981). Constructing a therapeutic reality. In G. Gerenson & H. White (Eds.), *Annual review of family therapy* (Vol. 1, pp. 129–147). New York: Human Services Press.

Minuchin, S. (1984). *Family kaleidoscope.* Cambridge: Harvard University Press.

Minuchin, S., & Fishman, H. C. (1981). *Family therapy techniques.* Cambridge: Harvard University Press.

Minuchin, S., Montalvo, B., Guerney, B., Rosman, B., & Schumer, F. (1967). *Families of the slums.* New York: Basic Books.

Mischel, W. (1973). Toward a cognitive social learning reconceptualization of personality. *Psychological Review, 80,* 252–283.

Mischel, W. (1977). On the future of personality measurement. *American Psychologist, 32,* 246–254.

Mischel, W. (1979). On the interface of cognition and personality: Beyond the person-situation debate. *American Psychologist, 34,* 740–754.

Mosak, H. H. (1972). Lifestyle. In A. G. Nikelly (Ed.), *Techniques for behavior change* (pp. 77–81). Springfield, IL: Charles C. Thomas.

Mosak, H. H., & Kopp, R. R. (1973). The early recollections of Adler, Freud, and Jung. *Journal of Individual Psychology, 29,* 157–166.

Mosher, D. L. (1968). The influence of Adler on Rotter's social learning theory of personality. *Journal of Individual Psychology, 24,* 33–45.

Murphy, G., & Kovach, J. K. (1972). *Historical introduction to modern psychology* (3rd ed.). New York: Harcourt Brace Jovanovich.

Murray, E. J., & Jacobson, L. I. (1978). Cognition and learning in traditional and behavioral therapy. In S. L. Garfield & A. E. Bergin (Eds.), *Handbook of psychotherapy and behavior change* (2nd ed.) (pp. 661–687). New York: Wiley.

Napier, A. Y., & Whitaker, C. A. (1978). *The family crucible.* New York: Harper & Row.

Naranjo, C. (1970). Present-centeredness: Technique, prescription, and ideal. In J. Fagan & R. Rondall (Eds.), *Gestalt therapy now* (pp. 47–69). Palo Alto, CA: Science and Behavior Books.

Neisser, U. (1976). *Cognition and reality.* San Francisco, CA: W. H. Freeman.

Neisser, U. (Ed.). (1982). *Memory observed: Remembering in natural contexts.* San Francisco, CA: W. H. Freeman.

Nemiah, J. C. (1984). Psychoanalysis and individual psychotherapy. In T. B. Karasu (Ed.), *The psychiatric therapies* (pp. 321–346). Washington, DC: American Psychiatric Association.

Nikelly, A.G. (Ed.). (1971). *Techniques for behavior change.* Springfield, IL: Charles C. Thomas.

Nikelly, A.G., & Dinkmeyer, D. (1972). The process of encouragement. In A. G. Nikelly (Ed.), *Techniques for behavior change* (pp. 97–101). Springfield, IL: Charles C. Thomas.

Nikelly, A. G., & O'Connell, W. E. (1972). Action-oriented methods. In A. G. Nikelly (Ed.), *Techniques for behavior change* (pp. 85–90). Springfield, IL: Charles C. Thomas.

Nikelly, A. G., & Verger, D. (1972). Early recollections. In A. G. Nikelly (Ed.), *Techniques for behavior change* (pp. 55–60). Springfield, IL: Charles C. Thomas.

Novaco, R. W. (1976). Treatment of chronic anger through cognitive and relaxation controls. *Journal of Consulting and Clinical Psychology, 44,* 681.

Novaco, R. W. (1977). Stress inoculation: A cognitive therapy for anger and its application to a case of depression. *Journal of Consulting and Clinical Psychology, 45,* 600–608.

Novaco, R. W. (1978). Anger and coping with stress. In J. P. Foreyt & D. P. Rathjen (Eds.), *Cognitive behavior therapy: Research and application* (pp. 135–173). New York: Plenum.

Novaco, R. W. (1983). *Stress inoculation therapy for anger control: A manual for therapists.* (Available from Raymond W. Novaco, University of California, Irvine)

Novaco, R. W. (1985). *Anger, stress, and coping with provocation: An instructional manual.* (Available from Raymond W. Novaco, University of California, Irvine)

Novaco, R. W., Cook, T., & Sarason, I. (1983). Military recruit training: An arena for stress coping skills. In D. Meichenbaum & M. Jaremko (Eds.), *Stress reduction and prevention* (pp. 377–418). New York: Plenum.

O'Leary, K. D. (1984). The image of behavior therapy: It is time to take a stand. *Behavior Therapy, 15,* 219–233.

Orgler, H. (1972). *Alfred Adler: The man and his works.* New York: Mentor. (Original work published 1963)

Orne, M. T. (1966). Hypnosis, motivation and compliance. *American Journal of Psychiatry, 122,* 721–726.

Orne, M. T. (1971). The simulation of hypnosis: Why, how and what it means. *International Journal of Clinical and Experimental Hypnosis, 19,* 183–210.

Orne, M. T. (1972). Can a hypnotized subject be compelled to carry out otherwise unacceptable behavior? *International Journal of Clinical and Experimental Hypnosis, 20,* 101–117.

Papp, P. (Ed.). (1977). *Family therapy: Full-length case studies.* New York: Gardner Press.

Parloff, M. B., Waskow, I. E., &Wolfe, B. E. (1978). Research on therapist variables in relation to process and outcome. In S. L. Garfield & A. E. Bergin (Eds.), *Handbook of psychotherapy and behavior change* (2nd ed.) (pp. 246–282). New York: Wiley.

Passons, W. R. (1975). *Gestalt approaches to counseling.* New York: Holt, Rinehart & Winston.

Patterson, C. H. (1980). *Theories of counseling and psychotherapy.* New York: Harper & Row.

Patterson, G. R. (1982). *Coercive family process.* Eugene, OR: Castalia.

Patterson, G. R., Reid, J. B., Jones, R. R., & Conger, R. E. (1975). *A social learning approach to family intervention: Vol. 1. Families with aggressive children.* Eugene, OR: Castalia.

Pattie, F. A. (1967). A brief history of hypnosis. In J. E. Gordon (Ed.), *Handbook of clinical and experimental hypnosis* (pp. 10–43). New York: Macmillan.

Patton, M. J., Connor, G. E., & Scott, K. J. (1982). Kohut's psychology of the self: Theory and measure of counseling outcomes. *Journal of Counseling Psychology, 29,* 268–282.

Pavlov, I. P. (1928). *Lectures on conditioned reflexes* (W. H. Gantt, Trans.). New York: International Publishers.

Penfield, W. (1952). Memory mechanisms. *AMA Archives of Neurology and Psychiatry, 67,* 178–198.

Pentony, P. (1981). *Models of influence in psychotherapy.* New York: Free Press.

Pentz, M. A., & Kazdin, A. E. (1982). Assertive modeling and stimuli effects on assertive behavior and self-efficacy in adolescents. *Behaviour Research and Therapy, 20,* 365–371.

Perlin, M., & Grater, H. (1984). The relationship between birth order and reported interpersonal behavior. *Journal of Individual Psychology, 40,* 22–28.

Perls, F. S. (1969a). *Ego, hunger, and aggression.* New York: Vintage. (Original published 1947)

Perls, F. S. (1969b). *Gestalt therapy verbatim.* Lafayette, CA: Real People Press.

Perls, F. S. (1969c). *In and out of the garbage pail.* Lafayette, CA: Real People Press.

Perls, F. S. (1970). Four lectures. In J. Fagan & I. L. Shepherd (Eds.), *Gestalt therapy now* (pp. 14–34). Palo Alto, CA: Science and Behavior Books.

Perls, F. S. (1973). *The Gestalt approach* and *Eyewitness to therapy.* Palo Alto, CA: Science and Behavior Books.

Perry, N. (1979). Why psychology does not need alternative training models. *American Psychologist, 34,* 603–611.

Peyser, C. S. (1984). Berne, Eric L. In R. J. Corsini (Ed.), *Encyclopedia of psychology* (Vol. 1, p. 145). New York: Wiley.

Phares, E. J. (1976). *Locus of control in personality.* Morristown, NJ: General Learning Press.

Phares, E. J. (1979). *Clinical psychology: Concepts, methods, and profession.* Homewood, IL: Dorsey Press.

Phares, E. J. (1984). Social learning theory. In R. J. Corsini (Ed.), *Encyclopedia of psychology* (Vol. 3, pp. 339–341). New York: Wiley.

Polkinghorne, D. (1983). *Methodology for the human sciences: Systems of inquiry.* Albany: State University of New York.

Rappaport, J. (1977). *Community psychology: Values, research, and action.* New York: Holt, Rinehart & Winston.

Raskin, N. J. (1984). Client-centered therapy. In R. J. Corsini (Ed.), *Encyclopedia of psychology* (Vol. 1, pp. 219–221). New York: Wiley.

Raskin, N. J. (1985). Client-centered therapy. In S. J. Lynn & J. P. Gaske (Eds.), *Contemporary psychotherapies: Models and methods* (pp. 155–190). Columbus, OH: Merrill.

Reid, J. B. (Ed.). (1978). *A social learning approach to family intervention: Observation in home settings.* Eugene, OR: Castalia.

Richard, J. T. (1978). Multimodal therapy: An integrating model for behavioral medicine. *Psychological Reports, 42,* 635–639.

Rimm, D. C., & Lefebvre, R. C. (1981). Phobic disorders. In S. M. Turner, K. S. Calhoun, & H. E. Adams (Eds.), *Handbook of clinical behavior therapy* (pp. 12–40). New York: Wiley.

Rimm, D. C., & Masters, J. C. (1979). *Behavior therapy: Techniques and empirical findings* (2nd ed.). New York: Academic Press.

Robinson, D. N. (1981). *An intellectual history of psychology* (rev. ed.). New York: Macmillan.

Rogers, C. R. (1942). *Counseling and psychotherapy: Newer concepts in practice.* Boston: Houghton Mifflin.

Rogers, C. R. (1951). *Client-centered therapy.* Boston: Houghton Mifflin.

Rogers, C. R. (1957). The necessary and sufficient conditions of therapeutic change. *Journal of Consulting Psychology, 21,* 95–103.

Rogers, C. R. (1959). A theory of therapy, personality, and interpersonal relationships, as developed in the client-centered framework. In S. Koch (Ed.), *Psychology: A study of science* (Vol. 3, pp. 183–256). New York: McGraw-Hill.

Rogers, C. R. (1961). *On becoming a person.* Boston: Houghton Mifflin.

Rogers, C. R. (1975a). Empathic: An unappreciated way of being. *The Counseling Psychologist, 5,* 2–10.

Rogers, C. R. (1975b). In retrospect: Forty-six years. In R. I. Evans (Ed.), *Carl Rogers: The man and his ideas* (pp. 121–146). New York: Dutton.

Rogers, C. R. (1977). *Carl Rogers on personal power.* New York: Delacorte Press.

Rogers, C. R. (1980a). Client-centered psychotherapy. In A. M. Freeman, H. I. Kaplan, & B. J. Sadock (Eds.), *Comprehensive textbook of psychiatry* (3rd ed.) (Vol. 2, pp. 2153–2167). Baltimore: Williams & Wilkins.

Rogers, C. R. (1980b). *A way of being.* Boston: Houghton Mifflin.

Rogers, C. R., & Dymond, R. F. (Eds.). (1954). *Psychotherapy and personality change: Coordinated studies in the client-centered approach.* Chicago: University of Chicago Press.

Rogers, C. R., & Skinner, B. F. (1956). Some issues concerning the control of human behavior. *Science, 124,* 1057–1066.

Rosenberg, J. B. (1983). Structural family therapy. In B. B. Wolman & G. Stricker (Eds.), *Handbook of family and marital therapy* (pp. 159–185). New York: Plenum.

Rosenfeld, E. (1978). An oral history of Gestalt therapy: 1. A conversation with Laura Perls. *Gestalt Journal, 1,* 8–31.

Rosenthal, T. L. (1982). Social learning theory. In G. T. Wilson & C. M. Franks (Eds.), *Contemporary behavior therapy: Conceptual and empirical foundations* (pp. 339–363). New York: Guilford Press.

Rosenthal, T. L., & Bandura, A. (1978). Psychological modeling: Theory and practice. In S. L. Garfield & A. E. Bergin (Eds.), *Handbook of psychotherapy and behavior change: An empirical analysis* (2nd ed.) (pp. 621–658). New York: Wiley.

Rosenthal, T. L., & Reese, S. L. (1976). The effects of covert and overt modeling on assertive behavior. *Behaviour Research and Therapy, 14,* 463–469.

Rotter, J. B. (1954). *Social learning and clinical psychology.* Englewood Cliffs, NJ: Prentice-Hall.

Rotter, J. B. (1966). Generalized expectancies for internal versus external control of reinforcement. *Psychological Monographs, 80,* 1–28.

Rotter, J. B. (1970). Some implications of a social learning theory for the practice of psychotherapy. In D. J. Levis (Ed.), *Learning approaches to therapeutic behavior change* (pp. 208–241). Chicago: Aldine.

Rotter, J. B. (1978). Generalized expectancies for problem solving and psychotherapy. *Cognitive Therapy and Research, 2,* 1–9.

Rotter, J. B. (1980a). Interpersonal trust, trustworthiness, and gullibility. *American Psychologist, 35,* 1–7.

Rotter, J. B. (1980b). Some views on effective principles of psychotherapy. *Cognitive Therapy and Research, 4,* 271–306.

Rotter, J. B. (1982a). *The development and application of social learning theory: Selected papers.* New York: Praeger.

Rotter, J. B. (1982b). Social learning theory. In N. T. Feathers (Ed.), *Expectations and actions: Expectancy-value models in psychology* (pp. 241–260). Hillsdale, NJ: Erlbaum.

Rotter, J. B., Chance, J. E., & Phares, E. J. (1972). *Applications of a social learning theory of personality.* New York: Holt, Rinehart & Winston.

Rychlak, J. F. (1981). *Introduction to personality and psychotherapy* (2nd ed.). Boston: Houghton Mifflin.

Ryckman, R. M. (1985). *Theories of personality* (3rd ed.). Pacific Grove, CA: Brooks/Cole.

Sahakian, W. S., & Lundin, R. W. (1984a). Ellis, Albert. In R. J. Corsini (Ed.), *Encyclopedia of psychology* (Vol. 1, p. 426). New York: Wiley.

Sahakian, W. S., & Lundin, R. W. (1984b). Rotter, Julian B. In R. J. Corsini (Ed.), *Encyclopedia of psychology* (Vol. 3, p. 254). New York: Wiley.

Sahakian, W. S., & Lundin, R. W. (1984c). Strupp, Hans H. In R. J. Corsini (Ed.), *Encyclopedia of psychology* (Vol. 3, p. 379). New York: Wiley.

Salter, A. (1949). *Conditioned reflex therapy.* New York: Creative Age Press.

Salter, A. (1952). *The case against psychoanalysis.* New York: Henry Holt.

Samelson, F. (1980). J. B. Watson's Little Albert, Cyril Burt's twins, and the need for a critical science. *American Psychologist, 35,* 619–625.

Samelson, F. (1981). Struggle for scientific authority: The reception of Watson's behaviorism, 1913–1920. *Journal of the History of the Behavioral Sciences, 17,* 399–425.

Samuels, A. (1985). *Jung and the post-Jungians.* London: Routledge & Kegan Paul.

Schwartz, B. (1978). *Psychology of learning and behavior.* New York: Norton.

Schwartz, G. E. (1977a). Biofeedback and the self-management of disregulation disorders. In R. B. Stuart (Ed.), *Behavioral self-management: Strategies, techniques and outcomes* (pp. 49–70). New York: Brunner/Mazel.

Schwartz, G. E. (1977b). Psychosomatic disorders and biofeedback: A psychobiological model of disregulation. In J. D. Maser & M. E. P. Seligman (Eds.), *Psychopathology: Experimental models.* San Francisco: W. H. Freeman.

Schwartz, G. E. (1978). Psychobiological foundations of psychotherapy and behavior change. In S. L. Garfield & A. E. Bergin (Eds.), *Handbook of psychotherapy and behavior change* (2nd ed.) (pp. 63–99). New York: Wiley.

Seltzer, L. F. (1986). *Paradoxical strategies in psychotherapy: A comprehensive overview and guidebook.* New York: Wiley.

Selye, H. (1978). *Stress of life.* New York: McGraw-Hill. (Original work published 1956)

Shakow, D. (1976). What is clinical psychology? *American Psychologist, 31,* 553–560.

Shapiro, D. H. (1984). Self-control. In R. J. Corsini (Ed.), *Encyclopedia of psychology* (Vol. 3, pp. 285–288). New York: Wiley.

Shilling, L. E. (1984). *Perspectives on counseling theories.* Englewood Cliffs, NJ: Prentice-Hall.

Shostrom, E. L. (1964). A test for the measurement of self-actualization. *Educational and Psychological Measurement, 24,* 207–218.

Shostrom, E. L. (1974). *Personal orientation dimensions.* San Diego: Educational and Industrial Testing Service.

Shostrom, E. L. (1976). *Actualizing therapy: Foundations of a scientific ethic.* San Diego: EdITS Publishers.

Shulman, B. H., & Mosak, H. M. (1977). Birth order and ordinal position: Two Adlerian views. *Journal of Individual Psychology, 33,* 114–121.

Shulman, B. H., & Nikelly, A.G. (1972). Family constellation. In A. G. Nikelly (Ed.), *Techniques for behavior change* (pp. 35–40). Springfield, IL: Charles C. Thomas.

Sifneos, P. (1979). *Short-term dynamic psychotherapy: Evaluation and technique.* New York: Plenum.

Simkin, J. S., & Yontef, G. M. (1984). Gestalt therapy. In R. J. Corsini (Ed.), *Current psychotherapies* (pp. 279–319). Itasca, IL: F. E. Peacock.

Sirkin, M., & Fleming, M. (1982). Freud's "Project" and its relationship to psychoanalytic theory. *Journal of the History of the Behavioral Sciences, 18,* 230–241.

Skinner, B. F. (1953). *Science and human behavior.* New York: Macmillan.

Skinner, B. F. (1972). *Cumulative record: A selection of papers* (3rd ed.). New York: Appleton-Century-Crofts.

Skinner, B. F. (1978). *Reflections on behaviorism and society.* Englewood Cliffs, NJ: Prentice-Hall.

Skinner, B. F. (1987). Whatever happened to psychology as a science of behavior? *American Psychologist, 42,* 780–786.

Skynner, A. C. R. (1981). An open-systems, group-analytic approach to family therapy. In A. S. Gurman & D. P. Kniskern (Eds.), *Handbook of family therapy* (pp. 39–84). New York: Brunner/Mazel.

Smith, D. (1982). Trends in counseling and psychotherapy. *American Psychologist, 37,* 802–809.

Smith, M. B. (1984). Humanistic psychology. In R. J. Corsini (Ed.), *Encyclopedia of psychology* (Vol. 2, pp. 155–159). New York: Wiley.

Spanos, N., & Gottlieb, J. (1979). Demonic possession, mesmerism, and hysteria: A social psychological perspective on their historical interrelatedness. *Journal of Abnormal Psychology, 88,* 527–546.

Spivak, G., & Spure, M. D. (1974). *Social adjustment of young children.* San Francisco: Jossey-Bass.

Spivak, G., Platt, J. J., & Shure, M. D. (1976). *The problem-solving approach to adjustment.* San Francisco: Jossey-Bass.

Sprafkin, R. P. (1984). Social skills training. In R. J. Corsini (Ed.), *Encyclopedia of psychology* (Vol. 3, pp. 343–345). New York: Wiley.

Stampfl, T. G. (1970). Implosive therapy: An emphasis on covert stimulation. In D. J. Levis (Ed.), *Learning approaches to therapeutic behavior change* (pp. 182–204). Chicago: Aldine.

Stampfl, T. G., & Levis, D. J. (1967). Essentials of implosive therapy: A learning-theory-based psychodynamic behavioral therapy. *Journal of Abnormal Psychology, 72,* 496–503.

Strephansky, P. E. (1983). Perspectives on dissent: Adler, Kohut, and the idea of a psychoanalytic research tradition. *Annals of Psychoanalysis, 11,* 51–74.

Strong, S. R. (1978). Social psychological approaches to psychotherapy research. In S.

L. Garfield & A. E. Bergin (Eds.), *Handbook of psychotherapy and behavior change* (2nd ed.) (pp. 101–135). New York: Wiley.

Strong, S. R., & Claiborn, C. D. (1982). *Change through interaction.* New York: Wiley.

Strupp, H. H. (1971). *Psychotherapy and the modification of abnormal behavior.* New York: McGraw-Hill.

Strupp, H. H. (1973). On the basic ingredients in psychotherapy. *Journal of Consulting and Clinical Psychology, 41,* 1–8.

Strupp, H. H. (1976). Clinical psychology, irrationalism, and the erosion of excellence. *American Psychologist, 31,* 561–571.

Strupp, H. H. (1978). Psychotherapy research and practice: An overview. In S. L. Garfield & A. E. Bergin (Eds.), *Handbook of psychotherapy and behavior change* (2nd ed.) (pp. 3–22). New York: Wiley.

Strupp, H. H. (1980a). Success and failure in time-limited psychotherapy: A systematic comparison of two cases (Comparison 1). *Archives of General Psychiatry, 37,* 595–603.

Strupp, H. H. (1980b). Success and failure in time-limited psychotherapy: A systematic comparison of two cases (Comparison 2). *Archives of General Psychiatry, 37,* 708–716.

Strupp, H. H. (1980c). Success and failure in time-limited psychotherapy: With special reference to the performance of a lay counselor (Comparison 3). *Archives of General Psychiatry, 37,* 831–841.

Strupp, H. H. (1981). Toward the refinement of time-limited dynamic psychotherapy. In S. H. Budman (Ed.), *Forms of brief therapy* (pp. 218–242). New York: Guilford Press.

Strupp, H. H. (1982). Psychotherapy and (or versus?) researchers. In M. R. Goldfried (Ed.), *Converging themes in psychotherapy* (pp. 329–333). New York: Springer.

Strupp, H. H., & Binder, J. L. (1984). *Psychotherapy in a new key: A guide to time-limited dynamic psychotherapy.* New York: Basic Books.

Strupp, H. H., & Hadley, S. W. (1979). Specific versus nonspecific factors in psychotherapy: A controlled study of outcomes. *Archives of General Psychiatry, 36,* 1125–1136.

Suinn, R. M., & Richardson, F. (1971). Anxiety management training: A nonspecific behavior therapy program for anxiety control. *Behavior Therapy, 2,* 498–510.

Sulloway, F. J. (1979). *Freud: Biologist of the mind.* New York: Basic Books.

Sundberg, N. D., Tyler, L. E., & Taplin, J. R. (1973). *Clinical psychology: Expanding horizons* (2nd ed.). Englewood Cliffs, NJ: Prentice-Hall.

Taylor, I. (1975). A retrospective view of creativity investigations. In I. Taylor & J. Getzels, *Perspectives in creativity.* Hawthorne, NY: Aldine.

Taylor, W., & Barron, F. (Eds.). (1963). *Scientific creativity: Its recognition and development.* New York: Wiley.

Telch, M. J., Bandura, A., Vinciguerra, P., Agras, A., & Stout, A. L. (1982). Social demand for consistency and congruence between self-efficacy and performance. *Behavior Therapy, 13,* 694–701.

Thoresen, C. E., & Mahoney, M. J. (1974). *Behavioral self-control.* New York: Holt, Rinehart & Winston.

Thorndike, E. L. (1911). *Animal intelligence.* New York: Macmillan.

Tolman, E. C. (1949). *Purposive behavior in animals and men.* Berkeley: University of California Press.

Truax, C. B., & Carkhuff, R. R. (1967). *Toward effective counseling and psychotherapy: Training and practice.* Chicago: Aldine.

Tryon, W. W. (1981a). A methodological critique of Bandura's self-efficacy theory of behavior change. *Journal of Behavior Therapy and Experimental Psychiatry, 12,* 113–114.

Tryon, W. W. (1981b). The practice of clinical behaviorism: An overview. *Journal of Behavior Therapy and Experimental Psychiatry, 12,* 197–202.

Turk, D. C., & Salovey, P. (1985a). Cognitive structures, cognitive processes, and cognitive-behavior modification: I. Client issues. *Cognitive Therapy and Research, 9,* 1–17.

Turk, D. C., & Salovey, P. (1985b). Cognitive structures, cognitive processes, and cognitive-behavior modification: II. Judgments and inferences of the clinician. *Cognitive Therapy and Research, 9,* 19–33.

Turner, R. M., & Ascher, L. M. (1979). Controlled comparison of progressive relaxation, stimulus control, and paradoxical intention therapies for insomnia. *Journal of Consulting and Clinical Psychology, 47,* 500–508.

Turner, R. M., & Ascher, L. M. (1982). Therapist factors in the treatment of insomnia. *Behaviour Research and Therapy, 20,* 33–40.

Turner, S. M., Calhoun, K. S., & Adams, H. E. (Eds.). (1981). *Handbook of clinical behavior therapy.* New York: Wiley.

Ullmann, L. P. (1981). Cognitions: Help or hindrance? *Journal of Behavior Therapy and Experimental Psychiatry, 12,* 19–23.

Ullmann, L. P., & Krasner, L. (1969). *A psychological approach to abnormal behavior.* Englewood Cliffs, NJ: Prentice-Hall.

Ulrich, D. N. (1983). Contextual family and marital therapy. In B. B. Wolman & G. Stricker (Eds.), *Handbook of family and marital therapy* (pp. 187–211). New York: Plenum.

Upper, D., & Cautela, J. R. (Eds.). (1977). *Covert conditioning.* New York: Pergamon Press.

Vallis, M. (1984). A complete component analysis of stress inoculation for pain tolerance. *Cognitive Therapy and Research, 8,* 313–329.

Van De Riet, V., Korb, M. P., & Gorrell, J. J. (1980). *Gestalt therapy: An introduction.* New York: Pergamon Press.

Wachtel, P. L. (1977). *Psychoanalysis and behavior therapy: Toward an integration.* New York: Basic Books.

Wachtel, P. L. (Ed.). (1982a). *Resistance: Psychodynamic and behavioral approaches.* New York: Plenum.

Wachtel, P. L. (1982b). What can dynamic therapies contribute to behavior therapy? *Behavior Therapy, 13,* 594–609.

Walen, S. R., DiGiuseppe, R., & Wessler, R. L. (1980). *A practitioner's guide to rational-emotive therapy.* New York: Oxford University Press.

Wallace, A. (1961). *Culture and personality.* New York: Random House.

Wallace, R. K. (1970). Physiological effects of transcendental meditation. *Science, 167,* 1751–1754.

Watkins, C. E. (1982). A decade of research in support of Adlerian psychological theory. *Journal of Individual Psychology, 38,* 90–99.

Watson, J. B. (1970). *Behaviorism.* New York: Norton. (Original work published 1924)

Watzlawick, P., Beavin, J. H., & Jackson, D. D. (1967). *Pragmatics of human communication: A study of interactional patterns, pathologies, and paradoxes.* New York: Norton.

Wechsler, D. (1958). *The measurement and appraisal of adult intelligence* (4th ed.). Baltimore: Williams & Wilkins.

Weeks, G. R. (1985). *Promoting change through paradoxical therapy.* Homewood, IL: Dow Jones-Irwin.

Weeks, G. R., & L'Abate, L. (1982). *Paradoxical psychotherapy: Theory and practice with individuals, couples, and families.* New York: Brunner/Mazel.

Wells, R. A. (1982). *Planned short-term treatment.* New York: Free Press.

Wender, P. H. (1968). Vicious and virtuous circles: The role of deviation-amplifying feedback in the origin and perpetuation of behavior. *Psychiatry, 31,* 309–324.

Wertheimer, M. (1978). *A brief history of psychology.* New York: Holt, Rinehart & Winston.

White, L. A. (1949). *The science of culture.* New York: Farrar, Strauss & Young.

Whiteley, J. (1980). *A history of counseling psychology.* Pacific Grove, CA: Brooks/Cole.

Wilson, C. (1972). *New pathways in psychology: Maslow and the post-Freudian revolution.* New York: Taplinger.

Wilson, G. T. (1978). Cognitive behavior therapy: Paradigm shift or passing phase? In J. P. Foreyt & D. P. Rathjen (Eds.), *Cognitive behavior therapy: Research and application* (pp. 7–32). New York: Plenum.

Wilson, G. T. (1982). Psychotherapy process and procedure: The behavioral mandate. *Behavior Therapy, 13,* 291–312.

Wilson, G. T., & Franks, C. M. (Eds.). (1982). *Contemporary behavior therapy.* New York: Guilford Press.

Wolberg, L. R. (Ed.). (1980). *Handbook of short-term psychotherapy.* New York: Thieme-Stratton.

Wolman, B. (1973). *Dictionary of behavioral science.* New York: Van Nostrand Reinhold.

Wolpe, J. (1958). *Psychotherapy by reciprocal inhibition.* Stanford, CA: Stanford University Press.

Wolpe, J. (1969). *The practice of behavior therapy.* New York: Pergamon Press.

Wolpe, J. (1977). Inadequate behavior analysis: The Achilles heel of outcome research in behavior therapy. *Journal of Behavior Therapy and Experimental Psychiatry, 8,* 1–3.

Wolpe, J. (1978). Cognition and causation in human behavior and its therapy. *American Psychologist, 33,* 437–446.

Wolpe, J. (1981). The dichotomy between directly conditioned and cognitively learned anxiety. *Journal of Behavior Therapy and Experimental Psychiatry, 12,* 35–42.

Wolpe, J. (1982). *The practice of behavior therapy* (3rd ed.). New York: Pergamon Press.

Wolpe, J., & Lang, P. J. (1969). *A fear survey schedule.* San Diego: Educational and Industrial Testing Service.

Wolpe, J., & Lazarus, A. A. (1966). *Behavior therapy techniques.* London: Pergamon Press.

Woodward, W. (1982). The "discovery" of social behaviorism and social learning theory, 1870–1980. *American Psychologist, 37,* 396–410.

Woolfolk, A. E., & Woolfolk, R. L. (1979). Modifying the effect of the behavior modification label. *Behavior Therapy, 10,* 575–578.

Woolfolk, A. E., Woolfolk, R. L., & Wilson, G. T. (1977). A rose by any other name . . . : Labeling bias and attitudes toward behavior modification. *Journal of Consulting and Clinical Psychology, 45,* 184–191.

Woolfolk, R. L., & Lazarus, A.A. (1979). Between laboratory and clinic: Paving a two-way street. *Cognitive Therapy and Research, 3,* 239–244.

Woolfolk, R. L., & Richardson, F. C. (1984). Behavior therapy and the ideology of modernity. *American Psychologist, 39,* 777–786.

Worthington, E. (1978). The effects of imagery content, choice of imagery, and self-verbalization on the self-control of pain. *Cognitive Therapy and Research, 2,* 225–239.

Wynne, L. C., Ryckoff, I., Day, J., & Hirsch, S. (1958). Pseudo-mutuality in the family relations of schizophrenics. *Psychiatry, 21,* 205–220.

Yates, A. J. (1970). *Behavior therapy.* New York: Wiley.

Yates, A. J. (1975). *Theory and practice in behavior therapy.* New York: Wiley.

Zimbardo, P. G. (1975). Transforming experimental research into advocacy for social change. In M. Deutsch & H. Hornstein (Eds.), *Applying social psychology* (pp. 33–65). Hillsdale, NJ: Erlbaum.

Credits

Source Notes

This is an extension of the copyright page.

Chapter 2: 46, Figure 2–2, "Flow Chart of Psychotherapy," from *How to Do Psychotherapy and How to Evaluate It,* by John M. Gottman and Sandra R. Lieblum, copyright © 1974 by Holt, Rinehart and Winston, Inc., reprinted by permission of the publisher.

Chapter 3: 52–53, quote from E. G. Boring, *A History of Experimental Psychology,* 2nd Ed., © 1929, renewed 1957, p. 708. Reprinted by permission of Prentice-Hall Inc., Englewood Cliffs, NJ. **58–59,** quotes from *Behaviorism,* by J. B. Watson. Copyright 1970 by W. W. Norton. Reprinted by permission. **59,** quote reproduced, with permission, from the *Annual Review of Psychology,* Volume 31, © 1980 by Annual Review Inc. **61,** quotes from *Cumulative Record: A Selection of Papers,* 3rd Ed., by B. F. Skinner. Copyright 1972 by Appleton-Century-Crofts. Reprinted by permission of the author. **66,** quotes from *The Freud/Jung Letters,* by S. Freud and C. G. Jung. Copyright 1974 by Princeton University Press. Reprinted by permission. **79–80,** quote from *Personality and Psychotherapy,* by J. Dollard and N. E. Miller. Copyright 1950 by McGraw-Hill Book Company.

Chapter 4: 90, quotes from "The Many Faces of Self-Control, or Behavior Modification Changes Its Focus," by F. H. Kanfer. In R. B. Stuart (Ed.), *Behavioral Self-Management,* by R. B. Stuart. Copyright 1977 by Brunner/Mazel, New York. Reprinted by permission. **92,** quotes from *Behavior Therapy and Beyond,* by A. A. Lazarus. Copyright 1971 by McGraw-Hill Book Company. **99,** quotes from *Psychology of Learning and Behavior,* by B. Schwartz. Copyright 1978 by W. W. Norton and Company, Inc. Reprinted by permission, **101, 148,** quotes from "Applied Behavior Analysis," by D. M. Baer. In G. T. Wilson and C. M. Franks (Eds.), *Contemporary Behavior Therapy.* Copyright 1982 by the Guilford Press. **103,** Figure 4–2 from *Behavior Modification in Applied Settings,* by A. E. Kazdin. Copyright 1975 by The Dorsey Press. Reprinted by permission of Brooks/Cole Publishing Company, Pacific Grove, CA 93950. **104,** quotes from Julian B.Rotter, *The Development and Applications of Social Learning Theory: Selected Papers* (Praeger Publishers, New York, 1982), pp. 2–3, 4, 30, 49, 50–51, 243, and 325. Copyright © 1982 by Praeger Publishers. Reprinted with permission. **107,** Figure 4–4 from Albert Bandura, *Social Learning Theory,* © 1977, pp. 8–10. Reprinted by permission of Prentice-Hall, Inc.,

Englewood Cliffs, NJ. **109, 159,** Figure 4–4 and Table 5–2 from "Cognitive and Self-Control Therapies," by M. J. Mahoney and D. Arnkoff. In S. L. Garfield and A. E. Bergin, *Handbook of Psychotherapy and Behavior Change,* 2nd Ed. Copyright 1978 by John Wiley & Sons. **113,** Figure 4–5 adapted from *Behavioral Analysis Forms for Clinical Intervention,* by J. R. Cautela. Copyright 1977 by Research Press Company. Reprinted by permission. **114,** Figure 4–6 reprinted with permission from "The Behavior Inventory Battery: The Use of Self-Report Measures in Behavioral Analysis in Therapy," by J. R. Cautela and D. Upper. In M. Herson and A. S. Bellak, *Behavioral Assessment: A Practical Handbook.* Copyright 1976 by Pergamon Books Ltd. **122,** quote from *You Must Relax,* by E. Jacobson. Copyright 1962 by McGraw-Hill Book Company. **123,** Figure 4–8 from "Psychosomatic Disorders and Biofeedback: Psychobiological Model of Disregulation," by G. E. Schwartz. In J. D. Maser and M. E. P. Seligman (Eds.), *Psychopathology: Experimental Models.* Copyright 1977 by W. H. Freeman and Company.

Chapter 5: **137,** Figures 5–1 and 5–2 reprinted with permission from J. Wolpe, *The Practice of Behavior Therapy.* Copyright 1982 by Pergamon Books Ltd. **139,** Figure 5–2, the Gambrill & Richey Assertion Inventory, from "An Assertion Inventory for Use in Assessment and Research," by E. D. Gambrill and C. A. Richey, *Behavior Therapy,* 1975, 6, 550–561. *Copyright 1975 by the Association for the Advancement of Behavior Therapy.* Figure 5–2, the Willoughby Personality Schedule, from *The Practice ofBehavior Therapy,* by J. Wolpe. Copyright 1982 by Pergamon Books Ltd. **142–143,** hierarchy list from "Behavioral Treatment of Victims of Sexual Assault," by J. V. Becker and G. G. Abel. In S. M. Turner, K. S. Calhoun, and H. E. Adams (Eds.), *Handbook of Clinical Behavior Therapy.* Copyright 1981 by John Wiley & Sons. **153,** Figure 5–3 from "Self-Efficacy: Toward a Unified Theory of Behavioral Change," by A. Bandura, *Psychological Review,* 1977, *84,* 191–215. Copyright 1977 by the American Psychological Association. Reprinted by permission. **160,** list of cognitive distortions from *Feeling Good: The New Mood Therapy,* by D. D. Burns. Copyright 1980 by William Morrow.

Chapter 6: **183, 185, 190,** scattered quotes from *The Interpretation of Dreams,* by S. Freud (J. Strachey, Editor and Translator). Copyright 1972 by Avon Books.

Chapter 7: **218,** quote from *Psychotherapy in a New Key: A Guide to Time-Limited Dynamic Psychotherapy,* by H. H. Strupp and J. L. Binder. Copyright 1984 Basic Books. **223, 237, and 239,** Figures 7–1, 7–2, and 7–3 adapted from *Transactional Analysis in Psychotherapy,* by E. Berne. Copyright 1961 by Grove Press. Reprinted by permission of Random House, Inc. **240,** Figure 7–4 from "Transactional Analysis," by J. M. Dusay and K. M. Dusay. In R. J. Corsini (Ed.), *Current Psychotherapies,* 3rd Ed., pp. 392–446. Copyright 1984. Reprinted by permission of the publisher, F. E. Peacock Publishers, Inc., Itasca, IL.

Chapter 8: **258–259,** quote from *The Gestalt Approach/Eyewitness to Therapy,* by F. S. Perls.Copyright 1973 by Science and Behavior Books. **279,** quote from *Man's Search for Meaning,* by V. E. Frankl. Copyright 1963 by Washington Square Press. **282,** Figure 8–3 from *The Will to Meaning,* by V. E. Frankl. Copyright 1969 by the New American Library.

Chapter 9: **315,** Figure 9–1 from *Families and Family Therapy,* by S. Minuchin. Copyright 1974 by Harvard University Press. Reprinted by permission. **360,** lyrics from "Why I Am So Blue," by Albert Ellis. Copyright 1977 by the Institute for Rational-Emotive Therapy. Reprinted by permission.

Chapter 10: **367,** Figure 10–1 reprinted with permission from A. A. Lazarus, "Multimodal Therapy," in J. C. Norcross (Ed.), *Handbook of Eclectic Psychotherapy,* p. 69. New York: Brunner/Mazel, 1986.

Epigraphs

Page 1: Mandler, G. (1975). *Mind and emotion.* New York: Wiley, p. 2.

Page 13: Gilligan, C. (1982). *In a different voice: Psychological theory and women's development.* Cambridge, MA: Harvard University Press, p. 6.

Page 50: Boring, E. G. (1978). The psychology of controversy. In E. R. Hilgard (Ed.), *American psychology in historical perspective* (pp. 249–250). Washington, DC: American Psychological Association. (Original speech delivered 1928)

Page 73: Maslow, A. H., quoted in C. Wilson (1972). *New pathways in psychology: Maslow and the post-Freudian revolution.* New York: Taplinger, p. 130.

Page 73: Skinner, B. F., quoted in F. K. Matson (Ed.) (1973). *Without/within: Behaviorism and humanism.* Pacific Grove, CA: Brooks/Cole, p. 45.

Page 77: Neisser, U. (1976). *Cognition and reality.* San Francisco: W. H. Freeman, p. 1.

Page 86: Jung, C. G. (1973). *Letters.* Princeton, NJ: Princeton University Press, p. 288. Also quoted in D. H. Shapiro (1984). Self-control. In R. J. Corsini (Ed.), *Encyclopedia of psychology* (Vol. 3, pp. 285–288). New York: Wiley.

Page 97: Wolpe, J. (1982). *The practice of behavior therapy* (3rd ed.). New York: Pergamon Press, p. 18.

Page 100: Skinner, B. F. (1953). *Science and human behavior.* New York: Macmillan, p. 373.

Page 103: Rotter, J. (1982a). *The development and application of social learning theory: Selected papers.* New York: Praeger, p. 2.

Page 106: Beck, A. T. (1976). *Cognitive therapy and the emotional disorders.* New York: New American Library, p. 23.

Page 129: Salter, A. (1949). *Conditioned reflex therapy.* New York: Creative Age Press, p. 33.

Page 168: Wachtel, P. L. (1977). *Psychoanalysis and behavior therapy: Toward an integration.* New York: Basic Books, p. xvi.

Page 210: Strupp, H. H. (1978). Psychotherapy research and practice: An overview. In S. L. Garfield & A. E. Bergin (Eds.), *Handbook of psychotherapy and behavior change* (2nd ed.) (pp. 3–22). New York: Wiley, p. 19.

Page 250: Frankl, V. E. (1969). *The will to meaning.* New York: New American Library, p. 28.

Page 291: Ackerman, N. W. (1966). *Treating the troubled family.* New York: Basic Books, p. 60.

Page 333: Rotter, J. B. (1970). Some implications of a social learning theory for the practice of psychotherapy. In D. J. Levis (Ed.), *Learning approaches to therapeutic behavior change* (pp. 208–241). Chicago: Aldine, p. 237.

Page 379: Bateson, G. (1972). *Steps to an ecology of mind.* New York: Balantine, p. xxi.

Name Index

Subject Index

ABAB design, 115–116
Accountability, contextual family therapy, 306
Adlerian psychotherapy
  assessment in, 227–228
  behavior change, 228–229
  birth order, 227–228
  client-therapist relationship, 227, 231
  cognition, 230–231
  evaluation of, 230–231
  compared to Freudian psychoanalysis, 224
  history of, 223–224
  indivisibility of purpose, 224
  inferiority, 225
  insight, 228
  intervention process, 226–227
  neurosis, 225–226, 231
  personality, 224
  sample session, 229
  social interest, 225, 231, 233
Adult, transactional analysis, 235–236
Aggression, modeling of, 151n
Alignments, structural family therapy, 315
Anal stage, 180
Anger control, stress-inoculation training, 164–165
Animal Intelligence (Thorndike), 60
Anxiety
  anticipatory anxiety, 286
  as biological event, 99, 134
  early experiences and, 195
  humanistic-existential perspective, 204–205
  manifestations of, 99
  as manipulation, 195, 197
  moral anxiety, 184
  neopsychoanalytic perspective, 195–197
  neurotic anxiety, 183–184
  psychoanalytic view, 182–184
  realistic anxiety, 183
  signal anxiety, 183
Anxiety-evoking techniques, 144–146
  flooding, 144–145
  paradoxical intention, 145–146

Applications of a Social Learning Theory of Personality (Rotter, Chance & Phares), 337
Applied behavior analysis, 100–103
  concepts related to, 102–103
  operant learning, 100–103
  radical behaviorism, 100–101
Archaeopsychic ego state, transactional analysis, 235
Art and science. 26–30
  common purposes of, 26–27
  duality in, 29
  honesty in, 27–28
  insight in, 29
  parsimony in, 28–29
Assertive behavior, definitions of, 136
Assertiveness training, 132, 136–139
  assessment in, 138, 139
  behavioral rehearsal in, 138
  goal of, 137–138
  process of, 138
  rational-emotive therapy, 360
  unassertiveness, causes of, 136, 137
Assessment. *See also* Assessment tests; Behavioral assessment
  behavioral manifestations, identifying, 40–41
  biological vs. behavioral assessment, 39–40
  client's history, 40
  goals of, 39
Assessment techniques
  assessment tests, 42–44
  interview, 41–42
  life history data, 42
  situational observation, 44–45
Assessment tests, 42–44
  intelligence tests, 43
  objective tests, 42–43
  personality assessment, 43
  projective tests, 42
  psychopathology assessment, 43
Attentional processes, and modeling, 151
Automatic thoughts, 159–160